The Russian Empire.
A Multiethnic History

We work with leading authors to develop the strongest educational materials in history, bringing cutting-edge thinking and best learning practice to a global market.

Under a range of well-known imprints, including Longman, we craft high quality print and electronic publications which help readers to understand and apply their content, whether studying or at work.

To find out more about the complete range of our publishing please visit us on the World Wide Web at: www.pearsoneduc.com

The Russian Empire:
A Multiethnic History

ANDREAS KAPPELER

Translated by
ALFRED CLAYTON

An imprint of **Pearson Education**

Harlow, England · London · New York · Reading, Massachusetts · San Francisco
Toronto · Don Mills, Ontario · Sydney · Tokyo · Singapore · Hong Kong · Seoul
Taipei · Cape Town · Madrid · Mexico City · Amsterdam · Munich · Paris · Milan

Pearson Education Limited
Edinburgh Gate
Harlow
Essex CM20 2JE
England

and Associated Companies around the world

Visit us on the World Wide Web at
www.pearsoned.co.uk

First published 2001

© Pearson Education Limited 2001

The right of Andreas Kappeler to be identified as author of this work
has been asserted by him in accordance with the
Copyright, Designs and Patents Act 1988.

ISBN 0 582 23415 8

British Library Cataloguing-in-Publication Data
A CIP catalogue record for this book can be obtained from the British Library

Library of Congress Cataloging-in-Publication Data
A catalog record for this book can be obtained from the Library of Congress

10 9 8 7 6
05

Typeset by 7 in 11.5/13pt Van Dijck
Produced by Pearson Education Malaysia, Sdn Bhd
Printed in Malaysia, VVP

Contents

Appendices

Translator's Note

I am very grateful to Professor David Saunders of the University of Newcastle upon Tyne, who helped me with the transliteration of Russian names and references and, in the process, read through the whole manuscript and suggested a number of ways in which it could be improved.

How did Russia expand?
— militarily
Assimilation?
— peter → no

Chronology

Dates are based on the Julian Calendar, which was used in Russia until 1918.

For further details see Edgar Hösch and Hans-Jürgen Grabmüller, Daten der russischen Geschichte (Munich, 1981) and Daten der sowjetischen Geschichte (Munich, 1981).

1462–1505	*Ivan III*
1478	Muscovy conquers Novgorod
1480	Mongol and Tatar suzerainty over Muscovy formally terminated
1500–03	Muscovy conquers Lithuanian 'Severian principalities' and Chernigov
1505–33	*Vassilii III*
1514	The Grand Duke of Muscovy conquers Smolensk
1533–84	Ivan IV Grozny ('the Terrible')
1551	Foundation of Sviiazhsk and incorporation into the Muscovite state of the part of the Khanate of Kazan on the right bank of the Volga
1552	Muscovy conquers Kazan and annexes the whole khanate
1553–57	Armed resistance by the population of the Khanate of Kazan
1556	Annexation of the Khanate of Astrakhan
1557	Loose protectorate over the Great Nogai Horde
1558–82/83	Livonian War. Temporary conquest of parts of Livonia and Lithuania, after which Muscovy is defeated by Poland-Lithuania and Sweden
1570–72, 1581–84	Cheremis and Tatar uprisings against Muscovite rule

1579–82	Ermak's campaign against the Khanate of Siberia, beginning of the conquest of Siberia
1584–98	*Fedor Ivanovich*
1586	Foundation of the fortress of Ufa in the Urals
1586–87	Foundation of Tobolsk, Tiumen, the first Russian fortresses in western Siberia
1598–1605	*Boris Godunov*
1598/1605–13	Civil war (Smuta)
1610	Polish troops occupy Moscow, the Polish prince Władysław is crowned tsar
1611	Poland-Lithuania conquers Smolensk
1613–45	*Mikhail Romanov*
1617	Treaty of Stolbovo, East Karelia and Ingermanland are ceded to Sweden
1618	Truce of Deulino, Smolensk and the 'Severian Principalities' are ceded to Poland-Lithuania
1619–48	Advance beyond the Enisei and Lena to the Pacific. Iakutsk is reached in 1632, and Okhotsk in 1648
1637	Establishment of the Sibirskii Prikaz
1645–76	*Aleksei Mikhailovich*
1648–49	Uprising of Ukrainians led by the Dnepr Cossacks under Bohdan Khmelnitsky against Poland-Lithuania
1652–61	Foundation of the fortress of Irkutsk
1654	Agreement of Pereiaslav and Moscow between the Dnepr Cossacks and the tsar. Muscovite protectorate over Ukraine
1654–67	(Second) Northern War
1654	Russian conquest of Smolensk, establishment of Smolensk central office
1655	Muscovite military alliance with Kalmyks
1663	Establishment of Malorossiiskii Prikaz (Little Russian Chancellery)
1667	Truce of Andrusovo. Ukraine is divided. Russia acquires the left-bank Hetmanate with Kiev, and Smolensk
1670–71	Popular uprising under the leadership of Stepan Razin

1676–82	*Fedor Alekseevich*
1682–89	*Ivan and Peter Alekseevich*
1685	The Metropolitan of Kiev is placed under the jurisdiction of the Moscow Patriarchate
1687–1709	Hetman Mazepa in Ukraine
1689	Treaty of Nerchinsk between Muscovy and China
1689–1725	*Peter I, the Great*
1700–21	(Third) Northern War
1701	The Kiev College is transformed into an Academy
1703	Foundation of St Petersburg
1709	Battle of Poltava
1710	Conquest of Estonia and Livonia
1713/18	Degradation of Muslim Tatar nobility
1716/18	Foundation of the fortresses of Omsk and Semipalatinsk
1718–24	Introduction of poll tax and state peasant category
1719–22	First revision (census)
1721	Peace of Nystad
1722	Introduction of the Table of Ranks
1722	Foundation of the Malorossiiskaia kollegia (Little Russian College)
1722–23	Peter I's Persian campaign, conquest of parts of Azerbaidzhan (held by Russia until 1735)
1725–27	*Catherine I*
1727–30	*Peter II*
1730–40	*Anna (Ivanovna)*
1731–42	Kazakh khans swear oaths of loyalty to Russia
1734–40	Final subjugation of the Bashkirs, who offer bitter resistance
1740–41	*Ivan VI*
1740–55	Aggressive missionary policy towards animists and Muslims
1741	Bering's expedition reaches the coast of Alaska
1741–61	*Elizabeth*
1743	Peace of Åbo, new border with Finland
1755	Foundation of University of Moscow

1761–62	*Peter III*
1762	Abolition of noble service requirement
1762–96	*Catherine II*
1762–63	Manifesto to attract foreign colonists
1764	Abolition of the office of Hetman in Ukraine
1764–95	Stanisław August Poniatowski, last king of Poland-Lithuania
1765	Sloboda Ukraine becomes Russian province
1767–73	Commission for new legal code
1768	Greater Russian influence in Poland-Lithuania
1768–74	Russo-Turkish War. Russia acquires the areas to the north of the Black Sea
1771	Conquest of the Khanate of Crimea, which becomes Russian protectorate
1771	The majority of the Kalmyks emigrate to Middle Asia. Abolition of the Khanate of the Kalmyks
1772	First partition of Poland
1773–75	Popular uprising led by E. Pugachev
1775	Conquest, destruction and dissolution of the Zaporozhian Sich
1775	Promulgation of new provincial order
1783–85	Russian administrative reforms applied to the Baltic provinces (partially revoked 1796)
1783	Russian protectorate over east Georgian kingdom in Treaty of Georgievsk
1783	Annexation of the Khanate of the Crimean Tatars
1784	Acquisition of Kodiak Island off Alaska
1784	Foundation of fortress of Vladikavkaz
1785–91	Chechens and Dagestanis under Sheik Mansur wage guerilla war against Russia
1785	Charters to the Nobility and the Towns
1788	Establishment of 'Assembly of Muslim Clergy' in Ufa
1791	Polish Constitution of 3 May
1793	Second Partition of Poland
1794	Polish uprising under T. Kościuszko
1794	Introduction of double taxation for Jews
1795	Third partition of Poland

1796–1801	*Paul*
1799	Foundation of Russian America Company
1801	Annexation of Kingdom of Georgia
1801–25	*Alexander I*
1802	University of Dorpat re-opened
1803–05	Foundation of Universities of Vilna, Kazan and Kharkov
1803–11	Russian protectorate over principalities of west Georgia (complete incorporation by 1857)
1804–13	Russo-Iranian War, conquest of khanates in northern Azerbaidzhan
1804	Promulgation of statute on Jews
1807	Abolition of serfdom in Duchy of Warsaw
1808–09	Conquest and annexation of Finland, which becomes an autonomous Grand Duchy within Russia
1810	Annexation of Kingdom of Imeretia
1811	Forcible integration of autocephalous Georgian church into Russian Orthodox church
1812	Peace of Bucharest. Russia acquires Bessarabia, the north-eastern part of Principality of Moldavia
1812	Union of Old Finland, which had been Russian since 1721 and 1743, with Grand Duchy of Finland
1812	Establishment of Fort Ross in California (until 1841)
1812–13	Napoleon's Russian campaign
1815	Congress of Vienna, new partition of Poland. A 'Kingdom of Poland' with a constitution and a large measure of autonomy within the Russian Empire
1816	University of Warsaw opened (closed down in 1831)
1816–19	Abolition of serfdom in Estonia, Kurland and Livonia
1818	Bessarabia granted large measure of autonomy
1818	Alexander I opens first sejm of the Kingdom of Poland
1822	M. Speranskii reforms Siberian administration Statute on the administration of inorodtsy
1822	Annexation of Middle Horde, and, in 1824, of Small Horde of the Kazakhs
1824	Foundation of Latvian Literary Society

1825–55	*Nicholas I*
1825	Decembrist revolt
1825–46	Kazakh uprising led by Kenisari Kasimov
1826–28	Russo-Persian War, conquest of the Khanates of Erivan and Nakhichevan
1828	Resumption of Orthodox missionary activity in the east of the empire
1828	Autonomous status of Bessarabia curtailed
1829–64	Caucasian War
1830–31	November insurrection in Poland
1831	Foundation of Finnish Literary Society
1832	'Organic Statute of Kingdom of Poland', dissolution of Sejm and Polish army
1832	Uprising in Georgia
1833	Declaration of a state of siege in the Kingdom of Poland
1834	The Russian language is introduced in the administration, the courts and the schools in areas of Poland-Lithuania annexed up to 1795
1834	(Russian) University of Kiev opened in place of (Polish) University of Vilna, which was closed down in 1832
1834–59	Shamil, head of the Murids, founds a theocratic imamate, and leads anti-Russian resistance in the Caucasian War.
1836	Confirmation of independence and privileges of Armenian church
1838	Foundation of Estonian Scholarly Society
1839	Incorporation of Uniate church (with the exception of the Kingdom of Poland) into Russian Orthodox church
1839	Failed Russian expedition against Khiva
1840	Abolition of Lithuanian Statute in the 'Western Provinces'
1840	Publication of *Kobzar*, a volume of poetry by Ukrainian poet T. Shevchenko
1845	Annexation of Kazakh Inner Horde, and in 1848 of Great Horde

1845–47	Movement to convert Latvians and Estonians to Orthodox church
1846/47	Ukrainian national society of St Cyril and St Methodius in Kiev
1849	Russia rediscovers mouth of the Amur
1849–60	Second stage of agrarian reform in Baltic provinces
1853–56	Crimean War, Russia loses southern Bessarabia
1854	Foundation of fortress of Vernii (modern Almaty)
1854	Foundation of Khabarovsk
1855–81	*Alexander II*
1856	Relaxation of Russian policy towards Poland
1858/60	'Unequal' treaties of Aigun and Beijing with China determine borders in the Far East
1859	Final Russian victory over north Caucasian gortsy under Shamil
1860	Foundation of Vladivostok
1861	Manifesto on liberation of the peasants. Abolition of serfdom in Russia
1861/62	Attempted 'reform from above' under A. Wielopolski in Kingdom of Poland
1863/64	January uprising in Poland and Lithuania
1863	Convocation of Finnish Diet
1863	Ban on teaching and printing of works in Ukrainian (with the exception of belles lettres). Followed by bans on printing works in Belorussian and Lithuanian (using Latin script)
1863–90	Attempts initiated by N. I. Ilminskii to christianize the non-Christians in the east of the empire with the help of native-language schools
1864	Severe reprisals against participants in the January uprising. Beginning of repressive measures against Catholic church and monasteries and the use of the Polish language in the administration and schools even of Congress Poland
1864	Zemstvo reform in thirty-four provinces
1864	Agrarian reform in Congress Poland
1864	Judicial reform

1864	Conquest and eviction of west Caucasian Circassians
1864	Colonel Cherniaev's first campaign in Middle Asia
1864–70	Agrarian reform in Transcaucasia
1865	Conquest of Tashkent
1867	Sale of Alaska to the United States
1867	Establishment of Governor-Generalship of Turkestan
1868	Conquest of Samarkand, protectorate over Emirate of Bukhara
1868/69	Debate between Iurii Samarin and Carl Schirren about position of Baltic Germans in the Russian Empire
1869	Uprising by Kazakhs of the Small Horde
1869	Foundation of Russian University of Warsaw
1870	Municipal reform
1871	Abolition of special status of colonists
1873	Russian protectorate over Khanate of Khiva
1874	Introduction of conscription in Russian Empire
1875	Sakhalin becomes Russian
1875	Kholm, the last Uniate diocese in Russian Empire, is incorporated into Russian Orthodox church
1876	Tighter measures against the Ukrainian language in the circular of Ems
1876	Annexation of Khanate of Kokand
1877	Introduction of Russian municipal order in the Baltic provinces
1877/78	Russo-Turkish war, areas of Kars, Ardahan, Batumi and southern Bessarabia are ceded to Russia
1878	Grand Duchy of Finland receives a largely autonomous army
1879	Tekke Turkmen defeat Russians
1881	Conquest of Turkmen fortress of Gök Tepe, annexation of Turkmenistan
1881	In Treaty of St Petersburg Russia relinquishes large parts of upper Ili valley in Chinese Sinkiang which it had conquered in 1871
1881	Assassination of Alexander II

1881–94	*Alexander III*
1881	Pogroms against Jews in Ukraine and Warsaw
1881–99	Construction of Transcaspian Railway
1883	Foundation of Lithuanian journal *Aušra* (Dawn)
1883	Foundation of journal *Tercuman* by I. Gasprali
1884	Russia occupies Merv
1885	Introduction of Russian as teaching language in primary schools in the Kingdom of Poland
1887	Introduction of restrictions on number of Jews in grammar schools and tertiary education institutions
1889	Russian judicial reform and Russian as language of the courts in Baltic provinces
1890	Foundation of Revolutionary Armenian Federalist Party (Dashnaks)
1891	Statute on administration of steppe areas
1891–1903	Construction of Trans-Siberian railway
1892	Foundation of Polish Socialist Party (PPS)
1892–1904	Minister of Finance Witte presses ahead with industrialization of Russia
1893	German University of Dorpat is transformed into Russian university of Iurev
1894–1917	*Nicholas II*
1895	Pamir Agreement with Britain determines border in Middle Asia
1896	Closure of Armenian church schools
1897	First general census in Russian Empire
1897	Foundation of 'Bund', the General Jewish Workers' Association in Lithuania, Poland and Russia
1898	Andizhan insurrection
1899	February manifesto curtails autonomy of Finland
1900	Foundation of Revolutionary Ukrainian Party (RUP), from 1905 onwards Ukrainian Social Democratic Workers' Party
1901	Compulsory Military Service Law in Finland
1902	Foundation of Belorussian Revolutionary Hramada
1902–04	Peasants' Movement in left-bank Ukraine and in Georgian Guria
1903	Pogrom against Jews in Kishinev

1903	Property of Armenian church confiscated
1903	General strike in Baku
1904–05	Russo-Japanese War
1905, 9 Jan.	'Bloody Sunday' in St Petersburg, start of revolution in Russia. Mass strikes and demonstrations in Poland, 'western provinces' and Baltic provinces follow
March	Foundation of Association for Equal Rights for Jews
17 April/1 May	Tolerance edicts reduce discrimination against non-Christian faiths
9–11 June	General strike and fighting on the barricades in Łódź
14–25 June	Mutiny on battleship Potemkin and disturbances in Odessa
Aug.	First congress of Muslims in Nizhnii Novgorod
Oct.	General strike in Russia and Poland
17 Oct.	Tsar's October manifesto
18–25 Oct.	Pogroms against Jews in west of the empire
22 Oct.	Restoration of Finland's autonomy
Nov.	Latvian Conference of Village Delegates and All-Estonian Assembly
Dec.	Great Lithuanian Diet in Vilna
Dec.	Armed insurrection in Moscow
1906, Jan.	Second Congress of Muslims in St Petersburg, Foundation of Union of Muslims of Russia (Ittifak)
20 Feb.	Manifesto summons State Duma
23 Apr.	Assent to 'Fundamental Laws'
27 Apr.– 8 July	First Duma in session
20 June	Parliamentary reform in Finland
8 Nov.	Stolypin's agrarian law
1907, 20 Feb.– 2 June	Second Duma in session
1907	Reform of electoral law in Finland (introduction of active and passive right to vote for women) and elections for diet
1907, 1 Nov.– 1912, 9 June	Third Duma in session
1910	Introduction of Imperial law in Finland
1911	Zemstvo reform extended to six western provinces of the empire

1911–13	Ritual murder case against a Jew, Beilis, in Kiev
1912	Province of Kholm is detached from Kingdom of Poland
1914	Demonstrations marking 100th birthday of T. Shevchenko in Ukraine
1914, July	Start of First World War
1915	German offensive, Russia loses Lithuania, Kurland, Poland and western Belorussia
1915	Germans, Poles and Jews deported from western border areas of Russian Empire
1916, summer	Insurrections in various parts of Middle Asia
1916, Nov.	Proclamation of Kingdom of Poland by the Central Powers
1917, 23–7 Feb.	February Revolution
2 Mar.	Proclamation of Provisional Government, abdication of Nicholas II
4 Mar.	Formation of Ukrainian Central Rada in Kiev
17 Mar.	Provisional Government recognizes the independence of Poland
20 Mar.	Revocation of discriminatory special powers, also against inorodcy and Jews
1 May	First All-Russian Congress of Muslims in Moscow
10 June	Declaration of autonomy of Ukraine in 1st. Universal of Ukrainian Central Rada
July	Dissolution of Finnish Diet, which had declared itself to be the supreme power, by Provisional Government
Aug./Sept.	German offensive in the Baltic. Conquest of Riga
Sept.	Congress of Peoples of Russia in Kiev
24–6 Oct.	October Revolution, Bolsheviks seize power
2 Nov.	Declaration of the Rights of the Peoples of Russia
7 Nov.	Establishment of 'Ukrainian People's Republic' as part of Russian federation
Nov.	Elections to Constituent Assembly
23 Nov. / 6 Dec.	Declaration of independence by Finland, recognized on 18 Dec.
12 Dec.	Proclamation of Ukrainian Soviet Republic in Kharkov

1918, 5 / 6 Jan.	Dissolution of Constituent Assembly
11 Jan.	Declaration of independence by Ukraine issued by Central Rada
16 Feb.	Declaration of independence by Lithuania
24 Feb.	Declaration of independence by Estonia
3 March	Peace of Brest-Litovsk between RSFSR and Central Powers
22 Apr.	Declaration of independence by Transcaucasian Federative Republic
26–8 May	Declaration of independence by Georgia, Armenia and Azerbaidzhan
10 July	Constitution of Russian Federative Soviet Republic
7 Oct.	Proclamation of independence of Poland
11 Nov.	End of First World War
18 Nov.	Declaration of independence by Latvia
1921	Conquest of Georgia by Red Army
1922, 30 Dec.	Foundation of Union of Socialist Soviet Republics (USSR)
1924	Incorporation of Bukhara and Khiva (People's Republics since 1920) into Soviet Union from 1921 New Economic Policy accompanied by *korenizatsiia* ('indigenization', increase in the share of non-Russians in party and administration) and liberal policy on language
1929–33	First Five Year Plan. Accelerated industrialization, forcible collectivization, terror, nomads forced to become sedentary
1933	Famine, especially in Ukraine
1934	Proclamation of Soviet patriotism
1936	Stalinist Constitution with 11 Soviet republics
1936–38	Terror, the Great Purges
1939	Hitler–Stalin Pact, annexation of eastern Poland and eastern Galicia
1940	Annexation of Lithuania, Latvia, Estonia and Bessarabia
1941–45	'Great Patriotic War' against Germany
1941–44	Deportation of Germans, Kalmyks, Crimean Tatars and several Caucasian ethnic groups to Soviet Asia
1953	Death of Stalin

1956	20th Congress of Soviet Communist Party, liberalization of policy on nationalities
1972	Renewed inflexibility with regard to policy on nationalities
1985	Gorbachev introduces policy of perestroika
1986	Disturbances in Kazakhstan
1988	National conflicts break out in Transcaucasia and in Baltic republics, national movements spread throughout Soviet Union
1988–90	Soviet republics declare themselves to be sovereign
1990, March	Declaration of independence by Lithuania
1991, Apr.	Declaration of independence by Georgia
1991, Aug.	Unsuccessful coup by reactionary forces in Moscow is followed by declarations of independence by all the republics, and recognition of independence of Estonia, Latvia and Lithuania
1991, end of Dec.	Dissolution of Soviet Union, foundation of 'Commonwealth of Independent States', Gorbachev resigns

Introduction

THE COLLAPSE of the Soviet Union in the final decade of the twentieth century marked the end of the seventy-year existence of the multinational Communist imperial polity. It also brought to a close the history of more than four centuries of the Russian multi-ethnic empire. For this reason explanations that ascribe the demise of the USSR to nothing more than the crisis of the socialist system whilst failing to take into account the legacy of the Russian Empire are clearly insufficient. Seen from a wider perspective of this kind, the disintegration of the Soviet Union forms part of the universal process of the dissolution and dismemberment of multi-ethnic empires and the rise of nation states. This occurred in Europe in the nineteenth and early twentieth centuries in the case of the Ottoman and Habsburg empires, and elsewhere in the world in the course of the process of decolonization. It may thus be argued that the October Revolution and the Soviet era merely deferred the dismemberment of the Russian Empire for a few decades.

This book represents the first attempt to provide a comprehensive survey of the history of the Russian multi-ethnic empire. As I embarked on the project I set myself three main goals. The first of these was to place the problems of nationality and the disintegration of the Soviet Union into a larger historical context. In order to arrive at a more profound understanding of the Soviet multi-ethnic empire, its nations and ethnic groups and their emancipation from the central government, it is necessary to go back to what preceded it. The structures of the multi-ethnic empire, the patterns of interaction between the centre and the periphery, and the nature of inter-ethnic relations evolved over a number of centuries. Furthermore, national identity and national movements are the end results of protracted processes, and derive their legitimacy primarily from history. Thus the distinct political cultures of Estonians, Lithuanians, Ukrainians, Armenians and Tatars are the result of national movements that arose in the nineteenth and early

I

twentieth centuries. The tension between the political and military predominance of Russia on the one hand and its relative backwardness in socio-economic terms when compared with the western periphery of the empire is not a feature that first appeared within the Soviet empire. Current problems such as the Armenian–Azerbaidzhani conflict, Russian anti-Semitism, the Eurocentric feeling of superiority that Russians display towards the Muslims of Middle Asia, their rejection of Ukrainian nationhood, Poland's conflict-ridden relationship with Russia, and the relatively relaxed attitude of the Finns all have their origins in the time before the Revolution.

The second aim of this book is to broaden our view of the history of Russia, which is widely misconstrued as Russian national history. Until recently the inhabitants of the USSR tended to be referred to as Russians in the West. People had hardly ever heard of Lithuanians, Kazakhs and Georgians, not to mention Ossetians, Meskhetians or Gagauz. With its almost complete control over information, for decades the authoritarian system covered up the problems associated with the nationalities by means of propaganda that suggested a non-existent harmony, and by repression. The majority of western observers were quite willing to accept this state of affairs, either because they were only able to conceive of ethnically uniform nation states, or because they were prey to wishful thinking concerning the notion that national characteristics were obsolete in an age of supranational alliances. The fact that the Soviet Union was a multi-ethnic state first became more widely known after the collapse of the Soviet polity.

The political changes have led to a resurgence of interest in the Soviet multi-ethnic empire, and to the recent publication of a number of general surveys of the subject.[1] However, this has not had an impact on the received interpretation of the tsarist empire. Although Russians accounted for only 43 per cent of the population at the end of the nineteenth century, to this day the Russian Empire by and large still continues to be thought of as a Russian nation state. This is even more true of western than of Soviet and post-Soviet historiography. However, the interpretation of Russian history in terms of the nation state derives primarily from two sources. The first of these is nineteenth-century Russian historiography, which, in keeping with the zeitgeist, construed the history of Russia as that of a nation state. This exercised a great deal of influence on Soviet historiography, and also, through both the works of Soviet historians and of Russian émigrés, on European and

North American historiography. Second, since the nineteenth century, western historiography has displayed a strong bias in favour of the categories of the nation state, and Soviet historiography under Stalin returned at least in part to a Russian national interpretation. However, I believe that it is misleading to interpret the history of Russia in terms of the nation state. For this reason I have attempted to correct the Russocentric approach, to show that polyethnicity is an important and enduring factor in Russian history, and to demonstrate that the history both of Russia and of its regions and peoples remains incomplete without an understanding of the overall multi-ethnic context.

Third, this book seeks to make a contribution to a general history of multi-ethnic empires, which have been neglected by the kind of historiography that takes its bearings from the nation state.[2] In an age in which the model of the ethnically uniform nation state is experiencing a revival, it needs to be remembered that in the past multi-ethnic states tended to be the rule, and that, at least outside Europe, they continue to be so to this day. In fact, the ideal of the ethnically uniform nation state first arose in the nineteenth century, and it was the source of a great deal of misery for mankind. Studying the history of multi-ethnic empires can serve to remind us that there are alternative principles with regard to the structure of states and societies. It can also clarify the problematical nature of the (ethnically restricted) principle of the nation state. With its great ethnic diversity, which included Europe and Asia, four world religions and a whole gamut of lifestyles and economic patterns, the Russian multi-ethnic empire is particularly instructive in this regard. Since there is a dearth of detailed work on this subject, the example of Russia cannot be compared with other empires. I nonetheless intend to emphasize the aspects on which a comparative approach of this kind might be based. They are also the questions at the heart of this study:

1. What were the methods and procedures used when occupying and integrating territories which had populations that differed in ethnic and religious terms, and possessed distinct economies, social orders and cultures?
2. What was the reaction of the conquered peoples in general, and of their elites in particular? Did it include armed resistance, or was there a willingness to cooperate? How did foreign domination affect the political order, social structure, economy and culture of their regions?

3. What was the character of the multi-ethnic realm? What was the nature of its socio-ethnic, administrative and economic structure? Which areas witnessed an inter-ethnic division of labour, and what were the specific functions which the individual ethnic groups performed within the empire? How did the different cultures and religions interact?

4. How did modernization influence and change the old supranational empire and its ethnic groups, and, in particular, how were they affected by the national movements? And how did national emancipation interact with social revolution?

These aims and issues have shaped the structure of this book. Thus a brief discussion of the mediaeval background (Chapter 1) is followed by an account of Russian expansion to the east, the south and the west between the sixteenth and early nineteenth centuries. This turned the Muscovite state, which was initially confined to the forests of northeastern Europe, into a vast Eurasian empire (Chapters 2 and 3). Chapter 4 complements the chronological narrative with a systematic analysis of the structure of the old multi-ethnic empire at the end of the eighteenth and at the beginning of the nineteenth centuries. The events of the nineteenth century, which led to the transition to the modern world, are dealt with in three separate chapters on a thematic basis. Chapter 5 is devoted to the final stage in the expansion of the Russian Empire, which took place exclusively to the south and to the east, and led to the annexation of large tracts of land in Asia. However, the most important caesura was the new historical power of the national movements, which called into question the unity of the pre-national empire (Chapter 6). Russian policy on nationalities changed under the influence of modernization and the national challenge (Chapter 7), as did the character of the multi-ethnic empire, the structure of which at the end of the nineteenth century is once more described in a systematic manner (Chapter 8). Chapter 9 is devoted to the interaction of the national question and revolution, and leads via the revolutions of 1905 and 1917 to the collapse of the Russian Empire in 1918. The book concludes with a brief survey of the historic development of the Soviet multi-ethnic empire up to the time of its demise in 1991.

It may of course seem that I am being rather presumptuous in attempting to write a comprehensive history of the Russian multi-ethnic empire, for it is clearly impossible to do justice to all aspects of its development and to each of the more than a hundred ethnic groups. Thus the insufficiently researched questions of inter-ethnic contacts and mutual acculturation have been largely ignored.[3] The emphasis has been placed on the interaction between the state, the central government and the ruling elites and the non-Russian population of the peripheral regions. Furthermore, ethnic groups with upper classes, traditions of statehood and a high level of civilization, for example the Poles, the Tatars or the Georgians, and dispersed groups with specific functions, such as the Germans, Jews and Armenians, are given greater prominence than the mass of the other ethnic groups with less clearly differentiated social structures. However, the numerous 'smaller peoples' of Russia, whose history is less well known, but who were certainly not, as Engels once claimed, 'without a history', will be given a chance to make their voices heard.

A historical account of the Russian multi-ethnic empire has to deal with a series of methodological problems. Although the present approach is deliberately different from the predominantly Russocentric approach to the history of Russia, it is still Russocentric inasmuch as the questions that it asks pertain to the Russian state. From their national perspectives Poles, Yakuts, Estonians, Uzbeks, Chuvash and Georgians have little in common in historical terms apart from the experience of Russian rule. Yet it is impossible in this context to comply with the suggestion, despite the fact that it seems to be justifiable, that the present study should concentrate on the nations conquered by the Russians. This is the task of the various national histories. An account that takes in the empire as a whole has to take its bearings from the state which determined the unity of what we are concerned to investigate.

However, the ethnic groups of the periphery will be examined not only as the objects of Russian statecraft, but also as forces that played a significant role in determining the course of historical events. In this context it will only be possible to give a brief account of the history of the non-Russians before they were incorporated into the Russian empire, which in the case of Transcaucasia and Middle Asia reaches back much further than Russian history itself.

A comparative examination of the ethnic groups of the empire as a whole is of use inasmuch as it enables us to transcend the confines of national history, which always tends to consider the historical fate of its particular group to be unique. However, a comparison with other nations reveals both areas of common ground and differences, and these help to put the exclusively national interpretations into perspective. A comprehensive analysis of the incorporation of the various ethnic groups into the Russian Empire, of the socio-ethnic and economic structures of the various regions, of the individual national movements and of the policy on nationalities as it affected a single ethnic group is only possible in the context of a comparative investigation.

An approach that seeks to encompass the whole empire soon comes up against the fact that the information at our disposal is rather one-sided. The most important sources originate from the Russian centre, and are correspondingly biased, whereas non-Russian sources are few and far between and are usually devoted to a narrow range of subjects. Connected with this is the problem of the languages in which they were written. I was only able to draw on sources and accounts in Slav and western languages, and, with regard to the history of the majority of peripheral regions of the empire, was forced to rely on specialized studies by western historians with a knowledge of the languages involved, and on Soviet studies written in Russian. The insoluble linguistic problems also lead to another Russocentric component, which manifests itself in the Russian spellings of Georgian, Tatar, Buriat and Belorussian names.

Those who desire to complement the Russocentric approach to the history of Russia with a multi-ethnic one run the risk of incorrectly overestimating the importance of national phenomena. In the pre-national era – and in Russia this lasted until well into the nineteenth century – linguistic and ethnic identities and loyalties were less important than estate-based, religious, regional and dynastic ones. When the ethnic factor becomes the central subject of our investigation, there is clearly a danger of allowing the national interpretation to be projected on to the past in an unhistoric manner, and this is something to which the majority of national histories succumb. An important aim of the present book is to emphasize the supranational and multi-ethnic character of the old Russian Empire, and to contrast it with the Russocentric and nation state approach and the restricted perspective of the national historiographies. Furthermore, due recognition will be given to the contribution of non-Russians to the history of the Russian Empire, which is largely ignored by Russian national historiography. Finally, the pre-modern history of Russia's ethnic groups is also of significance in that it constitutes the pre-history of nations which, in the nineteenth and twentieth centuries, did not suddenly appear from nowhere.[4] The danger of overestimating national elements continues to exist in the modern age, and thus the interaction between social and national factors must be treated with great caution.

To the best of my knowledge a theoretical model that would make it possible to deal with these complex problems in a systematic manner does not exist. Approaches that derive from the experiences of the period in which the capitalist powers of western Europe ruled non-European territories cannot without further ado be applied to the Russian agrarian autocracy. This is true of both Wallerstein's model of the European world order, and the various theories of dependence and imperialism, which, furthermore, only cover a restricted period. However, this does not mean that such theoretical approaches, as in studies devoted to the history of European expansion and colonial rule, cannot be used as a tool with which to explain certain aspects of the history of the Russian empire.[5] Similarly, I have drawn on middle-range theories for specific questions, such as the different approaches to the subject of nationalism, and on John Armstrong's model of mobilized diaspora groups. In a more general theoretical context the present book responds to the paradigmatic change from political science and sociology to ethnology that has occurred in the last two decades.

The question of terminology is closely connected with methodological and theoretical problems. Since the colonialism model developed with reference to western Europe cannot easily be transferred to the Russian context, terms such as colony and colonial dependence will not be used without a close examination of the situation to which they might be applied. The frequent and wholesale use of the terms colonialism and imperialism when referring to Russia and the Soviet Union, especially by American scholars, conceals far more than it explains.

The terms nation and national (national consciousness, national movement, nationalities, etc.) are used only for the era of the modern nation, which began in the late eighteenth century and then spread, in a number of phases, through Europe and the rest of the world. In contrast to its use by Anglo-Saxon historians and in some recent work published in German, the term nationalism is not used as an all-embracing neutral concept for everything pertaining to the nation, but in the common German and Russian sense to signify an aggressive, exaggerated and chauvinistic national ideology. In the case of the pre-modern age – and in certain parts of the Russian empire this lasted well into the twentieth century – the terms ethnic group or ethnic (for example in combinations such as ethnic consciousness, etc.) are preferred.

The use of ethnonyms also constitutes a problem. Should the names of nations in common use today be projected on to the past, or should one use their historical titles? In view of this confusing plethora of names, which sometimes changed a number of times, and the often vacillating identity of the more than a hundred ethnic groups of the Russian empire, it has proved impossible to be strictly logical in this regard. As a rule I eschew the ethnonyms that were first introduced in the Soviet era. Thus the modern Komi are referred to as Zyrians (the ethnonym commonly used under the tsars), the Mari as Cheremiss, and so on. However, in cases where the old title might lead to misunderstandings, as in the case of the Kazakhs, who were referred to as Kirgiz in the Russian empire, or in that of the widely used term Tatar, which was also used for the modern Azerbaidzhanis, it has not been retained. Where an ethnic group gave itself a new name before 1917, I have used this. Thus Ukrainians are not referred to as Little Russians or Ruthenes. The Moldavians, who constitute the Romanian-speaking population of Bessarabia, are referred to as Romanians (on languages and ethnonyms see Table 1).

A comprehensive modern history of the Russian multi-ethnic empire does not exist, not even in Russian. The main reason for this is the constricted view of the nation state, which began to prevail at the very moment when modern historical scholarship came into being. By contrast, in the age of the Enlightenment, historians were still very much interested in Russia as a multi-ethnic empire. Johann Gottlieb Georgi's *Beschreibung aller Nationen des Russischen Reiches* [A Description of all the Nations of the Russian Empire], which describes the 'lifestyle, religion, customs, dwellings, clothes and other noteworthy matters' of more than sixty ethnic groups, went through several editions at the end of the eighteenth century.[6] The French historian Levesque considered it apposite to follow up his voluminous history of Russia with a two-volume *Histoire des différents peuples soumis à la domination des Russes* that was clearly modelled on Georgi's work.[7] Heinrich Storch, in his *Historisch-Statistisches Gemälde des Russischen Reiches* [Historical and Statistical Description of the Russian Empire], also places considerable emphasis on its multi-ethnic composition.[8] This multi-ethnic approach subsequently fell into disfavour. The great Russian historians of the nineteenth century, Karamzin, Soloviev, Kliuchevsky and Platonov, wrote national history, like the majority of historians in other countries.[9] As a result, the history of the Russian multi-ethnic empire became Russian history pure and simple.

At the beginning of the 1950s the work of two scholars of pre-Soviet Russian origin represented the first attempt in the west to write a comprehensive modern history of the multi-ethnic empire. *La Formation de l'Empire russe* by the Russian émigré Boris Nolde is still the only work that attempts to give a comprehensive account of the subject. Unfortunately it was never finished. However, its description of the early stages of Russian expansion continues to be of value on account of its close adherence to the sources.[10] Georg von Rauch, a Baltic German, concentrated on the contrast between 'the unity of the state and national diversity' and the notion that this might be supplanted by a federal structure.[11]

The *Geschichte der orientalischen Völker Rußlands* by the orientalist Emanuel Sarkisyanz was devoted largely to the pre-Russian period and cultural matters.[12] More than two decades later the American historian Edward Thaden published an illuminating account of the history of the western parts of the Russian empire, which ranged from the eighteenth century to the 1860s. It was preceded by a study of russification in the Baltic provinces and Finland towards the end of the tsarist era.[13] In 1982, in a case study devoted to the ethnic groups of the central Volga, I closely examined the origins of the Russian multi-ethnic empire.[14]

Several collections of essays by American scholars concentrate primarily on the Soviet Union, though some of the contributors also turn their attention to the pre-revolutionary multi-ethnic empire. The articles by Marc Raeff and S. Frederick Starr, which contain stimulating and perceptive observations and ideas on Russian policy on nationalities and on the tsarist multi-ethnic empire, are of especial interest.[15] Two volumes on 'Russian imperialism' and 'Russian colonial expansion' deal exclusively with the tsarist empire. However, although they contain some interesting articles, they do not form a coherent and comprehensive interpretation of the facts.[16]

In the lengthy surveys contained in the *History of the USSR*, Soviet historians included the regions which became part of the Soviet Union, though not Poland or Finland, which later became independent states. Non-Russians were not integrated into the history of the Russian empire. Rather, short sections devoted to their histories were appended to the main account, which had a pronounced Russian national bias.[17] Apart from this the work was divided between the historians at the centre and those in the republics, with the net result that comprehensive accounts of the multi-ethnic empire as a whole did not appear.

Furthermore, very little work was published on the historic regions (Middle Asia, the steppes, the Baltic provinces, the central Volga, etc.), which in the Soviet era were divided up into several administrative districts.[18] Admittedly, the historiographies of the various Soviet republics grew in institutional terms and became more professional after the death of Stalin. However, they remained under central control. Research on politically sensitive questions connected with the Russian multi-ethnic empire was made particularly difficult by the official ideology, which legitimated the conquests made under the tsarist empire. Thus the compulsory axioms of 'the friendship of the peoples' and 'the progressive union with Russia' are omnipresent in historical works from the 1950s to the 1980s. Non-Russian resistance movements were usually dismissed as being reactionary and feudal, and national movements denounced as reactionary and bourgeois. Many areas concerning relations between Russia and non-Russians remained taboo. In the 1920s and the early 1930s some publications still took a much more positive line in this regard, either on account of their approach to the subject, which interpreted Russian policy as colonialism and the tsarist empire as a 'prison of peoples', as Lenin put it, or on account of the publication of sources which, unlike in the years that followed, were not as yet carefully selected.[19] Since the advent of glasnost and perestroika, which historians greeted with some hesitation, no new studies of the Russian multi-ethnic empire have been published. However, it is noticeable that in the latter part of the 1980s non-Russian historians began to liberate themselves from the shackles of dogmatic uniformity. In the Russian centre, on the other hand, traditional Russocentric attitudes and prejudices have survived unscathed, and in an era of national reawakening in Russia speedy reorientation seems unlikely.

The history of the various ethnic groups and regions has received much greater coverage than that of the Russian multi-ethnic empire as a whole. This is particularly true of the Poles and the Finns, who, after the First World War, were able to establish independent states and historiographies. In the case of Poland, however, the politically sensitive nature of research into the former eastern territories of Poland-Lithuania, which had become part of the Soviet Union, meant that after 1945 it lagged far behind the research done on 'Congress Poland'. Whereas it is true that the national historiographies of the USSR produced a great deal of important work, especially on social and economic history, potentially explosive subjects such as subjugation and incorporation into the Russian Empire, national movements and policy on nationalities were either deliberately evaded or portrayed in a one-sided and ideological manner. For this reason it is generally necessary to consult works published in the west on these subjects. There are numerous publications on the history of the Baltic peoples, the Muslims of Middle Asia under Russian rule, the Jews and the Germans. However, the history of the Belorussians, the Romanians of Bessarabia and the Muslims of the Caucasus has been insufficiently researched. American historians have taken the lead in this area, and 'Studies of Nationalities in the USSR', an as yet incomplete series of publications edited by Wayne S. Vucinich, is of especial scholarly importance.[20]

Finally, there are some technical questions. The transliteration of names in dozens of languages and several alphabets poses an insoluble problem. In doubtful cases I have decided in favour of the Russian version that was current in the Russian empire and which has become commonly accepted among scholars, even if it means that thereby I may be accused of being Russocentric. Broadly speaking, Cyrillic names have been transliterated in accordance with the Library of Congress system, but hard and soft signs have been omitted except in bibliographical references, name-endings in -ii have been altered to -y, and technically inaccurate forms have been retained if they are familiar in English.

The list of sources consulted and the specialist literature includes all those works to which I make frequent reference. They are cited in abbreviated form in the footnotes. Suggestions for further reading are also given in the footnotes. I have given precedence to publications in German, English and French, though where necessary I have also included references to works published in Russian, Polish and Ukrainian.

I owe a debt of gratitude to numerous individuals and institutions. I was able to work on aspects of the subject within the framework of two research projects. The first of these, which was funded by the Deutsche Forschungsgemeinschaft, was devoted to analyzing the data relating to the nationalities of the empire that is contained in the Russian census of 1897. I also participated in the European Science Foundation project on 'Governments and non-dominant ethnic groups in Europe, 1850–1940'.[21] Parts of the manuscript were read by my colleagues Fikret Adanir, Manfred Alexander, Otto Dann, Uwe Halbach, Hans-Henning Hahn, Sirje Kivimäe and Gerhard Simon, and by Ernst-Peter Wieckenberg of Verlag C. H. Beck. I am indebted to all of them for their critical comments and for correcting points of detail. My thanks are due both to those who have provided me with financial support and to my fellow historians with whom I have engaged in scholarly discourse. Finally, I would like to thank my students at the University of Cologne for their stimulating written work and critical comments.

Notes

1   See for example Mark (1989); Nahaylo and Swoboda (1990); and Stölting (1990), cited in Chapter 10, note 7. Simon (1986) remains the standard work on the time before 1985.

2   For some valuable insights see Seton-Watson (1977), a general survey which also refers to Russia.

3   I have described the interaction of Russians and the ethnic groups of the central Volga elsewhere (Kappeler 1982b).

4   See Anthony D. Smith, *The Ethnic Origins of Nations* (Oxford, 1986).

5   See von Albertini (1976); Reinhard (1983–88); and Bitterli (1986).

6   Georgi (1776–80).

7   M. Levesque, *Histoire des différents peuples soumis à la domination des Russes ou suite de l'histoire de Russie* I–II (Paris, 1783).

8   Storch (1797–99).

9   See Seymour Becker, 'Contributing to a Nationalist Ideology: Histories of Russia in the First Half of the Nineteenth Century', *RH* 13 (1986), 331–53; Carl Reddel, 'S. M. Solov'ev and Multi-National History', *RH* 13 (1986), 355–66; Robert Byrnes, 'Kliuchevskii on the Multi-National Russian State', *RH* 13 (1986), 313–30.

10 Nolde I–II (1952–53).

11 von Rauch (1953). See also an essay by another Baltic German, Reinhard Wittram, 'Das russische Imperium und sein Gestaltwandel', *Historische Zeitschrift* 187 (1959), 568–93.

12 Sarkisyanz (1961).

13 Thaden (1984); (1981).

14 Kappeler (1982b).

15 Raeff (1971); Starr (1978). See also Marc Raeff, 'Un Empire comme les autres?', *CMRS* 30 (1989), 321–7.

16 Hunczak (1974); Rywkin (1988).

17 *Istoriia SSSR* (1966–68). On the historiography of the nationalities of the USSR in general see Tillett (1969); Albrecht Martiny, 'Das Verhältnis von Politik und Geschichtsschreibung in der Historiographie der sowjetischen Nationalitäten seit den sechziger Jahren', *JbbGO* 27 (1979), 238–72; Andreas Kappeler, 'Die Historiographien der nichtrussischen Völker der RSFSR in den siebziger Jahren', *JbbGO* 29 (1981), 53–79.

18 *Istoriia narodov* (1988) and Alishev (1990) are recent exceptions.

19 See for example Drabkina (1930); *Kolonial'naia politika* (1936).
20 To date the following have been published: Fisher (1978); Rorlich (1986); Olcott (1987); Raun (1987); Suny (1989); Allworth (1990).
21 Findings published in *Die Nationalitäten* (1991); Kappeler (1992b).

I

The Mediaeval Background

THE HISTORY of the Russian multi-ethnic empire begins in 1552 with the conquest of Kazan by the Muscovite tsar, Ivan IV, the Terrible. The majority of scholars both within and outside the former Soviet Union are of this opinion, and they are supported by Russian folk tradition. It is possible to adduce a number of good reasons for such views. The Khanate of Kazan was the first independent polity to come under Russian rule which possessed a historical tradition, dynastic legitimacy and an upper class which not only spoke a different language but also belonged to a different world religion and civilization, Islam. However, the date traditionally assigned to the transition from an ethnically fairly uniform to a multi-ethnic Russia obscures the fact that the population of the Muscovite state and that of the other eastern Slav principalities had always been diverse in ethnic and religious terms, and that some of the nationalities of the former Soviet Union had been under Russian control since the Middle Ages.[1]

The population of the first polity of the eastern Slavs, the Kievan Rus, included a considerable proportion of tribes who spoke Finnish and Baltic languages, a small number of Turkic-speaking soldiers, and, in the early period, Scandinavian Varangians. The early principalities into which the Kievan realm was divided in the twelfth century were not ethnically uniform either. As the Russian historian V. O. Kliuchevsky has pointed out, the new ethnic group of the Great Russians began to emerge at this time in the north-eastern part of Rus as a result of the interaction of eastern Slav and Finnish-speaking tribes.[2]

A vast empire centred on the city state of Novgorod and inhabited by numerous non-Slav ethnic groups arose between the eleventh and fourteenth centuries in the north-western part of the area settled by eastern Slavs. An inner circle of Finnish-speaking tribes to the north – Karelians, Vots, Izhora (Ingrians) and Veps – was ruled directly from Novgorod, and an outer circle was subject to loose tributary rule. They included the Finnish-speaking Lapps in the far north, and, further to the north-east, the Zyrians and Permiaks, who were also Finnish-speaking, the Ugric-speaking Ostiaks and Voguls, and the Samoyeds (see Table 1) Novgorod exacted tribute from the hunters and fishermen of the north-east, if necessary with military force. Its most important component consisted of costly furs, which were exported from Novgorod via the Hanseatic cities to western Europe. Furs, and sable in particular, drew Russian soldiers and trappers from Novgorod for thousands of kilometres to the northern Urals. Yet the inner socio-political structure and the animist value system of the remote tribes remained untouched. Loyal tribal chiefs were left in place, and were responsible for collecting tribute. This first great eastward movement of the Russians via the river system of the north preceded the similar conquest of Siberia.

On the other hand, the Finnish-speaking ethnic groups of the inner circle, which subsisted largely on agriculture and forestry, were directly subject to the rule of Novgorod. The areas in which they lived were gradually settled by Russian peasants, and came into the possession of secular and ecclesiastical landowners from Novgorod. They were also converted to the Orthodox faith: to this day the Orthodox church continues to constitute the main difference between Karelians and Finns. However, the integration of non-Slav ethnic groups did not always take the form of peaceful acculturation, and the sources also reveal that there was armed resistance to the rule of Novgorod. In addition to this, the King of Sweden laid claim to the Karelians, and thus they frequently became the victims of border conflicts between Novgorod and Sweden.

Between the twelfth and the fifteenth centuries, the Novgorod state already possessed a series of features which were to become characteristic of the later Russian multi-ethnic empire: a variety of motives for expansion, the two types of direct and indirect rule, and the stepwise incorporation of non-Russians that led from economic to administrative subservience, and thence to social, religious and cultural integration.

In the principalities of the north-east, and in the Grand Duchy of Muscovy, which advanced to become the predominant power in the fourteenth and fifteenth centuries, Russians lived side by side with Finnish-speaking ethnic groups. However, the majority of the aboriginal inhabitants (Merya, Muroma and Ves) were assimilated in linguistic and religious terms in a process of acculturation that took several centuries, and they disappear from the sources in the fourteenth century. Only the western Mordvinians on the eastern tributaries of the Oka, who had been subjugated by Russian princes in the thirteenth century, retained the status of an independent ethnic group in the Muscovite state. Since the fourteenth century, Muscovy had extended its influence in the north-east to the Zyrians and the Permiaks, who nominally owed allegiance to Novgorod. In this the mission to the Zyrians of Bishop Stephen of Perm, who was later canonized, played an important role. It was the first example of missionary activity helping the cause of Russian expansion. However, both the mission and the flexible methods of Christianization, which was carried out with the help of sermons in the Zyrian language, and of translations written in a newly devised Zyrian alphabet, were to remain the exception in the history of Russian expansion.

The conquest of Novgorod by Ivan III in 1478 finally imparted a multi-ethnic character to the Grand Duchy of Muscovy. Furthermore, the Viatka district, which was conquered in 1489, was inhabited not only by Russians, but also by Finnish-speaking Votiaks and Cheremis, by Besermians, who were probably descendants of settlers of Volga Bulgar origin, and by a small Tatar elite. The majority of the non-Russian ethnic groups are mentioned in the testament of Ivan III (1503–04), and, in his famous book on Russia, the Austrian diplomat Sigismund von Herberstein, who went to Moscow twice at the beginning of the sixteenth century, describes the Karelians, Lapps, the Samoyeds, the Permians (i.e. Zyrians and the Permiaks), the Cheremis (partly confusing them with the Votiaks), the Mordvinians and the Ugric-speaking ethnic groups of the Urals, whose language he already described as being related to that of the Hungarians.[3]

However, in numerical terms these non-Russian ethnic groups were only small peripheral entities. The vast majority of the inhabitants of the Muscovite state in the first half of the sixteenth century were Great Russians. It was more Russian and Orthodox in character than its successors, and in ethnic and religious terms was considerably more homogeneous than any of its neighbours (Lithuania, Livonia, Sweden, the Khanates of Kazan, Sibir and Crimea), or, for that matter, than Poland and Hungary, the great kingdoms of eastern central Europe.

The non-Russian ethnic groups, which were part of the Muscovite state before the middle of the sixteenth century, can be divided into four different types that are subsequently encountered on numerous occasions:

1. Ethnic groups that engaged in agriculture and forestry, which were integrated in administrative, economic and social terms, which had accepted the Orthodox faith, at least nominally, whose elite no longer existed, and whose territory was also settled by Russian peasants. This type included the Karelians, Veps and Izhora in the north-west, and the Zyrians and Permiaks in the north-east. It is noteworthy that these groups – especially the Karelians and the Zyrians (now known as Komi) – have preserved their ethnic identity to this day, after more than 700 years of Russian rule and acculturation. However, they have been Russified to a greater extent than most of the other nationalities of the former Soviet Union.

2. The hunters, fishermen and reindeer herdsmen of the northern and north-eastern periphery, where there were no Russian settlers and the climate was harsh. They were subject to a loose tributary rule that left their inner socio-political structures and animist religion untouched. Their most important function for the centre was an economic one. Tribute was paid in kind, and consisted largely of furs, and to some extent of fish and walrus tusks. In the first half of the sixteenth century this group included the Samoyeds, Lapps, Ostiaks and Voguls.

3. Somewhere between these two types were the Mordvinians, Cheremis, Votiaks and Besermians on the borders of the Khanate of Kazan. They engaged primarily in agriculture and forestry, and their areas had to some extent been integrated in administrative and economic terms, and had already been reached by Russian settlers. However, they retained a non-Russian elite and their animist value system.

4. The fourth type consisted of the small though in qualitative terms important groups of foreigners who were residents of the Muscovite state and performed specific functions for its rulers. First, there were Tatars who had entered the service of the Grand Duke. They either supplied highly effective cavalry units that considerably strengthened the Muscovite armies, or were given land near the border in order to guard it against incursions from the steppes. In this respect they were the direct predecessors of the eastern Slav Cossacks. Originally this was also a task assigned to the Khanate of Kasimov, which was founded in the middle of the fifteenth century on the river Oka. Although its Tatar rulers were vassals of the Muscovite Grand Duke, it managed for more than two

centuries to retain its traditional socio-political order and Islamic religion. If they decided to settle permanently in the Muscovite state, Tatar noblemen became members of its aristocracy. This type may be regarded as a precursor of the later Russian practice of co-opting foreign elites and assigning complementary functions to them. The category also included foreigners from western and southern Europe. Under Ivan III these were primarily Greek and Italian specialists who were active in the fields of administration and diplomacy, or worked in technical professions. They also included architects and painters.

The traditions of the early Muscovite multi-ethnic realm, which evolved in the Middle Ages, constituted an important group of preconditions for the multi-ethnic empire that came into being around the middle of the sixteenth century. A second cluster of preconditions is associated with the successful territorial expansion of the Muscovite state from the fourteenth century onwards, which is commonly known as 'the gathering of the lands of Rus'.[4] In less than two centuries the small and politically insignificant principality of Muscovy became the largest European state in terms of size, although the vast taiga and tundra areas in the north and the north-east, which had originally belonged to Novgorod, were very sparsely populated. In the course of 'the gathering of the lands of Rus' the Muscovite rulers developed the basic patterns of an expansionist policy which made use of a number of different methods. They included an astute kind of diplomacy which made frequent use of the technique of *divide et impera*, wooed the support of foreign elites, and secured their allegiance; a stepwise strategy that led from protectorates whose status was sealed by a declaration of loyalty to complete annexation at a later date; the acquisition by purchase of smaller territories; military conquest and brutal repression; the legitimation of annexations with political arguments, such as the charge of collaboration with Muscovy's foreign enemies, or historical ones, such as the claim that the territories of the former Grand Duchy of Vladimir were the 'patrimony' (votchina) of the Muscovite rulers. In the case of the incorporation of the territories of Novgorod, Viatka and Pskov, the Grand Dukes of Muscovy proceeded in a particularly brutal manner, destroying the socio-political order, which differed considerably from that of Muscovy, and resettling a large part of the aristocratic elite and the merchants in the central areas of the Muscovite state.

Flexible diplomacy and conquest were also in evidence in the course of the conflict with Poland-Lithuania. At the end of the fifteenth and at the beginning of the sixteenth centuries this led to the incorporation of a series of eastern Slav principalities that had been conquered by the Grand Duke of Lithuania in the fourteenth and early fifteenth centuries. An important expansionist element in this context was the fact that certain eastern Slav Orthodox princes voluntarily switched their allegiance to the Muscovite state. The Grand Duke of Muscovy, who now styled himself 'Ruler of all Rus', developed the gathering of the lands of Rus into a claim to the patrimony of the whole realm of Kiev. In this he received support from the Metropolitan of the Orthodox Church, who resided in Moscow. The ensuing conflict with Poland-Lithuania for control of those areas inhabited by Orthodox eastern Slavs was a foregone conclusion. It was to determine the shape of later Russian foreign policy up to the partitions of Poland at the end of the eighteenth century and the events of 1939. The annexation of the 'Severian' principalities on the Desna, and of the principality of Smolensk at the beginning of the sixteenth century first brought Ukrainians and Belorussians under Muscovite rule. However, contemporary sources do not as yet refer to ethnic differences between the eastern Slavs, who are all referred to as Rus.

A third cluster of mediaeval preconditions for the multinational Russian empire derives from the fact that for a number of centuries the north-eastern Rus were part of the Golden Horde. With the decline of the vast Mongolian empire in the fifteenth century there began a struggle for its inheritance. This question is dealt with at the start of the next chapter, which, in analogy to the familiar concept of 'the gathering of the lands of Rus', is entitled 'The Gathering of the Lands of the Golden Horde'.

Notes

1   This chapter is primarily based on Kappeler (1986), which also contains suggestions for further reading. See also Ia. A. Kizilov, *Zemli i narody Rossii v 13–15 vv.* (Moscow, 1984); Janet Martin, 'Russian Expansion in the Far North: Tenth to Mid-Sixteenth Century', in Rywkin (1988), 23–43.

2   V. O. Kliuchevsky, *Sochineniia* I (Moscow, 1956), pp. 292–315.

3   *Dukhovnye i dogovornye gramoty velikikh i udel'nykh knyazei 14–16 vv.* (Moscow and

Leningrad, 1950), pp. 356 f.; Herberstein (1984), pp. 171 f., 198 f., 206–11, 286–92. The passages omitted in this shortened version in Herberstein, *Moscovia* . . . (Vienna, 1557), p. M IIIv.

4 See Stökl (1990), pp. 193–203; *Handbuch* I, pp. 635–52.

2

The Gathering of the Lands of the Golden Horde between the Sixteenth and Eighteenth Centuries

O N 2 OCTOBER 1552 a large Russian army commanded by the young tsar, Ivan IV, took the city of Kazan. A contemporary official Russian chronicle described the occasion thus:

> With the help of Our almighty Lord Jesus Christ and the prayers of the Mother of God . . . our Orthodox tsar and Grand Duke Ivan Vasilevich, crowned by God and autocrat of all Rus, fought the infidels, and, at last prevailing, took prisoner the tsar of Kazan, Ediger Mahmet . . . and he took possession of the tsardom and populous city of Kazan. The tsar caused the women and little children to be taken prisoner, but all those who carried arms were put to death on account of their treason.[1]

The conquest of Kazan was an unparalleled step in the history of the Muscovite state. Whereas it had been possible to justify 'the gathering of the lands of Rus' on historical, dynastic and religious grounds, the annexation of a sovereign state that had never belonged to Rus, and was a part of the Mongolian empire, the political system established by Genghis Khan, and the Islamic community, went against all the traditional legal concepts. Thus in contemporary sources and in numerous works of Russian historiography the conquest is legitimated with a series of arguments that are often quite implausible. For example, it is depicted as a defensive measure against the incursions of the Kazan Tatars, as punishment for their treason, as a crusade against the infidels (as in the chronicle cited above), and as a liberation (requested by emissaries) from the yoke of the Khanate of Crimea and the Ottoman Empire. In direct analogy to the gathering of the lands of Rus, the Khanate is even described as Muscovite patrimony (votchina), and as 'an ancient land of Rus', a statement that is 'proved' with reference to dynastic claims reaching back to Kievan days.[2] I shall return later to the question of the motives behind Muscovy's conquest of Kazan. However, before I do so the perspective needs to be widened.

The conquest of the Khanate of Kazan and, four years later, of the Khanate of Astrakhan, were epoch-making events in the history of Russia and of the whole of Eurasia. The predominantly eastern Slav, Orthodox and north-east European Muscovite state had finally turned into a multi-ethnic empire with several religions. By gaining control of the Volga waterway and thus dividing the Eurasian steppe into two parts, the Muscovite rulers assumed the mantle of the Khans of the Golden Horde. For this reason Russian ostpolitik in the centuries that followed can be described as 'the gathering of the lands of the Golden Horde'.

The conquest of Rus by the Mongols between 1237 and 1240, and the ensuing period of Mongol and Tatar rule, which lasted for more than two centuries, constituted a profound caesura in the history of the eastern Slavs as a whole and of Russia in particular. However, for the Khans of the Golden Horde, which was the westernmost part of the former Mongol empire and reached from the Crimea to the steppes of Middle Asia and from the Caucasus to the north of Russia, peripheral Rus was not of primary importance.[3] Thus they restricted themselves to indirect rule, though this was enforced with military means whenever the need arose. The political, social and religious structures remained unchanged. The Khan merely retained the right to appoint the Grand Duke, and the unending conflicts between the various branches of the Rurikid dynasty gave him an opportunity to intervene in the domestic affairs of Rus as a kind of referee. Rus was also required to pay tribute, and this weighed heavily on it.

As a rule both the Grand Dukes of Muscovy, who succeeded in disposing of their rivals in Tver in the fourteenth century, and the Metropolitans of the Orthodox church remained loyal to the Mongolian Khans, and pursued a pragmatic policy towards the Golden Horde. The border separating sedentary settlers and steppe dwellers, and Christianity and Islam, marked off the eastern Slavs from the Tatars, though within the framework of the Golden Horde they were also linked by permanent political and economic contacts. In fact, the symbiosis between Rus and the Tatars is only imperfectly reflected in contemporary sources, which are almost exclusively of ecclesiastical origin and proclaim a fundamental antagonism between the true believers, the Russians, and the Tatar infidels. The contrast between a policy of pragmatic cooperation and a doctrine of conflicting religions and lifestyles has been one of the basic features of the ambivalent relationship between the eastern Slavs and the steppe dwellers and Islam from the time of Kievan Rus to modern times.[4]

From the middle of the fourteenth century onwards the political system of the Golden Horde began to go into decline. As a result a whole series of successor states began to compete for the inheritance of the immense empire, and for control of the route across the steppes to the north of the Caspian Sea and the Black Sea. The most important rivals were the Great Horde, its formal successor on the lower Volga; the Khanates of Crimea and of Kazan; the Nogai Horde; and (smaller and less powerful) the Khanates of Astrakhan and Sibir. The Grand Duchy of Muscovy, which had itself been part of the Golden Horde, also participated in this struggle, as did Poland-Lithuania and (more unobtrusively) the Ottoman Empire. The first victory over a Tatar army in 1380 was a turning point for Muscovy, and in the years that followed the Grand Dukes played an astute part in the inheritance struggles. Here again they were able to secure the support of members of the elites of other successor states. Numerous Tatars of noble birth were given land, and in return they provided cavalry units and were accepted into the Muscovite aristocracy as equals.

The struggle for the inheritance of the Golden Horde followed the rules laid down by the Mongols and the world of the steppes.[5] They included respect for the dynasty of Genghis Khan; respect for foreign religions and cultures; frequently changing coalitions based on personal allegiance; and levying tribute and appointing rulers as a sign of submission. But they did not include demands for the surrender of sovereignty or for integration into another territory. However, the steppe code of conduct was at variance with the principle of patrimony that had arisen in sedentary Muscovy. Thus, when rulers of the steppe swore oaths of allegiance to the Muscovite Grand Duke, they were interpreted in Muscovy as acts of eternal submission, whereas they may simply have been intended to demonstrate temporary subservience, or even construed merely as alliances. The Muscovites treated secession from Muscovy as treason, whereas the steppe dwellers believed they were exercising their right to enter into new alliances. The irreconcilable nature of such fundamentally different traditions was to play an important role in the relations between Russia and the steppe right up to the nineteenth century. It is a role that is often overlooked in the kind of historiography dominated by representatives of 'sedentary' cultures.

In the second half of the fifteenth century, Muscovy entered into an alliance with Crimea against the Great Horde, which received support from Poland-Lithuania. In 1480 this enabled Muscovy to free itself formally from the rule of the Golden Horde, and, a few years later, to install an acquiescent member of the Genghis Khan dynasty as ruler of Kazan. The Grand Duke subsequently made this the one-sided basis for the claim that Kazan was under Muscovite suzerainty. At the beginning of the sixteenth century, the growing power of Muscovy and the final decline of the Great Horde led to a new set of alliances. The Crimean Khan now allied himself with Poland-Lithuania against Muscovy, and in 1521 installed a member of his dynasty as ruler of Kazan. This led to an even more intense struggle for the inheritance of the Golden Horde. The Crimean Tatars made incursions into areas controlled by Muscovy, and Muscovy intensified its efforts to regain control of the Khanate of Kazan, which now owed allegiance to the Khanate of Crimea.

1. The Foundations of the Russian Multi-ethnic Empire: The Conquest of the Khanates of Kazan and Astrakhan

The Khanate of Kazan occupied a special position among the successor states of the Golden Horde.[6] Its socio-political organization certainly corresponded to the pattern established by the Golden Horde, with a theoretically omnipotent ruler from the dynasty of Genghis Khan and a Tatar aristocracy, which in practice curtailed his power considerably. However, it was not a steppe polity with a population of nomads, and in the main consisted of arable land and forests. 'These Tatars', the Austrian diplomat Herberstein noted in the first half of the sixteenth century, 'are more human than the others, live in houses, till the soil, engage in trade, and seldom go to war'.[7] The traditions of non-nomadic Islamic civilization on the central Volga reached back to the tenth century, when the Volga Bulgars founded a kingdom that played an important role in political terms and as a pivot of trade between the orient and the Baltic. Thus the Khanate of Kazan was the heir of two traditions, that of the Volga Bulgar state, and that of the Golden Horde.

The population of the Khanate consisted primarily of five ethnic groups. The Turkic-speaking and Islamic Kazan Tatars formed the social and political elite: they served in cavalry units or in the administration, and in return were given grants of land. Kazan, the sizeable capital, which had a population of about 20,000, was the centre of the Volga trade, and was inhabited by Tatar merchants, craftsmen, clergymen and scholars. The literature, historiography and architecture of the Kazan Tatars formed an outpost of Islamic civilization on the eastern fringe of Europe. Whilst it is true that there was also a class of Tatar peasants, the majority of the rural population of the Khanate consisted of non-Tatars. South of the Volga lived Turkic-speaking Chuvash and Finnish-speaking eastern Mordvinians, who were primarily farmers, fishermen and forest bee-keepers. Mostly to the north of the Volga lived the Finnish-speaking Cheremis and southern Votiaks, for whom hunting also played an important role. Representatives of all four non-Tatar ethnic groups had to pay tribute, known as iasak, to the Khan. Members of the upper class were responsible for its collection. Otherwise they were left largely to their own devices, and lived in communities that were characterized by tribal and clan relationships and religious ideas of an animist kind.

Thus the Khanate of Kazan did not differ significantly in its economic habits and socio-political organization, and with regard to the level of economic and cultural development, from the Muscovite state. However, this qualitative equality went hand in hand with quantitative inferiority. The Khanate, the territory of which was rather small, possessed considerably fewer economic and human resources and was ethnically and politically less uniform than the Muscovite state, which in the first half of the sixteenth century had advanced to become a great power that had consolidated its position externally and internally.

Despite this considerable increase in power, Muscovite policy towards Kazan remained within the framework of traditional steppe politics, even after the escalation of 1521. By using military and economic pressure (for example, a trade boycott) and the well-tried method of attracting the support of part of the Tatar elite, Muscovy sought to reinstall a khan who was well-disposed towards it and thereby to secure the allegiance of Kazan. This proved successful in 1532, 1546 and 1551, though on each occasion the Muscovite pretender was soon ousted. The decisive steps leading up to annexation were first taken in 1551, when the fortress of Sviiazhsk was constructed on the territory of the Khanate, and when the part of the Khanate which lay on the right bank of the Volga was incorporated into the Muscovite state. It was only in the spring of 1552, after a final attempt to install a puppet khan had failed, that the decision was taken to conquer Kazan and to annex the whole of the Khanate.

A mere two years later Muscovy installed a ruler of its choice in Astrakhan. When the latter joined forces with the Khan of Crimea, a Russian army conquered the city. In 1556 Muscovy then proceeded to annex the Khanate of Astrakhan. Primarily inhabited by Tatars, this khanate was organized on lines that resembled those of the other states that succeeded the Golden Horde. However, it was much smaller and weaker than the Khanate of Kazan. The Khan of Astrakhan was dependent on the Nogai Tatars, who led nomadic lives on the steppe and were divided into rival clans. One of the Nogai hordes was actually in league with Muscovy (see below, Section 3). The city of Astrakhan, which was situated on the Volga delta, was extremely important, both in strategic terms and as a centre of trade. By conquering Astrakhan, the tsar not only gained control of the whole of the Volga waterway, but also secured an opening to the Caspian Sea and thus to the markets of Iran. He was now in a position to close off the route across the steppes from the Crimea to Middle Asia. Furthermore, and this is emphasized in the chronicles, Astrakhan was not far from Sarai, the former capital of the Golden Horde: its possessor was able to consider himself to be the heir of the great Mongol empire.

But why, we are once again prompted to ask, did Muscovy, in the 1550s, break the rules of steppe politics in the context of the struggle for the inheritance of the Golden Horde and begin to annex the territories of its rivals? Historians have given a number of rather different answers to this question. There can be no doubt that military and strategic considerations played a role, as did economic factors (the Volga trade, and reserves of land for the Muscovite service nobility). Of crucial importance for the qualitative leap that led to conquest and annexation was the new self-image that the young tsar and his court began to develop at this time. It revolved around a sense of their imperial mission, and this found expression both in the tsar's coronation in 1547, and in legends that traced claims to legitimacy back to Kiev, Byzantium and even to Rome. This imperial ideology was not, as historians used to claim in the past, based on the doctrine of 'Muscovy, the third Rome' and on the idea of a *translatio imperii* from Constantinople to Moscow, but on the emphasis placed on the development of Rus itself, of the Rurikid dynasty and its successful policy of expansion in the 'gathering of the lands of Rus'. The sense of empire was increased by the struggle for the inheritance of the empire of the Golden Horde. Possession of Kazan and Astrakhan, the seats of legitimate rulers of the Genghis Khan dynasty, who were called tsars in Russia, considerably enhanced the nimbus and the imperial pretensions of the tsar of Muscovy. And the new self-confidence also had a religious dimension. During the minority of Ivan IV the Orthodox church had increased its influence considerably. The new Metropolitan Makarii and the protopope Silvester were among the leading personalities at the Muscovite court. As Archbishop of Novgorod, Makarii in particular had pursued a policy of aggressive Christianization, and after 1549 the Metropolitan had issued several calls for a crusade against 'the impious sons of Hagar', the 'treacherous, accursed and ungodly Kazan Tatars'.[8] Thus the campaign against Kazan and the conquest of the city – at least in the version given in the chronicles – took the form of a crusade against Islam. In these years with a weak ruler and a powerful church, the pendulum of the ambivalent attitude to the steppe and to Islam swung from the pragmatic approach that had long been predominant to aggressive confrontation.

Muscovite policy initially pursued the aggressive aims that have already been mentioned. The call by the tsar's influential adviser, the protopope Silvester, to convert the Muslims and animists of the Khanate to Christianity, and to use force if necessary, was obeyed. Thus the male population of the town of Kazan was put to death, mosques were razed to the ground, and Orthodox churches erected in their stead. The khan and other Tatars of noble birth were deported to the interior of the Muscovite state and baptized. If they refused, they were put to death by drowning.

Yet Muscovy altered its policy as early as 1555. Guri, the newly appointed archbishop of Kazan, was, it is true, also ordered to baptize the Tatars. However, it was emphasized that this was to be done without the use of force.[9] As a result, missionary activity among the ethnic groups of the central Volga region practically came to a standstill for more than a century. In other areas Muscovy also switched from an aggressive to a flexible policy. There are two possible explanations for this. First, in 1553 the tsar's serious illness led to an internal political crisis, as a result of which Ivan IV began increasingly to emancipate himself from his advisers. In this way the traditionally pragmatic policy of the state once again triumphed over the aggressive and intolerant church. However, events in the conquered Khanate of Kazan made restraint seem advisable. Tatars and non-Tatars (especially the Cheremis) rose up against the foreign rule imposed upon them once the Russian troops had left, and attempted in a series of uprisings that lasted for five years to regain their independence. Muscovy was able to crush the rebellions by 1557 only after several lengthy campaigns and the implementation of carrot-and-stick policies.

The methods with which Muscovy, in the decades that followed, incorporated the Khanates of Kazan and Astrakhan, the first independent states with political traditions and a civilization that differed from that of Rus, also served as a model for the later 'policy on nationalities'. They made use simultaneously of the traditions of steppe politics, of the 'gathering of the lands of Rus', and of the Novgorod and Muscovite policy towards non-Slav ethnic groups. Since little is known about the policies pursued in the case of Astrakhan, I shall concentrate on the former Khanate of Kazan.[10]

It is necessary to distinguish between two basic policies. The repressive variety was designed to secure the loyalty of new subjects, and this was a top priority. Revolts were consistently put down with military force. This happened in 1570–72 and 1581–84, when the Cheremis and Tatars once again rose up against Muscovite rule. At the same time Muscovy established a system of fortresses in order to control the areas concerned and to defend them against possible attacks from without. The need for this was demonstrated by repeated incursions by Crimean and Nogai Tatars, and by an Ottoman campaign against Astrakhan in 1569. In addition to numerous fortresses on the territory of the former Khanate, three were built in the 1580s to protect the Volga route to Astrakhan. Shortly after the conquest of Kazan the Muscovites built a line of border defences that were designed to protect the right bank of the Volga against incursions from the steppe. In the seventeenth century this was extended further south and complemented by the 'Trans-Kama' line on the left bank of the Volga. Further measures designed to pacify the non-Russians are first documented in the seventeenth century. They were forbidden to possess weapons or even metal objects of any kind, and they had to give hostages (amanaty) who were required to live in the Russian administrative centre. The direct incorporation of the khanate into the Muscovite system of local government districts (uezd) can to some extent be explained by security concerns, and the Russian voevods who were in command of these administrative units also had military functions. But up to a point the khanate as a whole retained a special status, and was governed from a separate central department (Prikaz Kazanskogo Dvortsa).

The Muscovite policy of incorporation was also governed by economic considerations. The city of Kazan was taken over by Russians, and Russian merchants were ordered to settle in it. Only a small number of Tatars were permitted to live in a single suburb. In this way the latter were deprived of their economic and cultural centre and driven into rural areas. The towns of the khanate became Russian enclaves in a non-Russian environment. The Archbishop of Kazan and Russian monasteries were given grants of land, fishing rights and trade privileges. The land that had belonged to the khan or to aristocrats who had been executed or deported, or had fled, was given to Russian noblemen who had served the tsar, and to free peasants. Muscovy's interest in the Volga trade, the bees of the forest, the rich Volga fisheries and the salt lakes of Astrakhan is clearly apparent in the sources.

However, the fierce resistance movements had taught the Muscovite government that only a policy of prudent restraint would be able to secure the loyalty of the inhabitants of the Khanate of Kazan and, in the long term, economic benefits. This flexible and pragmatic policy approach, which became even more apparent in the course of the incorporation of the Khanate of Astrakhan, was to remain the model for the pre-modern Russian 'policy on nationalities'. It was based on cooperation with loyal non-Russian elites and a far-reaching retention of the status quo. The continued use of existing traditions and institutions was designed to guarantee a smooth transfer of power and to underpin Muscovite legitimacy.

The ownership of land and the forest bee and beaver preserves of the surviving elite and the peasants were reconfirmed, as were their traditional privileges and tasks. Tatar horsemen and military units recruited from all five ethnic groups now served in the armies of the Muscovite tsar instead of in those of the tsars of Kazan or Astrakhan. The representatives of the non-Russian elite retained their functions in local government. The Tatar and Muslim landowning elite was co-opted into the Russian hereditary nobility, whereas the majority of the members of the animist elites, even though they had the status of 'service men' and were thus distinct from the mass of taxpayers, were not recognized by the Russian aristocracy as being of equal rank. A pattern which was to continue to be valid for many years to come began to emerge. Where a non-Russian elite had a social position that corresponded to that of the Russian aristocracy, it was deemed to be of the same rank. Where this was not so, as for example in the case of predominantly clan and tribal relationships, there was cooperation with the non-Russian elite, but it was not co-opted into the empire's nobility.

With regard to the lower classes who were required to pay taxes, Muscovy continued to make use of the Mongolian system of taxation known as iasak. The peasants now had to pay iasak (in money or in kind, and to the same extent as before) into the Muscovite exchequer instead of that of Kazan (or Astrakhan). The legal status of the non-Russian peasants also remained unchanged. Despite the increase in the number of Russian landowners, and despite a great manpower shortage, it was forbidden to transform non-Russians into serfs or kholops. This policy was destined to remain in force in the centuries that followed. The Tatar, Chuvash, Mordvinian, Cheremis and Votiak peasants of the former Khanate of Kazan remained in the special category of 'iasak men' and, as state peasants, were later placed under the direct control of the state and its officials. Furthermore, after the initial missionary offensive had been called off, the value systems of the new subjects remained untouched until the eighteenth century. In the course of time Muscovy even permitted thousands of Orthodox Russians to work on the estates of Muslim Tatars, whereas, as we have seen, Russian aristocrats were forbidden to transform non-Russian peasants into serfs.

The fundamentally pragmatic character of the policies thus pursued continued to predominate until the end of the seventeenth century. It is documented by the phrase that occurs repeatedly in the instructions Muscovy sent to the local voevods, who were told to treat non-Russians 'with benevolence, courteousness and caution'. On the whole this proved to be a success. Whereas it is true that, as the revolts during the time of unrest at the beginning of the seventeenth century and under Stepan Razin (1670–71) were to demonstrate, the protest potential among the ethnic groups of the central Volga was great, it proved possible to contain it, partly with the help of incorporated Tatar elites. The integration of the former Khanate of Kazan was also promoted by the mass immigration of Russian peasants, especially in the more fertile southern areas of the central Volga region. However, this led to new conflict potential in the shape of disputes concerning the ownership of land. It became more and more apparent that the basically pragmatic policy and flexible restraint advocated by the central government were not always implemented by the representatives of the regional adminis-tration. Cases of corruption, arbitrary rule and blatant discrimination against non-Russians were legion.

Muscovy was in full military control of the former Khanate of Kazan by the second half of the seventeenth century, so that economic interests and the profit (pribyl) accruing for the tsar, figure more pro-minently in the sources. With the exception of certain minor aspects of local government, the former khanate's special administrative status gradually disappeared. However, the social integration of the elites and the lower classes was still incomplete. Whereas it is true that the Tatar elite was co-opted into the Muscovite nobility, its Islamic religion was an obstacle to complete integration. And in some respects the legal and social status of the other non-Russians continued to be anomalous.

In the first half of the eighteenth century, the Russian state as reformed by Peter the Great departed from the Muscovite methods of pragmatic flexibility and adopted a policy of forced integration with regard to the various ethnic groups of the former Khanate of Kazan.[11] The goal of transforming Russia into a systematized, regulated and uniform absolutist state based on the western European model left no room for the rights and traditions of non-Russians that had been respected in the past. As a first step it was decided to end cooperation with the Muslim elites. Between 1680 and 1682, and then finally in 1713, Muslim landowners were ordered to convert to Christianity. Non-compliance with the injunction led to the confiscation of estates on which there were Christian Russian peasants.[12] This divided the Tatar elite. A small number, above all the wealthier landowners, converted to the Orthodox church. They retained their estates; their hereditary aristocratic status was confirmed (many of them even retained their traditional princely titles); and in the years that followed they were gradually russified. The majority, however, accepted the loss of their estates and remained faithful to Islam. In 1718 these Tatar aristocrats were demoted to a new population category that was comparable to that of Russian yeomen (odnodvortsy). It was subsequently assigned to the class of taxable state peasants who were not serfs.[13] The Tatars later described as *lashmany* were lumberjacks who were required to hew and transport timber for the naval construction programme. Many of them had lost their land and had turned their attention to trade instead.

The lower class of Mordvinian, Chuvash, Cheremis, Votiak and Tatar iasak men were deprived of their special status between 1718 and

1724, and were also incorporated into the category of state peasants. After having been accorded the same status as Russian peasants, their taxes and duties increased considerably. However, the state did not confine itself to social regularization. It now for the first time started to integrate in a systematic manner the animists and Muslims of the central Volga region in religious terms. Baptism already began to be encouraged under Peter the Great. In 1740 conversion to the Orthodox church was then enforced with the help of powerful economic pressure. Those who were baptized were not required to pay the poll tax for three years and generally freed from the duty of supplying recruits for the army. These burdens were then transferred to those who had not been baptized.[14] This measure in particular led to an avalanche of baptisms, and as a result the great majority of the Mordvinians, Chuvash, Cheremis and Votiaks became members of the Orthodox church. However, this kind of conversion to Christianity was only a formal act, and for a long time to come continued to be superficial. Although the forcible conversion to Christianity of the Islamic Tatars assumed an extremely aggressive character — 418 out of a total of 536 mosques were razed to the ground — it was largely unsuccessful, and in fact provoked fierce resistance.

For this reason the assault on Islam was called off as early as 1755, and after 1763 Catherine II repealed most of the discriminatory measures. From 1775 onwards, and under the banner of enlightened absolutism, she returned to the traditional cooperation with the Tatar elite, and in 1784 the Muslim aristocrats were once again incorporated into the Russian nobility, though without recovering the right to have Russian serfs.[15] The Tatar merchants were accorded trading privileges that were designed to enable them to open up the Kazakh steppe and Middle Asia in the Russian interest. In 1788 the Muslim clergy were reorganized in a special government department, the 'Assembly of Muslim Clergy', which was under the control of a mufti.

Thus the situation of the various ethnic groups in the former Khanate of Kazan had changed considerably by the end of the eighteenth century. In social terms they had largely been integrated into the Russian system of estates, and the Mordvinians, Cheremis, Chuvash and Votiaks had been brought into line with the Russians in religious terms. Nevertheless, the value systems and social relationships of the former animists remained largely intact, and the Islamic Kazan Tatars began to use their new freedom for an economic and cultural renaissance.

2. The Advance to Northern Asia: The Conquest and Penetration of Siberia

After the conquest of the Khanates of Kazan and Astrakhan Muscovy tried to expand westwards and reach the Baltic in the Livonian War. When, at the beginning of the 1580s, the attempt finally proved to be a failure, it began once more to turn its attention to 'the gathering the lands of the Golden Horde'. From Astrakhan it seemed logical to make another thrust into the steppes in the direction of the Caspian Sea and the Black Sea, and the tsar engaged in a great deal of diplomatic activity with this purpose in mind (see the following section). However, Russian forest dwellers had a great deal of respect for the open steppe, and in military terms they continued to be inferior to the nomadic cavalry until the eighteenth century.

Thus the east suggested itself as a second salient of expansion, and the path opened up after the fall of Kazan. To the east the Khan of Sibir, another successor of the Golden Horde, ruled over a wide and thinly populated area in the upper basin of the Ob. After the conquest of Kazan one ruler of the khanate had even accepted the tsar as his overlord, though a few years later the new khan, Kuchum, terminated the alliance with Muscovy. Clearly, expansion to Siberia was another stage in 'the gathering of the lands of the Golden Horde'. At the same time it was a continuation of the mediaeval movement towards the east by both Novgorod and Muscovy, when, as a result of the quest for furs, the tribes in the north and the north-east had been subjected to loose tributary rule.

In the present context the conquest and exploration of Siberia, an event of epoch-making importance, can only be described briefly and with especial emphasis on the formation of the Russian multi-ethnic empire.[16] The ethnic groups that inhabited Siberia in the sixteenth and seventeenth centuries can be divided into northern and southern on the basis of where they lived and the kind of economic activity they engaged in. Thus the ethnic groups of the northern taiga (coniferous zone) and the tundra had an extensive economy adapted to the extreme climatic conditions. They were organized into clans, and to a certain extent into larger tribal communities. The nomadic hunters and fishermen of the taiga were primarily Manchu-speaking Tungus and palaeo-Asiatic Iukagir, the nomadic reindeer herdsmen of the tundra and forest tundra Samoyeds, Tungus and – in the east – palaeo-Asiatic

33

Chukchi, Kamchadals and Koriaks. Small groups of fishermen and hunters of walrus and seals were sedentary. The ethnic groups of the southern taiga and forest steppe, where the climate was not so adverse and the soil rather better, were largely nomadic herdsmen who kept horses and both large and small domestic animals. On the whole they were organized on a tribal basis. The most important ethnic group was that of the Mongol-speaking Buriats in the vicinity of Lake Baikal. This southern group, apart from a few Turkic-speaking groups of hunters and fishermen (for example the Teleuts in the Altai or the Shor, who were described as being Tatars), is usually reckoned to include the Iakuts, who were also Turkic-speaking, although they had already moved from the steppe to the central Lena in the Middle Ages. In the far north they adhered to the traditions of nomadic herdsmen, and to some extent they adapted themselves to the local Tungusic groups. None of these Siberian ethnic groups had any political organization to speak of, and were split up into small units. The only sizeable political entity was the Khanate of western Siberia, in which, in addition to the Siberian Tatars who lived mainly on the edge of the steppe, where they engaged in animal husbandry and agriculture, there also lived Ugric-speaking Ostiaks and Voguls, hunters and fishermen who were required to pay iasak. With the exception of the Islamic Tatars, all of the Siberian ethnic groups professed shamanist native religions.

The initiative for Russian expansion to Siberia did not at first come from the state, but from the Stroganov family. Since the end of the fifteenth century, and with the support of the Muscovite government, these entrepreneurs had built up a semi-autonomous economic area in the north of Russia that was largely devoted to trade in salt and furs. The quest for furs drew the attention of the Stroganovs to the forests on the other side of the Urals, which were teeming with suitable animals. In 1581–82 a troop of Cossacks in their pay (which was led by Ermak, a man later described as a hero in Russian folk tradition) conquered the capital of the western Siberian Khanate on the lower Irtysh. The motives for and precise circumstances of this campaign continue to be a matter for debate. After some hesitation, Muscovy followed and secured the Khanate with numerous fortresses (1586, Tiumen; 1587, Tobolsk; 1604, Tomsk). This interplay of private, state and military initiative was to remain typical of the conquest of Siberia.

In the first half of the seventeenth century, Russian trappers, adventurers, merchants, Cossacks and detachments supplied by the regional military administration moved farther and farther east along the Siberian river systems. In doing so they avoided the steppe, which was in the hands of the Kazakhs and Mongols. Furs in general, and valuable sable in particular, continued to be the most important incentive for such surprisingly fast expansion over more than 6,000 kilometres.[17] The ruthless advance led to the swift decimation of the fur-bearing animals in the more easily accessible areas, which in turn led to the exploration of more remote areas. This endangered the fragile ecological balance. Walrus tusks and precious metals were also much in demand. The tsar was clearly interested in these commodities, and for this reason followed promptly, erecting forts and securing a considerable share of the economic advantages in the form of tribute and duties. The Enisei had been reached by 1607. In 1632 the fortress of Iakutsk was erected on the Lena, and in 1639 the first Russian troops reached the Pacific, where the harbour of Okhotsk was established in 1648. From here Russian detachments ventured into the Amur basin, though they were soon forced to retreat on account of the resistance of the local inhabitants and the military response of the Manchu. Expansion in the south, on the edge of the steppe, progressed more slowly. Lake Baikal was reached in 1643, and the fortress of Irkutsk was erected between 1652 and 1661. Here again the Russians came across powerful military adversaries: the Mongols and the Manchu, who ruled China from 1644 onwards. At Nerchinsk in 1689 agreement was reached on the border between Russia and China, which remained in effect until the nineteenth century. In the first half of the eighteenth century, Russian expansion finally reached out to the farthest north-easternmost point of the Eurasian land mass, the peninsulas of Chukotka and Kamchatka.

The majority of the Siberian ethnic groups put up fierce resistance to the Russians. During the 'Time of Troubles', at the beginning of the seventeenth century, the Tatars of the former Khanate of Sibir organized large-scale rebellions with the aim of liberating themselves from Russian rule, and these spread to the Ostiaks and other ethnic groups in western Siberia. After they had been vanquished, there were repeated revolts among the Iakuts and Buriats, and the Iukagir, Chukchi, Kamchadal and Koriaks of the north-east. Organized in small communities and armed with inferior weapons, the Siberian ethnic groups were no match for the Muscovite soldiery, who comprised several hundred men at the most, and acted in a violent and brutal manner. However, the repeated outbursts of resistance strengthened the resolve of the Muscovite government to pursue a cautious policy of incorporation. Restraint also seemed advisable in order not to endanger the principal goal, which was the regular payment of iasak in the shape of furs. In this Muscovy had recourse to the well-tried methods of guaranteeing the status quo and of cooperation with foreign elites.

As a rule Muscovy confirmed the clan and tribal chieftains in their possessions and privileges, and conferred on them simple judicial duties and the task of local government. This mainly concerned the collection of iasak, which was usually paid with furs.[18] However, with the exception of the Siberian Tatars, representatives of the native elite were not co-opted into the hereditary nobility of the empire. Security was provided – as in the case of the central Volga – by fortresses manned by Russians, and by repressive measures such as the taking of hostages and prohibiting the possession of weapons. Adroit use was made of the well-tried method of playing off the various clans and tribes against each other. Detachments of non-Russians not infrequently helped the Russians to conquer other ethnic groups. In other respects the Russian administration left untouched the inner structures of the Siberian ethnic groups, who retained their economies, lifestyles and shamanist faith. At the beginning of the eighteenth century, Muscovy did not even object when the majority of the animist Buriats were converted to lamaist Buddhism by Mongol and Tibetan missionaries.

Muscovy's policy of restraint is reflected in the repeated admonishments to the Siberian voevods 'to approach non-Russians with benevolence and leniency, and not to levy the iasak harshly and with the use of force'. Often, however, the regional administrators and the Russian trappers, merchants, Cossacks and adventurers did not obey these instructions. Moscow was far away, and corruption, arbitrary administration, blackmail, illegal enslavement (especially of native women), robbery and acts of violence were a daily occurrence. 'Merciful lord', a group of Iukagirs wrote in a petition to the tsar in 1663, 'no longer allow your vassals and trappers . . . to continue to insult and rob us, to force us to buy their wares . . . and to beat us with sticks and lock us up, or . . . to tear down our yurts, and . . . to steal reindeer pelts from our stores and to take away our women and children!'[19] Clearly, government policy in theory and its practical implementation in the region diverged even more than in the case of the central Volga.

Initially Russian settlement in Siberia was restricted to the fortresses and small towns. However, in the course of the seventeenth century more and more Russian peasants were encouraged to go to Siberia, primarily in order to supply the garrisons with grain. At the beginning of the eighteenth century, the Russians already clearly out-numbered the non-Russian population of Siberia. However, the Russian peasants were concentrated almost exclusively on the fertile south-western Siberian black soil belt. Thus this region was already largely integrated into the Russian empire at this time, whereas the vast territories to the north and the east with their small populations of hunters, reindeer herdsmen, fishermen and nomadic herdsmen were exploited through a loose chain of fortresses and adminstrative centres. Initially greater social or cultural and religious integration was not envisaged.

In the eighteenth century, the Russian state made a determined attempt to incorporate the non-Russian ethnic groups in Siberia as it had done on the central Volga. However, it proved impossible to integrate the hunters, fishermen and nomadic herdsmen into the Russian social order, even though Orthodox missionaries were active in Siberia even before they turned their attention to the central Volga. As early as 1706 and 1710 Peter the Great had ordered the new Archbishop of Siberia to baptize the Ostiaks and Voguls with the help of material incentives and, if necessary, by force. Despite putting up fierce resistance, most of the respresentatives of the two Ugric-speaking ethnic groups converted to the Orthodox faith.[20] In the decades after an eparchy had been established in Irkutsk in 1731, numerous Iakuts, Tungus, north-western Buriats and even Chukchi and Koriaks were converted with the help of similar methods: 'From this time onwards . . . priests came from the town in the north', a Iakutian source records 'who travelled around, assembled the people at one place, poured water over and thus baptized them, and gave them Russian names. Valiant men with long pigtails bowed their heads in tears, and others, more recalcitrant, attempted to flee to the upper reaches of the rivers.'[21] Even more than in the case of the central Volga region, forcible Christianization in Siberia was merely a formal act, and the non-Russian ethnic groups continued to be influenced by shamanism both in their beliefs and their social relationships.

In the incorporation of Siberia into the Muscovite state the methods of indirect rule that had been developed in Novgorod mingled with methods of firmer military, administrative and economic links with the central government of the kind that Muscovy had tested in the central Volga region. That the central government initially saw Siberia in the same context as the Khanate of Kazan is demonstrated by the fact that Siberia was placed under the jurisdiction of the Moscow central office of the Kazan Prikaz. A separate chancellery for Siberia did not exist until 1637, when the Sibirskii Prikaz was established.

Russian expansion in Siberia has occasionally been compared to American expansion to the west, and in fact the parallels are clearly evident. Interpretations of the two historical processes, which were of global significance, were also based on similar patterns. Both the discovery of the wild west and that of the wild east were portrayed in heroic terms and legitimated by the descendants of European settlers. The brutal treatment of the native ethnic groups, whose traditional order was destroyed with armed force, alcohol and disease, and the thoughtless treatment of the environment (for example, compare fur-bearing animals and buffalo) have long been forgotten. Yet the problem is still on the agenda, as the recent debates in Russia (and in America) on the treatment of the environment, especially with regard to the exploitation of natural gas and oil resources, and the profound crisis of the native population demonstrate. However, the geographical differences between the United States and Siberia should not be overlooked. In fact, it seems more appropriate to make a comparison with Canada. Furthermore, the historical traditions of the Europeans who went overseas were different to those of the Russians, who had been in contact with the ethnic groups of the north for centuries. Whether, as is sometimes claimed,[22] this led to a less brutal and 'more humane' kind of interaction between Europeans and non-European hunters and nomads than in America remains a matter for debate.

3. The Stepwise Advance into the Steppe

Russian expansion into Siberia stood in the tradition of the eastern Slav settlement of land in the east which, ever since the time of the Kievan Rus, had extended to new forested areas. The open treeless steppe north of the Black Sea and the Caspian Sea continued to be strange, hostile and terrifying to the Russians, and Cossacks and Muscovite service men merely ventured to set up a number of bases along the rivers. The notion that the steppe formed the typical environment for Russians was first put about by songs and literature in the nineteenth century. Up to that time the steppe was the domain of nomad horsemen. Their lifestyle, which was based on nomadic grazing patterns that involved long-distance seasonal movements, was suited to the natural conditions of the steppe region. It went hand in hand with their outstanding military qualities and a decentralized and unstable socio-political order that was based on clan relationships. They had always maintained close contacts with the sedentary eastern Slavs. These were characterized on the one hand by raids and incursions carried out by the nomads, and on the other by intensive economic and diplomatic relations.

With the annexation of the Khanates of Kazan and Astrakhan Muscovy acquired a strategic position on the Volga that enabled it to exercise its influence on the steppe and to play an active role in the struggle for the inheritance of the Golden Horde. Yet Muscovy was unable to pursue its aims with military means because even in the sixteenth and seventeenth centuries the Russian armies were no match for the nomad horsemen on the steppe. Thus the tsar initially preferred to use political means in order to strengthen his position on the steppe little by little. Diplomatic relations with the nomad horsemen thus followed the traditional patterns of 'steppe politics', which were based on personal coalitions, and established a state of dependence through the imposition of tribute and the installation of rulers, but not through the annexation of territories. Muscovy made adroit attempts to drive a wedge between the various nomad horsemen and to obtain the support of individual chieftains or whole clans. However, the oaths of loyalty that they subsequently swore to the 'white tsar' were interpreted differently by the two sides. Whereas in the eyes of the nomads they merely sealed a temporary suzerainty that did not apply to other chieftains or clans, Muscovy, with its sedentary and patrimonial traditions, considered them to constitute claims to the whole political entity and its territory.[23] These conflicts continued to take place in an international context, and involved Poland-Lithuania, the Ottoman Empire and the Khanates of the Kazakhs. In the long term Muscovy was increasingly able to strengthen its position as heir to the Golden Horde. It was underpinned by the economic decline of the steppe, which was a result of the discoveries that were beginning to make the ancient trade route between Europe and Asia superfluous.

The Bashkirs

After the conquest of Kazan, Muscovy came into direct contact with the Bashkirs, who to a certain extent had owed allegiance to the Khanate of

Kazan.[24] The Bashkirs were Turkic-speaking Muslims who lived in the southern Urals between the Kama and the Iaik (Ural). They were not 'pure' nomads of the steppe: in the north and on the higher parts of the Urals certain tribes lived in the forest as hunters, fishermen and bee-keepers. In the west some of them also engaged in agriculture. However, the majority of the Bashkirs in the southern and eastern forest and grassy steppes were semi-nomadic and nomadic herdsmen. The Bashkirs were organized in clans and tribes, and clearly differentiated in social terms. Like other nomadic horsemen, they were superior to the troops of non-nomadic powers on the steppe, and made regular raids on the areas close to the Russian border. Unlike most of the other nomads who had been part of the Golden Horde, the Bashkirs did not form a single political unit, though they interacted closely with the Khanates of Kazan and Sibir in the north and the hordes of the Nogai Tatars and the Kazakhs in the south.

After the conquest of Kazan certain groups of Bashkirs accepted Muscovite suzerainty. However, for a long time the claims that the tsar based on this proved difficult to enforce. The fortress of Ufa had been established in the north of the Bashkir lands as early as 1586, but it was not until the middle of the seventeenth century that the trans-Kama line of fortifications was erected in the extreme north-west of the area inhabited by the Bashkirs 'as a shield against the Bashkirs and Kalmyks'.[25] Nevertheless the Bashkirs continued to be ruled in a rather loose manner. A number of tribal chieftains entered the service of Muscovy, and certain groups in the north and in the vicinity of the fortress of Ufa paid (a modest amount of) iasak to the tsar. It thus seems doubtful whether Soviet scholars were right to assign the 'voluntary unification' of the Bashkirs with Russia to as early as the second half of the sixteenth century.[26]

It was not until the second half of the seventeenth and the beginning of the eighteenth centuries that the state gradually began to levy taxes and demand services from the Bashkirs in a systematic manner.[27] At the same time more and more Tatars, Mordvinians, Chuvash, Cheremis and Russians left the central Volga region and settled in the central and southern Urals, where they transformed the pastures of the Bashkirs into arable land. As a result of this the Bashkirs, in the course of the eighteenth century, became a minority in their traditional homeland. The Bashkir aristocracy did in fact manage to subjugate the majority of the immigrant non-Russian iasak men, who are described as Teptiars and bobyli in the Russian sources. However, the classical conflict between sedentary peasants and nomads concerning the ownership of land occurred with increased frequency. This, together with the greater demands made by the state, was the background to the armed rebellions by the Bashkirs in 1662–64, 1676–82 and 1705–10, which were often directed against Russian settlers.

As usual the Russian state reacted to these rebellions with the stick – by taking hostages – and with the carrot – for example, by guaranteeing ownership of land. It was only in the 1730s that the government began to subjugate the Bashkirs in earnest. In the meantime the situation had changed considerably. The state, which had been reformed and strengthened in military terms by Peter the Great, now began in a systematic manner to streamline the empire and to utilize the resources of the peripheral regions. Thus the unused fertile arable land and the mineral resources of the southern Urals, the area inhabited by the Bashkirs, attracted the government's attention. Yet the primary reason for the Orenburg expedition, which began in 1734, was the fact that relations had recently been established with the Kazakhs, and this drew attention to the Middle Asian trade. The fortified border which was established between Samara on the Volga and the newly founded town of Orenburg on the Iaik between 1735 and 1740 cut the Bashkirs off from the steppe. They reacted with a number of large-scale armed insurrections, which were put down in the course of five years of brutal warfare. In this the troops were usually supported by immigrant non-Russian iasak men.

In the decades that followed there were a number of other Bashkir rebellions, though the southern Urals were now firmly under Russian military control. The area was subsequently incorporated into the Russian empire in administrative terms. Further integration followed the established pattern. The section of the Bashkir elite, which had not been wiped out in the Russian campaigns, and the Tatar Mishars (Meshcheriaki), who had moved to the area from the central Volga region, had their tenure, rights and privileges confirmed, and entered into the service of the Russian army in the form of cavalry units. The lower classes continued to have to pay iasak, though the Bashkirs had to pay less than the immigrants of other ethnic groups, and the non-Russian Teptiars and bobyli less than the Russian state peasants. Although tenure was specifically guaranteed, the struggle for Bashkir land persisted, and in the Bashkir areas there continued to be a great deal of potential for ethnic and social unrest. Unlike the non-Russians of the

Khanate of Kazan, the Bashkirs were not socially integrated into the Russian Empire in the eighteenth or the first half of the nineteenth centuries, and continued to have a special status. At the end of the eighteenth century they and the Mishars were assigned to a military caste similar to that of the Russian Cossacks, organized into an irregular 'Bashkir Army', and placed under the jurisdiction of an independent military administration. They served along the Orenburg frontier, and also in campaigns in the west, for example between 1806 and 1813.[28]

The Nogai Tatars

With the conquest of Astrakhan in 1556 Muscovy acquired a base in the middle of the steppes. Here the Turkic-speaking and Islamic Nogai Tatars, the successors of the 'Great Horde', led a nomadic existence in the central areas of the Golden Horde between the Volga and the Sea of Aral.[29] They were typical nomad horsemen with large herds and wide-ranging seasonal movements, and were loosely organized into clans and tribes which sometimes united to form one or more hordes. The destabilization brought about by the Muscovite conquests led the Nogai to split up into three hordes. The 'Small Horde' crossed the Volga and placed itself under the protection of the Khan of Crimea. In the east one of the hordes joined the Kazakhs, whereas the 'Great Horde' in the centre was shaken by power struggles between the various clans.

Muscovy had already established close diplomatic and commercial contacts with the Nogai Tatars at the end of the fifteenth century. After the conquest of the Volga khanates the Nogai Tatars of the Great Horde had become direct neighbours of Muscovy, and more and more dependent on it in economic terms. Muscovy played the warring clans off against each other, and in 1557 Prince Ismail swore an oath to the tsar that was interpreted as a sign of subservience in Moscow. Nogai Tatars served as mercenaries in the Russian armies, and certain aristocrats entered the service of the tsar. They included the ancestors of Prince Iusupov, who was granted large estates with thousands of Russian peasants on the upper Volga. However, Muscovy's relations with the Nogai Tatars remained unstable. Whereas, at the end of the sixteenth century, it was able to enforce the practice of giving hostages, and to appoint a prince of its choice in 1600, some of the clans were in the habit of rejecting their dependent status. The Great Nogai Horde was occasionally under Muscovite suzerainty, but continued to be independent even in the seventeenth century.

An internal crisis and the subsequent decline of the Great Nogai Horde were a foregone conclusion at the beginning of the 1630s when the Kalmyks occupied the steppe to the east of the Volga. The Nogai Tatars crossed the Volga and reorganized themselves in the steppe between the Kuban and the Dnestr in hordes that were under the suzerainty of the Khanate of Crimea. Thus the Nogai Tatars were the last nomad horsemen in the area to the north of the Black Sea.

The Kalmyks

The Kalmyk advance to the Volga was the last wave of the westward expansion of the central Asian nomad horsemen that had begun with the Huns, and reached its climax in the universal empire of the Mongols.[30] The Kalmyks were western Mongolian tribes which, as a result of the pressure exerted on them by the eastern Mongols and the Kazakhs, had wandered to the south-west in several waves in the first decades of the seventeenth century, taking possession of the steppes to the north of the Caspian Sea. Like the Nogai Tatars, the Kalmyks were 'pure' nomadic herdsmen, and disciplined and feared warriors. They were organized in family clans and in hordes or tribes (ulus) under the leadership of a *taysi*. On the Volga they at last united to form a khanate. The Kalmyks, like the other Mongols, were lamaists. They founded monasteries, were in touch with Tibet, and made use of the newly invented west Mongolian alphabet. Thus they constituted an outpost of Buddhism on the south-eastern fringe of Europe, and a foreign body in the middle of the Turkic-speaking and Islamic world of the steppe.

Muscovy attempted to acquire the allegiance of the Kalmyks at an early stage. In 1655 it reached an agreement which the Khan of the Kalmyks concluded with an oath of loyalty: 'We ulus men are all eternally obedient to the great ruler, the tsar and Grand Duke Aleksei Mikhailovich.'[31] For the government in Moscow – and for Soviet historiography[32] – this meant that the Kalmyks had become subjects of the tsar. For the Kalmyks, however, it was simply a voluntary military alliance in the context of the politics of the steppe. Muscovy needed these doughty warriors as a buffer in the south and as auxiliary troops against the Crimean Tatars, and in exchange was prepared to grant the

Kalmyk elite certain gifts and trading privileges. Yet it was impossible to gain control over the steppe, even if the Kalmyks occasionally gave hostages. The Khanate of the Kalmyks remained independent. This is also demonstrated by the fact that the oaths were continually repeated. Under Khan Ayuki (1670–1724) the Volga Kalmyks attained their greatest political and military power. Although they maintained relations with the Ottoman Empire and with China, the alliance with Russia persisted, and the Kalmyks served under Peter the Great as a power that guaranteed order in the steppes, even against the rebellious Bashkirs. They also served as auxiliary troops in the Northern and Persian wars.[33]

In the decades after the death of Ayuki, Russian pressure on the Kalmyks continued to increase. His successors were appointed from St Petersburg and required the Kalmyks to surrender their children as hostages. The governors of Astrakhan interfered in the internal affairs of the Khanate, and Russian, Ukrainian and German peasants took possession of the Kalmyk pastures. As a result their nomadic economy went into decline.[34] The Kalmyks' attempts to defend their land and their ancient rights were generally unsuccessful, so that they became more and more willing to return to their old homeland. When China, which had decisively defeated the western Mongols, invited the Kalmyks to occupy pastures in what was now depopulated Dzhungaria, more than two-thirds of them followed its summons. In January 1771 more than 100,000 Kalmyks under Khan Ubashi moved eastwards. However, only a fraction reached their destination. The others fell victim to attacks by the Kazakhs or the Kirgiz, or to the desert. The remaining Kalmyks in the steppes to the north of the Caspian Sea, especially to the west of the Volga, were now incorporated into the administration of the Russian empire. The Khanate was abolished, and every individual ulus was placed under the control of the governor of Astrakhan, whereas the Kalmyks who lived in the west were attached to the host of the Don Cossacks. The nomadic Kalmyks were not integrated into Russian society, and retained their traditional internal socio-political order even in the nineteenth century, although their autonomy was gradually curtailed and their grazing lands reduced in size.

The Crimean Tatars

Of the powers which had competed with Muscovy in the first half of the sixteenth century for the inheritance of the Golden Horde, only the

Khanate of the Crimean Tatars had not come under Russian rule by the eighteenth century. The Turkic-speaking and Islamic Crimean Tatars were in a position to control the wide steppes to the north of the Black Sea, not only on account of their outstanding military and organizational abilities, but also because of the support given to them by the Ottoman Empire.[35] The latter had gained control of the shores of the Black Sea towards the end of the fifteenth century, and on the Crimea had annexed the large city of Kaffa, which had been established by Genoese merchants, and certain other fortresses, including Tana (Azov) at the mouth of the Don. From this time onwards the Khanate of Crimea had owed a kind of allegiance to the Ottoman Empire, though until the seventeenth century it retained a great deal of independence and on the steppe continued to be a great power in its own right.

The Crimean Tatars and their allies, the Nogai Tatars, regularly carried out raids on the sedentary eastern Slav peasants who had settled near the border of the steppe. They robbed their possessions, laid waste their farmsteads, and took away thousands of people to be sold into slavery. In their conflict with Muscovy after 1521 Crimean Tatar armies also ventured deep into Russia itself, and in 1571 even burned Moscow to the ground. The Khans of Crimea exacted tribute from Poland-Lithuania and from Muscovy, thereby underlining their claim to the inheritance of the Golden Horde. Thus it does not come as a surprise that in Russian sources the Crimean Tatars are depicted as cruel and treacherous thugs who, being by nature murderous, avaricious and barbarous, attacked peaceful Christian settlers, killed them or sold them into slavery. The image of the perfidious traditional nomadic enemies of the Russians continued to play a role even in the twentieth century, and it is hardly an accident that the Crimean Tatars and the Kalmyks were among the nations deported to Asia at the end of the Second World War. However, the view of the nomads that tends to be held by sedentary societies is one-dimensional, and has rightly been criticized, for example by the American historian Alan Fisher.

Since the fifteenth century the Khanate of Crimea had been a multi-ethnic polity that was socially and politically differentiated, and displayed a high level of development in economic and cultural terms. Furthermore, it combined both nomadic and sedentary traditions. The Giray dynasty, which was descended from Genghis Khan, and the clans of the Tatar aristocracy ruled a territory which in addition to the peninsula included the whole of the steppe to the north and to the east of the Black Sea. In addition to the Crimean Tatars, most of whom were no longer nomads, the population of the Khanate included various groups of Nogai Tatars, who led nomadic lives on the continental steppes, and the sedentary urban population of the Crimea, which in addition to Tatars consisted of Armenians, Greeks (most of whom spoke Tatar) and Turkic-speaking Jews (Krymchaki and Karaim). The economy included nomadic herds, arable farming, viticulture and a brisk trade in slaves, farm animals and luxury goods. In keeping with Mongol and Ottoman tradition, the non-Islamic groups of the Khanate were not persecuted, although they had to pay fairly high taxes. The Crimea witnessed a flowering of Tatar culture, literature, historiography, architecture and Islamic educational institutions.

However, in the eighteenth century, the Khanate of Crimea was already well past its heyday. Its economy was in a state of crisis; its social and political stability had been undermined by internal conflicts; and it became more and more dependent on the Sultan. Russia's attitude to the Crimean Tatars was increasingly determined by its relations with the Ottoman Empire. From the time of Peter the Great onwards Russia had gone on the offensive, and, in analogy to its breakthrough to the Baltic, attempted to acquire access to the Black Sea. After a whole series of unsuccessful campaigns through the steppe, Russia finally began to gain the upper hand militarily as the eighteenth century progressed. This already became evident in the war of 1736–39, when Russian troops defeated the Crimean Tatars, and for a short time even ventured on to the Crimea itself. The decisive event was the Russo-Turkish war of 1768–74, as a result of which the Ottoman Empire was dislodged from the northern shore of the Black Sea. The Khanate of the Crimean Tatars now stood alone against the might of the Russian empire.

The annexation of the Crimea occurred in three stages which corresponded to the incorporation of other successor states of the Golden Horde, though they followed at much shorter intervals.[36] The Crimea was conquered in 1771, and in the following year the Ottoman protectorate over the Khanate of Crimea was replaced by a Russian one, although this guaranteed the existence of the Khanate as a 'free territory dependent on no one'.[37] Four years later Russia appointed a new khan who implemented a series of reforms aimed at achieving greater social equality. When the Tatar aristocracy rebelled against this, Catherine II once again ordered Russian troops to invade the territory. The last khan was deposed in 1783. With this the Khanate of the Crimean Tatars lost its political autonomy, and was incorporated into the Russian empire. The majority of the urban Greeks and Armenians had been resettled some years earlier in the area north of the Sea of Azov, where they had founded the colonies of Mariupol and Novyi Nakhichevan. In the course of the conquest of the Khanate of Crimea, Russia adroitly played off the nomadic Nogai Tatars against the Crimean Tatar ruling class, and many Nogai Tatars moved to the area of Kuban to the north of the Caucasus.[38] Thus the steppe to the north of the Black Sea, which had been the home of the Nogai Tatars, became available for the settlement of Ukrainian, Russian and foreign peasants (see the following section). In the steppe to the north of the Caucasus, which now also came under Russian control, the majority of the Nogai Tatars remained faithful to their nomadic lifestyle even in the nineteenth century. Some of them returned to the steppe to the north of the Crimea, and gradually became sedentary. This sizeable group of Nogai Tatars emigrated to the Ottoman Empire after the Crimean War.

The methods which were used to incorporate the Khanate of Crimea initially resembled those that had been employed two centuries earlier in the case of the Khanate of Kazan. In the wake of military occupation and administrative integration, St Petersburg attempted to win over the Crimean Tatars by pursuing policies which were both cautious and prudent. Thus the annexation document of 8 April 1783 states: 'We promise devoutly and unshakeably in our name and in that of our successors to the throne to treat you as the equals of our native subjects, to preserve and defend your persons, goods, holy places, and your natural religion . . . and to grant each of your estates the rights and privileges that prevail in Russia.'[39] The administrative structure of the Khanate was taken over and placed under the control of a Russian governor. The Russian authorities now worked together with the Tatar elite, whose landed property and privileges they guaranteed. In return the Tatars were required to serve the tsar either in the army or in the regional government. The Muslim Tatar aristocrats were also – unlike the elites of the other states of the steppe, but like the Kazan Tatars, who were also sedentary – co-opted into the hereditary nobility of the empire. However, they had to produce evidence of their noble origins, which not infrequently caused delays when it came to granting them full aristocratic rights.[40] The Tatar peasants also retained their land and their status as free state peasants who were not dependent on land-owners. In the age of enlightened absolutism, tolerance towards Islam was self-evident. Attempts were made to secure cooperation with Islamic religious leaders, whose land and property (vakif) was guaranteed. They were integrated into the state bureaucracy – as in the Volga-Urals region – by means of a 'Tauric Muslim Administration', both in order to exercise control over them and to use them in the interests of Russia.

This pragmatic and flexible policy was a success.[41] Although the Crimean Tatars had lost their ancient independence, there were no armed uprisings against Russian rule. However, as early as the 1780s many thousands of Tatars voted with their feet and emigrated to the Ottoman Empire. This wave of emigration was destined to continue in the following decades, reaching a climax during and after the Crimean War. Between 1783 and 1860 more than half of the Crimean Tatars left their homeland. From the beginning of the nineteenth century there was an influx of eastern Slav peasants and foreign colonists into the Crimea, and thus the Tatars became a minority in the peninsula after the middle of the century. The Russian government now did what it could to encourage the colonization of the Crimea, and in the process the Tatars lost some of their land. Furthermore, the authorities pushed ahead with administrative integration, and all the more important administrative tasks were assigned to Russians. The Tatars were also driven out of the Crimean towns. It is true that they were able to retain their social organization and cultural and religious identity. However, by the middle of the nineteenth century they had lost political power altogether, and had been considerably weakened in demographic and economic terms. The last sovereign successors of the Tatar overlords had become third-class subjects of the Russians.

4. Opening up the Steppe:
The Cossacks and the German Colonists

The total subjugation of the Bashkirs, the abolition of the Khanate of the Kalmyks, and the annexation of the Khanate of Crimea meant that the fertile area of the steppe to the north of the Black Sea and the Caspian Sea, which had hitherto been under the sole control of the nomadic horsemen, could now be settled by peasant farmers. Whereas it is true that eastern Slav Cossacks had ventured into the steppes since the sixteenth century, they had only settled along the rivers. The Cossacks, who had emerged at the frontier to the steppe, were a mixture of eastern Slavs, Tatars and other ethnic groups. However, from the seventeenth century onwards they were clearly influenced by the Orthodox church, and by Russian and Ukrainian culture. I will return to the Ukrainian Cossacks on the Dnepr in the next chapter, and will describe the Russian Cossacks briefly at this point, for I believe that they had the makings of an independent ethnic group.

The Cossacks had settled along the Don, the Volga, the Iaik (Ural) and the Terek since the sixteenth century. They were primarily Russian and Ukrainian peasants who had fled to escape from increased taxation and the extension of serfdom to the steppe frontier, where for a time they were beyond the reach of the state and the landowners.[42] They lived in fortified camps along the rivers, and worked as fishermen, hunters, forest bee-keepers and, at a later stage, herdsmen. This was supplemented by regular raids against the nomads of the steppes, attacks on merchants and payments from Muscovy. Russia used the Cossacks in its conflicts with the nomads of the steppe, employing them as frontier guards, scouts, robbers and occasionally as mercenaries. However, the individual Cossack hosts retained a high level of independence. They resembled the nomads of the steppe in that the Russians considered them to be unreliable allies. Thus Cossacks were the leaders of, and the troops at the heart of, the great popular uprisings in the seventeenth and eighteenth centuries.

In addition to having a specific way of life adapted to the conditions of the steppe, the Cossacks also developed a socio-political order that was totally different from that of the Russian autocracy. Under this democratic military constitution the most important decisions were taken by an assembly made up of all the Cossacks, the circle (krug). It also elected the ataman or leader. Social differentiation among the Cossacks, especially those on the Don, increased from the seventeenth century onwards, for more and more peasants flocked to the steppe frontier. In the course of the eighteenth century, the Russian government succeeded in obtaining the loyalty of the elite, and thus in controlling these unruly Cossacks. Nevertheless, in the eighteenth century the host of the Don Cossacks remained clearly distinct from the rest of Russia in administrative and socio-political terms.[43] However, as the nomad horsemen were gradually integrated into the Russian empire, the Cossacks were deprived of their most important function. Their autonomy was slowly whittled away, and they began to be 'transformed into peasants'. Yet even in the nineteenth century the Cossacks on the

Don survived as a separate military organization with a clearly distinct identity. Georgi's *Beschreibung aller Nationen des Russischen Reiches* (1776–80) mentions six groups of Cossacks, and a later Russian description of the ethnic groups of the empire still lists the Cossacks separately.[44] However, they never developed into a separate nation.

The Russian government made use of eastern Slav Cossacks and peasants, and foreign colonists in order to open up and settle the wide expanses of the steppe.[45] With this it continued the European (and especially German) tradition of establishing colonies in the east: since the Middle Ages peasants and townspeople from central Europe had accepted similar invitations from eastern European rulers. On the other hand, it also followed the patterns of the absolutist policies of *peuplierung* (or population growth). Specialists from western Europe had been invited to Russia as early as the fifteenth century, and since the time of Peter the Great their number had increased considerably.[46] They settled in towns, and above all in the new capital, St Petersburg. There were also colonies of foreign specialists in the towns of the south and the east, such as the Armenian merchants who traded with Asia in Astrakhan. Under the Empress Elizabeth, Orthodox emigrants from the Ottoman Empire were resettled in order to protect the Ukrainian steppe frontier. From the early 1750s onwards the military settlements of 'New Serbia' and 'Slavo-Serbia' were populated primarily by Romanians, Serbs and Bulgars.

The decisive impetus for the settlement of the newly pacified areas of the steppe by foreigners came from two declarations which were issued by Catherine II in 1762 and 1763.[47] Foreign colonists were promised land, a small amount of money, and loans, and told that 'everyone shall be freed of all taxes and dues . . . for thirty years'. Furthermore, they would never be required to serve in the army, were guaranteed 'the right to practise their religion according to the statutes and customs of their churches' and granted internal self-government. Most of those who took up the tsarina's offer were German. The settlers who emigrated to Russia in the next fifty years, especially from south-west Germany, were the ancestors of the numerous Germans who live in the former Soviet Union to this day. A first wave of more than 30,000 settlers emigrated before 1775 to the steppe to the west of the lower Volga, which was now safe from attacks by the Bashkirs, and increasingly safe from attacks by the Kalmyks. These first Volga Germans included members of the Herrnhut fraternity, who in 1765 founded a model colony in Sarepta to the south of Tsaritsyn.

At the same time the Ukrainian steppe frontier was reorganized and called 'New Russia' (Novorossiia). After the dissolution in 1775 of the Zaporozhian Sich, the last autonomous stronghold of the Dnepr Cossacks, and the annexation of the Khanate of Crimea in 1783, the door was open for Ukrainian, Russian and foreign settlers. From the 1780s onwards Mennonite German immigrants from West Prussia settled on the lower Dnepr. However, it was not until 1803, when official proclamations were issued in greater numbers, that tens of thousands of German settlers streamed into the fertile areas of New Russia and laid the foundations of the community of Black Sea Germans. In addition to Germans, numerous Bulgars, Greeks and Romanians who had emigrated from the Ottoman Empire, and small groups of Swiss, Swedes, Corsicans and Italians settled in this region at the end of the eighteenth and at the beginning of the nineteenth centuries. In 1804 this massive influx of people led the government of Alexander I to reduce the tax-free period to ten years, to make it more difficult to enter Russia, and to accept colonists only if they were experienced farmers or vine growers, silk-worm cultivators, stock breeders or village craftsmen.[48] In 1819 official invitations designed to attract colonists ceased altogether. At the same time many foreigners settled in the new towns of New Russia, especially in Odessa, which was founded in 1794.

In the first half of the nineteenth century the colonists continued to be a self-contained legal and social group with privileges that were denied to the majority of the Ukrainian and Russian peasants. The reasons why the colonists were in a better economic position than the latter were the fact that they owned more land, and that they enjoyed self-government, taxation privileges and exemption from military service. Specific laws of inheritance, which made it impossible to divide or reassign parts of a property, and better economic and educational preconditions meant that German estates in the Black Sea area, especially those of the Mennonites, were as a rule more prosperous than those of the Bulgars and the Greeks, and also of the Volga Germans, most of whom had adopted the Russian system of periodically re-assigning land among the members of a rural commune. Yet the German colonies with their Protestant or Catholic populations remained enclaves within an Orthodox world. They fulfilled the hopes placed in them inasmuch as they were successful in agriculture and trade, but had little impact on the eastern Slav peasantry.

5. Summary

The 'gathering of the lands of the Golden Horde' came to a conclusion of sorts at the end of the eighteenth century with the dissolution of the Khanates of the Kalmyks and of the Crimean Tatars. The steppes from the Dnestr to the Iaik (Ural) were now under Russian control, and the frontiers of the Mongolian steppe and of China had been reached in the east. Russia had become the unchallenged heir of the great Eurasian empire of the Golden Horde.

This struggle for its inheritance lasted for more than three centuries. The first phase took place in the framework of the traditional politics of the steppe. With the conquest of Kazan it turned into imperial expansion that aimed to incorporate the territories of the Golden Horde into the Russian empire in a manner that resembled the earlier gathering of the lands of Rus. The forested part of Siberia reaching to the Pacific was conquered in the course of a few decades, and in this Muscovy also took its bearings from Novgorod's mediaeval expansion towards the north-east. The third phase, the struggle for mastery of the steppe, and the attendant access to the Caspian Sea and the Black Sea, lasted rather longer. After the incorporation of Astrakhan in 1556 Russia advanced slowly for more than two centuries until, in 1783, it was able to eliminate its most powerful rival, the Khanate of Crimea. This final step was rendered more difficult by the fact that the Crimean Tatars were supported by the other Eurasian great power that laid claim to the inheritance of the Golden Horde. The involvement of the Ottoman Empire turned Russia's gathering of the lands of the Golden Horde into something that affected European politics as a whole.

The methods that Russia employed in the conquest of the individual territories varied according to the military and political power of its adversaries.[49] A stepwise approach in the manner of traditional steppe politics tended to be the rule. The first goal was to set up a loose protectorate, which was concluded by means of an oath, by installing a loyal ruler. From the Russian point of view this established a client status to which it could always refer in the future, whereas the other side saw it at the most as a personal and temporary act of submission. In the course of the gradual process of conquest Russia made adroit use of the methods of *divide et impera* by pitting non-Russians against each other and winning over parts of the enemy elite. But in the end military force usually proved to be the decisive factor:

rings of fortresses that encircled the enemy, and campaigns of conquest and pillage.

Almost everywhere the Russian armies met with bitter resistance, and this flared up repeatedly even after an area had been conquered. Whereas the Kazan Tatars and Cheremis, the Tatars, Ostiaks, Voguls, Iakuts, Buriats and Chukchi of Siberia and the Bashkirs resisted conquest and fought against their incorporation, the Kalmyks and Nogai and Crimean Tatars reacted with the nomadic form of protest: they simply went away. This fact alone demonstrates that the axiom referring to 'the voluntary union with Russia', which was current in the former Soviet Union for decades, was a lie.[50]

The methods which were used to incorporate the conquered territories were based on mediaeval patterns, especially those that had been developed by Novgorod, on 'the gathering of the lands of Rus', and the rules of steppe politics. In all of this the incorporation of the Khanate of Kazan served as a model for the areas inhabited by non-Russians, which until 1637 were in fact administered jointly by a central authority in Moscow. It is possible to distinguish two basic policies. Initially the pacification of the newly acquired territories had absolute priority. All resistance was crushed with the use of military force; and the construction of fortresses, the taking of hostages and the ban on the possession of weapons were designed to ensure the loyalty of the non-Russians. The second goal – deriving economic profit from a certain territory – was subordinated to the goal of pacifying it in military terms. And it did not become evident to the same extent everywhere. However, it is clearly apparent in the rush for furs in Siberia, the interest displayed in the fisheries and markets of the Volga khanates, in the natural resources of the Urals, and also in the fact that colonists began to clamour for the rich arable land on the steppe frontier.

When a territory had finally been pacified, Russia usually proceeded to implement cautious and flexible policies. A significant element in this was that on the whole it respected the status quo. Whereas it is true that annexation implied that the former ruler was replaced with someone entrusted with the task by the tsar, below this level the administrative and legal order, tenure of land, and value systems were left largely unchanged. For example, Russia adopted the iasak tax system from the Golden Horde, and also guaranteed the personal freedom of those peasants, herdsmen or hunters who paid iasak. Unlike Russian peasants, they could not become serfs. However, the cautious policies pursued by the government were not infrequently contradicted by its administrative officials on a regional level.

The second basic principle of the cautious policy of incorporation was cooperation with the non-Russian elites. Their privileges were confirmed, and in return they had to keep the lower classes in order and do military service. It was easiest for Russia to cooperate with elites who resembled the Russian nobility with regard to socio-political status, that is, who formed a sedentary, landowning military estate. They were co-opted into the hereditary nobility of the empire. This was certainly true of the Tatar elites of the Khanates of Kazan and Crimea, who also possessed the aura of being descendants of the ruling elite of the Golden Horde. It was more problematical to recognize the nomad aristocracy, whose lifestyle and culture were significantly different from those of the Russians. True, there was cooperation with Bashkirs, Nogai Tatars and Kalmyks, but as a rule they were not recognized as hereditary nobility. And this certainly did not come into question in the case of the leaders of the Siberian clans and tribes. In Russian thinking a hierarchy ranging from those who were sedentary to nomads of the steppes and hunters began to emerge in the eighteenth century. The upper and lower classes of sedentary societies were now subjected to much more intense integrative pressure than the nomads, who continued to be excluded.

The gradual adaptation to Russian social patterns was also underpinned by the settlement of the central Volga and the Crimea by eastern Slav peasants. This led to a great deal of conflict. Even more profound changes came about as a result of the striking conflict between arable farmers and nomads concerning the latter's summer pastures, which helped to accelerate the economic decline of the nomadic herdsmen.

In addition to its fundamental adherence to the pragmatic and flexible policy of incorporation, the state occasionally resorted to coercion. This happened as early as the 1550s, when the church for a time implemented an aggressive crusading policy. This repressive attitude resurfaced in the first half of the eighteenth century, when the absolutist state modelled on western Europe turned its back on pragmatic Muscovite policy, and, in its striving for systemization and uniform social conditions, attempted to convert numerous animists and Muslims to the Orthodox faith by force, abolished the special status of sedentary non-Russians in the east, and incorporated them into the

Russian estates. However, Catherine II subsequently returned to the traditional policy of cooperation with the Tatar elite.

In a western European context, the question arises of whether one ought to see the gathering of the lands of the Golden Horde as part of the process of European colonial expansion.[51] There are numerous obvious parallels in regard to the motives and methods of expansion and incorporation; these range from the mixture of strategic and economic aims to the techniques of *divide et impera* and indirect rule, and to specific forms of repression. The similarities between the conquest of Siberia and of Canada are particularly noticeable, and in fact the colonial model seems particularly apt in the case of Siberia.

Yet there are important differences. In early Russian expansion to the east, the economic aspect and missionary activity played a smaller role than in the case of western European maritime powers. The decisive difference was the fact that the distance between Russians and non-Russians was not as pronounced as the relationship between western Europeans and the colonial peoples in America, Asia and Africa. First, there was geographical distance. The foreign ethnic groups were not separated by wide oceans, but, again with the exception of the ethnic groups in eastern Siberia, were neighbours of the Russians. In addition there were differences in regard to 'historical distance'. Whereas the western Europeans actually discovered their colonies, the eastern Slavs were in close contact with the nomads and hunters to the east and to the south, and for centuries were even part of the same system of government. Respect for the Golden Horde and its aristocracy meant that the Tatar elite was held in high esteem and that its members were treated as equals. The long period of interaction was also the reason why the cultural distance to alternative lifestyles and the religious distance to Muslims and animists was considerably smaller than in western Europe. However, the gradual westernization of Russia in the eighteenth century and the adoption of Eurocentric values by the state and the elite led to a situation where the distance to nomads and Islam became greater than in Muscovy. Yet with the partial exception of Siberia, Russia's expansion to the east between the sixteenth and eighteenth centuries did not correspond to the western European model of colonial expansion.

Increased Russian preoccupation with the west meant that from the second half of the seventeenth century onwards the significance of the 'gathering of the lands of the Golden Horde' gradually declined as motivation for expansion. There are nonetheless links with Russian expansion in Asia in the nineteenth century, and these are particularly obvious in the case of the Kazakhs, who had already accepted a kind of loose protectorate in the eighteenth century. Yet here the decisive phase, the annexation of the Kazakh steppe, first occurred in the nineteenth century and under changed circumstances (see Chapter 5, Section 3). However, first it will be necessary to describe Russian expansion to the west, which in the seventeenth and eighteenth centuries went hand in hand with the 'gathering of the lands of the Golden Horde'.

Notes

1   *Polnoe sobranie russkikh letopisei* XXIX (Moscow, 1965), p. 108.

2   Frank Kämpfer, 'Die Eroberung von Kasan 1552 als Gegenstand der zeitgenössischen russischen Historiographie', *FOG* 14 (1969), 7–161; Jaroslaw Pelenski, *Russia and Kazan: Conquest and Imperial Ideology (1438–1560s)* (The Hague and Paris, 1974).

3   Charles J. Halperin, *Russia and the Golden Horde. The Mongol Impact on Mediaeval Russian History* (Bloomington, 1985); Bertold Spuler, *Die Goldene Horde. Die Mongolen in Rußland 1223–1502*, 2nd edn (Wiesbaden, 1965).

4   In addition to Halperin (1985), see also Mark Batunsky, 'Muscovy and Islam: Irreconcilable Strategy, Pragmatic Tactics', *Saeculum* 39 (1988), 63–81. However, Soviet historiography with its strong Russian national slant interprets the relationship to the Mongols as being fundamentally antagonistic in a manner that resembles the ecclesiastical sources.

5   Edward Louis Keenan, 'Muscovy and Kazan, 1445–1552. A Study in Steppe Politics', Ph.D. thesis, Harvard, 1965; Edward Louis Keenan, 'Muscovy and Kazan: Some Introductory Remarks on the Patterns of Steppe Diplomacy', *SR* 26 (1967), 548–58; Kappeler (1992a).

6   This chapter is based on Kappeler (1982b), pp. 39–198. See also Nolde I (1952), Chapters 1–3; and Alishev (1990). On the Khanate of Kazan see Rorlich (1986), pp. 3–31; *Istoriia Tat.* (1968), pp. 68–100; Mikhail Khudiakov, *Ocherki po istorii Kazanskogo khanstva* (Kazan, 1923).

7   Herberstein (1984), pp. 224 f.

8   Andreas Kappeler, 'Die Moskauer "Nationalitätenpolitik" unter Ivan IV.', *RH* 14 (1987), 263–82. The quotation comes on p. 267.

9   *AAE* I, no. 241, pp. 259 f. See Lemercier (1967), pp. 369–82 for a different interpretation of early missionary policy.

10   On the following see Kappeler (1982b), pp. 137–98, Alishev (1990), and I. P. Ermolaev, *Srednee Povolzh'e vo vtoroi polovine XVI–XVII vv. (Upravlenie Kazanskim kraem)* (Kazan, 1982).

11 See Kappeler (1982b), pp. 244–92, 370–3, and Nolde I (1952), pp. 100–8, 120–7.

12 *PSZ* I, 2734 (vol. 5, pp. 66 f.).

13 *PSZ* I, 3149 (vol. 5, pp. 533 f.).

14 *PSZ* I, 8236 (vol. 11, pp. 248–56). See also Lemercier (1967), pp. 382–91.

15 *PSZ* I, 15396 (vol. 22, pp. 51 f.).

16 This section is primarily based on Lantzeff and Pierce (1973); Nolde I (1952), pp. 130–90; Wood (1991); *Istoriia Sibiri* I–II (1968); S.V. Bakhrushin, *Izbrannye raboty po istoriia Sibiri XVI–XVII vv. C.2: Istoriia narodov Sibiri v XVI–XVII vv.* (Moscow, 1955) *Nauchnye trudy* III; *Etnicheskaia istoriia* (1982); Levin and Potapov (1964); B. O. Dolgikh, *Rodovoi i plemennoi sostav narodov Sibiri v XVII v.* (Moscow, 1960). See also the source material in *Russia's Conquest of Sibiria 1558–1700, To Siberia* I (1985), and David N. Collins, 'Russia's Conquest of Siberia: Evolving Russian and Soviet Historical Interpretations', *European Studies Review* 12 (1982), 17–44.

17 See Fisher (1943).

18 George V. Lantzeff, *Siberia in the Seventeenth Century. A Study of the Colonial Administration* (Berkeley, 1943); Fedorov (1978).

19 *Kolonial'naia politika Moskovskogo gosudarstva v Iakutii XVII v. Sbornik arkhivnykh dokumentov* (Leningrad, 1936), pp. 109–11. See David N. Collins, 'Subjugation and Settlement in Seventeenth and Eighteenth-Century Siberia', Wood (1991), pp. 37–56.

20 Glazik (1954), 32–51; Nolte (1969a), pp. 34–6; Smolitsch (1991), pp. 270–8.

21 Cited in T. V. Zherebina, 'Itogi kreshcheniia iakutov v XVII–XVIII vekakh', in *Pravoslavie v Drevnei Rusi* (Leningrad, 1989), p. 103. See also Glazik (1954), pp. 84–101; *Istoriia Iak* II (1957), pp. 123–5; Fedorov (1978), pp. 81–99.

22 See, for example, Frances Svensson, 'Comparative Ethnic Policy on the American and Russian Frontiers', *Journal of International Affairs* 36 (1982), 83–103.

23 See Yaroshevsky (1989).

24 On the Bashkirs see Donnelly (1968); Nolde I (1952), pp. 166–8 and 191–235; 'Bashkiry', *ES* 3 (5) (1891), 225–40; *Ocherki Bashk* I(1) (1956); Apollova (1964).

25 Kappeler (1982b), pp. 173 f.

26 See, for example, *Ocherki Bashk* I(1) (1956), pp. 56–66; *Istoricheskoe znachenie dobrovol'nogo prisoedineniya Bashkirii k russkomu gosudarstvu. Materialy nauchnoi konferentsii* (Ufa, 1982).

27 See also N. F. Demidova, 'Upravlenie Bashkiriei i povinnosti naseleniia Ufimskoi provintsii v pervoi treti XVIII v.', *IZ* 6 (1961), 211–37; U. Kh. Rakhmatullin, 'Krest'ianskoe zaselenie Bashkirii v XVII–XVIII vv.', in *Krest'ianstvo i krest'ianskoe dvizenie v Bashkirii v XVII–nachale XX vv.* (Ufa, 1981), pp. 3–25.

28 Baumann (1987), pp. 491–5; LeDonne (1984), pp. 283–90; *Ocherki Bashk* I(1) (1959), pp. 33–7, 64–70.

29 Kochekaev (1988), pp. 17–119; A. A. Novosel'skii, *Bor'ba Moskovskogo gosudarstva s tatarami v pervoi polovine XVII v.* (Moscow and Leningrad, 1948); Kappeler (1992a).

30 On the Kalmyks see *Ocherki ist. Kalm.* (1967); Charles Andrew Riess, 'The History of the Kalmyk Khanate to 1724', Ph.D. thesis, Indiana University, 1983; Michael Khodarkovsky, 'The Arrival of the Kalmyks and the Muscovite Southern Frontier, 1600–1670', *RH* 15 (1988a), pp. 225–54; Sarkisyanz (1961), pp. 252–62.

31 *PSZ* I, 145 (vol. 1, pp. 356–8, and especially p. 356). See also Michael Khodarkovsky, 'Kalmyk-Russian Relations, 1670–1697. Development of a Pattern of Relations between Nomadic and Sedentary Societies', *CAS* 2(3) (1983), 5–36.

32 *Dobrovol'noe vkhozhdenie Kalmytskogo naroda v sostav Rossii: Istoricheskie korni i znachenie* (Elista, 1985). This was published to commemorate the 375th anniversary of the Kalmyks' 'entry' into the Russian state, which is dated 1609 (*sic!*).

33 Michael Khodarkovsky, 'Uneasy Alliance: Peter the Great and Ayuki Khan', *CAS* 7(4) (1988b), 1–45.

34 Michael Khodarkovsky, 'Russian Peasant and Kalmyk Nomad: A Tragic Encounter in the Middle of the Eighteenth Century', *RH* 15 (1988c), 43–69.

35 The standard work on the Crimean Tatars is Fisher (1978).

36 Alan W. Fisher, *The Russian Annexation of the Crimea 1772–1783* (Cambridge, 1970); Nolde II (1953), pp. 115–95.

37 *PSZ* I, 13943 (vol. 19, pp. 708–12, and especially p. 708).

38 Kochekaev (1988), pp. 142–260; Nolde II (1953), pp. 219–29; L. N. Cherenkov, 'Tavricheskie nogaitsy (Poslednii kochevoi narod Prichernomorskoi etnokontaktnoi zony)', *Etnokontaktnye zony* (1989), pp. 44–53.

39 *PSZ* I, 15708 (vol. 21, p. 898).

40 See Iablochkov (1876), pp. 583 f., 619.

41 In addition to Fisher (1978) see also Edward Lazzerini, 'The Crimea under Russian Rule. 1783 to the Great Reforms', in Rywkin (1988), pp. 123–38, and E. I. Druzhinina, *Severnoe Prichernomor'e v 1775–1800 gg* (Moscow, 1959), pp. 92–146.

42 See Günther Stökl, *Die Entstehung des Kosakentums* (Munich, 1953); Peter Rostankowski, *Siedlungsentwicklung und Siedlungsformen in den Ländern der russischen Kosakenheere* (Berlin, 1969); *Istoriia Dona s drevneishikh vremen do Velikoi Oktiabr'skoi sotsialisticheskoi revoliutsii* (Rostov, 1965), pp. 94–193; Edward D. Sokol, 'Don Cossack Host', *MERSH* 9 (1978), 218–21; Edward D. Sokol, 'Volga Cossacks', *MERSH* 42 (1986), 225–30; idem, 'Yaik Cossacks', *MERSH* 44 (1987), 144–51.

43 LeDonne (1984), pp. 291 f.

44 Georgi IV (1780), pp. 501–21; Ziablovskii (1815), pp. 106–23.

45 On the following see Roger P. Bartlett, *Human Capital. The Settlement of Foreigners in Russia 1762–1804* (Cambridge, 1979); Hans Auerbach, *Die Besiedelung der Südukraine in den Jahren 1774–1787* (Wiesbaden, 1965); Detlef Brandes, 'Die Ansiedlung von Ausländern im Zarenreich unter Katharina II., Paul I. und Alexander I.', *JbbGO* 34 (1986), 161–87.

46 See Erik Amburger, *Die Anwerbung ausländischer Fachkräfte für die Wirtschaft Rußlands vom 15. bis ins 19. Jahrhundert* (Wiesbaden, 1968); Fleischhauer (1986), pp. 22–60.

47 On the Germans see (in addition to the works mentioned above) Karl Stumpp, *Die Auswanderung aus Deutschland nach Rußland in den Jahren 1763 bis 1862* (Tübingen, n.d.) [the proclamation of 1763 is given on pp. 14–18]; Bonwetsch (1919); Fleischhauer (1986), pp. 97–132, 156–76; Kabuzan (1984), pp. 868–70; Ehrt (1932).

48 *PSZ* I, 21163 (vol. 28, pp. 137–40).

49 See also Kappeler (1982a); Raeff (1971); Starr (1978); Scharf (1988); and Apollova (1964).

50   Tillett (1969), especially pp. 331–57.
51   See Reinhard (1983–88); *Dokumente* (1984–8); Bitterli (1986)

3

Westward Expansion from the Seventeenth Century to the Beginning of the Nineteenth Century

THE EXPANSION of the Muscovite state to the east and to the south always went hand in hand with expansion in the west. Thus the gathering of the lands of the Golden Horde was preceded by the gathering of the lands of Rus, which soon developed into a conflict with the Grand Duchy of Lithuania concerning possession of areas inhabited by Orthodox eastern Slavs. Furthermore, the imperial conquest of the Khanates of Kazan and Astrakhan (1552–57) was succeeded in 1558 by expansion to the Baltic. In the course of the Livonian War, which lasted for twenty-five years, large parts of Livonia and of the Grand Duchy of Lithuania were temporarily under Russian rule. However, the defeat of Russia and the partitioning of Livonia between Poland-Lithuania and Sweden demonstrated that in the west Russia had come up against great powers that were its match. This experience was repeated at the beginning of the seventeenth century, when Polish and Swedish troops occupied large parts of the Muscovite state. For this reason Russian expansion towards the west between the seventeenth and early nineteenth centuries was at the expense of Poland-Lithuania and Sweden. It took place within a European political framework, and led from the three Northern Wars (1558–83, 1654–67, 1700–21) to the 'coalition of the three black eagles' with Austria and Prussia in the four partitions of Poland.[1]

In addition to the different external preconditions of expansion to the east and to the west, the areas annexed by Russia possessed considerably diverging internal structures. In the west Russia, which was centralist and autocratic, was confronted with the task of integrating societies which possessed a corporate organization, different estates and regional traditions. The basic dilemma of Russian policy on nationalities became clearly evident for the first time, since Russia, which was superior in military and political terms, was annexing areas whose socio-political organization, economy and culture were more advanced than those of the metropolis. Russians were well aware of this. In the eighteenth century these elements of western structures formed the models for a new, westernized Russia, and the territories acquired in the west to some extent became the areas in which it experimented with reform. However, there was an insoluble contradiction between the task of integrating the western periphery into the socio-political system of tsarist autocracy, and the desire to use it as a model for a reform of this system.

1. Ukraine: Reunification or Coerced Integration?

A large part of Ukraine came under Russian rule in the middle of the seventeenth century.[2] The agreement of Pereiaslav, which Muscovy concluded in 1654 with the hetman of the Dnepr Cossacks, Bohdan Khmelnytsky, and the ensuing gradual integration of a part of Ukraine into the Russian empire have been and continue to be the subject of controversial debates. The majority of Ukrainian historians see the act of 1654 as an alliance between two independent partners who at the most envisaged a temporary Muscovite protectorate, but not incorporation into the Russian state. In contrast to this (and ever since the great jubilee celebrations of 1954) it has been an axiom among Soviet historians that it represented the liberation from the Polish yoke of eastern Slav brothers who had been separated from them after the decline of the Kievan state.[3] It is not an accident that so much attention was paid to the incorporation of Ukraine into the Soviet Union. The Ukrainians were by far the largest non-Russian nation of the multi-ethnic empire, and Ukraine was and continues to be of extraordinary economic and strategic importance. Furthermore, the similarity between the languages, membership of the Orthodox church, and what is in part a common history have always made the Ukrainians seem a special case to Russian eyes, in so far as they were not simply regarded as being part of the Russian nation. Until recently historians and public opinion in western Europe were hardly aware of the existence of the Ukrainian nation with its 45 million people.

The complicated and disputed problems of Ukrainian ethnogenesis cannot be discussed in this context. At any rate, the process had been completed by the seventeenth century, and the eastern Slavs in the south-eastern part of Poland-Lithuania, who usually referred to themselves as Rus, were at pains to draw a distinction between themselves and the Great Russians or Muscovites.[4] Ukraine, which had belonged almost entirely to the Polish half of the republic of nobles since the Union of Lublin (1569), was successively integrated into the kingdom in administrative, economic and social terms. However, there were significant differences between Galicia in the west, which had already been part of Poland since the fourteenth century, and the large areas in the east and in the south that had been a part of the Grand Duchy of Lithuania until 1569, and had preserved a considerable degree of independence. Whereas the peasant lower classes retained their Orthodox faith and eastern Slav language everywhere, the eastern Slav nobility was co-opted into the szlachta, the privileged noble estate of the kingdom, and – especially in its upper echelons – had on the whole converted to Catholicism, and had gradually been polonized.[5] Part of the urban Ukrainian population had been acculturated, and part of it had been replaced by Poles, Germans, Jews and Armenians. The Union of Brest, which was concluded in 1596 in the course of the Counter-Reformation, had created a Uniate church that owed allegiance to the Pope, and had thus divided the Kiev metropolitanate. Partly as a reaction to the challenge of Catholicism, Ukraine witnessed a proto-national intellectual renaissance. The first eastern Slav institution of higher education, the Kiev Collegium founded by Metropolitan Petro Mohyla, became a centre of Ukrainian culture that combined Orthodox traditions with western, Polish and Latin influences. After the Union of Lublin the process of social, religious, linguistic and cultural assimilation with Poland went hand in hand with increased pressure on the Ukrainian peasants by the Polish (and polonized Ukrainian) landowners, and they fled in growing numbers to the areas adjoining the steppe in the south.

Here, on the lower Dnepr, a Cossack community that was loosely allied with Poland-Lithuania had been emerging since the sixteenth century. Its way of life and socio-political organization resembled that of the Russian Cossacks on the Don, the Volga, the Iaik and the Terek.[6] At the beginning of the seventeenth century the host of the Dnepr Cossacks with its fortified centre, the Zaporozhian Sich, which lay beyond the rapids, was an important military and political factor on the steppe frontier (in eastern Slav this was called ukraina, hence the name,

Ukraine). Cossacks served in Polish campaigns against Muscovy and raided the Ottoman Empire in their boats. When Poland attempted to gain control over the Cossacks, they reacted with a series of armed uprisings. In this the mass of underprivileged Cossack recruits proved to be the driving force, and they joined forces with the Ukrainian peasants. In the first instance the Cossack elite demanded the confirmation of its autonomy and privileges, though it also supported the religious claims of the Orthodox clergy.

In 1648–49 an uprising under Bohdan Khmelnytsky (c 1595–1657), a member of the lower nobility, turned into a large-scale Ukrainian revolt against the Polish aristocracy, the Polish administrators and the Catholic clergy. Among its victims were several thousand Jews, who lived in the towns or were in the service of the Polish magnates as stewards, tenants, innkeepers or tax collectors. After a number of successful campaigns the Cossacks were able to impose the military organization of the Zaporozhian host on a large part of Ukraine, and to create an independent political entity headed by hetman Khmelnytsky and an elite (starshyna) consisting of Cossack officers. Since Poland was not willing to accept the secession of Ukraine, and since the Dnepr Cossacks were no match for a great power such as Poland, they were forced to look around for allies. One possibility was the Khanate of Crimea and the Ottoman Empire that supported it. In 1648 Khmelnytsky decided to choose this option. However, the Crimean Tatars proved to be rather unreliable allies.

Muscovy was another possible ally. After 1648 the Ukrainian Cossacks repeatedly offered to accept the tsar as their overlord if he agreed to come to their assistance. But although Muscovy, in the context of the gathering of the lands of Rus, had for a long time laid claim to the inheritance of Kiev on dynastic grounds, and in this was supported by the church, it initially rejected the overtures of the Cossacks. True, Muscovy had recovered from a serious crisis, the civil war (smuta), at the beginning of the seventeenth century. Yet it did not feel inclined to embark on a conflict with Poland-Lithuania. It was only after much hesitation that tsar Aleksei summoned an imperial assembly (zemskii sobor), and this agreed to establish links with the Dnepr Cossacks. In January 1654 hetman Khmelnytsky and the Zaporozhian Cossacks swore 'eternal fealty' to the tsar in Pereiaslav, and in March the agreement – with minor adjustments – was ratified in Moscow. The tsar guaranteed the privileges and the independent judicial system of the

Cossack host, its right to self-government, which included the free election of the hetman, and even a certain, albeit limited, freedom of action with regard to foreign policy. In a separate agreement the tsar also confirmed the privileges and right to self-government of the gentry, the metropolitan and the towns of Ukraine.[7]

When the Cossacks in Pereiaslav asked the Muscovite emissary, Vasilii Buturlin, to swear a reciprocal oath he was indignant and refused. The tsar could grant privileges, but could not swear to honour them. This episode, which is transmitted in Buturlin's report, highlights the different views and attitudes of the two sides. The Cossacks, who had been moulded in the tradition of Poland-Lithuania and the politics of the steppe, viewed the agreement of Pereiaslav as a kind of military pact, which, it is true, implied subordination, but also preserved the independence of the hetmanate, and could be terminated at any time. Muscovy, on the other hand, regarded the act of Pereiaslav as the first step towards the incorporation of Ukraine. In the agreements of 1654 the tsar already referred to himself as 'autocrat of Great and Little Russia', and described 'Little Russia' as his patrimony (votchina) and its inhabitants as his subjects. The term 'Little Russia' (Malorossiia), which was of ecclesiastical and Byzantine origin, subsequently became the official Russian word for Ukraine. In the first instance the Dnepr Cossacks were welcome as military allies able to protect the south-western frontier, and this was why Muscovy was prepared to grant autonomy to the hetmanate. Thus the agreement of Pereiaslav – and this has tended to be overlooked by what has largely been Eurocentric research – stood in the tradition of the numerous agreements which Muscovy concluded with nomadic political entities in the context of the gathering of the lands of the Golden Horde, agreements which were always interpreted differently by the two partners.

The war between Russia and Poland-Lithuania, which began in 1654, and also involved Sweden, shook the alliance between the Dnepr Cossacks and the tsar. As early as 1656 Muscovy concluded a truce with Poland-Lithuania, whereas Khmelnytsky entered into an alliance with Sweden.[8] In 1658, after the death of the hetman, the Dnepr Cossacks, in the treaty of Hadiach, even reverted to the overlordship of the King of Poland – under favourable conditions. However, a large Muscovite army put an end to this alliance only a year later. Muscovy used the opportunity to alter the conditions of the 1654 agreement to its own advantage, and curtailed the Cossacks' room for manoeuvre in the sphere of foreign policy. Furthermore, Russian garrisons were sent to Ukraine. However, Polish influence remained strong, especially on the right bank of the Dnepr, so that the Cossack hetmanate was split up into two parts.

This division was sanctioned by the truce of Andrusovo, which Muscovy concluded with Poland-Lithuania in 1667. The area on the right bank of the Dnepr was assigned to Poland, whereas the area on the left bank went to Muscovy. Kiev, which lay on the right bank of the Dnepr, was assigned to Muscovy for only two years, though in fact it subsequently remained Russian. It was agreed that the Zaporozhian Sich on the lower Dnepr should be under the protection of both powers, and should continue to defend the steppe frontier. The Cossacks on the left bank reacted to the partitioning of Ukraine with an uprising, whereas the hetman on the right bank, Petro Doroshenko, attempted in vain to achieve reunification with the support of the Ottoman Empire. Although this was not destined to be the last attempt of this kind, the division of Ukraine was thus a fait accompli. Henceforth the Ukrainians lived in seven differently structured areas. In addition to the two hetmanates there was Galicia, which was solidly integrated into the Kingdom of Poland; Carpatho-Ukraine in the extreme west, which was part of Hungary; and Bukovina, which formed part of the Ottoman empire. The Zaporozhian Sich retained its freedom of action at the edge of the steppe (which included coalitions with the Crimean Tatars and the Ottoman Empire), its traditional lifestyle and economic patterns, and its military democracy, which included the Cossack Council, the ataman and – at least at the centre of the Sich – celibacy. Ukrainians increasingly settled in what was known as Sloboda Ukraine (or Slobidska Ukraina) in the east of the hetmanate. Here, at the south-western frontier of the Muscovite empire, a separate Cossack organization came into being. Its constituent regiments were under the direct control of the Muscovite voevod in Belgorod.

Despite the restrictions alluded to above, the hemanate on the left bank of the Dnepr (together with the Kiev bridgehead) retained most of its autonomy within Russia.[9] Its military and administrative division into ten regiments and its Cossack institutions remained intact. The parliament of the Cossacks, the Council of the Host or General Assembly, which now included clergymen and representatives of the urban population, elected 'His Serene Tsarist Majesty Hetman of the Zaporozhian Host', though the smaller committees, the council of officers (rada starshyny) and the general starshyna, were more important when it came to making decisions. In addition to the administration, the actual organization of the host continued officially to comprise 30,000 Cossacks. The hetmanate also retained much of its independence in economic terms. Russia confirmed the privileges of the Cossack elite, the 'noble comrades of the host' (znatni viskovi tovaryshy), which also included remnants of the Ukrainian and polonized nobility. Its members were granted landed estates and serfs, and thus the Cossack military elite was gradually transformed into a landowning nobility. Moscow supported these tendencies, which brought about an adaptation to the status of the Russian nobility and facilitated cooperation with the Ukrainian elite.

On the whole the tsar confined himself to exercising control over the hetmanate. This was done by the Little Russian Chancellery (Malorossiiskii Prikaz), which was established in 1663, and the small Russian garrisons stationed in a number of Ukrainian towns. In addition to this, in 1685 the Kievan metropolitanate was finally placed under the control of the Patriarch of Moscow. Despite these integrationist tendencies, at the end of the seventeenth century the hetmanate was only loosely dependent on Russia. This is suggested by the fact that the Malorossiiskii Prikaz was part of the Foreign Ministry in Moscow, and that a customs barrier continued to exist between the hetmanate and Russia. However, the hetmanate's sovereignty was certainly restricted, especially with regard to foreign policy.

The hetmanate on the left bank of the Dnepr flourished one last time under hetman Ivan Mazepa. The ancient Kiev Collegium, which was granted the status of an academy in 1701, continued to be the leading eastern Slav institute of tertiary education. It now began increasingly to have an influence on Russia (see Chapter 4). Furthermore, there were more and better elementary and secondary schools than in Russia. At the beginning of the eighteenth century, Mazepa, who skilfully played off his enemies against each other, managed to reunite the separated parts of Ukraine along the Dnepr. In the (third) Northern War Ukraine then became the theatre of the military conflict, and Mazepa and the Zaporozhian Sich took the side of Sweden. The Russian government reacted promptly to this by destroying the Sich and deposing Mazepa. After Peter the Great had inflicted a decisive defeat on his Swedish enemy, Charles XII, and the latter's ally Mazepa at the battle of Poltava, he began to draw the hetmanate more closely into

Russia. As a first step, the Russian garrisons in Ukraine were considerably enlarged. At the same time Ukraine began to be exploited in economic terms by means of taxes and customs duties. The 'Little Russian College', which consisted of Russian officers, was established in 1722. Unlike the Malorossiiskii Prikaz, it was not attached to the Foreign Ministry, but to the Senate. It was located in Ukraine, at the court of the hetman, and was given considerable administrative and judicial responsibilities. As a result, a hetman was no longer appointed on a regular basis.

The years after the death of Peter the Great gave the hetmanate a breathing space. In 1727 a hetman was once again appointed, and Ukrainians began to be admitted to the Little Russian College. At the same time St Petersburg continued the policy of cooperating with the loyal Cossack elite, which was increasingly integrated into the nobility of the Russian empire. This process of assimilation was supported by the fact that Russian nobles were granted estates in Ukraine on the left bank of the Dnepr. Despite significant constraints and renewed setbacks between 1734 and 1750, the hetmanate was able to retain its special administrative and social status until the second half of the eighteenth century. There was even a final upsurge under the last hetman, Kyrylo Rozumovsky (1750–64).

In the reign of Catherine II the autonomy of the hetmanate finally came to an end.[10] The empress denied 'Little Russians' independence of any kind, in particular on account of the fact that their elite was gradually being absorbed into the Russian nobility. Apart from this she considered the pre-absolutist estate-based organization of the hetmanate, and of the Zaporozhian Sich in particular, as an impediment to the modernization of Russia, and as a potential danger for tsarist autocracy. A greater degree of integration also seemed appropriate in view of the fact that, in the wake of Russia's thrust into the steppes to the north of the Black Sea, Ukraine had acquired greater economic and strategic importance. In 1764 the office of hetman was finally abolished. An order issued by Catherine II at this time makes it abundantly clear how much she disliked the hetmanate: 'When Little Russia no longer has a hetman, one should try to make people forget both the era and the names of the hetmans.'[11] Yet here again the Russian government proceeded in a stepwise manner. Thus the special administrative status of the hetmanate was only abolished at the beginning of the 1780s, when the Russian provincial administration and the Russian system of taxation were introduced. As early as 1765 Sloboda Ukraine had become a normal province of the Russian empire. In 1775, when, after the victory over the Ottoman Empire, the steppe had been secured, Russian troops destroyed the Zaporozhian Sich. The Zaporozhian Cossacks were reorganized, and later resettled on the Kuban. The Cossack host of the former hetmanate was abolished and transformed into regular units of the Russian army. Steps were now taken to ensure the social integration of Ukraine. In 1785 a part of the Cossack elite was co-opted into the nobility of the empire. However, those who were lower down the social scale first had to prove that they were of noble descent in lawsuits that sometimes went on for decades. The other social groups were systematized on Russian lines. The free Cossacks, who were a characteristic of the hetmanate, were gradually incorporated into the category of state peasants, whereas the Ukrainian peasants, who were largely dependent, but not serfs, were degraded to the status of serfs, and the Ukrainian clergy brought into line with the Russian clergy. Linguistic homogeneity also made some progress, for the upper class gradually began to speak Russian, which was also the official administrative language. Conversely, Ukrainian sank to the level of the spoken language of the peasants. The far-reaching integration of the hetmanate into the Russian empire under Catherine II elicited a certain amount of protest, as is shown by the opinions expressed by Ukrainian deputies sent to the Legislative Commission in 1767–68, though on the whole it met with little resistance. This was primarily due to the fact that the Russian government had succeeded in co-opting and partly assimilating the Ukrainian elite, which was thus largely neutralized.

By the end of the eighteenth century the autonomy of the hetmanate had vanished, with the exception of a few residual vestiges of its administrative and social structure. In the eyes of the Russian government, Ukraine on the left bank of the Dnepr had become part of the Russian core, and the Ukrainian polity created by the Dnepr Cossacks had been eliminated. However, the hetmanate of the Dnepr Cossacks, especially its initial phase, has survived in Ukrainian tradition as a 'Golden Age'. It has often been asked why Ukrainians failed to maintain the sovereign state they fought for and established in the middle of the seventeenth century. Attempts to answer this fateful question concerning the Ukrainian nation have cited foreign policy factors – the struggle of the great powers for mastery of eastern Europe – and domestic reasons – the political and social instability of the hetmanate and the 'collaboration' of the Cossack elite with the Russian government. But as was pointed out at the beginning of this section, the fact that the unusual degree of autonomy which the hetmanate enjoyed until the beginning of the eighteenth century was totally abolished within the space of a few decades also had something to do with the special relationship of the Russians with the Orthodox Ukrainians who spoke a language related to theirs. This later had an influence on Russian policy in the nineteenth and twentieth centuries.

2. The First Step to Belorussia: Smolensk

In 1654, the year in which the Ukrainian Cossacks swore allegiance to the tsar, Russian troops conquered the city of Smolensk on the upper Dnepr. Smolensk had formed part of the Grand Duchy of Lithuania since the beginning of the fifteenth century. It had been occupied by Muscovite troops in 1514, and had then reverted to Poland-Lithuania in 1611. Thus, before the Smolensk district once again came under Russian control in the middle of the seventeenth century, it had already once been part of the Muscovite state for almost a century. This tradition, and the fact that in the Soviet era Smolensk formed part of the Russian (and not of the Belorussian) republic, have contributed to a state of affairs in which the conquest of Smolensk is hardly ever discussed in the context of the rise of the multi-ethnic empire, although until the beginning of the nineteenth century the majority of the inhabitants in the area were Belorussian peasants, whereas in the seventeenth century its social and political elite consisted of Polish or polonized nobles.

The conquest of Smolensk occurred during the second Northern War, in the course of which large parts of Lithuania were occupied by Russian troops.[12] In Smolensk the garrison and the rest of the population received guarantees that they had the right to leave the city, but most of the citizens swore an oath of allegiance to the tsar. Although Moscow guaranteed the possessions, rights and privileges of the nobility and the urban population, numerous nobles, service men and townspeople from the newly conquered territories were resettled in the interior of the Muscovite realm as the war continued. Thus 300 Smolensk nobles and Cossacks were sent to the recently erected Trans-Kama line of fortifications a long way to the east.[13] Close contacts with

Lithuania and the presence of a sizeable Belorussian colony in Moscow contributed to the westernization of Russia in a manner that was reminiscent of the influence of Ukraine.

After it had been conquered, the Smolensk district was incorporated into the Russian administrative structure. At the same time a Moscow central office (Prikaz kniazhestva Smolenskogo) responsible for 'the principality of Smolensk' was established. It resembled the existing offices for the Khanates of Kazan and Sibir, and the Malorossiiskii Prikaz that was set up a few years later.[14] In ecclesiastical terms the area was now placed under the control of Moscow. The Uniate archbishopric of Smolensk was abolished, and an Orthodox bishopric founded in its place. Although Catholics were given guarantees that they could practise their religion, in practice they were soon subject to constraints.[15]

After Poland-Lithuania had finally ceded the area of Smolensk to Muscovy in the truce of Andrusovo (1667), the property rights of the nobility were reconfirmed: 'The great rulers have shown mercy to the szlachta of Smolensk, Belsk and Roslavl, and they command that they and their heirs are to possess their estates [maetnosti, from the Polish majętność] . . . in accordance with their imperial commands and the grants and privileges of the Polish kings . . . '[16] The minor Smolensk nobility, from which, amongst others, came Grigorii Potemkin, the statesman and favourite of Catherine II, conserved certain idiosyncratic traits such as the everyday use of Polish. For a long time townsmen insisted on privileges such as the right to own land, and exemption from the poll tax.[17]

In the eighteenth century the special status of the Smolensk szlachta and its relations with Poland-Lithuania were gradually curtailed.[18] They were no longer permitted to call their estates maetnosti, to send their sons to Jesuit colleges in Lithuania or to invite Catholic priests into the country. In 1761 the special administrative status of the Smolensk szlachta was abolished, and after the partitions of Poland it gradually merged with the Russian nobility. This was reinforced by the fact that Great Russian areas which had been part of Russia uninterruptedly since the fifteenth century were added to the east of the Smolensk province, and that more and more Russian nobles were given estates there. Despite this gradual process of russification the Belorussian peasants in the western part of the area continued to constitute the majority of the population until the nineteenth century, and to this day Belorussian national historiography considers large parts of the region around Smolensk (in Belorussian, Smalensk) to be an integral part of Belorussia.[19]

3. A Window to the West: Estonia and Livonia

The incorporation of eastern Ukraine and of the area of Smolensk had confronted Russia with what to some extent were central European structures and traditions. However, Peter the Great first opened an obvious 'window to Europe' by breaking through to the Baltic. Whereas it is true that, in the 'Bronze Horseman', Pushkin called the new capital, St Petersburg, the window to Europe, the metaphor is even better suited to Estonia and Livonia, which Russia conquered in 1710. Since the Middle Ages this area on the Baltic had acquired a central European character on account of the Teutonic Knights, German colonization to the east, and subsequently Swedish rule. Although the Baltic provinces turned out to be a foreign body in the Russian empire, in the eighteenth century the estate structure of the nobility and the urban population corresponded to the reformist ideas that Peter the Great hoped to apply to the whole of Russia. This for the first time revealed the dilemma of Russian policy on nationalities in the west, the contradiction between the absolutist ideals of the unification and systematization of the empire, and the function which societies structured on central European lines performed for the westernization of Russia in acting both as bridges and models.

The ancient province of Livonia, which the Order of the Fraternity of the Sword (Schwertbrüderorden) had founded at the beginning of the thirteenth century, was divided up between Poland-Lithuania and Sweden in 1561. In 1629 the south, with the exception of Lettgallia, also came under Swedish control, whereas the Duchy of Kurland remained under that of Poland.[20] The two parts – smaller Estonia with Reval and Narva in the north, and larger Livonia with Riga and Dorpat in the south – enjoyed a special autonomous status in the Kingdom of Sweden. The corporations of the nobility (Ritterschaften) – provincial diet and diet council – and of the towns – town council and guilds – had been able to retain their rights of self-administration and privileges, albeit under the control of Swedish governors. The German and partly Swedish aristocracy owned the land and in return did military service. In contrast to free Swedish peasants, the Estonian and Latvian peasants, who constituted the majority of the population, were tied to the land as serfs who belonged to the German nobles. The German population of the towns carried on a flourishing trade with Holland on the one hand, and Lithuania and Russia on the other. Estate self-government was also linked to the Lutheran church and its German clergy. Furthermore, the central European character of the region was reflected in the educational system. A university had been founded in Dorpat in 1632, more than a century before the first Russian university, and it remained in existence, despite a number of long interruptions, until 1710. In addition to the existing primary schools and grammar schools in the towns, rural schools were established towards the end of the seventeenth century for the 'non-German' population.

Ever since the sixteenth century, Russia had attempted to conquer the adjoining area on the Baltic and its prosperous towns, which controlled some of Russia's trade with the west. Some parts of Livonia and Estonia were in fact taken in the first two Northern Wars (1558–83, 1656–61), though Russia was always forced to retreat from the Baltic coast. Thus it was wholly natural that Peter the Great should have attempted once again to conquer Estonia and Livonia in order to promote his two central aims. These were to transform Russia into a European great power, and to modernize it. The loss of its richest provinces would decisively weaken Sweden, Russia's most important rival in north-eastern Europe, whereas the economic and human resources and the central European character of the region's infrastructure would help to achieve the second of his two goals.[21]

The convoluted course of the (third) Northern War (1700–25) cannot be described in this context. Peter conquered Swedish Ingermanland early in his reign, and established the future capital of St Petersburg here at the mouth of the Neva in 1703. However, not until 1710, after the victory of Poltava, was Russia in a position to conquer Livonia and Estonia with the help of Denmark and Poland. Although Livonia had originally been promised to Poland-Lithuania, Peter kept it, and it remained under Russian control. On the other hand, Kurland remained Polish, though as a result of dynastic marriages it came under Russian influence. Using familiar and well-tried methods, Peter managed to obtain the support of a part of the Baltic German nobility (for example, the former speaker of the Livonian Ritterschaft, Johann Reinhold von Patkul, and the Estonian noble Gerhard Johann von Löwenwolde) because they believed that their self-government and privileges were being threatened by Swedish absolutism and attendant measures designed to promote integration and regularization. Thus, in addition to stating that he had the right to make such conquests and adducing ancient claims, Peter justified the annexation of Livonia and Estonia as a liberation from Swedish oppression: 'We . . . believe that not only the esteemed nobility, but also the City of Reval will appreciate their liberation from the Swedish yoke, under which they have been forced to groan for so long.'[22] It must be said, however, that the majority of Baltic German nobles and of the townspeople resisted the Russian armies with grim determination.

After the conquest in 1710 Russia concluded treaties of capitulation with the corporations of the nobility and the towns. These formed the basis of the distinctly special status of Estonia and Livonia within the Russian Empire which was accorded international recognition at the Peace of Nystad in 1721. On this occasion the basic principles of the Russian policy of incorporation – preservation of the status quo and cooperation with the foreign elite – were applied in a model manner. The Swedish provinces of Livonia and Estonia were turned into two provinces of the Russian Empire, and the Governor(-General)s, who were in part recruited from among the ranks of the Baltic Germans, constituted practically the only connection with St Petersburg. The regional administration and the judicial system remained in the hands of the corporations of the nobility and the towns, whose privileges were confirmed: 'The status provincialis is restored in full, and the corporations of the nobility shall retain their ancient and customary rights and duties.' Peter the Great's general confirmation states:

> Herewith we declare to our loyal nobles and diet in Livonia, and to their heirs, that all previously and legally acquired privileges brought to our attention . . . statutes, feudal rights, immunities, jurisdictions, freedoms . . . rightful possessions and property . . . are graciously confirmed and ratified by us and our rightful heirs herewith and in pursuance thereof.

The existence of the Lutheran faith and the state church were guaranteed, as was the use of German as the administrative and judicial language: 'That in the country and also in all the towns the Protestant religion hitherto practised in Livonia . . . shall without let and hindrance . . . be preserved in pure and steadfast form.[23]' Thus the status quo was not merely confirmed. The Baltic German elite was in fact better off than under Swedish rule, for the control of the centre diminished, and what were known as reductions, which had reduced the amount of land owned by the nobles and increased the amount owned by the king of Sweden, were repealed.

In the case of the Baltic Germans, the special interests of Peter the Great's Russia, which were briefly alluded to above, help to explain the strict adherence to the principles of indirect rule with the aid of the native elite. The idea was to tap the economic, administrative, military and intellectual abilities of the German elite in Estonia and Livonia for the purposes of war and the modernization of Russia. For this the traditional structures did not have to be changed, for they constituted a kind of prototype of a European Russia. In fact Peter the Great's reforms were to a large extent modelled on the example of Sweden.[24] But apart from this, for Russia cooperation with the Baltic German nobility was also fairly simple because the social order was largely the same as the one which existed in Russia itself. This explains why the Estonian and Latvian peasants dependent on the German gentry are not even mentioned in the treaties of capitulation.

In the course of the eighteenth century the new Baltic provinces settled down within the framework of the Russian Empire. The Russian government lent its support to the entrenched oligarchical rule of the German Baltic nobility by allowing the nobles to form closed corporations and to monopolize the provincial diets, and by permitting the noble ownership of land to increase, and serfdom of the Russian variety to be applied to Estonian and Latvian peasants. In economic terms the area recovered from the destruction caused by the war (and by the plague), and Riga became the leading harbour for Russia's trade with the rest of the world. Some Baltic Germans also emigrated into the Russian interior, especially to St Petersburg, and made an important contribution to the modernization of Russia (see Chapter 4). On the other hand, there was an influx of immigrants from Germany into the area, though (as yet) there were no Russian settlers in the Baltic provinces.

The virtually unclouded cooperation between Russia and the Baltic German elite experienced its first crisis under Catherine II.[25] The empress had at first confirmed the privileges and rights of the Baltic Germans, and then attempted unsuccessfully to carry out agrarian reforms in the Baltic provinces. She subsequently curtailed the provinces' autonomy, though not as rigorously as in the case of Ukraine. The administrative code introduced in 1783 partly abolished the estate-based bodies, or deprived them of some of their powers, and the simultaneous introduction of the poll tax put an end to their financial autonomy (and led to a peasant uprising). The Charters to the Nobility and the Towns issued in 1785 brought social conditions into line with those of Russia, and abolished the monopoly of the corporations of the nobility and the estate institutions of the towns.

These attempts to bring about a more pronounced administrative, economic and social integration of the Baltic provinces were of a transitory nature. In 1796, after Catherine's death, the new tsar, Paul, revoked most of his mother's measures and gave new guarantees protecting the traditional self-government, rights and privileges of the nobility and the towns. It is significant that the poll tax was not abolished. It weighed heavily on the peasants, as did the duty to provide recruits for the armed forces, which Paul extended to the Baltic provinces.[26] The loyal German Baltic elite continued to perform the function of being a guarantor of stability in the region and a complementary elite in the bureaucracy, the armed forces and the cultural life of the Russian empire as a whole. In the first half of the nineteenth century the Baltic provinces continued to be a world of their own. They were still characterized by their pre-modern socio-political structure, and still constituted a window on Europe on account of their educational system and culture, and their role as a go-between.

4. The Four Partitions of Poland

The partitioning of Poland constituted an act of violence that was without parallel in the earlier history of Europe. It infringed on legal norms and adversely affected the stability of the ancient political order of Europe.[27] The Kingdom of Poland-Lithuania, a sovereign and equal member of the European system of states which had been in existence for centuries, was abolished by and divided up between its neighbours Prussia, Russia and Austria. In the history of Russian expansion there were certain precedents for the annexation of a sovereign polity – the incorporation of the Khanate of Kazan, which had occurred more than two centuries earlier, and, after the first partition of Poland, that of the Khanate of Crimea. Yet in the context of European politics the abolition of Poland-Lithuania was on a different level than that of the two Tatar polities.

In the course of the four partitions of Poland between 1772 and 1815 the Russian Empire acquired a large territory of more than 450,000 square kilometres with significant human and economic resources, and thus strengthened its supremacy in eastern Europe. But Poland, as Rousseau had already predicted in his *Considérations sur le gouvernement de Pologne*, which was published in 1772, was easier to swallow than to digest.[28] The wide expanses of Poland-Lithuania were a foreign body in Russia on account of their historical traditions, their socio-political organization, their religion and their culture, and Polish resistance ensured that the Polish question remained a permanent problem in international politics well into the twentieth century, and a destabilizing factor within autocratic Russia.

The Kingdom of Poland-Lithuania had been a multi-ethnic state since the Middle Ages, and in the eighteenth century formed a colourful ethnic and religious mixture.[29] Since reliable sources do not exist, there are considerable differences between the data pertaining to the various ethnic groups given in the national historiographies. Roman Catholic Poles constituted only about 40 per cent of the population, and in the eastern areas of the Grand Duchy of Lithuania and Ukraine, which were ceded to Russia, their share of the population was considerably smaller. Here the Ukrainians and Belorussians were in the majority, and in Poland-Lithuania taken as a whole they also constituted about 40 per cent of the population. The majority of them belonged to the Uniate church which owed allegiance to the Pope, though a minority had remained faithful to the Orthodox church. About 5 per cent of the total population were Catholic Lithuanians, about 4 per cent largely Lutheran Germans (primarily in the west). The Latvians in Kurland (Lutherans) and in Polish Livonia or Lettgallia (Catholics) formed a considerably smaller group. More numerous were the Jews, who made up 7–9 per cent of the population of Poland-Lithuania (including a small group of Karaim). They constituted the largest Jewish community in Europe. Whereas the Jews retained their own language, Yiddish, two other small minorities, the Armenians, who were in full communion with the Roman Catholic church, and the Muslim Tatars were gradually polonized. Up to the seventeenth century the Grand Duchy of Lithuania employed as its official administrative language an eastern Slav written language that was similar to Belorussian. This was superseded by Polish, which came into general use in the eighteenth century.

The political, social and cultural elite, Poland-Lithuania's political nation, was the nobility (or szlachta). It consisted of Poles and of eastern Slav or Lithuanian aristocrats who had been polonized over the centuries, but had to a certain extent preserved a special regional consciousness. In comparison with other countries the Polish nobility, which amounted to more than 7 per cent of the total population, and about 20 per cent of the Polish population, was a very large group.[30] It was strongly differentiated in social and economic terms. More than 40 per cent of the nobles possessed no land of their own, and 40 per cent owned only small estates. Both on the vast estates of the small group of magnates, and on the estates of the middle nobility, the church and the crown, the majority of peasants were serfs who were required to labour for their masters. In the centre and in the west most of them were Poles, whereas in the eastern territories the vast majority were Ukrainians, Belorussians and Lithuanians. In right-bank Ukraine, which had formed part of the hetmanate of the Dnepr Cossacks founded by Khmelnytsky in 1648, Cossack organizational structures had already been abolished by the end of the seventeenth century. Its elite was subsequently incorporated into the Polish nobility, and the Ukrainian peasants once again came under the control of the Polish magnates.[31] However, the social, ethnic and religious tensions remained, and were demonstrated by the uprisings of the Ukrainian haidamaks, bandits who sought to redress social injustice in the Cossack tradition. They were opposed to the Polish nobility, to Catholic priests and to Jews, and in the end it only proved possible to quell the insurrection by calling on Russian military assistance.

Poland-Lithuania had numerous towns, most of which were fairly small. A significantly large number was owned by the magnates, and this was a sign that the nobility dominated the urban population. The Polish and German citizens of the towns possessed an estate organiz-ation based on German law, whereas Ukrainians, Belorussians and Lithuanians were at the most present in the lower urban orders. In Poland the sizeable Jewish community had enjoyed wide-ranging privileges, communal self-government (through the institution of the kahal) and the right to practise its religion since the Middle Ages.[32] Jews enjoyed personal liberty, had to pay taxes and were protected by the king. However, they did not have any political rights in the nobles' republic. Most of them lived in the towns, working as merchants, shopkeepers, moneylenders and craftsmen. They formed a community that in legal, cultural and religious terms and with regard to its lifestyle was quite distinct from the other ethnic groups, and strongly differentiated in social and economic terms. An increasingly large number of Jews became dependent on Polish magnates. They worked in the country as estate managers, or became tenants and innkeepers. Thus in Poland-Lithuania Jews and Christians lived in close proximity, engaging in economic competition in the towns, which sometimes led to animosity, and as social antagonists in the country, where Jews interacted with the Ukrainian, Belorussian and Lithuanian peasants as representatives of the nobles.

The Polish-Lithuanian multi-ethnic polity possessed in its most extreme form an estate-based constitution in which the estates – which meant the szlachta – were clearly more powerful than the king. Thus its system of government was diametrically opposed to that of autocratic and absolutist Russia. The noble assemblies, the provincial diets (sejmiki) and the national diet (sejm) made decisions concerning important issues, such as the levying of taxes and the election of the king, and they upheld traditional principles of unanimity (liberum veto) in the Chamber of Deputies of the Sejm, of equality and of the individual 'Golden Freedom' of the nobles. The steady increase in the power of the magnates, which undermined these principles, and the decline of Poland-Lithuania in economic and foreign policy terms, which began in the middle of the seventeenth century, resulted in a functional crisis of its libertarian constitution. This provided foreign powers with numerous ways of becoming involved in the country's internal affairs. And the relationship between the Catholics and other religious denominations deteriorated. Whereas Poland-Lithuania had been a shining example of tolerance in the sixteenth century, non-Catholics were increasingly discriminated against as the Counter-Reformation progressed. The religious conflicts went hand in hand with social problems, and Poland's neighbours, Russia and Prussia, were able to use these in order to intervene as protectors of Orthodox and Lutheran 'dissenters'.

The Partitions of 1772, 1793 and 1795
Poles, Ukrainians, Belorussians, Lithuanians

The conflict between Russia and Poland-Lithuania, which began at the end of the fifteenth century and lasted until the eighteenth century, was a continuation of the power struggle for the mastery of Rus which the Grand Dukes of Muscovy and Lithuania had conducted since the fourteenth century. In the sixteenth century the initiative was first taken by Muscovy, though after the defeat of Ivan IV in the Livonian War it passed to the King of Poland, who in 1610 occupied Moscow and had his son crowned as tsar. In the middle of the seventeenth century the tide turned once again, and Poland was forced to cede to Muscovy left-bank Ukraine and Smolensk. In the Great Northern War of 1700–21 Russia finally advanced to become the greatest power in eastern Europe, and established hegemonic control over Poland-Lithuania, in the internal conflicts of which it intervened on numerous occasions.[33] The Kingdom became the military training field and foreign policy toy of the great powers. Russia, which was once again an ally of Prussia after the Seven Years War (1756–63), succeeded, in 1764, in securing the election of Stanisław August Poniatowski, a Russian candidate, as king, and in 1768 in establishing a permanent protectorate over Poland-Lithuania. When large sections of the nobility opposed this in the Confederation of Bar, a civil war ensued, and this led to the intervention of Russian troops. The other two eastern European great powers, Prussia and Austria, looked on these developments with suspicion, especially since they were also accompanied by Russian successes against the Ottoman Empire, and pressed for some kind of compensation at the expense of Poland.

In the first partition of 1772 the kingdom lost about a third of its territory and population, and Russia acquired the eastern areas of Belorussia and Polish Livonia. This territory, which reached to the Western Dvina and the upper Dnepr, was primarily inhabited by Belorussian (and in Polish Livonia, Latvian) peasants, an urban population of which the Jews were the largest single group, and a thin layer of Polish nobles. The Poles reacted to the shock of the partition by introducing reforms in the fiscal and educational fields, in the army and in the political system, which culminated in the constitution of 3 May 1791. This, the first written representative constitution in Europe, was a challenge to the absolutist neighbouring powers in the age of the French revolution. Russia was also alarmed because the noble republic had rejected its protectorate status in 1788. Russian troops supported by a new (weak) noble confederation marched into Poland-Lithuania in order to combat 'the French pestilence' in 1792.[34] The second partition of 1793 took away more than half of the Kingdom's remaining territory, leaving nothing but a rump state dependent on Russia. A liberation struggle led by Tadeusz Kościuszko ended in 1794 with the Poles being defeated. Many of them subsequently emigrated and fought for the liberation of Poland from afar, especially from France. The end of the uprising led to the third 'general, final and irrevocable partition' in 1795, and two years later the three powers involved in the partitions recognized 'the necessity of eliminating anything capable of reviving memories of the existence of the Kingdom of Poland . . . and undertook never to incorporate the term "Kingdom of Poland" into their titles, and indeed to abolish it forever'.[35]

In the second and third partitions Russia acquired almost all of the areas inhabited by Lithuanians, Belorussians and Ukrainians up to the Memel, the western Bug and the Dnestr, and the Duchy of Kurland (but not predominantly Ukrainian eastern Galicia, which went to Austria, and the south-western part of Lithuania, Suvalkiia, which went to Prussia). The majority of the population in almost all of the areas acquired by Russia was not Polish, and the Russian government justified the annexation of the new territories in a number of ways, including the wish to complete the 'gathering of the lands of Rus', 'of the lands and towns which had once belonged to the Russian Empire, had been populated by their fellow Slavs (edinoplemenniki) and illuminated by the orthodox Christian faith'.[36] This was later taken up by Russian and Soviet historiography, which interpreted the partitions of Poland as 'a historically progressive reunification' of virtually all of the orthodox eastern Slavs within the Russian Empire.[37]

The incorporation of the vast territory annexed in the three partitions of Poland with its more than 7 million people, and its political, social, economic, ethnic and religious diversity posed new problems even for the Russian state with its rich store of experience in regard to expansion.[38] In practical terms Russian policy distinguished between four regions: eastern Belorussia and Polish Livonia, which had already become Russian in 1772 (the later provinces of Vitebsk and Mogilev); right-bank Ukraine (Podolia, Volhynia and the parts of the province of Kiev which first became Russian in 1793); Lithuania proper (the later provinces of Vilna, Minsk and Grodno); and the Duchy of Kurland. With its Baltic German elite and Latvian peasantry the Duchy of Kurland was subsequently added to the Baltic provinces of Livonia and Estonia as a third administrative unit. The privileges of the nobility and the institutions of self-administration, which were to some extent different from those of the other two governments, were confirmed.[39] Kurland will be discussed below in the context of the Baltic provinces.

Russian policy towards the areas that had been part of Poland-

Lithuania changed in the decades after the first partition. Whereas under Catherine II – as had been the case with Ukraine and the Baltic provinces – an attempt was made to achieve greater homogeneity and unity within the empire, the short reign of Paul (1796–1801) showed greater respect for the traditional structures of the peripheral areas. This meant that the districts which had been Russian since 1772 were subject to longer and more intense integrational pressure than the main section, which was only annexed in 1793 and 1795. Russia's continual military involvement in the west made it impossible, between 1798 and 1815, to embark on a forcible integration of the territories that had once been part of Poland-Lithuania. This was mirrored internally by the reforms carried out under the youthful Alexander I, which were partly the work of Polish magnates, and primarily of Prince Adam Jerzy Czartoryski (1770–1861), who was Russian Foreign Minister from 1804 to 1806.

When it came to integrating the Polish-Lithuanian areas, Russian policymakers were confronted with the same problems they had faced in the case of the eastern Ukraine, the area of Smolensk and the Baltic provinces. How could regions with a distinct estate organization, legal system and political tradition be incorporated into the Russian Empire? Here again it was of crucial importance to reach a modus vivendi with the elite. This was particularly difficult in the case of the Polish nobility, in view of the fact that it was not only the elite in social, economic and cultural terms, but had also been the political nation of the kingdom and was unable to come to terms with the loss of its independence and participation in the political process. On the other hand, the non-noble population, the townspeople and the Lithuanian, Belorussian and Ukrainian peasants did not really play a role as the partners of Russian policymakers. Only the status of the Jews (see below) had to be clarified.

After Russian troops had secured the new territories in military terms, the question first had to be resolved of whether 'the areas annexed from Poland' (oblasti ot Polshi prisoedinennye) were to remain an autonomous unit as had been the case with the Cossack hetmanate. The idea of establishing a Grand Duchy of Lithuania that was loosely associated with Russia, which was mooted in 1811 by Michał Ogiński, stood as little chance in the age of Catherine II as the idea of a special status on the lines of the Baltic provinces. The new territories were immediately incorporated into the system of provinces created in 1775, and the institutions relating to the state as a whole, in particular the Sejm, were abolished. Initially Catherine did not guarantee her new subjects any special rights, promising instead that they 'would enjoy all the rights, freedoms, and privileges which her old subjects possess'.[40] But on the regional level Russia was forced to fall back on the experience of the Polish nobles, and filled most of the administrative posts with Poles. Polish continued to be the language of the administration and the courts, and Russia confirmed the use of the Lithuanian Statute, the judicial code of the Grand Duchy of Lithuania, which stemmed from the sixteenth century. However, in eastern Belorussia, which was regarded as a Russian area, the Russian language and Russian courts were introduced as early as 1778, and Russian officials appointed to the more important posts. Yet even here the local administrative level remained in Polish hands. Under tsar Paul the noble provincial diets (sejmiki) were revived, though after 1802 their responsibilities were once again gradually curtailed. In December 1796 Paul confirmed that the provinces of Belorussia, Lithuania and right-bank Ukraine (and the Baltic provinces, Old Finland and the former hetmanate) would be governed 'on a special basis, in accordance with their rights and privileges'.[41] However, this applied only to a limited extent to eastern Belorussia and the province of Kiev, the capital of which had belonged to Russia since the seventeenth century.

As in its earlier expansionist moves, Russia sought to cooperate with the regional elite. This was not particularly difficult in view of the fact that the social position of the Polish landowning nobility corresponded to that of its Russian counterpart. Thus loyal Polish nobles were co-opted into the nobility of the empire. Russia confirmed their ownership of land and of the serfs which were attached to it, and employed them in the administration on a local level.[42] However, there were problems on account of their sheer number, and their social differentiation. In the Russian Empire about 150,000 Russian nobles were confronted with a considerably larger number of mainly Polish nobles from the areas that had belonged to Poland-Lithuania![43] The question arose of whether the mass of the poorer members of the szlachta, who owned no serfs and often no land either, and thus did not fit in with the Russian idea of the landowning nobleman, could also be co-opted into the hereditary nobility.

Polish noblemen, like their Russian counterparts, had to prove that they were of noble descent in order to be accepted into the nobility. The process of scrutinizing such credentials and the lawsuits which followed often lasted for decades, and this makes it difficult to put the results into perspective. The problem has been insufficiently researched, though a recent Polish study has revealed that many landless Polish nobles, most of whom were dependent on magnates, were demoted to taxable status immediately after the partitions.[44] True, some of them attempted to prove that they were of noble descent, though as a rule they were unsuccessful. In addition to the Russian authorities, the Polish magnates were also against according noble status to the landless szlachta. Thus, contrary to the commonly held view, before 1831 numerous poor Polish aristocrats had been demoted, paid taxes and had to supply recruits. Despite the reduction in their numbers, the Polish aristocrats co-opted into the nobility of the empire continued to constitute a far larger group in relation to the total population than the Russian aristocrats. Not counting the more than 200,000 members of the szlachta of the Kingdom of Poland (which became Russian in 1815), Poles constituted 66 per cent of the Russian hereditary nobility in 1795 (according to the pre-modern Russian censuses called 'revisions'). In 1816 they made up 64 per cent, in 1850 55 per cent.[45] However, decisive power continued to be wielded by the small group of magnates, and the Russian government succeeded in persuading many of them to cooperate with it. In the process common interests came to the fore, for example, in the preservation of the social status quo in the face of the radical movements of the republicans, and in economic progress, especially in the case of Ukraine, where the new Black Sea ports offered a substitute for the traditional export channels for grain that had been occupied by Prussia.

Russia also confirmed the estate organization of the towns, and subsequently combined it with the new municipal order laid down in the Charters of 1785. The situation of the serfs did not change in any way. Their rights, which had never been numerous, were curtailed even further in keeping with Russian practice, and under Russian rule their burdens increased on account of the imposition of the poll tax, and the duty to supply recruits for the army.

In the acts of partition Russia promised its new subjects that it would 'guarantee unrestricted freedom to practise their religion publicly'.[46] The Roman Catholic church, to which all Poles and Lithuanians, and about a quarter of Belorussians belonged, was reorganized by the Russian government without the prior consent of the Pope under the bishopric (and later archbishopric and metropolitanate) of

Mogilev. As in the case of the Muslims, the government cooperated with leading clergymen in order to exercise control over the Catholics.[47] The Orthodox church, the protection of which had already been an important Russian goal even before the partitions of Poland, was also reorganized and given active support. From the 1770s onwards the Orthodox hierarchy attempted to bring back into its fold the Uniate Belorussians and Ukrainians 'who by force and by guile had been led into the union with the Romans'.[48] The tolerance of enlightened absolutism did not apply to the Uniate church, the members of which were renegade heretics in Russian eyes (or had at the very least been forced to renounce their true religion by the Poles). Catherine II ordered Uniate bishoprics to be dissolved, and by 1796 – partly under duress – at least 1.8 million members of the Uniate church were received into the Russian Orthodox church. They included a very large number of Ukrainians from the southern areas, whereas the majority of Belorussians and Ukrainians in Volhynia remained loyal to the Uniate church. They were organized into several bishoprics and formed a division of the Roman Catholic church. Not until the reign of Nicholas I did the pressure on the Uniate church again increase. This finally led to its dissolution and incorporation in the Orthodox church in 1839.

In the areas of culture and education the newly acquired territories continued to be Polish in character. In fact, when, at the start of the nineteenth century, Russia embarked on a reorganization of its educational system, the Polish model and well-educated Polish aristocrats played a crucial role in the process. Two Poles, Prince Adam Czartoryski (Vilna) and Prince Seweryn Potocki (Kharkov), became the administrators of a whole educational district. The University of Vilna, which was reestablished in 1803, was the centre of a flourishing Polish cultural life in which among others the young poet Adam Mickiewicz participated.[49] And in Ukraine the school inspector Tadeusz Czacki created a centre of Polish learning in the lycée of Krzemieniec. But in the 1820s the Russo-Polish relationship began to go sour. A symptom of this was the trial of a secret student brotherhood at the University of Vilna to which Mickiewicz belonged.

In the eastern half of the kingdom, which was ceded to Russia in the course of the three partitions, the status quo was at first largely preserved. Whereas Poland-Lithuania had lost its centuries-old independence, and was controlled from St Petersburg in military and administrative terms, the predominant position of the Polish aristocracy persisted in the regional administration, in the judicial system, in the social structure and in culture. This was only partly true of eastern Belorussia and the province of Kiev. The majority of the population, the Ukrainian and Belorussian peasants who had in part reconverted to the Orthodox church, continued to be serfs of the Catholic Polish landowners. In the second and third decades of the nineteenth century there was a marked tendency towards curtailing the power of the Polish nobility. However, there was only a real change of course after the uprising of 1830–31.

Congress Poland

The Congress of Vienna reestablished a 'Kingdom of Poland'. However, this was not a restoration of the old Poland-Lithuania. In fact, it amounted to a fourth partition of Poland.[50] Russia, being the most important victor, received the main part of the Duchy of Warsaw, which Napoleon had created out of the predominantly Polish provinces of the Prussian and Austrian sections (without the district of Białystok, which Russia acquired in 1807). However, with the Grand Duchy of Poznań and Toruń (Posen und Thorn), Prussia was able to appropriate important parts of the Duchy of Warsaw in 1815, and the ancient capital of Cracow received the status of a free city. Thus for the Kingdom of Poland, often referred to as Congress Poland, there remained an area around Warsaw, which was about a seventh of the area and a fifth of the population of the former Poland-Lithuania. To this territory, about three-quarters of the population of which was Polish (in addition to Jews, Germans and Lithuanians), Russia could not make historical claims, even in the context of a generous interpretation of the historical facts, as it had done in the earlier partition areas primarily inhabited by Orthodox eastern Slavs.

For large sections of the Polish nobility the establishment of the Kingdom of Poland, whose name had been abolished forever by the partitioning powers eighteen years earlier, was linked with hopes of a restoration of the old Polish-Lithuanian noble republic. Such hopes had already been kindled in 1807 when Napoleon had set up the Duchy of Warsaw. However, they were dashed by the constitution on French lines that was forced upon the Duchy, and then by the defeat of the Grande Armée, in which tens of thousands of Poles had served. Yet some of the Napoleonic reforms, such as the guarantee of basic civil rights and the abolition of serfdom (without land) were subsequently of significance.

Hopes of a Poland-Lithuania under Russian protection emanated from the circle of Polish aristocrats who assembled in St Petersburg around the young tsar Alexander I under the leadership of Prince Adam Czartoryski. Such plans were linked to the overall aim of reforming Russia, in which Poland was to play a pioneering role.

The status which the Kingdom of Poland received in the constitution of 1815 was certainly bound to raise such hopes.[51] It is of course true that Article 1 stated that 'it was forever united with the Russian Empire', and that the tsar was the hereditary King of Poland. However, Alexander I granted the kingdom a constitution that took its bearings from the two constitutions of 1791 and 1807, and was the most liberal in Europe at the time. Basic civil rights and freedoms were guaranteed – ninety years earlier than in Russia – and a representative constitution with the traditional tripartite division of the sejm into king, senate and house of representatives came into force. This was a continuation of the Polish tradition, and also involved the more prosperous urban population, the peasants and the clergy. 'The Polish nation shall for all time receive a national representative institution [représentation nationale]' (Article 31). The kingdom was granted almost complete autonomy within the Russian empire, its own army with Polish officers and a kind of self-government in which only Poles were permitted to hold public office. Polish became the official language of the administration, the army and the educational system. The Catholic religion was guaranteed. Thus the Kingdom of Poland possessed numerous attributes of a sovereign state which was merely linked to Russia through the monarch. Only foreign policy remained the prerogative of the tsar.

The position of Congress Poland in the Russian Empire was thus rather similar to that of the Ukrainian hetmanate after 1654. However, the hetmanate had its own elected ruler. On the other hand, Alexander I, unlike tsar Aleksei 161 years earlier, swore to respect the Polish constitution: 'All our successors in the Kingdom of Poland . . . will swear the following oath: "I swear and promise before God and on the Gospel, to preserve and to implement the constitution with all my powers"' (Article 45). This was a novelty in the history of Russian expansion, for two reasons. Never before had a Russian ruler allowed himself to be bound by an oath sworn to his subjects, and never before had he guaranteed a constitution. The Kingdom of Poland, a constitutional monarchy with a liberal political, judicial and social order, was a foreign body in the Russian empire.

There were many motives for this — from a Russian point of view — unusual concession. They included the lack of legitimation of Russian rule, the need to take into account the views of other European powers, and the striving for independence of the Polish nobility, with whom Russia wished to cooperate. In addition to this it planned to use the newly acquired territory with its democratic traditions as a model for a projected reform of Russia: 'The organization which already exists in your country has enabled me to grant you without delay the organization which puts into practice the principles of these liberal institutions . . . and whose salutary influence will with God's help, as I hope, be spread over every region which providence has entrusted to me' (Alexander I's speech to the first Sejm in 1818).[52] However, historians differ when it comes to assessing the seriousness with which Alexander I swore such oaths and made such promises. Even the constitution of 1815 gave the ruler the ability to intervene and exercise control; for example, through the appointment of senators and ministers, through his sole right to initiate laws, through his right to convoke the sejm and to veto its decisions, and through the important office of imperial viceroy. Apart from this the office of imperial commissar, which was not envisaged by the constitution, was instituted and was given to a Russian, N. N. Novosiltsev, whereas the Grand Duke Constantine, the brother of the tsar, was made commander-in-chief of the Polish army. It is difficult to decide whether Alexander I really saw the constitution of 1815 as a way of curtailing autocratic power, or whether, acting in the tradition of Peter the Great and Catherine II, he merely wished to use it as a means of rationalizing and modernizing Russia, and of achieving a more efficient autocratic organization.[53] The contradiction between being an autocratic ruler in Russia and a constitutional monarch in Poland was bound to lead to conflict, or, as Alexander I's Corsican adviser Pozzo di Borgo put it in a prescient manner as early as 1814 : 'The title of the King of Poland can never be harmonized with that of tsar and autocrat of all Russia . . . A ruler could never bring together these differing functions without perhaps earning the displeasure of one or other of the nations concerned, or perhaps of both nations.'[54]

However, for the first few years many Poles were more pleased about the fact that the Polish state had been resurrected, and hoped for a reunification of the Kingdom with Lithuania. This harmonious mood still marked the opening of the first sejm in 1818. And the cultural and economic renaissance of Congress Poland gave reason for hope. The Polish educational system flourished, and in 1816 a university was founded in Warsaw. The practical abolition of the customs barriers with Russia created markets for the agricultural sector and for the textile industry, and economic reforms laid the foundations for the industrialization of Poland.

Yet a number of areas of conflict surfaced at an early stage. Many Poles were disappointed by the fact that no more than a small Poland had reappeared in 1815, and now expected the tsar to bring about a reunification of all the areas of the former kingdom under Russian control. Alexander I himself nourished such hopes with vague promises, and with his liberal cultural policy in Lithuania and in Ukraine. Yet people waited in vain for practical steps aimed at reuniting Poland with Lithuania and Ukraine. On the contrary, the policy towards the areas acquired in the first three partitions, especially in regard to the eastern part of Belorussia, developed in the direction of greater integration with the Russian empire. Thus the unbroken political consciousness of the Polish nobility collided increasingly with Russian policies. There were conflicts with regard to the interpretation of the constitution, and the Polish army in particular became a divisive issue. In Poland there were conflicts between liberals and conservatives, and in Russia between the government and the nationally conscious society that was gradually beginning to emerge. Many members of the Russian nobility, and officers and bureaucrats, had already advised Alexander I before the Congress of Vienna not to reestablish Poland. They believed that the concessions of 1815 went much too far. The growing conservative and nationalist forces in the following decade (including the historian N. M. Karamzin), but also the representatives of the emerging liberal intelligentsia (including the later Decembrists) were against giving Poland a special status.[55] Subsequently Russian conservatives and liberals were to find common ground in their distaste for and rejection of the Poles. In the 1820s the harmony that had existed in 1815 was already a thing of the past. As the liberal opposition increased and organized itself in the shape of secret societies, the Russian government reacted to the 'ingratitude of the Poles' by adopting sterner measures. Sensitivity towards revolutionary movements was further increased by the Decembrist uprising. Nicholas I (1825–55) then turned his back on his brother's liberal policies of reform.

Many Poles were unable to accept the loss of their state's independence, and the gradual transformation of Russian policy weakened the camp of those who wished to cooperate with the Russian empire. The mass of the Polish upper class, including Adam Czartoryski, thus supported the uprising which broke out after the revolutions in France and Belgium in November 1830.[56]

The deposition of Nicholas I and the Romanov dynasty, which was declared in January 1831, made war with Russia unavoidable. The Poles were entirely unable to reckon with outside help, and did not have the slightest chance against the might of the Russian army. The November uprising is also discussed below in connection with the Polish national movement (Chapter 6).

The consequences for Congress Poland were serious. A large section of the political, military and intellectual elite emigrated to western Europe, and attempted in the 'great emigration' to work for the liberation of Poland from abroad. As always, the Russian government reacted to the uprising with great severity. In the eyes of the Russians 'the traitorous Poles' had also forfeited their right to enjoy a special status. The Kingdom of Poland lost its sovereignty as a state and was incorporated into the Russian empire. However, the aggressive policy of integration towards Poland pursued by the Russia of Nicholas I cannot in fact be understood in the context of the pre-modern Russian multi-ethnic empire. For this reason I shall discuss it in Chapter 7.

The Integration of the Jews

A large number of Poles, Ukrainians, Belorussians and Lithuanians came under Russian rule as a result of the four partitions of Poland. So did the large Jewish community.[57] Only thus did the Jewish question reach Russia, where, in the nineteenth and twentieth centuries, it was destined to become an explosive issue. Russia came into contact with Jews much later than most other European countries. Before 1772 it was not acquainted with them, and there were hardly any anti-Jewish stereotypes in Russian society. Neither Muscovy nor the Russia of Peter the Great had a Jewish population worth mentioning. Whenever larger groups settled in Russia, they were as a rule expelled, even as late as 1742. It was no accident that this occurred at the same time as acts of repression against Muslims and animists. The incorporation of hundreds of thousands of Jews, an ethnic and religious diaspora group with a specific socio-economic structure possessed by neither of the social groups which were constitutive for Russia (nobility and peasants), thus confronted the Russian government with problems that were altogether new.

The government of Catherine II first pursued the traditional method of respecting the status quo. In a manifesto issued in 1772 the Jews of eastern Belorussia were guaranteed 'all the freedoms which they now enjoy with regard to their religion and their property', 'for the humanity of Her Imperial Highness makes it impossible for her to exclude only them from her general benevolence for all'.[58] The kahal, the Jewish communities' institution of self-government, was preserved, and so were its fiscal, administrative, judicial, cultural and religious functions. This seemed apposite not only for fiscal reasons, but also because, since the Jews did not posses an elite comparable to the nobility with which it might have been possible to cooperate, it was necessary to persuade the kahal to work together with the government, and to act as an authority capable of exercising control over its members.

On the other hand Catherine II hoped to achieve a uniform and well-ordered polity, and at the same time wished to exploit the specific economic abilities of the Jews in the modernization of the empire. For this reason the legal status of the Jews as an independent ethnic and religious group was abolished, and in the 1770s and 1780s the Jews were integrated into the estate structure of the empire. Since they were neither nobles nor peasants, rich Jews were incorporated into the estate of merchant guilds as members with equal rights, and poorer Jews into the estate of the meshchane (petit bourgeois). In this way they were given the same duties and rights as the Christian members of the urban estates. Thus enlightened and absolutist Russia did not initially discriminate against the Jews, attempting instead to integrate them by granting them equality in administrative and legal terms. This was done in order to make the best possible use of their abilities, and, in the long term, to assimilate them. In this respect Russian law, at least until the second partition of Poland, differed from the less liberal laws of most other European countries.

However, these enlightened theories soon clashed with social realities and Polish-Lithuanian traditions. This became apparent with regard to the question of the Jews in rural areas who worked as inn-keepers, tenants and administrators, and who, in the eastern part of Belorussia, were more numerous than the urban Jewish population. Jews who lived in rural areas were also assigned to the urban estates, and thus to the urban communes. This liberated them from their former dependence on the Polish nobility, but at the same time made their position more insecure. On more than one occasion Jews were forbidden to work as innkeepers or to be tenants, though for a long time it was impossible to implement this strictly. From the 1780s onwards more and more decrees were issued to resettle rural Jews in the towns. It proved impossible to implement such decrees in the short term. However, in the first quarter of the nineteenth century there were numerous instances of brutal mass resettlement, so that the number of Jews who lived in rural areas declined considerably. With these measures the government sought to regulate society in the envisaged manner, which was to assign the Jews wholly to the urban sphere. However, it changed its strategy at the beginning of the nineteenth century, and with the lure of privileges encouraged Jews to settle as colonists in 'New Russia', though this was not a great success. The government's most important motive for these radical measures was to eliminate the traditional position of the Jews in the villages, where they exercised power over eastern Slav peasants as administrators and tenants. After all, the subservience of Orthodox Christians to non-Christians was no longer tolerated in the case of the Muslims either. The peasants – and this was the predominant view – had to be protected against the Jews. This disengagement of Jews and non-Jews in rural areas was aided and abetted by anti-Jewish prejudices taken from the Polish tradition; for example, the notion that Jewish 'parasites and exploiters' had a harmful influence on eastern Slav peasants. From the end of the eighteenth century onwards such ideas gradually found their way to Russia, where they were adopted both by conservatives, for example, the poet Derzhavin, and liberals, such as the Decembrist Pestel.[59]

Soon there were also problems in the towns. These were partly due to the dual administrative assignment of Jews to both the civil administration and the kahal. As a result the administrative and judicial (but not the fiscal, cultural and religious) tasks of the kahal were gradually curtailed. As in the former Poland-Lithuania, sections of the Christian urban population protested against the equal status accorded to the Jews, and their partially privileged treatment. The Russians were primarily afraid of economic competition, and the Poles were against the inclusion of the Jews in urban self-government. The majority of Jews were also opposed to integration into Christian society. Thus the government took note of such 'complaints about certain abuses and grievances to the disadvantage . . . of the inhabitants of those provinces in which the Jews reside',[60] and used them to further its economic aims.

These were the most important reasons why, in the Russian empire, the rights of the Jews had already been curtailed by special laws even before the second and third partitions of Poland. The statute of 1804 assembled the ordinances relating to the Jews for the very first time, albeit in an unsystematic way.[61] It defined a pale of Jewish settlement (cherta osedlosti), outside of which Jews were not permitted to take up permanent residence. This comprised the formerly Polish areas, and also left-bank Ukraine and New Russia (and for a time the provinces of Astrakhan and the Caucasus). These restrictions on the Jews' freedom of movement, which remained in effect until the end of the tsarist period, went back to a petition submitted by Moscow merchants who feared Jewish competition. The government may also have agreed to it in order to direct the activities of Jews towards the areas to the north of the Black Sea which were then in the process of being opened up. An unmistakable act of discrimination against the Jews was the double tax burden imposed upon them (but not on the Karaim) in 1794. This signified that as a religious group they were being singled out for unfair treatment. Peter the Great had already adopted similar measures in the case of the Old Believers. Yet Muslims, Buddhists and animists were not discriminated against in terms of taxation. However, in practical terms the double tax burden was abolished soon after the proclamation of the statute. On the other hand, the fact that the Jews had the right, like the merchants, but unlike the Christian meshchane, to escape from the duty to provide recruits for the army by paying an agreed sum of money was something of a privilege.

The statute of 1804 also contained certain cultural constraints. Jews were henceforth required to keep their accounts in Russian, Polish or German, and Jewish officials in the municipal administration had to be able to read and write one of these languages, and were not permitted to wear Jewish clothes. On the other hand the statute confirmed the religious freedom and the economic privileges of the Jews, and their participation in urban administration. It also guaranteed access to state schools and universities (at this time still few and far between), and the existence of their own system of schools, which were now also supposed to teach Russian, Polish or German. The government's desire to utilize the specific abilities of the Jews in the modernization of Russia transpires in the sections which hold out the promise of privileges to Jews who were active as manufacturers and as factory workers. This proved to be a success inasmuch as Jewish entrepreneurs subsequently played an important role in the development of the textile industry in the west of Russia. Many of the other ordinances of the Jewish statute of 1804 were largely ignored and never implemented.

In Congress Poland Jews were not bound by the Russian ordinances.[62] Jews were not mentioned in the 1815 constitution, though it soon became abundantly clear that they were being denied equality with Christians. In the ensuing debates Russian bureaucrats, such as Novosiltsev, displayed a greater willingness to accommodate the Jews than the majority of the Poles, who were in the grip of strong anti-Semitic prejudices, and viewed the Jews as economic rivals. The Poles triumphed, and proceeded to link the emancipation of the Jews to their civilizational progress, something they first intended to encourage, partly with the help of enlightened Jews. In practice this meant that Jews could only obtain equal rights after they had been polonized. Thus the legal restrictions promulgated in the Duchy of Warsaw in 1808 (annulment of political rights for a period of ten years) were transferred to the Kingdom of Poland, and tacitly prolonged. Subsequently other laws diminishing the rights of the Jews and excluding them from urban society were enacted. At the end of 1821 the kahal was abolished and replaced by a new authority (headed by the rabbi of the community) which was confined to religious matters. And economic restrictions reduced the Jews' function of mediating between the town and the country. All in all the Kingdom of Poland missed the opportunity to initiate the emancipation of the Jews that was suggested by its liberal constitution.

The situation of the Jews in the Russian Empire did not change fundamentally in the first half of the nineteenth century. After 1815 an unsuccessful attempt was made to encourage Jews to be baptized, and in 1825 the Jewish pale of settlement was slightly reduced by excluding the provinces of Astrakhan and the Caucasus, and a zone of fifty versts from the empire's border (which was designed to prevent smuggling). In 1815 the statute of 1804 was to all intents and purposes confirmed. However, under Nicholas I the intrusions of the state increased considerably.[63] For example, in 1827 it abolished the Jews' right not to have to furnish recruits for the armed forces in exchange for a stipulated sum of money. On the face of it this simply meant that Jews were being placed on a par with non-Jews. However, the manner in which Jews between the ages of twelve and eighteen were press-ganged, and, as so-called cantonists, subjected to an extremely hard preparatory drill which was then followed by twenty to twenty-five years of military service, amounted to discrimination. Jews resisted these draconian meas-ures by running away, by self-mutilation, and by submitting petitions. The measures were also aimed at encouraging young Jews to be baptized, and were only repealed in 1856. In 1843 the decree of 1825, which ordered Jews to be moved away from areas close to the border, was implemented with great brutality, and a year later the kahal was officially abolished. However, its religious, cultural and social functions remained largely intact. On the other hand the government's radical intrusions shook the social stability of Jewish society, and, together with the enlightenment movement (Haskalah), which received support from the government, contributed to its transformation.

In the initial decades after the partitioning of Poland, Russian policy towards the Jews was full of contradictions. On the one hand it aimed from the start to integrate the Jews into the social structure of Russia in order to make use of their economic abilities and to assimilate them. However, the equality that had initially been granted to them was soon curtailed, and the strategy thus reversed. Jews were able to attain the same legal status as Christians only if they were willing to be assimilated, that is, if they were prepared to convert to Christianity. Discriminatory laws and everyday practice prevented Jews from becoming part of Christian society. An important aim was to eliminate those Jewish influences on Christians which were deemed to be detrimental. Further-more, some kind of segregation corresponded to the wishes of many Jews and non-Jews. But in the first half of the nineteenth century neither government policy nor the attitude of the population possessed the character of a determined, ideological or racist hatred of Jews. Both harsh discrimination and the development of Russian anti-Semitism were to take place in the second half of the century.

5. Autonomy for Finland

Finland as a whole came under Russian rule between the third and fourth partitions of Poland.[64] This territorial acquisition also occurred within the context of European politics. In the course of its successful campaigns against Sweden Russia had already occupied Finland on two occasions (1713–21 and 1742–43), though the country was only annexed in 1808–09 in the wake of the alliance concluded with Napoleon at Tilsit. Sweden was compelled to cede its eastern province to Russia in the Treaty of Frederikshamn. The incorporation of Finland into the Russian Empire can be compared either with the almost simultaneous integration of Poland, or with the integration of Estonia and Livonia, which had also belonged to Sweden a century earlier.

Finland had been part of the Kingdom of Sweden since the Middle Ages, though, unlike the Baltic provinces, which were acquired at a later date, it never possessed a special status. In contrast to the Baltic provinces the aristocracy and urban population spoke Swedish, and Swedish was also predominant as the language of the administration. The Finnish peasants, who made up more than 85 per cent of the population of Finland, were Swedicized if they ventured to climb the rungs of the social ladder. Their legal status was different to that of the Latvian and Estonian peasants of the Baltic provinces, for, like Swedish peasants, they were freemen. The population of Finland belonged to the Lutheran state church, which maintained an educational system on a fairly high level. A university had existed in Åbo (Turku) since 1640, and at the end of the eighteenth century it witnessed the rise of scholarly interest in the Finnish language and Finnish folklore.

Finland was a remote and economically backward Swedish province that the government in Stockholm tended to neglect. Although the four estates – nobility, clergy, burghers and peasants – sent representatives to the riksdag, they did not possess an estate organization in Finland itself. The growing pressure from the king and the perpetual wars with Russia which were fought on Finnish soil were the reasons for the growth of a regional consciousness among Finland's elite, which was directed against the King of Sweden. Thus certain 'Finlandish' nobles – 'Finlandish', in what follows, is the term I use for members of the Swedish-speaking elite in order to distinguish them from the Finnish-speaking Finns – turned to nearby St Petersburg. A leading role was played by Colonel G. M. Sprengtporten, who was in the service of Russia from 1786, and developed plans for an autonomous Finland as a Russian protectorate. In 1788, during another war initiated by Sweden, a club of Russophile officers mooted similar plans. Thus in Finland, as in the Baltic provinces, and in contrast to Poland, Russia was from the very beginning able to reckon with the support of a section of the native elite.

An area of Finland known as Old Finland had already come under Russian rule in the first half of the eighteenth century. In 1721, after Russia had occupied the whole of Finland in the Great Northern War, Sweden ceded to it not only Estonia, Livonia and Ingermanland, but also parts of Karelia and Vyborg. A number of other areas on the border were added to this in 1743 in the wake of another Russo-Swedish war. In 1721 Russia had merely guaranteed the practice of the Lutheran religion to this territory, which was now organized as the province of Vyborg. However, in 1743 it confirmed 'the privileges, customs and rights that had prevailed under Swedish rule'.[65] Thus Old Finland was granted an autonomous status which in some respects resembled that of the Baltic provinces, and Baltic Germans were often entrusted with administrative duties. German began to be used increasingly in addition to the official languages, Russian and Swedish.

The Grand Duchy of Finland, which was incorporated into Russia in 1808–09, was granted an even greater measure of autonomy. As early as 1808 Alexander I gave his word to the Finlanders that he would respect the status quo, and a parliament convened for the first time early in 1809. On 15 March 1809, before the opening of this first assembly of the Finnish estates in Borgå (Porvoo), the tsar guaranteed 'the religion, the traditional laws, the rights and privileges which each estate in this grand duchy in particular and subjects resident within it . . . have possessed hitherto by virtue of their judicial system'.[66] The autonomy granted to the Grand Duchy of Finland was considerably greater than it had been under Swedish rule. This manifested itself in the fact that the Grand Duchy had its own parliament and an administrative and judicial system staffed exclusively by Finlandish bureaucrats. This was merely presided over by a governor-general as a representative of the tsar, and not placed under the direct control of the central Russian authorities. Furthermore, Russian military structures were not introduced into Finland, which thus did not have to supply recruits and was permitted to maintain a (small) army of its own. The fact that the Grand Duchy of Finland also remained separate from Russia in economic terms was demonstrated by its customs barrier, its bank and its coinage. Finland was linked to Russia through the person of the tsar (Grand Duke) and his dynasty, and in the domain of foreign policy.

In the incorporation of Finland, Russia once again – and in a part-icularly apposite manner – made use of the method of guaranteeing the status quo and cooperating with foreign elites. The position of the Grand Duchy of Finland most nearly resembled that of the Ukrainian hetmanate (in the seventeenth century) and the Kingdom of Poland, which was established a few years later. By contrast, the Baltic provinces possessed less autonomy. And unlike Congress Poland, which in 1815 received a liberal representative constitution, Finland's socio-political order continued to be determined by the traditional estates, as in the Baltic provinces. Unlike Poland, the tsar did not go so far as to tie himself down to a constitution with an oath. Finlandish public opinion and historiography, when attempting to reject Russian claims to the contrary, subsequently interpreted the act of 1809 as the formal foundation of the state and as a legally guaranteed constitution, though such an exegesis, as the majority of Finnish historians now believe, goes too far.[67] The manifesto signed by Alexander I in Borgå does of course contain a number of unclear and ambiguous concepts. However, at least the basic Russian text seems to provide a guarantee of traditional estate autonomy and privileges, such as earlier Russian tsars had given to the Ukrainian Cossacks or the Baltic Germans.[68]

Yet the problem was not an acute one in the first half of the nineteenth century. The majority of the Finlandish upper class were content with the *de facto* autonomy they had been granted, for it was considerably more far-reaching than under the King of Sweden. This was underpinned by the fact that in 1812 Old Finland, which had been Russian since 1721 and 1743, was reunited with the Grand Duchy. In contrast to the Poles, who hoped in vain that Alexander I would reestablish their sovereign state, the Finlanders had obtained what was to all intents and purposes self-rule in an enlarged territory. True, the tsar did not convene a new parliament until 1863. However, Nicholas I confirmed the special status of the Grand Duchy of Finland. For this reason the Finlandish upper class subsequently remained loyal to Russia. And under Russian rule Finland experienced an economic and cultural upsurge. This new orientation found expression in the fact that the capital and the university were moved from Åbo (Turku), which lay across the Gulf of Bothnia from Stockholm, to Helsingfors (Helsinki), which lay on the Gulf of Finland. Helsingfors came under the economic and cultural influence of the nearby Russian capital, St Petersburg. A number of Finlanders entered the service of Russia itself as officers or civil servants. Political relations with St Petersburg were pragmatic, for neither side wanted conflict. Finlandish politicians, both in St Petersburg and in

Finland itself, took into account the internal situation in Russia, avoided provocation and also took certain measures against the opposition movements during the reign of Nicholas I. Thus the Swedish-speaking elite in Finland – unlike the Poles, though in a manner that resembled that of the Baltic Germans – became a model partner for the Russian government.

In the nineteenth century the Grand Duchy of Finland, despite the lack of constitutional guarantees, possessed a degree of internal autonomy which, in the other peripheral areas, was only seen (temporarily) in the case of the Kingdom of Poland. How are we to explain the fact that (after 1831) Finland of all places was granted such an extraordinary special status? For one thing we should bear in mind the uncertain foreign policy situation in 1809, which made it imperative to secure the north-western flank of the empire. Subsequently it continued to be in the Russian interest to have a peaceful country with a loyal population in this strategically important position near the capital. On the other hand Finland was not attractive in economic terms. It was only possible to make use of the specific abilities of the upper class, which in turn could only be done by means of a policy of cooperation. And finally, as was the case with the Kingdom of Poland and had earlier been the case with the Baltic provinces, Finland, with its estate order, its free peasantry and its Lutheran educational system based on western precepts, served as a model for the whole of Russia during the period of reform.

The large measure of autonomy which the Grand Duchy of Finland was granted for the first time in its history in 1809 laid the groundwork and set the scene for the creation of the Finnish state and nation. In his speech in Borgå, Alexander I had spoken of the fact that Finland 'now had a place among the nations',[69] though he could not know that Finland would later seek this place outside of Russia. On the other hand, 1809 saw the advent of the pragmatic cooperation with Russia which, despite serious setbacks and interruptions, continues to characterize to this day the special status of Finland as a small state in the shadow of Russia, a great power.

6. Bessarabia: Romanians or Moldavians?

At the beginning of the nineteenth century Russian expansion westwards made three final steps beyond the area settled by eastern Slavs. In the north-west, Russia seized the whole of Finland from the Kingdom of Sweden. In the west large parts of Poland came under the rule of the tsar in 1815. And, finally, in 1812 the Ottoman Empire was forced to cede to Russia the territory bordered by the rivers Dnestr, Pruth and the lower reaches of the Danube, which thereafter was known as Bessarabia. Russia lost the three territories during or after the First World War. Only Romanian Bessarabia was brought back into the Soviet fold by Stalin – as were Estonia, Latvia and Lithuania – and reorganized as the Moldavian Soviet Republic. Its name stood for a deliberate plan, for, although the results were not very convincing, in the years that followed a great deal of effort was expended on trying to create a Moldavian nation with an identity of its own that was distinct from Romania.[70]

The area between the Dnestr and the Pruth had never been a historical entity, though for a long time it had formed a part of the principality of Moldavia, which straddled the Pruth.[71] After a period of prosperity in the late Middle Ages, the principality of Moldavia had become a vassal state of the Ottoman Empire. By contrast, the Budzhak steppe along the Black Sea coast was directly ruled by the Khanate of Crimea, and the Ottoman fortresses were under the control of Istanbul. The loose tributary rule to which the Danubian principalities were subject became oppressive only in the eighteenth century under Phanariot rule. The complex administration which sought to maximize the amount of taxes collected, and which was thoroughly corrupt, was dominated by a handful of families loyal to the Sultan. They comprised a number of Greeks from Istanbul, and a number of grecicized Romanians. The leading social groups were the relatively numerous and socially strongly differentiated Romanian-speaking nobility (the boyars) and the Orthodox clergy. The Romanian-speaking peasants were free in legal terms, though the majority, known as ţaran, possessed no land of their own, and were thus obliged to pay a tithe to the noble landowners and perform labour services. On the other hand, most of the gypsies (Roma) were serfs. The small towns, which were also inhabited by Jews, Greeks and Armenians, did not play an important role. In fact, around 1800 the eastern part of the principality of Moldavia was a remote, war-torn and economically rather poverty-stricken peripheral area of the Ottoman Empire.

Russia had already had relations with the mediaeval principality of Moldavia. When, during the Russo-Turkish wars in the eighteenth century, Russian troops occupied the area on a number of occasions, they were supported by the Orthodox clergy and a section of the Romanian aristocracy.[72] Furthermore, since Russia had claimed to be the protector of the Sultan's Orthodox subjects after 1774, it gained considerable political influence in Moldavia and Wallachia. During the Napoleonic wars, and as a result of the Sultan's support for France, Russia once again occupied the Danubian principalities at the end of 1806. In the Treaty of Bucharest, which terminated this new Russo-Turkish war in May 1812, the principality of Moldavia was divided, and the territory to the east of the Pruth and the lower Danube was ceded to Russia. Although the long Russian occupation weighed heavily on the population, Russia was once again supported by a large section of the Moldavian elite. The incorporation of Bessarabia into the Russian empire was at least to some extent voluntary.

In the light of these preconditions and the precarious situation in 1812, it was natural that Russia, which was being threatened by Napoleon's Grande Armée, once again sought to cooperate with the native elite, and that it confirmed the legal, administrative and social status quo. Later Alexander I wrote, 'It is my intention to grant Bessarabia a self-rule which is consonant with its rights, customs and laws. All the estates of its inhabitants have the same right to this inheritance of their ancestors.'[73] In 1818, after some years of improvisation, the autonomous status of Bessarabia within the Russian empire was confirmed.[74] The administration, the legal system and even the system of taxation of the new district (oblast) were based on the existing order, and all functions were performed by the region's nobility, with the exception of those of the (Russian) military governor-general and his staff. The social order was retained. The landed property and privileges of the boyars were confirmed, and they were co-opted into the imperial nobility. The peasants continued to be free personally, though dependent on the noble landowners. Furthermore, the Orthodox church was reorganized within the eparchy of Kishinev. Thus the statute of 1818 granted Bessarabia a degree of autonomy which the deputy governor, F. Vigel, compared to the status of the Grand Duchy of Finland and the Kingdom of Poland.[75]

The north-western areas of Bessarabia, which continued to be dominated by Romanian-speaking boyars, differed from the Budzhak steppe near the Black Sea. After its population of Nogai Tatars and Turkish soldiers had been deported, Russia deliberately encouraged colonists to settle in the virtually uninhabited area, and tens of thousands of

Romanians, Bulgars and Gagauz (Turkic-speaking Orthodox Christians) from the Ottoman empire responded to the call. Among them were pro-Russian Romanian boyars, who were given grants of land and attempted to transform the peasants into serfs. Russian civil servants were given grants of land, and numerous Ukrainian and Russian peasants also settled in the south of Bessarabia. They were joined, as in the adjoining area of Novorossiia, by German colonists and Jews. Thus the multi-ethnic character of the area in fact increased under Russian rule.

The Bessarabian administrative structure, which was based on Ottoman practice, was introduced after 1812 and finalized in 1818, did not remain in force for long. The Russian authorities soon realized that the legal and administrative traditions of the Ottoman period, on which autonomy was based, did not – as was the case in the Baltic provinces or Finland – fit in with their vision of an estate-based order. The tax system, which the peasants found ruinous, and the large number of abuses of the system of noble self-administration provoked their displeasure, and in 1828, when a new Turkish war focused attention on Bessarabia, the very large measure of autonomy it had enjoyed was considerably curtailed. The administrative structure was brought into line with the order which prevailed in Russia, the role of the Romanian nobility in the areas of administration, taxation and the judiciary was reduced, and Russian officials under the Governor-General of New Russia began to perform the most important functions. Bessarabia nevertheless retained a certain administrative special status as a border area as late as the second half of the century and the traditional private legal system, which was still Byzantine in character, remained in force. The social status quo also remained unchanged: 'The inhabitants of Bessarabia of all estates, namely the clergy, the aristocracy . . . the merchants and meshchane, the cyrans or tillers of the soil, the gypsies who belong to the state and the landed gentry, and the Jews are granted all the rights and privileges which they have enjoyed up to the present day.'[76] The Romanian-speaking boyars, who were recognized as constituting a hereditary nobility, continued to be the dominant class; the peasants continued to be personally free, though economically dependent, and were not required to supply recruits for the army; and the special status of the unfree gypsies and the Jews was confirmed. However, the difficult task of adapting the numerous traditional population categories of Bessarabia into the Russian estate-based order continued to be addressed in the following decades.

In this period the south-western part of Moldavia, on the other side of the Pruth, and Wallachia, both of which continued to form part of the Ottoman Empire, witnessed the growth of the Romanian national movement, which, after the Crimean War, led to the formation of a Romanian nation state. The perspectives of the Romanians now changed in a fundamental way. What had been seen as liberation from Phanariot and Ottoman rule in 1812 could now be interpreted as Russian oppression. As a result Russia was saddled with the problem of Romanian irredentism.

7. Summary

Russian expansion in the west came to an end in 1815. From the middle of the seventeenth century onwards the tsarist empire had progressed as far as the Baltic and the Gulf of Bothnia, the mouth of the Danube, and the very heart of Poland. Whereas Russian expansion to the east had occurred within the framework of Eurasian steppe politics, 'the gathering of the lands of the Golden Horde', expansion to the west was part of European politics, the three Northern Wars, the partitions of Poland, the struggles against Napoleon and the Ottoman Empire. Whereas it is true to say that the areas of Poland-Lithuania which Russia acquired in the seventeenth century and as a result of the first three partitions were largely inhabited by orthodox eastern Slavs, the traditional 'gathering of the lands of Rus' was no longer the primary driving force behind the expansion. At the most it served to legitimate it.

There have been numerous attempts to explain the motives for Russian expansion between the sixteenth and nineteenth centuries. They have been accounted for in a variety of ways – as Russia's 'urge to the sea' (Kerner), as an ancient tradition of Russian imperialism which was based on the lack of natural boundaries and a resulting desire for security, or as a Messianic belief rooted in the doctrine of the Third Rome.[77] Even if such generalized explanations are not altogether erroneous, a historian will tend to remain sceptical. Rather, he will point to the internal preconditions of the Russian state, and the favourable external possibilities for expansion at the expense of weaker powers, which continually presented themselves. However, in the face of such persistent territorial growth the question arises of the purpose of such expansion. It is scarcely possible to conduct a cost–benefit analysis that takes into account all of the factors concerned. Yet Russia, as Rousseau prophesied, had bitten off more than it could chew, especially after the absorption of the Kingdom of Poland. The ensuing digestive disorders were destined to cause a great deal of misery for the Poles, and also for the Russian state and Russian society as a whole.

The non-Russians in the west put up considerably less resistance to Russian rule than the ethnic groups in the east and the south. On occasion the process of being integrated into Russia was to some extent a voluntary one, as in the case of the eastern Ukraine and Bessarabia. For the majority of non-Russians it merely signified a change of ruler, and not of the social and political order, and this made it easier to accept Russian governance. The Ukrainian Cossacks constituted an exception to this rule in that on several occasions up to the time of Mazepa they tried to escape from the Russian straitjacket by means of shifting coalitions. Another is that of the Poles, a significant number of whom were not prepared to accept the loss of a state which for centuries had been sovereign and independent.

Expansion to the west confronted the autocratic Russian state with estate-based forms of organization and regional traditions. Nevertheless, it initially had recourse to the pattern of incorporation which Muscovy had developed in 'the gathering of the lands of the Golden Horde'.[78] Here again top priority was accorded to securing the new territory in military and political terms, obtaining the loyalty of its non-Russian subjects and ensuring social and political stability. In addition to this there was the question of the profit Russia expected to derive from its new acquisition, though in the west this tended to be a matter of human resources. If it did not endanger these primary goals, an attempt was also made in the west to consolidate Russian rule by means of the existing state of affairs (for example, by guaranteeing the status quo), and to cooperate with the non-Russian elites.

Here, in contrast to the areas to the east and the south, which were partly inhabited by nomads, hunters and gatherers, there were always noble elites with which Russia could cooperate and which it could co-opt into the nobility of the empire: the Baltic Germans, the Polish landowning nobility, the Swedish-speaking nobility in Finland, the Romanian boyars in Bessarabia and also the Ukrainian Cossack nobility after it had been progressively integrated into the Russian nobility in the eighteenth century. Since Russia had very few specialists at its disposal, it was dependent on the non-Russian elites. Their task was to control and administer the peripheral areas and their populations, and to contribute their specific abilities to the administration, the army and the cultural life of the empire. In exchange Russia confirmed their privileges, estate rights and property. Initially the social and legal standing of the urban population and the peasants also remained unchanged. The idea was that merchants and entrepreneurs, including those who were Jewish, should place their skills at the disposal of Russia. On the other hand, the Russian government was not particularly interested in the peasant masses. Thus Russia took little note of ethnic groups such as Belorussians, Lithuanians, Latvians, Estonians, Finns or even Ukrainians.

The practice of religious tolerance also took its bearings from the Muscovite tradition.[79] In the seventeenth century Russia had accepted the Islamic faith of the Tatars and the Bashkirs, and the lamaist religion of the Buriats and the Kalmyks. Similarly, it now guaranteed the Lutheran faith in the Baltic provinces and in Finland, and the Catholic and Jewish faiths in Poland-Lithuania. At times this tolerance did not apply to the members of the Uniate church, who were considered to be defectors from the true faith. This was a special case. The use of the languages predominantly employed in the administrative and educational systems was guaranteed – German in the Baltic provinces, Swedish in Finland, Polish in the areas obtained through the partitions (with the exception of eastern Belorussia) and Romanian in Bessarabia. And in eastern Ukraine Ukrainian initially continued to be used, though in the course of the eighteenth century it was ousted by Russian. This was partly due to the fact that the elites were being acculturated and to measures adopted by the Russian government, which was no longer prepared to accept 'Little Russian' as a 'high' language. Although a policy of forced integration was already becoming apparent in the case of the Ukrainians and Belorussians, with whom Russians were related in linguistic and religious terms, I believe it to be a mistake to describe this as a policy of russification by applying the principles of the nation state and the later tsarist policy of assimilation to the time before the middle of the nineteenth century. Linguistic, ethnic, and – with the exception of a few short periods – religious categories still continued to play a subordinate role. In addition to political loyalty, the crucial factor was membership of a social class or an estate. A loyal noble was as a rule accepted by the Russian government as an equal, no matter if he was a Lutheran Baltic German, a Catholic Pole or a Muslim Tatar. On the other hand, there was no question of a partnership with Orthodox eastern Slav peasants.

Differing guarantees were given with regard to the administrative and political status quo of the areas in the west. A large measure of autonomy, limited only by the link with the Romanov dynasty and with regard to foreign policy, was enjoyed by the hetmanate of the Dnepr Cossacks in the second half of the seventeenth century and the Kingdom of Poland and the Grand Duchy of Finland at the beginning of the nineteenth century. In fact, the three territories were only to some extent deemed to belong to the Russian empire, and their special status can in part be traced back to foreign policy considerations. Until 1828 Bessarabia enjoyed a degree of autonomy that was almost on the same level, whereas the Baltic provinces were undoubtedly part of Russia in administrative terms, even though they possessed a large measure of self-rule. In western Belorussia, in Lithuania and in Ukraine on the right bank of the Dnepr the judicial and administrative status quo existed merely on a regional level, whereas eastern Belorussia and Ukraine on the left bank of the Dnepr retained only certain vestiges of their old administrative structures after 1764. The special administrative status of the western areas of the empire was also reflected at the beginning of the nineteenth century in the fact that — with the exception of the provinces of Smolensk, and Kharkov, which were deemed to have been integrated — they were placed together in a special section of the senate.[80] When compared with the areas in the south and the east, administrative incorporation was altogether more cautious in the west. In the case of the former there had also, it is true, been the type of the largely sovereign vassal — for example, the Khanate of the Kalmyks and the Great Nogai Horde. However, after the areas had finally been annexed, they were incorporated far more quickly into the Russian administrative organization.

These differences can to some extent be explained by the more intensive Russian colonization in the east and in the south, and by foreign policy considerations, though more pertinently by the model character that the socio-political order of certain areas in the west had for the new Russia. This was true of the corporate organization of the Baltic German and Finlandish estates, and of the constitutional experiment of the Kingdom of Poland, though not of the Ukrainian hetmanate. Whereas it is true that the hetmanate also possessed certain estate-based features, and influenced Russia in the cultural sphere, its political system, which was based on the military democratic Cossack constitution, never formed a model for the Russian autocracy. Rather, it was considered to be a potential danger and a perpetual source of unrest. Similarly, the constitution of the Polish noble republic, which was considered to be anarchical, did not constitute a model for absolutist Russia in the form in which it continued to exist to some extent on a regional basis. Nor did the Ottoman administrative model in Bessarabia. As a result, administrative autonomy was gradually curtailed in these areas.

In the west and in the east Russia promoted the gradual administrative and social integration of areas inhabited by non-Russians, though in different regions and at different times it pursued this policy with various degrees of intensity. The tradition of the Muscovite empire was to respect ancient rights. This was true of the hetmanate, which, like other peripheral areas of the steppe, remained for a long time in a state of loose dependency. Similarly, until the beginning of the eighteenth century Muscovy had preserved the order established on the middle Volga in the middle of the sixteenth century (after a brief aggressive phase had come to an end). Thus the policies pursued by Peter the Great, which were influenced by the west and sought to eradicate anomalies and systematize the state, led to the demotion of the Muslim elite, the abolition of the special status of the iasak men and, for the first time since 1555, called for missionaries to be sent to convert the animists (in Siberia). The systematic and forcible Christian-ization of the animists between 1740 and 1755, and a new and aggressive policy on Islam followed. At the same time, and as early as 1702, Peter had given assurances that the non-Orthodox Christian denominations would be tolerated, and had granted a large degree of autonomy to the Baltic provinces which was not revoked by his successors. In fact, it was actually extended to cover Old Finland. On the other hand – and this was partly the result of Mazepa's revolt – he curtailed the autonomy of the Cossack hetmanate. The guiding principle of his policies was based on the ideal, adopted from the west, of the 'well-ordered police state' (Raeff). Anything which fitted in with this ideal was to be retained, and whatever seemed to constitute an obstacle to the modernization of Russia had to be brought into line with the Russian order. This also applied to the tradition of tolerance, which was attacked by an important political thinker, Pososhkov, as an element that contributed to Russian backwardness. In 1719 Pososhkov con-trasted the activities of Catholic missionaries in America and China with the inability of the Russians to preach the word of God in their own empire: 'When we look at what they are trying to do, should we not be ashamed?'[81]

The policies espoused by Catherine II pursued the same goals as those of Peter the Great, though the methods employed were different.[82] Under the banner of enlightened absolutism, she returned to traditional tolerance, and accepted for the benefit (and under the control) of the state the Muslim Tatars and also (for the first time) the Jews, who nevertheless were soon confronted with a number of discriminatory measures. But at the same time she also tried to implement the newly systematized Russian administrative and social order in the western peripheral areas. 'Little Russia, Livonia and Finland [i.e. Old Finland] are provinces governed by privileges confirmed to them . . . One must, as in the case of Smolensk, induce them to become Russian [obruseli] with the help of methods that are not unduly oppressive, and persuade them to stop looking at the forest like wolves',[83] she wrote in 1764. In the case of the hetmanate, the district of Smolensk, and the Khanate of the Kalmyks, she forced the pace of integration after the Ukrainian Cossacks and the Kalmyk horsemen had lost their military significance for Russia. By and large the elites in Ukraine and Smolensk were successfully integrated. However, the measures designed to achieve uniformity and homogeneity in the Baltic provinces and in Poland-Lithuania were largely repealed after her death.

The reign of Alexander I witnessed a repeat of Peter's experiment in that he permitted Finland and the Kingdom of Poland to become models for a reformed Russia, and also confirmed the special status of the other areas in the west. On the other hand, this turning to the west went hand in hand with the rather inflexible policy of integration in Transcaucasia, which was regarded as part of Asia (see Chapter 5). Under Nicholas I the integrational tendencies in the west once again became more pronounced, in part even before 1830 (in the case of Bessarabia and the Jews), but especially as a result of the November uprising in Poland. On the other hand, the loyal Baltic Germans and Finlanders were spared such treatment. In fact, they served as pillars of the establishment under Nicholas I. More than ever the government saw the preservation of political and social stability as its top priority. Whilst it cooperated with loyal landowning elites, it reacted to secession and resistance movements (the Ukrainian Cossacks, the Bashkirs and Tatars in the Pugachev uprising, and the Poles) with decisive resolve and severity. It was precisely on account of the growing fear of revolution among the Russian elites that traditional thinking on security continued to be more important than an uncompromising policy of integration.

The first half of the nineteenth century was a transitional period in which tendencies that were to become characteristic of the second half of the century began to emerge. Increasingly Eurocentric attitudes gradually transformed the policy of expansion in Asia into one of colonialism (see Chapter 5). And the national movements of the Poles, and subsequently those of the Russians and other ethnic groups, called into question the estate-based and supranational order of the dynastic multi-ethnic empire (see Chapter 6). The policies pursued by the tsarist government were in reaction to this, and it intensified its efforts at integration (see Chapter 7). But before proceeding to examine these problems, I will give a brief and systematic account of the pre-modern Russian multi-ethnic empire.

Notes

1   On this and the concepts cited here see Klaus Zernack, 'Das Zeitalter der nordischen Kriege von 1558 bis 1809', *Zeitschrift für historische Forschung* I (1974), pp. 55–79, and the articles by Zernack and Michael Müller in *Handbuch* II.

2   On the history of Ukraine in general see Subtelny (1988), Polonska-Vasylenko (1988), Krupnyckyj (1943), Hrushevsky (1941), *Istoriia Ukr.* (1977–79).

3   See Basarab (1982).

4   Frank E. Sysyn, 'Ukrainian-Polish Relations in the Seventeenth Century. The Role of National Consciousness and National Conflict in the Khmelnytsky Movement', in Peter J. Potichnyj (ed.), *Poland and the Ukraine. Past and Present* (Edmonton and Toronto, 1980), pp. 58–82 (also deals with the following); Teresa Chynczewska-Hennel, 'The National Consciousness of Ukrainian Nobles and Cossacks from the End of the Sixteenth to the Mid-Seventeenth Century', *HUS* 10 (1986), 377–92.

5   On the first half of the seventeenth century see the following case study: Frank E. Sysyn, *Between Poland and the Ukraine. The Dilemma of Adam Kysil (1600–1653)* (Cambridge, Mass., 1985).

6   V. A. Golobutskii, *Zaporozhskoe kazachestvo* (Kiev, 1957); Zbigniew Wójcik, *Dzikie Pola w ogniu. O kozaczyźnie w dawnej Rzeczypospolitej*, 3rd edn (Warsaw, 1968); Władysław A. Serczyk, *Na dalekiej Ukrainie. Dzieje kozaczyzny do 1648 roku* (Cracow, 1984).

7   On the agreement of 1654 see Basarab (1982), which reproduces the most important sources; *Vossoedinenie Ukrainy s Rossiei. Dokumenty i materialy v trekh tomakh*, vol. III (Moscow, 1954); Hedwig Fleischhacker, 'Die politischen Begriffe der Partner von Pereyaslav', *JbbGO* 2 (1954), 221–31; Michajlo Brajčevskij, *Anschluß*

oder Wiedervereinigung (*Kritische Anmerkungen zu einer Konzeption*) (Munich, 1982) (reproduces sources).

8   C. Bickford O'Brien, *Muscovy and the Ukraine. From the Pereiaslavl Agreement to the Truce of Andrusovo, 1654–1667* (Berkeley, Los Angeles, 1963).

9   On the following see Kohut (1982), who provides a good overview, especially on the period after 1654; Hans Schumann, 'Der Hetmanstaat (1654–1764)', *JbbGO* (Old Series) 4 (1936), 499–548; Leo Okinshevich, *Ukrainian Society and Government 1648–1781* (Munich, 1978). On the legal status of the hetmanate within Russia in the seventeenth and eighteenth centuries see Nolde (1911), pp. 287–331.

10   See Kohut (1982).

11   *SIRIO* 7 (1871), 348.

12   On this and, following see L. Kubala, *Wojna Moskiewska. R. 1654–1655* (Warsaw 1910); Mal'tsev (1974), pp. 138–46, 163–77.

13   G. Peretiatkovich, *Povolzhe v 17 i nachale 18 veka* (*Ocherki iz kolonizatsii kraia*) (Odessa, 1882), pp. 154 f. and 162–64.

14   *PSZ* I, 135 (vol. 1, p. 349); N.V. Ustiugov, 'Evoliutsiia prikaznogo stroia russkogo gosudarstva v XVII v.', in *Absoliutizm v Rossii* (as Apollova) (Moscow, 1964), pp. 134–67, here pp. 155–7; Mal'tsev (1974), pp. 135–8.

15   See Nolte (1969a), pp. 114–16; Pelesz, vol. II (1880), pp. 321–6; Kharlampovich (1914), pp. 170 f; *PSZ* I, 398 (vol. 1, p. 659).

16   *PSZ* I, 983 (vol. 1, p. 490). See also *SIRIO* 32 (1881), 319; Iablochkov (1876), pp. 323 f.

17   See the instructions for the Legislative Commission of 1767 in *SIRIO* 134 (1911), 60 f., 79 f., 110 f.

18   See Iablochkov (1876), p. 469; K. Rovinskii, 'Delo o tridtsati shesti nezakonnykh brakakh. Epizod iz zhizni Smolenskoi shlakhty v XVIII veke', *Russkii Arkhiv* 47(2) (1909), 161–81.

19   See, for example, *Byelorussian Statehood* (1988), p. 125, map on pp. 390 f.; John P. Stankevich, *Ethnographical and Historical Territories and Boundaries of Whiteruthenia* (*Kryvia, Byelorussia*) (New York, 1953).

20   For general surveys of the subject see Wittram (1954); Spekke (1951); Raun (1987); *Istoriia Est.* I (1961); *Istoriia Latv.* I (1952); Thaden (1984), pp. 5–17; August Seraphim, *Die Geschichte des Herzogtums Kurland* (*1561–1795*), 2nd edn (Reval, 1904).

21   See Wittram (1964), also with regard to the following.

22   Eduard Winkelmann (ed.), *Die Capitulationen der estländischen Ritterschaft und der Stadt Reval vom Jahre 1710 nebst deren Confirmationen* (Reval, 1865), p. 23.

23   C. Schirren (ed.), *Die Capitulationen der livländischen Ritter- und Landschaft und der Stadt Riga vom 4. Juli nebst deren Confirmationen* (Dorpat, 1865), quotations on pp. 37, 38, and 47 f. See also Winkelmann (ed.), cited in note 22. Summary in Wittram, vol. I (1964), pp. 344–54; Haltzel (1977), pp. 3–12; Nolde (1911), pp. 332–407. See also the Russian texts in *PSZ* I, 2277, 2278, 2279 (vol. 4, pp. 500–26), 2297, 2298, 2299 (vol. 4, pp. 552–75), 2301, 2302, 2303, 2304 (vol. 4, pp. 575–80), 2495 (vol. 4, p. 810), 2501 (vol. 4, p. 819), 3819 (vol. 6, pp. 420–31). See also (and with regard

to the following) Hasso von Wedel, *Die estländische Ritterschaft vornehmlich zwischen 1710 und 1783. Das erste Jahrhundert russischer Herrschaft* (Königsberg and Berlin, 1935).

24 Claes Peterson, *Peter the Great's Administrative and Judicial Reforms: Swedish Antecedents and the Process of Reception* (Stockholm, 1979).

25 Thaden (1984), pp. 18–31; LeDonne (1984), pp. 325–34; de Madariaga (1981), pp. 61–6 and 315–24; Friedrich Bienemann, *Die Statthalterschaftszeit in Liv- und Estland* (1783–1796). *Ein Beispiel aus der Regentenpraxis Katharinas II*, repr. of 1886 edn (Hannover-Döhren, 1973); Otto-Heinrich Elias, *Reval in der Reformpolitik Katharinas II. Die Statthalterschaftszeit 1783–1796* (Bonn-Bad Godesberg, 1978).

26 *PSZ* I, 17584 (vol. 24, pp. 20 f.)

27 On the partitions of Poland see Müller (1984), which has a comprehensive bibliography. See also Robert Howard Lord, *The Second Partition of Poland, A Study in Diplomatic History* (Cambridge, Mass., 1915).

28 'Vous ne sauriez empêcher qu'ils ne vous engloutissent, faites au moins qu'ils ne puissent vous digerer.' Jean-Jacques Rousseau, *Considérations sur le gouvernement de Pologne et sur sa réformation projettée, Œuvres complètes*, vol. III (Paris, 1964), pp. 959 f.

29 On the history of Poland-Lithuania see Rhode (1980); Hoensch (1983); Davies, vol. I (1981); Gierowski (1988). With regard to the situation before the partitions and the proposed reforms see Jörg K. Hoensch, *Sozialverfassung und politische Reform: Polen im vorrevolutionären Zeitalter* (Cologne and Vienna, 1973).

30 Emanuel Rostworowski, 'Ile bylo w Rzeczypospolitej obywateli szlachty', *Kwartalnyk historyczny* 94 (1988), 3–40.

31 On the subject of the Ukrainians see the literature cited in note 2 above.

32 On the history of the Jews in Poland–Lithuania see Haumann (1990), pp. 17–65; Dubnow, vol. I (1916); Bernard D. Weinryb, *The Jews of Poland. A Social and Economic History of the Jewish Community in Poland from 1100 to 1800* (Philadelphia, 1973); Jacob Goldberg, 'Poles and Jews in the 17th and 18th Centuries. Rejection or Acceptance', *JbbGO* 22 (1974), 248–82.

33 On the events leading up to this and the first three partitions see Müller (1984).

34 The second partition was primarily justified as a battle against the spread of French revolutionary ideas in Poland. See Martens, vol. II (1875), pp. 228 f. See also *PSZ* I, 17108 (vol. 23, pp. 410 f.).

35 Quotations in Martens, vol. II (1875), pp. 291 and 303 f.

36 *PSZ* I, 17108 (vol. 23, p. 410).

37 See, for example, *Istoriia SSSR*, vol. III (1967), p. 550.

38 On the following see Thaden (1984), pp. 32–71; Nolde (1911), pp. 420–34; LeDonne (1984), pp. 314 f., 334–8; Winiarski (1924), pp. 135–51; U. L. Lehtonen, *Die polnischen Provinzen Rußlands unter Katharina II. In den Jahren 1772–1782. Versuch einer Darstellung der anfänglichen Beziehungen der russischen Regierung zu ihren polnischen Untertanen* (Berlin, 1907); Henryk Mościcki, *Dzieje rozbiorowe Litwy i Rusi. T. i. 1772–1800* (Wilno, 1913); *Historia* III (1981), pp. 833–60; *Historya* I (1972), pp. 444–53; Kosman (1979), pp. 200–4.

39 *PSZ* I, 17319 (vol. 23, pp. 664–85); Wittram (1954), pp. 123 f. and 137 f.; Haltzel (1977), pp. 11–13.

40 *PSZ* I, 13850 (vol. 19, p. 555); 17108 (vol. 23, p. 411); 17356 (vol. 23, p. 730); 17418 (vol. 23, p. 846).

41 *PSZ* I, 17634 (vol. 24, p. 229).

42 *PSZ* I, 17327 (vol. 23, p. 695).

43 See the statistics in Kabuzan and Troitskii (1971), pp. 157 and 162–5; Zhukovich (1915), January, pp. 76–94, and May, pp. 130–46.

44 Irena Rychlikowa, 'Deklasacja drobnej szlachty polskiej w Cesarstwie Rosyjskim. Spór o "Pułapkę na szlachtę" Daniela Beauvois', *Przegląd historyczny* 79 (1988), 121–47. Also see the information given in Ulashchik (1965), pp. 68–91, and Tadeusz Korzon, *Wewnętrzne Dzieje Polski za Stanisława Augusta (1764–1794)*, vol. I, 2nd edn (Kraków and Warszawa, 1897), pp. 87–152. In regard to earlier scholarly opinion, see Beauvois (1985), pp. 99 f.; Romanovich–Slavatinskii (1912), pp. 96 f. and 496–501.

45 See Kabuzan and Troitskii (1971), p. 158; Jerzy Jedlicki, 'Szlachta', *Przemiany społeczne w Królestwie polskim 1815–1864* (Wrocław, 1979), pp. 27–56.

46 *PSZ* I, 13850 (vol. 19, p. 555); *Recueil* (1862), p. 328.

47 See Kumor (1980).

48 Quotation in *PSZ* I, 17333 (vol. 23, p. 699). See Ammann (1950), pp. 441–7 and 472–5; Pelesz, vol. II (1880), pp. 548–60, 583–95 and 793–831; Smolitsch (1991), pp. 394–402. With regard to the organization of the church see Amburger (1966), pp. 181–5.

49 See Blackwell (1959), pp. 52–61.

50 On Congress Poland see, in addition to the more general literature listed in note 29, Thackeray (1980); Blackwell (1959); Leslie (1956), Chapters 1–3; *Historia* (1981), pp. 168–579; *Przemiany* (1979); Szymon Aszkenazy, *Rosya–Polska 1815–1830* (Lwów, 1907), pp. 63–117; Wandycz (1974), pp. 53–67 and 74–91; Davies, vol. II, (1981), pp. 306–33; Thaden (1984), pp. 71–80.

51 *Konstitutsionnaia khartiia 1815 goda i nekotorye drugie akty byvshego tsarstva polskogo (1814–1881)* (St Petersburg, 1907), pp. 64–86 (French original) and pp. 87–108 (Polish translation).

52 *Recueil* (1862), p. 374.

53 See, for example, Thackeray (1980), pp. 30–3.

54 N. Tourgeneff, *La Russie et les Russes*, vol. I (Paris, 1847), pp. 443–61. The quotation (in French) appears on p. 450.

55 Documents cited by Thackeray (1980), especially pp. 7, 11–13, 33–5, 45–50. See also Blackwell (1959).

56 With regard to the November revolution and its consequences see, in addition to the literature already referred to above, Leslie (1956) and Wandycz (1974), pp. 105–26.

57 On the following see Klier (1986); Rest (1975); Hildermeier (1984), and in more general terms Dubnow, vol. I (1916), pp. 242–413; vol. II (1918), pp. 13–110; Baron (1964), pp. 7–41; Haumann (1990), pp. 66–82.

58 *PSZ* I, 13850 (vol. 19, p. 555).

59 For a detailed discussion of the subject see Klier (1986), pp. 63 f., 86 f., 92, 95–115, 186 f.; Dubnow, vol. I (1916), pp. 410–13.

60 Statute of 1804, cited in Rest (1975), p. 229.

61 *PSZ* I, no. 21547. See the German translation in Rest (1975), pp. 229–40.

62 See Hensel (1983); Artur Eisenbach, *Kwestia równouprawnienia Żydów w Królestwie Polskim* (Warszawa, 1972), Part 1.

63 Michael Stanislawski, *Tsar Nicholas I and the Jews. The Transformation of Jewish Society in Russia, 1825–1855* (Philadelphia, 1983).

64 For general information on Finland see Jutikkala (1964); Wuorinen (1965); Thaden (1984), pp. 81–95; Peter Scheibert, 'Die Anfänge der finnischen Staatswerdung unter Alexander I.', *JbbGO* (Old Series) 4 (1939), 351–430; Peter Scheibert, 'Volk und Staat in Finnland in der ersten Hälfte des vorigen Jahrhunderts', thesis (Breslau, 1941); Päiviö Tommila, *La Finlande dans la politique européenne en 1809–1815* (Helsinki, 1962).

65 *PSZ* I, no. 8766 (vol. 11, pp. 863–74, quotation on p. 869). In addition to the general literature mentioned above see Nolde (1911), pp. 411–20.

66 K. Ordin, *Pokorenie Finliandii. Opyt opisaniia po neizdannym istochnikam*, vol. II (St Petersburg, 1889), pp. 335–41. See the English translation of the most important texts in Kirby (1975), pp. 12–18. The central passage is given in Russian and German in Schweitzer (1978), p. 18.

67 See, for example, Hösch (1991), pp. 25–9. The traditional view is still defended by Jutikkala (1964), pp. 253–64.

68 See the English translation of the Russian and Swedish text in Kirby (1975), pp. 14 f. See also Schweitzer (1978), pp. 18–26; and Nolde (1911), pp. 475–542.

69 Kirby (1975), p. 18.

70 See Nicholas Dima, 'Moldavians or Romanians?', in Ralph S. Clem (ed.), *The Soviet West. Interplay between Nationality and Social Organization* (New York, 1975), pp. 31–45; Walter Feldman, 'The Theoretical Basis for the Definition of Moldavian Nationality', in Clem (ed.), pp. 46–59.

71 On the history of this area see Babel (1926); R. W. Seton-Watson (1934); *Istoriia Mold.* (1982); Andrei Otetea (ed.), *The History of the Romanian People* (Bucharest, 1970); Zelenchuk (1979).

72 On this and the rest of the chapter see Jewsbury (1976); Nolde, II (1953), pp. 259–99; *Istoricheskoe znachenie prisoedineniia Bessarabii i levoberezhnogo Podnestrov'ia k Rossii* (Kishinev, 1987); Alexandre Boldur, *La Bessarabie et les relations russo-roumaines (La question bessarabienne et le droit international)* (Paris, 1927), pp. 15–26 and 48–57.

73 Cited in Nolde (1911), p. 437, and Nolde, II (1953), p. 289.

74 *PSZ* I, 27357 (vol. 35, pp. 222–81).

75 Cited in Nolde (1911), p. 441, and Nolde, II (1953), p. 289.

76 *PSZ* II, 1834 (vol. 3, pp. 197–204). The quotation appears on p. 198.

77 Robert J. Kerner, *The Urge to the Sea* (Berkeley, 1942); O. Halecki, 'Imperialism in Slavic and East European History', *The American and East European Review* 11 (1952), 171–88; Henry R. Huttenbach 'The Origins of Russian Imperialism', in Hunczak (1974), pp. 18–44.

78 On the following see Raeff (1971); Starr (1978); Kappeler (1982a); Thaden (1984); Scharf (1988); von Rauch (1953), pp. 25–68.

79 See Nolte (1969a); Nolte (1969b); Scharf (1988).

80 A. M. Chetvertkov, 'K voprosu o pravovom polozhenii zapadnykh natsional'nykh raionov v sostave Rossiiskoi imperii v pervoi chetverti XIX v.', in *Vestnik Moskovskogo gosudarstvennogo universiteta*, Seriia 11, Pravo, 6 (1986), pp. 64–70.

81 I. T. Pososhkov, *Zaveshchanie otecheskoe* (St Petersburg, 1893), pp. 320–8.

82 See Marc Raeff, 'Uniformity, Diversity, and the Imperial Administration in the Reign of Catherine II', *Osteuropa in Geschichte und Gegenwart. Festschrift für Günther Stökl zum 60. Geburtstag* (Cologne, 1977), pp. 97–113.

83 *SIRIO* 7, 348.

4

The Pre-modern Russian Multi-ethnic Empire

By the Grace of God We, Catherine II, Empress and Autocrat of all the Russias, of Moscow, Kiev, Vladimir, Novgorod, Tsarina of Kazan, Tsarina of Astrakhan, Tsarina of Siberia, Tsarina of the Taurid Chersonese [the Crimea], Lord of Pskov and Grand Duchess of Smolensk, Princess of Estonia, Livonia, Karelia, Tver, Iugra, Perm, Viatka, Bulgaria [this refers to the land of the Volga Bulgars], etc.

THE VERY first lines of the imperial title (as it appears in an official document of 1785) refer to the most important stages of Russian expansion and the heterogeneous nature of the Russian empire. The empress went on to emphasize this in the same document:

> The All-Russian empire is unique in the world on account of its far-flung lands, which, ranging from the eastern limits of Kamchatka as far as and beyond the western Dvina, which flows into the Baltic near Riga, embrace within their boundaries 165 degrees of longitude. From the mouths of the Volga, the Kuban, the Don and the Dnepr, which flow into the Caspian Sea and the Black Sea, to the Arctic Ocean, the empire embraces 32 degrees of latitude.[1]

The vast multi-ethnic empire that had arisen as a result of centuries of expansion was characterized by great ethnic, religious, social, economic, administrative and cultural diversity. The policy of the government, which as a rule was flexible and pragmatic, respected — though to differing extents — the status quo in newly acquired territories, so that numerous aspects of foreign social, economic and administrative structures and independent non-Orthodox and non-Russian cultures survived within the framework of the Russian empire. Loyalty to the tsar and his dynasty served to link this varied assortment of territories and societies. If this was endangered, instruments of coercion were employed, and these could even lead to military intervention.

In this chapter I attempt for the first time to provide a survey of the structure of the pre-modern Russian multi-ethnic empire. In view of the dearth of previous work on the subject, it cannot of course be a comprehensive picture. Thus I have decided to concentrate on certain aspects. The first section examines the ethnic division and the social (or socio-ethnic) structure of the whole empire and its regions. The second section sheds some light on the inter-ethnic economic division of labour and on specific functions that were performed by non-Russians in various areas. Thirdly, religions and cultures are described with special reference to education and acculturation processes. The fourth section is devoted to the resistance of non-Russians to Russian rule; and, finally, the character of the Russian multi-ethnic empire is compared to that of other similar states. In chronological terms the whole epoch from the seventeenth century to about 1830 forms the subject of the investigation, though I discuss only those ethnic groups and territories which have already been introduced in the preceding chapters. Thus the areas of Transcaucasia and the Kazakh steppe, which will be dealt with in the context of colonial expansion in Asia, are omitted, even though to some extent they already came under Russian rule in the first half of the nineteenth century.

1. Ethnic Division and Social Structure

In numerical terms the ethnic composition of the Russian Empire before the first general census of 1897 can be ascertained only approximately. True, the revisions (or censuses of the tax-paying population carried out from 1719 onwards) included ethnic criteria, at least in the eighteenth century. However, not all of the peripheral areas and not all of the ethnic groups were included, and the data collected in the peripheral areas in particular were rather unreliable. Furthermore, parts of the non-taxable population, especially the nobles and members of the army, were excluded. The data of the revisions that have survived in the archives have been examined by the Soviet historian V. M. Kabuzan, who in a series of publications has given a critical account of the sources and adduced others to complement them.[2] Since I was unable to examine the voluminous material in the archives, the following remarks are based largely on the data contained in these studies.[3]

At the end of the sixteenth century non-Russians (the Tatars and the other ethnic groups of the middle Volga and the ethnic groups of the north) probably constituted slightly more than 10 per cent, and Russians about 90 per cent of the Muscovite population. In the seventeenth century they were joined by the Ukrainians of the Hetmanate and the Belorussians of Smolensk in the west, and the ethnic groups of Siberia and the steppes in the east. In 1718–19, the year of the first revision, Russians, according to Kabuzan, made up 70.7 per cent of a total population estimated to number 15.7 million (see Table 3, also with regard to the following). Of the non-Russians, who thus constituted almost 30 per cent of the population, the Ukrainians (almost 13 per cent) were far and away the most numerous. Together the three eastern Slav ethnic groups represented no less than 86 per cent of the total population. The ethnic groups of the middle Volga (including the Tatars with about 2 per cent) and the Baltic provinces (Estonians amounted to 2 per cent) each totalled between 4 and 5 per cent. The nomads of the steppes, who were only loosely linked to Russia, made up 3 per cent of the total, and the ethnic groups of the north and in Siberia both amounted to about 1 per cent. Thus the population of Peter the Great's Russia was still very much dominated by Russians, particularly when one takes into account the fact that the majority of the 2 million Ukrainians lived in the autonomous Hetmanate.

By the end of the eighteenth century the picture had changed considerably. According to the information in the fifth revision of 1795, which Kabuzan has reconstructed with the help of other sources and deductions based on later data, the Russians now made up only 53 per cent of a total population which had grown to about 37 million. The share of the Ukrainians (8.16 million) had now risen to 21.8 per cent, and that of the Belorussians to more than 8 per cent, so that the three eastern Slav ethnic groups together constituted about 83 per cent of the total population. The remaining 17 per cent was made up on the one hand of ethnic groups which had already belonged to Russia in 1719, and whose proportion had declined as a result of the increase in the territory (with the exception of the Latvians, whose numbers rose considerably as a result of the acquisition of Kurland); and on the other of the new groups of Lithuanians, Poles,[4] Jews, Crimean Tatars and Germans, which each constituted less than 2 per cent of the total population. Thus the decisive numerical shift occurred between 1719 and 1795 in favour of the Ukrainians and Belorussians, who, at the end of the eighteenth century, with a proportion of about 30 per cent, were almost twice as numerous as all of Russia's non-eastern Slav ethnic groups taken together.

The territorial changes of the next two decades reduced the proportion of Russians even further, and by 1834 (the eighth revision) they already constituted less than half of the population of Russia (with Congress Poland and Finland, but without Transcaucasia). Above all the proportion of Poles, which now probably amounted to more than 7 per cent, had risen, as had that of the Finns (about 1.8 per cent), the Jews (about 2.5 per cent), the Lithuanians and the Germans. Finally, there were new groups: the roughly 400,000 Romanians in Bessarabia (1835), and the Bulgarian, Gagauz and Greek colonists. In the eighteenth century and at the beginning of the nineteenth century the centre of gravity of the Russian empire had shifted markedly to the west, and this was also reflected in its ethnic composition. But in the nineteenth century colonial expansion then caused it to shift back towards the east.

However, the population figures and percentages given above are only of limited use. For one thing, in the pre-democratic age they tell us nothing about the political and social significance of the various ethnic groups. In 1719 the Estonians and Latvians were ten times more numerous than the Baltic Germans, and in 1795 there were five times as many Belorussians in Russia as Poles. Despite their obvious numerical inferiority, it was the Baltic Germans and the Poles who determined political and social life in their regions. Secondly, the overall figures for Russia tell us nothing about the ethnic composition of the various different areas. Therefore I will now give an account of the socio-ethnic structure of the peripheral areas of Russia.[5]

To some extent in the reign of Peter I, and then without exception in that of Catherine II, the inhabitants of the Russian empire were divided into the estates of nobility, clergy, urban population and peasantry. The nobility included both hereditary and non-hereditary nobles, and it was possible to progress to both categories by means of a career in the bureaucracy or the army. The urban estates consisted of the meshchane (petit bourgeois), who included the mass of the craftsmen and tradesmen, and a small group of merchants, who were divided into three guilds on the basis of their wealth. The peasant estate included serfs who were dependent on a landowner; palace or appanage peasants who lived on the estates of the imperial family; and personally free state peasants, a category created by Peter I which included the free Russian peasants of the north and of Siberia, the non-Russian iasak men, and demoted minor service men. After 1764 it also included the former serfs who lived on lands belonging to monasteries or the church.

Ethnic diversity had existed in most parts of the empire since the Middle Ages. Only the Russian core area around Moscow had possessed a largely uniform ethnic structure since the fourteenth century. And the complexity of the ethnic mosaic was increased by perpetual migration. In this connection we should recall the wanderings of the nomads (the Nogai Tatars and the Kalmyks), the settlement of foreign colonists, the migration of Ukrainian peasants and Cossacks, and many of the Volga ethnic groups (the Tatars, the Mordvinians and the Chuvash) to the east and the south. Since the Middle Ages the Russians had also displayed a great deal of horizontal mobility. Russian peasants went in search of new and if possible more fertile land, and fled to escape from a serfdom that was becoming increasingly oppressive. However, monasteries and landowners soon followed in their footsteps. Before the sixteenth century they could venture only into the forests of the north: Russians first began to settle in the middle Volga region after the fall of the Khanate of Kazan. From the middle of the seventeenth century onwards they began increasingly to settle the steppe frontier, and from the eighteenth century onwards the steppes of the southern Urals, the lower Volga and New Russia.[6] The structure of the following survey of the socio-ethnic composition of the Russian regions is based on the proportion of the Russian population.

1. The administratively autonomous peripheral regions in which very few Russians had settled constitute the first regional type. The small Russian population was restricted to a handful of civil servants, garrisons and the occasional settler in the areas bordering on Russia proper. This category included the *Grand Duchy of Finland*, the borders of which, after 1812, were only about 30 kilometres from the capital, St Petersburg. Nevertheless, in 1834 it still had a Russian proportion of only 2.2 per cent.[7] In 1834 about 86 per cent of the 1.4 million inhabitants were Finns (primarily free peasants), whereas the political, social, economic and culturally dominant Swedish-speaking population comprised about 12 per cent. The picture was very similar in the *Baltic provinces* of Estonia and Livonia, where in 1719 Russians comprised only 0.3 per cent of the population, and in 1795 (with Kurland) only 1.1 per

cent. The Baltic Germans, who comprised the noble upper class (1 per cent of the population) and the urban upper and middle classes, were, at 6.6 per cent (78,500 in 1795), numerically even smaller in comparison to the Latvians and Estonians than the Swedes in comparison to the Finns. The more important respect in which the Baltic provinces differed from Finland was the hereditary serfdom of the Latvian and Estonian peasants. In 1795 70 per cent of the peasants in the Baltic provinces were dependent on the landowners. By comparison, the all-Russian average was 60 per cent.

This category also includes the areas of Poland-Lithuania annexed in the first three partitions, *Belorussia-Lithuania* (the provinces of Vitebsk, Mogilev, Minsk, Vilna and Grodno), and *Ukraine on the right bank of the Dnepr* (the provinces of Kiev, Volhynia and Podolia). In 1795 the Russians in Ukraine on the right bank of the Dnepr comprised a mere 0.1 per cent of the population, and after 1834 only 0.3 per cent and in Belorussia-Lithuania about 1 per cent. Although the two large areas annexed between 1772 and 1795 did not have autonomous status in the Russian empire, the Polish or polonized nobility continued to dominate social, cultural and to some extent political life. As a result of the unclear ethnic distinction between Poles and partially polonized Belorussians, Ukrainians and Lithuanians, the figures adduced by scholars differ significantly. Whereas Kabuzan – on the basis of the Russian sources – gives the number of Poles in 1795 as 6.7 per cent (Belorussia-Lithuania) and 7.8 per cent (Ukraine on the right bank of the Dnepr), Polish scholars have come up with much higher percentages (between 10 and 20 per cent).[8] The (predominantly Polish) nobles comprised at least 6 per cent of the total population, which indicates that the nobility in the formerly Polish areas constituted a share of the total population that was ten times greater than in Russia proper.[9] In Belorussia-Lithuania this Polish or partly polonized upper class was faced with Belorussian (64 per cent, though considerably less according to Polish sources), Lithuanian (15 per cent), Ukrainian (5 per cent) and Latvian (3 per cent) peasants who lived in homogeneous settlements; and in Ukraine to the right of the Dnepr with almost exclusively Ukrainian peasants (88 per cent). On the other hand, the Jews (about 5 per cent[10]) lived initially in both urban and rural areas, though, as the nineteenth century progressed, largely in the towns. In this region 85 per cent of the peasants were serfs attached to landed estates.

At the end of the eighteenth century the social structure of the west and the south of the province of *Smolensk* (which had already been conquered in the seventeenth century), where Belorussians constituted the vast majority of the population, differed from the rest of Belorussia-Lithuania. Here the formerly Polish or polonized aristocracy had been largely russified, so that a Russian upper class now confronted the non-Russian Orthodox peasants. Furthermore, the eastern and northern districts of the province were exclusively Russian.

The socio-ethnic structure of the three regions examined above (with the exception of Smolensk) shows that they had in common the fact that under Russian rule a non-Russian elite was on the whole able to retain its position, and that peasants who belonged to another ethnic group continued to be its serfs. The unusual feature in Finland was that the peasants were free, and in the case of the formerly Polish areas that the ethnic group (the Poles) which predominated in the nobility was very much differentiated in social terms, and faced competition in the towns from another group (the Jews). In the Baltic provinces and in the formerly Polish areas the retention of serfdom and the far-reaching congruence of ethnic and social divisions created a potential for inter-ethnic strife which made it possible for the Russian government to assume the role of mediator, and thus to play off the various groups against each other.

2. In the largely autonomous *Kingdom of Poland* there were practically no Russians either. Here, however, the Poles constituted not only the politically and socially predominant noble class in 1817, but also the majority of the peasants, who had been personally free since 1807, and a large part of the urban population. The Lithuanian (7 per cent) and Ukrainian (6 per cent) peasants were most numerous in one of the peripheral areas, whereas the majority of the Jews (8.6 per cent) and the Germans (4.2 per cent) lived in the kingdom's towns. Although the towns had a multi-ethnic character, the Kingdom of Poland was more uniform in ethno-social terms than the three regions discussed above.

The same was true of the Ukraine on the left bank of the Dnepr, most of which formed part of the autonomous Hetmanate until 1764. Here the Russians made up 2.2 per cent of the population in 1719, and about 5 per cent in 1795. The Ukrainians clearly constituted the vast majority, with 96 per cent (1719) or 93 per cent (1795). In the province of Poltava they even reached 99 per cent. They comprised the nobility

(1.3 per cent of the population), the large rural Cossack middle class, the peasants, some of whom had first sunk to the level of serfs after the dissolution of the Hetmanate, and also a large part of the urban population. However, the social structure of the Ukraine on the left bank of the Dnepr gradually lost some of its ethnic homogeneity. The Cossack upper class was russified, and in Sloboda Ukraine (province of Kharkov) the number of Russian peasants and landowners increased. Furthermore, Russian merchants and, from the end of the eighteenth century onwards, Jews settled in the towns. *Central Bessarabia*, which had 78 per cent Romanians (boyars and peasants), and an ethnically diverse urban population, can also be assigned to this basic category.

3. The nomads, hunters and gatherers in the southeast, the east and the north also had an ethnically self-contained social structure. Although it is true that the vast regions of *the north, Siberia and the steppes* were intensively settled by Russians, among the ethnic groups which had retreated to the areas of the tundra, the taiga and the steppe the traditional clan and tribal structures remained intact. This was true of the handful of hunters and reindeer herdsmen of the far north and Siberia, who in 1719 comprised about 50,000 people (Lapps, Samoyeds, Ostiaks, Voguls, Tungus, etc.), and the more numerous Iakut herdsmen and nomadic Buriats. In 1795 there was a total of 360,000 non-Europeans in Siberia, half of whom were Buriats and Iakuts. On the other hand, there were 819,000 Russians, above all free state peasants who were not dependent on private landowners. They lived mainly on the thin strip of fertile arable land in south-west Siberia, and later also in southern east Siberia. In this type of socio-ethnic structure Russians and non-Russians interacted on an economic, administrative and fiscal level, though they lived in their own ethnically homogeneous societies.

4. A mixed social structure consisting of Russians and non-Russians also existed in regions into which Russian settlers had migrated after they had been annexed. The first category (also in historical terms) were the areas in *the north and north-east*, which had already been colonized by Russian peasants, monasteries and landowners in the Middle Ages. The non-Russian peasants had been almost totally integrated in administrative and social terms, placed on a par with Russian peasants and converted to the Orthodox church, though they had retained at least a part of their ethnic identity. This was more true of the Karelians and Zyrians, who lived in the sparsely populated north,

than of the Izhora (Ingrians) in the province of St Petersburg, and the Veps. Almost half of the Karelians in Russia had lived in the Tver region since the seventeenth century, that is, in an area that was traditionally Russian.

5. In the seventeenth century a particularly complicated socio-ethnic structure came into being in the *Middle Volga* region, which was settled by Russians after the conquest of Kazan. The noble upper class consisted of Russians and Muslim Tatars, and the urban population largely of Russians. On the other hand, the peasant lower classes can be subdivided into the Chuvash, Tatar, Mordvinian, Cheremis, Votiak and (occasionally) Russian iasak men, and the exclusively Russian serfs dependent on landowners and monasteries. It is noteworthy that the iasak men, unlike the Russian peasants, were personally free, with fewer taxes and duties and more land and cattle than the latter. As early as 1719 the Russians constituted the largest single group in all the provinces of the middle Volga region. Their share initially increased in the first half of the eighteenth century in the more fertile southern parts of the region, but then remained constant because settlers primarily made their way to the lower Volga and to the southern Urals. Living in compact settlements, the Chuvash (310,000 in 1795), Cheremis (140,000) and Votiaks (127,000) continued to form the majority of the population in their traditional forest areas, whereas the c 400,000 Tatars and 260,000 Mordvinians were spread over a larger area that was also inhabited by Russians.[11] The eighteenth-century policy of regularization largely eliminated the Tatar upper class, though it also encouraged the formation among the Tatars of an economically active class of merchants and entrepreneurs. The peasant categories were standardized, though the Russian serfs continued to be at the bottom of the regional social pyramid.

6. The region of *the southern Urals*, which was inhabited by Bashkirs, forms a special category. In the course of the eighteenth century it was increasingly settled by Russians and by ethnic groups from the middle Volga region. The Bashkirs, who according to Kabuzan had numbered about 172,000 in 1719, though Akmanov puts their number at 380,000 in 1730, had been reduced to about 200,000 as a result of the heavy losses sustained in the course of numerous uprisings. In the eighteenth century they continued to be the landowning upper class in many areas, though their position was gradually undermined by Russian landowners

and settlers. At the end of the eighteenth century the region's social pyramid, beneath the Russian nobility, and beneath the Bashkir and Tatar (about 50,000 in 1795) service men (sometimes referred to as meshcheriaki), who retained a special status as a military estate, was based on the special group of more than 100,000 Tatar, Mordvinian, Cheremis and Chuvash teptiars (especially in the north), more than 40,000 primarily Tatar iasak peasants, and more than 300,000 Russian state peasants and serfs (especially in the south), who had to pay more taxes and render more services than the non-Russians.[12] Although the Bashkirs were able to retain their special status, they had become a minority in numerical terms.

7. *The peripheral areas of the steppe*, which were newly settled after the nomadic herdsmen had been evicted, constitute the last of the categories in this list. The steppes on the lower Volga were the domain of the Kalmyks, who were in the majority before 1771 with a population of about 200,000. After their mass emigration, the area was settled primarily by Russian peasants, though also by Ukrainian, Tatar and Mordvinian peasants, and German colonists. Yet the Russian nobility was predominant in social terms. The pastures of the decimated Kalmyk nomadic horsemen were considerably reduced in size. The steppes to the north of the Caucasus were inhabited by about 100,000 Nogai Tatars, and Russian and Ukrainian Cossacks and peasants in well-nigh separate societies. Russians and Kalmyks had also settled in the area of the Don Cossacks, and here the Ukrainian proportion of the population rose to about a third. The percentage of Ukrainians was about the same in the Russian black earth provinces of Voronezh and Kursk.

Towards the end of the eighteenth century and early in the nineteenth century the steppe to the north of the Black Sea was resettled after the Nogai Tatars had been driven out of the area. In 1815 about 1.5 million people were already living in what was known as *New Russia* (the provinces of Ekaterinoslav, Kherson and parts of the province of Taurida). About three-quarters were Ukrainian state peasants and serfs, and the rest were Russian peasants and German, Jewish, Greek, Romanian and South Slav colonists. The new towns, including rapidly expanding Odessa, were very diverse in ethnic terms, and the number of Jews increased markedly. In New Russia, where a 'new' multi-ethnic society arose in which a majority of peasants were not serfs, the Russian minority in the nobility and the urban population set the tone. The category of the multi-ethnic settlement of the steppe also includes *southern Bessarabia* (Budzhak), which was primarily inhabited by Romanian, Ukrainian and Russian peasants, and by German, Bulgarian and Gagauz colonists.

In the first few decades under Russian rule *the Crimea* had a socio-ethnic structure which resembled that of the middle Volga: a Tatar and increasingly also Russian nobility, an ethnically diverse urban population, Tatar state peasants and Ukrainian and Russian state peasants and serfs. They were joined at the beginning of the nineteenth century by colonists, most of whom were German. The latter formed a new rural middle class. Whereas at the end of the eighteenth century the c 160,000 Crimean Tatars still made up the great majority of the population, this kind of immigration and several waves of Tatar emigration in the nineteenth century led to a dramatic decline in the Tatar proportion of the Crimean population.

A survey of the socio-ethnic structure of the periphery of the Russian empire reveals a very complex state of affairs. Ethnic groups cannot be assigned unequivocally to specific classes. This also applies to the Russians, the state people, who, it is true, dominated the noble elite in the regions of the east and the south, but at the same time also included the class of serfs, who were underprivileged when compared with non-Russian peasants. This substantiates the notion that ethnic and religious criteria were not of decisive importance for the social structure of pre-modern Russia.

It is true that the majority of the empire's elite, the hereditary nobility, the bureaucracy, the officers and the rich landowners, were Russian and Orthodox. However, the elite also accepted non-Russians, at first Muslim Tatars, then Protestant Baltic Germans and Finlanders, Catholic Poles and numerous foreigners. In fact, in the first third of the nineteenth century the non-Russians were considerably more numerous than the Russians in the Russian hereditary nobility, primarily on account of the incorporation of a large part of the Polish szlachta, most of whom, admittedly, were rather poor. In the case of the sedentary ethnic groups of the periphery the old non-Russian elites stayed in power as a rule, and were often able to preserve some administrative autonomy, even if, in places where Russians settled in greater numbers, they had to compete with the Russian nobility. The nomadic elites also retained their positions of power, though like the other classes of their ethnic groups they were not integrated into the Russian social order.

For a long time the towns of the western periphery enjoyed a special status that went back to ancient civic rights, and displayed some ethnic diversity. The Jews were particularly numerous in the areas in the pale of settlement. Russians predominated in the towns of the south and the east, though here Armenians, Greeks, Germans and other diaspora groups also played an important role (see below, Section 2).

In Russia the vast majority of the rural population was dependent on the landowners. As a rule Russian nobles had Russian (and a handful of Belorussian or Ukrainian) serfs, whereas non-Russian nobles often possessed peasants belonging to other ethnic groups and religions. Sometimes there were also Russian peasants on their estates. This, for example, was the case with the Muslim Tatars in the seventeenth century. Since the social status quo was preserved, the peasants of the western periphery retained their legal and social status, which (with the exception of the Finns) resembled that of Russian serfs, whereas the personally free non-Russian peasants in the east and the south were generally classified as state peasants, and therefore, like the colonists, Cossacks and nomads, who enjoyed a special status, were in a better position in legal, economic and social terms than Russian peasants. Thus Russian peasants were to some extent discriminated against in legal terms when compared to non-Russian peasants. This remarkable feature of the socio-ethnic structure had already made an appearance in even more pronounced form in the Muscovite realm, where the lowest social category of slaves (kholops) consisted almost entirely of Russians, whereas in most other societies slaves were racial, ethnic or religious outsiders.[13] This once again underlines the fact that in the pre-modern era ethnic categories were of little importance to the Russian elite and government.

The complicated socio-ethnic structure of the pre-modern Russian multi-ethnic empire was a crucial precondition for the national movements of the nineteenth century, which are discussed in Chapter 6. As a rule social and ethnic antagonisms reinforced each other, though they were not necessarily directed against the Russians who dominated the centre. Rather, they were often directed against the foreign upper and middle classes in the various regions, who were either largely Russian (as in the east and in the south), Polish magnates, Jewish merchants or Baltic German barons.

2. The Inter-ethnic Division of Labour and the Specific Functions of non-Russians in the Russian Empire

Two interpretational models have been used to analyze the economic structure of the pre-modern Russian multi-ethnic empire. According to pre-revolutionary Russian historians and Soviet historiography since the 1930s, the union with Russia of areas inhabited by non-Russians was a fundamentally positive occurrence.[14] From the point of view of many non-Russian historiographies and Soviet historiography before Stalin, it was a matter of colonial exploitation of the non-Russian periphery by the Russian centre. Comprehensive analyses capable of demonstrating the veracity of either of these two theories have yet to appear, and in this context we can merely give a short account of the economic significance of the non-Russian peripheral areas.[15] Greater emphasis is then placed on the question of the specific and often complementary functions that were performed by non-Russians within the framework of the Russian Empire.

For the majority of the Russian and the non-Russian population of the empire agriculture was the predominant economic activity in the eighteenth and early nineteenth centuries.[16] The methods of production were traditional, the harvests were small and the continual expansion of agricultural land in the south and the south-east favoured an extensive approach. Arable farming in the Baltic provinces, where Baltic German landowners carried out a number of improvements, and (after having overcome the initial difficulties) as practised by the German, and especially Mennonite, colonists in the south of Ukraine, differed from this picture on account of its higher level of productivity. The great differences in soil quality between the fertile chernozem areas in the south and the podzol areas in the north led to an inter-regional division of labour and a flow of grain from the south to the north. In addition to the Russian chernozem areas most of the regions inhabited by non-Russian agriculturalists (the Baltic provinces, Belorussia-Lithuania, the Kingdom of Poland, Ukraine, the middle Volga, the southern Urals) produced a grain surplus. A significant part of it was turned into spirits, whereas the share of the grain that was sold and exported to other regions or abroad remained relatively small until the beginning of the nineteenth century.[17]

Forest husbandry had always played an important role in the lives of the Russians and non-Russians who lived in the woodlands of the north and the east. They included the ethnic groups of the middle Volga, who specialized in forest bee-keeping, paid some of their taxes in the shape of wax and honey, and participated as auxiliary workers in cutting down the forests for the production of potash, and for the construction of the navy. The small ethnic groups of the far north and Siberia caught sable and other fur-bearing animals, the pelts of which made their way to Russia via the iasak. In the seventeenth century they contributed about 10 per cent of the state's income, and were to a large extent exported.[18] The nomadic Kalmyks, Nogai Tatars, Bashkirs and Buriats continued to specialize in animal husbandry, and in exchange for grain and manufactured goods supplied Russia with horses, skins, wool and tallow. Similarly, animal husbandry played a larger role in Ukraine, in the Baltic provinces and in the newly opened steppe areas of New Russia and the lower Volga than in Russia proper.

From peripheral areas originally inhabited only by non-Russians Russia obtained a sizeable proportion of its metals, the mining and utilization of which witnessed an important upsurge in the eighteeenth century. In addition to Karelia (iron) and Siberia (silver, gold and copper), the southern Urals became the main centre for the mining and smelting of iron and copper. The Bashkirs, to whom the land had once belonged, were evicted, and the forests cut down. However, the region's non-Russians were at the most employed as auxiliary labour, whereas workers were recruited from among the Russians. In the early stages of these metallurgical activities foreign specialists such as the Dutchmen Winius, Marselis and Hennin played an important role,[19] though subsequently most of the entrepreneurs were Russian. The textile manufactories of Ukraine on the left bank of the Dnepr and the central Volga region were also largely in the hands of Russian entrepreneurs, whereas in the Baltic provinces they were run by Baltic Germans, and in the formerly Polish areas initially by Polish nobles, and subsequently by Jews. In the first half of the nineteenth century new industries such as sugar refineries or cotton mills were often set up by foreigners, who were usually German or English, or by Polish and Jewish entrepreneurs.[20] Trade and industry in the Kingdom of Poland, which in economic terms became the most dynamic region of the Russian empire after 1815, was, at least until 1830, in the hands of Poles, Jews and Germans. In certain industries Armenians and Tatars played a pioneering role in the east of the empire.

Domestic trade in the Russian heartland was dominated by Russian merchants, whereas foreign trade in the west and in the south was in the hands of foreign merchants. However, non-Russian ethnic groups in Russia, who to some extent cooperated with foreigners, also participated in domestic and foreign trade – Baltic Germans in the north-west, Ukrainians and the Greeks of Nizhyn in eastern Ukraine, after the partitions of Poland mainly Jews and to a lesser extent Poles in the west, and Greeks, Armenians and Tatars in the south and the east. Since the seventeenth century, Russian merchants had protested unceasingly, though with little success, against the privileges granted to foreigners and non-Russians, and this helped to spread protonational ideas among the Russian commercial community.[21] The abolition of customs barriers in the middle of the century helped to incorporate the peripheral areas into the all-Russian market,[22] and the territories incorporated in the decades which followed, with the exception of the Grand Duchy of Finland, were also gradually integrated in economic terms.

A partial division of labour between the regions and the ethnic groups came into being. In the case of Siberian furs this was clearly a matter of colonial exploitation, and, similarly, the mining activities in the Urals were also largely disadvantageous to the Bashkirs. On the other hand, the economic interaction between the pastoral nomads and the Russians was a tradition that went back centuries, and had originally been advantageous to both sides. The basis of the nomads' economy was undermined only after the advent of Russian settlers had led to a reduction in the size of their grazing areas. Whether Ukraine's economic interaction with Russia, which began in the middle of the eighteenth century, was advantageous at the time or not remains a subject for debate, though subsequently there were increasing signs of one-sided dependence.[23] However, the Baltic provinces, Finland, and also the Kingdom of Poland, which were more highly developed in socio-economic terms than the Russian centre, were quite capable of profiting in economic terms from their position. This also held true of the Polish magnates in Ukraine, of various groups of non-Russian merchants and entrepreneurs, who on the whole were able to defend their traditional privileges against the demands of Russian merchants, and of foreign (and especially German) colonists. In any case, until the nineteenth century Russia derived little in the way of profit from the majority of the non-Russian peripheral areas if one takes into account the fiscal privileges of certain non-Russians and the high levels of expenditure for the administration and the armed forces.[24] All this shows that the heterogeneous economic character of the pre-modern Russian empire rules out generalizations such as, for example, the notion that Russia had a fundamentally beneficial influence on the peripheral areas, or that they were economically backward on account of their colonial dependency status.

In addition to their role in the economy, non-Russians also performed important functions in other areas. In the pre-modern period it was a fundamental fact that Russia had far too few well-educated experts in order to be able to solve the huge task of modernization which Peter the Great had set the country. As a result of this state of affairs, which was described as maloliud'e or maloliudstvo (dearth of people), the government was forced to rely on the cooperation of non-Russians. I have already emphasized on a number of occasions that under Russian rule the non-Russian elites retained important functions in their areas in the administration, the judiciary and the police organizations. For the upper classes which were co-opted into the hereditary Russian nobility this, since Catherine II's reforms, was partly within the framework of the new estate-based local administration, and partly, as for example in the Baltic provinces, in Finland and in the Kingdom of Poland, within the traditional corporate structures. On the other hand, the upper classes of the nomadic and Siberian ethnic groups, which remained outside the empire's estate-based order, retained their tribal and clan organizations. Russia, whose regions were under-administered by European standards, could not have controlled and administered large newly acquired territories using Russian personnel.[25]

The second area in which non-Russians began to perform important tasks at an early stage was the *armed forces*. The army had played a central role in Russia since the beginnings of the Muscovite state, not only in the wars which were waged almost without interruption, but also as an instrument of control and an arm of the administration, especially in the peripheral areas.[26] In the Muscovite empire the cavalry had been strengthened on a regular basis by detachments of nomadic horsemen. Muscovy initially enlisted the services of Tatars from the successor states of the Golden Horde, who were later joined by Bashkirs and Kalmyks. Troops of mounted Kalmyks were still fighting on the Russian side in the Seven Years' War and in the 'Patriotic War' against Napoleon, and two Kalmyk cavalry regiments entered Paris on their camels in 1814. They were partly responsible for the fact that in the west Russian armies were not infrequently regarded as barbaric and Asiatic.[27] Furthermore, in the sixteenth and seventeenth centuries up to a quarter of the Muscovite army consisted of irregular units from sedentary ethnic groups, for example Volga Tatars from Kazan and Kasimov, and Mordvinians and Cheremis. They were also employed to guard the steppe frontier.[28] Subsequently the Russian Cossack armies which lived on the steppe frontier were reinforced by non-Russians (Kalmyks, Ukrainians, Tatars, Bashkirs, Buriats and Tungus). The Ukrainian Dnepr Cossacks, who had the status of an independent army, also served Russia by protecting the border in the south-east. Moreover, larger detachments participated on the Russian side in the wars of the seventeenth and eighteenth centuries. And thousands of Ukrainians who were known as cherkasy entered the service of the tsar directly in the second half of the seventeenth century.[29]

When, in the seventeenth and eighteenth centuries, Russia began to replace its traditional cavalry with a modern army capable of holding its own against its western counterparts, the dearth of trained specialists once again became apparent. The establishment of the 'troops of the new order' initially proceeded under the command of foreign officers. In 1679, no less than forty-two out of sixty-six high-ranking officers were foreigners, and in Moscow's foreigners' suburb officers were very much in the majority. We should mention the Scots, Leslie, Bruce and Gordon, and Lefort, a native of Geneva, who rose to a prominent position under Peter the Great.[30] In fact, Peter the Great, who enlarged the Russian army even further, enlisted the services of more foreign officers (they included a German, Burchard Christoph Münnich, who was subsequently the only non-Russian to become president of the War College). Yet at the same time he speeded up the training of Russian officers. At the start of the Great Northern War in 1700 foreigners comprised a third of the officer corps. Their number later shrank to an eighth, though the percentage in the upper ranks was much higher. Thus in 1730 thirty-seven out of 114 high-ranking officers were foreigners. In addition to several Scotsmen they were of French, German, Polish and Swedish origin.[31] In the course of the eighteenth century the foreigners were replaced by numerous Baltic Germans who had often been educated in the St Petersburg Cadet Corps. In 1762 41 per cent of the 402 high-ranking officers and half of the four highest ranks were non-Russians, and three-quarters of these were Baltic Germans and Germans.[32]

In the decades which followed other foreigners, for example the Prussian Diebitsch, the Hessian Klinger (who in his youth had been a friend of Goethe) or the Georgian Bagration, and numerous Baltic German, Finnish and Polish aristocrats entered the service of Russia. In the reign of Nicholas I non-Russians were still present in large numbers.[33] The percentage of Protestants (primarily Baltic Germans and Finlanders) was particularly large among the high-ranking officers, whereas the percentage of Catholic Poles, whom the Russian government regarded with increasing mistrust, was much higher among the junior officers, and lower among the high-ranking officers. In contrast to Muslims, Jews were not given commissions.[34]

The multi-ethnic composition of the army was not a peculiarly Russian phenomenon. The officer corps of other pre-modern empires such as Prussia and Austria were just as cosmopolitan. However, Russia, to an even greater extent than other countries, had to rely on non-Russian officers. In the eighteenth century they contributed to the modernization of the Russian army by transferring western military technology and tactics, and introducing Prussian drill. Yet it would be wrong to overestimate the contribution made by the non-Russians. Thus it was easier to introduce technical innovations than to inculcate values such as a Prussian sense of duty. There were quite a number of adventurers among the non-Russian officers. Furthermore, non-Russians sometimes succumbed to the influence of Russian traditions. Nevertheless until the middle of the nineteenth century the officer corps continued to be cosmopolitan, and had a high proportion of Germans.[35]

It hardly comes as a surprise that Russians occasionally protested against the preferment of non-Russians, whether foreigners or subjects of the tsar, in the army. In the second half of the eighteenth century the Russian Lieutenant General Rzhevsky asked, 'Why do we need so many foreign officers?', and pointed out that this diminished the chances of promotion for able Russians. Under Nicholas I there was Russian opposition to German officers: 'Germans are disliked in our army . . . They are intriguers and egoists, and support each other like the links of a chain.'[36] Such voices, which were also raised against the numerous Polish officers, who were often considered to be unreliable, articulated an important theme in Russian national consciousness which resounded in the years that followed: Russians were at a disadvantage to privileged non-Russians who were perceived as a barrier to mobility. However, it had little or no effect until the second half of the nineteenth century.

The second pillar of power in the Russian empire, apart from the army, was the *bureaucracy*. Although absolutist Russia expanded its administrative structures, it was once again confronted with a dearth of highly trained Russian cadres, so that pre-modern Russia was forced to rely on the specific skills of non-Russians. The Muscovite state, when setting up its central administration under Ivan III, had already made use of the services of knowledgeable immigrants, especially of Greeks and Tatars.[37] The areas acquired from Poland-Lithuania from the middle of the seventeenth century onwards constituted a new source of recruits, especially eastern Ukraine and the Kievan Academy, which was capable of training Orthodox cadres. From the Smolensk area came the baptized Jew Shafirov, whose son carved out a successful career under Peter the Great. And the Ukrainians Feofan Prokopovych and Stefan Iavorsky were among the tsar's most important advisors. Throughout the whole of the eighteenth century, members of the Ukrainian upper class, such as A. K. Rozumovsky, A. A. Bezborodko, P. V. Zavadovsky and V. P. Kochubei, rose to hold important offices in the state.[38]

An even more important role in the modernization of the Russian administration was played by western Europeans and Baltic Germans, who were recruited by Peter the Great and, even if they were not of noble origin, were brought into the Russian nobility via the Table of Ranks. In the collegiate administration, Russians were as a rule appointed to the posts of president, yet non-Russians, such as the Baltic Germans Magnus Wilhelm Nieroth, Hermann von Brevern or Johann Benckendorff, were assigned to them in an advisory capacity. In addition to Münnich, Heinrich Ostermann, who was also of German origin, the Baltic German Reinhold Gustav von Löwenwolde and Ernst Johann von Biron (Bühren), a native of Kurland, all became particularly prominent figures after the death of Peter. In the course of the eighteenth century the Baltic Germans gained in importance at the expense of German-speaking foreigners. In the reign of Catherine II there were, for example, the influential statesmen Johann Jakob Sievers and Otto Heinrich Igelström. And Alexander I entrusted important tasks to aristocratic Poles, such as Adam Jerzy Czartoryski and Seweryn Potocki, and Finlanders, such as Gustav Armfelt.

All of the groups mentioned above possessed a good western education, and to an extent had gained some experience in the administration of their regions, which served as models for Russia. Ethnic and religious criteria were of no importance, and therefore non-Russian civil servants did not have to adopt the Russian language or convert to the Orthodox church. However, this only applied to Christians, whereas Jews or Muslims, although they to some extent possessed the required educational qualifications, were not accepted in the bureaucracy. Orthodox non-Russians such as Ukrainians or Romanians cannot be deduced from the statistics, for government departments only recorded an individual's membership of a religious community, and not of an ethnic group.

Whereas the share of foreigners among the high-ranking civil servants at the beginning of the nineteenth century was still about 8 per cent, it declined even further under Nicholas I.[39] Yet two of his most important ministers, foreign minister Karl Nesselrode and finance minister Georg (Egor) Kankrin, were of German origin. On the other hand, the Baltic Germans now attained their greatest influence in the bureaucracy, and under Nicholas I they contributed nineteen of the 134 members of the State Council. In the middle of the century not even 4 per cent of all civil servants were Lutherans (and most of these were Baltic Germans). However, they included about an eighth of the incumbents of the 350 top posts, twelve out of 113 members of the governing senate, nine out of fifty-five members of the State Council and nine out of forty-eight governors. Estimates concerning the share of Germans in the Russian military and civil elite are higher still.[40] In the reign of Nicholas I, particularly prominent Baltic Germans included the first head of the Third Section (of the secret state police), Alexander Benckendorff, and Karl Lieven, the minister of education.

What political influence did the Germans and Baltic Germans who were to be found in such large numbers in the upper echelons of the Russian bureaucracy really have? They usually contributed good professional knowledge to their government departments, and were predominant in certain areas. However, the core of Russia's political elite continued to be Russian even after the implementation of Peter the Great's policy of westernization. Even in the period after Peter's death, which, from the perspective of Russian proto-nationalism, was denounced as 'government by Germans', the ancient Russian nobility continued to be the dominant force, whereas the significance of foreigners as a group was always restricted, even though the role of individuals was substantial.[41] It was no different in the reign of Nicholas I, despite the alarm expressed by national-minded Russians such as Mikhail Pogodin or Iurii Samarin, or by the 1844 publication entitled *La Russie envahie par les Allemands*.[42] It was not the Germans who ruled the Russian state. Rather, the latter used Germans, who were dependent on the tsar's benevolence, as instruments in the pursuit of its goals. Furthermore, Baltic Germans and Germans were acculturated by the Russian milieu, and they did not transform Russia's bureaucracy into a Prussian one, even if this may have been what Nicholas I wanted, and what appeared to be the case to certain Russians who were in competition with 'Germans'.

Around the middle of the nineteenth century the share of Poles in the Russian civil service was about 3 per cent, and among high-ranking civil servants it was even as high as 6 per cent.[43] However, many of these Poles worked in special institutions that dealt only with Poland or in the west of the empire, and thus made an appearance in the central administration only at the beginning of the nineteenth century. The Russian government, especially after the November revolution of 1830–31, regarded the Polish nobility with mistrust. Clearly, the kind of good education which some Poles had certainly received was not the only criterion for admission into the higher civil service. It had to go hand in hand with loyalty to the tsar and his dynasty. Of the educated elites of the Russian empire these dual requirements were met best by the Baltic Germans, whereas the Finlanders, whose qualifications were similar, tended to pursue military rather than civil service careers. In addition to constraints imposed by maloliud'e (the dearth of educated Russians), there may have been another reason why non-Russians played such an important role in the armed forces and the civil service, namely that the government hoped to use loyal and privileged foreign groups who were wholly dependent on the tsar in order to counterbalance the Russian nobility. This was not only true of the reign of Nicholas I, but to some extent also of the preceding centuries in which noble Tatars had had prominent positions at the Muscovite court. Thus it was perhaps no accident that the first head of the political police (Benckendorff) and his second-in-command (von Fock) were Baltic Germans, and one could, if one were so minded, see a connecting link with the numerous non-Russian specialists in the early Soviet secret police.

Diplomacy had been a special domain of non-Russians since Muscovite times, when in the west Greeks, such as Georgios Trachaniotes, and in the east and the south Tatars served as valuable intermediaries.[44] With the growth of diplomatic ties with western Europe in the eighteenth century such tasks were often assigned to foreigners, especially Germans and Baltic Germans. It is symptomatic that Jakov Bruce and Heinrich Ostermann signed the Treaty of Nystad as the Russian representatives. Subsequently diplomats came from Baltic German families such as Stackelberg, Meyendorff, Krüdener and Pahlen. There were also a handful of Poles and Orthodox Christians who had emigrated from the Ottoman Empire, such as the Romanian Prince Antioch Kantemir.[45] In diplomacy, western education, a knowledge of languages and international family connections played a special and important role. Thus in 1853 nine out of nineteen envoys and ambassadors belonged to the Lutheran church.[46]

In the eighteenth century non-Russians also played an important role in the *hierarchy of the Orthodox church*. With their high level of education, which also included Latin and Polish elements, the Ukrainian graduates of the Kievan Academy fitted better into a westernized Russia than the traditional Russian clergy, who resisted Peter the Great's reforms. Of the 127 bishops consecrated between 1700 and 1762 not less than seventy-five (60 per cent) were Ukrainian, and only thirty-eight (30 per cent) Russian. Most of the others were Greeks, Serbs and Romanians from the Ottoman Empire.[47] But the Ukrainian hierarchs with their partly western education did not have an easy time in the Russian eparchies, and after 1760, as the educational level of the Russian clergy gradually improved, the preferential treatment of Ukrainians was less in evidence.

The work of foreigners and non-Russians who acted as intermediaries in the fields of *culture, science and scholarship* was of very great importance. In the educational system and in the fields of science and scholarship their percentage was even larger in the eighteenth and early nineteenth centuries than in the other areas mentioned above. In this context it would be appropriate to include an account of the colourful story of the numerous cultural contacts which went back to the fifteenth century, but I restrict myself to pointing out certain salient features. Mention must be made of the individual foreign specialists who had come to Russia since the Middle Ages, and had worked in an innovative manner in various fields.[48] From the second half of the seventeenth century onwards the influence of Ukrainians and Belorussians on Russian culture and learning was profound. Until the first half of the nineteenth century eastern Slavs with a Western education from the formerly Polish-Lithuanian areas, above all graduates of the Kievan Academy such as Epifanii Slavynetsky, Simeon Polockii, Stefan Iavorsky and Feofan Prokopovych, provided an important intellectual link between Russia and the Roman Catholic west. It was not an accident that P. V. Zavadovsky, a Ukrainian graduate of the Kievan Academy, was appointed to head the Schools Commission which was established in 1782, or that in 1802 he became the first Minister of Popular Enlightenment.[49]

Peter the Great stepped up the recruitment of foreign specialists, and subsequently whole areas such as medicine or engineering became the domain of western foreigners, and later of Baltic Germans and Poles. Thus in the eighteenth century over half of the members of the newly founded Academy of Sciences and, with the exception of the Ukrainian Kirill Rozumovsky, all of its presidents had German names.[50] The higher education system, which was reorganized at the beginning of the nineteenth century, was to a large extent established by Polish aristocrats such as Adam Czartoryski and Seweryn Potocki, who were able to utilize the insights of the Polish 'Commission for National Education', and by German, Baltic German and Polish scholars. In any case, the German University of Dorpat and the Polish University of Vilna functioned as transmitters of western scholarship and ideas, not to mention the Universities of Warsaw and Helsingfors in the largely autonomous territories of the Kingdom of Poland and the Grand Duchy of Finland.[51]

Compared to the transmission of western culture and scholarship, intermediaries to the oriental and Islamic world were of lesser importance. The religious barrier prevented an intensive reception of Islamic or Buddhist cultural influences in Russia. However, even here non-Russian subjects of the tsar also functioned as intermediaries. For example, Kalmyks and Tatars were of importance to the Foreign Ministry as translators. In the eighteenth century and in the first half of the nineteenth century Tatar mullahs and merchants, partly at the behest of the Russian government, began to infiltrate the peoples of the steppes and then also the sedentary civilizations of middle Asia in economic, political and intellectual terms. This intermediary activity served to prepare the way for Russian commercial and possibly even political expansion, though in the medium term it also had an effect on the national awakening of the ethnic groups in middle Asia.[52]

We come to the following conclusions. In Russia the elite was cosmopolitan, as in other pre-modern empires. The dearth of educated Russians meant that the Russian government was compelled to make use of the services of non-Russians. Initially they were primarily foreigners, though from the middle of the eighteenth century onwards they were increasingly non-Russian subjects of the tsar who performed complementary functions in commerce, the armed forces, the bureaucracy, the diplomatic service and scholarship and culture, making a crucial contribution to the modernization of Russia. It is true that Russians occasionally protested against the privileges accorded to non-Russians. However, as long as the latter were irreplaceable, protests met with little success.

This picture of the functions of non-Russians corresponds at least in part to the model of the *'mobilized diaspora groups'* proposed by the American political scientist John Armstrong.[53] He observed that in many multinational empires governments cooperated with the elites of ethnic diaspora groups, who perform specific functions which cannot be performed by the predominant ethnic group. He divided mobilized diaspora groups into two subcategories, the 'archetypical diaspora', for whom religion and religious myth play a special role (the Jews being a classical example), and the 'situational diaspora', which is also scattered and dispersed, though it has a large mother country to back it up (for example, the Germans in eastern Europe, or the Chinese in south-east Asia). Intensive communication networks and language skills mean that the diaspora groups are able to specialize in acting as intermediaries, introducing innovations and working as merchants, entrepreneurs, moneylenders, physicians or diplomats, functions which cannot be performed by the dominant ethnic group. They are dependent on the protection of the government, and run the danger of being sacrificed as scapegoats as a result of the social mobilization of the lower classes of the dominant ethnic group.

Armstrong has applied his model to the case of the Baltic Germans, who in his opinion were the central mobilized diaspora group in the Russian empire in the eighteenth and nineteenth centuries.[54] He rightly makes a distinction between the three subcategories of the nobility, which devoted itself to the armed forces and the bureaucracy, the commercial urban population, which devoted itself to trade, and the educated middle-class literati, who devoted their energies to culture and scholarship. However, in this category he also includes the German urban population of Russia proper (outside the Baltic provinces), which was linked to the Baltic Germans through the Lutheran church, and represented a mobilized diaspora group with the corresponding functions. I have already described the most important functions which Germans and Baltic Germans had to perform within the framework of the Russian empire until the middle of the nineteenth century. They were loyal to the tsar and his dynasty, and enjoyed their protection. It is true that there were links with Germany and its many fragmented states, and these simplified the economic, diplomatic and cultural intermediary activities of the Baltic Germans and the German urban population. However, they were not of a political nature. Conflicts first began to occur after the appearance of national ideas, which surfaced in the 1840s.

In addition to the German-speaking population, which can be regarded as the most important diaspora group in the centre and the north-west of Russia, there was a series of other ethnic groups which performed similar functions in their regions. The Jews were prevented from playing such a role throughout the empire by discriminatory restrictions and their own traditionalist attitudes, and they were thus compelled to concentrate on economic activities in the pale of settlement and in the Kingdom of Poland. Here Jews were predominant in the retail business and in certain trades such as tailors, hauliers or barbers, whereas they relinquished their monopoly in the liquor trade. Growing competition led to large-scale impoverishment. There was a small upper class of wealthy Jews, who were active as moneylenders and merchants. In this their contacts with Jews in other countries proved to be advantageous. According to a contemporary report (the reliability of which has, it is true, been called into question), in the middle of the nineteenth century Jews comprised three-quarters of the merchants in eight of the fourteen provinces of the pale of settlement. They were also well represented among the merchants of the first guild. Jewish entrepreneurs were active in the manufacture of cloth, in part as the successors of Polish aristocrats, and later in the new sugar refineries. In their factories, in contrast to the numerous Polish and Russian firms which were based on forced labour, they generally employed Jewish wage-earning workers, and their activities made a crucial contribution to the modernization of industry in the west of Russia.[55]

Some Armenians, who, like the Jews, are distinct from all other ethnic groups on account of their exclusive religion (and sacred script), had lived from the eleventh century onwards in communities scattered over wide areas of Asia and Europe. Since the Middle Ages they had played an important role in trade between Poland-Lithuania or Rus and the Orient.[56] Armenian communities, which were granted trade privileges and religious freedom (and to some extent tax concessions and self-rule) by the Russian government, established themselves in the capital cities of Moscow and St Petersburg; in Astrakhan (on the lower Volga); in New Nakhichevan, the colony founded on the lower Don by Armenians who had emigrated from the Crimea; and in Grigoropol in Bessarabia. In addition to the Orient trade, which was primarily conducted from Astrakhan, where a colony of Indian merchants also played a part, Armenians in the eighteenth century and at the beginning of the nineteenth century were also active as entrepreneurs. For example, they played a pioneering role in the cotton and silk manufactories in Astrakhan and Moscow. A few Armenians also served as officers in the Russian army. The rich Lazarev family, which was ennobled in 1784, had come to Moscow from Iran. It pursued wide-ranging trade and entre-preneurial activities, and was also a notable patron of the arts. The Lazarev Institute for Oriental Languages, which was founded in Moscow in 1815, made a striking contribution to Russia's cultural interchange with Asia. Thus by the beginning of the nineteenth century, Armenians had taken on some of the tasks that were typical of mobilized diaspora groups in the Russian empire. However, their complementary functions in the Ottoman and Iranian empires were actually far more important. After the annexation of Transcaucasia their significance as a mobilized diaspora group in Russia increased considerably.

Whereas scholars have as a rule taken note of the complementary activities of Jews and Armenians, they have tended to overlook the Volga Tatars, who in fact were also a typical mobilized diaspora group. In the European part of the Russian empire they had formed an exclusive religious minority since the sixteenth century, and, in addition to their core area, were dispersed throughout the whole of the east of Russia. The policy of discriminating against the Muslim elite, which, from the first half of the eighteenth century onwards, excluded it from the ranks of the landowning nobility, and thus from careers in the armed forces and the bureaucracy, made it turn its attention to trade. In the second half of the eighteenth century and at the beginning of the nineteenth century Tatar merchants from Kazan and Orenburg played an increasingly important role in regional domestic trade and in foreign trade with the Kazakhs and the khanates of middle Asia. They were granted trade privileges by the government, and self-administrative bodies in the shape of 'Tatar Town Halls' (tatarskaia ratusha) in Kazan and a suburb of Orenburg. In the first quarter of the nineteenth century Tatars comprised about a third of the guild merchants in the province of

Kazan. They were headed by wealthy families such as Iunusov, Apanaev, Yusupov and Akchurin. Tatar merchants also played a not inconsiderable role as entrepreneurs in the production of leather and soap, and, as in the case of the Armenians, a pioneering part in the cotton industry in Russia. In this field they transmitted middle Asian expertise to Russia. In any case, their complementary functions resulted largely from their economic, political and cultural intermediary activities between Russia and middle Asia, a task for which, as Muslims, they were predestined.[57]

Greeks were also active in Russia as a mobilized diaspora group. Together with the Armenians and the Jews they were among the ethnoreligious minorities which performed important complementary functions in the Ottoman empire. Since the Middle Ages Greeks had repeatedly come to Ukraine and Russia within the framework of ecclesiastical relations, and had played a significant role as cultural and diplomatic intermediaries.[58] The Greek merchants of Nizhyn in Ukraine, who had been granted privileges by the Ukrainian hetman and then by the Russian tsar, were active in the eighteenth century as trade intermediaries between Russia and the Ottoman empire, and also as founders of cotton manufactures.[59] With the development of New Russia these activities shifted to the new towns on the Black Sea, where Greek colonies were established. The Greeks of Odessa in particular played an important role, both as pioneers of the Russian Black Sea trade, and later as a cultural and political centre of the diaspora that was of significance for the Greek national movement. For this reason the 'situational diaspora' of the Greeks highlights certain links between ethnic minorities and Russian foreign policy. A number of Greeks pursued careers in the Russian navy and diplomatic service. The most famous figure was Ioannis Kapodistrias, who was Secretary of State in the Russian Foreign Ministry between 1815 and 1822, and was elected to be the first Greek president.[60]

Future research will demonstrate whether or not other ethnic groups in the pre-modern empire performed the functions of mobilized diaspora groups. One such group would be the gypsies, although Armstrong explicitly excludes them from the category. Whereas it is true that they did not have the typical mobilized diaspora tasks of elites, they had, in Bessarabia, to name but one example, clearly defined economic tasks.[61]

It has become apparent that in the pre-modern Russian empire non-

Russian mobilized diaspora groups performed a whole series of complementary functions which Russians were incapable of. Whereas in the centre Baltic Germans and Germans played an outstanding role in the bureaucracy, the armed forces, and in science and scholarship, Jews in the west, Greeks in the south, Armenians and Tatars in the east and, once again, Baltic Germans and Germans in the north-west developed important intermediary activities in trade, early industrialization, culture and diplomacy. There is also the question of how the complementary functions of the mobilized diaspora groups developed as Russia proceeded to modernize itself in the nineteenth century. As we have seen, their privileges and special status were repeatedly criticized by Russians, who saw them as competitors and as a barrier to advancement. This pressure increased as a result of the social mobilization of Russians in the nineteenth century. How did the Russian government react to this? Did it sacrifice the mobilized diaspora groups once it no longer needed their services? I shall return to these questions in Chapters 6–8.

3. Religious and Cultural Diversity

At the end of the eighteenth century Heinrich Storch, a scholar who lived in Russia, wrote:

> No other state in the world has such a mixed and diverse population. Russians and Tatars, Germans and Mongols, Finns and members of Tungusic tribes live here separated by vast distances and in the most varied regions as citizens of a single state, joined together by their political order, but differing with regard to their physical appearance, language, religion, lifestyle and customs in the strangest of contrasts.

He came to the conclusion 'that the inhabitants of the Russian empire comprise at least eighty distinct nations, which differ essentially from each other on account of their descent, their customs and their language . . . Yet to see such an extraordinary number of peoples and ethnic groups united in a single body of a state is a most rare occurrence, a second example of which we would look for in vain in the history of the world.'[62] Even if this observant scholar exaggerated slightly, it is still a fact that, even before the colonial conquests of the nineteenth century, the Russian empire displayed great cultural diversity. In the pre-modern age the most important feature in cultural terms was one's faith, which determined group identity to a far greater extent than language. Being multilingual was widespread among the upper and middle classes. But one could only have one religion. And the educational system was still largely in religious hands.

The ethnic groups of the pre-modern Russian empire included adherents of four world religions: Christianity, Judaism, Islam and Buddhism. In addition to this there were also adherents of nature religions. The Christians were by far the largest group in numerical terms, comprising about 91 per cent of the total population in 1719, and about 94 per cent in 1815. They included the members of the Orthodox church (including an unspecified number of Old Believers), who were the most numerous, comprising about 87 per cent of the population in 1719, and still about three-quarters of the population in 1815. The following belonged to the Orthodox church around 1815: all of the Russians; the vast majority of the Ukrainians; some of the Belorussians; the Romanians of Bessarabia; the Greeks, Bulgars and Gagauz; the Karelians, Ingrians, Veps and Zyrians who had been baptized in the Middle Ages; and the Chuvash, Mordvinians, Cheremis, Votiaks, Iakutians and other small Siberian ethnic groups which had all been Christianized in the eighteenth century.[63]

The Orthodox church was the Russian state church. From the very beginning of the Muscovite empire it had been closely connected with its rulers, and from the eighteenth century onwards was wholly under the control of the state. The formerly independent Kievan metropolitanate had already been placed under the control of the patriarch of Moscow at the end of the seventeenth century, whereas the Romanians in Bessarabia were gathered together in the eparchy of Kishinev in 1813.[64] The large group of exclusively Russian Old Believers remained outside the church, and was tolerated from the eighteenth century onwards. However, its members were subject to discrimination.

The history of Russian expansion shows quite clearly that since Muscovite times the state tolerated non-Orthodox faiths within the framework of its habit of guaranteeing the status quo.[65] Although it welcomed Orthodox missionary activity, it did so only when this did not endanger its goals, which were social and political stability, and economic returns. The state only departed from this practice in the middle of the sixteenth and in the first half of the eighteenth centuries, supporting the baptism of Muslims and animists with the help of economic inducements and coercive measures. In 1702, at the same time as the most massive wave of forced conversions was commencing in the east, Peter the Great, in his tolerance manifesto, proclaimed that there would be religious freedom for foreigners who wished to enter the service of Russia. In 1710 he guaranteed religious freedom in the Baltic provinces. After 1755 the enlightened absolutist government went back to tolerating the non-Orthodox inhabitants in the east of the empire. But Catherine II reinforced government control over the non-Christian religions, and attempted to instrumentalize their adherents for the good of the state.

Tolerance did not apply to those who had fallen from the true faith, for example, the Uniate Ukrainians and Belorussians who came under Russian rule in 1654, and more particularly in 1772. Only the Orthodox church was permitted to engage in missionary activity, and a member of the Orthodox church was not permitted to convert to another faith. On the other hand, conversion to the Orthodox church was encouraged with the help of certain inducements. Since the Middle Ages the members of the Orthodox community were often equated with Russians, though from the very beginning it also included other ethnic groups. In contrast to this Orthodox Russian core there were the inovertsy, those who believed in other faiths. For a long time the state also separated the latter from the Orthodox spatially by permitting them to live only in their own suburbs outside the towns proper. Baptism made it possible for this and other restrictions to vanish, and the discriminations against, but also the privileges accorded to those of other faiths disappeared. Whereas it is true that individuals were gradually russified as a result of being baptized, this was not the case with larger ethnic groups.

Up to the end of the seventeenth century the Russian Orthodox church had a decisive influence on Russian culture and, over and above this, on the thinking of the lower and middle classes. Despite attempts at secularization under Peter and Catherine, the elementary school system remained in the hands of the church, at least in rural areas, though the network of parish schools was very patchy, and the level of literacy among Russians continued to be very low.[66] In the eighteenth and early nineteenth centuries only the Russian nobility and a part of the clergy and urban population received an adequate education in newly established schools. The eight Russian universities which existed before 1830 had considerably more non-Russian than Russian professors and students. Two of them were Polish-speaking (Vilna and Warsaw), one was German-speaking (Dorpat), and one was Swedish-speaking (Helsingfors).

Although the Ukrainians of the Hetmanate were also Orthodox, their culture had since the seventeenth century been subjected to much more powerful influences from the west, especially from Poland. To this day numerous buildings in the style of the Ukrainian baroque bear witness to this. The western influence was most obvious in the educational system based on the model of the Jesuit schools, in which Latin played an important role. At its head was the famous Kievan Academy which, as we have seen, for a time became a college producing cadres for the whole of Russia. Heinrich Storch wrote at the end of the eighteenth century that it was a university with 1,500 students.[67] In addition there were the colleges of Chernyhiv and Kharkiv, which not only trained the clergy, but also the sons of the nobility and the middle classes. And the net of elementary schools was also denser than in Russia, so that in the eighteenth century the Ukrainians had a considerably higher literacy level than the Russians. But this advantage slowly diasappeared with the integration of the Ukraine, the gradual Russification of its elite, the adaptation of the other classes and the growth of a secular educational system in Russia.

As a result of the partitions of Poland numerous adherents of the *Uniate church*, which acknowledged the supremacy of the Pope whilst retaining the Slavonic rite, came under Russian rule. As we have seen, the Russian authorities made life difficult for Uniate Ukrainians and Belorussians, and as late as the end of the eighteenth century very many of them were forced to convert to the Orthodox church. At the beginning of the nineteenth century the Uniate eastern Slavs, who still numbered several million, were initially incorporated into the organization of the Roman Catholic church. However, the dissolution of the Uniate church came as early as 1839 (with the exception of a residual organization in the diocese of Kholm). Most of the Uniate Belorussians and Ukrainians in Russia were illiterate peasants dependent on the Polish Catholic upper class.[68]

Roman Catholics were few and far between in Russia before the partitions of Poland. There were on the one hand individual foreign specialists, most of them officers from Scotland, France, Italy and Poland, who lived in the two capitals. Here, since the time of Peter the Great, they also had their own churches. On the other hand, as early as the seventeenth century there were Polish or polonized noblemen in Smolensk and (as a result of resettlement) in other parts of Russia, though as a rule they soon became members of the Orthodox church. It was only between 1772 and 1815 that the adherents of the Roman Catholic church, who comprised about 10 per cent of the population, became the largest non-Orthodox religious community in Russia. They were primarily Poles, together with Lithuanians, and some Belorussians, Latvians and German colonists. The Catholics in the Russian empire were organized without the permission of the Holy See in the Archbishopric of Mogilev, and at the beginning of the nineteenth century – with the exception of the Catholic church of the Kingdom of Poland, which was organized within the Archbishopric of Warsaw – placed under the control of the 'Roman Catholic Religious College', which was part of the St Petersburg 'Central Administration of the Religious Affairs of Foreign Faiths'.[69]

The culture and the educational system of the areas which had once been part of Poland-Lithuania (with the exception of Kurland) were also Polish in character under Russian rule, and this had the effect of acculturation on Lithuanians, Belorussians and Ukrainians. To all intents and purposes the three-level school system which was based on ancient traditions, and had been reformed in the last years of the republic, was retained. It consisted of a relatively dense network of church and secular elementary schools, numerous middle schools which traced their origins back to Jesuit or Piarist colleges and, at its head, the Academy of Vilna, which had become a university in 1803. It was joined in 1805 by the lycée of Krzemieniec, and in 1816 the University of Warsaw. The first two decades of Russian rule witnessed a flowering of the Polish educational system and of Polish culture in the Kingdom and in Lithuania.[70] At any rate, the level of literacy and the percentage of people with secondary and tertiary education was considerably higher among the Poles than among the Russians, Belorussians and Lithuanians.[71]

From the sixteenth century onwards several groups of *Protestants* came under Russian rule. Foreign specialists and prisoners from Livonia formed the most important element in the Moscow foreigners' suburb (Nemetskaia Sloboda), which later found its continuation in the large German colony in St Petersburg. After the Great Northern War the Lutheran Estonians, Latvians, Baltic Germans and Finns of Old Finland became Russian subjects, and after the third partition of Poland so did the Latvians and Germans of Kurland. They were later joined by the German colonists, most of whom were Protestant, the Germans in the Kingdom of Poland and the Finns and Swedes in Finland. Unlike the Catholics, the Protestants in Russia were heterogeneous, with the members of the Reformed church forming a small minority. Although they comprised only about 5 per cent of the population, their qualitative significance was considerably larger. The Protestant churches in the Baltic provinces, in Finland, and in the Kingdom of Poland continued to be independent churches based on a particular country, whereas the Germans in the towns and the colonies established communities and churches which at the beginning of the nineteenth century were linked in organizational terms by means of consistories. In 1832 the state also reinforced its control over the Protestants in Russia, and, with the exception of those in Finland and Poland, but not the Baltic provinces, placed them under the control of the Lutheran chuch in St Petersburg.[72]

Russia's Lutherans lived in worlds of their own, which were central European in character, and, despite their denomination, had little to do with each other. They all had in common a high level of education (going by the average Russian standards), and through church instruction this also reached the peasant lower classes. As early as the end of the Swedish period the Estonian-speaking and Latvian-speaking parish schools in Estonia and especially in Livonia had reached a high percentage of the rural population, and at the end of the eighteenth century the level of literacy of the peasants in northern Livonia is estimated at having been no less than two-thirds.[73] In the second decade of the nineteenth century reforms gave a new and added impetus to popular education. In the towns, in addition to German elementary schools, there was a whole series of secondary schools including the ancient Cathedral School in Riga, where Herder taught for a time. At the top of the educational pyramid there was the German University of Dorpat, which was reestablished in 1802. It played an important role in the training of cadres.

In the Russian empire only the Grand Duchy of Finland with its dense network of Finnish-speaking parish schools, which also provided for a high percentage of the peasants, and its Swedish University of Helsingfors, possessed an educational level comparable to that of the Baltic provinces. In the eighteenth century and at the beginning of the nineteenth century the German schools in Moscow and above all in St Petersburg developed into educational institutions which were on a high level, and also attracted the children of noble Russians. Although the German colonies on the Volga and in southern Ukraine all had schools, they only developed slowly in the first post-immigration decades.[74] Of the numerous sects we should briefly mention the *Mennonites*, who came to Russia from West Prussia, and in New Russia founded communities closed to outsiders which flourished in both economic and cultural terms.[75]

Of members of other Christian denominations we must also mention the *Armenians*, whose colonies in Russia formed communities belonging mainly to the Armenian Gregorian church, and partly to the Armenian Uniate church, which were accorded recognition by the Russian government.[76]

The *Jews*, who lived in the pale of settlement in the west of the empire, also formed groups closed to outsiders whose culture and daily and communal life were largely determined by their religion. They continued to be organized in the traditional communities with a self-administrative body, the kahal, in which rabbis played an important role. The spiritual life of the Jews had been characterized since the eighteenth century by the conflict between the popular Hassidic faith and rabbinical orthodoxy. In the first decades of the nineteenth century the enlightenment movement (haskalah) began to make itself felt, though for many years to come older traditions predominated in culture and the educational system. The elementary school, the kheder and the higher Talmud school, the yeshivah, gave Jewish boys a religious education, which concentrated on the reading of Hebrew texts. A handful of schools were centres of rabbinical scholarship and widely influential. Although a high percentage of Jewish boys attended a school, it is not easy, in view of the formal character of the teaching, to say anything about the Jews' standard of literacy. However, it was certainly higher than that of the other ethnic groups of the region.[77] In addition to the vast majority of Yiddish-speaking Jews, there were also small groups who used other languages, for example, the Krymchaki, who spoke Crimean Tatar.[78] They should not be confused with the adherents of the Jewish sect of the *Karaim*, most of whom also spoke Tatar. This small group of people lived in the Crimea and in Lithuania in communities which were tolerated by the Russian state and, unlike the Jews, were not discriminated against.[79]

At the end of the eighteenth century the *Muslims* comprised only about 4 per cent of the population of Russia. Their share did not increase significantly until the nineteenth century. The Volga Tatars were the first larger group belonging to a non-Christian world religion to live under Russian rule from the middle of the sixteenth century onwards. They were later joined by the Siberian Tatars, the Bashkirs and the Crimean Tatars. All these groups belonged to the Sunni branch of Islam. Yet Islam was less strongly entrenched among nomads with their tribal traditions than among the Volga and Crimean Tatars. The latter had been sedentary for a long time, and their culture and community life were determined by Islamic law and religious traditions. The Muscovite state showed tolerance to the Muslims in Russia, and in a very pronounced manner in the autonomous Khanate of Kasimov on the Oka river. Its tolerance was also demonstrated by the remarkable fact, for a Christian realm, that until the end of the seventeenth century tens of thousands of Russian peasants were dependent on Muslim Tatars. After the intense missionary campaign at the beginning of the eighteenth century had come to nothing, the enlightened absolutist government once again accorded tolerance to the Muslims, though at the same time it reinforced the state's control by creating a 'Religious Assembly' in Ufa and a corresponding institution in the Crimea, each of which was headed by a mufti appointed by St Petersburg.[80]

The Muslim community in Russia resembled that of the Jews, for it was moulded by ancient religious traditions. The Islamic clergy had a leadership role, and were also responsible for the educational system. The Koran school (makhtab), which was attached to every mosque, taught Tatar boys the rudiments of reading Arabic, though this was often confined to memorizing religious texts. The Islamic secondary schools (madrasa), which existed in certain towns, provided a thorough religious education. Those who wished to obtain a higher education had to go abroad, for example to Bukhara. At the end of the eighteenth and at the beginning of the nineteenth centuries the Kazan Tatars witnessed a kind of intellectual renaissance. This was seen, for example, in the shape of the encouragement of Tatar printing presses. As in the case of the Jews, it is difficult to determine the level of literacy of the Volga and Crimean Tatars in view of the debatable quality of the Koran schools. However, contemporary observers emphasized that it was higher than that of the Russians in the region.[81]

It is a little-known fact that *Buddhism* was also to be found among the ethnic groups within the Russian empire. In the process of the 'gathering of the lands of the Golden Horde', Russia encountered descendants of the founders of the empire, the Mongols, who in the sixteenth and seventeenth centuries had been converted to lamaism via Tibet. Two groups of Mongol tribes came under Russian rule: the Kalmyks, who in the seventeenth century occupied areas on the lower

Volga, and the Buriats in south-east Siberia. The Kalmyks had already become lamaists in western Mongolia, whereas the Buriats to the south of Lake Baikal were converted by Tibetan and Mongolian lamas in the first half of the eighteenth century, that is, whilst they were already under Russian rule. The northern Buriats remained shamanists. Russia subsequently displayed tolerance to lamaism, though in the second half of the eighteenth century it also increased its control over this religious community through a Buriat and Kalmyk head lama whose status was confirmed by St Petersburg. Culture and the religious education system were sustained by the monasteries. In the case of the Buriats there were about twenty in the first half of the nineteenth century, most of them large wooden structures based on Tibetan models, whereas at this time the Kalmyks had more than a hundred smaller monasteries which as a rule were housed in tents and took part in the Kalmyks' nomadic wanderings. The monasteries maintained schools which to some extent also taught secular subjects. Since the monks alone comprised about 10 per cent of the population of the two ethnic groups, it may be assumed that their level of literacy was higher than that of the Russians.[82]

A number of Finnish-speaking ethnic groups in European Russia and the majority of the ethnic groups in Siberia were adherents of *nature religions*. The Muscovite empire displayed tolerance towards them, and it was only under Peter the Great that most of them were converted to the Orthodox church with the help of economic incentives and coercion. In formal terms, at the end of the eighteenth century only a handful of ethnic groups in the far north and in the east of Siberia, such as the Samoyeds and the Chukchi, had not been baptized. However, the traditional animist customs and traditions also continued to determine the culture and the social relationships of those who had just been baptized. This was even true of the Chuvash and the Cheremis, who lived in the middle of European Russia.[83]

Thus it is clear that, although the vast majority of the population of the Russian empire belonged to the Orthodox church, the mass of the Orthodox Russians had a lower level of literacy than the majority of non-Orthodox non-Russians, the Lutheran Germans, Estonians, Latvians and Finns, the Catholic Poles and the Jews, and most probably the Muslim Tatars and the lamaists in the east. Although the Russian secondary and tertiary educational systems were greatly expanded at the end of the eighteenth and at the beginning of the nineteenth centuries, this was not a centre-periphery educational cleavage of a kind characteristic of colonial empires. There was also a foreign policy aspect in Russia's religious diversity, for at least the Catholics, lamaists and Muslims were suspected of having divided loyalties on account of their allegiance to Rome, to Lhasa and to the Islamic centres abroad (and especially in Istanbul). Conversely they were able to serve as the pace-makers of Russian influence, especially in the neighbouring states to the east.

Language as an identity factor was of subsidiary significance and came after religion. It is possible to divide the languages of pre-modern Russia into roughly two categories. On the one hand there were languages which were spoken and written by the upper class, and were vehicles of high cultures, and on the other there were non-written languages which were only spoken by the lower classes who were ruled by elites from another ethnic group. Russia recognized the written languages of the non-Russian elites, and they included Polish, German, Swedish, Greek, Armenian, Mongolian, Hebrew and Yiddish, Volga Tatar, Crimean Tatar and Arabic. These languages were used on various levels as teaching languages in schools, and they were also printed. The largely non-written languages of the other ethnic groups were ignored by the Russian government. It also allowed the non-Russian elite languages and cultures to influence the peasant nations. Thus the Tatar influence on the Chuvash, Cheremis, Mordvinians and Bashkirs, the Polish on the Lithuanians, Belorussians and Ukrainians, the Swedish on the Finns, and the German on the Estonians and Latvians continued unabated.[84]

Certain of the empire's ethnic groups were traditionally bilingual, with a sacred written language and an everyday language which was only in part used in writing. This was true of Church Slavonic in the case of the Russians and Ukrainians, of Armenian, of Hebrew in the case of the Jews, of Arabic in the case of the Muslims, and Tibetan or Old Mongolian in the case of the lamaists. The fact that these languages all had their own alphabets helped to distinguish those who used them from the Russians in cultural terms, and to support the cohesion of these ethno-religious communities. The idioms of the Lutheran peasant peoples (the Latvians, the Estonians and the Finns) were a special case: they were the languages used in teaching in the elementary schools, and – to a limited extent – were written languages. Finally, the Ukrainians had developed their own written language in addition to Church Slavonic. However, it gradually disappeared because it was not recognized by the Russian government, and because the Ukrainian elite was russified.

Not a great deal of research has been done on the questions of mutual acculturation among the various ethnic groups, assimilation processes and, more important still, Russification in the pre-modern Russian empire. It is possible to state that, whereas there were many kinds of cultural interaction between the ethnic groups, the assimilation of a larger number of people by another ethnos was rare before the middle of the nineteenth century.[85] On the whole the various ethnic groups in the rural areas and the ethno-religious groups also found in the towns lived separated from one another, and retained their traditional cultures: 'It is nonetheless to be admired that the majority of the dispersed Finnish tribes, despite the location of their lands, have retained . . . so much that is peculiar to them', wrote Johann Gottlieb Georgi in the 1770s about the ethnic groups of the middle Volga region.[86] Exceptions were small Finnish-speaking ethnic groups such as the Ingrians and Vots and some of the western Mordvinians, who had lived for centuries in scattered settlements in largely Russian surroundings, and Belorussians and Ukrainians who lived in areas inhabited by Russians.[87] If members of the peasant peoples moved to a town and began to climb the social ladder, they were usually subject to upwardly mobile assimilation by the ruling ethnic group. Thus Latvians and Estonians were germanized; Lithuanians, Belorussians and Ukrainians were polonized or russified; and the ethnic groups which had been converted to Christianity were russified. On the other hand, the peasants who had been converted to Christianity usually retained their own language and culture. This is exemplified by the group of baptized Tatars, some of whom had already been converted to Christianity in the sixteenth century, although they still spoke Tatar in the nineteenth century, and formed a distinct ethnic group recognized neither by the Russians nor by the Muslim Tatars.[88]

Thus, whereas in the pre-modern period the non-Russian rural population was only slightly russified, the non-Russians who had been co-opted into the nobility were subject to a greater degree of assimilation. From the Middle Ages onwards members of non-Russian elites had repeatedly joined the Russian nobility, and of the 125 Russians who together with fifty-four foreigners and Baltic Germans formed the military and political elite of the empire in 1730s, at least a quarter (if we exclude the eastern Slav nobles from Lithuania) was of non-Russian origin. The vast majority were descended from Tatars, for example, the descendants of the ruling family of the Great Nogai Horde, Iusupov and

Urusov, who had entered the service of Russia in the sixteenth century.[89] The Volga Tatar nobles who were converted to the Orthodox church at the beginning of the eighteenth century were quickly russified, for example, the Engalychev, Kildishev, Kugushev and Tenishev families.[90] In the course of the eighteenth and early nineteenth centuries most of the members of the Smolensk szlachta and the Ukrainian Cossack upper class who had been co-opted into the nobility were russified. They were followed by some of the Germans and Baltic Germans who served at the centre.[91] But most of the Baltic German, Polish and Finlandish members of the elite who came from the west of the empire retained their ethnic identity, quite apart from the non-Russian upper classes in the peripheral areas.

Despite the existence of certain assimilation processes, the elite of the pre-modern Russian empire continued to be cosmopolitan. In addition to members of the Orthodox church, it included Protestants, Catholics and, in the regions, Muslims. In linguistic terms French and German were predominant in addition to Russian, in the west also Polish and Swedish, and in the east Tatar. The majority of high-ranking nobles were multilingual. Karl Nesselrode is a classic example of the cosmopolitan character of the Russian elite. Born in Lisbon as the son of a German Catholic father and Jewish Protestant mother, and baptized in the Church of England, he was for more than four decades Russian foreign minister, without in the process having learnt to speak Russian properly.[92]

Russia's capital city was a mirror image of the country's complex religious and linguistic structure. In the eyes of a Russian patriot of German descent, 'From the time of its foundation St Petersburg, the most important link of a Russia attaching itself to Europe, displayed a terrible mixture of languages, manners and customs.'[93] In addition to the bureaucratic and military elite of the empire, which apart from Russians also comprised Baltic Germans, Germans, Poles and Finlanders, there were in St Petersburg fairly large communities of Germans, with numerous churches and schools, of Poles (with a church and a school), Finlanders, Estonians and even of Tatars (with their own mosque). In the first half of the nineteenth century foreigners made up about 9 per cent of the population, and non-Russians from Russia itself about 5 per cent.[94] But many other towns and cities were multi-ethnic and multi-religious, for example, Moscow, the towns in the west with their Jewish communities, the ethnically especially colourful towns in the south and the east such as Odessa (which had Jews, Greeks, Bulgars, Romanians, Germans and Armenians), Astrakhan (with its Tatar, Armenian, Indian, Persian and Greek communities)[95] or Kazan. Catherine II also noticed this when she visited Kazan in 1767, and later wrote to Voltaire: 'Il y a dans cette ville vingt peuples divers, qui ne se ressemblent point du tout. Il faut pourtant leur faire un habit qui leur soit propre à tous.'[96]

4. Non-Russian Resistance

The picture of the formation and structure of the pre-modern Russian multi-ethnic empire that I have painted in the previous chapters is a little too harmonious. True, in comparison to the age of nationalism Russian policy towards the non-Russian ethnic groups was for long periods of time remarkably pragmatic, flexible and tolerant. The same is true of the cooperation of Russians and non-Russians in the adminis- tration, army, business and commerce and culture. But from the perspective of numerous non-Russians – especially of the ethnic groups which, before joining Russia, had possessed a politically independent polity – the situation looked quite different. Russian rule was seen as brutal foreign domination which sought to force on non-Russians a foreign administrative and social order, and also, in the long term, a foreign religion and culture.

A first indication of the potential for protest is given by the resistance which the ethnic groups mounted against annexation by Russia. As the two chapters on Russian expansion have shown, armed resistance in the east among the 'heirs of the Golden Horde' was much stronger than in the west. The non-Russians of the Khanate of Kazan reacted to the conquest of their state with a bitter struggle for liberation that was only put down after five years by large Muscovite armies; and they made two attempts in the following decades to exploit periods of weakness of the Muscovite state and shake off Russian rule through violent popular uprisings. Numerous ethnic groups in Siberia, such as the Iakuts, Buriats, Koriaks and Chukchi, responded to conquest and Russian rule with long periods of armed resistance. For a whole century the partly nomadic Bash- kirs resisted integration into the Russian empire in a series of revolts, and in the last rebellion of 1755 proclaimed that they were waging a 'holy war'. The nomadic Nogai Tatars, the Kalmyks and the Crimean Tatars sought to escape from mounting Russian oppression by means of a mass exodus.

The Russian authorities used brutal force to put down any kind of insurrection. Security interests, the maintenance of Russian rule, and the loyalty of Russia's new subjects had absolute priority. At the time of a particularly aggressive policy in the east, which among other things also deployed the weapon of forcible Christianization, this could verge on ethnocide: 'Proceed against the unruly Chukchi with armed force and extirpate them utterly. Only those who are prepared to become subjects of His Imperial Majesty shall be taken prisoner and taken from their homes' (1742).[97] There were also what can only be described as campaigns of extermination against the Bashkirs between 1735 and 1740, which led to them being decimated. Once the insurrections of the non-Russians had been quelled, the government did not as a rule come to the conclusion that repression had to be continued in order to ensure their loyalty. Rather, it realized that a more flexible policy was necessary. Thus resistance by non-Russians was an important factor which ensured that Russian policy on the whole continued to be one of restraint.

However, the potential for protest among the ethnic groups in the east continued to be great. Thus it comes as no surprise that the ethnic groups of the middle Volga and the Urals were the first to join great popular uprisings of the seventeenth and eighteenth centuries which were started and led by Russian Cossacks. Chuvash, Mordvinians and Tatars made a significant contribution to the rebellion of Stepan Razin (1670–71), and in the last popular uprising of 1773–75, the Pugachev revolt, non-Russians, primarily Bashkirs and Tatars, but also Votiaks, Chuvash and Mordvinians, comprised the numerically largest group. The fact that numerous Russians took part in these rebellions shows that in the first instance the issue was no longer the liberation of the non-Russians from foreign oppression, but a joint social and political protest against the centralist state and its regional representatives. But neither were the great pre-modern popular uprisings, as Soviet historiography has claimed, primarily the work of Russian peasants and directed against serfdom.[98]

The non-Russians in the west put up less resistance to Russia than the ethnic groups in the east. The reasons for this can probably be found in their social order, lifestyle and value systems. Nomadic or semi-nomadic animist or Muslim groups who lived in tribal units had a higher anti-Russian protest potential than sedentary Christian societies with a noble upper class and serfs. In contrast to most of the upper classes in the east, the Christian elites were recognized as equals, and as a rule the

Russian government succeeded in securing their loyalty by co-opting them into the nobility and guaranteeing their self-administration, owner-ship of land and privileges. Thus in the Baltic provinces, in Finland and in Bessarabia there was hardly any resistance to Russian rule. For the years after 1709 this is also true of Ukraine on the left bank of the Dnepr (excluding the Zaporozhian sich), whereas in the epoch of the largely autonomous Hetmanate there were repeated attempts to secede from Moscow. The Poles, who, like most of the ethnic groups in the east, had a long tradition of political independence, were an exception to this rule. Although the Polish aristocrats were also able to preserve their social status quo, many were unable to come to terms with the loss of statehood and sovereignty, and pursued the aim of reestablishing the Polish-Lithuanian kingdom. The uprising under the leadership of Tadeusz Kosciuszko in 1794 and the November revolution in 1830 constituted the largest resistance movements in the west of the empire. Russia suppressed them with military force, as it did the revolts in the east, and then attempted with both repression and concessions to secure the Poles' loyalty. But large numbers of them preferred to emigrate, and thus the Polish question remained on the agenda.

Large-scale armed uprisings were only the tip of the iceberg, which consisted of a whole gamut of forms of resistance to Russian rule. The refusal to pay taxes and render services, deserting from the army, fleeing to areas not (yet) controlled by the Russian state, and local small-scale rebellions were just as frequent among non-Russians as among Russians. Disputes concerning land and property became increasingly numerous, either between (usually non-Russian) old settlers, and new settlers (often Russian), or between nomads and sedentary Russians and non-Russians. Although the centre repeatedly emphasized that the regional administration should treat non-Russians with 'mildness and caution', innumerable petitions enable us to deduce that especially non-Christian and newly baptized non-Russians suffered a great deal from the arbi-trary rule of Russian administrators. There were particularly strident protests against forcible Christianization in the second third of the eighteenth century.

It is difficult to determine the potential and aims of non-Russian resistance, for only a fraction of it is recorded in the sources. The only opportunity to obtain a glimpse of the complaints of numerous ethnic groups is provided by the consultative 'Commission for a New Legal Code' of 1767. Among the more than 500 delegates who assembled in

Moscow to discuss the proposals there were also many non-Russians, including representatives of the nobles and the urban population of the Hetmanate (thirty-four, with ten Cossacks), of Sloboda Ukraine, New Russia, the Baltic provinces (fourteen), Old Finland, the province of Smolensk, and representatives of the Tatar, Chuvash, Mordvinian, Cheremis, Votiak, Bashkir and a handful of Siberian state peasants and service men (forty-eight). Although in fact only the 'non-nomadic peoples' had been invited, there were also two representatives of the Kalmyks and two of the Buriats. The serfs, who comprised the vast majority of the population in the centre and in the west, were either absent altogether, or represented merely by the owners of the estates.[99]

The common denominator of the specific wishes of the non-Russians, which have survived in the instructions and discussions, was the preservation of the status quo, which in a large number of ways was being called into question by the systematizing intrusions of the absolutist state. Thus the representatives of the Baltic German, Ukrainian and Smolensk upper class and urban population, and those of the Tatar merchants defended their traditional special rights and privileges, which had been confirmed by earlier rulers, whereas Russian delegates called for their abolition. The Muslim Tatar service men and the Ukrainian Cossack elite demanded equality with the Russian nobility. The non-Russian state peasants complained about new taxes and services, and demanded a guarantee for their landed property that was being endangered by Russian settlers. Representatives of the newly baptized and animist ethnic groups protested against the methods of forcible Christianization, and Tatars against anti-Muslim discrimination.[100] It is true that the wishes articulated in the 1767 Commission were certainly not representative of all social groups, and only for individual estates. However, their principal thrust, the maintenance or restoration of 'ancient rights', corresponds to the aims of the Pugachev revolt, which erupted a few years later. It is of course true that the latter also included social revolutionary elements.

The potential for protest among the non-Russians of the Russian empire was considerable, and in the pre-modern epoch represented a destabilizing element in the system of governance with which the Russian government had to reckon, more in fact than with the resistance of the Russians. It is true that most of the ethnic groups which had been part of the Russian empire for some time no longer pursued the goal of regaining their independence, though they resolutely defended the rights and guarantees that Russia had given them. In the nineteenth century, expansion to new areas once more raised the level of potential for protest. The wars of liberation conducted by the nomads and the mountain peoples of the Caucasus perpetuated the tradition of resistance in the east, whereas in the west the Poles continued to work for the restoration of the Polish-Lithuanian state. New destabilizing elements were the national movements of the non-Russians, and the revolutionary movement of the Russians themselves.

5. The Character of the Pre-modern Russian Multi-ethnic Empire

The Russian empire as it had evolved by the beginning of the nineteenth century was characterized by a great diversity which cannot be described using simplistic labels such as 'Russian unitary state', 'Orthodox realm', or 'colonial empire'. Its ethnic, religious, cultural, socio-economic and socio-political variety was noticed by contemporary observers such as Heinrich Storch, who kept coming back to this subject in his *Historisch-Statistisches Gemälde des Russischen Reiches*.

> This so numerous and so thoroughly intermingled mass of people offers a spectacle which must prove exceptionally interesting to every thinking observer. The physical, political, and moral state of the same forms a large and instructive picture in which all modifications are visible . . . a commentary on the history of mankind which explains the gradual development of culture by means of the most vivid and striking examples.[101]

The question of the character of Russia as a multi-ethnic empire, to which a large number of contemporary observers in the second half of the eighteenth century and at the beginning of the nineteenth century devoted themselves, was subsequently rarely asked, and the fictitious ideal type of the nation state also began to be applied to Russian history. This incorrect interpretation, which continues to influence thinking to this day, can fall back on a number of arguments. Whereas it is true that the imperial state, the Muscovite and the 'Russian empire' (Rossiiskaia Imperiia), were distinct in terminological terms from the ethnos 'Russian' (russkii), it cannot be denied that the concept 'Russia' (Rossiia) assigned a special role to the ethnic group of the Russians, and that the ideology of the state also absorbed certain aspects of Russian ethnic consciousness.[102] The religious element was even more important than the ethnic one. Since the Middle Ages the difference between Russians and the infidel Muslims, Roman Catholics and animists constituted a factor which contributed to the Russian identity. The Muscovite empire, after the fall of Constantinople, was the only bulwark of the Orthodox church, and even the westernized Russia of the eighteenth century could not dispense with the Orthodox church as an integrational ideology.

Thus Russian ethnic consciousness and the Orthodox faith were certainly among the integrational elements of pre-modern Russia. However, they were not constitutive principles of the Russian empire and its society. This has been demonstrated by the analysis of Russian policy towards the non-Russians and the structure of the empire. Priority was given to stabilizing Russian power and securing the loyalty of non-Russian subjects to the ruler and his dynasty. The cohesion of the multi-ethnic empire could not be ensured by an ethnically or religiously exclusive ideology. Thus the principles of the dynasty, of the autocratic, divinely legitimated ruler and his empire defined the state and its institutions, whereas the estate principle was of fundamental importance for the various social groups.

Projecting the exclusive national principle on to the past obscures the fact that human beings of the pre-modern (and also of the modern) age did not merely have a single identity and loyalty. Rather, they had (and have) a variety of situational identities. The nobles of the Russian empire were indebted to the tsar of Russia and his dynasty, and they were members of their estate. Subordinated to these primary loyalties, as a rule, were loyalties to a region and to a religious community. On the other hand, membership of a linguistic or cultural community played an even more minor role. In the upper and middle classes dual ethnic identities and multilingualism were frequent. What integrated the Russian aristocracy from the eighteenth century onwards was neither the Russian language and culture nor the Orthodox faith. It was their noble descent, their service for the ruler and a lifestyle based on western education. The state cooperated with noble elites of various religions, but not with Orthodox peasants. The Baltic German noble was initially a member of the nobility of his region and a loyal subject of the tsar, then a member of the Lutheran church, and only then a member of the German linguistic and cultural community. The Russian, Ukrainian or Polish peasants and urban inhabitants were stranger to the Russian,

Ukrainian or Polish nobleman than a member of his estate who belonged to another ethnic or religious group. For the middle and lower classes membership of an estate-based social group, region and religious community played a greater role than membership of an ethnic group. For nomads, hunters and gatherers their lifestyle and economic system and the resulting social and cultural traditions were more important than religion or language.

Russia shared the priority of dynastic and estate-based principles at the expense of ethnic and linguistic ones with other pre-modern multi-ethnic empires. The Utopian call for an ethnically uniform nation state has obscured the fact that fundamentally every state had and has a multi-ethnic population. It is merely a question of the size of the various ethnic groups, and the extent to which the dominant ethnic group managed to acculturate the other ethnic groups. If one compares the Russian empire from this angle with other pre-modern states, it becomes apparent that west European states (for example, France or the United Kingdom) integrated their ethnic minorities to a far greater extent than Russia. This is also true to a lesser extent of Poland-Lithuania and the Habsburg empire in the eighteenth century. Heinrich Storch was no doubt thinking of all these examples when he emphasized Russia's unique status: 'It may well be true that there are a few European countries in which there is more than one nation, or where one still sees traces of the erstwhile difference between the original and later inhabitants. But almost everywhere in these states the ruling people has as it were devoured the conquered one.'[103]

Why did this heterogeneous character survive, especially in centralist, autocratic and absolutist Russia? Here one has to name a whole series of factors – the sheer size of the territory, which, as a result of continual expansion, was becoming ever larger, made migration easy, prevented the growth of densely populated districts and provided areas which were secluded and isolated; the fact that the administration only reached parts of the empire; and, maloliudstvo, the dearth of Russian cadres. To sum up this chapter I should like to highlight three explanations: 1. The backwardness of the Russians in comparison to the non-Russians of the empire; 2. the ancient traditions of multi-ethnic symbiosis which went back to the Middle Ages; and 3. the resistance of the non-Russians.

1. In contrast to the majority of the other European multi-ethnic empires, the Russian 'state people' was not superior to many other

ethnic groups of the empire with regard to its economic development, socio-political organization or level of education. This was true not only of the relationship to the ethnic groups of the societies of the Baltic provinces, Finland, the Hetmanate and Poland-Lithuania, which, at least in part, possessed central European structures, but, at least up to the second half of the eighteenth century, also with regard to the sedentary Muslims (the Volga and Crimean Tatars) and the militarily superior nomads with their lifestyle and economic systems which were superbly suited to the steppes in which they lived. On top of this was the fact that the Russian government as a rule did not favour the Russian lower classes. Rather, it not infrequently permitted their economic and legal position to be inferior to that of the non-Russians, whose social status quo and privileges were usually guaranteed. For this reason an acculturation to the Russian ethnos was certainly not attractive for the mass of non-Russians. The same is true of the conversion of individuals to the Orthodox church, which, as is demonstrated by the example of baptized Tatars, usually led to a deterioration in their status. There were exceptions in the case of some of the non-Russian nobility, which was able to retain or enhance its social status by conversion to the Orthodox church (Tatars) and acculturation to the Russians (Tatars, Ukrainians). In this specific relationship between the 'state people' and the other ethnic groups the Russian empire differed not only in comparison to west European multi-ethnic empires, but also to Poland-Lithuania and the Habsburg empire. In this respect, as in the heterogeneous nature of its structure, it was probably closest to the Eurasian Ottoman empire.

2. That the multi-ethnic and multi-religious character of the Russian empire survived into the nineteenth century can also be traced back to the traditions of dealing in a pragmatic manner with other cultures and religions. Here again there are parallels to the Ottoman empire. From mediaeval times Russian princes and merchants had worked together closely with Muslims and nomads of the steppe. The traditions of tolerance and of pragmatic relationships with those who belonged to other religions had already been established in the great empire of the Golden Horde. The Orthodox church was subsequently unable to persuade the state to adopt its vision of Christianization. Russia was spared the aggressive missionary policy of the Roman church and the religious wars of the western states. When in the eighteenth century the

new Russian state began to imitate the example of the west in this respect as well, and proceeded to the practice of forcible Christianization, the experiment was terminated after a short time, for it clearly destabilized the governance of certain areas. Whereas the vision of conversion to the Orthodox faith played a certain role, albeit usually a subsidiary one, linguistic assimilation was not a Russian policy goal. Instead of encouraging the Russification of non-Russians, the authorities allowed non-Russian elites such as the Poles, the Baltic Germans or Tatars to polonize, germanize or tatarize the non-Russians who were dependent on them.

3. The fact that the ethnic diversity of the Russian empire survived can also be traced back to the resistance of non-Russians (above all to the non-Christian ethnic groups in the east). Their self-contained social and value systems remained largely intact well into the nineteenth century, even after centuries of Russian rule, and despite close interaction with Russians. Whenever the Russian state attempted to tamper with the traditional structures, the Muslims, lamaists and animists, whether sedentary, nomads or hunters, repeatedly put up stiff resistance, and thus forced the government to return to pragmatism and tolerance.[104]

All this makes it clear that the 'colonial empire' label does not aptly describe the character of the pre-modern Russian empire. True, it is possible to point to colonial elements, for example in the relationship to the ethnic groups in Siberia and, from the eighteenth century onwards, to the nomadic herdsmen of the steppe, and also to some extent to the Ukrainian Hetmanate. However, the lack of a level of development in the metropolis which was superior to the periphery, the limited bias in favour of Russians in comparison to the colonial peoples, and in general the priority of political and strategic aims over economic ones do not fit into the picture of a colonial empire. The west of Russia corresponded even less to the colonial model.[105] Here the political and military predominance of the centre went hand in hand with the economic, social and cultural superiority of the periphery. Yet in the nineteenth century, expansion in the east, which forms the subject of the next chapter, did in fact reinforce the colonial character of Russia.

Russia represented a variant of the pre-modern European multi-ethnic empires, and was characterized by great structural heterogeneity, by staggered levels of development in which the state people lagged behind numerous other ethnic groups, and by an ambivalence between old traditions that had arisen in the Eurasian context and new models adopted from the West. In the nineteenth century, western influences increased with the challenge of nationalism and modernization. However, the pre-modern traditions did not entirely disappear, and their influence can be felt to this day.

Notes

1 *Zakonodatel'stvo* (1987), p. 23

2 Kabuzan (1990, 1963, 1971); Bruk and Kabuzan (1980, 1981, 1982). See also Kabuzan and Troitskii (1971); Kabuzan (1984); V. M. Kabuzan, 'Gosudarstvennye krest'iane v XVIII – 50-kh godakh XIX veka. Chislennost', sostav i razmeshchenie', in *ISSSR*, vol. I (1988), pp. 68–83; V.M. Kabuzan, *Zaselenie Novorossii (Ekaterinoslavskoi i Khersonskoi gubernii) v XVIII–pervoi polovine XIX veka (1719–1858 gg.)* (Moscow, 1976).

3 With regard to specific areas and ethnic groups see also Zelenchuk (1979); Weinryb (1972), pp. 3f.

4 Kabuzan's figures for the Poles and the Jews are obviously too low. See below, note 8.

5 I base my remarks on the literature cited in the previous chapters, and in notes 2 and 3 above.

6 On this subject see Bruk and Kabuzan (1984); Kabuzan (1971).

7 With regard to the figures for the various regions see the literature listed in note 2.

8 Compare the figures given in Bruk and Kabuzan (1980) and Kabuzan (1990), pp. 216–17 with those in Wandycz (1974), p. 17; *Historia*, vol. III (1981), pp. 834f.; Zhukovich (1915), January, May.

9 See Kabuzan and Troitskii (1971); Kabuzan (1990).

10 See Kabuzan (1990), pp. 221–4.

11 Compare the figures given in Kabuzan (1990) with those in Kappeler (1982b), p.330.

12 I. G. Akmanov, 'O chislennosti naseleniia Bashkirii v XVII–pervoi polovine XVIII v.', *Sotsial'no-demograficheskie protsessy v rossiiskoi derevne (XVI–nachalo XX v.)*. Vyp. I (Tallin, 1986) pp. 57–63; A. Z. Asfandiiarov, 'Zaselenie Bashkirii nerusskimi krest'ianami v kontse XVI – pervoi polovine XIX v.', ibid, pp. 102–8; B. S. Davletbaev, 'K voprosu o sotsial'noi strukture bashkirskogo obshchestva po dannym revizskikh materialov', ibid, pp. 208–13; LeDonne (1984), pp. 288–90. See also *Ocherki Bashk.* I(1) (1956), pp. 255–7 and 271.

13 Richard Hellie, *Slavery in Russia, 1450–1725* (Chicago and London, 1982), pp. 385–96.

14 See Tillett (1969).

15 The reader is referred to the literature on the various regions cited in the previous

chapters. See also the corresponding sections in *Istoriia SSSR* III, IV (1967); *Handbuch* II; Kahan (1985).

16 N. L. Rubinshtein, *Sel'skoe khoziaistvo Rossii vo vtoroi polovine XVIII v (istoriko–ekonomicheskii ocherk)* (Moscow, 1957) especially Chapter 6.

17 See B. N. Mironov, *Khlebnye tseny v Rossii za dva stoletiia (XVIII–XIX vv.)* (Leningrad, 1985) especially pp. 67–99; Mironov (1981).

18 See Fisher (1943), especially pp. 118–22.

19 With regard to the following see also Blackwell (1968); Erik Amburger, 'Der fremde Unternehmer in Rußland bis zur Oktoberrevolution im Jahre 1917', in Amburger, *Fremde und Einheimische im Wirtschafts- und Kulturleben des neuzeitlichen Rußland. Ausgewählte Aufsätze* (Wiesbaden, 1982), pp. 97–115.

20 For a general account see Rieber (1982), pp. 54 and 62–5.

21 Rieber (1982), pp. 52–79.

22 Mironov (1981), especially pp. 238–41.

23 The arguments are summed up by Kononenko (1958), pp. 21–32. See also Blackwell (1968), pp. 65 f, 70 f.; M.E. Slabchenko, *Khoziaistvo Getmanshchiny v XVII–XVIII stoletiiakh*, vols. I–III (Odessa, 1922–3); A.P. Ogloblin, *Ocherki istorii ukrainskoi fabriki. Predkapitalisticheskaia fabrika* (Kiev, 1925).

24 See Starr (1978), pp. 28 f., who gives a tentative cost-benefit analysis.

25 See Frederick Starr, *Decentralization and Self-Government in Russia, 1830–1870* (Princeton, 1972), Chapter 1.

26 Starr (1978), pp. 12 f., emphasizes the role of the army in the context of imperial politics.

27 See Kappeler (1992a), pp. 97–9; Duffy (1981), pp. 58, 82, 164; Keep (1985), pp. 215 f.

28 See A. V. Chernov, *Vooruzhennye sily russkogo gosudarstva v XV–XVII vv. S obrazovaniia tsentralizovannogo gosudarstva do reform pri Petre I* (Moscow, 1954), pp. 95, 131; Keep (1985), pp. 77–9; Kappeler (1986), pp. 147 f.; Kappeler (1982b), pp. 100 f., 103, 172, 174.

29 Keep (1985), p. 75; LeDonne (1984), pp. 279f., 296.

30 Wittram, vol. I (1964), pp. 49 f., 63 ff.; Keep (1985), pp. 80–92; Erik Amburger, 'Die weiteren Schicksale der alten Einwohnerschaft der Moskauer Ausländer-Sloboda seit der Zeit Peters I.', *JbbGO* 20 (1972), 412–26.

31 See M.D. Rabinovich, 'Sotsial'noe proiskhozhdenie i imushchestvennoe polozhenie ofitserov reguliarnoi russkoi armii v kontse Severnoi voiny', in *Rossiia v period reform Petra I* (Moscow, 1973), pp. 133–71, especially pp. 138f and pp.154–8; Wittram, vol. II (1964), p. 9; Duffy (1981), pp. 18f.; Keep (1985), p. 241; Amburger (1966), p. 515; Meehan-Waters (1982), pp. 24–9, 172–202.

32 Duffy (1981), pp. 146 f.; Amburger (1966), p. 515; Meehan-Waters (1982), pp. 24–9, 172–202.

33 Curtiss (1965), pp. 204–11; Amburger (1966), pp. 335, 514; Fleischhauer (1986), pp. 140–50; Screen (1976).

34 See Stein (1967), pp. 457–9, 462, 467.

35 See Duffy (1981), pp. 145 f., 233–5.

36 Curtiss (1965), pp. 205 f. (citation 209); Keep (1985), pp. 86 and 242.

37 Kappeler (1986), pp. 148 f.

38 On this and the following subjects see Saunders (1985), pp. 65–111. Also see Amburger (1966); Wittram, vol. II (1964), pp. 92–6, 104–23; Meehan-Waters (1982), pp. 24–9, 172–202.

39 On the following see, in addition to Amburger (1966), Walter M. Pintner, 'The Social Characteristics of the Early Nineteenth-Century Russian Bureaucracy', *SR* 29 (1970), 419–43, especially pp. 436–8; Walter M. Pintner, 'The Evolution of Civil Officialdom, 1755–1855', in *Russian Officialdom. The Bureaucratization of Russian Society from the Seventeenth to the Twentieth Century* (Chapel Hill, 1980), pp. 190–226; Walter M. Pintner (1965), p. 56, A.2 (p. 65); Zaionchkovskii (1978), pp. 130–40; W. Bruce Lincoln, 'The Composition of the Imperial Russian State Council under Nicholas I', *Canadian-American Slavic Studies* 10 (1976), 369–71; Fleischhauer (1986), pp. 190–92 and 199–205; Igor N. Kiselev and Sergei V. Mironenko, '"Russia's Bureaucratic Ruling Elite". Towards a Social Portrait of Russia's Higher Bureaucracy During the First Quarter of the 19th Century', *Historical Social Research* 16 (1991), 144–54, here p. 152.

40 See, for example, Armstrong (1978), pp. 75–7. However, cf. Kiselev and Mironenko, 'Russia's Bureaucratic Ruling Elite', p. 152.

41 See Meehan-Waters (1982), which comes to this conclusion.

42 See, for example, Riasanovsky (1959), pp. 144–6.

43 For remarks concerning Polish civil servants in Russia see Bazylow (1984), pp. 61, 70, 202.

44 Kappeler (1986), p. 149.

45 Amburger (1966), pp. 442–64.

46 Zaionchkovskii (1978), p. 141.

47 Erich Bryner, *Der geistliche Stand in Rußland. Sozialgeschichtliche Untersuchungen zu Episkopat und Gemeindegeistlichkeit der russischen Orthodoxen Kirche im 18. Jahrhundert* (Göttingen, 1982), pp. 25–51; Kharlampovich (1914), Chapter 7.

48 Erik Amburger, *Die Anwerbung ausländischer Fachkräfte für die Wirtschaft Rußlands vom 15. bis ins 19. Jahrhundert* (Wiesbaden, 1968).

49 See Kharlampovich (1914), Chapters 4–6, 9, 10; Saunders (1985); Amburger (1966), pp. 188–91.

50 Amburger (1966), p. 473. See also the other studies by Amburger cited above, and Fleischhauer (1986), pp. 37 f., 46–50, 80 f., 90–97, 176–80.

51 Stefan Truchim, *Współpraca polsko-rosyjska nad organizacją szkolnictwa rosyjskiego w początkach XIX wieku.* (Łódź, 1960); Bazylow (1981), especially pp. 57–61, 68–72, 156f., 201–5; Reinhard Wittram, 'Die Universität Dorpat im 19. Jahrhundert', *ZfO* I (1952), 195–219.

52 Alishev (1990), pp. 193–6; Serge A. Zenkovsky, 'A Century of Tatar Revival', *ASEER* 12 (1953), 303–38; Fisher (1968).

53 Armstrong (1976).

54 Armstrong (1978). On the German population of the towns see also the studies by Amburger and Fleischhauer (1986), pp.193 f., 205–15.

55 Weinryb (1972); Rieber (1982), pp. 56–62; Blackwell (1968), pp. 230–7; Baron (1964), pp. 90–10; Hensel (1983); Kahan (1983); Zhukovich (1915), February, pp. 302 f., May, pp. 173–5.

56 See *Histoire* (1982); Gregorian (1972), pp. 169–75; Nolte (1969a), pp. 92–5 and 52–4; Rieber (1982), p. 70; Golikova (1982), pp. 159–208 and Kahan (1985), pp. 259–62 on the significance of the Armenians in Astrakhan; Zelenchuk (1979), pp. 219–25.

57 See Kappeler (1982b), pp. 373–5, 459–74; Alishev (1990), pp. 124–68; Rieber (1982), pp. 71 f.; G. A. Mikhaleva, *Torgovye i posol'skie sviazi Rossii so sredneaziatskimi khanstvami cherez Orenburg* (Tashkent, 1982); Kh. Kh. Khasanov, *Formirovanie tatarskoi burzhuaznoi natsii* (Kazan, 1977).

58 Edgar Hösch, 'Probleme der russisch-griechischen (balkanischen) Beziehungen im 16. und in der ersten Hälfte des 17. Jahrhunderts', *FOG* 38 (1986), 257–75.

59 Rumjana Mihneva, 'Les "Grecs" et le commerce entre les Balkans et la Russie (milieu XVIIe – milieu XVIIIe s.). Des privilèges à la crise', *Études balkaniques* I (1990), 80–99.

60 G. L. Arsh, 'Grecheskaia emigratsiia v Rossiiu v kontse XVIII – nachale XIX veka', *SE* 3 (1969), 85–95; Theophilos C. Prousis, 'The Greeks of Russia and the Greek Awakening 1774–1821' *Balkan Studies* 28 (1987), 259–80; Stephen K. Batalden, *Catherine II's Greek Prelate Eugenios Voulgaris in Russia, 1771–1806* (Boulder, 1982). In general see Ioannis K. Hassiotis, 'Continuity and Change in the Modern Greek Diaspora', *Journal of Modern Hellenism* 6 (1989), 9–24.

61 See Zelenchuk (1979), pp. 213–19; Ziablovsky (1815), p. 134; Zhukovich (1915), May, p. 167.

62 Storch, vol. I (1797), p. 39.

63 With regard to the following remarks I refer the reader to the literature on the various ethnic groups cited in Chapters 2 and 3, and list only a few selected studies which deal with specific questions.

64 See Smolitsch (1964), pp. 357–89.

65 See Nolte (1969a, 1969b); Scharf (1988).

66 Smolitsch (1964), pp. 538–633; Alston (1969), pp. 3–30.

67 Storch (1795), p. 92.

68 See Pelesz, vol. II (1880); Amburger (1966), pp. 184 f.; Ziablovsky (1815), p. 287.

69 Ammann (1950), pp. 457–63; Amburger (1966), pp. 181–3. Concerning the earlier period see Nolte (1969a), pp. 110–22; Ziablovsky (1815), pp. 285 f.

70 Wandycz (1974), pp. 92–102; Daniel Beauvois, *Lumières et société en Europe de l'Est. L'université de Vilna et les écoles polonaises de l'Empire russe (1803–1832)*, vol. I, (Lille/Paris, 1977).

71 Cf., for example, the numbers of schools, teachers, and pupils in the various regions in Ziablovsky (1815), pp. 135–8, and, with regard to the Kingdom of Poland, in Ryszarda Czepulis-Rastenis, 'Szkolnictwo', *Przemiany* (1979), pp. 173–97.

72 See Amburger (1961) and (1966), pp. 177–81 for a general survey of the subject. With regard to the earlier period see Nolte (1969a), pp. 95–110.

73 Raun (1979), especially p. 118. See the details of the schools of the various provinces given in Storch (1795).

74 Bonwetsch (1919), pp. 68–81.

75 Ehrt (1932); S.V. Sokolovskii, 'Etnicheskie kontakty i razmyvanie etnoizoliruiushchikh bar'erov u mennonitov Novorossii (konets XVIII – nachalo XX v.)', in *Etnokontaktnye zony* (1989), pp. 70–85.

76 Amburger (1966), p. 186. Concerning the earlier period see Nolte (1969a), pp. 92–5.

77 Baron (1964), pp. 135–57; *Die Nationalitäten* I (1991), pp. 357–65.

78 M.S. Kupovetskii, 'K etnicheskoi istorii krymchakov', *Etnokontaktnye zony* (1989), pp. 53–69.

79 See *Die Nationalitäten* I (1991), pp. 328 f. (with bibliography).

80 See Nolte (1969a), pp. 54–89; Kappeler (1982b), pp. 213–18, 351–3, 475–8; Fisher (1968); *Die Nationalitäten* I (1991), pp. 364–73.

81 See for example the comments of German observers concerning the educational system of the Kazan Tatars, K.F. Fuks, *Kazanskie tatary v statisticheskom otnoshenii* (Kazan, 1844), pp. 113–21; Erdmann, vol. I (1822), pp. 80–7.

82 Nolte (1969a), pp. 36–52; Sarkisyanz (1961), pp. 255–63, 379–86; Fedorov (1978), pp. 95–103; Hundley (1984), pp. 151–6; *Lamaizm v Buriatii XVIII-nachala XX veka. Struktura i sotsial'naia rol' kul'tovoi sistemy* (Novosibirsk, 1983); A.I. Karagodin, 'Kalmytskoe dukhovenstvo v XVII-pervoi polovine XIX vv.', *Voprosy istorii lamaizma v Kalmykii* (Elista, 1987), pp. 5–23; *Ocherki Kalm.* (1967), pp. 72–9, 428 f.; *Die Nationalitäten* I (1991), pp. 226 f. See also Erdmann's eyewitness account of the Kalmyks, II(2) (1826), pp. 331–8, 347 f.

83 Nolte (1969a), pp. 20–36; Kappeler (1982b), pp. 353–5, 478 f.

84 See *Die Nationalitäten* I (1991), pp. 174–300; Franklin A. Walker, 'Patriotic Rhetoric, Public Education, and Language Choice in the Russia of Tsar Alexander I (1801–1825)', *Canadian Review of Studies in Nationalism* 12 (1985), 261–71.

85 See the conclusions reached by Bruk and Kabuzan (1980), pp. 25–34; (1980), pp. 20f.; Kappeler (1982b), pp. 361–4, 489–500; or A. Richter's remarks concerning the Karelians in *ES* 16 (1895), 228.

86 Georgi, vol. I (1776), p. 2.

87 Kappeler (1982b), pp. 500 f.; Bruk and Kabuzan (1981), pp. 21, 30.

88 Kappeler (1982b), p. 498; Iu. G. Mukhametshin, *Tatary-kriasheny. Istoriko-etnograficheskoe issledovanie material'noi kultury. Seredina XIX – nachalo XX v.* (Moscow, 1977).

89 Brenda Meehan-Waters, 'The Muscovite Noble Origins of the Russians in the Generalitet of 1730', *CMRS* 12 (1971), 28–75; Kappeler (1992a), pp. 98 f., 102 f. See also Troitsky (1974), pp. 209–18, and, on a more general level, Iablochkov (1876); N.A. Baskakov, *Russkie familii tiurkskogo proiskhozhdeniia* (Moscow, 1979).

90 Kappeler (1982b), pp. 335–8.

91 John A. Armstrong, 'Acculturation to the Russian Bureaucratic elite: The Case of the Baltic Germans', *JBS* 15 (1984), 119–29; Duffy (1981), p. 147.

92 Riasanovsky (1959), pp. 44–6.

93 *Vospominaniia F. F. Vigelia*. Ch.2. (Moscow, 1864), p. 29.

94 Iukhneva (1984), Chapter 1; Bazylow (1984), *passim*, including p. 91.

95 On the first quarter of the eighteenth century see Golikova (1982), pp. 159–208. On the end of the eighteenth century and the beginning of the nineteenth century see the accounts given by Erdmann, vol. II(2) (1826), pp. 139–62, and Storch (1795), p. 98.

96 *SIRIO*, 10, 204.

97 *Kolonial'naia politika tsarizma na Kamchatke i Chukotke v XVIII veke. Sbornik arkhivnykh materialov* (Leningrad, 1935), p. 163.

98 See Kappeler (1982b), pp. 178–87, 307–21; Andreas Kappeler, 'Die Rolle der Nichtrussen der Mittleren Volga in den russischen Volksaufständen des 17. Jahrhunderts', *FOG* 27 (1980), 249–68.

99 A. V. Florovsky, *Sostav zakonodatel'noi kommissii 1767–74 gg* (Odessa, 1915); Georg Sacke, *Die Gesetzgebende Kommission Katharinas II. Ein Beitrag zur Geschichte des Absolutismus in Rußland* (Berlin, 1940); Madariaga (1981), pp. 139–83.

100 I. Telichenko, 'Soslovnye nuzhdy i zhelaniia malorossiian v epokhu Ekaterinskoi kommissii', *Kievskaia starina* 30 (1890), 161–91, 390–419; *Kievskaia starina* 31 (1890), 94–122, 213–15; Kohut (1982), pp. 125–90; Alexander von Tobien, 'Die Livländer im ersten russischen Parlament (1767–1769)', *Mitteilungen aus der livländischen Geschichte* 23 (Riga, 1924–6), pp. 424–84; *SIRIO* 32 (1881), p. 319 (Smolensk); Kappeler (1982b), pp. 298–307; Fedorov (1978), pp. 163–9.

101 Storch vol. I (1797), p. 302.

102 See Michael Cherniavsky, 'Russia', in Orest Ranum (ed.), *National Consciousness, History, and Political Culture in Early Modern Europe* (Baltimore, 1975), pp. 118–43; Andreas Kappeler, 'Bemerkungen zur Nationsbildung der Russen', in idem (ed.) (1990), pp. 19–35.

103 Storch, vol. I (1797), p. 40.

104 See also Starr (1978), pp. 26–8.

105 In general terms, see David Morison, 'Kolonialherrschaft', in *Sowjetsystem und demokratische Gesellschaft* 3 (Frankfurt, 1969), pp. 689–709; Rudolf von Albertini (ed.), *Moderne Kolonialgeschichte* (Cologne, 1970), Reinhard, vol. I (1983). See also above, Chapter 3, Section 5.

5

Colonial Expansion in Asia in the Nineteenth Century

SINCE THE Middle Ages the eastern Slavs had interacted with the nomad horsemen and Muslims of Asia. For Russia, Asia signified the world of the steppes and the world of Islam. Yet Russia's relations with its Asiatic neighbours had always been ambivalent. On the one hand there were military conflicts with the nomad horsemen, and the ideological antagonism between the Russian Orthodox church and Islam. On the other hand there was intense economic, political and cultural interaction with the steppe and the Muslims, and a pragmatic policy towards the overlord of Rus, the Golden Horde. Nomads of the steppe and Muslims were always recognized as being equal partners, even though they were infidels. In the 'gathering of the lands of the Golden Horde', this traditional relationship was also applied to Muscovy's Muslim and nomad subjects, and as a rule pragmatic cooperation got the better of antagonistic polarization.

In the second half of the seventeenth and the first half of the eighteenth centuries Russian economic and military pressure on the steppe increased. At the same time Russia adopted from the west a eurocentric feeling of superiority towards Asia. The distance between Russia and the Asiatic peoples increased, and terms such as Islam, nomadic life, Asia and the Orient now acquired connotations that were definitely negative. Religion became the most important line of cleavage, and 'non-believers' (inovertsy) became the collective term for the non-Christian subjects of the empire.[1] In imitation of the Western model, there was an attempt to Christianize the animists and Muslims, using force if necessary. And Russia now adopted a sterner attitude towards rebellious nomads such as the Bashkirs and Kalmyks.

Catherine II's enlightened absolutism led to another change of course. Partly as a result of the fierce resistance put up by non-Christians, there was a return to a pragmatic and flexible political stance. However, this did not signify a return to earlier attitudes towards the Asiatic peoples. In fact, the eurocentric belief that Russia had a 'mission civilisatrice' in Asia became even stronger.[2] As the steppe began to be settled by eastern Slavs and colonists, the nomads became the prime objects of such civilizing activities, and lifestyle now replaced religion as the most important line of cleavage. In the context of what was considered to be the logical development of humanity from hunter and gatherer via nomadic herdsman to a sedentary existence, the untamed, destructive and morally inferior nomads were gradually to be introduced to 'higher' European civilization. This was linked to the practical goal of turning the northern part of the steppe into arable land. In order to civilize the savage nomads, the Russians not only promoted eastern Slav colonization, but also the educational and missionary activity of the Muslim Tatars among the Kazakhs. Islam was instrumentalized as a tool of the new policy.

This strict distinction between settlers and nomads became evident in the invitation to the Legal Commission of 1767, which excluded the participation of nomadic peoples, but admitted sedentary Muslims and animists. Thus the nomads were explicitly regarded as second-class citizens. The commission discussed the passing of laws specific to 'the nomadic peoples', and in 1798 a projected statute for non-sedentary Russian subjects was unveiled with the long-term goal of turning the nomads into full (i.e. sedentary) citizens. Here they were for the first time described by the term 'inorodtsy' (foreign-born, allogeneous), which subsequently took the place of the term 'inovertsy' (of a different faith).[3]

In 1822 an enlightened reformer, M. M. Speransky, first established the legal framework for the new estate of the inorodtsy. In order to contain arbitrary administrative excesses, Speransky, who was Governor-General of Siberia from 1819 to 1822, drew up, together with G. S. Batenkov, a new administrative code for Siberia and a 'statute concerning the administration of the inorodtsy'.[4] The new legal category of the inorodtsy comprised three groups based on their level of civilization: the hunters, gatherers and fishermen of the far north (brodiachie), with the exception of the Chukchi, who were given a special status; the nomads (kochevye), the largest of the groups; and the 'sedentary inorodtsy', who were deemed to constitute a transitional stage to full citizenship. The aim of the reforms was to raise the ethnic groups in Russia who were deemed to be backward in civilizational terms to the higher level of sedentary Russians. Speransky believed that this could only come about gradually and as a result of free will.

Initially he considered it to be essential to give the inorodtsy a legal status of their own which took into account their way of life and their economic habits, and to protect them against the abuses of the Russian administration.

On lower levels the 1822 statute guaranteed the inorodtsy a very large measure of self-administration based on the clan and tribal order. The lowest level were the 'clan administrations' (rodovye upravleniia), the second the 'inorodtsy authorities' (inorodnye upravy) and the third the 'steppe councils' (stepnye dumy). Only the lowest level was envisaged for the hunters and gatherers. Nomads could also be assigned to the second level, whereas the steppe councils were intended for the larger ethnic groups of the Iakuts and the Buriats. These institutions were assigned tasks associated with local administration, police duties, justice (based on local common law) and the collection of taxes. They were placed under the control of the elders or chieftains, who were usually identical with the clan or tribal upper class. Thus Speransky's reforms were motivated by the traditional principles of guaranteeing the status quo and cooperating with non-Russian elites. This was also seen in the fact that the members of the upper class received the title of 'honoured inorodtsy', and that their privileges were guaranteed. But with a handful of exceptions they were not subsequently co-opted into the empire's hereditary nobility. Furthermore, the duties of the inorodtsy differed. As in the past they had to pay iasak (in the shape of furs or money), though only the nomads also had to pay regional taxes (zemskie povinnosti). With the exception of the Buriat Cossacks, all inorodtsy were exempt from the duty to supply recruits for the army. All in all, the tax burden on the inorodtsy was smaller than that on Russian peasants. Apart from this they received assurances which guaranteed their religious, trade and commercial freedoms.

The inorodtsy statute of 1822 combined the traditions of the pragmatic Muscovite policy on minorities with the enlightenment aims of paternalistic concern and the 'mission civilisatrice'. However, this reform programme soon came up against the Siberian realities of administrative despotism, corruption, and the absence of any kind of control, and was only partly implemented. Of equal importance was the fact that it created a legal category which excluded certain non-Russians from the circle of the 'natural' (prirodnye) inhabitants of the empire. Although the inorodtsy enjoyed a series of privileges, they were second-class citizens nonetheless. Thus the Russian government possessed an instrument with which it could divide the empire's non-Russians into two groups in a hierarchic manner. For this reason it was a question of which ethnic groups, apart from those in Siberia, it would class as inorodtsy in the course of colonial expansion, and which it would not.

The inorodtsy concept was gradually applied to ethnic groups which did not belong to the same legal category. In Russian journalism the word inorodtsy was initially used to describe the non-Russians in the east, and subsequently began to be used more frequently for all of the empire's non-Russians. In this context the term no longer had its original neutral meaning, and served instead as a pejorative way of distinguishing between the state people, the Russians, who were now in the grip of nationalism and strangers who belonged to another 'rod', a foreign clan, lifestyle and perhaps even race.

1. Russia and the Ancient Transcaucasian Cultures: Georgians, Armenians and Muslims

The ethnic groups in Transcaucasia, the area which, from a Russian point of view, lay beyond the Caucasus, can look back on a tradition of civilization and statehood which is much older than that of the eastern Slavs. Even though they were sedentary and belonged to sophisticated civilizations, and despite the fact that a considerable number were Christians, the Russians made no distinction between the inhabitants of Transcaucasia who lived under Persian or Ottoman rule in the eighteenth and nineteenth centuries, and regarded them as Asiatics to whom Russia had to bring the blessings of European civilization. This eurocentric feeling of superiority on the part of the Russians collided with the self-esteem of the Georgians, Armenians and Turkic-speaking Muslims (Azerbaidzhanis) which emanated from their various traditions.

Transcaucasia was part of the ancient Persian, Greek and Roman world, and its traditions of statehood reached back to before the birth of Christ.[5] As early as the fourth century AD the Armenians, whose language is an independent branch of Indo-European, and the Georgians, who speak a South Caucasian language, became Christians, and developed unique civilizations with their own alphabets, literatures and a style of architecture that was based on Byzantine models. Armenia, which was largely independent, witnessed a final flowering in the tenth and eleventh centuries before it was conquered by the Byzantine empire and the Seljuk Turks. The mediaeval kingdom of Georgia reached its political and cultural peak in the twelfth and early thirteenth centuries, and here the Mongols put an end to the Golden Age. The history of the Muslims in Transcaucasia was closely linked with Iran. Although they were turkicized in linguistic terms as the Middle Ages progressed, they remained in touch with Iranian culture, partly on account of their common allegiance to the Shiite form of Islam. It is difficult, in the pre-national age, to describe Azerbaidzhanis in terms of a homogeneous ethnic group. The ethnonym first came into common use in the 1930s. For this reason I refer to them as Turkic-speaking Muslims. Other ethnic groups also lived in Azerbaidzhan, for example, the Iranian-speaking Talyshians and (nomadic) Kurds, and, in the north, Caucasian-speaking mountain tribes. Those who spoke Georgian (Kartvelian) were split up into numerous smaller groups such as the Kartlians, Kakhetians, Imerelians, Khevsurians, Pshavians, Mingrelians, Lazi and Svanetians. The last three ethnic groups are often credited with independent languages of the South Caucasian group. There were also Georgian-speaking Muslims (Adzharis), and the Muslim Abkhaz, who belonged to the West Caucasian language group. The historic regions of Armenia and Azerbaidzhan, and the areas settled by the Armenians and Turkic-speaking Muslims, went far beyond Transcaucasia, and included large parts of eastern Anatolia and the north-west of Iran.

However, conditions in the eighteenth century were no longer on the level of former glories.[6] Since the thirteenth century Transcaucasia had witnessed an economic and cultural decline and had been fought over by foreign powers. And since the sixteenth century western Georgia and western Armenia had been part of the Ottoman Empire, whereas Azerbaidzhan and eastern Armenia had been Iranian. However, the khanates of Karabakh, Gandsha, Sheki, Shirvan, Derbent, Kuba, Baku, Talysh, Nakhichevan and Erivan (Erevan), which were under Persian overlordship, and the eastern Georgian kingdom, a union of Kartli and Kakhetia which had existed since 1762, possessed a very large degree of autonomy, as did the kingdom of Imeretia and the principalities of Mingrelia, Abkhazia and Guria in Ottoman western Georgia.

In the case of the Georgians the social elite was the nobility, which was numerous and hierarchically structured. Its upper echelons possessed far-reaching privileges and power over the Georgian serfs. The Armenians, on the other hand, had only retained a small nobility of their own (meliki), which was able to survive in small principalities (melik) in the Khanate of Karabakh. Azerbaidzhan and eastern Armenia were dominated by the Muslim nobility of the begs (beys), which had acquired privileges in the khanates through military and bureaucratic service. As in other Muslim states the majority of the (Armenian and Muslim) peasants were not personally and directly dependent on the landowning upper class. Whereas Georgians and Muslims were predominant in rural areas, the urban middle class throughout Transcaucasia consisted mainly of Armenians. Around 1800 Armenians comprised almost three-quarters of the population of Tiflis, the most important city in Georgia. As in the case of the Jews and Tatars, the Armenians, who had in part been forced out of the upper class, and were dispersed in demographic terms, had turned their attention to economic activities (trade, crafts-manship), and played the role of a mobilized diaspora group. There were Armenian colonies not only in Transcaucasia, Persia and in the Ottoman Empire, but also in Russia, western Europe, India and China.

In view of the political and demographic fragmentation of the Armenians, the church played a decisive role in the maintenance of their cultural traditions and ethnic identity. The Apostolic Gregorian church had maintained its ancient claim to independence and thus imparted to the Armenians in a manner that resembled the Jews the nimbus of a chosen people. The Georgian church was part of the Orthodox community, though it was autocephalous, that is, it had its own head. Both churches were tolerated in the Iranian and Ottoman empires, and represented an important unifying bond for Armenians and Georgians. The Armenian and Georgian churches and the Muslim clergy ran the educational system, promoted culture and also played an important economic role. The specific socio-ethnic and socio-religious structure of Transcaucasia constituted a potentially dangerous hotbed of inter-ethnic conflict, though in the pre-national age this did not become an issue.

Russia had been in touch with the ethnic groups of the Caucasus area since the Middle Ages, and numerous noble Georgians and Armenians entered the service of Russia, especially in the eighteenth century. They included Prince Bagration, the hero of the war of 1812. Peter the Great's Persian campaign brought large parts of Azerbaidzhan under Russian rule in 1723, though Russia was forced to relinquish them as early as 1735. In the course of opening up the steppe areas after the victory over the Ottoman Empire in 1774, Russian pressure on the Caucasus area resumed in the reign of Catherine II, and in 1783 the east Georgian King

Erekle II, who was being threatened by Iran and the Ottoman Empire, placed himself under Russian protection.[7] When the Persians invaded eastern Georgia in 1795 in order to recover it, Russia, the suzerain power, did not honour its obligations, and merely proceeded to conquer some of the khanates of Azerbaidzhan a year later. However, after the death of Catherine II Russian troops once more withdrew. The final annexation of eastern Georgia occurred in 1800–01. The new Georgian king, Giorgi, who died shortly afterwards, sent a petition to the tsar asking him to incorporate Georgia into the Russian Empire. Paul I seized the opportunity, and 'the lands of the Georgian tsardom were accepted as direct subjects of the Imperial All-Russian Throne'. However, it was only Alexander I, after he had succeeded his assassinated father to the throne, who clarified what this actually meant. The Bagratid dynasty was deposed and the kingdom of Georgia abolished. This unilateral and direct annexation, which ran counter to previous agreements with the Georgians, was legitimated in the manifesto of 12 September 1801 with high-sounding phrases about the need to defend Russia's new subjects against domestic discord and external enemies. 'Not for the increase of our power, not because of greed, not in order to extend the borders of what is already the greatest empire in the world, have we taken upon ourselves the burden of the administration of the Georgian tsardom.'[8] The western Georgian principalities, which were part of the Ottoman Empire, also placed themselves under Russian protection between 1803 and 1811, though with the exception of the Kingdom of Imeretia they were for several decades able to retain a large measure of autonomy under their native princely families.

The Russo-Iranian war of 1804–13 led to the incorporation of the khanates in the northern part of Azerbaidzhan into the Russian Empire.[9] Southern Azerbaidzhan around Tabriz remained Persian, a division that has continued to the present day. Another war against Persia secured these new acquisitions, and enlarged them by the addition of the Khanates of Erivan and Nakhichevan in eastern Armenia (1828).[10] Thus Persia was driven out of Transcaucasia, though the larger, south-western group of Armenians was still part of the Ottoman Empire. The incorporation of eastern Armenia into the Russian Empire led to a mass influx of Armenians from Iran and the Ottoman Empire to Transcaucasia. Within the space of a few years this led to a situation where the Armenians, who under the Persians had been a clear minority amongst the Muslim majority, became the majority in the core areas of Russian

Armenia.[11] In 1878, in the wake of a war with the Ottoman Empire, Russia also annexed the areas of Kars and Batumi, which were in part inhabited by Armenians and Adsharis, from which Muslims subsequently emigrated, and to which Armenians also immigrated from the Ottoman Empire.

Thus the conquest of Transcaucasia resembled the territorial acquisitions in the west and south-west in that it was closely linked to Russia's conflicts with other great powers, in this case Iran and the Ottoman Empire. The weakening of its two neighbours to the south facilitated the Russian advance. British and French diplomats now began to take a greater interest in Transcaucasia, and started to perceive Russia as a colonial rival in Asia. Russian interests in Transcaucasia were primarily of a military and strategic nature, though economic goals (natural resources and trade routes) also played an important role. Whereas the majority of the Muslims viewed incorporation into Russia as violent colonial conquest, the incorporation of Transcaucasia was represented in contemporary Russian politics and public opinion (and Russian and Soviet historiography) as the liberation of the Christian Georgians and Armenians from the rule of backward Islamic masters. It was a fact that wide circles of Georgians and above all Armenians, and many ecclesiastical leaders, repeatedly sought to place themselves under the protection of the tsar, and also took part in the military conflicts, so that their union with Russia, as in the case of Bessarabia, has not incorrectly been described by Russian and Soviet historiography as having been voluntary. However, they expected Russia not only to liberate them from foreign domination, but also to grant them political and cultural autonomy. On the whole such hopes were not fulfilled, so that from a Georgian and Armenian perspective the union with Russia is interpreted to this day in an ambivalent way.

The incorporation of Transcaucasia into the Russian Empire did not proceed in a straightforward manner. Rather, the policies pursued veered between a repressive approach and a pragmatic one. This was partly dependent on the person of the regional military viceroy, who had been given far-reaching powers, and who at the same time was concerned up to the 1860s with the task of securing the Caucasus area in military terms.[12] Under Nicholas I the hard centralist approach increasingly gained ground, and Russian policy was now concerned if possible to achieve a complete integration of Transcaucasia, which was regarded as a colony inhabited by uncivilized Asiatics. Transcaucasia, as the State Council stated in 1833, should be linked 'to Russia . . . as one body, and its population be brought to speak, think, and feel Russian'.[13] As a result of dashed hopes, repressive policies and the incompetence of the regional bureaucrats, who had no knowledge of local conditions and were eurocentric and arrogant, there were numerous insurrections by Georgian aristocrats and peasants (in 1812, 1819–20, 1832 and 1841) and the Muslims (in the 1830s), the latter in part influenced by the 'Holy War' of the Muslims of the Caucasus mountains. Ongoing resistance, and in particular the considerably more vigorous liberation struggle of the ethnic groups of the Caucasus mountains (see below, Section 2), the failure of forcible integration, and the absence of economic profit from the Transcaucasian colony led to the realization, under the first namestnik (or viceroy), M. Vorontsov (1845–54), that only traditional flexible and pragmatic policies and cooperation with the non-Russian elites would in the end secure the Caucasus area for Russia.

The administrative incorporation of the Transcaucasian areas did not proceed in the same way everywhere.[14] Most of the territories were first integrated into the Russian administrative system after a phase of far-reaching autonomy under native vassals. This phase varied in length. In eastern Georgia it lasted from 1783 to 1801, in most of the Azerbaidzhani khanates about fifteen years, in western Georgia in the case of Mingrelia and Abkhazia more than fifty years (until 1857 or 1864). However, in the case of Imeretia, whose king, Solomon II, had put up bitter resistance, and had even called upon Napoleon to help him against Russia, it lasted only from 1804 to 1810. The khanates of Gandsha, Baku and Erivan were transformed directly into Russian administrative units. In the middle of the nineteenth century the Russian gubernia or province system was finally introduced in Transcaucasia. The provinces of Tiflis, Kutais, Erevan, Shemakha and Derbent were now headed by civil servants appointed by St Petersburg, and not by native rulers. However, local anomalies persisted in the judicial system and in the local administration.

Here again relations with the native upper class were of paramount importance. The annexation manifesto of 1801 had already promised the Georgian nobility that it would receive the same status as Russian nobles.[15] This was also facilitated by the fact that its legal and social position corresponded to that of the Russian nobility. The foremost class of the princes was co-opted into the Russian nobility at an early stage, although the Russian authorities hesitated for a long time before recognizing the status of all of the numerous nobles, who constituted about 5 per cent of the population. It is true that in 1827 Georgian nobles were accorded the same status as their Russian counterparts, though as elsewhere they were required to submit proof of their noble rights. This dragged on for decades, and those who were unable to prove their status were degraded to the category of state peasants. The reforms implemented by the new viceroy Vorontsov first attempted in a consistent and successful manner to establish a partnership with the Georgian nobility, which was drawn more into the regional adminis-tration. And the estate-based organization of the nobility was also introduced in the provinces of Tiflis and Kutais. Finally, in the 1850s the hereditary noble rights of numerous Georgians were recognized. Others were still excluded, and continued to try to prove their noble status.[16]

It was even more difficult to co-opt the Azerbaidzhani nobles, who were Muslims, and did not possess serfs.[17] Despite the colonialist pre-judices, there never seems to have been any question of assigning the Azerbaidzhanis to the legal category of the inorodtsy. However, the time of enlightened absolutism in which Muslim Tatars were co-opted into the nobility with full rights was past, and at first the Russian government did not grant any privileges to the Muslim upper class. It was only under Vorontsov that Russia, in 1846, recognized the hered-itary landowning rights of the begs, who were deemed to include the minor Armenian nobles (meliki), and drew them into the regional administration. Whilst they were granted a tax-exempt status, the question of whether they should be fully co-opted into the nobility of the Russian empire, and whether they should also be granted other noble rights, remained unresolved until the revolution. It is true that what were known as 'Beg Commissions' recognized the property rights of most of the Muslim nobles and their status as 'the highest Musulman estate'. Nevertheless the begs continued to constitute a special noble category with restricted rights.[18] In this way the Russian government also reached its goal of turning the Transcaucasian elites into loyal partners. Thus numerous Georgians, Armenians and Muslims embarked on careers in the Russian army and bureaucracy.

Cooperation with the Transcaucasian elites led to the gradual assimilation of the legal and social system to the Russian model. The once rebellious and hierarchically structured noble layer was transformed, especially in Georgia, into a loyal and uniform official service nobility. Whilst the peasants lost traditional rights, here again the Muslim peasants were not degraded to the status of serfs. The Armenian merchants, whose privileges Russia had confirmed, increased their predominant economic position. In cooperation with the government they performed important functions as a mobilized diaspora group in the development of long-distance trade and craftsmanship. Armenian immigration from the Ottoman Empire continued throughout the nineteenth century, so that the proportion of Armenians increased even further in eastern Armenia and in Transcaucasia as a whole.

Russian policy on the three religious communities in Transcaucasia was inconsistent. The Georgian church, which had been autocephalous for centuries, was forcibly integrated into the Russian Orthodox church as early as 1811, and from 1817 placed under a Russian exarch.[19] On the other hand, the independence and the privileges of the Armenian church and its monasteries were confirmed in the statute of 1836, though at the same time they were placed under Russian control. The Katholikos of Echmiadzin, the spiritual head of all Armenians, continued to be the true leader of the Armenians in Russia. The traditional Armenian church schools witnessed an upsurge under Russian rule. In Georgia Vorontsov supported secular (Russian) schools and Georgian culture, which finally turned its back on the Iranian model and began to move towards Europe. 'The late prince', Vorontsov's widow later recalled, 'loved the Georgians very much, revered their great history, and hoped they would have a better future. He was in the habit of saying that this small Georgia would be the most beautiful, colourful, and strongest brocade in the embroidery of Russia.'[20] With regard to the Muslims of Transcaucasia, Russia adhered to the traditional patterns of tolerance and control. It confirmed the ownership of land and the privileges of the clergy, who continued to play a predominant role in culture and in the educational system. In 1862 the Shiites were granted a spiritual organization under a sheikh, which, as elsewhere, also functioned as an instrument of control.

The preservation of an indigenous elite and the traditional civilizations created important preconditions for the national movements which, in the second half of the nineteenth century and at the beginning of the twentieth century, were destined to inspire the Georgians, the Armenians and the Azerbaidzhanis. An inherited feature of the traditional socioethnic structure was the fact that the national movements were not only directed against Russia, but also against other ethnic groups. The self-confident pride of its peoples, which is rooted in history, and the inter-ethnic tensions continue to determine the situation in Transcaucasia to this day.

2. The Long War against the Mountain Peoples of the Caucasus

Transcaucasia was conquered in the course of several campaigns against Iran and the Ottoman Empire, and thereafter, despite numerous uprisings, Russian rule was no longer in doubt. However, for the whole of the first half of the nineteenth century it proved impossible to pacify the mountainous region of the Caucasus itself (to the north). As the most important land road to Transcaucasia traversed the central Caucasus, and because forays by ethnic groups of the Caucasus repeatedly ravaged and destabilized certain areas of Georgia, the subjection of the Caucasians was not only a question of prestige, but also of strategic significance. Therefore Russia attempted to attain this goal by deploying a large part of its military might, though it took decades before it broke the resistance of the vastly outnumbered Caucasians. This successful war of liberation, which lasted for decades, is a unique event in the history of Russian expansion. The Caucasian warriors and their famous leader Shamil thus became legendary both in Russia and abroad. Between 1854 and 1860 alone more than thirty books on this subject were published in western Europe.[21] The fact that small Muslim ethnic groups managed to oppose Russian might for such a long time subsequently continued to be a symbol of anti-colonial resistance – even during the recent war in Afghanistan.

The Caucasus region is characterized by an extraordinary ethnic diversity which is unique in the world. The most important of the more than fifty ethnic groups from west to east are as follows.[22] In Dagestan, in the mountains and on the narrow coastal strip along the Caspian Sea alone there are more than thirty ethnic groups. They include the Caucasian-speaking Avars (who have no connection whatsoever with the steppe people of the sixth to eighth centuries), Darginians, Lesgians and Lakians, the Iranian Tatians, the mountain Jews, who also spoke Tatian, and the Turkic-speaking Kumykians and Nogai Tatars, who lived primarily in the valleys and plains. In the bordering mountainous areas of the central Caucasus to the west there follow the Caucasian-speaking Chechens and Ingushetians, then, on the upper Terek, the Iranian-speaking Ossetians, and, in the high mountains around Elbruz, the Turkic-speaking Balkarians and Karachai. The Circassians, who are assigned to a Caucasian linguistic group of their own, inhabited the whole of the western Caucasus up to the Black Sea. Their eastern branch was formed by the Kabardinians, who lived in the foothills to the west of the Terek. The ethnic groups of the Caucasus mountains also included Abkhaz and some Georgians (Svanetians and Khevsurians) in the south-west, whose history took place within the context of Georgia.

This linguistic variety – as in other mountainous areas – corresponded to a colourful diversity of archaic and exotic manners and customs which were repeatedly described by travellers. Both can be traced back to the geographical facts, which encouraged the isolation of the various communities. And the ethnic groups of the Caucasus also differed with regard to their economic lifestyles and socio-political organization. In the mountains animal husbandry (sheep and cows) based on transhumance predominated, and in the valleys and foothills there was arable farming, and to some extent nomadic animal husbandry. Whereas in parts of Dagestan and in Azerbaidzhan there existed khanates and sultanates with a hierarchical social structure, polities did not arise in the other areas of the Caucasus. However, there were great differences between the communities, which were based on tribes, clans and groups. They ranged from a very differentiated and graded social structure in the case of the Kabardinians and – slightly less pronounced – in the case of the Ossetians, to the virtually non-hierarchical, patriarchal and egalitarian order based on village communities of the Chechens, Ingushetians, Karachai, Balkaris, certain ethnic groups in Dagestan and the majority of the Circassians.

But in addition to this great diversity there were also important common features which formed the basic precondition for successful Caucasian resistance to Russia.[23] For one there was religion: almost all of the ethnic groups of the Caucasus were Sunni Muslims. The sole exception were the Ossetians, of whom only a minority were Muslims, whilst the majority were Orthodox Christians. However, the degree to which the Caucasians had been converted to Islam differed. Whereas in Dagestan Islam had for a long time been deeply ingrained, and Arabic served as a literary language, in the case of the western Circassians, who had been converted much later, it was rather superficial. Common aspects were also seen in the lifestyles and the customs of the Caucasian mountain peoples. They were rooted in tribal relationships with the unusual judicial system of adat, which linked vendetta and hospitality as social institutions, and protected values such as respect for old age and for one's ancestors. Like other mountain peoples, such as the Albanians and Montenegrins in the Balkans, the Caucasians had a warrior ethos with a specific code of honour which compelled men to fight, and also to rob. They felt superior to outsiders. As the collective term 'gortsy' (mountain folk) demonstrates, the Russians also viewed the ethnic groups of the Caucasus as a single entity.

Russia came into contact with Caucasian ethnic groups in the context of the 'gathering of the lands of the Golden Horde'.[24] In the middle of the sixteenth century, after the conquest of Kazan and Astrakhan, a number of Kabardinian princes sought the protection of the Muscovite tsar. This political alliance, which Soviet historiography has interpreted as an act of submission by Kabardinia, was enhanced by Ivan IV's marriage to a Kabardinian princess and the fact that certain Kabardinian princes entered the service of Russia. The distinguished Russian princely family of Cherkassky was descended from them. At the same time Russia began to establish a military presence in the foothills of the Caucasus by building a fort on the Terek and settling Cossacks in the area.

However, Russia began to advance in a systematic manner only in the eighteenth century. From the 1730s onwards it established new forts, which were later linked to form the 'Caucasian Line' from the Black Sea to the Caspian Sea. It also established a number of Cossack armies: the Terek Cossacks in the east; the Kuban Cossacks (1777–81), who were moved from the Don to the western foothills of the Caucasus; and the Black Sea Cossacks in the vicinity of the new fortress of Ekaterinodar (1792–94), who had been recruited from the remnants of the Zaporozhian Sich. The victory over the Ottoman Empire in 1774, the annexation of the Crimea, and the protectorate over Georgia (both in 1783) provided new themes for Russian expansion. A number of khanates in Dagestan were placed under Russian protection in order to secure the link with Transcaucasia. Work on the Georgian Military Highway commenced, and the Kabardinians and Ossetians, who controlled this, the only road over the Caucasus, were formally placed under Russian suzerainty. In 1784 Russia built the fortress of Vladikavkaz, the name of which, 'Ruler of the Caucasus', stood for a political programme.

Yet eighty years were to pass before this programme materialized. From the end of the eighteenth century onwards the mountain peoples reacted to the Russian advance by repeatedly attacking both the fortresses and the Cossacks. The Russian presence in the foothillls endangered not only their security and mobility, but also their economic existence, which depended on winter pastures in the plains, and trade with the foothills region. The fundamental resistance of the various ethnic groups and tribes became particularly effective on account of Sufic Muridism.[25] In the Middle Ages the mystical teaching of Sufism had already developed into religious brotherhoods, a type of organization, which, in various parts of the world, became the catalyst of Muslim resistance. In Asia – and also in the Caucasus – the Naqshbandi order, which had been founded in Bukhara in the fourteenth century, acquired a special significance. Muridism, the unquestioning obedience of the pupils (the Murids), towards their Sufic teacher, formed the backbone of these organizations. They derived their integrational power from attempts to introduce Islamic law in place of tribal common law (adat), and from the principle of the 'jihad' or 'ghazavat' ('Holy War'), which was directed against unfaithful Muslims and against the infidels. In the Caucasus it was used to ward off Russian aggression.

Although the sources are silent on this point, it seems probable that even the first resistance movement, which united several Caucasian ethnic groups under the banner of the 'Holy War' against Russia, was organized by a Sufic brotherhood. Under the leadership of Sheik Mansur, the Chechens and some of the mountain Dagestanis conducted a guerilla war against the Russians in 1785 and 1786.[26] With the new Russo-Turkish war Mansur shifted his activities in 1787 to the western Circassians, where he cooperated with the Ottoman Empire. In 1791, after the end of the war, he was captured by Russian troops and incarcerated in the fortress of Schlüsselburg, where he died in 1794. What were clearly Sufic organizations subsequently arose in the Caucasus in the 1820s. Their first recorded leader was Imam Gazi Muhammed, who with the help of Muridist slogans succeeded in uniting the ethnically heterogeneous tribes of Dagestan and the Chechens against Russia. He died in 1832 whilst fighting Russian troops. Two years later his pupil Shamil became the next imam.

Shamil (1797–1871), an Avar with an Islamic education, was to remain in power for a quarter of a century. His outstanding political, organizational and military abilities, and his charismatic aura turned him into the most important leader of anti-Russian Islamic resistance in the nineteenth century. In the 1840s, with his theocratic imamate, he created a highly effective centralized political organization in the eastern Caucasus, and combined the slogans of the Holy War and the introduction of the sharia with egalitarian goals which were also directed against the Caucasian elites, some of whom cooperated with Russia.

The majority of the ethnic groups in Dagestan and the Chechens formed the core of the imamate, though it proved impossible to integrate the Ossetians, the Kabardinians and the Circassians on a permanent basis. Nevertheless, the guerilla war led by Shamil tied the Russian armies down for a period of twenty-five years.

Nicholas I had already sketched out Russian aims in 1829 when he congratulated his general Paskevich on his victory over the Turks: 'Now that you have concluded such a glorious undertaking, another, to my mind no less glorious, stands before us, which with regard to the immediate advantages is perhaps far more important – the final pacification of the mountain peoples or the extirpation of the rebels.'[27] The best Russian generals (including Ermolov, Paskevich and Vorontsov) attempted repeatedly to turn the project into a glorious affair, though instead of glory they garnered one failure after another. Russia lost tens of thousands of soldiers in the Caucasus, and up to a sixth of the state's income. In an ever more brutal and merciless war the goal of 'extirpation' became increasingly apparent. Since the Russian armies were no match for the partisans in the mountains, they destroyed and burned down villages, fields and forests, and drove away the livestock. Whilst this made the economic situation difficult for the Caucasians, it also meant that the conflict continued to escalate. Vorontsov in particular also attempted to cooperate with non-Russian upper classes. In this he was partly successful, though it reinforced the egalitarian tendencies of the resistance. It was only after the end of the Crimean War that the new Caucasian viceroy Bariatinsky proceeded systematically to overcome the resistance of the Caucasians. Shamil was captured in 1859 and taken to Russia, where he was granted an audience with the tsar and greeted with amazement by the public. He then lived in honourable exile in Kaluga. In 1870 he was even permitted to leave the country, dying in Medina in 1871.

With this the resistance of the eastern Caucasians was broken, though the Circassians in the western Caucasus continued to resist the Russian troops. The Circassian tribes, who operated independently of Shamil, and were only in part adherents of Muridism, had for decades repeatedly and successfully warded off the Russian troops. In this they received some support from the Ottoman Empire, which had for a long time maintained relations with the Circassians.[28] After the defeat of Shamil, Russia moved against the Circassians in a brutal manner, and by 1864 it also controlled the western Caucasus. Since Russia wished to colonize and secure the Black Sea coast and the area of the foothills with

Christian settlers, most of the Circassians were either killed or expelled. Others chose to emigrate rather than to live under Russian rule. In the 1860s and 1870s almost all of the surviving Circassians (at least 300,000) emigrated to the Ottoman Empire. In 1897 only 44,746 Circassians remained in the Russian Empire.[29] Furthermore, the majority of the Abkhaz, whose language was related to that of the Circassians, emigrated in several waves to the Ottoman Empire in the course of the nineteenth century, in addition to tens of thousands of Chechens, Kabardinians and Nogai Tatars.[30] The little-known mass emigration of the Caucasians and Crimean Tatars from Russia to the Ottoman Empire was a tragedy which in some respects foreshadowed the mass expulsions of the twentieth century.

'The subjection of the western Caucasus, which has been completed by means of a series of glorious and heroic deeds and lengthy and protracted exertions, brought the lengthy Caucasian War to an end', Alexander II announced in July 1864. And he shortened the term of duty of the Cossacks involved, 'who have protected our borders unceasingly against the larcenous attacks of the "gortsy" '.[31] The government now proceeded to incorporate the Caucasus in administrative terms, and the military administration was replaced by a civil administration as early as 1860. The east was referred to as the Terek district, and the west as the Kuban district, whereas the greater part of Dagestan, after the khanates had been abolished between 1859 and 1867, was appended to Transcaucasia as a self-contained unit.[32] Initially the authorities were in doubt as to whether the mountain peoples of the Caucasus should be assigned to the legal category of inorodtsy, or whether they should be incorporated into the Russian system of estates.[33] Their integration subsequently followed the pattern established by the Muslims of Transcaucasia. Once again Russia tried to obtain the cooperation of loyal elites which had not emigrated. However, such nobles only existed in the case of socially differentiated ethnic groups, such as the Kabardinians and Kumyks, and were absent in the case of those with an egalitarian social structure, such as the Chechens. Members of the non-Russian upper class were involved in the local administration, and to some extent were given land. As in Azerbaidzhan, commissions were given the task of examining their landowning rights and privileges, and, as before, they decided to recognize the upper class as the 'highest estate of the gortsy', and in Dagestan as begs, though not as full-scale nobles.[34] However, a number of Caucasians were co-opted into the hereditary nobility as a result of service in the army and the administration. Furthermore, the Islamic clergy with their Koran schools (especially in Dagestan), and the traditional social order of the Caucasians remained largely intact under Russian rule. Problems arose primarily as a result of the increased settlement of Russians and Ukrainians in the plains and valleys, and especially in the western Caucasus. That the resistance of the Caucasians had not been totally overcome became apparent when the Chechens and Dagestanis staged another uprising during the Russo-Turkish War of 1877–78.

There was a great deal of discussion about the Caucasus war in the first half of the nineteenth century in the Russian public.[35] The 'gortsy' keep appearing in Russian literature, for example, in the work of Griboedov, Pushkin, Lermontov and Tolstoy. They are sometimes portrayed in glowing Romantic colours as noble, nature- and freedom-loving savages. However, in the long term the negative image of unreliable brigands and Muslim fanatics gained the upper hand. It persisted into the Soviet era, and thus it is no accident that in the Second World War Stalin ordered not only the Crimean Tatars, the Kalmyks, and the Germans, but also four of the Caucasian peoples who had put up a great deal of resistance to Russia – the Chechens, the Ingushetians, the Karachai and the Balkars – to be deported to Middle Asia. In Soviet historiography the anti-colonial protest of the 'gortsy' was always hotly debated and repeatedly reinterpreted.[36] In the Caucasus the figure of Shamil continued to be a symbol of freedom and of anti-colonial resistance, and to this day the Sufic brotherhoods are widespread among the Caucasians.

3. The Stepwise Advance into the Kazakh Steppe

The vast areas of steppe which stretch for almost 3,000 kilometres between the southern Urals and the Caspian Sea in the west and the mountains of the Altai and Tienshan ranges in the east, and for more than 1,500 kilometres between southern Siberia and the oases of middle Asia, constitute the area settled by the Kazakhs.[37] The single most important factor in Kazakh history was the nomadic lifestyle: the Kazakh language uses the same term to refer to both Kazakhs and nomads. The Kazakhs had a pasture-based economy which involved seasonal migration: in the hot summers they moved to the northern edge of the steppe (in southern Siberia and the southern Urals), and in the cold winters to the more southerly areas which in part were already semi-deserts. In the mountainous regions of the land of the seven rivers in the east they also practised transhumance. Their most important possessions were herds of horses, sheep, goats and, more rarely, of cattle and (in the south) of camels. Their socio-political organization was tribal: the clans guaranteed social cohesion, and organized the communal migrations in mobile auls. There were regular incursions and raids on other nomads and sedentary groups. And patriarchal common law and animist ideas such as a cult of ancestors and animals went deeper than adherence to Islam. The Kazakh encounter with Russia is yet another instance, in the wake of the Nogai Tatars, Bashkirs and Kalmyks, of the conflict between nomadic herdsmen and sedentary farmers of arable land.

The Turkic-speaking ethnic group of the Kazakhs was first mentioned in sources from the fifteenth century onwards in connection with the Kazakh khanate. Until early Soviet times the Russians referred to them as Kirgiz, whereas the real Kirgiz were called Kara-Kirgiz. Closely related to the Kazakhs were the Karakalpaks, who were also nomads. In the fifteenth century the clans of the Kazakhs split off from the Khanate of the Uzbeks, and formed an independent khanate in the steppe, which subsequently developed into three hordes – the Little or Younger Horde in the west, the Large or Older Horde in the land of the seven rivers (Semireche) in the east and the Middle Horde in the intervening central steppe areas. These wide-ranging power structures based on Mongolian models were loose tribal confederations. In addition to the khans elected by the various hordes there was a powerful clan aristocracy consisting of sultans and begs (beys). Traditional opponents of the Kazakhs in the steppes were the mighty western Mongols (Oirats), who also included the Kalmyks. In the first decades of the eighteenth century Oirat armies repeatedly descended upon Kazakhstan, and defeated the Kazakhs on numerous occasions. This threat led certain Kazakh khans to ask their sedentary neighbour in the west, the Russian tsar, for help against their nomad enemy in the east.

Russia's encounter with the Kazakhs can be construed as part of the 'gathering of the lands of the Golden Horde', which in the eighteenth century crossed the frontier to the steppes in order to integrate the nomads in the south (Bashkirs, Kalmyks and Nogai Tatars).[38] The traditional summer grazing grounds of the Kazakhs were reached from both southern Siberia and the southern Urals, and were secured by the fortresses of Omsk (1716) and Semipalatinsk (1718) on the Irtysh (which were later connected by a line of fortifications) and by the Orenburg line. At the same time the government encouraged trade relations with the Kazakhs, partly in the context of Russian trade with Asia in general. The khans' call for help then gave Russia the opportunity to extend its political influence in the time-honoured manner. Between 1731 and 1742 the khans of the Little and Middle Hordes, and even a number of clan chieftains of the eastern Great Horde swore an oath of allegiance to the tsar.[39] As in other cases the nomads of the steppe regarded this kind of subservience as a temporary alliance between two rulers which the leaders of the clans did not consider to be of a permanent nature. For example, in the second half of the eighteenth century, khans of the Middle and Great Hordes placed themselves under the protection of the Manchu emperor after China had conquered the western Mongols in 1757. Although it is true that in the eighteenth century the Kazakh hordes were not technically part of the Russian Empire, the oaths of allegiance, from a Russian point of view, constituted legally binding acts which formed the basis for claims to sovereignty. They were also seen by Soviet historiography as the cornerstone of the 'voluntary union of the Kazakhs with Russia'.

However, the incorporation of the Kazakhs into the Russian Empire in fact occurred in the first half of the nineteenth century, when Russian pressure increased. At the same time what were now four Kazakh hordes (after the establishment of the Inner or Burkey Horde between the Urals and the lower Volga in 1801) experienced internal crises. In 1822 the khan of the Middle Horde was deposed, and his territory assigned to the Siberian administration, and placed under the inorodtsy statute created by Speransky. The Little Horde followed in 1824, and the Inner Horde in 1845, whereas by 1848 the Great Horde, to which the Khan of Kokand also laid claim, had been dissolved step by step. New forts such as Kokchetav and Akmolinsk and fortified lines were erected in order to control the Kazakhs and to delimit their pastures.

At the end of the eighteenth century the Kazakhs had repeatedly rebelled against Russian suzerainty. They also took part in the Pugachev uprising, and subsequently reacted to the growing pressure and the abolition of the hordes with increased resistance. Kazakhs attacked Russian garrisons, Cossacks, settlers and merchants, and in the Middle Horde there was a mass insurrection in 1825. In 1837 Kenisary Kasymov

(1802–47), a grandson of Ablay, the last significant khan of the Middle Horde, became its most important leader. He attempted to unite the Kazakhs against Russia, and to reestablish the khanate. Twenty years passed before Russian troops were in a position to quell the uprising of the Middle Horde in 1846. However, there were further insurrections in the 1850s. In Kazakh tradition Kenisary Kasymov became a heroic figure comparable to Shamil. Here again Soviet historiography veered between interpreting this uprising as a progressive social and national revolutionary event, or as a reactionary and aristocratic one.[40]

By about the middle of the nineteenth century Russia had annexed the vast area of the Kazakh steppes. With fortresses such as Irgiz, Turgay and Aralsk to the north of the Aral Sea (1845–47), Perovsk on the lower Syr-Darya (in place of a fortress of the Khan of Kokand, 1853) and Verny (the modern Almaty) at the foot of the Tienshan (1854) it secured the new areas in military terms. On the basis of the three hordes the government first created the administrative units of the 'Kirgiz of Orenburg', the 'Siberian Kirgiz' (centred on Omsk) and Semipalatinsk. After the conquest of southern Middle Asia the Kazakh steppe was again divided up in administrative terms. The southern areas on the Syr-Darya and the land of the seven rivers were added to the Governor-Generalship of Turkestan, which was established in 1867, whereas the principal section in the north was divided into two areas (oblasti) and in 1868 assigned to the Governor-General of Orenburg and the Governor-General of Western Siberia (or, after 1892, of the Steppes). In 1891 a special statute regulated the local administration.[41] Kazakhs were also employed in the district administration headed by Russians. In the local administration, with 'councils of elders', and with regard to the judicial system (based on common law) they remained largely autonomous. Here again Russia cooperated with the non-Russian elite, though the Kazakh begs were no longer, as had still been the case with the upper class of the Caucasian Muslims, practically (if not wholly) co-opted into the Russian nobility. As had been the case with the 'Siberian Kirgiz' in 1822, all Kazakhs were now assigned to the legal category of inorodtsy envisaged for nomads. In other words, they were not deemed to be fully fledged citizens. For the natives this also brought with it certain advantages, for example, in addition to self-administration it meant that they did not have to do military service. In 1869 some of the Kazakhs of the Little Horde reacted to the new administrative order with an insurrection, which was put down in a brutal manner by a Russian punitive expedition.

As in the inorodtsy statute of 1822, Russian policy towards the Kazakhs pursued the goal of introducing backward nomads to the 'higher stage' of a sedentary lifestyle. The territorial administrative order, the monetary taxes, and new land laws impeded the mobility and also the economic system of the Kazakhs, which was based on barter and pasturage. In the cultural and economic spheres the Russian government, from the end of the eighteenth century onwards, initially employed Kazan Tatars in order to 'civilize' the Kazakhs. Tatar and Russian merchants achieved a considerable increase in trade with the latter, who now became important customers for Russian industrial products. At the same time Tatar mullahs succeeded in strengthening Islam among the nomads, who were still very much under the influence of animism. When the authorities noticed that the Tatars, whilst bringing western influences to bear on the Kazakhs, were at the same time the source of undesirable Islamic and protonational movements, they tried, using the system of the Orientalist Ilminsky, to withdraw them from the influence of the Tatars in mixed Kazakh and Russian schools.[42] But in the medium term these measures contributed less to their integration into the Russian empire, and more to the rise of a Kazakh national movement.

As in the case of other nomads, the settlement of pastureland by Russian and Ukrainian arable farmers became the decisive destabilizing factor for the Kazakhs.[43] For a long time the steppe frontier was colonized in a desultory manner, and primarily by Cossacks. However, from the 1860s onwards the area under cultivation kept shifting farther south. In the steppes statute of 1891 the land owned by the Kazakhs was drastically reduced, and in the following two decades hundreds of thousands of settlers from European Russia streamed into northern Kazakhstan. They occupied the most fertile pastures in the northern part of the steppes, which in the period of drought in the summer were essential for the survival of the herds. This curtailed the seasonal movement between different pastures, and thus the nomadic herdsmen were driven to the drier areas in the south. This not only created serious economic problems for the Kazakhs, but also shattered their social structure, which was based on the nomadic lifestyle. For this reason a number of Kazakhs chose to become sedentary. Yet the majority remained faithful to their traditional lifestyle, and put up resistance to the surveyors, administrators, soldiers and peasants. The potential for conflict between the nomadic Kazakhs and the sedentary eastern Slavs continued to increase. It was destined to erupt once again in a large-scale uprising in 1916 (see below, Chapter 9). Under Soviet rule the confrontation between the sedentary and nomadic inhabitants remained, and in the 1930s Stalin brought Russia's 'mission civilisatrice' to a conclusion by using brutal force to compel the Kazakhs to become sedentary.

4. The Conquest and Incorporation of Southern Middle Asia

The history of inner Asia was shaped by the contrast between and the complementary symbiosis of nomadic herdsmen and the inhabitants of river valleys and oases. South of the Kazakh steppes there are great deserts (Kara-Kum, Kyzyl-Kum) through which the Syr-Darya and the Amu-Darya flow into the Aral Sea. The two rivers, which the Greeks called Jaxartes and Oxus, have their sources in the high mountains of the Tienshan and Pamir, which, together with slightly lower ranges to the west, form the region's southern perimeter. This area with its deserts, oases and mountains I refer to in what follows as Middle Asia, whereas I use the term Central Asia for a larger area which also includes Sinkiang, Afghanistan and Mongolia, and the term Turkestan for the Russian administrative unit.

The oases and river valleys of Middle Asia had become the seat of high cultures which were based on intensive arable farming (with irrigation) and on trade.[44] Urban centres had arisen at the crossroads of the caravan routes, which included the Silk Road to China: Samarkand and Bukhara in Transoxiana or Mawarannahr between the Syr-Darya and the Amu-Darya, Tashkent to the north-east of them, Merv in Khorasan in the south-west, and Urgench and Khiva in Khoresm to the south of the Aral Sea. With regard to cultural influence, the two most important factors were Iran and Islam. In antiquity Middle Asia formed part of the Persian Empire, and Alexander the Great's advance to the Syr-Darya brought it in touch with Hellenism. After its conquest by the Arabs Middle Asia, in the tenth century, experienced under the Samanid dynasty a flowering of Iranian Islamic high culture, and their capital city of Bukhara became a centre of Muslim scholarship.

The political history of Middle Asia was determined to a significant extent by the incursions of nomad horsemen. Subsequently the Mongols and their successor states had a lasting influence on the area. Middle Asia flourished under the great conqueror Timur at the end of the fourteenth century and at the beginning of the fifteenth century, and Samarkand became the brilliant capital of the Timurid empire. A century later there followed the last of the conquerors from the steppe, the Uzbek Shaibanids. In the seventeenth and eighteenth centuries this dynasty presided over an economic and cultural decline which was compounded by the fact that the transcontinental caravan trade had become less important than the maritime routes, and that the Middle Asian Sunni Muslims were becoming increasingly isolated from the Iranian Shiites. The period of Uzbek rule was also accompanied by a gradual turkicization of the sedentary population of Middle Asia, which, in addition to Persian, also used an eastern Turkic written language, Chagatai.

Thus the ethnic and linguistic situation in Middle Asia was always in a state of flux. The urban population was often bilingual, and tribal or regional identities, religion and lifestyle (whether nomadic or sedentary) were often more important than ethnic and linguistic criteria.[45] The various ethnonyms were also ambiguous and subject to change, so that projecting today's names for peoples into the past can be misleading. Thus the distinction between the terms 'Sarts' and 'Tadzhiks', which were used for the sedentary population, was not always clear. As a rule only the largely nomadic descendants of the tribes which immigrated under the leadership of the Shaibanids were considered to be Uzbeks, whereas in the Soviet era other Turkic-speaking or turkicized sedentary ethnic groups were also referred to as Uzbeks.

The central areas were primarily inhabited by Persian-speaking and partly turkicized Tadzhiks, and by various Turkic-speaking ethnic groups, of whom the Uzbeks were the most important. In the mountains in the east there lived nomadic herdsmen, the Turkic-speaking Kirgiz (whom the Russians called Kara-Kirgiz), and in the Pamir mountains a few small ethnic groups which spoke eastern Persian dialects. Some of them were Ismailis. In the west, in the Kara-Kum desert between the Caspian Sea and the Amu-Darya, and to some extent in Iran and in Afghanistan, the Turkmen lived nomadic lives. Their language, like that of the Azerbaidzhanis and the Ottoman Turks, belongs to the Oghuz group of Turkic languages. The southern tribes of the Kazakhs and the Karakalpaks also formed part of the Middle Asian region.

Before it was conquered by Russia, there were three polities ruled by Uzbek dynasties in Middle Asia: the Emirate of Bukhara in the centre, the Khanate of Khiva in ancient Khoresm to the south of the Aral Sea in the north-west, which ruled the majority of the Karakalpaks, and the Khanate of Kokand in the south-east, which held sway over the majority of the Kirgiz.[46] The Turkmen were in part under the suzerainty of Khiva and Bukhara, and in part under that of Iran, though in practical terms independent. The three Middle Asian polities with their despotic rulers possessed a differentiated administration with a complicated system of taxation. The frequent wars between the khanates and the continual internal conflicts between various viceroys and between the sedentary and the nomadic population were a source of instability. In the river valleys and oases the inhabitants practised arable farming (with a host of irrigation systems), and in the mountains and deserts animal husbandry. In the towns, some of which had tens of thousands of inhabitants, trade and a large variety of crafts flourished. The upper class consisting of khans, emirs, sultans and other nobles was Uzbek. Although the Persian- and Turkic-speaking arable farmers had to pay numerous kinds of taxes, they were personally free. Slaves were recruited from among foreign prisoners of war, such as Persians and Russians. Culture was dominated by the conservative (Sunni) Islamic clergy, as was the educational system consisting of the Koran schools (maktab), and the middle and higher schools (madrasa). In addition to this Sufic brotherhoods also played a certain role. Islam was not as well entrenched among the Turkmen and Kirgiz as among the sedentary groups. Their social structure was defined primarily in tribal terms, and displayed very little differentiation. The nomadic Turkmen herdsmen were mainly engaged in raising sheep, horses and camels. They were renowned as brave warriors, and feared as marauding robbers. A number of Turkmen tribes had become sedentary in the oases. Most of the Kirgiz led nomadic lives with their herds of sheep and horses in the high mountains of the Tienshan.

Russia had maintained trade links with the Islamic centres of Middle Asia since the sixteenth century; these were in the hands of Middle Asian merchants and Volga Tatars.[47] For a long time non-Muslims did not have access to the markets of Middle Asia. A number of military expeditions against Khiva which set out from the Caspian Sea came to grief in the desert as early as 1717, and then again in 1839. It is true that a number of explorers and emissaries established more contacts in the first half of the nineteenth century. However, up to the middle of the nineteenth century the khanates of Middle Asia remained a little-known, remote and exotic part of Asia. It was only after the final incorporation of the Kazakh steppes and the construction of fortresses on its southern border that, in the 1850s, Russia became a direct neighbour of the Middle Asian khanates. The Crimean War and the final subjection of the Caucasian mountain peoples delayed further expansion southwards by another ten years. Thus the conquest of Middle Asia only began in 1864 after the resistance of the Circassians had finally been crushed.

As in other cases of colonial expansion, there were underlying economic, strategic and political motives. At the beginning of the 1860s the American Civil War led to a situation where the Russian textile industry was no longer being supplied with sufficient quantities of cotton. Thus Russia was forced to look around for alternative suppliers of this important raw material. And the fact that it had an interest in controlling the Middle Asian trade routes and in acquiring markets for Russian industrial products, which were difficult to sell in central and western Europe, was repeatedly articulated. However, the notion that Russian expansion was largely motivated by economic factors has been rejected by most Soviet and western scholars, who point to the fact that at this time Russian policy was determined by political and strategic considerations, and not primarily by economic ones.[48]

After Russia's defeat in the Crimean War the conflict with Britain shifted to Asia. 'Only in Asia can we take up the struggle with Britain with some chance of success', the diplomat N. P. Ignatiev stated as early as 1857.[49] In the nineteenth century the British attempted to gain control over Afghanistan from India, and it was here that the two colonial powers met face-to-face. In Russia defensive ideas were linked with expansionist ones. For example, General Skobelev is reputed to have said: 'Give me 100,000 camels, and I will conquer India.'[50] The humiliating defeat in the Crimean War had proved detrimental to the prestige of the elite, and especially of the military leadership, and made them look for various kinds of compensation. Thus it was suggested that Russia should demonstrate its imperial might in Asia and attain a position which equalled that of the western colonial powers. Such ideas were certainly fairly common in St Petersburg, though there were also differences of opinion, and quite a number of people who spoke out against the conquest of Middle Asia. In such a situation individual generals on the periphery were able to take the initiative. Occasionally prompted by a personal craving for fame, they conducted attacks which were sometimes unauthorized, though subsequently sanctioned by the government. That such actions were also justified by referring to Russia's need for security was part of the traditional arsenal of legitimation of colonial expansion.

In 1864 foreign minister Gorchakov, who was not one of the warmongers, explained the mechanisms of expansion as follows:

> The situation of Russia in Middle Asia is that of all civilized states which come into contact with semi-savage and itinerant ethnic groups without a structured social organization. In such a case the interest in the security of one's borders and in trade relations always makes it imperative that the civilized state should have a certain authority over its neighbours, who as a result of their wild and impetuous customs are very disconcerting. Initially it is a matter of containing their attacks and raids. In order to stop them, one is usually compelled to subjugate the adjoining ethnic groups more or less directly. Once this has been achieved, their manners become less unruly, though they in turn are now subjected to attacks by more distant tribes. The state is duty-bound to protect them against such raids, and punish the others for their deeds. From this springs the necessity of further protracted periodic expeditions against an enemy who, on account of his social order, cannot be caught . . . For this reason the state has to decide between two alternatives. Either it must give up this unceasing work and surrender its borders to continual disorder . . . or it must penetrate further and further into the wild lands . . . This has been the fate of all states which have come up against this kind of situation. The United States in America, France in Africa, Holland in its colonies, Britain in eastern India – all were drawn less by ambition and more by necessity along this path forwards on which it is very difficult to stop once one has started.'[51]

This subjective explanation of expansion as an as it were elementary necessity is familiar from the legitimation of other colonial powers. In the context of a policy determined by Russia's 'mission civilisatrice' and questions of prestige, there could, in the eyes of the Foreign Minister, be chain reactions which left policymakers with very little leeway. However, such experiences were more the result of the confrontation with the nomads of the steppe, and could not be applied automatically to the sedentary inhabitants of Middle Asia. Gorchakov's remarks are insufficient as an objective explanation of Russian expansion, though they shed light on its ideological preconditions, the perception of Asia by the Russian centre.

In May 1864 Colonel Cherniaev and 2,600 men left Verny, and a smaller detachment Perovsk. Both moved southwards.[52] In the same year he occupied the town of Chimkent, which belonged to the Khanate of Kokand. Acting in defiance of orders from St Petersburg, in 1865 Cherniaev also conquered the great trading centre of Tashkent. However, Alexander II immediately gave his assent to the arbitrary undertaking. As early as 1867 the northern areas of the Khanate of Kokand were organized into the Governor-Generalship of Turkestan centred on Tashkent. The first Governor-General, General von Kaufmann, moved westwards the following year, routed a numerically larger army of the Emir of Bukhara, and conquered Samarkand, but not – probably in deference to British interests – Bukhara, which was of symbolic importance. In 1873 the Russians conquered the feared, though militarily weak Khanate of Khiva. In 1875, when an insurrection by Kirgiz and Uzbek nomads (which turned into a Holy War against the Russians) broke out in the Khanate of Kokand, a Russian army overran the southern part of the Khanate of Kokand in the course of several campaigns in 1875 and 1876.

The last region of Middle Asia to be conquered was the westernmost area of the Turkmen. In 1869 the base of Krasnovodsk was established on the eastern shore of the Caspian Sea, where a number of Turkmen tribes already lived under Russian rule. However, the conquest of Turkmenistan began only a decade later. In 1879 a Russian army suffered an unpleasant defeat at the hands of the Tekke-Turkmen. Subsequently a large Russian army with 20,000 camels under General Skobelev moved against the Turkmen and in January 1881 stormed their fortress of Gök-Tepe, an action in which fewer than 300 Russians died and probably more than 8,000 Turkmen. This brutally crushed the embittered resistance of the Turkmen. The oasis of Merv was also conquered in 1884, and in the following year so was Kushka, which lay on the road to Herat.

The conquest of Merv, which was seen as the key to Afghanistan, finally awakened fears in Britain of further Russian expansion in the direction of Iran and India. The press spoke of 'mervosity' and an imminent Russo-British war. But energetic British action stopped Russia's expansion, and in several border treaties the two powers divided up Middle Asia. These finally led to the Pamir treaty of 1895. One result of these treaties was the fact that Turkmen, Tadzhiks, Uzbeks and Kirgiz were divided up among different states. In this respect nothing has changed to this day.

Another wave of Russian expansion had been directed against Sinkiang (eastern Turkestan) at the beginning of the 1870s.[53] An insurrection against Chinese rule organized by General Yakub Beg of Kokand provided the pretext for Russian involvement, and in 1871 Russian troops occupied the upper Ili valley. However, six years later the rebellious Uigurs were defeated by the Chinese, and, after lengthy negotiations with China, Russia declared in 1881 that it was willing to withdraw with the exception of a small strip of territory in the west, one of the rare cases in which Russia relinquished a conquered territory.

In contrast to expansion in the Caucasus and in the Kazakh steppes, the conquest of Middle Asia did not present Russia with any particularly serious military problems. True, the khanates had resisted conquest in military terms. However, only nomadic groups such as the Turkmen did this with any degree of success. It was said that a total of only about 1,000 Russian soldiers died, whereas their opponents suffered a far greater number of casualties. The badly armed and politically divided Muslims of Middle Asia did not stand a chance against European military power. Thus Russia had finally moved into the circle of the European colonial powers. This was like balm to its elites' craving for prestige, and Dostoevsky spoke for many when, after the conquest of Gök-Tepe in 1881, he painted a shining picture of Russia's future in Asia: 'In the whole of Asia Skobelev's victory will resound, to its farthest borders . . . May in these people numbering millions, as far as India and indeed in India, grow the conviction of the invincibility of the white tsar.'[54]

How was this large new territory in Asia absorbed into the Russian empire? In contrast to the Caucasus and to Kazakhstan, not all of the conquered area was actually incorporated.[55] The Emirate of Bukhara and the Khanate of Khiva merely became Russian protectorates, and remained independent under international law. However, their territory was considerably reduced in size, and wound its way across Middle Asia as a relatively small strip from the Aral Sea to the Pamir mountains. In treaties with Russia the emir and the khan had to make far-reaching concessions. Bukhara and Khiva were opened up to Russian merchants, and later incorporated into the Russian customs union. They had to pay high war reparations, which placed a heavy burden on their economies. The two rulers had 'political agents' assigned to them for purposes of control, and in foreign policy terms they were completely dependent on St Petersburg. However, internally the socio-political structure was preserved. The emir and the khan continued to rule unchecked over their subjects. Only the slave trade was outlawed. Islam continued to form the basis of society and culture, and 'noble Bukhara' retained its famous Arabic and Persian schools.

Thus the Emirate of Bukhara and the Khanate of Khiva were under the control of and dependent on Russia in military, political and economic terms. Nevertheless, until after the revolution they retained their formal sovereignty. Nowhere else in the nineteenth century did Russia exercise indirect rule of this kind, which was British practice in India. Even the Grand Duchy of Finland, the Kingdom of Poland and the khanates of Azerbaidzhan and the principalities of western Georgia, which continued temporarily to be ruled by the old dynasties, were parts of the Russian empire. Thus it was not only the advantages of the protectorate, which made real rule with minimal costs possible, but also foreign policy considerations, especially deference to Britain and to the reputation of Bukhara in the Islamic world which on this occasion prompted Russia to exercise restraint.

The Khanate of Kokand was initially retained, though after the uprising of 1875 it was attached to the Governor-Generalship of Turkestan, which had been founded in 1867 and enlarged by incorporating parts of the Emirate of Bukhara (with Samarkand) and of the Khanate of Khiva.[56] However, the Transcaspian area, which was primarily inhabited by Turkmen, was initially placed under the control of the Caucasian administration, and only added to Turkestan in 1897, even though it was separated from it physically by the polities of Bukhara and Khiva. The Governor-General of Turkestan, who resided in Tashkent, was invested with far-reaching powers. Thus General Konstantin von Kaufmann, the first incumbent of the post, exercised a crucial influence on the new socio-political order in Middle Asia. A military administration and a strong military presence guaranteed the loyalty of Russia's new subjects. All in all, von Kaufmann favoured the well-tried policy of non-intervention. The status quo was largely preserved with regard to local administration, the judicial system and ownership of land (including the important water rights). However, taxes were gradually standardized, and a limited agrarian reform implemented, which weakened the landowning nobility in favour of the peasants.

Whereas it is true that the old elite took on certain tasks as elected officers in the local administration and the judicial system, it seems that there was never any question of co-opting the Uzbek aristocrats into the

Imperial nobility. However, Russia did enlist the services of Turkmen cavalry units, and a few tribal chieftains became officers in the Russian army. The English observer Curzon considered this to be an example of Russia's 'remarkable talent for fraternizing with the vanquished'.[57] Yet neither the nomads nor the sedentary inhabitants of Middle Asia were regarded as fully fledged citizens of Russia. As a rule the sedentary inhabitants were referred to as 'natives' (tuzemtsy), and in practical terms their position corresponded to that of the inorodtsy.[58] Thus the inhabitants of Middle Asia remained colonial peoples segregated from the Russians. Nor was the upper class integrated in social terms. On the other hand they had the benefit of certain privileges such as being exempt from military service. The fact that sedentary ethnic groups with an ancient tradition of high culture were assigned to the inorodtsy contradicted the original definition of this legal category, which was based on the nomadic lifestyle. It showed quite clearly Russia's increasing distance in the nineteenth century not only from the non-sedentary ethnic groups, but from all Asiatics.

In keeping with this tendency to segregation, there were few attempts to do missionary work in Middle Asia or to russify the population in linguistic terms. Rather, the Russian authorities deliberately preserved the conservative Muslim clergy, guaranteeing their large estates (waqf), and retaining their schools. The Orthodox church was expressly forbidden to engage in missionary work, and a planned bishopric of Tashkent was never established. The Governor-General hoped to guarantee the political and social stability of Middle Asia with the support of the Islamic establishment.[59]

Of greater significance for Middle Asia than the policy of political, social and cultural 'non-interference' were the changes in the economic structure.[60] In the course of the accelerated process of industrialization economic goals modelled on those of the western colonial powers gained the upper hand towards the end of the nineteenth century. Thus the Middle Asian colonies were supposed to fit in with the economic needs of the mother country. The most obvious example of this was the cultivation of cotton, which was designed to ensure that the Russian textile industry would get the supplies it required. Whereas in 1885 cotton had been planted on only 14 per cent of the cultivated land in the Fergana valley, by 1915 it was already approaching 40 per cent. The native kinds of cotton were gradually replaced by better quality American varieties. At the same time large projects were designed to increase and improve the irrigation systems, though not a great deal of this materialized. As a rule the cotton was seeded and pressed in Middle Asia. In other words, the first stage in the manufacturing process took place locally. Then, however, it was transported to the centres of the Russian textile industry. No attempt was made to establish a cotton manufacturing industry in Middle Asia. The transport problem was solved by the construction of railways. Yet work on the first railway, the Transcaspian, started in 1881 for strategic reasons. It led from the Caspian Sea to Merv (1886), then through the territory of the Emirate of Bukhara to Samarkand (1888), reaching Tashkent in 1898 and Andishan in the Fergana valley in 1899. The Orenburg–Tashkent line, which established a direct link with Russia in 1906, proved to be far more important for the transportation of cotton.

Thus in its concentration on cotton Russian economic policy in Middle Asia was certainly colonial in character. In some areas, such as the Fergana valley, which before the First World War had to import grain, and where there were profound social changes, it was even already possible to speak of monoculture. Yet all in all, in 1913 cotton had been planted on only 15 to 20 per cent of the (irrigated) land in Turkestan which was available for agriculture. At any rate, in 1910 cotton is said to have comprised more than half of the total value of the agricultural output of Turkestan. In retrospect it is clear that the Russian economic policy of the day laid the foundations for the serious economic and eco-logical problems which have arisen as a result of the cotton monoculture in Middle Asia.

But in general terms Russian influence on the non-Russians of Middle Asia was slight. The sedentary and nomadic Muslims continued to live within their traditional social orders and value systems. The Russian presence was restricted to a small class of administrators, to garrisons, and to the new Russian quarters which were clearly separate from the Oriental quarters in certain large cities, above all in Tashkent. Only the fertile foothills in the north of Kirgizia were gradually settled by eastern Slav peasants, as had been the case with the Kazakh steppes. However, the oases and river valleys of the south were already densely populated, and the Russian and Ukrainian arable farmers would pro-bably have found it difficult to come to grips with the foreign irrigation system. Thus the proportion of Russians in Middle Asia and in Transcaucasia remained rather small – an ethnodemographic pattern that has remained to this day.

Taken as a whole, Russian policy in Middle Asia followed the traditional methods of pragmatic flexibility, though abuses by the Russian regional authorities were not infrequent. The non-Russian population considered Russian rule to be foreign domination by infidels, and again and again there were spontaneous rebellions. These were usually of a local character, for example, the cholera rebellion of 1892 in Tashkent. Only on rare occasions, as in the Andishan insurrection of 1898, did they become supraregional 'Holy Wars'. In such cases, as in the Caucasus, Sufic brotherhoods played an important role in the organization.[61]

For Russia the conquest and partial incorporation of Middle Asia signified a further shift of its centre of gravity to Asia. It is true that the demographic and economic weight of Middle Asia at the end of the nineteenth century was still rather small, and it is true that Russia continued to be primarily interested in Europe. However, the fact that the Russian Empire now included fairly large groups of sedentary Muslims in the heart of Asia, and that it possessed colonies within its own boundaries, influenced Russia's self-image as a Eurasian power. As a result of their national emancipation and demographic explosion the Muslims of Middle Asia became increasingly important as the twentieth century progressed.

5. Reaching Out to America and the Far East

In the eighteenth century Russia had expanded into the steppes, and in the nineteenth century it continued to expand southwards, to the Caucasus, and to Middle Asia. At the same time it continued to expand into the forests of the north-east from Kamchatka and eastern Siberia. In view of the fact that the Manchu empire still constituted a formidable opponent in the eighteenth century, it was for the time being only possible to reach out across the sea to Alaska.

A Russian expedition under the command of Bering, a Dane, was the first to reach the North American continent. This was followed from the 1740s onwards by stepwise expansion from Kamchatka via the Aleutians to the islands of Kodiak (1784) and Sitka (1799) off the coast of Alaska.[62] As in Siberia, the most important incentive was the search for new sources of furs. However, here the favoured animal was the sea otter and not the sable. Expansion was in the hands of trappers and adventurers, but it also attracted Russian merchants, who were quick to establish trading companies. They included Grigorii Shelikhov, at whose suggestion the Russian American Company was established in 1799, albeit after his death. It was modelled on the British Hudson's Bay Company and the East India Company, and combined private enterprise with the support of the government. The state conferred privileges on the Company, and even assigned certain responsibilities to it, a unique occurrence in the history of Russian expansion. It received a twenty-year monopoly over the fur trade from the 55th parallel to the Bering Strait, and was assigned the task of erecting Russian forts in Alaska and of expanding maritime trade with Japan and China.

The first director of the Russian American Company, Alexander Baranov, turned Novo-Arkhangelsk on Sitka into the centre of Russian America. Up to the 1830s about 800 Russians settled in Alaska, especially on the islands. The local Aleutians and Eskimos, who repeatedly destroyed the Russian forts, were hostile. They were exploited, enslaved as hostages or required to do forced labour, and their numbers began to dwindle. Some were forced to convert to the Orthodox faith or sent to Russian schools. 'Ten American boys were brought to Irkutsk and taught to play various musical instruments.'[63] It was difficult to provide the settlers with food and supplies. For this reason the Russians began to contemplate colonies further south, where they could engage in arable farming. They reached what was still Spanish California as early as 1806, and in 1812 the Company built a fort at Bodega Bay, about 100 kilometres north of San Francisco, which was named Ross after Russia (Rossiia). From this base there were expeditions to Mexico and Hawaii.

However, Russian expansion in America soon came up against opposition from the British and the Americans, whose maritime power was superior in the northern Pacific, and who also became rivals as trappers and whalers.[64] Fort Ross was sold in 1841, and in Alaska the position of the Russians also deteriorated. The fact that the fur-hunting grounds were quickly exhausted, and the problem of supplies could not be solved meant that fewer and fewer Russian settlers came to the area. Since the pressure of the Western powers increased during the Crimean War, and Russia proceeded to new conquests in the Amur region and in Middle Asia, the government came to the conclusion that it was unable to hold on to the remote, thinly populated and not particularly profitable areas in America. Thus in 1867 Russia sold Alaska and the Aleutians to the United States for $7.2 million after it had rejected a higher offer from its arch-enemies, the British. Russia's surrender of its American possessions was repeatedly discussed in the age of Soviet–American conflict. Whereas American historians emphasize that Russia wished to rid itself of Alaska, some Soviet historians regretted the sale and explained that it was due to the pressure exerted by the western powers. 'A Russian would never have dreamt of selling Russian America, a land that is so liberally drenched in the blood and sweat of those who discovered and opened it up. And Russian America would have remained Russian . . . '[65]

From Kamchatka and Alaska, Russian ships also sailed to China. In 1849, 200 years after the Russians had first sighted it, the naval officer Nevelskoi rediscovered the mouth of the Amur. The following year he hoisted the Russian flag and founded the base of Nikolaevsk.[66] In St Petersburg there was opposition to this unauthorized occupation of Chinese sovereign territory. However, the tsar, after whom the fort had been named, is said to have retorted: 'Where the Russian flag has once been raised, it shall not be taken down again.'[67] This principle of Russian expansion was first destined to be broken by his successors in Alaska and in the Ili valley.

However, the initiative for expansion into the Amur region did not come from the government. As in the seventeenth century, it came from military commanders on the periphery. In those days Moskvitin, Poiarkov and Khabarov had conquered the Amur basin, and the Muscovite government had later given them its blessing. Now it was the Governor-General of eastern Siberia, Nikolai Muraviev, who organized campaigns of conquest of his own accord. He was initially disowned by St Petersburg, though finally celebrated as a hero and accorded the honourable cognomen of Amursky. Muraviev occupied the Amur region in 1854, and established a fortress at the mouth of the Ussuri which he called Khabarovsk in honour of his predecessor. Neither the handful of Tungusic and palaeo-Asiatic ethnic groups of the region nor China offered any resistance. A small Franco-British fleet which attempted to intervene was defeated.

This highlights the fact that the international context was quite different to that in the seventeenth century. Whereas in those days China, newly resurgent under the Manchu dynasty, had stopped the Russian advance, and had recovered the Amur region in the Treaty of Nerchinsk, it was now no longer a match for Russia. China's defeat in the Opium War against Britain and France (1840–42) and the Taiping rebellion (1850–64) revealed its weakness for all to see. Russia, like the other European powers, took advantage of the situation, and, in the Treaty of Aigun (1858) and in the Peace of Peking (1860) forced China to cede not only the territory to the north of the Amur, but also the coastal strip to the south which reached as far as the Korean border. The island of Sakhalin had been occupied in 1853. It was ceded to Russia in 1875, whilst the Kuril islands went to Japan. In 1860 a town was founded near the border with Korea which soon became important as a harbour and a naval base. By analogy with Vladikavkaz it was given the symbolic name of Vladivostok (ruler of the east).

The newly acquired territory was divided into three areas for administrative purposes, and in 1884 these were combined to form the Amur Governor-Generalship.[68] As in Siberia, the relatively small native population was assigned to the inorodtsy category, and organized correspondingly. However, not all of them paid iasak. The Manchurian-Tungusic tribes which, inter alia, were known as Gold (now Nanai), Oroch, Ulch, Udegei and Negidal, the Gilyaks, who belonged to the Palaeo-Asiatic language group, and the linguistically and ethnically completely isolated Ainu on Sakhalin lived in small clan communities as fishermen, hunters and occasionally as reindeer herdsmen.[69] A number of them were converted to the Orthodox faith, though they all remained loyal to their animist ideas of religion. The ruthless exploitation of natural resources by the Russians and numerous epidemics led to the demographic stagnation of the ethnic groups in the Amur region in the nineteenth century. The Russian presence in the Amur area was initially designed to provide military protection against foreign enemies. Thus the Amur Cossack army was founded in 1858, and the Ussuri army in 1889. Settlement by eastern Slav peasants at first proceeded at a rather sluggish rate, and only increased at the beginning of the twentieth century as a result of the opening of the Trans-Siberian Railway. At the same time more and more Koreans and Chinese came to the coastal province as peasants, tradesmen and seasonal workers.

The conquest and incorporation of the area in the Far East must be seen in the context of imperialist competition between the great European powers in the Far East. The rivalry between Russia and Britain also played an important role in this context. The fact that the name of Vladivostok stood for Russian imperialism in the east became clearly apparent at the end of the nineteenth century when the Far Eastern area became the springboard for expansion into Manchuria.[70] The founding of the

Russo-Chinese Bank (1895), the construction of the Chinese Eastern Railway (1896–1903), the associated Russian protectorate over the northern part of Manchuria and the establishment of the ice-free harbours of Port Arthur and Dairen (1898) were the most important stages. At the same time they were the last offshoots of Russian expansion eastwards, which in 1905 was brought to an end by the new Asian great power, Japan.

6. Summary

Whereas Russian expansion in the west had come to an end in 1815, it continued in the east throughout the whole of the nineteenth century, and added vast Asian territories to the tsarist empire. Expansion in Asia was to some extent a continuation of the 'gathering of the lands of the Golden Horde'. The conquest of Siberia led to distant Alaska, to the Amur area and to Manchuria. After Russia had gained control of the steppes to the north of the Black Sea and Caspian Sea, it expanded to the south, to the Caucasus and to the east, into the Kazakh steppes, and from here to the deserts and oases of Middle Asia. As in previous centuries, expansion came to a halt whenever it ran up against a great power that was Russia's equal: Britain, France, the United States and Japan.

In the nineteenth century Russian expansion in Asia became an international affair. For this reason the Caucasus, Middle Asian, Alaskan and Far Eastern theatres were linked to each other and European politics, and especially with the Oriental question. The growing confrontation with Britain became an important impetus in Russian expansion. As had been the case in earlier centuries, Russian policies were primarily determined by considerations of strategy and power politics. Russia expanded in places where there was an imbalance of power in its favour. It is true that economic goals were regularly stated in the nineteenth century, and Russia placed hopes in the Asiatic colonies as suppliers of natural resources and as markets for its goods. However, economic motives probably played a decisive role in expansion only in the fur rush in Alaska, and subsequently in the 'peaceful penetration' of Manchuria at the end of the nineteenth century. In the course of the speedy industrialization of Russia, economic factors also played a more important role at this time in Middle Asia (cotton), Kazakhstan (colonization) and Transcaucasia (oil).

For this reason the methods of Russian expansion were not primarily economic ones. Exceptions to this were the Russian–American Company, and the instruments employed in Manchuria. That these two enterprises in particular should have failed shows clearly Russia's economic weakness and its inferiority to the industrialized states of western Europe. On the other hand, the traditional methods of military expansion were successful. The army played a crucial role in the Asian expansion of the nineteenth century, either at the centre, in the person of ambitious generals on the periphery, or subsequently in the administration of the newly acquired territories. Whilst Transcaucasia was annexed in the context of wars with Iran and the Ottoman Empire, and with the active help of the Armenians and Georgians who sympathized with Russia, the Caucasus, Kazakhstan and Middle Asia were conquered in colonial wars. As in earlier centuries the tribally organized and mobile ethnic groups of the steppe, the desert and the mountains resisted with especial ferocity. The resistance of the Caucasian 'gortsy', the Kazakhs and the Turkmen was crushed with brutal force. The Russian policy of violence reached a sorry climax in the mass slaughter and expulsion of the Circassians.

The incorporation of the new territories in Asia possessed the traditionally ambivalent character. On the one hand, the pragmatic tradition continued to exist in St Petersburg. It was to a great extent determined by security considerations, largely respected the status quo with regard to socio-political and economic organization and value systems, and sought to achieve the social, and also, in the long term, the cultural integration of the foreign societies by means of cooperation with the non-Russian elites. On the other hand, in the nineteenth century the Russians' eurocentric feeling of superiority with regard to nomads, Muslims and Asiatics in general – and at least initially to the Christian Georgians and Armenians – became increasingly pronounced and displayed less and less understanding for foreign social orders, economic styles and value systems. Like the western European colonial powers, from whom this consciousness was copied, Russia had to fulfil a civilizing mission in Asia; it was to bring to 'primitive' non-Russians the blessings of 'higher' European culture. In the inorodtsy statute of 1822 the hunters, gatherers and nomads had been excluded from the circle of citizens with equal rights. The original goal, which was to protect the inorodtsy and then to integrate them step by step, was increasingly obscured by segregation, discrimination and a kind of racism influenced by western concepts that was implicit in the term 'of foreign origin'.

In keeping with this ambivalence the incorporation of the new Asiatic territories did not proceed in a consistent manner. In Transcaucasia the military administration had at first shown little understanding for the proud elites and their high cultures. However, by the 1840s the prevailing view was that the old methods of cooperation were far more efficacious. In the case of the 'gortsy', the nobles who remained after war and expulsion were at least to some extent also co-opted into the empire's upper class. Thus whereas the ethnic groups of the Caucasus were not deemed to be inorodtsy, the nomadic Kazakhs, Kirgiz and Turkmen were ideal types of this legal category, and for this reason their elites were not co-opted into the nobility. Although the Middle Asiatics of the oases and river valleys did not correspond to the definition, they were in *de facto* terms assigned to the inorodtsy category. This was the first time that sedentary inhabitants who belonged to high cultures were excluded from the circle of the 'natural' inhabitants of Russia. This development mirrors the change in the Russian policy on nationalities in Asia from paternalism and pragmatism to colonialism. That the old and cautious approach had not quite disappeared even in the second half of the nineteenth century is demonstrated among other things by the fact that, in contrast to the steppe, the territory of Middle Asia was not annexed completely, being given in part the legal status of independent protectorates.

Towards the end of the nineteenth century the settlement of the periphery of the steppes and foothills by eastern Slav peasants became increasingly important. The occupation of their winter pastures shook the basic economic structures of the Kazakhs, Kirgiz and Caucasians. As had been the case with the Nogai Tatars, Bashkirs and Kalmyks, this encounter between sedentary arable agriculturalists and nomadic herdsmen led to serious conflicts. On the other hand, eastern Slav peasants hardly settled in Transcaucasia and Middle Asia, where the economic and social structures remained largely intact.

In the nineteenth century, expansion in the west and in the east did not occur at the same speed. The government of Alexander I, which can be seen as the climax of liberal experimentation in the west, embarked on the annexation and ruthless integration of Transcaucasia, and the era of the liberator of the serfs, Alexander II, witnessed the brutal suppression of the Caucasian 'gortsy' and the military expansion to Middle

Asia and the Far East. On the other hand, under Nicholas I, the policeman of Europe and the gravedigger of Polish freedom, there was a change of course to a pragmatic Transcaucasian policy. Thus an orientation to Europe not infrequently went hand in hand with expansion and aggression in Asia – both in the political sphere and with regard to ideology. This had already been seen in the age of Peter the Great. And it was repeated once again under Finance Minister Witte at the end of the nineteenth century.

In comparison to the seventeenth and eighteenth centuries, the colonialist elements in Russia's expansion in Asia became more pronounced.[71] This is evident not only in the gradually increasing importance of economic goals, but above all in the greater distance between Russians and Asiatics. Whilst it is true that Russian expansion, in contrast to its west European maritime counterpart, remained a continental kind of expansion, the new subjects in Transcaucasia and Middle Asia, who were separated from Russia by high mountain ranges and deserts, were no longer direct neighbours. Russia had maintained no permanent relations with them, and they did not share a common history. In addition to this there was the ideological distance, the growing eurocentric feeling of superiority of the Russians towards the Asiatics. However, even now not all of the regions fitted equally well into the colonial pattern. Thus Transcaucasia, whose upper class was increasingly integrated into the Russian nobility, can only to a certain extent be regarded as a colony after the middle of the nineteenth century. The areas on the edge of the steppe and the mountains were colonies of settlers, whereas Middle Asia was a classical example of a colony ruled by Europeans. And the concept of imperialism can also be applied to Russia, at least by the end of the nineteenth century, when it took an active part in the competition between the European powers for Asian markets.[72]

In the nineteenth century Russia's centre of gravity shifted to the east, and this meant that the problem of 'Russia and Asia' became more acute.[73] Although Russia was now one of the European colonial powers in Asia, Russian politics and public opinion continued to be orientated primarily towards Europe. In some respects Asia was a subsidiary theatre of action, which primarily acquired its significance as a function of European politics. On the other hand, awareness of Russia's backwardness, compared to western Europe, meant that Russia's 'mission civilisatrice' in Asia also had a compensatory role: 'In Europe we were only poor recipients of charity and slaves, but we come to Asia as masters. In Europe we were Tatars, but in Asia we are also Europeans. Our mission, our civilizing mission in Asia will entice our spirit and draw us thither once the movement has gained momentum' (Dostoyevsky 1881).[74]

The Soviet Union took over Russia's Asiatic heritage, the ambivalent attitude to Asia, the colonial empire with its strategic positions in Middle Asia and the Far East and its resources, but also with its burdens, which included its far more heterogeneous character, which was the result of its economic patterns, social structures and values. The heritage of the Russian colonial empire also included the decolonization of the empire, which, lagging behind that of the other European powers, first came about at the end of the twentieth century.

Notes

1   Nolte (1969b), pp. 502 f.; Kappeler (1982b), p. 356. See also Andreas Kappeler, 'Die zaristische Politik gegenüber den Muslimen des Reiches', *Die Muslime* (1989), pp. 117–29; Bennigsen (1972).

2   On the following see also Yaroshevsky (1989); Yaroshevsky, 'Imperial Strategy in the Kirghiz Steppe in the Eighteenth Century', *JbbGO* 39 (1991), 221–4; and, although the emphasis is slightly different, Mark Batunsky, 'Islam i russkaia kultura XVIII veka. Opyt istoriko-epistemologicheskogo issledovaniia', *CMRS* 27 (1986), 45–70; Becker (1986); Batunsky (1990).

3   Fedorov (1978), pp. 156–81.

4   *PSZ* I, 29126 (vol. 38, pp. 394–416). On the following see Marc Raeff, *Siberia and the Reforms of 1822* (Seattle, 1956); Hundley (1984); Fedorov (1978), pp. 178–202; Dameshek (1986), pp. 31–45; Jadrinzew (1886).

5   With regard to the whole chapter see Suny (1989); Lang (1962); Salia (1983); *Histoire* (1982); *Istoriia Azer.* I (1958). On the earlier period see also Sarkisyanz (1961), pp. 26–85, 141–56; and the first three articles in Suny (1983).

6   On the following see Lang (1957); Atkin (1980), pp. 8–45; Atkin (1988).

7   *PSZ* I, no. 15835 (vol. 21, p. 1013).

8   *PSZ* I, 19721 (vol. 26, pp. 502 f.); 20007 (vol. 26, pp. 781–6, quotation on p. 783). On the incorporation of Georgia see Lang (1957), pp. 158–266; Atkin (1980), pp. 46–65.

9   *PSZ* I, 25466 (vol. 32, pp. 641–5). See also Atkin (1980); Galoian (1976), pp. 125–80; Khadzhi Murat Ibragimbeili, *Rossiia i Azerbaidzhan v pervoi treti XIX veka (iz voenno-politicheskoi istorii).* (Moscow, 1969).

10 *PSZ* II, 1794 (vol. 3, pp. 125–30).

11 George A. Bournoutian, 'The Ethnic Composition and the Socio-Economic Condition of Eastern Armenia in the First Half of the Nineteenth Century', in Suny

(1983), pp. 69–86; I. Shopen, *Istoricheskii pamiatnik sostoianiia Armianskoi oblasti v epokhu eia prisoedineniia k Rossiiskoi imperii* (St Petersburg, 1852).

12 On the following see Rhinelander (1975); Rhinelander, 'Russia's Imperial Policy. The Administration of the Caucasus in the First Half of the Nineteenth Century', *Canadian Slavonic Papers* 17 (1975), 218–35; Rhinelander, 'Viceroy Vorontsov's Administration of the Caucasus', in Suny (1983), pp. 87–104; Suny (1989), pp. 63–95; Lang (1957), pp. 251–84; Atkin (1980), pp. 145–61; Swietochowski (1985), pp. 4–14; Milman (1966), pp. 49–141; Makhmedov (1987); I.P. Petrushevsky, 'Sistema russkogo kolonial'nogo upravleniia v Azerbaidzhane v pervoi polovine XIX v.', *Kolonial'naia politika* (1936), pp. 6–32; Gregorian (1972); *Histoire* (1982), pp. 447–51; Parsamyan (1972), pp. 71–124.

13 *Kolonial'naia politika* I (1936), p. 280.

14 Amburger (1966), pp. 412–22.

15 *PSZ* I, 19721 (vol. 26, p. 502); 20007 (vol. 26, p. 783). On the following see Rhinelander (1975); Rhinelander, 'Viceroy Vorontsov's Administration of the Caucasus', in Suny (1983), pp. 87–104; Suny (1989), pp. 63–95; Stephen F. Jones, 'Russian Imperial Administration and the Georgian Nobility: The Georgian Conspiracy of 1832', *SEER* 65 (1987), 53–76.

16 *SZ* IX, kn. I (1899), Art. 53 (with footnote), 68, 69, 147, 190. See also Korelin (1979), pp. 47 f.

17 This is dealt with in detail in the unpublished thesis by Makhmedov (1987).

18 *SZ* IX, kn. I (1899), Art. 85, note 2; Art. 189. See, for example, the list of the various Transcaucasian noble categories (princes, nobles, beki, highest Muslim estate, meliki), in part also gathered into one estate, in Svod (1893).

19 *PSZ* I, 24696 (vol. 31, pp. 767–71); 25709 (vol. 32, pp. 1013–16); Smolitsch (1964), pp. 369 f.

20 Akaki Zereteli, *Aus meinem Leben* (Zurich, 1990), p. 117.

21 See Halbach (1991); Thomas M. Barrett, 'The Remaking of the Lion of Dagestan: Shamil in Captivity', unpublished conference paper (1988).

22 On the individual ethnic groups see Wixman (1980); Bernard Geiger et al., *Peoples and Languages of the Caucasus. A Synopsis* ('s-Gravenhage, 1959); Sarkisyanz (1961), pp. 86–140; Wixman (1984); Bennigsen and Wimbush (1985), pp. 146–206; Akiner (1983), pp. 122–236; Volkova (1974); *Istoriia narodov* (1988).

23 On this point see, for example, Wixman (1980), pp. 99–120.

24 On the following see Firuz Kazemzadeh, 'Russian Penetration of the Caucasus', in Hunczak (1974), pp. 239–63; Paul B. Henze, 'Fire and Sword in the Caucasus: The 19th Century Resistance of the North Caucasian Mountaineers', *CAS* 2(1) (1983), 5–44; Nolde, II (1953), pp. 301–63; Hoetzsch (1966), pp. 34–43; Fadeev (1960), Chapters 1 and 3; *Istoriia narodov* (1988), especially pp. 131–218; *Istoriia Dagestana*. II (1968), pp. 9–28 and 79–118.

25 See Halbach (1989).

26 Alexandre Bennigsen, 'Un Mouvement populaire au Caucase au XVIIIe siècle. La "Guerre Sainte" du sheikh Mansur (1785–1791), page mal connue et controversée des relations Russo-Turques', *CMRS* 5 (1964), 159–205.

27 Cited after Fadeev (1960), p. 340. On the Caucasus war see also Curtiss (1965), pp. 152–75.

28 Paul B. Henze, 'Circassia in the Nineteenth Century. The Futile Fight for Freedom', in *Passé turco-tatar* (1986), pp. 243–73; Ramazan Traho, 'Circassians', *CAS* 10 (1/2) (1991), 1–63; T. Tatlok, 'The Ubykhs', *Caucasian Review* 7 (1958), 100–9; Sarkisyanz (1961), pp. 104–6.

29 *Die Nationalitäten* I (1991), p. 233. Estimates concerning the number of Circassians who emigrated in the 1860s go as far as 2 million (Kemal H. Karpat, 'The Status of the Muslim under European Rule: The Eviction and Settlement of the Cerkes', *Journal of Muslim Minority Affairs* I (1978–9), 7–27, here p. 11).

30 Volkova (1974), pp. 220–2; *Istoriia narodov* (1988), pp. 202–12; Wixman (1980), pp. 76–9; Alan W. Fisher, 'Emigration of Muslims from the Russian Empire in the Years After the Crimean War', *JbbGO* 35 (1987), 356–71; Z. V. Anchabadze, *Ocherk etnicheskoi istorii abkhazskogo naroda* (Sukhumi, 1976), pp. 84–9.

31 *PSZ* II, no. 41048 (vol. 39, pp. 583 f.).

32 *Istoriia narodov* (1988), pp. 277–84; *Istoriia Dagestana.* II (1968), pp. 119–39.

33 'Uchrezhdenie upravleniia Stavropol'skoi gubernii', *SZ* II (1857), Chapter 2, kn. 2, Art. 105, 107, 128. But see also *PSZ* II, no. 35201 (vol. 34, p. 320).

34 Kh. S. Akhmedov, 'Tsarskaia administratsiia i vopros o sosloviakh v checheno-ingushskom obshchestve vtoroi poloviny XIX – nachala XX vv.', *Razvitie feodal'nykh otnoshenii u narodov Severnogo Kavkaza* (Makhachkala, 1988), pp. 267–72; F. P. Troino, 'Tsarizm i gorskie narody Severnogo Kavkaza v 60–90e gg. XIX v.', *Izvestiia Severo-Osetinskogo nauchno-issledovatel'skogo instituta* 25 (Ordzhonikidze, 1966), pp. 107–24. With regard to Dagestan, see also *Svod* (1893).

35 Halbach (1991).

36 Tillett (1969), pp. 130–70, 194–221, 259–69; Khadzhi Murat Ibragimbeili, 'Narodno-osvoboditel'naya bor'ba gortsev Severnogo Kavkaza pod rukovoditel'-stvom Shamilia protiv tsarizma i mestnykh feodalov', *Vist* 6 (1990), 151–60.

37 Olcott (1987) is of fundamental importance for this section. See also Hambly (1966); Sarkisyanz (1961), pp. 310–39; Demko (1969), *Istoriia Kazakh* I–II (1975–9).

38 See I. Stebelsky, 'The Frontier in Central Asia', *Studies*, I (1983), pp. 143–73, and especially pp. 151–61.

39 Sources in *Kazakhsko-russkie otnosheniia v XVI–XVIII vekakh (Sbornik dokumentov i materialov)* (Alma Ata, 1961). See also Alan Bodger, 'Abulkhair, Khan of the Kazakh Little Horde, and his Oath of Allegiance to Russia of October 1731', *SEER* 58 (1980), 40–57. With regard to trade see N. G. Apollova, *Ekonomicheskie sviazi Kazakhstana s Rossieiu v XVIII – nachale XIX v* (Moscow, 1960).

40 Tillett (1969), pp. 110–29, 149–67, 230–7.

41 Amburger (1966), pp. 401–9; 'Polozhenie ob upravlenii oblastei Akmolinskoi, Semipalatinskoi, Semirechenskoi, Ural'skoi i Turgaiskoi', *SZ* 2 (1892).

42 On Ilminsky see below, Chapter 7.3.

43 See Demko (1969); Pierce (1960), pp. 107–38; N. E. Bekmakhanova, *Formirovanie mnogonatsional'nogo naseleniia Kazakhstana i Severnoi Kirgizii. Posledniaia chetvert' XVIII–60-e gody XIX v. M.* (1980); Bekmakhanova (1986).

44 On the following see Hambly (1966); Sarkisyanz (1961), pp. 160–227, 332–41.
45 See Bert G. Fragner, 'Probleme der Nationswerdung der Usbeken und Tadshiken', *Die Muslime* (1989), pp. 19–34; Bennigsen and Wimbush (1985), pp. 45–125; Akiner (1983), pp. 266–383; Wixman (1984); *Die Nationalitäten* (1991), pp. 252–83; Karl H. Menges, 'Peoples, Languages, and Migrations', in Allworth (1989), pp. 60–91; Allworth (1990), pp. 30–43.
46 Hambly (1966), pp. 186–96; Wheeler (1964), pp. 40–7; Bacon (1966), pp. 47–91; Hayit (1971), pp. 21–38; *Istoriia Uzbek.* I (1967), pp. 607–86; *Istoriia tadzhik* (1964), pp. 57–126; *Istoriia Kirg.* (1963), pp. 282–326; *Istoriia Turkm.* (1957), pp. 7–92; Lorenz (1988), pp. 120–37; Carrère (1988), pp. 7–36.
47 See Allworth (1989), pp. 1–59; Hayit (1971), pp. 39–49.
48 Geyer (1977), pp. 73–81; Hoetzsch (1966), pp. 76–9; Lowell Tillett, 'Russian Imperialism and Colonialism', in Samuel H. Baron and Nancy W. Heer (eds), *Windows on the Russian Past* (Columbus, 1977), pp. 105–21 (which provides details of the most important Soviet studies).
49 Cited after A. L. Popov, 'Iz istorii zavoevaniia Srednei Azii', *IZ* 9 (1940), 202. See also Hoetzsch (1966), pp. 102–22.
50 Cited after Hoetzsch (1966), p. 113.
51 S. S. Tatishchev, *Imperator Aleksandr II. Ego zhizn' i tsarstvovanie*, vol. II (St Petersburg, 1903), pp. 115–16. See also Hoetzsch (1966), p. 27.
52 On the following see Pierce (1960), pp. 17–45, and the summary in Hambly (1966), pp. 217–28; Hélène Carrère d'Encausse, 'Systematic Conquest, 1865 to 1884', in Allworth (1989), pp. 131–50; Hoetzsch (1966), pp. 79–122; David MacKenzie, *The Lion of Tashkent. The Career of General M. G. Cherniaev* (Athens, 1974); David MacKenzie, 'The Conquest and Administration of Turkestan', in Rywkin (1988), pp. 208–34; Hayit (1971), pp. 74–114.
53 Immanuel C. Y. Hsü, *The Ili Crisis. A Study of Sino–Russian Diplomacy 1871–1881* (Oxford, 1965).
54 F. M. Dostoevsky, *Tagebuch eines Schriftstellers*, cited after *Polnoe sobranie sochinenii*, vol. 27 (Leningrad, 1984), p. 32. Another German translation in *Tagebuch eines Schriftstellers* (Munich, 1963), pp. 583 f.
55 On the following see Seymour Becker, *Russia's Protectorates in Central Asia: Bukhara and Khiva, 1865–1924* (Cambridge, Mass., 1968); Carrère d'Encausse (1988), pp. 37–53.
56 On the following see Pierce (1960), pp. 48–91, 141–52, a short summary also in Hambly (1966), pp. 221–33; Wheeler (1964), pp. 65–78; Seymour Becker, 'Russia's Central Asian Empire 1885–1917', in Rywkin (1988), pp. 235–56; Hélène Carrère d'Encausse, 'Organizing and Colonizing the Conquered Territories', in Allworth (1989), pp. 151–71; Amburger (1966), pp. 409–11; 'Polozhenie ob upravlenii Turkestanskogo kraia' in *SZ* II (1892); Galuzo (1929); *Istoriia Uzbek.* II (1968), pp. 39–68.
57 Curzon (1967), pp. 127–9.
58 *Die Nationalitäten* I (1991), pp. 437–9.
59 On the religious background see Batunsky (1987).

60 Pierce (1960), pp. 163–99; Ian Murray Matley, 'Agricultural Development', in Allworth (1989), pp. 266–81; Ian Murray Matley, 'Industrialization', in Allworth (1989), pp. 309–30; Lorenz (1989), pp. 237–41; Jörg Stadelbauer, *Bahnbau und kulturgeographischer Wandel in Turkmenien. Einflüsse der Eisenbahn auf Raumstruktur, Wirtschaftsentwicklung und Verkehrsintegration in einem Grenzgebiet des russischen Machtbereichs* (Berlin, 1973). See the detailed comments by a contemporary observer, Curzon (1967).

61 Pierce (1960), pp. 221–33; Halbach (1989), pp. 227–9.

62 On the following see *To Siberia* vol. II *Russian Penetration of the North Pacific Ocean 1700–1797. A Documentary Record* (1988), pp. 31–70; vol. III *The Russian American Colonies 1798–1867. A Documentary Record*, (1989), pp. 27–80, both volumes with numerous sources translated into English; S. B. Okun, *The Russian-American Company* (New York, 1970) (reprint of 1951 edn, transl. from the Russian); Alekseev (1982), pp. 86–132; short summary in Alton S. Donnelly, 'Russian–American Company', *MERSH* 32 (1983), pp. 38–44.

63 *Dokumente*, II (1984), pp. 517–21, quotation on p. 519 (a comment made by N. A. Shelikhova in 1798).

64 See James R. Gibson, 'Diversification on the Frontier: Russian America in the Middle of the Nineteenth Century', *Studies* (1983), pp. 197–238; James R. Gibson, 'Tsarist Russia in Colonial America: Critical Constraints', in Wood (1991), pp. 92–116.

65 Cited in Alekseev (1982), p. 132. See also Ronald J. Jensen, *The Alaska Purchase and Russian–American Relations* (Seattle and London, 1975).

66 On the following see Hoetzsch (1966), pp. 50–60; Walter Kolarz, *Rußland und seine asiatischen Völker* (Frankfurt am Main, 1956); Alekseev (1982); Dieter Landgraf, *Amur, Ussuri, Sachalin 1847–1917* (Neuried, 1989).

67 Cited by Hoetzsch (1966), p. 53.

68 Amburger (1966), pp. 407 f. On the following see also Kurt Spiess, *Periphere Sowjetwirtschaft. Das Beispiel Russisch-Fernost 1897–1970* (Zurich and Freiburg im Breisgau, 1980), pp. 16–30 and 97–114.

69 Levin and Potapov (1964), pp. 685–787; *Etnicheskaia istoriia* (1982), pp. 223–57; *Die Nationalitäten* I (1991), pp. 288–97; Wixman (1984).

70 See Geyer (1977), pp. 143–69; B. A. Romanov, *Russia in Manchuria (1892–1906)* (repr., New York, 1974); R. K. I. Quested, '"Matey" Imperialists' ? *The Tsarist Russians in Manchuria 1895–1917* (Hong Kong, 1982).

71 See above, Chapters 3.5 and 5.5, and Reinhard, vols I–III (1983–8); von Albertini (1976).

72 See Geyer (1977).

73 See Nicholas V. Riasanovsky, 'Asia Through Russian Eyes', in Vucinich (1972), pp. 2–29, and Hoetzsch (1966), pp. 123–38.

74 F. M. Dostoevsky, *Polnoe sobranie sochinenii*, 27 (Leningrad, 1984), pp. 36 f. (*Diary of a Writer*, 1881).

6

The National Challenge

IN THE NINETEENTH century, European multi-ethnic empires were rocked by national movements, and were gradually transformed. The foundations on which the Russian empire was based – the dynastic idea of empire, the tsarist autocracy, and the estate-based order – began to be undermined by the modern national principle of the community of political will and the ethnic cultural community which transcended estate boundaries, and by the notion of the sovereignty of the people. The modern nation became the primary object of identity and loyalty, the principle that gave order to the modern world. It required political participation, self-determination and autonomy, had as its distant goal the nation state that as a rule was ethnically homogeneous, and thus threatened to blow apart the supranational dynastic empires.

The national movements were both a product and a component of the fundamental economic, social, political and cultural process of transformation which has engulfed Europe and the rest of the world since the eighteenth century, and for which the (eurocentric) concept of modernization has become the accepted term. Modern societies require the complementary communication of individual social and regional groups, a greater degree of homogeneity and mobility of the population, and the political participation of wider sections of society.[1] The national movements were both the result and the cause of social and political mobilization, increasing communication and the vertical integration of societies across traditional estate and regional boundaries. Their most important precondition was the social mobilization of society in the wake of the decline of the estate-based feudal order. The mobilizing factors included the abolition of serfdom, industrialization and urbanization, the spread of literacy, schools, and the press. However, the correlation between the national movements and the social, political, economic and cultural modernization of society was not a mechanical one. The basic framework of the system of government, for example, the degree of centralization, or of political and cultural oppression, must be taken into account just as much as external intellectual and political influences.

The Czech historian Miroslav Hroch has divided the surprisingly similar course of the majority of European national movements into three phases.[2] In Phase A a small group of educated people develops a learned interest in the language, history and folklore of the ethnic group. This phase of cultural awakening is followed by the phase of national agitation (Phase B). A group of patriots now pursues the aim of instilling national consciousness into wider circles of the population, mobilizing them and integrating them into a national community. If this proves successful, the national movement proceeds to Phase C, the mass movement in which a large part of the community is influenced by national consciousness and espouses the goal of political autonomy. These three phases can be observed in almost all European national movements, though they did not take place simultaneously. On account of its relative socio-economic backwardness and its autocratic style of government, national movements appeared later in Russia than in the rest of Europe, and in fact within the Russian Empire the phases always shifted from west to east. Furthermore, the traditional dynastic and imperial principles possessed great integrational power, and ideas of nationhood were slow to begin to compete with them.

Of fundamental importance for the character of the various national movements is the distinction which has to be made between what were known as the 'great' or 'ancient' nations, and the 'small' or 'young' nations.[3] The 'ancient' nations had an elite of their own and an unbroken tradition of statehood, high culture and high language. In the Russian Empire this applied primarily to the Russians, whose national movement pursued the aims of reforming the existing state, integrating the Russian ethnic group into a nation, and closing the gap between the elite and the masses and between high and folk culture. The Poles, the Georgians, the Crimean Tatars and also, with certain reservations, the Muslims of Asia, who had lost states dominated by their own elites only towards the end of the eighteenth century, or in the nineteenth century, and had retained an elite and a high culture, must also be assigned to the category of 'ancient nations'. These national movements usually pursued political goals, especially the reestablishment of their state, and were thus primarily directed against foreign rule by the Russians. Moreover, their elites were confronted with the task of integrating the rest of the population into one nation.

The 'young' or 'small' nations on the other hand had an 'incomplete' social structure. As a rule they lacked an elite of their own, and often they did not have an urban middle class. When peasants climbed the social ladder, they were subject to assimilation by the dominant ethnic group. The 'young' nations had either never formed a political entity of their own, or their mediaeval traditions of statehood had come to an end at the beginning of the modern age. As a rule they possessed neither a literary language of their own, nor a high culture. The 'young' nations were peasant peoples ruled by elites from a different ethnic group. They had, it is true, occasionally articulated social protest, though it was only through the national movements that they (once again) returned to the stage of political history. Their aims were primarily of a social nature, and initially directed less against the state and more against the foreign elite. The task of their national movements was to overcome the deficits mentioned above, in other words to create a complete social structure, a high culture of their own, and to bring about political autonomy. In the Russian Empire this category included most of the ethnic groups in the west (Ukrainians, Belorussians, Lithuanians, Estonians, Latvians, Finns) and the ethnic groups in the north and the east which had been part of Russia for some considerable time.

The distinction between 'ancient' and 'young' nations, and between 'great' and 'small' is reminiscent of ideal types. In reality there was a whole row of intermediate forms, for example, in the case of the ethnic groups which had managed to retain the remnants of an ancient elite and high culture. The mobilized diaspora groups of the Jews and the Armenians, which possessed an urban elite and a high culture, but not a nobility or a political entity, constitute special cases.

In what follows the national movements in the Russian Empire will be examined in a comparative way up to 1905. On the basis of Hroch's work, I place particular emphasis on the question of which broader social class, in addition to the intelligentsia, which almost always supplied the leadership, constituted the backbone of the national movement in Phase B. Its interests and its mentality – and this is the gist of my argument – had a decisive influence on the goals and programmes of the national movement, and thus also on the political culture of the nascent nations. In terms of ideal types, one could distinguish noble, middle-class and peasant national movements from this point of view. However, it is doubtful whether the national movements of the Asian ethnic groups can be adequately described with the help of these categories, which derive from European experience.

1. The Polish Noble Nation as Forerunner

The first national movement to shake the Russian Empire, and the one which shook it most forcefully, was that of the Poles.[4] It challenged not only the government, but also large sections of Russian society, and had an influence on the Lithuanians, Belorussians and Ukrainians, who had been dependent on the Polish aristocracy for centuries, and had been influenced by Polish culture. The pioneering Polish role was repeated in the crisis of the Soviet empire at the end of the twentieth century.

The Poles formed an 'ancient' nation with a tradition of statehood reaching back many centuries. This had only come to an end with the partitions of 1793 and 1795. They had an elite, a high culture and a literary language. The 'szlachta' had been the political nation of the noble republic. Despite being equal in regard to legal status, its members were strongly differentiated in social and economic terms. The noble nation comprised about 20 per cent of the ethnically Polish population and constituted the broad basis of national consciousness. This noble patriotism was already political in character in the eighteenth century, and was reinforced by the shock of the first partition. The ensuing reform movement, which was influenced by the Enlightenment and the French Revolution, led to the political mobilization of the noble nation. The fundamental problem, which was to enlarge the nation by including non-noble classes, was also discussed, though it remained unresolved. Thus the Polish national movement did not need a Phase A. Instead it started directly with Phase B, political agitation. The cultural concerns for language, literature, history and folklore typical of Phase A unfolded at the same time, and in the age of romanticism created the basis for an ethnic national consciousness. Yet the main goal of the Polish national movement was indubitably a political one: the restoration of the Polish state, the multi-ethnic noble republic, within its old borders. In the following I confine myself to the Polish national movement in the part of Poland which belonged to Russia, and pass over its interaction with activities in Prussia and Austria.

After the noble nation had failed to achieve its political goals within the context of the autonomous Kingdom of Poland, insurrectionism gained the upper hand and culminated in the two great uprisings of 1830–31 and 1863–64. They mobilized the majority of the noble nation, and also certain groups of non-nobles, and for this reason were mass movements. However, when hopes of foreign intervention were not fulfilled, and the more powerful Russian armies crushed the rebellions, the national movement on each occasion reverted to Phase B. The leaders and most important supporters of the rebellions came from the nobility, whereas the majority of the non-nobles, above all the peasants, were not prepared to fight for the aims of a noble Poland. Whilst it is true that Polish radicals realized at an early stage that a national mobilization of the peasants and their integration into the Polish nation made agrarian reform imperative, they failed to make much headway with such ideas in the noble upper class.

Yet the defeat of 1831 and the repressive measures of the Russian government accelerated the transformation of the szlachta. The social decline of the majority of nobles continued, and the group of intellectuals who emanated from the nobility gained in importance. More than 10,000 Poles, most of them members of the political leadership class, emigrated and continued the struggle 'for our and your freedom' from abroad. In addition to the political radicals, the patriotic work of Chopin or of poets such as Mickiewicz and Słowacki, who proclaimed a Polish Messianic creed, aroused enthusiasm for Poland among Europe's liberals. In the 'Great Emigration' the national movement polarized into the aristocratic wing under Adam Czartoryski and that of the democrats, who developed a revolutionary programme.[5]

Radical forces were behind a new uprising which broke out at the beginning of 1863 after reformist measures introduced by Russia had again raised hopes and led to political conflict.[6] The January rebellion was largely the work of nobles and intellectuals, though they were joined by sections of the urban population and the peasantry. Despite the fact that they had already been promised land in January 1863, it again proved impossible to mobilize the mass of the peasants. Quite a number of peasants, as had already been the case in Galicia in 1846, actually turned against the rebels. This was particularly true of the Ukrainians and Belorussians, though less of the (Catholic) Lithuanians, some of whom joined in the insurrection.

Russian public opinion had already largely condemned the November uprising of 1830, and subsequently national ideologues, such as the historian M. Pogodin, reinforced this anti-Polish mood. As a result the reaction to the uprising of 1863 was even more severe. For this reason the Russian government was able to rely on a large measure of Russian societal support when it put down the January insurrection with military force, took merciless and punitive measures against its ringleaders and initiated a repressive policy on Poland.[7]

The shock of the renewed defeat at the hands of the Russian armies, the disappointment at the lack of foreign support, the hard repressive measures, and the ensuing policy of Russification led to a reorientation of the Polish national movement. As a result of the abolition of serfdom and the accelerating pace of industrialization and urbanization of Congress Poland, the Polish noble nation was transformed into a modern nation. Partly under the influence of Poles in the Prussian part of the partitioned territories, the noble and military traditions of insurrection were replaced by 'work on the foundations', or 'organic work', which strove for a modernization of Polish society in the economic and educational spheres. In 'Warsaw positivism' it is possible to discern certain middle-class tendencies in the political methods of the national movement, even though it continued to proceed under the leadership of the nobility and the noble intelligentsia. The stated aim of re-establishing the noble republic was now joined increasingly by an ethnic national consciousness which, in order to resist Russification and the persecution of the Catholic church, made use of the Polish language and the Catholic faith as integrational factors. There did not seem to be a contradiction between political national consciousness, which wished to resurrect the multi-ethnic Polish state, and ethnic national consciousness. After all, the Ukrainians, Belorussians and Lithuanians had never been regarded as independent nations.

The integration of the majority of the Poles, the peasants, could only be achieved by solving the agrarian question. Here the initiative did not come from the national movement, but from the Russian government. The serfs in the so-called western provinces, most of whom were non-Polish, had been freed in 1861 on the basis of the Russian model. However, in November 1863 they were granted better conditions than the Russian peasants. The agrarian reform of 1864 in Congress Poland was even more generous, and even assigned land to those who had hitherto been without it. The aim of the government was to win over the peasants, and to weaken the nobility. Initially these measures proved to be a success, though in the medium term the emancipatory measures introduced by Russia made it possible to integrate the peasants into the

Polish nation. Their national mobilization was subsequently encouraged by the policy of Russification, and above all by the persecution of the Catholic church. The Polish-speaking urban middle classes had already been integrated gradually into national society. However, this led primarily to their acculturation to the nobility, and did not make them more securely middle class. The industrialization of Congress Poland also led to the gradual creation of a proletariat and (earlier than in Russia) of a socialist movement which competed with the national movement among the Polish workers.

Thus the Polish national movement, in the decades after the January uprising, succeeded in gradually transforming the noble nation into a modern nation which was beginning to include all classes of society. Towards the end of the nineteenth century, and earlier than in Russia, two national political parties with different programmes came into being. Józef Piłsudski's Polish Socialist Party (PPS) attempted to combine socialist and national aims. In this it harked back to the romantic noble tradition which wished to restore the ancient Jagiellonian kingdom by means of military uprisings. The national slogan 'through independence to socialism' managed to mobilize many of the workers, which demonstrates how great the integrational power of the noble insurrectionary tradition continued to be. Another section of the noble intelligentsia sought an alliance with the middle classes. The National Democrats led by Roman Dmowski was the first middle-class nationalist party in the Russian Empire. It developed a nation-state programme tainted with traces of chauvinism which was directed against the national aspirations of the non-Poles and against the Jews.[8]

Thus, even under the difficult conditions of Russian autocracy, the Polish national movement, towards the end of the nineteenth century, had created a mass base with numerous organizations and its first political parties. Both of the main political movements were still in favour of political independence, and the social reorganization of Polish society was subservient to this goal. Although the nobility had largely relinquished its leading social position in Russia, it retained its political leadership role. The noble nation remained the ideal of Polish society, and this was largely adopted by the non-noble classes. Thus the nobility moulded the mentality and the political culture of the Poles well beyond the nineteenth century.

In the Russian Empire the Polish national movement played a pioneering role. After 1815, and even more so after the two uprisings, it mobilized public opinion in Russia and thus had an influence on the course of the Russian national movement (see below, Section 6.4) and Russian policy on nationalities (see Chapter 7). At the same time it had a profound influence on the emancipatory national movements of the Lithuanians, Ukrainians and Belorussians, who until the end of the eighteenth century had largely been ruled by the Polish nobility in the Kingdom of Poland-Lithuania. The national movements of the peasants in the western part of the empire are discussed in the following section.

2. The National Emancipation of the Peasant Peoples

In the west of the Russian Empire there was a whole series of 'young' nations which lived under the rule of elites from other ethnic groups. They did not possess their own high culture and literary language, and had no (or no living) tradition of statehood. The Ukrainians, Belorussians, Lithuanians, Latvians, Estonians and Finns were almost exclusively peasants, and they were hardly regarded as communities in their own right by the Russian state and the upper classes. At the beginning of the nineteenth century it would have seemed fanciful to prophesy that a hundred years later these ethnic groups would have their own elites, their own literary languages and high culture, and that they would demand political self-determination.

Apart from the basic similarities of the 'young peoples', which justify a comparative analysis in this section,[9] there were important differences between the six ethnic groups. The Cossack Hetmanate provided the Ukrainians, and the Grand Duchy of Lithuania the Lithuanians (and to some extent the Belorussians), with starting-points for a tradition of statehood. These were completely missing in the case of the other three ethnic groups, though the establishment of the Grand Duchy of Finland in 1809 created the political and administrative framework for a political nation. Of even greater importance were the differences in the speed of the social mobilization of the various ethnic groups. These were the result of economic development, the abolition of serfdom and the spread of literacy. On this basis it is possible to divide the six ethnic groups roughly into two groups, and these can also be assigned to different historical spheres of influence: the Lutheran Finns, Estonians and Latvians with their central European (Swedish or

German) character, and the Lithuanians, Belorussians and Ukrainians, who were closely involved in the fate of Poland-Lithuania. To include the Lithuanians in this group might seem contradictory in view of their linguistic relationship with the Latvians and their religion, which differed from that of the eastern Slavs. However, it makes more sense than the usual grouping of the three Baltic peoples, which first came about as a result of their common fate after the First World War.

The common Lutheran religion was a fundamental reason why, around 1800, the Finns, Estonians and Latvians already had a dense network of native-language elementary schools and the highest literacy rate among all the ethnic groups of the Russian Empire.[10] The abolition of serfdom also occurred earlier than in Russia. Whilst the Finnish and Swedish peasants had always remained free, the majority of Estonians and Latvians had been serfs dependent on Baltic German landowners. In the era of the experimental reforms under Alexander I, the Estonians and Latvians received their personal freedom in 1816–19, and acquired full legal rights. However, since the landowners were still in possession of the land, the peasants continued to be dependent on them. The second stage of the agrarian reform, which made it possible to acquire land, followed from the 1840s to the 1860s, and led – together with a system whereby smallholdings were inherited undivided, which stood in contrast to the customs observed in Russian villages – to the formation of a class of prosperous Estonian and Latvian peasants and a large number of householders and agricultural labourers. The Latvian, Estonian and Finnish peasants, most of whom were literate and lived on a sound economic footing, were in a position to provide a social base for the national movements. The Catholic Latvians of Lettgallia constituted an exception to this. They were only freed in 1861 together with the peasants in Lithuania, and became part of the national movement at a considerably later date.

Phase A of the national movement, the cultural awakening of the Finns, the Estonians and the Latvians, began – after a handful of precursors in the eighteenth century – in the first half of the nineteenth century.[11] At first members of the Swedish and German elite, for example clergymen or scholars at the Universities of Åbo and Dorpat, began to take an interest in the language and the rich folk culture of the three peasant peoples. For this purpose they founded cultural societies, the Latvian Literary Society (1824), the Finnish Literary Society (1831) and the Estonian Scholarly Society (1838). Of importance for the foundation of a national consciousness and a literary language was the publication of the Kalevala epos (from 1835 onwards), which was assembled from Finnish folk poetry, and the Estonian Kalevipoeg (1857–62), written in the spirit of Romanticism on the basis of this model.

The Finnish national movement was the first to reach Phase B, which it did as early as the middle of the century. The Estonians and Latvians followed suit, though only in the 1860s. The aims of the national movements were at first primarily cultural ones, above all the question of securing the recognition of the languages of the people as official and educational languages, which was achieved step by step, though only in Finland; or the establishment of native-language secondary schools, for which money was collected. In the case of the Latvians and the Estonians the choral clubs and the mass singing festivals were especially effective in terms of mobilization and integration. Newspapers and magazines in Finnish, Estonian and Latvian were important sources of national agitation, and editors such as the Finn J. V. Snellman, the Latvian K. Valdemárs or the Estonian C. R. Jakobson became leaders of the national movements. In Phase B all three national movements split into radical and moderate wings, whereby a section of the radicals who were in conflict with the Swedish-speaking and Baltic German upper class sought temporarily to cooperate with Russia.

The Finns also led the way in regard to the transition to a mass movement. Up to the 1880s the language question continued to predominate, and here the Finnish patriots, the Fennomanes, competed with the Svekomanes, the Swedish movement of the upper class. In the 1890s Russian policies, which sought to curtail the autonomy of Finland, led to large-scale political mobilization, and in 1899 the 'Great Address' to the tsar, which was directed against the February manifesto, was signed by a very large number of Finlanders (more than 500,000, it was claimed). The national movements of the Latvians and Estonians, which reached Phase C towards the end of the nineteenth century, was primarily directed, as would also become apparent in the revolution of 1905, against the Baltic Germans. Finns, Latvians and Estonians settled in increasing numbers in the towns, where they obtained their first electoral majorities. These political currents gradually developed into political parties, whereby the middle-class national groups appeared earlier and more noticeably in Finland and Estonia, and the Social Democratic groups in the province of Livonia, which was more intensively industrialized and socially divided.

From which social groups did the activists of the three national movements come? In the case of the Estonians and the Latvians, in addition to a few (mainly Latvian) university graduates, only teachers and vergers came into question as non-German-speaking intellectuals who were in close touch with the peasants, and in the main also of peasant origin. They were joined in growing numbers by peasants and urban craftsmen. The Finnish movement was initially in the hands of clergymen (like the teachers, they lived mainly in rural areas), low-ranking civil servants, students and members of the urban intelligentsia, some of whom came from the Swedish-speaking elite. The number of teachers and peasants increased only at a later stage.

The programmes of the national movements were in keeping with the classes which supported them. Initially the goals everywhere were of a cultural nature. In this the use of Finnish at the expense of Swedish, and of Estonian and Latvian at the expense of German in education, administration and the courts was of primary importance, whereas religion did not have a great mobilizing effect, for the peasants and the upper class were Lutheran, and religious freedom had in principle never been infringed upon by Russia. On the other hand, the congruence of ethnic and social antagonisms constituted a prime mover of the national movements, so that social revolutionary and populist demands formed an important part of the national programmes. This was above all true of the Estonians and Latvians, who were primarily opposed to the privileges and the vast estates of the Baltic German nobility. It was less true of the Finnish peasants, who had always been free and in possession of political rights, and were not confronted with a self-contained upper class of wealthy landowners. Demands for political autonomy remained in the background until 1905 in the case of the Estonians and Latvians, whereas in Finland the constitutional question had dominated the national debate since the end of the nineteenth century, and increasingly integrated Swedish-speaking and Finnish-speaking citizens against Russia.

At the beginning of the twentieth century the Finns, the Estonians and the Latvians had created the basis of modern nations. A new intelligentsia and middle class which had arisen from the peasantry challenged the traditional German and Swedish elites, and gradually integrated the peasants into national society with the help of national organizations and a well-developed educational and publishing system. The newly created high cultures reached a high level within a short space of time, as is shown by the works of the Latvian poet Janis Rainis or of the Finnish composer Jean Sibelius. Initially the question of political autonomy suggested itself only in Finland, where, within the framework of the autonomous Grand Duchy, the political nation of the Finlanders, which comprised Swedes and Finns, had arisen next to the ethnic nation of the Finns.

The second group of peasant peoples in the west of the Russian Empire, the Lithuanians, Belorussians and Ukrainians, had been part of the Kingdom of Poland-Lithuania for long periods of their history, and the Polish or polonized eastern Slav and Lithuanian nobility had remained the leading social class even in the nineteenth century over the greater part of their settlement area.[12] This was not true in the case of eastern and southern Ukraine, where the Russian and russified Ukrainian nobility was predominant. Poles and Russians did not consider the Lithuanians, Belorussians and Ukrainians to be independent communities, and treated them as constituent parts of their own nation. For this reason the three ethnic groups were drawn into the Polish–Russian conflicts, and their national movements had the difficult task of emancipating themselves simultaneously from the Polish upper class and from Russia.

For the Ukrainian, Lithuanian and Belorussian peasants the abolition of serfdom came in 1861, that is, later than in the case of the Estonians and the Latvians. However, the Lithuanians in the western province of Suwałki had been personally freed (without receiving land) together with the Poles of the Duchy of Warsaw as early as 1807. Subsequently, in 1864, they were given rather generous grants of land like all the peasants in Congress Poland. It was not an accident that here in particular there arose a class of prosperous peasants which subsequently produced part of the national intelligentsia. In the case of the Ukrainians of the former Hetmanate there was a large group of former Cossacks who had never been serfs. Despite all these differences between the various regions, the abolition of serfdom created a uniform class of poor smallholders in all three ethnic groups. The primary education of the Orthodox Ukrainians and Belorussians and of the Catholic Lithuanians, unlike that of the ethnic groups of the north, which owed a debt to Protestantism, had not improved, so that their level of illiteracy was much higher.

Despite the unfavourable social and cultural preconditions, the national movement started earlier among the Ukrainians and Lithuanians, and, in a more modest manner, even among the Belorussians, than among the Estonians and Latvians.[13] In their ·case, if one discounts certain precursors at the end of the eighteenth century, Phase A, cultural reawakening, began at the beginning of the nineteenth century. The reason for this was that a handful of nobles had survived. Imbued with local patriotism, they kept alive the memory of the Cossack Hetmanate and the Grand Duchy of Lithuania. Thus, in addition to the Polish and Russian scholars of the Universities of Vilna and Kharkov (and later Kiev), members of the thoroughly polonized Lithuanian and eastern Slav minor nobility, and of the partly russified Ukrainian nobility in the former Hetmanate, began to take an interest in the language and culture of the people, and also in history, a typical sign of local patriotism. It was also of importance for the Ukrainian national movement that the greatest Ukrainian poet, the former serf Taras Shevchenko, published his popular patriotic works during this early phase, and for the Lithuanian national movement that Bishop M. Valančius spent decades promoting the cause of Lithuanian culture.

Among the Lithuanians, the Ukrainians and the Belorussians the cultural phase took far longer than in the case of the Finns, the Estonians and the Latvians, and Phase B, political agitation, began with a great deal of delay. In addition to the modernization backlog mentioned above, this can also be explained by the repressive Russian policy which began after the January uprising, in other words, a mere two years after the abolition of serfdom. This considerably hampered the cultural development and the political organization of the three national movements (see Chapter 7). For this reason it was important that there were Ukrainians and Lithuanians (but not Belorussians) who were able to promote the national cause under more favourable political conditions beyond the Russian borders. However, the Lithuanians in the eastern part of East Prussia were no more than a small group who, on account of their Lutheran religion, were distinct from the Catholic majority in Russia. Nevertheless, Tilsit and Memel became the seats of national organizations, such as the 'Lithuanian Literary Society', the place where Lithuanian publications were printed and a sanctuary for refugees. The significance for the Ukrainian national movement of what were referred to as the 'Ruthenes' in Austrian eastern Galicia was much greater. Here, as early as 1848, and then finally in the 1860s, Phase B unfolded under the leadership of the Greek-Catholic clergy, with a broad organizational network and a Ukrainian press. Interaction with Galicia was especially important for the Ukrainian national movement in Russia during the decades of political repression, and a not inconsiderable number of Ukrainian patriots from Russia, for example the historian M. Hrushevsky worked for a time in Lvov.

The Ukrainians in Russia undertook several attempts to embark on Phase B. The 'Brotherhood of Saint Cyril and Methodius', which was founded in Kiev in 1846, developed the first Ukrainian national programme. However, its handful of members and sympathizers were arrested only a year later. They included the historian M. Kostomarov and the poet Shevchenko, who, on account of his ten-year exile in Kazakhstan, and his early death, which occurred shortly afterwards, became a martyr of the national cause. The leading members of the 'Brotherhood' were able once again to disseminate their ideas in 1861– 62 in the St Petersburg magazine *Osnova* (Foundation), which was published partly in Ukrainian. At the same time groups of teachers and students at the University of Kiev ('Hromady') attempted to use a more liberal phase of Russian politics to develop a national movement. However, the Russian government suppressed them rigorously. This pattern was repeated in the middle of the 1870s. The Ukrainian national movement in Russia finally reached Phase B in the 1890s, at a time when Ukraine was already in the process of becoming industrialized.[14] For this reason the first large national organization was a political party which attempted to combine social revolutionary, social democratic and national programmes. This, the Revolutionary Ukrainian Party, which was founded in 1900, was followed shortly afterwards by two moderate parties which had emerged from the Hromada movement. However, these organizations did not become widely known, and it was the revolution of 1905 which first provided an opportunity to engage in political agitation on a larger scale. Whereas the Ukrainian national movement in Galicia had already become a mass movement by the beginning of the twentieth century, the Ukrainians in Russia first reached this stage in 1917.

The course of the Belorussian national movement, which has been insufficiently researched, resembles that of its Ukrainian counterpart. A series of ephemeral attempts at political agitation – the first by K. Kalinoŭski as early as the January uprising in 1863, another by middle school pupils in Minsk and students in St Petersburg – soon fizzled out. Phase B first began with the foundation of the populist Belorussian Revolutionary (later Socialist) Party (Hramada) in 1902. With their weak social mobility and low level of cultural identity, the Belorussians lagged behind the other five peasant peoples in the west of the Russian Empire with regard to the intensity and the popularity of their national movement.

It also took the Lithuanian movement a long time before it reached its political phase in 1883, the year in which the magazine *Aušra* (Dawn) first appeared in Tilsit. Published by a physician, J. Basanavičius, it was followed by a whole series of other national periodicals of a moderate clerical, liberal and radical kind. Here the first and most important political party was that of the Social Democrats, which had been founded in 1895, and combined socialist goals with national and separatist demands. In 1902 it was followed by a liberal Democratic Party. After a tardy start the Lithuanian national movement thus progressed considerably faster than its Ukrainian and Belorussian counterparts, and (according to Hroch) had already reached Phase C in the 1890s. It had certainly reached this stage in the revolution of 1905.

The greater effectiveness of the Lithuanian national movement, when compared to the Ukrainians and Belorussians, was due, amongst other things, to the fact that it was supported by a large part of the lower Catholic clergy, who functioned as mediators to the peasants, mobilizing them against the policy of Russification. On the other hand, the Orthodox clergy, who were very much part of the state church, only participated occasionally in the Ukrainian movement. In the light of the rudimentary (and non-native-tongue) educational system, teachers did not play a great role in the three ethnic groups before 1905. Scholars disagree on the question of the significance of the regional nobility for the national movements. It seems that the Shemaitic minor nobility and the descendants of the Cossack nobility were of importance in that they transmitted national values. Thus the greater part of the small secular intelligentsia, of the students, middle-school teachers and (in Lithuania) doctors, who in all three cases provided the majority of the leaders of the radical national movement, came from the nobility (and also from the Orthodox clergy and the Lithuanian peasantry). The grammar schools and universities forged the cadres of the national movement.

The programmes of the movements were very much shaped by cultural concerns, and concentrated on promoting the language of the people and the educational system. This was especially important in the case of the Ukrainians and Belorussians, who were regarded as part of the Russian nation by the government and the majority of Russian society. They were only able to define the fact that they were different from the Russians through their languages, and not through their religious denomination. However, the difference in religious denomination coincided with social antagonisms to the Polish nobility and the urban Jewish population. Membership of the Uniate church was the most important focal point of the Ukrainian national movement in Galicia. Yet in Russia, where it was banned in 1839, it only constituted a defining feature of nationality in the case of certain Belorussians. In contrast, the Lithuanians were clearly distinct from the Russians and Poles on account of their language, though only from Russia with regard to their Catholic religion. As in the case of the Poles, the anti-Catholic policy of the tsarist government reinforced the anti-Russian religious component of the Lithuanian national movement, whereas the secular intelligentsia distanced itself from the Polish nobility through language and social slogans. The Lithuanian movement was clearly divided into a clerical and a secular wing. Under the influence of the Polish, Jewish and Russian socialist movement, all three movements, in order to mobilize the peasants, attempted to combine national and revolutionary agrarian aims. In the case of the Ukrainians and the Belorussians, however, the Russian revolutionary movement became a successful rival of the national movements, and many young intellectuals joined Russian parties in order to help them to bring down the tsarist regime. In the case of the Ukrainians the predominant populist movement, which already found expression in the work of Shevchenko, and later in that of the important theorist M. Drahomanov, was complemented at a relatively late stage by a conservative tendency which took its bearings from the old upper class and the tradition of statehood.

By 1905 the Lithuanians, Ukrainians and Belorussians had not progressed as far on the path towards becoming a modern nation as the Finns, the Estonians and the Latvians. They were still largely peasant-based, the towns remained Polish, Jewish and Russian, and the intelligentsia with a national consciousness was a small group. Only in the case of the Lithuanians had a section of the clergy joined the national movement, thereby increasing its influence on the peasants. Despite the various bans, the Lithuanians had also managed to create a high language and provide secret tuition, whereas the Ukrainians and Belorussians found it rather more difficult to press the claims of their languages against Russian, which was closely related to them. However, despite what was still a small base, Ukrainian and Lithuanian high cultures had already reached their first peaks, which were documented by the work of the poets T. Shevchenko, L. Ukrainka and J. Maironis.

In the course of the nineteenth century the national movements of the six peasant peoples in the west of the Russian Empire developed at different speeds. The delay was due to both social preconditions, such as the time and circumstances of the abolition of serfdom, and the level of education, and the differing political circumstances, above all, in the Polish context, the considerably more repressive Russian policy. All six ethnic groups claimed political sovereignty after the Russian Revolution and set up nation states. The Finns have been able to keep their state to this day, whereas the Estonians, the Latvians and the Lithuanians lost theirs in 1940 as the result of the Hitler–Stalin pact. The Ukrainians lost their state after a few years, the Belorussians after a few months. It is noticeable that this pattern corresponds to the degree of nation-formation of these ethnic groups before the First World War. Although foreign policy factors often played a decisive role in addition to the internal preconditions, this coincidence is not an accident.

The national movements of the Estonians, the Latvians, the Lithuanians, the Ukrainians and the Belorussians, which were directed against the Soviet centre at the end of the twentieth century, displayed numerous parallels to their predecessors in the nineteenth century. This, for example, was evident in forms of organization, such as the 'singing revolution' in the case of the Estonians and Latvians, in focal points, such as the Catholic clergy in Lithuania, in the different national programmes, in the specific inter-relationship between the Ukrainians in Galicia and those in the east and in the way in which the Ukrainians and the Belorussians distanced themselves from the Russians.

The Christianized ethnic groups on the middle Volga, in the Urals, in northern Russia and in Siberia resembled the 'young' peasant peoples in the west of Russia in typological terms. They also lived almost exclusively in rural areas in self-contained village or clan communities, and did not possess a written language and high culture, did not have their own tradition of statehood, and no more than remnants of a degraded upper class. In contrast to the peasants in the Baltic region and in Poland-Lithuania, the vast majority of them had never been serfs, and had belonged to the category of state peasants. In most of the tribes animism continued to play an important role with regard to their value concepts and social relationships after they had been Christianized. Thus their social and political opponents were not so much the landowning upper classes. Rather, they were the Russian bureaucrats and priests.

Protonational protest had expressed itself as early as the first half of the nineteenth century in apostasy from the Orthodox church, as for example in the case of the Cheremis, or in nativist Messianic movements, as in the case of the Mordvinians.[15] However, their 'national awakening' subsequently began with Russian scholars and the first members of an intelligentsia educated in Russian schools, such as the Zyrian I. Kuratov.[16] Important impulses also came from N. I. Ilminsky's missionary programme, which first created (Cyrillic) alphabets for numerous languages and founded native-language schools (see Chapter 7.3). From these schools came 'national revivalists' such as I. Iakovlev, the Chuvash who was encouraged by Lenin's father. Together with Russian ethnographers and linguists they sparked off the cultural phase of the national movements by studying the manners and customs of the various ethnic groups and by publishing educational books and the first literary works in the languages of the peoples. These ethnic groups, which in socio-economic and socio-cultural terms had hardly been touched by modernization, had taken their first steps towards nation building around 1900. Certain groups such as the Iakuts were already on the brink of Phase B by the time of the 1905 revolution, whereas others, such as the Mordvinians, the Votiaks and most of the small peoples of Siberia, had hardly been affected at all by the national movement.

3. The Georgian and Armenian National Revolutionary Movements

The mixture of ethnic and religious groups in the south and the east of the Russian Empire can only to some extent be analyzed using the models of 'ancient' and 'young' nations, and of noble and peasant national movements derived from the European context. Whereas it is true that they were affected by national movements virtually without exception in the course of the nineteenth and early twentieth centuries, these assumed specific forms corresponding to the specific social, political and cultural and religious circumstances, and this in turn makes it imperative to enlarge the typology. The Christian ethnic groups of Transcaucasia approximated most nearly to the European patterns.

In the Russian Empire the Georgians, together with the Poles, represent the type of the ancient noble nation: a very numerous, socially differentiated class of nobles, on whom the peasant serfs were dependent, living traditions of statehood and an ancient Christian high culture.[17] After the Georgian nobles, like their Polish counterparts, had unsuccessfully revolted against Russia on several occasions, they were integrated into the Russian nobility and state by the reforms of Vorontsov. Loyalty towards the tsarist regime bore fruit during the abolition of serfdom in 1864–71, which was more favourable to the nobility than in Russia, let alone than in Poland. The Georgian peasants received their personal liberty, but were granted the use of only a part of the nobles' land. The consequences for the peasants were low levels of land ownership, growing dues and taxes and continuing dependence on the landowners. Thus, as in Russia, the abolition of serfdom did not bring with it a genuine social emancipation of the peasants.

Since the Georgians did not possess an urban middle class worth mentioning, their national movement, right into the twentieth century, remained largely a matter of the nobility and of the intelligentsia which emanated from the nobility.[18] In the years between 1830 and 1850 the Georgian nobility reacted to Russian rule and to the challenge of Russian culture, which had been reinforced by Vorontsov's reforms, with a romantic kind of patriotism which led to a revival of interest in the Georgian language, and of Georgian literature, folklore and history. After the incorporation of the Georgian into the Russian church, the Georgian language became particularly important as a criterion of demarcation, especially since it was continually discriminated against by the Russian authorities.

In the 1860s the cultural Phase A merged into the political Phase B, which was initially in the hands of a rather conservative noble national movement. For decades its most important representative was Prince I. Chavchavadze, an important writer and publicist, the chairman of the 'Society for the Promotion of Literacy in Georgia', and in numerous other functions 'the uncrowned king of Georgia'.[19] The gradual economic decline of the nobility and the economic and political pre-dominance of the Armenian middle class in the cities, especially in Tiflis, prompted the sons of the nobility to look for more radical answers. These were supplied by the Russian intelligentsia at the universities, and ranged from a kind of liberalism based on the western model to revolutionary agrarian populism, and finally to Marxism.

A number of young Marxists, including the later President of

Georgia, N. Zhordaniia, returned to Georgia from university at the beginning of the 1890s. A decade later the Georgian Social Democrats had become the most important focal point of the national liberation movement. In contrast to the Georgian Party of Social Federalists founded in 1903, which sought to achieve national autonomy, they had managed not only to organize the small Georgian proletariat, but also to secure the support of many educated people, and even of numerous Georgian peasants. The majority joined the Mensheviks after 1903, whereas a minority, including the young I. Dzhugashvili (the later Stalin), joined the Bolsheviks. It is surprising that the majority of the Georgian noble nation should have supported not a national movement, but a basically internationalist and revolutionary one which in the first instance was not dedicated to the national liberation of Georgia. After all, a revolution would have adversely affected the nobility in particular. However, the Georgian nobility, which was socially in decline, obviously considered Marxism to be a suitable weapon in its struggle with its opponents, the Armenian middle class and the Russian bureaucrats. The progressive radicalization of the noble intelligentsia has striking parallels with Russia: the 'repentant aristocrats', who were separated from the mass of the peasantry by a deep social and cultural gap, had to atone for their sins by serving the people.

At the beginning of the twentieth century the Georgians were subjected to intense national and social mobilization. Nevertheless, they continued to be divided into a poor peasant majority and a nobility which was as socially predominant as it had always been. Led by the Mensheviks, the national movement, which was fragmented into several factions, was confronted with the difficult task of bridging this gap.

The Armenians, the second of the Christian peoples of Transcaucasia, were fundamentally different from the Georgians. They possessed only a small nobility (most of it in Nagorny Karabakh), and their elite comprised the rich merchants of the towns and the clergy, whereas the majority of the peasants continued to be dependent on Muslim masters even after the agrarian reform of 1870.[20] In addition to this there was the fact that the majority of Armenians did not live in Russian Armenia, but in the rest of Transcaucasia, in the Ottoman Empire and in diaspora communities dispersed throughout Asia and Europe.

A national renaissance had already begun in the eighteenth century as a result of numerous cultural activities in the diaspora, for example those of the Mekhitarists in Venice and the Armenian community in

Madras in India. This movement within the church became secular in the course of the nineteenth century, and the high language and literature, and the press and educational system were gradually modernized. The proponents of Phase A of the national movement were, in addition to the clergy and the urban middle classes, the new secular intelligentsia, which was increasingly influenced by Russian ideas.[21]

In 1878 disappointment at the fact that the European powers had not guaranteed the Armenians in the Ottoman Empire the autonomy they had been promised led to the politicization of the national movement. Armenian students who had been influenced by the Russian revolutionary movement, especially by the 'Narodniki', founded the Socialist organization Hnchak (Bell) in Geneva in 1887, and the 'Revolutionary Armenian Federation' (Dashnaktsutiun) in Tiflis in 1890. The principal aim of both of these national revolutionary organizations was the liberation of the Armenians in the Ottoman Empire. Their socialist programme remained vague and was overlapped by a great deal of revolutionary activity. Following the example of the Russian and Bulgarian terrorists, they organized attacks and revolts in the Ottoman Empire, which in turn led to anti-Armenian acts of repression such as the massacres of 1894–96.

It was only as a result of the policy of Russification, which came to a head in 1903 with the confiscation of the property of the Armenian church, that the Armenian revolutionaries also turned against the tsarist regime. On the wave of a spontaneous national and religious protest movement, which was also supported by the Katholikos, they organized demonstrations and attacks on Russian bureaucrats. Whereas the Union of Armenian Social Democrats, which had been founded at the beginning of the twentieth century, attracted only a few supporters on account of its internationalist aims, the national revolutionary Dashnak Party (Dashnaks), which was allied to the Russian social revolutionaries, managed after 1903 to create a mass movement in Transcaucasia which had as its stated aim the liberation not only of the Armenians in the Ottoman Empire, but also of those in Russia. For this reason the Armenian national movement was of the 'insurrectionary type' (as defined by Hroch) which was widespread in the Ottoman Empire.[22]

Thus the Armenians had also reached Phase C of the national movement well before the revolution of 1905. Its moving force was not the leading social group, the largely loyal middle class with its pro-Russian national conservative or liberal orientation, but the small secular intelligentsia, which successfully mobilized wider classes and gradually transformed the religious community into a modern nation. The specific terrorist character of its national populism was based, as in the case of the Bulgarian Haiduks, on ancient traditions of guerilla warfare, though it was also influenced by Russian terrorism. As regular attacks by Armenian groups demonstrate, it has survived to this day.

The question arises of whether the Armenians as a mobilized diaspora group represent a specific type of national movement. A comparison with the Jews and the Tatars shows that in all three ethno-religious groups a middle class and clergy existed as possible focal points, though the national movements nonetheless assumed different characters. Whilst the Jews in Russia reacted to increasing discrimination and the start of the pogroms with socialism and Zionism (see Chapter 7.4), the Tatars must be examined together with the other Muslims in Russia.

4. Islamic National Consciousness

The Muslim ethnic groups which lived in the Russian Empire in the second half of the nineteenth century were a heterogeneous mixture with regard to their ethnic composition, economic organization and political and cultural traditions. The Volga Tatars, Azerbaidzhanis and Middle Asians, who had been sedentary for many centuries, stood in contrast to nomadic herdsmen such as the Kazakhs and the mountain peoples of the Caucasus. Whereas the Volga Tatars had already belonged to Russia for three centuries, the Middle Asians first came under Russian rule after 1860. Whilst it is true that the vast majority of the Muslims in Russia spoke a Turkic language, language was less important for their ethnic identity than lifestyle and religion. The question was, which role would Islam play once these peoples had been confronted with modernization and the national principle? Would it be merely that of a factor of their national consciousness, or would it be that of a primary integrational ideology which overlapped other identities?

The Volga Tatars were the first Muslims in Russia to be influenced by the national movement, which was in the hands of merchants and Islamic clergy who were in close contact with the Muslims of Russia's eastern regions.[23] Ideas for a national rebirth also came from the University of Kazan, which had been founded in 1804. A printing press for Tatar publications (in Arabic script) was set up, and the university introduced tuition in Tatar and encouraged Oriental studies. Repeated waves of apostasy among the baptized Tatars were evidence of the unbroken dynamism of Islam. National revivalists such as Sh. Merdzhani and K. Nasiri subsequently laid the foundations for research into Tatar history and folklore, for a new Volga Tatar literary language, and a Tatar publishing system which flourished throughout the nineteenth century. The small Volga Tatar intelligentsia, most of whom were descended from merchants or mullahs, countered renewed missionary attempts and in general met the challenge of Russo-European modernism with an Islamic reform movement which sought to renew Islamic Tatar culture without endangering its identity in the process. Islam, the theory went, was to adapt to the modern world primarily with the help of a reformed Tatar-speaking educational system.

Subsequently a Crimean Tatar developed a 'new method' of teaching (usul al-jadid), a term which lent its name to Jadidism, the Muslim reform movement in Russia.[24] In 1883, after having lived in Moscow, Paris and Istanbul, Ismail Bey Gaspirali (Gasprinsky), who came from an impoverished Crimean Tatar noble family, founded the journal *Tercuman* (Interpreter) in Bakhchisarai, which in the following three decades spread his ideas throughout Russia and beyond. The ossified Islamic school was to adopt the methods and thinking of the west, and Jadidism sought to achieve a synthesis of Islamic culture, modern science and technology and western ideas of progress. Lessons were no longer to be exclusively in Arabic, and Gaspirali countered the Volga Tatar reforms – not only in his *Tercuman* – with the idea of a common language based on modernized Ottoman Turkish, which was designed to facilitate the integration of the Muslims in Russia under the slogan 'Unity of Language, Thought, and Action'.

By the beginning of the twentieth century, Jadidism had numerous adherents, primarily among the Volga and Crimean Tatars, but also among the Bashkirs and the Muslims of Azerbaidzhan, whereas the Muslims of Middle Asia, who maintained less intense contacts with Russia, remained faithful to conservative Islam. Jadidism, which might be described as forming Phase A of a religious national movement, was largely unpolitical and Gaspirali and his supporters remained loyal subjects of the tsar. Yet the Crimean Tatar reformer had already formulated the two concepts which were to become important in the political phase of the Muslim national movement, pan-Islamism and pan-Turkism, which in Russia were not mutually exclusive, and in fact reinforced each other. On the other hand, there were signs even before 1905 of the beginnings of centrifugal ethnic national movements.

Around 1900 the Volga Tatars were the spiritual leaders of the Muslims in Russia. Numerous Jadidist schools and Tatar printers turned Kazan into a centre of reformist Islam with a charismatic power that went far beyond the borders of Russia.[25] Within Russia itself the Tatars exercised a particularly powerful influence on the Bashkirs, who used Tatar as their high language, and who did not have an independent national movement before 1905. In Kazan Tatar intellectuals began to form circles with political goals after 1885, and as early as the beginning of the twentieth century these were already in favour of a synthesis of Islam and socialism. They were opposed by moderate liberal and pan-Islamic groups which in 1905 joined forces to form the Union of Muslims (Ittifak). Tatar national tendencies also continued to flourish. In conservative form they had begun to appear from 1862 onwards in the Sufic sect of the Waisites, who, harking back to their Volga Bulgar heritage, rejected the authority of the official clergy and the Russian state.[26] Yet the conflicts between the pan-Islamic and Tatar national movements were still to come.

The pattern of events was similar in the case of the Crimean Tatars, and the predominant movement of the Jadidist followers of Gaspirali was gradually challenged by more radical 'Young Tatars'. As a result of the linguistic and historical links with the Turks in the Ottoman Empire, the interaction with the latter's reform movement was particularly close.

On the other hand, the Muslims of Azerbaidzhan, who were even more closely related to the Turks in linguistic terms, were divided into an Ottoman orientation (especially among the Sunnis), and the traditional Persian orientation (among the Shiites).[27] A small secular intelligentsia which had its origins mainly in the upper class of landowners and merchants and had been moulded by Russian schools, had already begun to initiate Phase A of the national movement around the middle of the nineteenth century. Its most important member, the writer F. A. Akhundov, helped the vernacular known as 'türki' to hold its own against Persian and classical Azeri, and from the 1870s onwards the first periodicals in this language began to appear in Baku. Jadidism also had its supporters here, and from the 1890s onwards the first political groups of a pan-Turkic, pan-Islamic, liberal and socialist character appeared, though only the Islamic programmes struck a chord with large sections of the population. Thus the Muslims of Azerbaidzhan, an 'ancient nation' with its own elite, had already embarked on Phase B of the national movement before the revolution of 1905. The question was: which of the competing directions would gain the upper hand, and what would be its relationship to the Volga Tatars, the other strongly mobilized Muslim group?

Since the eighteenth century the Kazakhs had been under the economic and spiritual influence of the Volga Tatars, whose mullahs had strengthened Islam among the nomadic herdsmen, and towards the end of the nineteenth century had also disseminated Jadidism. From the 1860s onwards a number of Kazakh intellectuals who had been to Russian schools began to oppose the cultural predominance of the Tatars. Their first representative, Ch. Valikhanov, who came from a high-ranking noble family, proposed a radical secular programme orientated on Russo-European culture.[28] Valikhanov had served as an officer, was acquainted with influential Russians such as Dostoevsky, and wrote his orientalist works in Russian. The enlighteners who followed him subsequently created a Kazakh literary language which was designed to replace Tatar, and published the first literary works in Kazakh. At the same time there were tendencies directed against the authorities and the greater influx of settlers which hoped to establish a Kazakh identity by combining Islam and nomadic traditions.

All these currents had merely reached the northern areas of the steppe, whereas the Kazakhs in the south continued to be influenced by the Islamic centres of Middle Asia. Here Jadidism and the concept of the nation found little resonance before 1905, and in both Russian Turkestan and the realms of Bukhara and Khiva the old literary languages (Chagatai and Persian) and the traditional support for conservative Islam and its educational system continued to predominate.[29] The Muslim mountain peoples of the Caucasus continued to be characterized by their tribal structures and Sufic communities, and were also largely impervious to outside influences. Yet as early as the second half of the nineteenth century in certain ethnic groups there appeared, in addition to the traditional folk singers, intellectual 'awakeners' influenced by Russia, especially in the case of the Ossetians, the majority of whom were Christians.[30]

Among the Muslims in Russia there were in the second half of the nineteenth century numerous varieties of national and religious rebirth. As a rule the impetus came from the west, primarily from Russia, and to some extent from the Ottoman Empire. The movements spread among the various ethnic groups with varying degrees of intensity. The Islamic reform movement initiated by the Muslims in Russia exercised an influence far beyond the borders of the tsarist empire, reaching as far as India and Egypt. Until the end of the nineteenth century cultural aims (language, education, literature, the reform of Islam) predominated. However, the movements then became more political, and this was considerably intensified in the revolution of 1905 (see Chapter 9). Tension between pan-Islamism and specific nationalisms began to become apparent even in the decades preceding 1905, and it was destined to remain topical throughout the whole of the twentieth century.

In the course of the nineteenth century the lamaist Buriats also developed a 'religious national consciousness' which was comparable to that of Islam.[31] They responded to the threat posed by Christian missionaries and eastern Slav colonization with a movement which sought to achieve a renaissance and modernization of traditional Buriat culture. Folk poetry, chronicles and fiction were published both in the ancient Mongol literary language and in a newly devised Buriat written language which employed the Cyrillic alphabet. This cultural movement was in the hands of lamas and individual intellectuals raised in Russian schools such as the teacher and ethnologist M. Khangalov, who was influenced by the Russian narodniks. At the beginning of the twentieth century the movement was reinforced by protests against the policy of colonization and administrative reforms, and had spread to a considerable section of the Buriats, especially the lamaists of Trans-Baikalia.

5. The National Awakening of the Russians

In addition to the non-Russian ethnic groups of the Russian Empire, the Russians themselves were also affected by the national movement in the nineteenth century. The Russians formed an 'ancient' nation with a nobility, a high culture and a literary language, and – unlike the other nationalities of the empire – a state.[32] However, Russia was not a Russian nation state, but a multi-ethnic empire legitimated in dynastic and estate terms, and whilst it is true that the imperial patriotism which integrated it had certain elements in common with the ethnic consciousness of the Russians (the Orthodox church, a common history and culture), the supranational traits predominated. During the reign of

Nicholas I E. Kankrin, the Minister of Finance, suggested renaming Russia 'Romanoviia' after the ruling dynasty, or 'Petroviia' after Peter the Great, and among the three fundamental principles of Russia coined at the same time by S. Uvarov, the Minister of Education, the Orthodox religion and autocratic government were more important than the rather vague 'narodnost' (nationality).[33] The main goal of the government continued to be the maintenance of the territorial, political and social status quo in the multi-ethnic empire, and for this it needed the traditional supranational ideology of integration. Thus the dynamic national concept, which wished to mobilize and integrate the lower social classes, and proclaimed the notion of loyalty to the nation instead of to the ruler, was forced by its very nature to oppose the autocratic system. Subsequently, it is true, there was some interaction between the two political models. However, official imperial patriotism and societal Russian national consciousness cannot be regarded as being identical.

Modern Russian national consciousness arose in the eighteenth century, initially as a reaction to the westernization of Russia and the undue degree of foreign influence in the wake of Peter the Great's reforms. Subsequently it was also influenced by the Enlightenment and Romanticism.[34] An intelligentsia that gradually detached itself from the nobility now no longer, as in the past, sought Russian identity and culture in the state and in religion, but in the Russian language, Russian history and in the Russian people. In the case of the Russians one also sees the elements which are typical of Phase A of a national movement – the creation of a standardized literary language and of Russian literature, the publication of folk poetry and historical works. The noble intelligentsia attempted to bridge the profound gap between traditional folk culture and the westernized high culture of the elite with an ethnically based type of national consciousness.

In the 'Patriotic War' against Napoleon imperial patriotism and ethnic national consciousness mingled and spread to wider sections of the population. A national conservative current took its cue from this closing of ranks with the state, and N. M. Karamzin became its most important proponent. He and other historians began to regard the Russian empire as a nation state, and to criticize Alexander I's concessions to the Poles. As a result of the November uprising in 1830, the Polish question became the catalyst of a type of Russian national consciousness which was loyal to the state, and sought to combine ethnic and political elements.[35]

But after 1815 an increasingly large section of the Russian intelligentsia turned its back on the state, and moved towards the societal national movement with its political aims. The intellectual and political movements of the ensuing decades have been analyzed by Soviet and western historians largely in teleological terms, that is, as revolutionary (or reactionary) movements. In doing so they have overlooked the fact that at the same time they were all national movements which pursued the goal of restructuring Russia on the basis of the western model, of supporting the introduction of civil rights, of mobilizing the lower classes and integrating them into a Russian national society.[36] These aims were impeded by the autocratic political system, the system of serfdom and widespread illiteracy. Thus the national movement quite logically linked national with social and political demands, and was directed against the state which resisted the implementation of such changes.

In the programmes of the Decembrists, whose attempted uprising failed in 1825, national goals such as the transformation of Russia into a democratic and centralist nation state based on the French model already played a great role.[37] The next generation of the intelligentsia reacted to the challenge of the modernization of Europe and to the new ideas which emanated from it with the question of Russian identity.[38] The answer of the Slavophiles was to return to the Orthodox church and the idealized Rus before the time of Peter the Great. That of the Westernizers was to make demands for middle-class and liberal reform. Both Slavophiles and Westernizers wanted to integrate the Russian peasants into the nation and idealized their commune constitution, both were in favour of civil rights and against serfdom. Both branches of the national movement – and in this they resembled the noble national consciousness of the Poles – acquired a Messianic character, and assigned to the Russians a special role among the nations of Europe.

The defeat in the Crimean War, the abolition of serfdom, political reform, the renewed confrontation with the Polish national movement in the January uprising and in general the accelerated modernization of Russia all led to a considerable intensification and polarization of the Russian national movement from the 1860s onwards.[39] The radicals once again turned their attention to overcoming the cleavage between themselves and the lower classes, and the narodniki 'went to the people' in order to mobilize the Russian peasants. This agrarian socialist movement had an obviously national streak in its idealization of the peasants and their repartitional commune. It was no different in the case of the liberals, who continued to pursue the goal of the democratic transformation of Russia, and in doing so called into question the traditional special rights of the non-Russians in the west.

An extreme kind of Russian nationalism also came into being in the aftermath of the Polish uprising of 1863. Its most important spokesman was the influential journalist M. N. Katkov. It was linked with a kind of pan-Slavism oriented towards imperial foreign policy, which found eloquent expression in N. Ia. Danilevsky's work *Russia and Europe*.[40] The proponents of this integral nationalism were sections of the elite, of the intelligentsia, and the rising urban middle classes, though at the time of the Polish uprising in 1863–64 and of the Balkan war of 1877–78 it proved possible to mobilize wider sections of the population. As a rule the extreme nationalists were loyal to the state, the imperialist foreign policy and assimilatory policy on nationalities of which they supported. However, their goal, the nation state, constituted a challenge for the autocratic system.

Thus the government regarded all the wings of the Russian national movement, which called into question traditional legitimacy and the autocratic system's monopoly on power, with reserve and suspicion. The revolution of 1848 had made the government acutely aware of the democratic and emancipatory potential of the national principle. Furthermore, traditional dynastic imperial patriotism was still deeply ingrained in the mass of the population. The Russian peasants were integrated by their 'belief in the tsar', loyalty to the autocratic system and to the Orthodox church, not by an ethnic national consciousness.[41] On the other hand, nationalist currents had also made their way into the bureaucracy and the army, and had an influence on policymakers. Faced with the dual challenge of the revolutionary movement and the national aspirations of the non-Russians, it seemed apposite to co-operate with the proponents of extreme Russian nationalism in order to divert attention from the social and political conflicts in Russian society. Thus the Russian government increasingly attempted after 1863, and especially after 1881, to make use of nationalism in order to stabilize its rule. This showed itself above all in its policy on nationalities (see Chapter 7). Partly influenced by aggressive kinds of nationalism in other European states, traditional imperial patriotism gradually acquired the character of imperial nationalism. However, despite all the concessions which it was prepared to make, relations between the tsarist state and the Russian national movement remained ambivalent.

As a result of the influence of modernization, the challenge of the west, and of the national movements of the non-Russians, national ideas also spread amongst Russians in the nineteenth century. However, this did not lead to a monolithic national movement. Rather, it led to a whole series of alternatives. In the second half of the century revolutionary currents began to be more important than national ones. This was partly due to the fact that the repertoire of national thinking gradually became discredited among the democratic intelligentsia. It was increasingly losing its function as an emancipatory and democratic force in the other ruling nations of Europe, and was being employed for the purposes of systemic stabilization. But in Russia none of the national groupings entered into a stable coalition with the state, which on the whole adhered to the pre-national dynastic and estate-based imperial patriotism. The contradictions between state and society, and between the elite and the lower classes were simply too great to allow the national movement to perform its task in Russia of integrating the various social groups into a nation.

6. Summary

Almost all of the ethnic groups in the Russian Empire were affected by national movements in the course of the nineteenth century. From the end of the eighteenth century it is possible to observe Phase A, cultural awakening, in the west, and later in the south and the east, whereas as a rule Phase B, political agitation, was reached with some delay only in the second half of the nineteenth century, and in part as late as the revolution of 1905. Before 1905 there were mass national movements only among the Poles, Russians, Finns, Estonians, Latvians, Lithuanians, Georgians and Armenians.

The national movements made their greatest impact in the case of the 'young' peasant nations in the west, which were transformed into modern nations with an elite and a high culture of their own, whereas the Christianized ethnic groups in the east and north of Russia reached Phase A at the most. The intelligentsia of the 'ancient' nations, most of whom came from the elite, mobilized new sections of society and integrated them to form a modern nation. In the first instance this was achieved by the Poles, and to some extent by the Armenians and Georgians, whereas in the case of the Russians dynastic imperial patriotism inhibited the spread of ethnic national consciousness, and the cleavage between the elite and the lower classes prevented the formation of a modern nation. The Muslims and Lamaists in Asia responded to the challenges of the national principle and modernization with reform movements of a religious nature which also assumed a national character.

It is certainly possible to apply Hroch's three-phase schema, though, in the case of the 'ancient' nations, modifications are necessary. In typological terms the distinction between the peasant national movement of the 'young' peoples and the noble national movement proves to be especially useful for the west of the Russian Empire. The movements of the 'ancient' nations (of the Poles, the Russians and above all of the Georgians and Armenians) can also be termed 'revolutionary'. In the case of the Russians, there was also an increasingly aggressive 'imperial nationalism' which emanated from the supranational imperial patriotism. On the other hand, Russia's Muslims and Lamaists must be assigned to the category of 'religious national movement'.

The explosive power of political self-determination was present, at least in a rudimentary form, in all of the national movements. They possessed a strong democratic and emancipatory potential which called into question the basic tenets of the tsarist autocracy. This became clearly apparent in the 'springtime of the peoples' which Russia experienced in the revolution of 1905 (see Chapter 9.1). Yet the state was forced to respond even earlier to the national challenge, which wished to replace loyalty to the ruler with loyalty to the nation. It did so primarily with its policy on nationalities, which in turn had an effect on the national movements. This forms the subject of the next chapter.

Notes

1   Karl W. Deutsch, *Nationalism and Social Communication. An Inquiry into the Foundations of Nationality*, 2nd edn (Cambridge, Mass., 1966); Ernest Gellner, *Nations and Nationalism* (Oxford, 1983). See also Lemberg (1964); Heinrich August Winkler (ed.), *Nationalismus* (Königstein im Taunus, 1978); Otto Dann, 'Der moderne Nationalismus als Problem historischer Entwicklungsforschung', in Dann (1978), pp. 9–21.
2   Hroch (1963); Hroch (1985).

3   In addition to Hroch see also Seton-Watson (1977), pp. 6–9; Józef Chlebowczyk, *On Small and Young Nations in Europe* (Wrocław, 1980).

4   On the Polish national movement see Tadeusz Łepkowski, *Polska – narodziny nowoczesnego narodu 1764–1870* (Warszawa, 1967). Short summary in 'La formation de la nation polonaise moderne dans les conditions d'un pays démembré', *APH* 19 (1968), 18–36; Stefan Kieniewicz, 'Le développement de la conscience nationale polonaise au XIXe siècle', idem, pp. 37–48; Kurt Georg Hausmann, 'Adelsgesellschaft und nationale Bewegung in Polen', in Dann (1978), pp. 23–47; Peter Brock, 'Polish Nationalism', in Peter F. Sugar and Ivo J. Lederer (eds), *Nationalism in Eastern Europe* (Seattle and London, 1969), pp. 310–72; Davies, vol. II (1981), pp. 3–79; Andrzej Walicki, *Philosophy and Romantic Nationalism: The Case of Poland* (Oxford, 1982). In general terms see Hoensch (1983); Rhode (1980); Wandycz (1974).

5   Hans-Henning Hahn, 'Die Organisationen der polnischen "Großen Emigration" 1831–1847', in Otto Dann and Theodor Schieder (eds), *Nationale Bewegung und soziale Organisation*, vol. I, *Vergleichende Studien zur nationalen Vereinsbewegung des 19. Jahrhunderts in Europa* (Munich and Vienna, 1978), pp. 131–279.

6   R. E. F. Leslie, *Reform and Insurrection in Russian Poland 1856–1865* (London, 1963); Stefan Kieniewicz, *Powstanie styczniowe* (Warsaw, 1972).

7   See below, Chapter 7.2.

8   Hans Lemberg, 'Polnische Konzeptionen für ein neues Polen in der Zeit vor 1918', in Theodor Schieder (ed.), *Staatsgründungen und Nationalitätsprinzip* (Munich and Vienna, 1974), pp. 85–104.

9   Compare the trail-blazing studies by Hroch (1968, 1985) with empirical research concerning the Finns, Estonians and Lithuanians, to which I return in the following.

10 On the following in general see Jutikkala (1964); Wuorinen (1965); Thaden (1981); Wittram (1954); Raun (1987); Kruus (1932); Spekke (1951).

11 On the national movements see Hroch (1968, 1985); Loit (1985), mainly about the Estonians; Alapuro (1988); Pentti Renvall, 'Zur Organisations- und Sozialgeschichte der finnisch-nationalen Bewegung im 19. Jahrhundert', in Theodor Schieder (ed.), *Sozialstruktur und Organisation europäischer Nationalbewegungen* (Munich and Vienna, 1971), pp. 155–67; Hösch (1991), with details of recent Finnish literature; Toivo U. Raun, 'The Latvian and Estonian National Movements, 1860–1914', *SEER* 64 (1986), 66–80; Trapans (1979); Andrejs Plakans, 'Peasants, Intellectuals, and Nationalism in the Russian Baltic Provinces, 1820–90', *Journal of Modern History* 46 (1974), 445–75.

12 In general on the following see Hellmann (1966); Čeginskas (1959); Ochmański (1967); Subtelny (1988); Krupnyckyj (1943); Vakar (1956); *Historyia* I, II (1972); Wasilewski (1916).

13 In general on the national movements see Hroch (1968), (1985); on the Lithuanians some contributions in Loit (1985); Manfred Hellmann, 'Die litauische Nationalbewegung im 19. und 20. Jahrhundert', *ZfO* 2 (1953), 66–106; Jerzy Ochmański, *Litewski ruch narodowo-kulturalny w XIX wieku (do 1890 r.)*, (Białystok, 1965);

Leonas Sabaliunas, *Lithuanian Social Democracy in Perspective 1893–1914* (Durham and London, 1990); Vladislas Kaupas, *Die Presse Litauens. Unter Berücksichtigung des nationalen Gedankens und der öffentlichen Meinung*, vol. I (Klaipeda, 1934); A. Bulat, 'Litovtsy', in Kasteliansky (1910), pp. 426–44; Wandycz (1974), pp. 239–59, 303–7; on the Ukrainians Andreas Kappeler, 'Ein "kleines Volk" von 25 Millionen: Die Ukrainer um 1900', in *Kleine Völker* (1991), pp. 33–42; Kappeler (1992b); Ivan L. Rudnytsky, 'The Role of the Ukraine in Modern History', in *SR* 22 (1963), 199–216; Ivancevich (1976); on the Belorussians Anton Novina, 'Belorussy', Kasteliansky (1910), pp. 382–95; Jan Zaprudnik, 'National Consciousness of the Byelorussians', *Byelorussian Statehood* (1988), pp. 9–31; Peter Scheibert, 'Der weißrussische politische Gedanke bis 1919', *Jomsburg* 2 (1938), 335–54; Wasilewski (1925) on the Lithuanians and Belorussians.

14 On this see Boshyk (1981).

15 Kappeler (1982b), pp. 386–92.

16 See Sarkisyanz (1961); *Ocherki Komi* (1955), pp. 275–85; *Istoriia Chuvash.* (1966), pp. 217–30; *Istoriia Sib*, III (1968), pp. 423–31.

17 On the following see Suny (1989); Lang (1962); Salia (1983).

18 On the Georgian national movement see Suny (1989) and Z. Avalov, 'Gruziny', in Kasteliansky (1910), pp. 469–93.

19 See Fairy von Lilienfeld, 'Die Heiligsprechung des Ilia Chavchavadze durch die Georgisch–Orthodoxe Kirche am 20.7.1987', in *Kleine Völker* (1991), pp. 66–75.

20 See in general *Histoire* (1982); Gregorian (1972); Parsamyan (1972).

21 On the Armenian national movement see also Anahide Ter Minassian, 'Nationalisme et socialisme dans le mouvement révolutionnaire arménien (1887–1912)' in Suny (1983), pp. 141–84.

22 See Hroch (1985), pp. 28 f.

23 On the following see Bennigsen and Lemercier-Quelquejay (1960), pp. 26–41; Rorlich (1986), pp. 48–103, a summary of which is contained in 'Eine oder mehrere tatarische Nationen', *Die Muslime* (1989), pp. 63–79; Dzhamaliutdin Validov, *Ocherk istorii obrazovannosti i literatury tatar (do revoliutsii 1917 g.)* (Moscow, 1923); Ia. G. Abdullin, *Tatarskaia prosvetitel'skaia mysl' (Sotsial'naia priroda i osnovnye problemy)* (Kazan, 1976). For a more general account see Hans Bräker, 'Die muslimische Erneuerungsbewegung in Rußland', in *Rußlands Aufbruch* (1970), pp. 181–98; Zenkovsky (1960), pp. 8–40; von Mende (1936), pp. 21–91; Bennigsen and Lemercier-Quelquejay (1981), pp. 30–42.

24 See Edward J. Lazzerini, 'Reform und Modernismus (Djadadismus) unter den Muslimen des Russischen Reiches', *Die Muslime* (1989), pp. 35–47; Edward J. Lazzerini, 'Ismail Bey Gasprinskii (Gaspirali): the Discourse of Modernism and the Russians', in Edward Allworth (ed.), *Tatars of the Crimea. Their Struggle for Revival* (Durham and London, 1988), pp. 149–69; Alan W. Fisher, 'Ismail Gaspirali, Model Leader for Asia', in Edward Allworth (ed.), pp. 11–26; Bennigsen and Lemercier-Quelquejay (1964), pp. 35–42.

25 Bennigsen and Lemercier-Quelquejay (1960), pp. 52–8; *Ocherki Bashk.* I(2) (1959), pp. 263–77.

26 Halbach (1989), pp. 229–31.

27 Swietochowski (1985), pp. 23–36; Bennigsen and Lemercier-Quelquejay (1964), pp. 27–31; *Istoriia Azerb.*, II (1960), pp. 271–87, 314–405; Audrey Altstadt-Mirhadi, 'The Azerbaijani Bourgeoisie and the Cultural-Enlightenment Movement in Baku: First Steps Toward Nationalism', in Suny (1983), pp. 197–207.

28 Kermit E. McKenzie, 'Chokan Valikhanov: Kazakh Princeling and Scholar', *CAS* 8(3) (1989), pp. 1–30.

29 Hélène Carrère d'Encausse, 'The Stirring of National Feeling', in Allworth (1989), pp. 172–9; Hayit (1971), pp. 185–9.

30 *Istoriia narodov* (1988), pp. 336–80.

31 L. Shternberg, 'Buriaty', in Kasteliansky (1910), pp. 601–24; Sarkisyanz (1961), pp. 379–87; Hundley (1984), pp. 151–75; Egunov (1963); *Istoriia Buriat.* (1954), pp. 448–6.

32 With regard to the whole chapter see Rogger (1961/62); Andreas Kappeler, 'Bemerkungen zur Nationsbildung der Russen', in Kappeler (1990), pp. 19–35.

33 See Riasanovsky (1959) for Kankrin's comment, p. 139. With regard to Uvarov's three principles see source excerpt in German in *Die Orthodoxe Kirche* (1988), pp. 503–5.

34 Hans Rogger, *National Consciousness in Eighteenth-Century Russia* (Cambridge, Mass., 1960).

35 See Riasanovsky (1959).

36 This idea already appears in Lemberg, vol. I (1964), pp. 228–31.

37 Hans Lemberg, *Die nationale Gedankenwelt der Dekabristen* (Cologne and Graz, 1963).

38 Nikolay I. Zimbajew, 'Zur Entwicklung des russischen Nationalbewußtseins vom Aufstand der Dekabristen bis zur Bauernbefreiung', in Kappeler (1990), pp. 37–54; Nicholas V. Riasanovsky, *Russia and the West in the Teaching of the Slavophiles. A Study of Romantic Ideology* (Cambridge, Mass., 1952).

39 On the following see Geyer (1977), especially pp. 43–54.

40 See Edward C. Thaden, *Conservative Nationalism in Nineteenth-Century Russia* (Seattle, 1964); Katz (1966); Lukashevich (1965); Picht (1969); Michael Boro Petrovich, *The Emergence of Russian Panslavism 1856–1870* (New York, 1956).

41 See Daniel Field, *Rebels in the Name of the Tsar* (Boston, 1976); Jeffrey Brooks, *When Russia Learned to Read. Literacy and Popular Literature 1861–1917* (Princeton, 1985), pp. 214–45.

7

The Reaction of the State: Policy on Nationalities 1831–1904

U P TO THE first decades of the nineteenth century, Russian policy towards the non-Russian peoples of the empire adhered fundamentally to traditional patterns. Securing the power of the state without and within was given priority. When rebellions endangered this goal, the government intervened vigorously and with military force. When the non-Russian elites demonstrated their loyalty to the tsar and maintained the socio-political stability in their territories, they were accepted as partners. The government cooperated with them, guaranteed their privileges, and adhered to the well-tried practice of flexible pragmatism and tolerance. Under Alexander I this policy was applied in particular to the regions in the west, which were to serve as models for reform in the rest of Russia. However, eurocentric ideas brought about a greater cleavage between the Russians and the ethnic groups in the east and in the south.

In the course of the nineteenth century a number of new factors appeared on the scene, and these changed the traditional policy patterns. The two most important ones have already been discussed in the previous chapter. The national movements of the non-Russians, first and foremost that of the Poles, and national consciousness in sections of Russian society began to jeopardize the basis of the dynastic legitimation of the multi-ethnic empire and its estate-based and pre-national policies. To this was added the increasingly urgent need to modernize the empire, something that was linked to an administrative, judicial and social process of systematization and regularization. Finally, Russia was affected by changes in the rest of Europe, where the model of the ethnically uniform nation state was gaining ground. That this could also be applied in multi-ethnic empires was demonstrated by the policy of germanization which followed the unification of Germany, and the policy of magyarization which occurred after the Austro-Hungarian 'Compromise' of 1867.

Russian policy was influenced by these new forces, and the tendency towards swift administrative, social and cultural integration became stronger, and culminated towards the end of the nineteenth century in what was known as the policy of russification. However, the widely held view among historians that there was such a thing as a simple and one-dimensional policy of russification which began at the latest under Nicholas I needs to be differentiated in what follows in both regional and chronological terms.[1] Furthermore, it needs to be asked to what extent, as the title of this chapter suggests, there was in fact a *single* Russian policy on nationalities. In the following I shall make sparing use of the term 'policy on nationalities', and will use the concept of 'russification' not as it is normally used, that is, to describe the policy of integration as such, but only with regard to its linguistic and cultural aspects. It needs to be remembered that conservative forces continued to be powerful, and that the tsarist autocracy, despite its many concessions to national currents and political pressure, sought to preserve the pre-national dynastic and estate-based political structure, which alone was capable of maintaining socio-political stability.

1. The Stabilization of Power through Repression under Nicholas I

The government of Nicholas I (1825–1855) was characterized by the priority of the need to uphold the system, though this did not exclude controlled reforms.[2] The key events of the Decembrist revolt (1825), the revolutions of 1830 in France, Belgium and above all Poland, and the revolutions of 1848 increased the emperor's fear, and that of the power elites, of revolutionary turmoil, and the desire to preserve Russia from the debilitating influences of western liberalism, nationalism and socialism. Within this framework the government strengthened bureaucratic controls and cooperated more closely with conservative forces, such as the Orthodox church. Religion once more gained in importance as a line of cleavage between Russians and non-Russians.

On the basis of these premises the severe reaction to the November revolt in Poland was only logical. It signified a continuation of traditional policies in that it punished the disloyal Polish elite, which had repaid the magnanimity of the Russian tsar as revealed in the liberal constitution of the kingdom with ingratitude, and had called into question the political status quo established in 1815. Intervention in Poland was also supported by a large section of educated Russian society, and even Pushkin defended the introduction of Russian troops in 1831 by stating that Russia had to defend its position of leadership in the Slav world against the Poles: 'Who will triumph in the unequal strife, the haughty Pole or the trusty Russian? Will the Slav rivers flow into the Russian sea? Or will it dry up? That is the question.'[3]

Russia first dealt with the rebels insofar as they had not emigrated to western Europe.[4] Numerous estates were confiscated and granted to Russians, and many nobles were now required to do military service in Russia. Then the Russian government rescinded most of the concessions that it had made to the Kingdom of Poland under Alexander I. The Constitution of 1815 was suspended, the Sejm and the Polish Army were abolished, and the University of Warsaw closed down. Although it is true that in the Organic Statute of 1832 the special administrative status of the Kingdom and civil freedoms were theoretically confirmed,[5] in practice Nicholas I, his viceroy I. F. Paskevich and the top Russian bureaucrats now ruled with the help of emergency powers. The integration of the Kingdom of Poland into the Russian Empire began to be implemented in the next two decades, which saw the introduction of provincial subdivisions, of the Russian currency, weights and measures, of the Russian penal code, the Russian police corps, of Russian censorship, and direct supervision of the schools. The Catholic church in Poland was now discriminated against in favour of its Orthodox counterpart. A strong military presence, which found symbolic expression in the newly built Warsaw citadel, ensured Russia's control over Poland.

In Congress Poland there continued to be vestiges of autonomy, a largely Polish civil service, the special status of the szlachta, a largely Polish legal system, the use of Polish as the official language and the Uniate church. However, the Polish areas annexed between 1772 and 1795 (where the uprising had been supported primarily by Poles) were incorporated even more firmly into the Russian Empire after 1831. This included the abolition of the Lithuanian Statute and the introduction of Russian law, the ending of regional self-rule, the introduction of the Russian language in the administration, the judiciary and schools (though here Polish soon made a comeback), the centralization of the educational system, the closure of the University of Vilna, the opening of the Russian University of Kiev and the suppression of numerous Catholic monasteries. The Polish nobility, which, especially on the lower levels, differed from the Russian model, was brought more into line with the Russian nobility, and many of the landless minor nobles who had not yet been degraded were gradually assigned to the tax-paying category of 'odnodvortsy' (smallholders).[6] On the other hand, the social status of the middle-rank nobility and loyal magnates was preserved. Despite its numerical reduction, the Polish nobility remained the socially predominant force not only in Congress Poland, but also in large parts of the 'western provinces' even after 1831. The fact that the noble elite was not deprived of its power and degraded despite these severe anti-Polish measures highlights the systemic maintenance priorities of policy under Nicholas I.

The Lithuanians, Belorussians and Ukrainians now gradually came to the notice of the Russian government, and there were attempts to contain the influence of the Catholic church and Polish culture on these peasant peoples. This aim was supported by the above-mentioned measures, which were designed to promote the use of Russian instead of Polish, and by the final suppression of the Uniate church in the 'western provinces' in 1839.[7] All of the Belorussians and Ukrainians in the 'western provinces' who had been in communion with the Catholic church were now incorporated into the Orthodox church. Some attempts were also made to convert Lithuanian and Belorussian peasants who were Catholics, though these met with little success. The social position of the Ukrainian, Belorussian and Lithuanian peasants remained unchanged. The majority continued to be serfs dependent on Polish nobles. This also meant that, in spite of the attempts at containment, the influence of Polish language and culture continued to predominate in the reign of Nicholas I, not only in the Kingdom of Poland, but also in the 'western provinces'.

That the government of Nicholas I was primarily concerned with preserving the status quo, and not with cultural and linguistic russification, also becomes apparent in policy towards other regions. Nevertheless, in the Baltic provinces it encouraged attempts by the newly founded Orthodox bishopric of Riga to convert the Latvians and Estonians. Between 1845 and 1847 about 100,000 Latvian and Estonian peasants, who hoped that this might improve their economic and social situation, converted to the Orthodox church. Plans to promote the Russian language and Russian teachers in the schools were implemented to a much smaller extent. The predominant position of German culture and of the Baltic German elite (here and in the empire's bureaucracy and military) was preserved, and the codification of provincial law completed in 1845, which confirmed their traditional privileges, emphasized that Nicholas I wished to continue to cooperate with the loyal conservative Baltic Germans.[8] The same was true of Finland, whose internal autonomy, which was based on a consensus with the loyal elite and on a constitutional guarantee, was not changed.[9] It was also true of the Armenians.

In the reign of Nicholas I the church and the Orthodox faith once again became important pillars of conservative state policy. The effect of this was felt in more severe policies towards the Jews, and in a revival of missionary activity. The reversion to Islam of baptized Tatars, and a great sacrificial animist feast staged by the Cheremis were the reasons why the Holy Synod, in 1828, resumed its missionary activities, since 'unity in faith' also made for 'unanimity' in the state.[10] Whereas it is true that the state reaffirmed the ban on Orthodox Christians who wished to convert to another religion, and on non-Orthodox missionary work, it gave only lukewarm support to the church in its missionary attempts among the ethnic groups of the middle Volga, the far north and Siberia, so that it met with little success. Plans to introduce certain reforms among the state peasants of the middle Volga were met with vociferous protests, especially from the Chuvash and Cheremis. They were also directed against decrees concerning the mandatory planting of potatoes.[11] The disturbances were put down by force, though they demonstrated that any change in the status quo brought with it certain risks.

There were no significant changes under Nicholas I in the policy towards the Crimean Tatars and the foreign colonists. However, in 1828 the autonomy of Bessarabia was substantially curtailed, and subsequently the Romanian language was banished from the administration and the schools.[12] This measure, which was unusual for the 1840s, should probably be seen in the context of the strengthening of the church, which wanted the tsar's Orthodox subjects to attend Russian-speaking schools. A similar policy of assimilation was also pursued in the case of the Georgians, even though it was precisely in the 1840s that policy on Transcaucasia shifted from a centralist strategy of integration to the traditional kind of flexible pragmatism (see above, Chapter 5.1).

All in all the reign of Nicholas I did not signify a fundamental change in policy towards the non-Russians of the empire. Top priority continued to be accorded to social and political stability, and to cooperation with loyal non-Russian elites. However, upholding the system was considerably more important than in the first two decades of the century. This became evident in support for or at least tolerance of church activities. It also meant that the government responded to rebellions with great severity. Moreover, the reaction to the November uprising of 1830–31 also included a policy to promote the cultural and linguistic integration of the Poles and the peasant peoples dependent on Polish nobles. These new Russian national elements were supported by large parts of the bureaucracy and educated society. However, under Nicholas I they did not become the determining policy-making factor. Rather, they were subordinated to the traditional dynastic and estate-based legitimation of the autocratic system, and towards the end of his reign they had once again become more moderate.

2. The Policy of Forced Integration in the West after 1863

When, after the death of Nicholas I, his son Alexander II ascended to the throne in 1855, great hopes were placed on him. The young emperor certainly fulfilled some of these expectations, and has thus gone down in Russian history as the liberator of the serfs and as a reformer. However, in the national history tradition of some of the empire's non-Russian ethnic groups, the image of Alexander II is a negative one. The tsar is remembered not as a liberator, but as an oppressor.

The course of events was once again determined by the Polish question.[13] After 1856 the government of Alexander II made a number of concessions to the Poles, especially to those in the Kingdom. There was an amnesty for those who had taken part in the November uprising, the state of siege was lifted, the vacant position of the Archbishop of Warsaw was filled, and an institution of higher education was re-established (the Medical Academy in Warsaw). The government attempted to return to cooperation with the loyal Polish elite and, as in Russia, to discuss with it the question of the abolition of the serfdom. For this purpose an 'Agricultural Society' was founded, and within a short space of time it became a large national organization with a membership of 4,000. The relaxation of Russian pressure and the hopes that were thus awakened led to a rapid upsurge in the national revolutionary movement, and in 1861 there were bloody clashes in

Warsaw between demonstrators and Russian security forces. Russia then attempted to regain control of the situation by introducing moderate reforms.

Marquis A. Wielopolski, who had been appointed head of a Polish civilian government, announced a programme designed to restore a measure of autonomy to the Kingdom of Poland which took its bearings from the Organic Statute of 1832, and included Polish self-administration and a Polish school system. However, Wielopolski was unable to secure broad support for this plan within Polish society, and the January uprising of 1863 put an end to the attempt at 'reform from above' in Poland.

The Russian reaction to the January uprising repeated the scenario of 1831. The retention of power and systemic stabilization once again received top priority, and the methods of oppression were considerably more severe under the reformist tsar than under his conservative father. In Congress Poland and in the 'western provinces' about four hundred rebels were executed, about 2,500 were sentenced to hard labour, and about 20,000 deported to Russia and Siberia or sent to join penal companies. About 3,500 estates belonging to Polish nobles were confiscated.

Russian policy towards Poland in the ensuing decades pursued the goal of solving the Polish question once and for all through repression and forced integration. As had already been the case after 1830, this received support from a majority of the Russian public, which was seized by a new wave of hatred for Poles. A few demonstrations of solidarity, for example, by Alexander Herzen, were confronted by a far greater number of anti-Polish utterances. Whereas Slavophile pan-Slavs such as Ivan Aksakov and Iurii Samarin, whilst portraying the Polish national movement and the foreign Latin cultural principle as a dangerous challenge to Russian leadership claims, did not call into question the existence of the Polish nation in a cultural sense, Russian nationalists such as M. N. Katkov simply called for action to be taken against the rebellious Poles: 'Between these two related nationalities (the Russians and the Poles) history has always placed the fateful question of life and death. The states were not simply rivals, but enemies who could not live next to each other, enemies to the end.'[14]

In the years after 1863 the last vestiges of the Kingdom of Poland's special status were abolished step by step. Even the name Poland was eradicated, for from this time on the region was called the 'Vistula region' (Privislinskii krai). The Polish authorities were abolished, Polish bureaucrats were replaced with Russian ones and Polish as an official language was replaced by Russian. Whereas the judiciary was brought into line with the Russian system, Polish civil law, which was based on the Code Napoléon, was retained. Russian policy was primarily directed against the Polish nobles, the most important supporters of the uprisings. With the reforms of 1864, which were favourable to the peasants, it proved possible to weaken the social and economic position of the majority of the landed nobility, whereas the magnates were less affected by the measure. With this policy, which was propagated by liberals such as N. A. Miliutin, Russia departed from the well-tried estate-based principle of cooperation with foreign elites, and for the first time tried to play off the peasant lower classes against the aristocracy in a systematic manner. In the medium term this attempt did not prove to be a success, partly on account of the uncompromising attitude towards the Catholic church, which also mobilized the Polish peasants against Russia.

The repression of the Catholic clergy, who were deemed to be the second main pillar of national resistance, also went against the traditional policy of tolerance and cooperation with non-Orthodox ecclesiastical organizations controlled by Russia.[15] Most of the bishops were dismissed, the property of the church was secularized, monasteries were closed down and there was a ban on contacts with Rome. Conversely, the Orthodox church received a great deal of support. In 1875 Kholm, the last Uniate diocese in Russia, was incorporated into the Orthodox church, and its members were forced to convert to the Orthodox faith. The goal of cultural russification was now added to that of administrative integration. For the first time Russia now proceeded to mount a systematic assault on what had hitherto been accepted as a high language. It was decreed that in middle and upper schools (with the exception of religious instruction) Polish was to be replaced by Russian, and in 1879 the use of Polish in school buildings (even during the breaks) became a punishable offence. In 1885, under Alexander III, Russian was also introduced in elementary schools as the language of instruction. The University of Warsaw, which had been founded in 1869, was solely Russian speaking, and was largely boycotted by the Poles. This linguistic russification, from which only the Catholic church was exempt, did serious damage to the Polish educational system.

In the 'western provinces', which now tended to be divided into a 'north-western region' (Lithuania-Belorussia) and a 'south-western region' (Ukraine on the right bank of the Dnepr), Russian policies were directed primarily against the Catholic clergy and the Polish nobility, whose position had already been weakened after 1831. In his memoirs N. M. Muraviev, the Governor-General of Vilna who was responsible for implementing this policy, stated, 'I decided to cut through the Gordian knot, the corrupting influence of the *pane* on the rural population.'[16] The local modifications to the abolition of serfdom in favour of the peasants of 1863 and the ban on the purchase of land by Poles or Catholics served the same purpose, as did the decision not to introduce the zemstvo self-government system, which would have assigned new tasks to the regional nobility. The repressive measures against the Catholic church and the elimination of the Polish language in the administration, the educational system and even on invoices and business signs were designed to put an end to the hitherto unbroken predominance of Polish culture and the Polish language, and their influence on the Lithuanian, Belorussian and Ukrainian peasants. Their places were to be taken by the Orthodox church, the Russian language and Russian culture. There was no question in St Petersburg of providing support for the languages of the peasants.

This was the background to the russification measures connected with the Lithuanian, Belorussian and Ukrainian languages, which were primarily directed against the Polish nobility.[17] Furthermore, the Russian government and the majority of the Russian public were now of the opinion that the 'western provinces' had been 'Russian since time immemorial' and that 'the Russian nationality and the Orthodox church' had to be 'restored throughout the land'.[18] The Belorussians and Ukrainians, and even the Lithuanians, were deemed to be 'western Russians' and 'Little Russians', that is, parts of the Russian people who had to be protected against the Poles. With the Polish uprising the national and cultural revivalist movements of the Ukrainians, Belorussians and Lithuanians, which for a long time had been regarded sympathetically by the Russians, suddenly acquired a political significance, and were described by the Russian press as a 'Polish' or 'Jesuitical intrigue', or as the work of 'fanatical Polish agitators'.[19]

The government reacted by banning all three languages. As early as the summer of 1863, interior minister P. Valuev, in a secret circular, banned the printing of books in Ukrainian, with the exception of literature, but including religious and educational works, as well as tuition in Ukrainian. His reasons, which emphasized the connection with the 'political plans of the Poles', also reflected the opinion of large sections of Russian society. 'There has never been, there is not, and there cannot be an independent Little Russian language. The dialect spoken by the man in the street is Russian, and has merely been corrupted by the influence of Poland.'[20] This was followed a short time later by a ban on the printing of works in Belorussian, and of Lithuanian publications using 'Latin-Polish letters', as well as imports of such works (from East Prussia). Lithuanian publications using Cyrillic letters were permitted. However, the Lithuanians considered them to be a symbol of the Orthodox church, and they did not come into widespread use.

At the same time the Catholic church was subject to discrimination, and about 60,000 Catholics, most of them Belorussians, were converted to the Orthodox faith. In 1876 the resurgent Ukrainian movement, which was the result of a certain amount of liberalization, prompted the government to reinforce the language ban in the circular of Ems, which forbade the import of publications in Ukrainian (from Galicia), as well as theatrical performances and lectures in Ukrainian. Although these were primarily anti-Polish measures, the publications ban had an adverse effect on the Ukrainians, Lithuanians and Belorussians: for decades it impeded popular education and communication in the national language, something which was of crucial importance for the national movements.

Under Alexander III (1881–1894), whose reign was characterized by political reaction and 'defensive modernization', policy towards the Poles, Lithuanians, Belorussians and Ukrainians remained fundamentally unchanged. On the one hand the conservative government for a time sought once again to cooperate with loyal Polish nobles, and retracted certain measures. Thus there was an amnesty for the Poles deported in 1864, and the ban on dictionaries and theatrical performances in Ukrainian was lifted. On the other hand the Russian authorities now first began in a resolute way to implement forced integration with measures such as the dismissal of Polish bureaucrats, the encouragement of Russian ownership of land in the 'western provinces', or the introduction of Russian as the language of instruction in Polish village schools. The police quelled every kind of opposition with great severity. Thus the resistance of the Lithuanian population to the destruction of the monastery church of Krazhiai, which was carried out at the orders of the Russian authorities, was put down with much bloodshed. There was no change in direction during the first ten years of the reign of Nicholas II (1894–1917). However, a modified policy began to become apparent in 1904, when the government once again permitted the printing of Lithuanian publications which used Latin letters. It was then forced to make fundamental concessions a year later as a result of the revolution.

From 1863 onwards the policy towards the Poles, the Ukrainians, the Belorussians and Lithuanians openly pursued the goal of cultural and linguistic russification for the first time in Russian history. Acting in accordance with a large section of public opinion that had been mobilized by Russian national ideas, the government jettisoned the majority of its traditional political principles. The question arises of whether this marked a fundamentally new era in Russian policy on nationalities. In order to provide an answer to this, we must include the other ethnic groups in Russia in the analysis.

The 1860s also saw the introduction of changes in the Baltic provinces.[21] However, it was not the government, but the Russian national press, which, having been mobilized by the January uprising and the rise of Prussia, opened the attack on the special status of the Baltic Germans. The debate reached its climax in 1868 when a Slavophile, Iurii Samarin, published the first instalment of his work on the 'border areas of Russia' (okrainy Rossii), and a Dorpat historian, Carl Schirren, responded a year later with a 'Livländische Antwort' (Livonian Reply). Samarin mounted a vehement attack on the outmoded privileges and supposedly separatist tendencies of the Baltic Germans, and their germanizing influence on the Estonians and Latvians. He demanded that the Russian government should abolish their special rights, that it should promote the Russian language and the Orthodox church, and that it should liberate the Estonian and Latvian peasants from oppression by German nobles. With equal eloquence Schirren defended the historic rights of the Baltic Germans (but not of the Latvians and Estonians). His apology for the ancient estate-based order and the superiority of German and western culture also included some national and russophobic remarks.[22]

The government regarded with displeasure the attack on the estate-based order in the Baltic provinces, which corresponded to its own principles, and on the Baltic German elite, with which it had always cooperated closely. As early as 1867 Alexander II had assured the Baltic German nobility that 'he spat on this press, which was trying to place it on the same level as the Poles'.[23] Samarin, who had already been imprisoned in the 1840s for a few days because of an earlier attack on the Baltic Germans, and had been admonished personally by Nicholas I (significantly, he had published his new book not in Russia, but in Prague), was reprimanded, as was Schirren, who was deprived of his professorship. Despite the fact that the Minister of Education, D. A. Tolstoi, was in favour of a cultural russification of Poland, and succeeded in promoting the Orthodox church and the teaching of Russian, the educational system based on the vernacular and above all the German university of Dorpat remained, and the government even tolerated the reversion to Protestantism of thousands of converted Estonians and Latvians. At the same time administrative pressure on the Baltic provinces increased. In 1867 Russian was introduced as the official language of state institutions, and the adoption of the Russian municipal statute of 1870, which occurred in 1877, created new municipal self-government bodies in which Estonians, Latvians and Russians were henceforth represented in far greater numbers than had previously been the case. On the other hand, the judicial and zemstvo reforms were not introduced in the Baltic provinces until 1881.

Yet it is first possible to speak of a systematic policy of standardization in the Baltic provinces in the reign of Alexander III, who was strongly influenced by the Procurator of the Holy Synod, K. P. Pobedonostsev. As early as 1881, when he ascended the throne, the emperor had for the first time failed to confirm the Baltic privileges. A commission headed by Senator N. A. Manasein then introduced a series of measures which undermined the special status of the Baltic provinces. Russian, as the official language, was introduced in many more areas, such as the internal operation of municipal administration; the Russian police system was introduced in 1888, and the Russian judicial reforms (with Russian as the language of the courts) in 1889. There was greater pressure on the Lutheran church, and especially on the Orthodox Estonians and Latvians who had returned to the Lutheran faith, and the clergy who had encouraged them to take this step. Nor was the highly developed school system spared. In schools Russian became the language of instruction at all levels, with the exception of religious instruction and the two lowest classes of primary schools (Volksschule). The corporations of the nobility (Ritterschaften) reacted to this by closing numerous schools. In 1893 the German university of Dorpat was transformed into the Russian university of

Iurev. Only the theological faculty continued to use German. Despite massive protests from the Baltic Germans, hardly any of these measures were rescinded until 1905, not even under Nicholas II. Nevertheless, here the period of forced integration came to an end in 1895.

Thus in the 1880s and the early 1890s the special status of the Baltic provinces, which had been established in 1710, was considerably curtailed. However, it was not completely abolished. The zemstvo reform was not introduced, and the German-speaking and self-governing corporations of the nobility remained, albeit with reduced competencies. The Lutheran church was also able to hold its own, and the leading social and economic position of the Baltic Germans remained unchallenged. The process of standardization, which began later and was implemented in a less rigorous manner, did not have as profound an effect here as in the case of the Poles, Ukrainians and Lithuanians. However, it provoked resistance from the Baltic German elite, which was bent on protecting its ancient privileges. The German national and anti-Russian tendencies which surfaced among the educated 'literati' reinforced Russian fears of German irredentism in the Baltic provinces.

Many Latvians and Estonians regarded Russia as an ally in their struggle against the Baltic German elite, whose power they hoped to break by means of administrative reforms. Leading figures of the Latvian and Estonian national movements sought support in St Petersburg, and tens of thousands of peasants signed petitions demanding the introduction of reforms, the abolition of Baltic German privileges and the partitioning of the estates. The subsequent introduction of the reforms weakened the Baltic German upper class, and brought a series of improvements for the Estonians and Latvians. However, there were negative reactions to linguistic russification, which also affected the Estonian and Latvian primary schools. Yet at this point russification was no longer a threat to the national identity of the Estonians and Latvians.

Russian policy towards the Baltic provinces was essentially contradictory. On the one hand it wished to introduce reforms against the wishes of the conservative Baltic Germans, and promoted the emancipation of the Estonians and Latvians. On the other hand it wished, especially during a period of modernization, to prevent socio-political destabilization, and this, in the Baltic provinces, could only be achieved with the help of the Baltic German elite. In the 1880s the government was influenced even more strongly by Russian national groups, who, as a result of the deterioration of Russia's relations with the German Empire, were against granting privileges to the Baltic Germans at the expense of Russians, Estonians and Latvians. However, the national principle called into question the dynastic and estate-based legitimation of the autocratic system, to which the majority of the Baltic German upper class continued to adhere for reasons of ancient loyalty. The Russian government was aware of the dangers which emanated from relinquishing the traditional priority of securing its power with the help of foreign elites. Yet it was only the revolution of 1905 which made the Russian ruling elite and the Baltic German upper class realize that they needed each other.

Finland became the object of the Russian policy of standardization far later than Poland and the Baltic provinces.[24] Alexander II, and subsequently Alexander III, continued the well-tried consensus-based cooperation with the Finlander elite. It is true that the two monarchs still did not give constitutional guarantees on the special status of Finland, though they made a whole series of new concessions. In 1863, the year of the Polish uprising, the Finnish diet was convoked for the first time since 1809, and its statutes, which were promulgated in 1869, permitted it to embark on a great deal of legislatory activity. Finland received a currency of its own in 1865, and in 1877 this was converted to the gold standard, and thus separated from the rouble. The reforms were not imposed on Finland. In fact, in 1878 the Grand Duchy received a largely independent army. Even in the 1880s, at the time when the administrative and cultural integration of the Baltic provinces was proceeding apace, there were further concessions.

At the end of the nineteenth century the Finlanders had not only progressed a long way towards becoming a modern nation, Finland also possessed a number of attributes of independent statehood, and as a rule its upper class interpreted the concessions made by the tsar as constitutional guarantees. From 1889 onwards the Russian national press began to attack Finland's unique status, and in the 1890s the Russian government began to bring Finland into line with the interests of the whole state. Thus in 1890 Finland's independent postal service was abolished. On the other hand, plans to unite its customs and currency with Russia, two other visible symbols of its independent statehood, never materialized. In 1894 Nicholas II, like his predecessors, swore an oath to protect Finland's basic rights. However, in the years that followed the pressure on Finland increased. In 1899 the Ministry of War's demand that the Finlandish army should be integrated into the Russian army then led to Nicholas II's February manifesto, which withdrew from the diet any responsibility for laws affecting the interests of the Russian Empire. This in turn called into question the autonomy of Finland.[25] In the years that followed the Finlander army was disbanded, and the use of Russian introduced in the upper echelons of the administration, and in the Senate. In 1903 Governor-General N. I. Bobrikov, who had been installed in 1898, was given dictatorial powers. The new Russian policy, which, after nine decades, diverged from the principles of pragmatic consensus, was perceived in Finland as a breach of the constitution, and led to violent resistance. This reached its climax in the assassination of Bobrikov in 1904. Russia continued to attempt to implement the programme of the February manifesto after 1905, so that the gap between the Finlanders, who had been mobilized in national and political terms, and Russia grew ever wider.

Thus all of the areas in the west inhabited by non-Russians became the targets of a policy of forced integration in the course of the nineteenth century. However, a comparative analysis shows a considerable difference in the timing of the various phases, for the policy of standardization in Finland began almost 70 years later than in Poland. There were also considerable differences with regard to the motives and methods, and the extent and intensity of assimilation to Russia. Before embarking on an overall examination of the 'policy of russification', I intend to include the ethnic groups of the south and the east and the Jews in the comparison.

3. Traditional and Innovative Elements in Policy towards the Ethnic Groups in the East and the South

The ethnic groups in the south and the east of the Russian Empire were extremely diverse with regard to language, religion, lifestyle, economic patterns and social structure. Whereas the Volga Tatars had been subjects of the tsar since the sixteenth century, the Turkmen had been part of the Russian Empire only since the 1880s. For this reason it is self-evident that Russian policy towards these ethnic groups could not be uniform in the second half of the nineteenth century. In what follows I examine the question of the extent to which there were tendencies towards centralization, increased integration and cultural russification. Since I have already discussed the policy towards the Kazakhs and the Muslims in Middle Asia during this epoch in Chapter 5, I shall largely exclude them here.

Around the middle of the century new waves of apostasy among baptized Volga Tatars, and unrest among the Tatars during the Crimean War led to counter-measures by the government. The Tatar self-governing body in Kazan (tatarskaia ratusha) and tuition in Tatar at the grammar schools were abolished, the Centre for Oriental Studies at the University of Kazan was transferred to St Petersburg and there were compulsory resettlements and compulsory baptisms.[26] When the government had been forced to admit that both the mission and the violence had once more proved to be a failure, policy again shifted to a course of action designed to integrate foreign elites with the help of flexible methods. The new feature, for the first time since Stephen of Perm in the fourteenth century, was that an attempt was made to attract non-Christians to the Orthodox church through instruction in their native langauges or, since this was more topical, to strengthen the baptized non-Russians in their faith and to shield them against the influence of Islam.

The most important advocate of this new method of integration was N. I. Ilminsky, an orientalist, who was active in Kazan from 1846 onwards, initially at the Theological Academy, and subsequently at the University.[27] In the course of his many travels he had become acquainted with the languages and the everyday life of the Volga Tatars, Bashkirs, Kazakhs and Turkmen, and with the Islamic centres in the east. In 1863 he established in Kazan a model school for baptized Tatars, with tuition in the Tatar language, and subjects which were mainly Christian in character. In reaction to a new wave of apostasy on the part of baptized Tatars four years later, he also founded a missionary society, the 'Brotherhood of Saint Gurii', named after the first archbishop of Kazan, which also primarily had the goal of strengthening baptized non-Russians in the Orthodox faith by means of tuition in their mother tongues. In 1870 Ilminsky's system received the assent of D. A. Tolstoi, the Minister of Popular Education, who stated categorically that 'the final goal of the education of all the inorodtsy . . . must be their russification and their amalgamation with the Russian people'.[28]

Ilminsky and his co-workers, who were often of non-Russian origin, created Cyrillic alphabets for numerous languages which had hitherto not possessed a script, such as Chuvash, Cheremis, Votiak, Kazakh, Iakut or the languages of the present-day Chakassians and Altaians, but also for Tatar, Buriat and Kalmyk as alternatives to the Arabic and Mongol alphabets. Numerous Christian texts were translated into these languages and subsequently published, as were dictionaries, grammars and schoolbooks. Numerous native-language schools were established in the Volga-Urals region, in Siberia and in Kazakhstan in order to nurture new elites on which Russia could rely. In 1872 a teachers' seminary for non-Russians was founded in Kazan under the direction of Ilminsky. In 1904 the students included twenty-six Mordvinians, twenty-three Chuvash, twenty-two Tatars, seventeen Cheremis, fifteen Votiaks, seven Koreans, six Kazakhs, three Bashkirs and three Zyrians, two Iakuts, and one Kalmyk and one Vogul.[29] In addition to this there were special central schools for the education of Tatar, Chuvash, Votiak and Cheremis teachers and priests. Ilminsky's system was imitated as far afield as Siberia and the Far East, and, through his pupil N. P. Ostroumov, also in Middle Asia, though here it was unable to make a great deal of headway against the traditional Muslim schools. Towards the end of the nineteenth century Ilminsky's methods came increasingly under fire from Russian national circles, which saw the Russian language and not the Orthodox faith as the decisive integrational element, and feared that the native languages would also arouse national aspirations among the non-Russians of the east.

Such fears were certainly justified. Whereas it is true that Ilminsky's missionary policy was successful in that it became possible to attach baptized animists more firmly to the Orthodox church, to convert tens of thousands of Tatars to Christianity, and to alienate the Kazakhs from the pan-Islamic movement, in the medium term it was of greater importance that the creation of written languages, of native-language schools, and of a small class of intellectuals laid the foundations for national movements in many ethnic groups, and that in the case of the Tatars the efficient missionary methods made a crucial contribution to the rise of the Islamic reform movement.[30] The Ilminsky system, which could be described by the slogan 'national in form, Orthodox in content' also continued to be influential after the October Revolution, for it seems likely that Lenin, whose father played an active role in the organization of Chuvash schools, derived from it certain ideas for his own policy on nationalities, which was based on the slogan 'national in form, Communist in content'.[31]

Russian policy towards the ethnic groups of the Volga-Urals region was not restricted to questions of missionary work and education, though in most of the other areas it remained essentially unchanged. However, in the second half of the nineteenth century assimilatory tendencies and eurocentric prejudices became more noticeable here as well. This is apparent in the demand for the 'complete fusion' of the baptized ethnic groups of the middle Volga with the 'predominant ethnic group' for the benefit 'of the Christian church and civilization',[32] or in the case of ten Votiaks, who in 1892 were accused of having perpetrated a heathen human sacrifice. In 1894 seven of them were found guilty of ritual murder, and sentenced to hard labour (katorga). Their sentences were overturned in 1896, but only after the writer V. G. Korolenko had mounted a press campaign in Russia.[33]

I have already described Russian policy towards the non-Russians in Asia in Chapter 5. The legal distinction between the 'natural' (prirodnye) subjects of Russia and the special category of the inorodtsy continued to be of fundamental importance. The ethnic groups of the middle Volga and the Urals were deemed to have been integrated, and this was the reason why in their case the reforms were all implemented. As a result the Bashkirs also lost their special status. They were now required to do the normal military service, and their upper class was co-opted into the Russian nobility.[34] On the other hand, Russia pursued a policy of non-intervention towards the inorodtsy, most noticeably in Middle Asia, and less consistently in the case of the ethnic groups of Siberia and the nomads, who were supposed to be gradually acculturated with the help of flexible methods.[35] In principle, the traditional discrepancy between the cautious pragmatism of the centre, which had been laid down in the still-valid inorodtsy statute of 1822, and the arbitrary acts of the regional administration persisted in the case of the ethnic groups of Siberia. However, administrative reforms introduced between 1898 and 1901 curtailed the autonomy of the inorodtsy in a number of Siberian provinces. For example, in the case of the Buriats the administration was partly brought into line with that of Russian peasant communities.[36] The mission to the Buriats was now to some extent supported by the government as well, though it was not a lasting success, especially in the case of the lamaists. For the nomad Kazakhs, Kirgiz, Buriats and Kalmyks the settlement of their pastures by eastern Slav peasants, which was encouraged by the Russian government, constituted a challenge that endangered their very existence.

Most of the reforms of the 1860s and 1870s were also introduced in Bessarabia and the Crimea, and reinforced the integration of these areas into the Russian empire. The Romanian language had already been displaced by Russian in Bessarabia as early as the reign of Nicholas I, Romanian was abolished in the 1860s as a school subject, and subsequently even as a language used in church services.[37] In practice Russian never became totally predominant, neither in schools nor in churches. However, the linguistic policy towards the Romanians of Bessarabia constituted an extreme type of russification. The underlying motives were probably the striving for standardization on the part of the Orthodox church, and also the fear of irredentist movements as a result of the foundation of the Romanian nation state.

In the course of the reforms the special legal status of the foreign (and primarily German) colonists living in the south of Russia and Ukraine was abolished.[38] In 1871 their self-administrative bodies were dissolved; Russian became the official language; and the colonists were incorporated into the category of peasants. Yet in the German communities numerous aspects of the administrative, legal and social special status remained *de facto*. However, in 1874 they were also deprived of the privilege of not having to serve in the armed forces, and were henceforth required to do the normal kind of military service. The Mennonites, who had once emigrated to southern Ukraine in order to escape from military service in their countries of origin, were permitted to serve in a non-military capacity. After the foundation of the German Empire, and especially from the 1890s onwards, at a time when Russo-German relations were deteriorating, the German colonists, like the Baltic Germans, were reviled in the Russian national press as nationalist conspirators, as people who exploited the Russians and as the spearhead of the 'German drive to the east'.[39] The government gave way to public opinion inasmuch as it restricted the purchase of land by German immigrants in Volhynia in 1887 and 1892, and introduced Russian as the language of tuition in the German primary schools in 1890s. Yet on the whole it remained true to its traditional role as protector of the loyal colonists.

From the 1860s onwards Transcaucasia continued to be integrated in administrative terms. Judicial reform (without juries) and (stepwise) municipal reform were introduced, and in 1883 the office of viceroy, which had been invested with far-reaching powers, was abolished.[40] The Georgian and Muslim nobility and the Armenian merchants had been incorporated into the Russian order of estates, and subsequently the two Christian peoples, though not the Muslims, became the targets of cultural russification.

The situation of the Orthodox Georgians, who had repeatedly rebelled against Russian rule, was worse than that of the loyal Gregorian Armenians. The Georgian church was a part of the Russian Orthodox church, and as early as the reign of Nicholas I, who appointed only Russians as Georgian exarchs, its liturgy had gradually been brought into line with that used in the Church Slavonic Russian rite. Furthermore, the Georgian-speaking school system had largely been replaced by a Russian-speaking one. After a certain revival in the middle of the century, Georgian was systematically excluded from use in schools in the 1870s, and especially at the beginning of the 1880s.[41] In 1872 it was also replaced by Russian as the language of tuition in the theological seminary in Tiflis. The director of the seminary, who resisted the re-introduction of Georgian, which he called a 'language for dogs', was murdered in 1886. In 1882 the use of the term Georgia in print was forbidden. The national movement, which championed the Georgian language, and Georgian literature and culture, successfully opposed this repressive policy, which refused to recognize the Orthodox Georgians with their ancient high culture and written language as being the peers of the Russians.

On the other hand, the independent Armenian Gregorian church, whose clergy had played an active role in the Russian conquest of Transcaucasia, was recognized under Nicholas I as being the central cultural institution of the Armenians. It was only in the 1880s, after the end of the Russo-Turkish war, in which the Russian armies had received support from Armenians, that there was a campaign against the flourishing church school system. It began with the imposition of Russian control and the use of Russian as the language of tuition. Subsequently, after 1895, church elementary schools, welfare associations and libraries were closed down.[42] The Russian nationalist press began to carry polemical diatribes in which the Armenians, like the Jews, were branded as being exploiters, parasites and disloyal traitors. Finally, in 1903, when its possessions were confiscated, the Armenian church itself became the target of the policy of integration. The measure was aimed at the church as the most important source of Armenian culture. Now, as a result of the national revolutionary movement in the Ottoman Empire, Armenians were no longer regarded as loyal allies, but as a danger to order within Russia as well. Since the discriminatory measures were repealed in 1905, their assimilatory effect was negligible. However, their political effect was significant. The traditional russophile attitudes of the Armenians received a severe blow, and the mass protests against the ordinance of 1903 made a crucial contribution to the politicization of the Armenian national movement.

Although the Muslim population of Transcaucasia was affected just as much as Christians by general integrational measures, such as the introduction of judicial reform (with Russian as the language of the courts), no direct measures were taken against its religious and educational institutions. The different intensity levels of the measures directly designed to implement the policy of Russification provide an insight into the aims of Russian policymakers. As in the case of the Romanians in Bessarabia, the language and culture of the Orthodox Georgians were only to a certain extent recognized as being discrete, and for this reason they were subjected to a great deal of assimilatory pressure at an early stage. The Armenians only became the object of active cultural integration much later, and there were probably political motives for this. Yet in a way which resembled its actions in Middle Asia, the government did not interfere with the religion and the culture of the Muslims of Transcaucasia and the Caucasus. On the one hand these differences are a reflection of the different levels of development on the part of the national movements which were potentially capable of bringing down the system, and thus drew a response from Russian policymakers. But on the other hand they also mirror the interest in integrating more strongly those ethnic groups which were closer to the Russians in religious and socio-cultural terms than the Asiatic Muslims or the 'gortsy'. The latter were regarded as marauding savages who were kept under control by a repressive colonial administration. A network of Russian-language schools was only established in the case of the Christian Ossetians.

4. From Integration and Assimilation to Exclusion and Discrimination: The Jews as Scapegoats

Up to this point my description of the Russian policy on nationalities and of the national movements of the non-Russian ethnic groups has omitted to mention the Jews. The reason for this is that the Jews, being an ethno-religious mobilized diaspora group, constitute a special case. However, the Jewish question was at the centre of the debate at the end of the nineteenth century. The Jews became the most important issue in extreme Russian nationalism and, in mutual interaction with this, also of the policy on nationalities. At the same time the Jewish national movement became a mass movement.

Russia had initially attempted, as it had done with other ethnic groups, to integrate the Jews, with whom it first came into contact in the last three decades of the eighteenth century. However, the government soon began to introduce discriminatory laws, and under Nicholas I measures directed against the Jews by the state became more frequent.[43] As in other European countries, the question of Jewish emancipation came to the fore in the context of liberalization and reform under Alexander II.[44] There was a renewed debate about whether it was necessary to grant Jews equal rights in order to integrate and assimilate them, or whether, conversely, assimilation had to precede equality. Whereas equal rights for the Jews were decreed in the Kingdom of Poland in 1862, it was decided that in the rest of Russia there would be a compromise or emancipation step by step. This entailed reducing the degree of discrimination, but not abolishing it entirely. The Jewish pale of settlement – 15 provinces in the west, and ten in the Kingdom of Poland – remained, though in the reformist years merchants belonging to the first guild, people with academic degrees, guild craftsmen and in 1879 everyone who had graduated from a university or college had the right to settle in the Russian interior. Furthermore, some of the restrictions on the Jews who lived in rural areas were lifted, and they were once again able to become tenants and sell alcohol. All of the important reforms were also applied to the Jews, and only the municipal reform of 1870 contained supplementary discriminatory regulations which stated that Jews were permitted to have no more than a third of the deputies in the municipal self-governing body, and excluded them from holding the office of mayor. Although Russian policy was clearly a kind of compromise, it led to the social mobilization of the Jews. Many attended state schools. Moreover, there came into being a professional elite and a small class of wealthy bankers and entrepreneurs. A number of Jews were assimilated by their Russian surroundings, and some joined the Russian revolutionary movement.

The participation of a female terrorist of Jewish origin in the conspiracy that led to the assassination of Alexander II on 1 March 1881 was the pretext for large-scale anti-Jewish pogroms.[45] Ten years earlier there had already been a pogrom against the Jews in Odessa which had been initiated by the city's Greeks. Yet it was the anti-Jewish riots of 1881 which led to a decisive change in Russian policy towards the Jews. The pogroms occurred primarily in towns in Ukraine, where 40 Jewish men and women were killed, a considerably larger number were wounded and raped, and hundreds of Jewish shops and houses plundered and destroyed. In December there was also a pogrom against the Jews in Warsaw. To this day there continues to be controversy about whether these pogroms were organized by the Russian authorities or whether they were merely spontaneous. Recent research has been predominantly of the opinion that the government in St Petersburg was not involved, and that, whilst the pogroms were not directly organized by the local authorities, the latter tolerated the riots and thereby encouraged them. The 1881 pogroms emanated primarily from the urban lower classes and from Russian railway workers and day-labourers. These had come to Ukraine in search of work, where they came upon the numerous Jews who dominated the market as craftsmen and small traders, and were suitable scapegoats for those who wished to give vent to their anger about unsolved social problems. Whether merchants from Moscow were behind the pogroms, as certain sources seem to suggest, is now impossible to prove. From the towns, which were mainly Russian in character, the programs also spread to the rural areas, where Ukrainian peasants participated in them. This pattern of events refutes the widely held view that the 1881 pogroms were a continuation of the anti-Jewish massacres of the seventeenth and eighteenth centuries and that they can be traced back to the 'eternal tradition' of Ukrainian anti-Semitism.

The government used the 1881 pogroms as an opportunity to make its policy towards the Jews more repressive. Its ancient prejudices to the effect that the Jews exploited the eastern Slav lower classes had once again been confirmed. Since the latter had to be protected against Jews, the policy of progressive emancipation became obsolete. Russian policymakers no longer pursued the aims of integration, equality and assimilation, but of exclusion of and discrimination against the Jews. Nor, in contrast to all the other non-Russian ethnic groups in the west, did Russia, in the case of Jews, promote cultural russification. In fact, it adhered to the ban on Russian tuition in the Jewish religious schools. Moreover, the Orthodox church had virtually given up its missionary work among the Jews. Although baptism put an end to formal discrimination, it did not turn a Jew into a Russian. The increasing exclusion of Jews, which gradually began to include a racist component, was already mirrored in the fact that as early as the reign of Nicholas I they were assigned to the legal category of inorodtsy. Thus, like the nomads and the Muslims of Asia, Jews were second-class citizens, though they were denied the advantages of this status, such as self-government and freedom from military service.[46]

In May 1882, in order to protect eastern Slav peasants against Jews, the latter were forbidden to resettle in rural areas. This regulation also applied to the Kingdom of Poland, and thus curtailed the status of equality which had been granted to Jews two decades earlier. Towards the end of the 1880s there were other discriminatory measures. In 1887 restrictions were placed on the number of Jews permitted to study at grammar schools and institutes of higher education. Henceforth Jews in the pale of settlement were allowed to constitute a maximum of 10 per cent of the student body. In the rest of Russia they were restricted to a maximum of 5 per cent and in St Petersburg and Moscow to a maximum of 3 per cent. It was claimed that these laws were needed because Jews were introducing the revolutionary bacillus into the schools. As in the case of the Armenians, the stereotype of the exploiter was now joined by that of the revolutionary. These and other discriminatory measures did a great deal to impede the social betterment of the Jews. At the beginning of the 1890s, in the context of the counter-reforms, the rights in the zemstva and municipal self-government granted to the Jews under Alexander II were rescinded. Furthermore, other liberalization measures were also repealed. For example, in 1891 more than 10,000 Jewish craftsmen were expelled from Moscow. The expulsion of the Jews from Russia, an extreme form of exclusion, was, it is true, occasionally demanded, but only implemented inasmuch as after 1881 Jews were usually permitted to emigrate if they wished to do so. Between 1881 and 1914 about 2 million Jews left the Russian Empire, most of them going to North America.

After 1881 Russian policy changed and began to advocate discrimination against and segregation of Jews. However, sections of the ruling elite also continued to be in favour of a cautious emancipation of the Jews. The Ministers of Finance in particular repeatedly opposed the anti-Jewish policy supported by the Ministry of the Interior by pointing out the important role which Jews could play in the process of industrialization. That such voices failed to make themselves heard can also be explained by the marked increase in the number of people who hated Jews in Russian society towards the end of the nineteenth century. This gradually assumed the form of a kind of militant anti-Semitism which reached up into the highest circles of government.

After the reactionary shift of 1881 Russian policy sought to preserve the autocratic system, the estate-based order, and the predominance of the nobility by means of 'defensive modernization'.[47] Parallel to the forced industrialization of the 1890s, a reactionary kind of anti-capitalism with strong anti-Semitic overtones began to become increasingly common in Russia. To these reactionaries the Jews were the embodiment of the capitalist exploiter, who, after the process of industrialization, would also seize political power. The fact that numerous Jews had joined the socialist movement was used to depict Jews as the wire-pullers of the revolution. Hand in hand with this extreme form of Russian nationalism went the notion of cosmopolitan and international Jewish stockbrokers, and a Polish–Jewish conspiracy which wanted to take Russia down the disastrous path to liberalism and capitalism. The anti-Semitic legend of a Jewish conspiracy to seize power on a global scale was at the root of the 'Protocols of the Elders of Zion', which was fabricated by agents of the tsarist secret police in 1895. Hardly any of the elements in what Löwe has called a 'reactionary utopia' corresponded with the facts. They nonetheless had a certain effect on the urban lower classes in Russia, and it proved possible to instrumentalize them for purposes of group cohesion. The Jews became the welcome scapegoats for the social and economic problems which were the result of the accelerated pace of modernization.

However, the pogroms of 1881 and the anti-Jewish measures adopted by the government also marked a crucial turning-point for the long-term aims of the Jews themselves.[48] The failure of the emancipation and assimilation encouraged under Alexander II meant that socially mobilized Jews now turned to the national and revolutionary movement. As in the case of the other ethnic groups in the empire, the ground for the Jewish national movement had been prepared by a cultural renaissance, the enlightenment movement (Haskalah) and the rediscovery of Jewish culture and the Yiddish and Hebrew languages. As a result of the reforms, and with the Jewish intelligentsia moulded by Russian ideas, there was now a broad class of people who were susceptible to national and socialist slogans. A characteristic feature of the Jews in Russia was the fact that the emancipation movement was not part of a single current, and that it was split up into rival groups. Furthermore, the countervailing traditionalist forces retained their influence on the masses, be it in the shape of a rabbinate, which sought to protect the religious identity of the Jews against Russian influences, enlightenment and reforms, or in the shape of a mystical and other-worldy hasidism.

The national movement of the Jews in the narrower sense crystallized as Zionism, which began to emerge in Russia in the 1880s.[49] In addition to the main strand of political Zionism, which strove for the establishment of a Jewish nation state in Palestine, there was another strand which concentrated on the national and cultural consolidation of the Jews in the diaspora, whereas a third tried to combine Zionism and socialism. Numerous Jews from Russia attended the Zionist World Congresses, which were held regularly from 1897 onwards. In 1902 hundreds of organizations sent their delegates to Minsk for a conference of Zionists in Russia. It was of importance for the spread of Zionism that, in contrast to other national movements, it was tolerated until 1903 by the government, which was in favour of the stated aim of Jewish emigration.

In competition with Zionism was a workers' movement which arose among the Jews in the Russian Empire. It was already organizing strikes in the 1890s.[50] The 'General Jewish Workers' Union in Lithuania, Poland and Russia' (the 'Bund'), which opposed middle-class Zionism, already had about 25,000 members in 1903. It became the most important Jewish party. The 'Bund', which had been founded before the Russian Social Democratic Party, thought of itself as being part of the Russian Social Democratic community. Despite this fundamentally internationalist character, it addressed itself to specifically Jewish issues, such as the struggle against discrimination, and began to organize Jewish self-defence units. Furthermore, the 'Bund' declared that Jews constituted a nation and demanded for the Jewish nation personal cultural autonomy with Yiddish-speaking schools. These aims were rejected by the Russian Social Democrats and in 1903 this led to the 'Bund' temporarily leaving the RSDRP.

At the beginning of the twentieth century a solution to the Jewish question was further away than ever. The policies pursued by the government had increased the level of discrimination and exclusion; anti-Semitism was gaining ground in Russian society as a whole; and the Jews had initiated a national and socialist movement. The explosive nature of the situation was demonstrated by a new pogrom, which occurred in Kishinev in Bessarabia in 1903, in which more Jews were killed than in all of the 1881 pogroms together. Once again the government does not seem to have been directly involved. However, the Kishinev pogrom was not a spontaneous affair, having been planned by local anti-Semitic organizations which received support from the authorities. This scenario was to be repeated during the revolution of 1905.

5. Summary

After 1831 Russian policy towards the ethnic groups of the Russian Empire showed a tendency towards growing oppression and increased standardization and began increasingly to reject the traditional patterns of respect for the status quo, cooperation with loyal elites and tolerance, though it continued to adhere to the notion that the maintenance of power and the unity of the state were of paramount importance. 'To maintain the empire was an end in itself, the chief objective of Russian political life' (F. Starr).[51] Whereas this principle determined policy under Nicholas I, from the 1860s onwards administrative standardization and linguistic and cultural russification became more prominent. From the expulsion of Crimean Tatars and Circassians to the sharp reaction to the Polish insurrection of 1863, the renewal of Orthodox missionary activity, and the implementation of standardizing reforms under Alexander II, via the measures against the Baltic Germans, German colonists and Jews under Alexander III, which were in tune with the general reactionary trend, to the attacks on the traditionally loyal Finns and Armenians under Nicholas II there emerges a clear-cut image of steadily increasing and systematic russification. The notion that there was a consistent policy of russification designed to achieve complete administrative, social and cultural uniformity in the Russian Empire and to transform it into an ethnically uniform nation state is widespread in western research, and to some extent even projected back to the age of Catherine II. However, such sweeping generalizations fail to explain and do justice to the complexity of Russian policy, and they have increasingly been called into question in recent years.[52]

For a start, the concept of russification is negated by the fact that the policies pursued towards numerous ethnic groups were based not on integration, but on segregation and discrimination. This applies especially to the legal category of the inorodtsy, who were never regarded as being among the 'natural' inhabitants of the Empire. More than in the case of the nomads, hunters and gatherers, who were originally assigned to the inorodtsy category, this kind of exclusion became apparent with great clarity in the case of the sedentary Muslims of Middle Asia, and, from the 1880s onwards, of the Jews. An extreme form of segregation was expulsion (or at least a clear encouragement to emigrate) as applied to the Crimean and Nogai Tatars, the Circassians and other Caucasians and, in a less aggressive form, to the Jews. Other ethnic groups, such as the Muslims of Transcaucasia, were, it is true, subjected to administrative integration, but not to cultural russification.

Furthermore, the policy of cultural integration was not always the same everywhere. Whereas in the west and in the south an attempt was made to introduce the Russian language gradually into the administration, the judiciary and the educational system, Russian policy towards the ethnic groups of the middle Volga, the Urals, the steppe and Siberia was concerned to encourage native languages with the aim of ensuring the entrenchment of the Orthodox church. Finally, linguistic and cultural russification was pursued with differing degrees of intensity. The loyal Baltic Germans, German colonists and Armenians were only affected at a late stage, and the Finlanders only marginally. Whilst the Poles, and in their wake the Ukrainians, Belorussians and Lithuanians, were subjected to russification in the 1860s and 1870s, the government continued to cooperate with the loyal elites in the Baltic provinces and with the Armenian clergy. When the Baltic Germans came under pressure under Alexander III, the Finlanders were not subjected to measures designed to russify them. And when around 1900 the policy towards them became more severe, the government adhered to its traditional co-operation with the Muslim elite. Total russification in the sense of assimilation to the Russians was never seriously envisaged in regard to the ancient ruling nations, not even in regard to the Poles, who were mercilessly oppressed. Thus the all-inclusive concept of russification does not sufficiently explain the complexity of what really happened, as a contemporary observer remarked: 'Imperial policy in regard to the national question is as diverse and variegated in its manifestations as the population of the empire is diverse and variegated. To trace this diversity back to a logical system or to some kind of unity is impossible, for in the real world there was no such thing.'[53]

This insight does not absolve us from the task of seeking an explanation for the tendencies, which began to make an appearance from the 1860s onwards, of forced integration and also, for the first time, of a policy of linguistic and cultural russification. Such an explanation cannot simply posit a single reason by pointing to the Russian government's set and unchangeable aims. Rather, it must take into account the appearance of four new interdependent historical forces.

After suffering defeat in the Crimean War, one of these forces was the inescapable need to modernize Russia. This, as had already been the case under Peter I and Catherine II, was coupled with administrative systematization and standardization. Modernization was also directed against the ancient special rights and privileges of the non-Russian elites, especially when, in contrast to the eighteenth and early nineteenth centuries, they were no longer considered to be models and progressive, but were seen as a hindrance. Standardization also entailed the introduction of the Russian language in the administration and the educational system, which put non-Russians at a disadvantage to Russians. We will briefly consider the reforms of the 1860s and 1870s in order to examine the consistency with which this modernization and standardization was implemented in the various regions of the Russian Empire.

The abolition of serfdom was implemented everywhere with no more than a slight delay, though the different conditions under which it took place, as was apparent in the case of Poland and Georgia, were very much determined by political considerations. It proved impossible to create a single uniform category of peasants through the reforms, and until the revolution there were numerous agrarian arrangements in the Russian Empire. Similarly, the judicial reform of 1864, which modernized the courts on the basis of the western model, was applied to most of the peripheral areas and also to the Jews, though in part with considerable delay and with important restrictions.[54] Thus the jury system was not introduced in Poland, Transcaucasia and the Baltic provinces for political reasons. Similarly, in the peripheral regions with a non-Russian population, the municipal reform of 1870, which involved restructuring the system of self-government, was implemented much later and with added exemption clauses. General military service, an important integrational instrument, was introduced with some delay in the Caucasus area; it was not introduced at all in the case of the Asiatic inorodtsy or in Finland.[55]

The extent to which security considerations impeded the policy of standardizing the empire is seen most clearly in the case of the zemstvo reform of 1864, which envisaged giving greater powers to local self-government bodies under the supervision of the nobility. Apart from the areas inhabited largely by Russians, it was initially implemented only on the middle Volga, in the northern Urals, in eastern and southern Ukraine, in the Crimea and in Bessarabia. Initially the Jews who lived in these areas were fully included. It was not until shortly before the First World War that western Ukraine and the provinces to the north of the Caspian Sea followed suit. The zemstvos were not introduced in the Kingdom of Poland, in Belorussia/Lithuania, in the Baltic provinces, in Finland and in the whole of the Caucasus area, where the non-Russian nobility predominated everywhere, nor in Middle Asia and Siberia, where there were not enough nobles who had been accorded equal status.[56] Whereas it is true that the reforms of the 1860s and 1870s brought about a certain administrative integration of the peripheral areas and at the same time a series of progressive changes for the non-Russian lower classes, they were not automatically introduced in all of the areas inhabited by non-Russians. Rather, they were usually first introduced in an inner circle which was deemed to be fully integrated (the middle Volga area, the Urals, eastern and southern Ukraine, Bessarabia), and then, in carefully graded steps, in the areas in which a foreign elite predominated (the 'western provinces', Transcaucasia, the Baltic provinces and the Kingdom of Poland). They were hardly applied at all to autonomous Finland or to the inorodtsy in Asia.

The non-Russian national movements constituted the second new force which had a bearing on Russian policy. Together with the revolutionary movement, they were perceived as endangering the stability and the unity of the empire, and combated with repression and measures designed to introduce standardization and russification. In the case of the Poles, and also to some extent in that of the Armenians and Finlanders, Russian policy on nationalities was primarily a reaction to the national emancipation movements, which were considered to be disloyal. Since St Petersburg at first considered only the movements led by ancient elites to be dangerous, it occasionally provided support for the national movements of the peasant peoples. Conflicts also escalated because non-Russians affected by a national movement often reacted rather violently to integrational measures by the government.

In the course of the struggle with the national movements of the non-Russians, there was an increase in nationalism in Russian society, and from the 1860s onwards this had an influence on government policy. On the one hand parts of the bureaucracy and the armed forces were influenced by national ideas, and on the other the pressure exerted by the nationalist press increased. The latter was able to mobilize a considerable section of the educated public. Although the government also remained sceptical about the Russian national movement, it was an obvious idea to instrumentalize the integrational power of Russian nationalism and of anti-Semitism in order to neutralize the growing problems with which it was confronted as a result of modernization and industrialization, and the growing social tensions and opposition movements. Russian nationalism not only reinforced the attempts at linguistic russification, but also the support for the Orthodox church at the expense of other faiths. This coalition of state, church and Russian nationalism was personified by the influential Supreme Procurators of the Holy Synod, D. A. Tolstoy and K. P. Pobedonostsev. However, neither the church nor the extreme nationalists triumphed completely, and in principle the state adhered to the dynastically legitimated autocratic system.

Russian policy was influenced by a fourth factor: foreign policy considerations. For one thing, in an age of imperialism and extreme nationalism the example of other European countries had an influence on Russia. But the policy towards individual ethnic groups could also be influenced by foreign policy considerations: in the case of the Armenians and Crimean Tatars by relations with the Ottoman Empire, in the case of the Romanians of Bessarabia by concerns about the Romanian nation state and in the case of the Ukrainians by the connections to the Ukrainian Piedmont in Austrian eastern Galicia.

The intensity with which the various ethnic groups of the Russian Empire were subjected to standardization and integration can be summed up on the basis of a rough-and-ready scale. The Ukrainians and Belorussians were subjected to the greatest pressure: their elite had been largely integrated and they were deemed to be Russians. For this reason their national aspirations were considered to be apostasy from the Russian nation. On the second level were Orthodox non-Russians, who on account of their common faith also belonged to Russiandom in a wider sense of the word: the Romanians of Bessarabia, the Greek and Bulgarian colonists, the Georgians, and the baptized animists and Muslims. On the other hand, the Poles were clearly not Russians, nor could they be transformed into Russians. However, they were deemed to be enemies and traitors who had to be punished by means of severe repression and forced integration. For a long time the Lithuanians were placed in the same category as the Poles and from the end of the nineteenth century onwards Russian policy reacted to the Armenian national revolutionary movement as it had done to that of the Poles.

Whereas Russia pursued a policy of forced integration (also in linguistic and cultural terms) towards the above-mentioned ethnic groups, less pressure was exerted on others. This is the category to which one should assign the Baltic Germans (after 1885) and, to a lesser extent, the Estonians and Latvians, the German colonists and the Muslims of Azerbaidzhan. The nomads, hunters and gatherers in Asia were largely excluded on the one hand, though on the other subjected to increased pressure from Ilminsky's mission schools and eastern Slav colonization. At the bottom end of the scale one would have to place the policy of non-intervention towards the sedentary Muslims of Middle Asia. The Jews, who were excluded and discriminated against after 1881, were a special case and do not fit into this pattern.

The results of the new Russian policy, which was designed to integrate non-Russians more firmly, were ambivalent. It achieved its most important goal, for it maintained law and order in the Russian Empire: between 1864 and 1905 there were no large-scale uprisings among the non-Russians. It also gave a boost to the administrative standardization and centralization of Russia, even if certain special regulations continued to survive in the peripheral regions. Cultural russification meant that the national movements of the eastern Slavs and the Lithuanians were seriously impeded, whereas in the case of numerous ethnic groups elementary education in their native languages was prevented from expanding.

On the other hand, cultural russification and discrimination against those who were not of the Orthodox faith had a counter-productive effect. In addition to the educated elites, it mobilized wider sections of the population against Russia, especially among the Poles, Lithuanians, Armenians and Finns. Although it is true that the ancient elites were weakened by the policy of standardization, most of the upper classes were able to retain their social position and cultural identity. This was true of the Swedish-speaking elite in Finland, of the Baltic Germans, of the Polish magnates, of the Georgian nobles and of the Muslim beys in Azerbaidzhan. The following chapter surveys the multi-ethnic empire's structure, which was changed by national movements and modernization.

This constituted an important precondition for the social and national conflicts of the revolutionary epoch.

Notes

1   See the important publications by Thaden (1981, 1984), and the criticism of his use of the term russification by Schweitzer (1984) and Gert von Pistohlkors "'Russifizierung" in den baltischen Provinzen und in Finnland im 19. und beginnenden 20. Jahrhundert', *ZfO* 33 (1984), 592–606. A survey of the Russian policy on nationalities is given by von Rauch (1953), pp. 89–145; Hugh Seton-Watson, *The Russian Empire 1801–1917* (Oxford, 1967), pp. 409–18, 485–505; Hans Rogger, *Russia in the Age of Modernisation and Revolution 1881–1917* (London and New York, 1983), pp. 182–207; Violet Conolly, 'Die "Nationalitätenfrage" im Zarenreich', in *Rußlands Aufbruch* (1970), pp. 151–80.

2   See W. Bruce Lincoln, *Nicholas I. Emperor and Autocrat of all the Russias* (Bloomington and London, 1978); Riasanovsky (1959), especially pp. 224–33.

3   A. S. Pushkin, 'Klevetnikam Rossii' (To the Slanderers of Russia), in *Sochineniia*, vol. I (Moscow, 1962), p. 317. See also Thaden (1984), pp. 159 f.; Fleischhacker (1941); Władysław Bortnowski, *Powstanie listopadowe w oczach Rosjan* (Warszawa, 1964).

4   On policy towards Poland, in addition to the general accounts of Hoensch (1983); Rhode (1980); Wandycz (1974); *Historia* vol. III (1981) and Amburger (1966), pp. 426–8, see also Winiarski (1924), pp. 112–22 and 151–64; Thaden (1984), pp. 121–37 and 144–53.

5   *Recueil* (1862), pp. 911–20.

6   *PSZ* II, 4869 (vol. 6, 2, pp. 134–8), also in abbreviated form in *Recueil* (1862), pp. 881–4. See also Beauvois (1985), pp. 110–53.

7   On the Uniate church see Pelesz (1880); Smolitsch (1991), pp. 404–15. On the Lithuanians, Belorussians and Ukrainians see Hellmann (1966); Čeginskas (1959); Vakar (1956); Subtelny (1988); Ivancevich (1976).

8   See Wittram (1954); Haltzel (1977), pp. 12–13; Thaden (1984), pp. 169–91; Garve (1978).

9   Thaden (1984), pp. 201–19.

10 Kappeler (1982b), pp. 387–92, quotation on p. 389; Lemercier-Quelquejay (1967), pp. 397–402; Glazik (1954); Glazik (1959), pp. 120–7; Smolitsch (1991), pp. 280–312.

11 Kappeler (1982b), pp. 393–400.

12 Babel (1926), pp. 136 f.; V. F. Shishmarev, 'Romanskie iazyki iugo-vostochnoi Evropy i natsional'nyi iazyk Moldavskoi SSR', in *Voprosy moldavskogo iazykoznaniia* (Moscow, 1953), pp. 73–120, here p. 114; Zelenchuk (1979), pp. 167f.

13 On the following see Wandycz (1974); *Historia* vol. IV (1982); Thaden (1984), pp. 154–68 and 138–43; Fleischhacker (1941); Winiarski (1924), pp. 122–32 and 153–70; Amburger (1966), pp. 429–34.

14 Katz (1966), pp. 118–31, quotation on p. 121. See also Michael B. Petrovich, 'Russian Pan-Slavists and The Polish Uprising of 1863', *Harvard Slavic Studies* 1 (1953), pp. 218–48; Lukashevich (1965), pp. 76–89; Picht (1969), pp. 237–42; Fleischhacker (1941), pp. 93–114.

15 See also Simon (1969), pp. 203–17.

16 *Der Dictator von Wilna. Memoiren des Grafen M. N. Murawjew* (Leipzig, 1883), p. 59. See also Sambuk (1980).

17 On the following see Hellmann (1966), Čeginskas (1959); Vakar (1953); Sambuk (1980); Subtelny (1988); Ivancevich (1976); Roman Solchanyk, 'Language Politics in the Ukraine' in Kreindler (1985), pp. 57–105, here pp. 58–62; Fedir Savchenko, *Zaborona ukrainstva 1876 r.* (Munich, 1970) (repr. of 1930 Kiev ed.)

18 *Der Dictator von Wilna*, p. 13. See also p. 85.

19 M. Lemke, *Epokha tsenzurnykh reform 1859–1865 godov.* (St Petersburg, 1904), p. 300; Katz (1966), pp. 131–3.

20 Lemke, pp. 295–309, quotation on p. 303.

21 On the following see Haltzel (1977); Thaden (1981); Thaden (1984), pp. 191–9; Wittram (1954); Jarve (1978).

22 *Juri Samarins, Anklage gegen die Ostseeprovinzen Rußlands.* (Translated from the Russian) (Leipzig, 1869); C. Schirren, *Livländische Antwort an Herrn Juri Samarin* (Leipzig, 1869) (reprint, 1971).

23 Quotation after Haltzel (1977), p. 32.

24 On the following see Schweitzer (1978); Thaden (1981); Jutikkala (1964); Hösch (1991), including a summary of recent literature in Finnish.

25 English translation in Kirby (1975), pp. 80 f.

26 Kappeler, *Rußlands* (1982), pp. 403–6. On the following in general see also *Materialy po istorii Tatarii vtoroi poloviny XIX veka. Chast' I: Agrarnyi vopros i krest'ianskoe dvizhenie 50–70-kh godov XIX v.* (Moscow and Leningrad, 1936); Frank T. McCarthy, 'The Kazan Missionary Congress', *CMRS* 14 (1973), 308–32.

27 Isabelle Kreindler, 'Nikolai Ilminskii and Language Planning in Nineteenth-Century Russia', *International Journal of the Sociology of Language* 22 (1979), 5–26; Stephen J. Blank, 'National Education, Church and State in Tsarist Nationality Policy: The Il'minski System', *Canadian-American Slavic Studies* 17 (1983), 466–86; Jean Saussay, 'Il'minskij et la politique de russification des Tatars 1856–1891', *CMRS* 8 (1967), 404–26; Simon (1969), pp. 237–48; Bennigsen and Lemercier-Quelquejay (1960), pp. 33–6; Zenkovsky (1960), pp. 28–30; Rorlich (1986), pp. 44–7; Glazik (1959), pp. 131–43 (apologetic in character).

28 A. Kh. Makhmutova, *Stanovlenie svetskogo obrazovaniia u tatar (Bor'ba vokrug shkol'nogo voprosa. 1861–1917)* (Kazan, 1972), p. 23.

29 *Materialy po istorii Chuvashskoi ASSR. Vyp. 2* (Cheboksary, 1956), p. 263.

30 See above, Chapter 6, Sections 2 and 4.

31 Isabelle Kreindler, 'A Neglected Source of Lenin's Nationality Policy', *SR* 36 (1977), pp. 86–100.

32 *Sbornik dokumentov i statei po voprosu ob obrazovanii inorodtsev* (St Petersburg, 1869), passim, quotation on p. 5.

33 V. G. Korolenko, 'Multanskoe zhertvoprinoshenie', in V.G. Korolenko, *Sobranie sochinenii*, vol. 9 (Moscow, 1955), pp. 337–92; *Ocherki Udmurt.* (1958), pp. 179–82.

34 Baumann (1987); *Ocherki Bashk.*, I(2) (1959), pp. 140–64.

35 See Batunsky (1987).

36 On this see Jadrinzew (1886); Dameshek (1986); Glazik (1953), pp. 134–44; Sarkisyanz (1961), pp. 381 f.; Egunov (1963).

37 Babel (1926), pp. 187 f.; Zelenchuk (1979), p. 168; *Istoriia Mold.* (1982), p. 219. See also Gustav Weigand, *Die Dialekte der Bukowina und Bessarabiens* (Leipzig, 1904), p. 24; Seton-Watson (1934), p. 563.

38 Fleischhauer (1986), pp. 278–316; Long (1988), pp. 16–40; Neutatz (1993), pp. 27–62. On the Mennonites see Ehrt (1932); P. M. Friesen, *Die Alt-Evangelische Mennonitische Bruderschaft in Rußland (1789–1910) im Rahmen der mennonitischen Gesamtgeschichte* (Halbstadt, 1911).

39 Neutatz (1993); Ingeborg Fleischhauer, 'Zur Entstehung der deutschen Frage im Zarenreich' in A. Kappeler, B. Meissner and G. Simon (eds), *Die Deutschen im Russischen Reich und im Sowjetstaat* (Cologne, 1987), pp. 39–47; Fleischhauer (1986), pp. 329–57.

40 Amburger (1966), pp. 418–20; Milman (1966), pp. 181–95 and 204–34; John P. LeDonne, 'La réforme de 1883 au Caucase', *CMRS* 8 (1967), 21–35.

41 Lang (1962), pp. 108 f.; George B. Hewitt, 'Georgia: A Noble Past, A Secure Future' in Kreindler (1985), pp. 163–79, here pp. 168 f.; Ammann (1950), pp. 577 f.; R. Janin, 'Géorgie', *Dictionnaire de théologie catholique*, vol. VI (Paris, 1920), pp. 1239–89, here pp. 1264–70.

42 Gregorian (1972), pp. 194–204; Ronald Grigor Suny, 'Images of the Armenians in the Russian Empire' in Richard G. Hovannisian (ed.), *The Armenian Image in History and Literature* (Malibu, 1981), pp. 105–37.

43 See above, Chapter 3.3.

44 On the whole section see Rogger (1986); Löwe (1978) and in summarized form, idem, B. Martin and E. Schulin (eds), *Die Juden als Minderheit in der Geschichte* (Munich, 1981), pp. 184–208; Hildermeier (1984); Baron (1964), pp. 46–69; Dubnow, vols II–III (1918–20).

45 I. Michael Aronson, *Troubled Waters. The Origins of the 1881 Anti-Jewish Pogroms in Russia* (Pittsburgh, 1990); Omeljan Pritsak, 'The Pogroms of 1881', *HUS* 11 (1987), 8–43; Mina Goldberg, 'Die Jahre 1881–1882 in der Geschichte der russischen Juden', thesis, Berlin, 1934; Stephen M. Berk, *Year of Crisis, Year of Hope. Russian Jewry and the Pogroms of 1881–1882* (Westport and London, 1985).

46 See John D. Klier, 'The Concept of 'Jewish Emancipation' in a Russian Context' in *Civil Rights* (1989), pp. 121–44.

47 Here I follow Löwe (1978).

48 On the following see Baron (1964), pp. 135–86; Dubnow, vols II–III (1918–1920); Frankel (1981).

49 David Vital, *The Origins of Zionism* (Oxford, 1975); Gershon Swet, 'Russian Jews in Zionism and in the Building of Palestine', *Russian Jewry* (1966), pp. 172–208; J. Goldstein, 'The Attitude of the Jewish and the Russian Intelligentsia to Zionism in the Initial Period (1897–1904)', *SEER* 64 (1986), 546–56.

50 Ezra Mendelsohn, *Class Struggle in the Pale: The Formative Years of the Jewish Workers'
    Movement in Tsarist Russia* (Cambridge and New York, 1970); Henry J. Tobias, *The
    Jewish Bund in Russia from its Origins to 1905* (Stanford, 1970); Klaus Heller,
    *Revolutionärer Sozialismus und nationale Frage. Das Problem des Nationalismus bei russischen
    und jüdischen Sozialdemokraten und Sozialrevolutionären im Russischen Reich bis zur
    Revolution 1905–1907* (Frankfurt am Main, 1977).

51 Starr (1978), p. 31.

52 See the interpretations of Schweitzer (1986); Thaden (1981); Starr (1978); Rogger
    (1961–2); Raymond Pearson, 'Privileges, Rights, and Russification' in *Civil Rights*
    (1989), pp. 85–102; John D. Klier, 'The Polish Revolt of 1863 and the Birth of
    Russification: Bad for the Jews?', *Polin. A Journal of Polish-Jewish Studies 1* (1986),
    96–110. Löwe (1990) made a plea for a uniform policy on nationalities. See also
    note 1 above.

53 M. Slavinsky, 'Natsional'naia struktura Rossii i velikorossy', in Kasteliansky
    (1910), pp. 277–303, here p. 284.

54 Friedhelm Berthold Kaiser, *Die russische Justizreform von 1864. Zur Geschichte der
    russischen Justiz von Katharina II. bis 1917* (Leiden, 1972), pp. 465–7.

55 Robert F. Baumann, 'Universal Service Reform and Russia's Imperial Dilemma',
    War & Society 4(2) (1986), 31–49.

56 Kermit E. McKenzie, 'Zemstvo Organization and Role within the Administrative
    Structure' in Terence Emmons and Wayne S. Vucinich (eds), *The Zemstvo in Russia.
    An Experiment in Local Self-government* (Cambridge, 1982), pp. 31–78, here pp. 33 f.

8

The Late Tsarist Multi-ethnic Empire between Modernization and Tradition

THE INCREASINGLY fast pace of modernization which the Russian Empire experienced after the middle of the nineteenth century also changed its character as a multi-ethnic empire. The reforms, in particular the abolition of serfdom and the process of industrialization, mobilized new social and ethnic groups. The national movements, which were closely linked to modernization, gradually remodelled the horizontally divided estate-based societies into vertically integrated and culturally conscious nations which now began to make political demands.

The process of social and national mobilization which, by the end of the nineteenth century, had taken place in various parts of the Russian Empire (with differing degrees of intensity) strengthened its heterogeneous character. Expansion in the Caucasus and in Middle Asia also contributed to the fact that, as the nineteenth century progressed, the ethnic, religious, social and economic diversity of Russia continued to increase. Yet at the same time modernization and industrialization brought about greater standardization. From the 1860s onwards Russian policy-makers attempted to systematize the heterogeneous empire in administrative terms, and reacted to the national movements with a certain degree of cultural russification. The tendencies towards greater national homogeneity were confronted with conservative forces which continued to attempt to integrate the empire within the dynastic and estate-based framework.

This chapter is devoted to the structure of the Russian Empire at the end of the nineteenth century and the changes and continuities that become apparent when it is compared to the pre-modern multi-ethnic empire. As in Chapter 4, the emphasis is placed primarily on the socio-ethnic structure, the economic division of labour and culture. The documentary material available in the case of late tsarist Russia is much better than for the period around 1800, and for this reason some aspects of the structure of the multi-ethnic empire can be investigated with the help of statistical data only in this period. However, comprehensive studies of the late tsarist multi-ethnic empire do not exist,[1] and the numerous sources and studies devoted to single regions cannot be dealt with exhaustively in the present context. For this reason I have chosen to concentrate on evaluating what is beyond doubt the most important source, the material of the first and only general census of the Russian Empire, which was conducted in 1897.

The census data, which were published in 89 volumes, constitute the only source which makes it possible to compare the total population of the Russian Empire (without Finland and the protectorates of Bukhara and Khiva, which were still independent under international law), and which links ethnic and social factors.[2] In the present context it is of especial importance to note that ethnic categories (i.e. mother tongue, religion) were recorded separately and correlated with social categories, such as urban and rural population, social status, profession and educational level. Thus the data of the census make it possible to shed light on important social, economic and cultural aspects of the Russian multi-ethnic empire on a broad and empirical basis.

Whereas it is true that the value of the census of 1897 as a source was repeatedly called into question by contemporary commentators, recent research has shown that on the whole its data can be regarded as reliable. Yet it is necessary to treat its findings with a certain amount of caution in the case of some peripheral areas in Asia and in the west. More serious than this is the limited usefulness of some of the categories employed in the census. The data on membership of a specific estate category only enable us to make imprecise deductions about the social structure, and the 65 professions polled merely distinguish between sectors and not social standing. For example, this means that a member of the peasant category could be an urban industrial worker or craftsman, and that the category of metallurgy included craftsmen, workers, white-collar employees and businessmen.

The more than 130 language categories of the census are usually in line with modern nomenclature. Problems arise only in the case of the Turkic languages. Thus the ethnonym Tatar not only applies to the Volga, Crimean and Siberian Tatars, but also to the Muslims of Trans-caucasia (Azerbaidzhanis) and other smaller groups. Furthermore, the Turkic-speaking Muslims of Middle Asia were not categorized in a uniform manner, so that it is impossible to determine their ethnic differentiation in certain administrative districts. Third, the number of Bashkirs is evidently too high and that of the Tatars too low.[3] The question which asked people to state their native language was not always a precise indicator of the ethnic group to which they belonged, especially in view of the fact that certain groups, such as the urban population in Middle Asia or the minor nobility in the west of the empire, were bilingual. Yet on the whole the native language category recorded by the census provides a good idea (bearing in mind contemporary limitations) of Russia's ethnic structure.

1. The Changes in the Socio-ethnic Structure

The *ethnic composition* of the Russian Empire changed in the course of the nineteenth century to the disadvantage of the Russians and the eastern Slavs taken as a whole. As a result of expansion to the west, the south and the east, the Russian percentage of the total population of the empire (without Finland) sank from about 53 per cent (1795) to 44.3 per cent (1897) (though some scholars put the figure as low as 40 per cent to 43 per cent), and that of the eastern Slavs from 83 per cent to 66.8 per cent (see Table 3).[4] Thus non-Russians made up considerably more than half of a total population of more than 125 million. Yet officially the tsarist empire was said to be a state in which two-thirds of the inhabitants were Russians, for 'Little Russians' (Ukrainians) and Belorussians were not recognized as independent nations.

Almost half of the remaining non-eastern Slav third of the empire's population was made up of the ethnic groups in the west, starting with the Poles (7.9 million and 6.3 per cent, a figure that is too low[5]), the Jews (5.1 million and 4 per cent), and the Estonians, Latvians and Lithuanians (together 4.1 million and 3.3 per cent). To this should be added roughly 2.2 million Finns and 300,000 Swedes of the Grand Duchy of Finland who were not included in the census.[6] The Muslims of Middle Asia only numbered 7.2 million (5.8 per cent) in 1897, for the Emirate of Bukhara and Khanate of Khiva were excluded. The Caucasian ethnic groups made up 5.7 million (4.6 per cent), the groups of the Volga and Urals region 5.9 million (4.7 per cent). The 1.8 million Germans (1.4 per cent) must be divided up into the socially heterogeneous groups of the colonists, the Baltic Germans, the Germans in Poland and the German-speaking urban population of Russia.[7] The ethnic groups of the north and of Siberia, and the surviving remnants (after their mass emigration) of the Crimean Tatars and the nomads of the steppe in European Russia constituted only very small percentages. Although the late tsarist multi-ethnic empire was characterized by great ethnic diversity, the Russians continued to be the largest ethnic group by far, and the eastern Slavs clearly the predominant group, whereas the non-Slavs were split up into numerous heterogeneous ethnic groups. Despite the shift to Asia, the Russian Empire, with regard to its ethnic structure, continued to be very much European in character.

The Orthodox church was still a unifying force, and, if one includes the Old Believers, 71 per cent of the population continued to belong to it. The other *denominations and faiths* (see Table 2) were tolerated, though the Orthodox state church continued to enjoy its privileges, and in the second half of the nineteenth century became increasingly a Russian national force.[8] The second largest religious community of the Russian Empire was no longer the Roman Catholic church, as had been the case until the middle of the century, but the Muslims, who constituted more than 11 per cent of the total population (without Bukhara and Khiva). Roman Catholics followed with 9 per cent, Jews with 4.3 per cent, Lutherans with 2.7 per cent (without Finland), members of the Armenian-Gregorian church with 0.9 per cent, and the Buddhist lamaists with 0.4 per cent. There were also a number of smaller groups, including the animists.

Ethnic, linguistic and religious identities still continued to interact closely, and as a rule reinforced each other. This was most obvious in the case of the Armenians and the Jews, whose ethnic identity coincided with their religious identity. In the case of the sedentary Muslims religious identity was still more important than ethnic and linguistic identity. The majority of ethnic groups were homogeneous in religious terms. More than 98 per cent of the Russians, Ukrainians, Romanians, Greeks, Zyrians, Mordvinians, Chuvash and Iakuts were Orthodox, and almost all of the Kazakhs, Uzbeks, Kirgiz, Sarts, Tadzhiks, Chechens and Dagestanis were Muslims. More than 98 per cent of the Poles and Lithuanians were Catholics, almost all of the Finns and Swedes were Lutherans, and more than 96 per cent of the Kalmyks lamaists.

There were different religious denominations in the case of the Germans, of whom 13.5 per cent were Catholics, whilst many were members of smaller Protestant groups (including the Mennonites); the

Belorussians, of whom almost 18 per cent were Catholics (including former members of the Uniate church, and a number of Poles); the Latvians, of whom 18 per cent were Catholics and 4.5 per cent Orthodox; and the Ossetians, of whom about 11.7 per cent were Muslims. In a whole series of ethnic groups a small minority had converted to the Orthodox church, for example, about 13.2 per cent of the Lutheran Estonians, about 6–7 per cent and 24.6 per cent of the Muslim Volga Tatars and Circassians, 34.3 and 6.6 per cent of the animist Koriaks and Chukchi. In the case of other ethnic groups only a small minority had remained faithful to the old (animist) faith, as in the case of the Cheremis (27.6 per cent), Votiaks (7.5 per cent) and Ostiaks (5.3 per cent). Despite formal membership of a church, animist traditions persisted after baptism and had a crucial influence on ethnic consciousness.

Great differences between the various ethnic groups in Russia also become apparent when we consider their social characteristics. Thus according to the census, in the case of the Jews the proportion of the *urban population* was almost 50 per cent (if one includes the small shtetls, the figure was considerably higher), whereas not a single Iukagir lived in a town (see the figures in Table 4).[9] In the case of ethnic groups which for a long time had performed the function of mobilized diaspora groups within the Russian Empire, the degree of urbanization was considerably higher than the 13.4 per cent average.[10] In addition to the Jews, this was true of the Germans (23.4 per cent), the Armenians (23.3 per cent), the Greeks (18 per cent) and, to a lesser extent, of the Tatars, many of whom lived as traders in rural areas.[11] The sedentary Muslims of Middle Asia had a traditionally high percentage of townspeople. Poles and Russians had lived in towns since time immemorial, though the process of urbanization in the nineteenth century meant that the percentage of townspeople increased noticeably. Nevertheless, as regards the level of urbanization, the Russians came only eleventh among the empire's ethnic groups in 1897. Urbanization was also noticeable in the case of the Georgians and the Muslims of Transcaucasia, though not to the same degree. On the other hand, the above-average level of urbanization of the Latvians and Estonians, peasant peoples which had been mobilized in social and national terms, was remarkable. In the last third of the nineteenth century they had moved increasingly to the towns, and by 1897 had displaced the Germans as the largest group in Riga, Dorpat and Reval. All the other traditionally agrarian ethnic groups of the Russian Empire tended to stay away from towns, even at the end of the nineteenth century. For example, in the west the Lithuanians and Belorussians had a level of urbanization of no more than about 3 per cent. In the case of most of the Asiatic ethnic groups the figures were even lower: in the case of the nomads they were 0.04 per cent (Karakalpaks) and 1.7 per cent (Kazakhs), and in the case of the Christianized ethnic groups of the middle Volga and the ethnic groups of Siberia (with the exception of the Iakuts) it was under 1 per cent. Since a large part of the process of economic and cultural modernization occurred in the towns, a large proportion of the ethnic groups in Russia was only marginally affected by them. On the other hand, even at the end of the nineteenth century certain non-Russian groups continued to be more strongly represented among the urban population than the Russians.

This is also shown by the ethnic composition of the nineteen *large cities* of the Russian Empire with more than 100,000 inhabitants (Table 5). In ten towns situated in the western, southern and eastern peripheral areas, the Russians constituted less than half of the population. In Warsaw, Łódź and Tashkent they amounted to less than 10 per cent, in Riga 15.8 per cent and in Vilna 20 per cent. Only Moscow and Tula had populations of which more than 90 per cent were Russians. The majority of the Jews continued to be restricted to the pale of settlement, though there were smaller groups of them in all the major cities. In Kishinev and Vilna they were the largest ethnic group, and the second largest in Warsaw, Odessa, Łódź, and Ekaterinoslav. The Poles dominated in Warsaw and Łódź, and constituted the second largest group in Vilna. Larger groups of Germans lived in Łódź and Riga (where they were the second largest ethnic group after the Latvians). In all of the nineteen cities there were smaller groups of Poles and Germans. The Armenians were the largest ethnic group in Tiflis (before the Russians and Georgians) and the third largest in Baku (after the Muslims and the Russians), whereas their share of the population in the other cities with the exception of Astrakhan remained small. The Tatars made up more than 10 per cent of the population only in Kazan and Astrakhan. The Ukrainians also lagged behind the Russians, and occasionally behind the Jews, in the cities of Ukraine. Muslims predominated in Tashkent, with over 85 per cent of the population, and in Baku, with more than 40 per cent of the population.[12]

There were also great differences in regard to the *estate affiliation* of the ethnic groups in 1897 (Table 6). In this context it needs to be emphasized that the estates were legal categories which make it possible to come to no more than imprecise conclusions about the social structure at the end of the nineteenth century.[13] The ethnic groups of Middle Asia and Siberia, the vast majority of which were excluded as inorodtsy, and the Jews, the vast majority of whom were assigned to urban estates, remained special cases.

In 1897 the Georgians and the Poles still had a particularly high percentage of hereditary nobles which amounted to about 5 per cent, though in this context most of the hereditary nobles who were described as Lithuanians or Belorussians must also be counted as Poles. The Muslims of Azerbaidzhan (3 per cent)[14] and the Germans (1.4 per cent) also had a considerably higher proportion of hereditary nobles than the Russians. Thus it transpires that, despite the policy of standardization and russification, the non-Russian elites co-opted into the nobility had been able, even at the end of the nineteenth century, to retain their privileges, despite the fact that these had been considerably curtailed by the reforms, and, in the case of the Poles and the Trans-caucasians, were not comprehensive. On the other hand, in the case of personal nobility, which had been acquired through service to the government, the percentage was slightly higher than that of the Russians only in the case of the Georgians and the Germans. The inorodtsy and the Jews had practically no nobles, nor did the Latvians, the Estonians, the ethnic groups of the middle Volga and of the Urals. The proportion of non-noble urban merchants and 'honorary citizens' was highest in the case of the Armenians, the Jews and the Germans. It does not come as a surprise that 90 per cent of the traditionally agrarian ethnic groups belonged to the peasant category. The division into estates in itself indicates that certain ethnic groups continued to perform specific functions in the Russian Empire in the elite, and in the urban and rural population.

Thus, despite social mobilization and national movements, many of the 'young peoples' of the Russian Empire still possessed an 'incomplete' social structure at the end of the nineteenth century.[15] The majority of the small ethnic groups which had hardly been mobilized at all in national and social terms, and also the Ukrainians, Belorussians, Lithuanians and Romanians, consisted to 90 per cent and more of peasants. An urban petit bourgeois class had emerged only in the case of the Estonians, Latvians and Finns. Only the Russians and the Poles were 'ancient nations' with a noble upper class, an intelligentsia, an economically active urban population, a still numerically predominant lower class of peasants and a small (new) industrial proletariat. With certain reservations, the Georgians and the Muslims of Transcaucasia (who had only a small urban population) and the sedentary Muslims of Middle Asia (who did not have a legally recognized nobility) also belonged to this ideal type. The third type, which had a non-noble urban merchant elite, was represented by the Jews, the Armenians, the Greeks and the Volga Tatars. There was a predominantly urban lower class in the case of the Jews and a rural lower class in the case of the other three ethnic groups.

However, the picture remains rather imprecise if we look at the empire as a whole. For this reason, as in Chapter 4, I have decided to concentrate on the socio-ethnic structure of the most important *peripheral regions*.[16] The Russian percentage of the population, which changed continually as a result of migration, is once again used as a structural criterion.

1. The large regions in which Russians were still few and far between. The Grand Duchy of *Finland* had the lowest percentage of Russians (0.2 per cent). The majority of the population spoke Finnish (over 86 per cent), and about 13 per cent Swedish.[17] Whereas it is true that most of the rural and urban elite continued to consist of Swedish-speaking Finlanders, the Finns nonetheless, as a result of the process of urbanization, already comprised more than 70 per cent of the urban population in the 1890s. Ethno-social antagonisms continued to exist, especially since a significant percentage of the rural population did not own land. However, as a result of the increasing opposition to the Russian centre, these were to some extent neutralized by a national political closing of ranks on the part of the Finlanders.

After Finland, the lowest proportion of Russians in 1897 was to be found in the former *Kingdom of Poland*. The region, which had lost its autonomy, was now known officially as the Vistula Provinces. The 267,000 Russians who lived in Poland fufilled the role of an occupying power. Seventy-eight per cent of the Russians who were gainfully employed worked in the army. Russian officers and bureaucrats comprised a sixth of the hereditary and 30 per cent of the personal nobles in Poland. The remaining nobles were still Polish, though in the former Kingdom only 1.6 per cent of the Poles still belonged to the hereditary nobility. The Poles, who constituted 72 per cent of the total population, clearly predominated among the peasants as well. However, they were also the largest group in the towns (48.8 per cent), though here they vied with the Jews (35.4 per cent) and the Germans (5.3 per cent). This was demonstrated with particular clarity by the fact that more than half of the small estate of privileged merchants were Jews. The most important changes when compared to the beginning of the nineteenth century were the social decline of the Polish nobility, the great increase in the urban population and the over-proportional increase in the number of Jews (from 8.6 to 13.5 per cent of the total population).

The complicated socio-ethnic structure of the regions *Belorussia-Lithuania* and *Ukraine on the right bank of the Dnepr*, which Russia had acquired as a result of the partitions of Poland, did not change decisively despite the anti-Polish policy pursued by Russia during the nineteenth century. However, the proportion of Russians increased to 5.6 and 4.3 per cent, and that of the Jews to 14 and 12.5 per cent, whereas the proportion of Poles decreased considerably. Although Russians predominated in the army and the administration, and, after 1863, also took over a large amount of Polish-owned land, a section of the Polish magnates and medium-sized landowners were able to hold their own as a rural elite. In addition to the numerous poor Polish nobles, there was a smaller group of Lithuanian and Ukrainian minor nobles. The mass of the peasants was still made up of Ukrainians, Belorussians and Lithuanians. Among the urban population the Jews were the single largest group, with 52 per cent in Belorussia-Lithuania, and 40 per cent in Ukraine to the right of the Dnepr. Their predominance in the merchant estate was even more noticeable. Thus the traditional social structure – a Polish elite, an urban population which was significantly Jewish in character, a broad mass of Ukrainian, Belorussian and Lithuanian peasants – persisted, and, in the light of the numerous unresolved social problems, was a breeding-ground for inter-ethnic conflicts which were not primarily directed against Russians and the Russian government.

In the *Baltic provinces* the socio-ethnic antagonisms between the Latvian and Estonian lower class and the Baltic German upper class persisted. The Germans, who still only comprised 6.9 per cent of the population, continued to set the tone in the towns and the countryside, even though the number of Russian nobles and merchants increased in the second half of the nineteenth century. In 1897 the Russians, who included numerous industrial workers, made up 4.8 per cent of the total population. Whereas the Latvians and Estonians already comprised more than half of the urban population in 1897, they still only made up 11 per cent of the privileged merchant estate. Increased social and national mobilization reinforced the pressure exerted on the German elite by Latvian and Estonian farm labourers, householders and urban lower classes towards the end of the nineteenth century. Here again social protest was not primarily directed against the Russians.

In *Transcaucasia*, which had been conquered at the beginning of the nineteenth century, the Russians comprised 4.5 per cent of the population in 1897, and were to be found in the military, the administration and among the industrial workers (especially in Baku). Nevertheless, here again the traditional socio-ethnic structure remained largely intact. The Georgian and Muslim nobility predominated in the rural elite. Although their relative share of the urban population had declined to 30 per cent, the Armenians continued to be the leading economic group in the towns, and also in Tiflis, the most important centre; 53.8 per cent of the merchant estate were Armenians. They were competing not so much with Georgians and Muslims, who were moving to the towns in increasing numbers, but with Russian and foreign entrepreneurs. The mass of the Muslims, Georgians and also Armenians were peasants in the rural areas. As in the regions described above, the primary conflicts of interest in Transcaucasia were not between non-Russians and Russians, but between the native ethnic groups, particularly between Muslims and Armenians.

The largely Muslim population of the *Caucasian mountain areas* had also been partially integrated into the Russian system of estates. However, its traditional social order, which was based on tribal and religious constituents, remained intact, as did its potential resistance to Russian settlers and bureaucrats. In the area of Dagestan the Russians comprised only 2.3 per cent of the population. Moreover, three-quarters of the hereditary nobility consisted of members of Caucasian- and Turkic-speaking ethnic groups. However, in the Terek area in the central Caucasus Russians already comprised 29 per cent of the population in 1897, and also more than 70 per cent of the hereditary nobility.

Under Russian rule southern *Middle Asia* (including the southern part of the steppe region) remained a world of its own. Its population was assigned to the inorodtsy category, and its socio-ethnic structure remained fundamentally unchanged. True, the Uzbek political elite had been deposed and replaced by Russians, who in 1897 comprised 3 per cent of the population here, most of them in the north-eastern steppe and mountain area of the land of the seven rivers (Semireche) and in Transcaspia. In the southern arable areas there were still very few Russians. For example, in the Fergana area they made up only 0.5 per cent of the population. Although the tribal chieftains of the nomads and the mountain peoples, and the rural and urban nobility of the oases and the river valleys were not co-opted into the imperial nobility, as had been the case with the Muslim upper class in the Caucasus, they retained certain privileges. Under Russian rule the urban population of Middle Asia still consisted largely of Iranian- and Turkic-speaking Muslims. Finally, the encouragement given to the cultivation of cotton led to a progressive social differentiation of the peasants, especially in the Fergana valley.

The small ethnic communities (most of which had already been excluded as inorodtsy at an earlier stage) of the hinterland in *northern and eastern Sibiria*, to which only a handful of Russian settlers had penetrated, also retained their traditional social order. Yet in the case of a number of small and dispersed ethnic groups centuries of interaction with European settlers and the decimation of their economic resources were the origins of a serious social and cultural crisis which led to alcoholism, epidemics and a decline in their numbers.[18] The numerically larger Iakuts, who lived in a single area, were better able to hold their own. In 1897 they had a clear majority of 82.1 per cent in the Iakutsk area, compared to only 11.4 per cent Russians.

In all of the regions of the first type the Russians to all intents and purposes were present merely as a military and administrative elite, and to some extent also as industrial workers. Although the administrative autonomy of the peripheral regions was considerably curtailed in the course of the nineteenth century, particularly in Poland-Lithuania, Bessarabia, Transcaucasia and the Crimea, Russia still needed the regional elites, who, despite the policy of standardization and russification, were to some extent able to retain their social privileges. The relatively small number of Russians among the landowning nobility and the urban economic elite meant that social protest was not primarily directed against the Russians, especially in cases where the regional elite and the economically active urban population belonged to an ethnic group that was different to that of the rural lower classes. Coalitions between the lower and middle classes and the Russian centre against regional elites had now become possible. The social mobilization of the peasants meant that they exerted greater pressure on the urban population. Particularly explosive situations arose when the members of a foreign ethno-religious group (Jews, Armenians) dominated trade, commerce and the crafts, thereby preventing the lower classes from ascending the social ladder.

2. *Ukraine on the left bank of the Dnepr* was a special case. Here the proportion of the Russian population in 1897 was 13 per cent, which was considerably higher than in the areas discussed above. However, the Russians were concentrated in the peripheral areas in the north and the east. More important was the fact that the Ukrainian upper class of the Hetmanate had lost its predominant position at the end of the eighteenth century and in the nineteenth century. Russians were now predominant in the landowning nobility, and, next to the Jews, in the urban economic upper class. The reason for this, apart from the government's repressive policy towards Ukraine, was the fact that, in the course of the integration of the Cossack Hetmanate into the Russian Empire, a large section of the Ukrainian Cossack elite had been totally absorbed into the Russian upper class. In 1897, in the former Hetmanate (the provinces of Poltava and Chernigov), the majority of the nobles (especially the minor nobles) and the urban population were still Ukrainians, though this was not true of the merchant estate. Yet in the large cities of Kharkov and Kiev, which had also belonged to the Hetmanate, they were clearly a minority next to the Russians.

The situation was similar in *Bessarabia*, where Russians comprised only 8 per cent of the total population, but 55.8 per cent of the hereditary nobility. The old upper class, the Romanian boyars, had to a certain extent been absorbed into the Russian nobility, so that only 22 per cent of the hereditary nobility in Bessarabia was still Romanian. The Romanians (Moldavians), who were primarily peasants, constituted 47.6 per cent of the total population,[19] whereas the Jews formed the largest group in the towns. The Ukrainians, who comprised almost 20 per cent of the population, were mainly peasants who had immigrated from the adjoining regions.

3. On the other hand, there were few changes in the regions which had been part of Russia for centuries, and had for a long time been inhabited by Russians. Here the Russian proportion of the population was high, and as a rule they comprised the upper class in the towns and rural areas, and a considerable proportion of the peasants. These areas had for

a long time been firmly integrated into the Russian Empire in administrative, economic and social terms.

In *northern Russia*, in addition to a clear Russian majority, there were small Finnish-speaking ethnic groups (Karelians, Zyrians, Veps, Izhora). They were peasants, fishermen and hunters. Most of the Belorussian peasants in the west of the province of *Smolensk* were absorbed by the Russian majority in the course of the nineteenth century. The remainder were confronted with a Russian nobility and a Russian urban population.

In the region of the *middle Volga and the northern Urals* the Russians, who comprised 73 per cent of the population, were also considerably more numerous than the non-Russians. Whereas the majority of the Chuvash, Votiaks and Cheremis lived compactly in their ancient settlement areas, the Tatars and Mordvinians were dispersed over the whole of the Volga-Urals area. The Muslim Tatars were ethnically stable, whereas the Mordvinians were the target of intense russification. In the province of Kazan, at the centre of the former Khanate of Kazan, which for a considerable period of time had no longer been colonized by Russians, the non-Russians, who comprised more than 60 per cent, clearly continued to be in the majority (31.1 per cent Tatars, 23.1 per cent Chuvash and 5.7 per cent Cheremis). But in the region as a whole the Russians dominated the nobility and the urban population. The overwhelming majority of non-Russians were peasants. Only the Tatars also possessed a small and largely impoverished nobility, and a class of craftsmen, merchants, entrepreneurs and workers. On the *lower Volga* there was also a special rural group, the German colonists and in the steppe the numerically decimated nomadic Kalmyks.

In *south-western Siberia* Russian settlers constituted the overwhelming majority of the population at the end of the nineteenth century. For example, in the province of Tobolsk, Russians comprised almost 90 per cent of the population as opposed to the 4 per cent share of the Tatars and the 1.5 per cent of the Ostiaks. The small Turkic- and Finno-Ugric-speaking ethnic groups had been forced to retreat to more inaccessible areas. Only the Siberian Tatars with their social differentiation were to a certain extent able to hold their own.

4. The fourth basic type comprised the regions first settled in the course of the nineteenth century by Russians, Ukrainians and other ethnic groups, and where the socio-ethnic structure was still in a constant state of flux.[20]

New Russia, the area of the steppe to the north of the Black Sea (together with Bessarabia, the Crimea and the Don district), was the most important goal of Ukrainian, Russian, Jewish and German settlers in the first half of the nineteenth century. After the middle of the century they were increasingly supplanted by workers. In 1897 its population was made up of Ukrainians (42.9 per cent), Russians (29.8 per cent), Romanians (10 per cent), Jews (6.7 per cent), Germans (3.5 per cent), Tatars (2.1 per cent) , Bulgars (1.6 per cent) and numerous other ethnic groups. The Russians dominated the hereditary nobility and thus the rural elite, and, with 71.6 per cent, were clearly ahead of the Poles and the Ukrainians. In the urban population the Russians were again the largest group (48 per cent), ahead of the Jews (23 per cent) and the Ukrainians (15.5 per cent). Jews and Russians predominated in the merchant estate, whereas the Russians were predominant among the industrial workers. This group grew rapidly towards the end of the century. The German colonists played an important role as a wealthy rural middle class; in the last decades of the nineteenth century they increased their already sizeable estates by purchasing land from the nobility. The steppe to the north of the Black Sea, which was only sparsely populated until the second half of the eighteenth century, had become a domain of the eastern Slavs by the end of the nineteenth century, with the Russians predominant in the elite. The large towns were multi-ethnic in character, as is demonstrated by the ethnic composition of Odessa with its 404,000 inhabitants (see Table 5). Eastern Slavs also continued to settle in the Crimea. In 1897, after several large waves of emigration, the Crimean Tatars in the province of Taurida comprised only 13 per cent of the population, and on the peninsula only 34 per cent. Furthermore, the importance of the Crimean Tatar nobility had declined. Despite its markedly Russian character, New Russia possessed a fairly complicated socio-ethnic structure, and there were considerable social and inter-ethnic tensions in this economically dynamic peripheral region far away from the centre.

Until the eighteenth century the plains and hilly areas *to the north of the Caucasus* had also been a domain of nomad horsemen and Caucasian 'gortsy' into which Russian and Ukrainian Cossacks gradually advanced. After the conquest of the Caucasians in the middle of the nineteenth century, it became the most important European goal of Russian and Ukrainian settlers, who occupied the area which had become vacant on account of the extermination, expulsion and emigration of Muslim ethnic groups. In 1897 the eastern Slav population, which consisted in roughly equal parts of Russian and Ukrainians, and to a considerable extent of Cossacks, already comprised more than 90 per cent of the population in the province of Stavropol and in the Kuban district. Otherwise there were only small groups of Nogai Tatars, Circassians, Karachaians and Kabardinians. In contrast to the central and eastern Caucasus, brutal conquest had broken the resistance of the native ethnic groups in this area.

The immigration of Russians into the area of the *southern Urals*, which had already begun in the eighteenth century, continued with particular intensity, especially in the first half of the nineteenth century. As early as the 1850s the Russians constituted the majority of the population. The minority comprised the Bashkirs, the former masters of the region, and the Tatars (among whom I also count the Teptiars and Mishars), Mordvinians and Cheremis, who were also immigrants. Whereas the Russians in the province of Orenburg already comprised more than 70 per cent of the population, they only amounted to 38 per cent in the province of Ufa. Here the Bashkirs and the Tatars together still formed the majority. In the hereditary nobility the Tatars still constituted the largest group, and Tatar merchants continued to play an important role as intermediaries in the trade with Asia via Orenburg. The conflicts surrounding the pastures of the Bashkirs continued to smoulder, even if, when compared with the eighteenth century, they were potentially no longer quite as explosive.

At the end of the nineteenth century the *northern steppe in Kazakhstan* became the area which witnessed the most violent clashes between eastern Slav setttlers and the Muslim nomads of the steppes. The Russians and Ukrainians who, from the 1860s onwards, had migrated to the vast region of the steppes of Middle Asia already comprised 20 per cent of the population in 1897, and as much as a third of the population in the fertile northern peripheral areas, such as the Akmolinsk district. The nomadic Kazakhs, who still comprised more than three-quarters of the population, believed that their economic existence was being threatened by the occupation of their summer pastures. However, the settlement of northern Kazakhstan proceeded at a faster pace at the end of the nineteenth and at the beginning of the twentieth centuries, and, as a result of this, by 1911 the proportion of eastern Slavs had doubled, and the land owned by the Kazakhs had decreased considerably. Thus the potential for socio-ethnic conflict was constantly increasing.

In the second half of the nineteenth century and at the beginning of the twentieth century, *Siberia* became the most important goal for Russian settlers. The vast majority of the colonists remained in western Siberia, where they further reinforced the existing Russian predominance. Yet many settlers were attracted by eastern Siberia, and the newly annexed area on the Amur and the Pacific. However, in this area the construction of the Trans-Siberian Railway (1891–1903) first led to mass colonization. The Russians already constituted a third of the population in the Trans-Baikal area in 1897, and the conflicts over the land of the nomadic Buriats, who still comprised slightly more than a quarter of the population, intensified. In the Far East, on the other hand, the native Tungusic and Palaeo-Altaic ethnic groups were no more than small entities which were further reduced in size by epidemics. The largest ethnic minority next to the Russian and Ukrainian majority of 63 per cent was made up of immigrant Chinese and Korean workers. In the coastal area of Vladivostok they comprised about a quarter of the population.

Over the centuries the intensive colonization of the newly conquered and sparsely inhabited areas in the south and the east created a broad zone of settlements and colonies stretching from the Black Sea to the Pacific. The largely nomadic population of these regions was either killed and expelled (as in the western Caucasus), or gradually encircled by agrarian settlements which had the support of the government, and driven into more inaccessible areas. In this confrontation between arable farmers and nomads of the steppe (and in part hunters and mountain herdsmen) the opponents were not, as in the first type, members of various elites. Rather, the conflict over land was played out between the lower classes, and this made the inter-ethnic conflicts particularly explosive. The situation is reminiscent of the struggle between European settlers and Indians in North America.

For the Russians and Ukrainians the colonization of the peripheral regions in the south-east and the east was certainly a substitute for central and west European emigration overseas. Only a few ethnic groups in the west of the empire, such as the Jews, Poles, Lithuanians and Finlanders, participated in emigration overseas in larger numbers. However, at the same time, between 1860 and 1890 more than two million foreigners (primarily Germans, Poles, Armenians, Muslims, Koreans and Chinese) came to Russia from the adjoining states, and this helped to increase the percentage of non-Russians in the population.[21]

The process of the intensive settlement of new peripheral areas, which led to a situation where they were inhabited by an eastern Slav majority and controlled by a Russian elite, constitutes one of the important changes in the socio-ethnic structure of the Russian Empire in the course of the nineteenth century. But Russian pressure also increased in areas which were not the target of colonization. Political and administrative autonomy was abolished or curtailed, though, as the examples of Finland and Poland demonstrate, to various extents. In this way the political and social position of the Russian elite in the periphery improved. Typical for the new state of affairs was the fact that in the newly conquered areas in Middle Asia the nobility was no longer co-opted into the Russian nobility. Nevertheless the non-Russian nobility in the numerous peripheral areas of the west and the south was able to retain its position as the leading social class.

It is noteworthy that in 1897 the Russians, with just on 40 per cent, still comprised less than half of the empire's hereditary nobility.[22] The Poles, on the other hand, contributed no less than 29 per cent (or 39 per cent if one includes the at least partly polonized Belorussians and Lithuanians) of the hereditary nobility. The Georgians (5.9 per cent), 'Tatars' (mainly Azerbaidzhanis, 4.8 per cent) and Germans (2 per cent) also continued to be over-represented. However, assignment to this legal category did not accurately reflect their actual social position. The vast majority of Polish and Georgian nobles were poor and possessed little or no land. Furthermore, their privileges had been curtailed. Thus, although the numerically large non-Russian nobility (Poles, Georgians, Azerbaidzhanis) had declined in social terms, its leading class retained its socially predominant status. The fact that such a large number of non-Russians had at least been able to retain their membership of the privileged nobility at the end of the nineteenth century sheds light on that component of Russian policy which sought to preserve the social status quo.

As a result of the process of urbanization the Russians were also able to strengthen their position among the urban population. However, in the towns in the west and the south the mobilized diaspora groups of the Jews, Germans and Armenians continued to predominate, as did the Muslims in Middle Asia. But the new class of industrial workers, which is not included as a special category in the census, was largely Russian. Although the great legal disparities relating to the status of the rural population were abolished by the reforms, there continued to be differences with regard to the general state of agriculture, ownership of land and social rank. This meant, for example, that the mass of the Russian peasants, who continued to live in repartitional communes which were characterized by social uniformity and restricted mobility, and on whom the heritage of serfdom weighed heavily, were worse off than numerous non-Russian peasants in the west and the east, something that had already been the case in the pre-modern multi-ethnic empire.

Russians were now more predominant in the *political and military elite* at the centre of the Russian Empire, which had still been cosmopolitan in the first half of the nineteenth century. On the one hand the expansion of the educational system and Russian social mobilization had alleviated the 'dearth of people' (maloliudstvo) and on the other in the national age the Russian government and Russian society began to be suspicious of non-Russian bureaucrats and officers. In the light of this tendency it is surprising how high the percentage of non-Russians in the central elite continued to be.

Under Nicholas II (1894–1914), the 215 members of the State Council, which consisted of high-ranking civil servants, and a number of military men and academics, included at least 26 (12.1 per cent) who were non-Orthodox, and in the main members of the Lutheran church. And of the 568 top positions in the central and regional administration, in 1903 10 per cent had non-Orthodox incumbents (6.9 per cent were Lutheran, 3.2 per cent Catholics).[23] Germans from the Baltic provinces and from Germany, who were strongly represented in the Finance and Foreign Ministries, in the diplomatic service, and among the governors, continued to constitute the largest group. For example, from 1882 onwards the embassy in London was headed by Baltic Germans. Even before the First World War 10 to 15 per cent of the more than 6,000 ministerial civil servants were non-Orthodox, most of them Lutherans. However, the career patterns of high-ranking German civil servants demonstrate that the vast majority had now been through Russian educational institutions, which means that to some extent at least they had been russified. Furthermore, there were numerous high-ranking civil servants with German names who were Orthodox, and most of them had been more or less russified. Thus personalities such as Finance Ministers M. von Reutern (1862–78) and N. von Bunge (1881– 87), or Foreign Ministers N. Giers (1882–95) and V. Graf Lambsdorff (1900–06) can only be described as being German in a very limited sense of the word. Nevertheless they stood for the great tradition of the Germans

THE LATE TSARIST MULTI-ETHNIC EMPIRE

and the Baltic Germans in the Russian bureaucracy. In addition to the Germans there were, in various sections of the bureaucracy, such as the Ministry of Agriculture, a fair number of Poles, even though they were considered to be unreliable. As a rule Orthodox non-Russians, such as Georgians or Ukrainians, were not listed separately in the statistics. Occasionally members of other ethnic groups were also promoted to senior positions, for example, the Armenian Loris-Melikov, who was Minister of the Interior in 1880–81.

Germans, Baltic Germans, Finlanders and Poles were traditionally well represented among the officers of the Russian army, and in the nineteenth century they were joined by the Caucasians. In 1867–8 77 per cent of the officers were Orthodox, 14 per cent Catholic (mainly Poles), 7 per cent Protestant (Baltic Germans, Germans and Finlanders), 1 per cent Armenian and 1 per cent Muslim. Most of the last were probably Azerbaidzhanis, though there was also a handful of northern Caucasians.[24] No less than 27 per cent of the generals were Protestants. In 1903 the proportion of eastern Slav officers had risen to about 80 per cent (this figure included numerous russified Germans). But of the more than 4,000 captains 12.9 per cent were still Catholics, 4.2 per cent Lutherans (about 1 per cent were Finlanders), 63 Georgians (1.5 per cent), 48 Armenians (1.1 per cent) and 38 Muslims (0.9 per cent). Among the high-ranking officers the proportion of non-Russians was about the same, though the ethnic structure changed considerably. The higher the rank the greater the proportion of Lutherans and the lower the rank the greater the percentage of Poles, Armenians and Muslims whose careers were being impeded. Among the 2,679 colonels the Lutherans already amounted to 7.3 per cent, among the 1,468 generals 10.3 per cent, and among the top 132 generals 14.7 per cent, whereas the corresponding percentages for the Catholics were 5.9, 3.8 and 3.6.[25] Nine generals were Muslims, six Armenians and five Georgians. Thus around 1900 the officer corps continued to be multi-ethnic. In the lower ranks there were numerous Poles, and even Muslims continued to be accepted, in contrast to the Jews, who could practically rise to officer rank only as military physicians. In the upper ranks the Baltic Germans, Germans and Finlanders (who were especially numerous in the navy) continued to play an important role, even though their percentage had declined.

Despite the fact that national ideology began to cloud the relationship between Russians and non-Russians in the second half of the nineteenth century, Germans, Finlanders and to some extent Poles and Caucasians continued to be represented in the military and civil elite of the Empire. Thus until the First World War the tsarist government adhered to its principles, which were to value loyalty, specialist knowledge and noble descent more highly than religion or ethnic origins.

The intelligentsia, which was initially recruited from the ranks of the Russian nobility, was opposed to the autocratic regime, and from the 1860s onwards began to form oppositional and revolutionary groups. From the 1870s onwards more and more non-Russians joined this *anti-elite*. Thus only half of the Populists active between 1878 and 1887, who had a penchant for terrorism, were of Russian origin. Particularly well represented in the 1870s were the Ukrainians and in the 1880s the Jews. There were also a number of Poles and Germans. The Russian revolutionary parties continued this cosmopolitan tradition, which was especially noticeable in the case of the Mensheviks, in the leadership of which the Russians were clearly in the minority when compared with non-Russians (especially Georgians and Jews). Numerous Jews and Ukrainians also joined the Social Revolutionaries and many Jews the Bolsheviks, though in these parties the Russians had a clear majority.[26]

The non-Russians in the All-Russian revolutionary movement were as a rule more or less russified. The situation was different in the independent revolutionary parties, which were founded for example by Poles, Jews and Armenians, and in the national movements, which to some extent adopted socialist goals. All in all, a number of non-Russian ethnic groups, the Jews, the Poles, the Georgians and the Armenians, played a significant role within the counter-elite of the revolutionary intelligentsia.

Although ethnic criteria became increasingly important in the national age, and the geographical and social mobility of the population increased in the wake of the gradual process of modernization, the socio-ethnic structures of the Russian multi-ethnic empire changed rather slowly. The traditional estate elements and the horizontal structure of society remained intact in large parts of the country. Thus the tension between the pre-modern and pre-national order and the new social and national forces made a crucial contribution to the instability of the late tsarist empire.

2. The Economic Division of Labour and Competition in the Age of Industrialization

There were significant changes in the socio-economic structure of the Russian Empire in the nineteenth century, and especially in its final third.[27] Industrial development became more dynamic from the 1860s onwards, and in the 1890s made a qualitative leap with the highest growth rates in Europe. The prime movers of industrialization, which was energetically encouraged by the Russian state, were the construction of railways, capital formed by banking and financial institutions, foreign capital and a protectionist foreign trade policy. Mining and heavy industry constituted the central growth sector, though the textile and sugar industries, which had already reached a high level of development, also continued to expand. On the other hand, the development of agriculture lagged behind, though it proved possible to increase the production and the export of grain on a continual basis in the second half of the nineteenth century. The rapid economic development of the Russian Empire occurred within certain sectors and was not the same in the different regions. This leads us to ask to what extent the peripheral areas and the non-Russian ethnic groups participated in the process in the context of the multi-ethnic empire as a whole.

In its industrial development the former Kingdom of Poland had enjoyed a head start over the other regions of the Russian Empire since the beginning of the nineteenth century. The industrial revolution occurred here as early as the 1870s and 1880s, and with regard to the degree of mechanization, organization and productivity, the rapidly growing textile industry in Łódź and the surrounding area, and the heavy industry of the Dabrowa basin were well ahead of Russian industry. Exports to other regions of the Russian Empire increased steadily. This contributed to the close economic links between Russia and Poland, and drew protests from Russian industrialists. In the 'Kingdom' the entrepreneurs and industrial workers were Poles, Jews and Germans (and foreigners). There were hardly any Russians.

The Urals, the old Russian centre of heavy industry, retained its leadership in iron and steel production despite its antiquated technology and organization until the end of the 1880s. However, it was overtaken in the 1890s by the heavy industry of southern Ukraine which had been set up with the help of foreign capital and foreign entrepreneurs and specialists, and was based on the coalfields of the Donets basin and the iron ore deposits of Kryvyi Rih on the Dnepr. At the turn of the century just about half of the empire's iron and steel production came from this region, whilst the Urals still contributed 20 per cent and Poland 15 per cent. To all intents and purposes the industrialization of the Urals had proceeded without the participation of the Bashkirs. Similarly, the Ukrainians had little or no share in the rapid development of the south of their region, where foreign and Russian entrepreneurs and Russian workers clearly predominated.[28] It was primarily the sugar industry which expanded in Ukraine on the right bank of the Dnepr, with Jewish merchants and Polish nobles as entrepreneurs, whereas most of the seasonal workers were Ukrainian.

In addition to southern Ukraine and Poland, the cities of St Petersburg and Moscow (together with some of the surrounding provinces) developed into the most important industrial centres of the empire. In the other peripheral regions the swiftly growing metal and textile industries in the Baltic provinces, especially in Riga, were of importance, with mainly German companies and Latvian, Estonian and Russian workers, as was the timber processing industry in Finland. Finally, we should mention the oilfields in the Caucasus area, not only the district around Grozny in the northern Caucasus, but primarily the area of Baku, which towards the end of the century became the largest oilfield in the world. Foreign companies such as Nobel and Rothschild were once again involved, in addition to Russian and Armenian entrepreneurs and skilled workers. Azerbaidzhanis from Transcaucasia and Persia usually found employment as unskilled workers.

All in all the industrialization of the Russian Empire proceeded both in the regions of the Russian centre and in the peripheral areas. Yet the majority of the entrepreneurs were Russians and foreigners, and the majority of the workers Russians. Numerous non-Russian peripheral ethnic groups took little or no part in these developments. Apart from the Poles, Latvians and Estonians, exceptions were the mobilized diaspora groups of the Jews, the Germans and the Armenians, who were actively involved in the industrialization of their regions. The rise of industry in the peripheral regions of the Empire contributed to the intensification of economic interaction and the development of railway links with the centre, and, with the exception of Poland, to the immigration of Russian workers. In this way the industrial regions on the periphery were integrated more firmly into the Russian Empire.

Despite the rapid development of industry, the agricultural sector clearly continued to play a leading role in the Russian Empire. The traditional division of labour between the primarily grain-producing black-earth zone, and the other areas, which had always had a non-agricultural orientation, became even more pronounced. By increasing the amount of land under cultivation and increasing productivity it proved possible to step up the production of marketable grain in the last decades of the century, particularly in the newly developed fertile steppe areas of New Russia, the area to the north of the Caucasus, and the southern Urals. Most of the surplus wheat was shipped from the Black Sea ports, and made a significant contribution to the rapid growth of Russia's grain exports. Russian and Polish nobles and German colonists were primarily involved in the commercialization of arable farming, and to a lesser extent the Ukrainian and Russian peasants. It is noteworthy that, at least in the case of wheat production in European Russia, the peripheral areas inhabited mainly by non-Russians almost always attained a higher level of productivity than the Russian regions. In the 1890s the Baltic provinces were at the top of the list, followed by Ukraine, New Russia, the southern Urals and Belorussia-Lithuania.[29] The most important reasons for the high productivity of the old agricultural regions in the west, in which Finland and Poland, which are missing from the above list, should be included, was the existence of estates which were in the process of modernizing themselves and their agrarian order, the absence of uniform repartitional communes and the predominance of individual farmers.

The agricultural division of labour meant that certain regions which were primarily inhabited by non-Russians had specific tasks. Whilst the cultivation of sugar beet was concentrated in western Ukraine and in Poland, and tobacco plantations in Ukraine on the left bank of the Dnepr, New Russia became the most important producer of grain exports. The nomads of the steppes and the mountain population of the Caucasus and Middle Asia continued to concentrate primarily on animal husbandry. The cultivation of vines, rice and fruit was encouraged in all of the southern areas. In Middle Asia the production of cotton became increasingly important, though the goal of making the Russian Empire self-sufficient in this area was still a long way off in 1917. The small ethnic groups in the north and the east continued to ply their traditional trade of forestry. An ever greater division of labour and the intensification of the exchange of goods in the agricultural sector also contributed to the integration of the non-Russian periphery.

Since its economy was designed to supply the needs of the metropolis, Middle Asia in particular became a colony dependent on the centre.

To sum up. In the nineteenth century the largely Russian centre and a section of the Russians experienced a period of rapid economic development. Since industrialization and commercialized agriculture arose simultaneously in various regions in the west of the Empire, the traditional west–east gradient in the level of economic development persisted, albeit to a lesser degree. The traditional leading regions in the north-west of the Empire (Poland, the Baltic provinces and Finland) were joined by the steppe areas in the south-west, in the development of which Russians also played an important role. However, the areas in the east inhabited by non-Russians took little or no part in the development of industry and capitalist agriculture. Here the traditional economic patterns of nomadic animal husbandry on the steppes and the mountains, of arable farming based on irrigation in Middle Asia and of hunting, reindeer breeding and fishing in the far north and the Far East persisted, and to some extent the relationship to the Russian centre resembled economic colonialism.

With regard to the question of the inter-ethnic division of labour in the Russian Empire, the data of the 1897 census provide information about those employed in the various sectors of the economy, even though it is only of an imprecise nature.[30] The following figures refer as a rule to the returns of the occupational groups with dependents (Table 7), although the data for employees (without dependents) are occasionally adduced for purposes of comparison (Table 8). The most important kind of gainful employment, for all groups with the exception of the Jews and small groups of foreign immigrants, was *agriculture* (which in this context comprised arable farming, animal husbandry, forestry and fisheries). More than 96 per cent of the ethnic groups of the middle Volga (excluding the Tatars) and of Siberia were active in this sector. In the west of the empire the Romanians (92.9 per cent), the Belorussians (90.9 per cent), the Ukrainians (87.2 per cent) and the Lithuanians (85.8 per cent) had the highest percentages, whereas those of the Georgians and Azerbaidzhanis were slightly lower. The Greeks, Russians, Armenians, Latvians and Estonians came next, with figures of around 70 per cent, and were followed by the Poles (63 per cent) and Germans (57.7 per cent), whereas in 1897 only 3.8 per cent of the Jews were still employed in agriculture.

However, the overall figures given for the Germans must be

differentiated, for they comprised at least four distinct socio-economic groups. About three-quarters of the German colonists of the lower Volga, New Russia and Volhynia were employed in the agricultural sector, as opposed to only half of the Germans in Poland and less than 5 per cent of the Germans in the Baltic provinces and in central and northern Russia. In the case of the Armenians the percentage of those engaged in agriculture was much higher in their core areas than in the rest of Transcaucasia and in the diaspora.

The above statistics are mirrored in reverse in the figures of those employed in the industrial and craft, and trade and banking sectors. In 1897 no less than 34.5 per cent (excluding dependents 35.4 per cent) of the Jews worked in the *craft and industrial* sector. As a result of this, in Belorussia-Lithuania they comprised 60 per cent of those active in these economic sectors, and about 30 per cent in Poland and Ukraine. The lion's share went to small Jewish craftsmen in urban and rural areas, 45 per cent of whom were active in the clothing industry (tailors, cobblers, etc.). On account of the fact that they were crowded together to an unusual extent, Jewish craftsmen found it very difficult to make a living. They were competing with other Jews, with non-Jews, and with an increase in industrial production.

With regard to the proportion of those employed as craftsmen and in industry, the Germans came second with 20.9 per cent (excluding dependents 25.0 per cent). The figures for the Baltic provinces (37.3 per cent) and for Poland, central and northern Russia (about 30 per cent) were considerably higher. In this way two of the typical mobilized diaspora groups were clearly distinct from the other ethnic groups.[31]

In the case of the four following ethnic groups a proportion of industrial workers and craftsmen of 11 to 14 per cent (excluding dependents, 15–18 per cent) demonstrates their relatively high degree of social mobilization within the context of the Russian Empire. It is a remarkable fact that the Estonians and Latvians, who had once been peasant peoples, were on about the same level as the Poles and the Russians. This once again shows the speed of their social mobilization and differentiation. The Russians comprised 51.6 per cent (excluding dependents as much as 57.6 per cent) of the Empire's industrial workers and craftsmen, and were thus above average in this sector. The Armenians and Greeks had percentages corresponding to the Imperial average, whilst the ethnic groups of Middle Asia led the field of the Asiatic peoples. Yet their averages tell us little, for the traditional urban population of the Tadzhiks and Sarts had a proportion of craftsmen which, at 21.8 and 17.1 per cent (excluding dependents about 28 per cent), was far higher than that of the Russians.

With regard to the proportion of those employed in *trade and banking* the Jews, with 36.7 per cent (excluding dependents, 29.7 per cent), were still more obviously in the lead. They comprised no less than 44.8 per cent (36 per cent) of all those employed in this sector. In Belorussia/Lithuania the figure was as high as 92.9 per cent, in Poland 82.6 per cent and in Ukraine 80.8 per cent. For the Jews the most important sub-sector was trade in agricultural products (grain, livestock, etc.). As small retailers and money-lenders, and in regard to their traditional function of acting as intermediaries between the urban and rural populations, they enjoyed a virtual monopoly in large parts of the pale of settlement. Here again it must be remembered that most of these Jews were small retailers, hawkers and peddlers who were hardly able to feed their families with the meagre income derived from their trade. Only a small group became wealthy. Nevertheless, in the pale the Jews comprised the majority of the guild merchants. As merchants and bankers a number of Jews such as J. Günzburg, S. Poliakov, H. Epstein, J. Bloch and I. Brodsky acquired the capital which they then partly invested in companies active in the textile, sugar and oil industries, and in the construction of railways.[32]

The Greeks (6.7 and 11.7 per cent) and the Armenians (6.4 or 9.6 per cent), who performed intermediary economic functions in the south of the Russian Empire, followed, though with much lower percentages. The Tatars, who had played an important role in the east of the Empire from the eighteenth century onwards, though their significance had since declined, and the Azerbaidzhanis were also above the average. And the low average for the Germans tells us little, since the figures for the Baltic provinces (13.2 per cent) and for central and northern Russia (15.9 and 8.9 per cent) were much higher. The percentage of those employed in trade and banking reflects with even greater clarity than that of those employed as industrial workers and as craftsmen the inter-mediary role which mobilized diaspora groups continued to play in the Russian Empire. In the case of the Jews specialization had continued to increase in the nineteenth century as a result of the fact that they were either barred from working in agriculture, in the administration and in numerous other professions, or at least it was made very difficult for them to do so.

The Russians, however, with 2.5 per cent (excluding dependents 2.3 per cent) had a percentage of those employed in trade and banking which was considerably below the average, and they constituted only slightly more than a third of the inhabitants of the Russian Empire active in this sector. In contrast to this, the figures for the Tadzhiks and the Sarts in Middle Asia were once again rather high. In the case of all the other ethnic groups, including the Poles, Latvians, Estonians and Georgians, a considerably lower percentage was active in trade and banking. Thus the inter-ethnic division of labour was more pronounced in this area than in the craft and industry sector. However, the economic significance of the mobilized diaspora groups declined towards the end of the nineteenth century. The social mobilization of other ethnic groups meant that the latter began to see the predominance of the mobilized diaspora groups in certain areas as constituting an obstacle to social advancement, and that the government was no longer wholly dependent on their services, and no longer confirmed their traditional privileges. The social and economic antagonism between the ethnic groups which consisted primarily of urban and rural lower classes, and the mobilized diaspora groups of the Jews, Armenians, Germans and Greeks which dominated trade, banking and crafts led increasingly to inter-ethnic conflict.

3. The Growth of Literacy and the Creation of National Intelligentsias

The growth of literacy constituted an important aspect of the modernization process in addition to urbanization, industrialization and the expansion of communication and mobility. Here again the data of the 1897 census make it possible for the first time to compare all of the ethnic groups of the Russian Empire (excluding Finland). The census recorded the ability to read, and not the ability to write, which would have led to considerably lower results. Although the lack of other data makes it impossible to prove this directly, there is reason to believe that the figures relating to the reading skills of the non-Christian ethnic groups were too low. On the one hand this may have been due to the fact that the Muslim, Jewish and Buddhist schools to some extent simply taught their pupils to memorize certain things in parrot fashion. On the other hand, some of the Russians who conducted the census may simply not have recorded reading skills in Arabic, Tatar, Hebrew, Yiddish or Mongolian. It should also be borne in mind that the considerable upsurge which the educational system in the Russian Empire experienced, in particular at the end of the nineteenth century, had little impact on the census data. The following data concerning the degree of literacy (Table 9) refer to the proportion of people with reading skills in the population over the age of ten.[33]

Indisputably at the top of the list were the Estonians with a literacy level of 94 per cent, followed by the Latvians (85 per cent) and the Germans (78.5 per cent). In this group we should also include the Finns and the Swedes of the Grand Duchy of Finland who were not covered by the census. In 1900 the percentage of those with reading skills came to over 98 per cent.[34] Thus the ethnic groups which belonged primarily to the Lutheran faith were able to maintain the educational advantage which they had enjoyed since the eighteenth century. An even clearer picture emerges for the Baltic provinces, where 96.1 per cent of the Estonians, 95.2 per cent of the Germans and 92.1 per cent of the Latvians were able to read. This underlines the special status of the Baltic provinces and Finland with their central European traditions and structures. On the other hand it also highlights the significance of the Lutheran faith for the level of education. Of the Catholic Latvians who lived in Lettgallia (province of Vitebsk), only 57.7 per cent were able to read. The Germans who lived in other regions of Russia, some of whom were Catholic, had a lower level of literacy than the Baltic Germans. This was true not so much of the former colonists (around 87 per cent) than of the Germans in Volhynia and Poland (around 60 per cent). It is note-worthy that in the case of the Estonians and Latvians, more women than men were able to read, and that there was virtually no difference in the level of literacy of the urban and rural population. However, a large number of Estonians, Latvians and Finns was only partially literate. Thus, whilst it is true that almost all Estonians were able to read as early as 1881, less than half of them were also able to write.[35]

With a literacy level of 50.1 per cent, the Jews were a long way behind the largely Protestant ethnic groups. Since religious education in the cheder was in the first instance intended for men, the latter had a considerably higher percentage with reading skills (64.6 per cent) than women (36.6 per cent). Contemporary observers were of the opinion that the literacy level of the Jews was higher than these figures suggest.[36]

The next group comprised the two most important Roman Catholic ethnic groups of the Russian Empire, the Lithuanians (48.4 per cent) and the Poles (41.8 per cent). In both cases women were not far behind men. It is noteworthy that, according to the data of the census, the Lithuanians, a peasant people, had a higher percentage of people with reading skill than the Poles, an ancient nation and culture, with their numerous nobles and urban population. The level of literacy was only higher (62.6 per cent) in the case of the Polish urban population. It is of course conceivable that the figures for the Poles are slightly too low, though the main reason for this surprising state of affairs was probably the fact that Polish national education had suffered more under the repressive linguistic and ecclesiastical policies of the Russian government than that of Lithuania, which, with a dense network of secret schools and the support of the pro-national clergy, was able to develop even in the era of cultural repression. Thus the relatively high percentage of Lithuanians with reading skills was at one and the same time a product and an important factor of the national movement, which spread rapidly at the end of the nineteenth century. In the case of the Poles, whose native educational system had been expanded at the end of the eighteenth and the beginning of the nineteenth century, the degree of male literacy was now on the same low level as that of the Russians.

Of the Orthodox ethnic groups, the Greeks and Bulgars had a higher percentage of people with reading skills than the Russians, who, with 29.3 per cent, were just above the imperial average. However, in the case of the Russians, who until the middle of the century had lagged behind the ethnic groups in the west and to some extent those in the east, the dynamic increase in literacy was especially noticeable at the end of the nineteenth century and at the beginning of the twentieth century. In 1897 almost 70 per cent of the Russian male urban population was already able to read. The Belorussians (20.3 per cent) and the Ukrainians (18.9 per cent), who possessed no native schools, came at a considerable distance behind the Russians. In the eighteenth century the educational level of the Ukrainians had still been higher than that of the Russians. However, its development was hampered in the nineteenth century by the repressive policy on language, and by assimilatory tendencies. Among the relatively small Ukrainian and Belorussian urban population the level of literacy was considerably higher, reaching 52 and 60 per cent in the case of men. In the Orthodox ethnic groups, with the exception of the Georgians, the difference between the reading skills of men and women was very great. In the case of the Russians, women had a level of literacy that was three times lower than that of men, and in the case of the Ukrainians it was six times lower. The Armenians, who possessed an independent church, had a surprisingly low level of literacy (18.3 per cent). This may have been due to the campaign against the Armenian schools which began in the 1880s. However, 46 per cent of the economically active Armenian urban population was already able to read. The Romanians of Bessarabia, who were largely peasants with a language which had for a long time been subject to repression, had the lowest literacy level by far among the Christian ethnic groups (8.8 per cent).

In fact the majority of the Christianized peasant ethnic groups in European Russia had a higher percentage of people with reading skills than the Romanians. The list was headed by the firmly integrated Karelians (20.8 per cent) and Zyrians (17.9 per cent), and continued on a slightly lower level with the Mordvinians (11.6 per cent), the Chuvash (9.5 per cent), and the Cheremis (8.9 per cent). The Votiaks lagged behind with 6.8 per cent. Since almost all of the women of the Volga ethnic groups were illiterate, the percentage of men with reading skills was almost twice as high as the figures given above. However, the formally Christianized ethnic groups in Siberia had a considerably lower level of literacy. In the case of the Iakuts it was 0.9 per cent, and in 1897 only two of the 8,812 Chukchi stated that they were able to read. However, the percentage of those with reading skills in the case of the mainly lamaist Buriats was considerably higher, and probably even higher than the figure of 9.1 per cent given in the census.

With regard to their level of literacy, the Muslim ethnic groups can be divided into two groups. On the one hand there were the Volga and Crimean Tatars and the intensively tatarized Bashkirs with a percentage of people with reading skills which, ranging from 24 to 27 per cent, was only a little lower than that of the Russians. However, in the case of men the Russians were clearly ahead, though considerably more Tatar and Bashkir women were able to read than Russian women, a state of affairs which was not self-evident for Muslims. The Tatars' relatively high level of education does not come as a surprise in view of the fact that for a long time they had had a developed religious education system and a relatively high literacy level. In the second half of the nineteenth century they seem to have lost ground to the Russians despite the spread of Jadidist reforms. On the other hand, according to the census, the percentage of people with reading skills in the case of all of the

Muslims in the Asiatic areas was below 5 per cent. The data may well be accurate in the case of the nomadic Kazakhs (4.0 per cent), Turkmen (2.1 per cent) and Kirgiz (0.8 per cent), and the Caucasian mountain peoples (7.1 per cent, 10.8 per cent in the case of the Dagestanis, and 3.1 per cent in the case of the Chechens). In the case of the sedentary Muslims of Trancaucasia (3.3 per cent) and Middle Asia (2.1–4.8 per cent), who had possessed a dense network of religious schools for centuries, the figures were obviously too low, even if one takes into account the modest level of conservative Koran schools.

Taken as a whole, it is noticeable that, when grouping ethnic groups on the basis of educational attainment, religion was the primary factor. The Protestants were ahead of the Jews, Catholics, Orthodox, Muslims, Buddhists and animists. This sequence reflects the importance and the quality of the educational system, which was still markedly religious in character, among the various religious groups. The degree of urbanization, however, was only of subsidiary importance. This is demonstrated by the example of the Lithuanians, who were a long way ahead with regard to their level of literacy, whereas with regard to their level of urbanization they occupied one of the last places among the ethnic groups of the European part of the Russian Empire.

The census data concerning the ability to read Russian make it possible to say something about the effects of the partial russification of the educational system. As a rule the ethnic groups without elementary schools in their native languages, such as the Ukrainians, Belorussians, Romanians or Chuvash, could only read Russian. In the case of the Jews, the Greeks and the German and Armenian urban population, the number of persons with reading skills in Russian was considerably higher than the number of persons who possessed reading skills only in another language, as a rule their native language. This does not signify that the members of the mobilized diaspora groups could not read their native languages. Yet for their intermediary activities they were forced to rely to a greater extent than other ethnic groups on a command of Russian. The fact that in the case of the Poles almost half of those able to read could (also) read Russian points to the partial success of the particularly repressive local policy on schools. In the case of the Lithuanians, Estonians and Georgians, less than a third of those able to read could also read Russian; in the case of the Latvians less than half. However, among the urban population the proportion of those with Russian reading skills was considerably higher, which points to the acculturating effect of the urban environment. The proportion of those able to read Russian continued to be very small in the case of the Tatars and the other Muslims, whose educational system had hardly changed. Among the ethnic groups in the west of the Empire, the russification of the schools had been effective, and a knowledge of Russian had spread, especially among the urban population. But this does not mean that these persons could not read their native languages, or in fact that they had given up using them. Since there are no reliable data concerning those who could read in their native languages, and no data whatsoever concerning the oral use of these languages, it is unfortunately impossible to say anything in quantitive terms about the processes of assimilation.

The 1897 census also contains information about the percentage of people who had attended (but not necessarily graduated from) a secondary or tertiary educational establishment (Table 9). However, only educational establishments recognized by the state were included, in other words, non-Christian religious schools were excluded. The percentage of these people (here those over the age of ten), who in the following will simply be referred to as educated people, make it possible to draw certain conclusions about the potential for a national intelligentsia. Additional information can be garnered from the data on specific professional groups, especially those concerning the free professions (Tables 7 and 8). This term is used for the following activities: education and teaching, scholarship and art, work in a private legal capacity and in charitable institutions.[37] Since these categories also included the auxiliary staff of the institutions in question, such as servants, clerks or watchmen, the percentages in question do not only refer to educated people. Another professional category which absorbed a section of the intelligentsia was 'Administration, Courts, Police' (with an even higher percentage of uneducated people), whereas the category 'Church' also included the educated clergy.

Of all of the ethnic groups of the Empire, the Germans had the highest number of educated people by far (6.4 per cent) in 1897. The percentage was considerably higher still among the Baltic Germans (19.1 per cent) and the German urban population of central Russia, which to a large extent consisted of specialists (47.1 per cent). The Germans also headed the list with regard to the free professions and the administration. German specialists had played an outstanding role in the modernization of Russia since the eighteenth century. Although more and more Russians joined the ranks of the intelligentsia in the course of the nineteenth century, the Germans, including the Baltic German 'Literati' and numerous new immigrants who were specialists, had the highest percentage, in relative terms, of any ethnic group in the areas of medicine, science and scholarship, and art in 1897.

The ethnic groups with the second and third highest percentage of educated people were the 'ancient nations' of the Poles (2.8 per cent) and the Russians (2.3 per cent). They possessed a noble upper class which had traditionally been educated. In the case of the Russians, whose nobility was considerably smaller than that of the Poles, the intelligentsia emanated from additional social groups, the clergy and the urban population. Russians and Poles were also slightly overrepresented in the free professions. Since there was no longer a Polish university in the Russian empire, numerous Poles studied at Russian universities and specialist institutions of higher education. Polish doctors, lawyers, engineers and scholars (including, for example, the famous linguist Baudouin de Courtenay) were also active in the Russian interior, especially in St Petersburg.[38] It does not come as a surprise that the Russians had the highest percentage of those employed in the administration, since they were also very much in evidence among the bureaucrats in most of the peripheral areas. However, the fact that in this field the Poles were the second most numerous group demonstrates that the Russian state was still forced to rely on the cooperation of the educated Polish elite. As a result of repressive government policies, the religious elite of the clergy was rather small in the case of the Poles. In that of the Russians it was rather large, since Russian or russified priests were also active among non-Russians, for example the Ukrainians or the ethnic groups of the middle Volga.

The mobilized diaspora groups of the Armenians and Greeks had a percentage of educated people that was on a par with that of the Russians. The Jews, however, lagged a long way behind, according to the information supplied by the census, and were even below the Imperial average. The figures for the male population are particularly low. An explanation for this may be found in the restricted number of places available for Jews in higher schools, which especially affected boys.[39] Even if the figures were correct, they would not enable us to make a definitive statement about the low proportion of educated people among the Jews. Despite the restrictions, this seems to be contradicted by the relatively high percentage of Jewish pupils at middle schools and higher education institutions, and by the data on the free professions. In the school/teaching segment the Jews in fact quite clearly had the highest percentages, whereas in medicine and scholarship/art they were behind the Germans, and in the legal profession behind the Poles. However, they were clearly ahead of the Russians everywhere. Here the Armenians and Greeks had a below-average position. Their educated people addressed themselves primarily to economic activities, and the Armenians also to administrative tasks. In practice Jews were excluded from careers in the administration.

On account of their numerous nobles, the Georgians had a proportion of educated people that corresponded to the Imperial average. However, Georgian nobles were slow to embrace careers in the free professions or the administration. All the other ethnic groups included a small number of people who had attended the middle schools and higher education institutions recognized by the state, and were active in the free professions or the administration. This was also true of the Latvians and Estonians, who, whilst possessing the highest percentage of people with reading skills and a rapidly growing urban population, rarely attended higher educational institutions before 1900. In the free professions, the administration and the clergy the broadly educated Baltic Germans stood in their way. Teachers were the only larger group of educated Estonians and Latvians. The percentage of educated people and of those active in the free professions was even smaller in the case of the Ukrainians, Belorussians, Lithuanians and Romanians, who lived primarily in rural areas and were subject to assimilation when they ascended the social ladder. Nevertheless, even in the case of these traditionally peasant ethnic groups a small national intelligentsia gradually came into being. By 1897 more than 50,000 Ukrainians, 20,000 Belorussians, more than 3,000 Lithuanians and more than 3,000 Romanians had been to a secondary school. Even among the ethnic groups of the middle Volga, the north, and Siberia, which had extremely small numbers of educated people, certain groups such as the Zyrians and the Iakuts possessed a small national intelligentsia.

Since the religious secondary and tertiary educational institutions of the non-Christians were excluded in the census, it is not possible, on the basis of the extremely low percentage of educated people contained in the results, to infer the absence of a religious elite in the case of Muslims and lamaists. With the exception of a small secular intelligentsia (especially in the case of the Tatar diaspora), the intellectual elite in the case of Russia's Muslims and lamaists still consisted of clergy.

Although a process of secularization began everywhere in the course of the nineteenth century, the high cultures of the Russian Empire were still very much religious in character around 1900. This is true primarily of the Islamic cultures of southern Middle Asia and the Caucasus area, and of the small lamaist enclaves of the Buriats and Kalmyks, but also, though to a slightly smaller extent, of the culture of the Tatars, Armenians and Jews. All these ethnic groups retained their own scripts and sacred languages (Arabic, Mongol, Hebrew), though in addition they increasingly continued to develop their secular literary languages (Tatar, Azerbaidzhani, Yiddish).

Russian culture, which in the nineteenth century reached a pinnacle of achievement in literature, music and painting, and Russian science, which was increasingly integrated into developments in the rest of Europe, exercised a great attraction on the representatives of the secular non-Russian intelligentsia, who as a rule were educated at the state educational institutions, which, towards the end of the nineteenth century, were already extensively russified. The Russian influence was particularly strong on the Ukrainians and Belorussians, but also on the other Orthodox ethnic groups. However, the Protestant Germans and the Catholic Poles were also increasingly acculturated as a result of the fact that their native universities had been transformed into Russian-speaking ones. Careers were now more dependent on one's knowledge of Russian than had previously been the case. In addition to the institutions of higher education, there was yet another melting-pot, the Russian army, in which all of the tsar's subjects with the exception of the inorodtsy were required to serve, and, as the professional tables indicate, to a very large extent not in the area in which they lived.

Yet the ancient Christian high cultures of the Poles, the Georgians and Armenians continued to develop in the late tsarist empire. Despite the measures which discriminated against it, Polish culture continued to influence the Lithuanians, the Belorussians and the western Ukrainians, and German culture to influence the Latvians and the Estonians. In Finland, however, the replacement of the old Swedish high language by Finnish was already in full swing. The co-existence with what amounted to equal rights of various high languages and high cultures, which had been characteristic of the pre-modern multi-ethnic empire, had been replaced at the end of the nineteenth century in the European part of the Empire by a predominance of Russian. The tendency towards standardization was counterbalanced by the fact that together with the national movements of the 'young peoples' there arose new high languages and incipient high cultures. Thus in the medium term the co-existence of Russian, German, Polish, Hebrew-Yiddish, Armenian, Georgian, Tatar and Arabic high languages and high cultures was not replaced by the Russian language and Russian culture. Rather, it expanded to encompass an even greater variety of literary languages and high cultures.

4. The Character of the Late Tsarist Multi-ethnic Empire

The Russian Empire at the end of the nineteenth century continued to be characterized by great diversity with regard to patterns of economic activity, social organization and culture. After it had expanded further in the direction of Europe than ever before at the end of the eighteenth and at the beginning of the nineteenth century, its centre of gravity began to shift back to Asia in the nineteenth century as a result of expansion eastwards. The Russian proportion of the population declined, and that of the Muslims and nomads increased. Although isolated thinkers, such as the pan-Slavist N. Ia. Danilevsky, emphasized its special Eurasian status, the Russian Empire in the thinking of the government and the elite continued to be a European state.[40] The wave of modernization initiated by the state in the second half of the nineteenth century was designed to overcome Russia's relative backwardness when compared to the rest of Europe, and thus to bring about at least a partial adaptation to the advanced countries of the west, or, to put it another way, to introduce another bout of europeanization.

The abolition of serfdom, industrialization, urbanization, the commercialization of agriculture and the expansion of educational opportunites made the Russian multi-ethnic empire more dynamic and changed its character. Social mobility encompassed greater sections of society, modernization encouraged the economic integration of the peripheral areas and the process of standardizing the administrative and social structures. The migration of Russians increased their share of the population in particular in the steppe areas which had hitherto served the nomadic herdsmen as pastures and in certain industrial centres in the periphery. The Russian military and administrative elites now occupied all the top positions in all of the peripheral areas with the

THE LATE TSARIST MULTI-ETHNIC EMPIRE

exception of Finland. Russian language, Russian culture and the Orthodox church were increasingly wielded as weapons in the quest for greater homogeneity. However, social and national mobilization affected numerous non-Russian ethnic groups at the same time as it affected the Russians, and they gradually advanced to become modern nations with new elites, literary languages and high cultures. The contrary tendencies towards greater homogeneity and diversity reinforced political and social tensions in the late tsarist multi-ethnic empire.

However, in regional and sectoral terms the Russian Empire was affected by modernization in different ways and to varying extents. Its political system remained essentially unchanged, and so did its socio-economic base. The Russian Empire continued to be dominated by agriculture, the vast majority of the population continued to live in rural areas, to adhere to a traditional economy and to be illiterate. The dynastically legitimated autocracy and the traditional estate-based order remained important social linchpins, and, despite progressive secularization, religion retained its significance for culture and ethnic identity.

The structure of the late tsarist multi-ethnic empire was characterized by this mixture of new and traditional elements. This is also reflected in the status of the non-Russian elites which, in the course of expansion, had been co-opted into the nobility of the empire. It is of course true that the Polish, Georgian, Azerbaidzhani and Baltic German nobles lost their special political status (with the exception of Finland), and some went into social decline after the abolition of serfdom. However, as a numerically reduced elite they were largely able to assert their leading social and economic position in their various regions. It is true that, as a result of an increase in the educated Russian upper class, the Russian state was no longer as dependent on their collaboration as in earlier centuries, yet it was still not in a position to do without such cooperation. Thus Baltic Germans, Germans, Finlanders, Poles and Caucasians continued to perform important functions, not only in the local administration, but also in the central military and administrative elite. The particularly numerous degraded Polish nobility addressed itself to new tasks in scholarship and science, technology and culture.

Social and national mobilization also increased the pressure on the mobilized diaspora groups, which had perfomed complementary functions in business and commerce, the bureaucracy, science and scholarship, and culture in the pre-modern multi-ethnic empire, and on account of their specific abilities, especially their linguistic skills and communication networks, were of inestimable value for the state, though at the same time dependent on it.[41] Although it was not only the lower classes and nationalists who began to turn against the mobilized diaspora groups of the Jews, the Germans and the Armenians, but also the Russian government, which towards the end of the nineteenth century relinquished its traditional protective role, the groups to a large extent retained their specific functions. Jews, Germans (Baltic Germans and the German urban population), Armenians and, less obviously, Greeks and Tatars continued to be noticeably urbanized groups overrepresented in trade, the financial services sector and among craftsmen. They were also active as industrial entrepreneurs, even if they did not play the same kind of prominent role as foreigners. The Jews continued to be active in the west of the empire, the Germans in the north-west, the Armenians and the Greeks in the south and the Tatars in the east. At the centre Baltic Germans and Germans, including many new immigrants, contributed to the modernization of the empire as scientists, scholars, doctors and engineers. And Jews, despite being confined to the pale of settlement, played an important role in the banking sector. However, the significance of the mobilized diaspora groups was already in decline. Their tasks were increasingly being taken over by Russian cadres, and they were subjected to more and more pressure from the socially mobilized lower classes, and especially from the Russians. The rise of nationalism, and to a certain extent its emerging presence in foreign policy, destroyed the government's trust in their loyalty, and reinforced its prejudices against foreign ethno-religious groups. As the rise of anti-Semitism and the hatred of Armenians and Germans showed, they assumed the role of scapegoats in a Russia which was in the throes of modernization.

The capital city of St Petersburg continued to be a mirror image of the multi-ethnic empire, whereas Moscow was more Russian in character. The percentage of non-Russians in the population of St Petersburg remained constant in the second half of the nineteenth century, though their number increased rapidly together with that of the total population. In 1869 16.8 per cent of the city's 667,000 inhabitants were non-Russians. In 1900 the figure was 17.8 per cent out of 1.4 million. The proportion of the second largest ethnic group, the Germans, had declined (from 6.8 to 4 per cent), as had that of the Finns (from 2.7 to 1.4 per cent), whereas the percentage of Poles (2.2 and 3.5 per cent),

Belorussians (0.4 and 2.9 per cent), Estonians (0.6 and 1.3 per cent) and Jews (1.0 and 1.4 per cent) had risen.[42] However, the non-Russian inhabitants of St Petersburg, many of them women, were overproportionally represented in numerous areas. An especially large number of Germans were employed in certain trades (mechanics, bakers and watchmakers), or were active as entrepreneurs, merchants, doctors, teachers and engineers. Numerous Finns worked as craftsmen (especially as jewellers), factory workers and domestic servants, and most of the Estonians and Belorussians as workers and as domestic servants. The Poles of St Petersburg were traditionally officers, bureaucrats and students, and at the end of the century they were joined by members of the intelligentsia and workers. The Jews were initially active as merchants and craftsmen, and then increasingly as military doctors, physicians and lawyers. On the whole more non-Russians than Russians were to be found in professions which required qualifications. Thus the specific abilities of non-Russian ethnic groups were also utilized in the modernization of St Petersburg. Whereas it is true that in the capital, as everywhere in the empire, the importance and attraction of the Russian language and Russian culture increased, the various communities retained their religious and cultural enclaves.

All in all the structure of the Russian multi-ethnic empire remained complicated and irregular. On the one hand, its colonial character became more pronounced as modernization proceeded,[43] and the economic development of certain regions was increasingly adapted to serve the needs of the centre and its industries. In this regard some scholars make a distinction between classical overseas colonialism, and 'European' or 'internal' colonialism.[44] Middle Asia became the perfect example of a classical colony on account of the deliberate encouragement of the cultivation of cotton. With the growing migration of Russian peasants the colonial settlements expanded and led to the further displacement of nomadic herdsmen, mountain peoples and hunters, and to an even greater dependence on the centre. Thus the Asiatic areas of Russia can be described unreservedly as colonies, not only on account of their role as suppliers of raw materials and markets for finished products, but also on account of their relatively low socio-economic and socio-cultural level of development, and the exclusion of their indigenous population in legal terms. It is true that Transcaucasia subsequently also became dependent on the centre as an economic colony, at the latest with the rapid growth of the oil industry. However, with its nobility, which had been co-opted into the imperial nobility, its economically influential Armenian middle class and the relatively high educational level of the Christian ethnic groups, it no longer entirely fits the classical colonial pattern.

Since the 1920s Ukrainian scholars have assigned Ukraine to the category of 'inner colony'.[45] The construction of heavy industrial plants in southern Ukraine certainly resembled economic colonialism inasmuch as it was one-sidedly oriented towards the exploitation of natural resources and was controlled from without. However, I would describe the relationship of Russia to Ukraine as having been colonial only in a restricted sense, for the region, the socio-economic development of which was higher than that of Russia, also benefited from modernization. Nevertheless, the majority of the population, the Ukrainians, began increasingly to lag behind. The debate on Russian colonialism is further complicated by the fact that at the end of the nineteenth century Russia itself, as an economically backward power, was dependent on foreign capital, knowhow and foreign entrepreneurs.

Nor was the north-western periphery of the empire colonially dependent on Russia. Although the Russian centre, and the two capitals in particular, experienced a period of extremely rapid economic, social and cultural change, the Kingdom of Poland, Finland and the Baltic provinces were able to keep their lead with regard to the socio-economic and socio-cultural level of development. Whilst it is true that these regions were also tied more closely to the centre, their economies profited from the Russian market for their goods, and from imports of raw materials from Russia. With regard to the level of development of agriculture, most of the regions in the west and the south were similarly above that of the Russian centre and the east.

Even if one does not use the regions as a yardstick, and prefers to use the ethnic groups instead, it turns out that the Russians were certainly not the privileged 'master race' of the empire. It is true that they had narrowed the gap when compared with the pre-modern period. However, when it came to the degree of urbanization and literacy, they continued to lag far behind a whole series of other ethnic groups. It is true that there was now a large Russian intelligentsia, but there were still more Germans, Poles and Jews. The mass of the Russian peasants continued to enjoy worse living standards than most of the peasants in other regions of the empire, though in the case of certain ethnic groups in the west there was a larger rural proletariat without land. If one uses average life expectancy as an indicator of an ethnic group's standard of living, then the Russians, going by the calculations of a Soviet Ukrainian statistician in the 1920s, were not only behind the Latvians, Estonians, Lithuanians and Jews, but also behind the Ukrainians, Belorussians, Tatars and Bashkirs.[46] Thus the modernization of Russia and the Russians, in regional and social terms, happened in an even more uneven manner than in the case of most of the other regions and ethnic groups. Although it is true that the tsarist government encouraged the Russian centre and the Russian power elite, the mass of the Russians in the provinces continued to be a neglected majority.

Thus in the late tsarist multi-ethnic empire the political and military predominance of the Russian centre was, in terms of socio-economic and socio-cultural development, paralleled by a declining gradient from the north-west via Russia to the east of the empire; and the mass of the Russians lagged far behind a whole series of other ethnic groups with regard to economic level, educational attainment and the standard of living. These fundamental structural features were inherited by the Soviet Union.

This fact makes us ask once again who actually profited from the imperial expansion of Russia. The majority of non-Russians and many Russians complained (and continue to complain) that they were oppressed and exploited by the centre. Then as now only the state and the (predominantly Russian) power elite in the bureaucracy and the army are said to have profited from holding sway over the empire. There can be no doubt that the policy of expansion and the interminable task of securing Russian rule consumed immense human and material resources over the centuries, that they diverted attention from social, economic and political developments within Russia itself, encouraged extensive at the expense of intensive growth and thus constituted one of the reasons for Russia's backwardness. And what had Rousseau said about the Russian appetite for Poland? His remark turned out to be prophetic. Neither the tsarist empire nor the Soviet Union were able to digest the numerous gobbets that they had devoured with such haste.

Notes

1   The large surveys of Russian history only discuss multi-ethnic aspects in passing. Attempts at a comprehensive survey were made by Hoetzsch (1917), a

contemporary, and by Drabkina (1930), an interpretation that takes its bearings from economic factors.

2 For a detailed account of the 1897 census and its categories see *Die Nationalitäten* I (1991).

3 See also D. I. Ishakov, 'O nekotorykh aspektakh problemy mesta priural'skikh tatar v etnicheskoi strukture tatarskoi natsii', *Priural'skie tatary* (Kazan, 1990) pp. 4–12. For a general account of the linguistic category of the census see *Die Nationalitäten* I (1991), pp. 137–284.

4 Here and subsequently data from the 1897 census are taken from *Die Nationalitäten* II (1991). On the share of the Russians and eastern Slavs see vol. I, pp. 147f. and 167–71. Of studies restricted to single ethnic groups or regions which are also largely based on the 1897 census see Krawchenko (1985); Steven L. Guthier, 'The Belorussians: National Identification and Assimilation, 1897–1970', *Soviet Studies* 29 (1977), 37–61 and 270–83; Brutskus (1908, 1909); *Die sozialen Verhältnisse* (1906); Lukawski (1978); Zelenchuk (1979); Iu. I. Smykov and L. N. Goncharenko, 'Natsional'nyi sostav naseleniia Povolzh'ia v kontse XIX veka', in *Natsional'nyi vopros v Tatarii dooktiabr'skogo perioda* (Kazan, 1990), pp. 97–106; B. Ischchanjan, *Nationaler Bestand, berufsmäßige Gruppierung und soziale Gliederung der kaukasischen Völker* (Berlin, 1914); Bekmakhanova (1986); D. D. Nimaev, 'Etnodemograficheskie protsessy v Buriati v XIX – nachale XX v.' in *Buriatiia XVII – nachala XX v.* (Novosibirsk, 1989), pp. 69–84.

5 *Die Nationalitäten* (1991), pp. 172 f.

6 Kasteliansky (1910), pp. 627 f.

7 Since language was the criterion of the census, the term German was also used for German-speaking Swiss and Austrians.

8 For the data concerning the religious structure of the population see *Die Nationalitäten* II (1991), and, for a critique of the sources, vol. I, pp. 285–323. Supplementary census data from the Cologne NFR database (see *Die Nationalitäten*, I (1991), pp. 89–134).

9 The percentages of the urban population are from *Die Nationalitäten* II (1991), pp. 69–72. On the census concept of a town see vol. I, pp. 523–5.

10 On this concept see Chapter 4.2.

11 See D. M. Ishakov, 'Tatary v krupnykh gorodakh Povolzh'ia i Priural'ia v kontse XIX–nachale XX v. (Etnostatisticheskii ocherk)' in *Etnicheskie gruppy* (1987), pp. 82–90.

12 Hamm (1986) discusses eight of the major cities (Moscow, St Petersburg, Kiev, Warsaw, Riga, Odessa, Tiflis, and Baku).

13 However, recent research has once again upgraded the significance of the estate categories. See *Die Nationalitäten* I (1991), pp. 377–429; Gregory L. Freeze, 'The Soslovie (Estate) Paradigm in Russian Social History', *American Historical Review* 91 (1986), 19–34. See also *Handbuch* I (1987), pp. 1104–19. Data are taken from *Die Nationalitäten* II (1991).

14 Thus the 'highest Muslim estate' of the beki, which did not have all the same rights, was included in the hereditary nobility category (see the numbers in *Svod*, 1893).

15 With regard to these concepts see Chapter 6.

16 Once again I rely on *Die Nationalitäten* II (1991), which gives the data of the 1897 census concerning fifteen large regions. From time to time, in order to give a more balanced picture, I also have to fall back on the database 'Die Nationalitätenfrage im spätzaristischen Rußland' of the Seminar für osteuropäische Geschichte of the University of Cologne. It is archived in the 'Zentrum für historische Sozialforschung der Universität zu Köln' (Studiennummer 8054). On this see *Die Nationalitäten* I (1991), Chapter 2. See also the essay, based on the same sources, on the urban population of European Russia by N. V. Iukhneva, 'Materialy k etnicheskomu raionirovaniiu gorodskogo naseleniia Evropeiskoi Rossii (Po dannym perepisi 1897 g.)' in *Etnicheskie gruppy* (1987), pp. 112–26. For more information I refer the reader to the literature on the various regions listed in the previous chapters, and not repeated here.

17 Since the Grand Duchy of Finland was not covered by the 1897 census, the data are taken from Kasteliansky (1910), pp. 627–8; Raun (1984), pp. 454–6.

18 S. Patkanov, *O priroste inorodcheskogo naseleniia Sibiri. Statisticheskie materialy dlia osveshcheniia voprosa o vymiranii pervobytnykh plemen* (St Petersburg, 1911).

19 After Zelenchuk (1979, pp. 153–8), who corrects the census figures in favour of the Moldavians, 52.1 per cent.

20 On the migrations see Bruk and Kabuzan (1984); B. V. Tikhonov, *Pereseleniia v Rossii vo vtoroi polovine XIX v* (Moscow, 1978); Demko (1969); Bekmakhanova (1986).

21 *Handbuch* II (1987), pp. 1038–55. See the Zurich research project on Swiss emigration to Russia, and the summary in *Schweizer im Zarenreich. Zur Geschichte der Auswanderung nach Rußland.*(Zurich, 1985).

22 See Korelin (1979), pp. 48 f., even though he subsumes all eastern Slavs under the term Russian.

23 Zaionchkovskii (1978), pp. 200–9; Dominic C. B. Lieven, 'The Russian Civil Service under Nicholas II: Some Variations on a Bureaucratic Theme', *JbbGO* 29 (1981), pp. 366–403. See also the comments of Armstrong (1978) and Amburger (1966).

24 P. A. Zaionchkovsky, *Samoderzhavie i russkaia armiia na rubezhe XIX–XX stoletii. 1881–1903* (Moscow, 1973); Stein (1967), pp. 458 f.; Screen (1976).

25 The picture is confirmed by the figures for 1912. However, by this time the proportion of Orthodox officers had risen to 89 per cent, and of Orthodox generals to almost 86 per cent. See Peter Kenez, 'A Profile of the Prerevolutionary Officer Corps', *California Slavic Studies* 7 (1973), 121–58, here pp. 137 f.

26 Andreas Kappeler, 'Zur Charakteristik russischer Terroristen (1878–1887)', *JbbGO* 27 (1979), 520–47, here pp. 528–31; Leonard Shapiro, 'The Rôle of the Jews in the Russian Revolutionary Movement', *SEER* 40 (1961), 148–67; Lukawski (1978), pp. 193–212; David Lane, *The Roots of Russian Communism. A Social and Historical Study of Russian Social-Democracy 1898–1907* (Assen, 1969), pp. 39–51, especially p. 44; Maureen Perrie 'The Social Composition and Structure of the Socialist-Revolutionary Party before 1917', *Soviet Studies* 24 (1972–3), 223–50, here pp. 236–8.

27 On this chapter see in general terms *Handbuch* III (1981), pp. 102–49 and 213–43; Arcadius Kahan, 'Wirtschafts- und Sozialgeschichte Rußlands und Kongreßpolens', *Handbuch der europäischen Wirtschafts- und Sozialgeschichte* vol. V (Stuttgart, 1980); Roger Portal, 'The Industrialization of Russia', *The Cambridge Economic History of Europe*, vol. VI (Cambridge, 1966), pp. 801–72. With regard to the various regions and ethnic groups I rely on the specialist literature cited in the preceding chapters.

28 See Krawchenko (1985), pp. 17 f. and 39–44; Theodore H. Friedgut, *Iuzovka and Revolution*, vol. 1. *Life and Work in Russia's Donbass, 1869–1924* (Princeton, 1989).

29 A. S. Nifontov, *Zernovoe proizvodstvo Rossii vo vtoroi polovine XIX veka. Po materialam ezhegodnoi statistiki urozhaev Evropeiskoi Rossii* (Moscow, 1974), p. 276. See also Andreas Moritsch, *Landwirtschaft und Agrarpolitik in Rußland vor der Revolution* (Vienna, 1986), pp. 119–57, and tables.

30 The figures after *Die Nationalitäten* II (1991), with additional information from the Cologne NFR database. With regard to source criticism of the occupational categories see *Die Nationalitäten* I (1991), pp. 480–8. On the Jews see *Recueil* I (1906); and Brutskus (1908). See also Weinryb (1972) for the time before 1881.

31 On the term 'mobilized disapora group' see above, Chapter 4.

32 See Kahan (1983).

33 The data are taken from *Die Nationalitäten* II (1991). See the source criticism of the educational categories, vol. I, pp. 324–76.

34 See Aira Kemiläinen, 'Initiation of the Finnish People into Nationalist Thinking', *Nationality and Nationalism in Italy and Finland from the Mid-19th Century to 1918* (Helsinki, 1984), p. 112. See also Raun (1984), p. 455.

35 Raun (1979).

36 Brutskus (1909), pp. 47 f.; *Die sozialen Verhältnisse* (1906), pp. 41–52. But see also *Recueil* II (1908).

37 See the detailed description of the professional categories in *Die Nationalitäten* I (1991), pp. 466–88.

38 On this see Lukawski (1978); Bazylow (1984).

39 See *Die sozialen Verhältnisse* (1906), pp. 52–7; *Recueil*, II (1908), pp. 340–54.

40 See Mark Bassin, 'Russia between Europe and Asia: The Ideological Construction of Geography', *SR* 50 (1991), 1–17 (contains a bibliography).

41 Armstrong (1976). See above, Chapter 4.2.

42 Iukhneva (1984); Bazylow (1984). The ethnic nomenclature is particularly difficult in the case of St Petersburg, on the one hand because all non-Russians were subject to ongoing russification, and on the other because the two most important ethnic groups were of disparate origin. The Germans comprised German-speaking Swiss, Finlanders, Jews, etc., and the Finns also included the Finnish-speaking Izhora who lived in St Petersburg province. Moreover, the categories of the urban censuses and the 1897 census were not identical.

43 On the question of the colonial character of Russia see above, Chapters 2.5, 4.5, and 5.6 (with bibliography). See also Petr Grigorevich Galuzo, 'Das Kolonialsystem des russischen Imperialismus am Vorabend der Oktoberrevolution', *Zeitschrift für Geschichtswissenschaft* 15 (1967), 997–1013.

44 With regard to western Europe see Michael Hechter, *Internal Colonialism: The Celtic Fringe in British National Development, 1536–1966* (London, 1975).

45 On the debate surrounding the notion of the Ukraine as a 'European' or 'inner colony' of Russia, which was already being conducted in the Ukrainian Soviet Republic in the 1920s, see Kononenko (1958); Krawchenko (1985), incl. pp. 6–8 and 39 f.

46 M. Ptukha, *Smertnist' u Rosii i na Ukraini* (Kharkiv-Kyiv 1928), especially pp. 63–93.

9

The Nationalities Question
and the Revolution

A T THE BEGINNING of the twentieth century the Russian Empire was
confronted simultaneously with three tasks that European countries
which had progressed further in social, economic and political terms
had already had to face at different stages of their development. First,
there had never been a bourgeois revolution in Russia. There was no
constitution, nothing to guarantee basic civil rights, no political
participation of large sections of the population, no middle class able to
underpin the state. The power of tsarist autocracy remained unchecked,
at least in theory; the land-owning nobility continued to play an
important role; and the abolition of serfdom had not been completed.
The task of implementing liberal and democratic reforms was linked, as
in the revolution of 1848, with a second task, the national emancipation
of the non-Russian ethnic groups, which constituted almost 60 per cent
of the population. Third, in the wake of the increasingly fast pace of
industrialization, from the 1890s onwards the opposition intelligentsia
and the workers' movement placed on the agenda the task of bringing
about a socialist revolution.

The fact that these three tasks had to be dealt with simultaneously
led to an accumulation of social and political conflict. The state, the
traditional political system of the ancien régime, and the pre-modern
socio-economic structures (especially in the agricultural sector) were
all in a state of crisis. Tensions which were the result of the new forces
unleashed by industrialization and modernization increased, as did
tensions with western countries, and national tensions within the
multi-ethnic empire itself. The weakness of the state and the autocratic
system with its pre-modern legitimation and its restricted ability to
implement reforms became obvious in the Russo-Japanese War of
1904–05 and in the First World War.

This is not the place to analyze the Russian Revolution and the
complex web of historical forces which contributed to it.[1] For this

reason I will restrict my remarks to a brief account of the national factor. And this prompts me to pose two questions:

1. What was the significance of the national question for the revolution, and what contribution did the non-Russian ethnic groups make in the upheavals of 1905–06 and 1917?
2. What significance did the Revolution have for non-Russians and their national movements?

Neither of these questions has yet been examined in a comprehensive manner.[2] This is partly due to the fact that in the Soviet Union and in other countries the social and political factors which contributed to the revolution were given priority, and that national factors were considered to be of lesser importance. This approach is certainly justifiable. National conflicts do not occur in a vacuum, and are always linked to social, political and economic antagonisms. Yet national movements have a momentum of their own that should not be underestimated. The explosive force and the magnitude of ethnically related social, political and economic conflicts of interest were once again demonstrated by events in the Soviet Union after 1988. And to a certain extent these were reminiscent of what happened in 1905 and 1917.

1. The Revolution of 1905 as the Springtime of the Peoples

Fifty-seven years after the revolution of 1848 Russia was at last also confronted with two tasks: the bourgeois revolution, and national emancipation. In the era of industrialization liberal and democratic demands vied with the aims of socialism, and in the revolutionary and national movements the two elements were variously intermingled. The revolution of 1905 was at one and the same time a revolution of the intelligentsia, the workers, the peasants, the soldiers, and the different nationalities. The fact that the various strands did not coalesce to become a unified revolutionary movement, and that on the whole they pursued autonomous paths of their own, can be seen as one of the primary reasons for the failure of the revolution.[3]

The revolution began in the capital, and in the events leading up to it the movements of the liberal landowners and the radical thinkers in St Petersburg played an important role. At the same time there were important precursors on the periphery of the Russian Empire that are often overlooked. As early as 1895–1900 only three of the 59 street demonstrations recorded in the Russian Empire took place in the Russian territories, whereas 25 occurred in the Kingdom of Poland, nine in the Baltic provinces, nine in Ukraine, seven in Belorussia, and six in Finland.[4] After decades of relative peace, the peasants' movement re-emerged in Ukraine on the left bank of the Dnepr in 1902–04, and the peasant protest movement which occurred simultaneously in the socially and ethnically homogeneous Georgian area of Guria spawned a system of revolutionary self-government. The urban disturbances in 1903 and 1904 occurred first in Baku, and then spread to the whole of Transcaucasia, Ukraine and the Kingdom of Poland, where, towards the end of 1904, there were numerous demonstrations and protests against the mobilization of reservists.[5]

However, it was the events in St Petersburg, the mass strikes and the use of armed force to suppress a great workers' demonstration on 9 January 1905, which sparked off the revolution. Yet the more overtly political non-Russian periphery reacted more swiftly and with greater vehemence to 'Bloody Sunday' than did the areas inhabited by Russians.[6] Only a few days after 9 January, strikes broke out in the Kingdom of Poland and in Warsaw armed clashes led to at least 90 deaths.[7] The ensuing general strike also spread to the cities of the 'West Russian' provinces, brought hundreds of thousands of Polish and Jewish workers on to the streets, and lasted for about a month. It was accompanied by national demonstrations, above all by a boycott of the Russian-language state secondary schools. In the spring there were another general strike and demonstrations in Warsaw, and in June yet another general strike and bloody battles on the barricades in Łódź (there were, it seems, 500 victims, many of them Jews) and in other Polish cities. The numerous acts of terror perpetrated by Piłsudski's Polish Socialist Party (PPS) exacerbated the situation, and the Russian government, despite the ongoing war with Japan, felt compelled to reinforce the troops stationed in the Kingdom of Poland, which in fact already comprised 250,000 men.

In Transcaucasia the social and ethnic conflicts that had been on the increase since 1902 became even more widespread during the revolution.[8] The strikes started in Baku and spread to Tiflis, Batumi and other towns. In August soldiers brutally dispersed a meeting in the town hall of Tiflis and killed several dozen people. The Georgian peasants of the 'Gurian Republic' controlled large parts of the province of Kutaisi, and under the influence of the Mensheviks began to make radical social and political demands. However, in eastern Transcaucasia social protest began increasingly to be supplanted by inter-ethnic antagonism. This was seen most clearly in the bloody struggles between the Muslims of Azerbaidzhan and the Armenians, which, starting in Baku, shook Transcaucasia from February 1905 to the spring of 1906. There were thousands of victims.[9] The revolutionary movement in Transcaucasia, which had begun in 1903, was the first revolution in the Orient, and had an influence on the adjoining countries of Iran and the Ottoman Empire, where there was revolutionary unrest in 1906 and 1908.

The third peripheral area to which the revolution spread at an early stage was that of the Baltic provinces. In the cities the workers reacted to 'Bloody Sunday' in St Petersburg with strikes and mass demonstrations. In Riga, where the Latvian Social Democrats were very influential, there were armed clashes as early as January, and these left seventy-three people dead.[10] The Baltic provinces, and Livonia in particular, were among the regions with the largest number of strikes in the revolutionary year. In the spring and in the summer the protest movement spread to the countryside. Latvian and Estonian farm labourers went on strike, farmers refused to pay taxes and, especially in Kurland and southern Livonia, established a system of revolutionary self-government. The agrarian movement directed against the Baltic German nobility subsequently became more radical, and 563 noble estates were destroyed (primarily towards the end of 1905) – 38 per cent of all the estates in the southern (predominantly Latvian) and 19 per cent in the northern (predominantly Estonian) areas. Numerous landowners were evicted, and eighty-two Germans, including a number of clergymen, were killed. The government proclaimed martial law in Kurland as early as August 1905. Livonia and Estonia followed slightly later, in November and December.

From January 1905 onwards, when the 'Bund' organized numerous strikes, the activities of Jewish workers intensified and became more political, often in conjunction with Poles, Russians or Latvians.[11] Jewish workers also took part in the uprising in Odessa, where, in connection with the mutiny on the battleship *Potemkin*, a revolt broke out in June 1905 in which more than 1,000 people lost their lives. Particularly intense agrarian unrest involving large-scale strikes by farm labourers occurred in Ukraine on the right bank of the Dnepr.[12] In short, in the summer of 1905, at a time when Russia was relatively peaceful, the periphery in the west and in the south was shaken by unrest, and at least in the Kingdom of Poland, in Transcaucasia and in the Baltic provinces, a state of civil war was imminent.

But in the autumn of 1905 the initiative passed back to Russia, and it was largely a general strike organized by Russians which forced the government to make far-reaching concessions. The October manifesto held out the prospect of civil rights and freedoms and an elected parliament with legislative powers. In the last three months of 1905 the revolution in Russia reached its climax, with a massive increase in protests by the peasants, revolts by soldiers, with the activities of the St Petersburg soviet of workers' deputies and an attempted military coup in Moscow. However, the revolutionary movement in the non- Russian periphery also regained its momentum. Agrarian revolts shattered Ukraine and the Kingdom of Poland, reached a climax in the Baltic provinces, and spread from Guria to the whole of western Georgia. Here they were brutally suppressed towards the end of the year and at the beginning of 1906. The strike movement reached its greatest intensity in the autumn of 1905 and in 1906, not in Russia, but in the Kingdom of Poland. In December the PPS attempted to seize power in Warsaw, and continued to perpetrate acts of terrorism after the failure of the uprising.

However, a number of non-Russian ethnic groups, especially in the east of the empire, took little or no part in the revolution. This was primarily true of the majority of the Muslims, who used the new freedoms to establish a moderate Islamic movement. And the small ethnic groups of the Volga-Urals area and Siberia, most of whom had converted to the Russian Orthodox faith, took little or no part in the revolution initiated by Russians in certain towns. Furthermore, calm prevailed in the German colonies. In Finland the workers had taken part in mass strikes in the autumn of 1905, though they had soon called off their protests when the tsar promised to grant autonomy to Finland.

On the whole, however, the role played by non-Russian ethnic groups in the revolution of 1905 was more important than is generally assumed to have been the case in both Russian and western historiography. Whereas it is true that the most important decisions were made in the centre, the protest movements on the periphery made a significant contribution to the destabilization of the social and political system, and tied down a large section of the military. A quantitative survey of the strikes in 1905 shows that in the predominantly non-Russian periphery in the west a considerably higher percentage of workers was mobilized than in the Russian centre. The only exception was St Petersburg, though it also lagged behind Warsaw, Łódź and Riga.[13] The ethnic groups which played the most active role in the revolution were those whose territories had already been influenced by industrialization and modernization, and whose national movements had already acquired a mass character, though only in cases where the four most important components of the revolution – the agrarian movement, the workers' movement, the democratic movement of the intelligentsia and the national movement – coincided. This was something which, for example, did not apply to the Finlanders. As Otto Hoetzsch, a contemporary, realized,

> For the state the danger of this national movement thus unleashed did not only lie in the fact that these other nationalities, except the Baltic Germans, were without exception democratic and directly reinforced the revolutionary movement, but primarily in the fact that nationalism of this kind . . . threatened to tear apart the whole state.[14]

The specific significance of the national factor is difficult to determine. However, it certainly exacerbated the social and political conflicts. This was especially noticeable in the case of the Poles, who were pursuing the restoration of their independence, and with whom the mass movement had also, by European standards, reached a very advanced state of mobilization in 1905. In the peasant movements national goals did not have the same kind of significance.

That the protest movements on the periphery were also considered to be very dangerous by the government is demonstrated by the merciless punishment it meted out after they had failed, which was considerably harsher than in the case of the Russian rebels. In the Baltic provinces more than 2,000 people were killed in the course of punitive expeditions carried out jointly by Russians and Baltic Germans, and subsequently more than 600 others were sentenced to death. Of the death sentences imposed in the aftermath of the revolution, 25 per cent were in the Kingdom of Poland, more than 15 per cent were in the Baltic provinces and more than 5 per cent in tiny Guria.[15] At the same time the Russian government succeeded in using ethnic antagonisms for its own purposes. The violent uprising of the Latvians and the Estonians led the autocracy to close ranks with the Baltic German elite. In eastern Transcaucasia the government made successful use of 'divide and rule' methods, and the local authorities encouraged the inter-ethnic conflicts between Muslims and Armenians. And finally it was possible to instrumentalize the pogroms against the Jews, which flared up yet again, and were at the very least tolerated by the authorities, to divert attention from revolutionary activities.

The revolution of 1905 imparted significant impulses to all the national movements in the Russian Empire. The revolutionary situation in the country as a whole and the example of the mass movements of individual ethnic groups in particular had the same mobilizing effect as the weakness of the regime, which was also revealed by its defeat at the hands of Japan. The concessions which the government was forced to make as a result of the pressure exerted by the revolution were of crucial importance. With this Russia, after a period of repressive assimilation policies, once again returned to the traditional pattern of flexible prag-matism. A number of russifying measures, such as the ban on printing Lithuanian in Latin letters, had been repealed as early as 1904. They were followed in April 1905 by a tolerance edict, which, whilst confirming the predominant status of the Orthodox church, abolished discrimination against non-Orthodox denominations, and granted Orthodox Christians the right to join other Christian communities.[16] Thereupon 200,000 Belorussians who had been forced to join the Orthodox church and tens of thousands of baptized Tatars returned to their former religions. There followed a series of concessions in the area of language policy (for example, with regard to Polish, Lithuanian, Ukrainian, Armenian, German, Estonian and Latvian) and the abrogation of the ukaz against Finland and Armenia, which had been promulgated a few years earlier. Subsequently the most important document was the 'October Manifesto', which, by guaranteeing civil rights and freedoms, also permitted national organiz-ations, and national communication and agitation, and thus created the preconditions for the growth of the national movements. The elections to the first Duma, Russia's first elected parliament, contributed to the politicization of the national societies.

The national movements were now in a far better position to trans-mit political programmes to larger sections of the population and to construct a national society. Numerous new organizations and parties were founded, there was an upsurge in newspapers in the national languages and national demonstrations became increasingly common. In the Kingdom of Poland the strikes in schools had an especially far-reaching mobilizing effect. For seven months boys and girls boycotted the Russian state middle schools until, in September 1905, the government gave permission for the establishment of private Polish schools.[17] Subsequently, with the help of a school association (Polska Macierz Szkolna) a system of Polish schools was re-established next to the state system. The revolution of 1905, which, after 1794, 1830 and 1863, is sometimes described as the fourth Polish uprising, made a significant contribution to the politicization of the Polish masses. The Polish parties now at last became mass parties, especially the PPS, which had over 50,000 members in 1906. The conflicts between the different political wings now became increasingly serious, particularly after the October Manifesto. There were even armed clashes between socialist groups and supporters of the National Democrats. At the same time the polarization of the internationalist and national wings of the Socialists continued, and one wing of Piłsudski's PPS joined forces with Rosa Luxemburg's SDKPil (Social Democrats of the Kingdom of Poland and Lithuania), who were hoping to cooperate with the Russian Social Democrats.

New national parties arose among the Estonians, Latvians and Lithuanians, most of which demanded democratic reforms, and cultural and political autonomy. Mass meetings such as the congress of elementary school teachers and the conference of about 900 village delegates in the case of the Latvians, and the All-Estonian Assembly with about 800 delegates marked the climax, in November 1905, of national political mobilization. In Finland the revolution also reinforced political mobilization and at the same time led to differentiation between the Social Democrats and the Constitutionalists, whose restorationist demands had largely been met by the government's concessions. At the beginning of December the Lithuanians held a great provincial diet in Vilna at which about 2,000 participants spoke out in favour of national autonomy, the use of Lithuanian as an offical language and a constitutional assembly. At the same time the Lithuanians tried to introduce the use of Lithuanian into churches, though the Polish clergy resisted this.

The Jewish movement combined social and national elements. Since March 1905 the 'Bund for Jewish Emanicpation', which had been founded by Zionists and Liberals, agitated in the west of the empire for 'the complete implementation of the civil, political, and national rights of the Jewish people in Russia',[18] though apart from a few concessions, such as the question of access to higher education the October Manifesto again refused to introduce emancipation for the Jews. In fact, during the 'days of freedom' in the autumn of 1905 the Jews in Russia suffered the worst pogroms they had ever experienced.[19] In the previous months there had already been numerous acts of violence as a result of which, in Kiev, Zhitomir and Białystok, dozens of Jews had lost their lives. The large-scale pogroms in October and November, which took place mainly in Ukraine, affected about 600 Jewish communities. They led to widespread destruction, and to the murder of at least 1,000 Jews. The aim of the pogroms was anti-revolutionary, that is, as in the wake of the assassination of the tsar in 1881, the Jews were identified as being revolutionaries. This is also suggested by the fact that to a certain extent the pogroms emanated from monarchist processions, and were accompanied by violent attacks on students, demonstrators, workers and, in Baku, on Armenians. Once again the carriers were the urban lower and middle classes, and also to some extent peasants. Whereas it has been demonstrated that certain regional authorities participated in the pogroms, it is unclear whether the government in St Petersburg was involved. The Jewish self-defence groups formed under the direction of the 'Bund' put up some stiff resistance.

The consequences which the Jews drew from by far the worst wave of pogroms the Russian Empire had ever witnessed were different, as had been the case after 1881. On the one hand there was an upsurge in Jewish emigration overseas, and on the other an increase in the wing of the Zionist movement which sought to bring about the national consolidation of the Jews within the Russian Empire.[20] Whereas the pogroms weakened the internationalist character of the Jewish movement as a whole, the Jewish revolutionary movement, which sought to abolish tsarism and pursued socialist goals, gained momentum and a more pronounced national character. The 'Bund' was able to broaden its mass base, and new Jewish socialist parties were founded. Thus the advanced state of mobilization and the characteristic fragmentation of the Jewish movement persisted even after 1905.

The agitation and excesses against the Jews in 1905 were the first open sign of an extreme kind of Russian nationalism.[21] In a proto-fascist manner, the 'Union of the Russian People' and the 'Black Hundreds' combined loyalty to the autocracy and to the Orthodox church with a belief in the dominant position of the Russian nation, and with anti-capitalism, xenophobia and a hatred of Poles and Jews. However, other strands of the Russian national movement also received the chance to make themselves heard in 1905, including a constitutional wing which was supported in part by the parties of Popular Freedom (Cadets) and the Octobrists. At any rate, in 1905 Russian society was also caught up in the springtime of the peoples, and this was bound to have an effect on the policies of the government.

In Transcaucasia the bitter conflicts led to a further politicization of the national movements. The Armenians secured an annulment of the confiscation of Armenian church property, which had been decreed in 1903, and the re-establishment of Armenian schools. These concessions reconciled the clergy and the Armenian merchants with the tsarist state. On the other hand, the Muslim–Armenian civil war had led to a strengthening of the Dashnak national revolutionary party, which organized self-defence groups and, with tens of thousands of adherents, finally took over the political leadership of the Armenian national movement. In the case of the Georgians the Mensheviks strengthened their position in the course of the revolution as the crucial political force, something which encouraged a shift from an internationalist position to a more obviously Georgian national one. For larger sections of the Muslims of Transcaucasia the revolution of 1905 marked the start of a phase of political mobilization. Their protests were directed less against Russia, and more against the Armenian upper class in Baku and other towns. On the other hand, the liberal Muslim elites joined the pan-Islamic movement.

The concessions exacted by the revolution gave the Muslims in Russia the opportunity to initiate their own political movement.[22] In August 1905, despite an offical ban, representatives of the Muslim intelligentsia met on a boat on the Oka near Nizhnii Novgorod and founded an organization which, at the second congress in St Petersburg in January 1906, was given the title 'Union of the Muslims in Russia' (Ittifak). Its moderate political platform demanded democracy and civil and equal religious rights for the Muslims, and sought a cultural and religious renewal on the lines of Jadidism. Two wings emerged at the third congress of the Muslims in August 1906. The more powerful and moderate one under the leadership of the Tatars A. Ibragimov, I. Gaspirali and Iu. Akchura, who had already mapped out a pan-Turkish programme in 1904, and of the Azerbaidzhani A. Topchibashev was close to the liberal Russian Cadets, whereas the group represented by the Volga Tatar A. Ishaki had a more radical social revolutionary programme. The pan-Islamic movement was largely in the hand of Tatar intellectuals, whereas the other Muslims, especially those of Middle Asia, and the conservative clergy were weakly represented. After 1905 the national movements continued to develop in the various regions at the same time as pan-Islamism, especially among the Azerbaidzhanis, Volga Tatars and Kazakhs. The liberal reformist tendencies predominated, whereas Social Democratic circles such as the 'Himmat' group in Azerbaidzhan continued to be rather weak.

The political awakening of the Muslims was accompanied by a cultural movement. In the revolutionary years there was a dramatic upsurge in the press and in publishing.[23] Between 1905 and 1907 more than fifty newspapers and magazines in Arabic script appeared in Russia, thirty-one of them in the Tatar language (in Kazan, Orenburg, Astrakhan, Uralsk, Orenburg, Ufa and St Petersburg), thirteen in Azeri and two in Persian (all in Baku), three in Crimean Tatar (including Gaspirali's prestigious *Tercuman*) and one in Kazakh. At the instigation of Tatars, Jadidist periodicals were now published for the first time in Turkestan in a conglomerate Turkic language. The Muslim press discussed cultural and political questions, whereby the moderate reformist tendency predominated. At the same time Tatars and Azerbaidzhanis founded numerous national organizations with primarily cultural aims.

As in the case of the Muslims, the revolution of 1905 also marked the start of a new phase of the national movement in numerous other ethnic groups of the Russian Empire. This was especially true of the Ukrainians and Belorussians, whose national cultural development had repeatedly been stifled by the rigorous policy of russification. The small pro-national Ukrainian intelligentsia – frequently on the model of the Ukrainians in eastern Galicia – founded a series of new organizations such as a Society for Popular Enlightenment (Prosvita), which already had 150 local branches in 1906, a Ukrainian scholarly society, numerous, albeit usually ephemeral periodicals, the first daily newspaper (*Rada*) in Ukrainian and peasant cooperatives. The Ukrainian parties were now able to develop with greater freedom, though even in Ukraine they lagged behind the All-Russian parties. This was also true of the most important political party. Founded in 1900, the Revolutionary Ukrainian Party, which from 1905 onwards was called the Ukrainian

Social Democratic Workers' Party, was surpassed by the Russian parties, and by the Ukrainian Social Democratic Union (Spilka), which had seceded from it in order to join forces with the Russian Social Democrats.[24] As the peasant disturbances during the revolution demonstrated, it is true that the broad mass of the Ukrainians had been mobilized in social terms. However, they were largely ignorant of the national movement. Moreover, the government's concessions towards the Ukrainian movement were very restricted. It is true that the repressive language ordinances were repealed, and that the Academy of Sciences (with a majority of one vote) even confirmed the existence of Ukrainian as a language in its own right. However, even after 1905 the Russian Empire did not witness the establishment of a native Ukrainian educational system.

The Belorussian national movement was even less in a position than its Ukrainian counterpart to take a step towards becoming a mass movement in 1905. Yet here the proclamation of the October manifesto led to the foundation of new national organizations which demanded autonomy for Belorussia and native-language schools. The first legal periodicals in Belorussian, which began to be published in 1906, were of the greatest importance for the rise of a Belorussian consciousness. The weekly newspaper Nasha Niva (Our Field) occasionally reached a circulation of 3,000, and printed works by young poets such as Ianka Kupala and Iakub Kolas, who came from the ranks of the Belorussian peasantry. However, in the towns of Belorussia Russian, Polish and Jewish culture continued to predominate.

The revolution and the October manifesto led to a political awakening of the German colonists, who founded numerous journals and associations, and called for a re-germanization of the partly russified school system. Among the Romanians of Bessarabia the small national intelligentsia founded a cultural society and a Democratic Party, campaigned for the use of their native language in the schools and published newspapers in Romanian.

For many of the small ethnic groups in the east of European Russia and in Siberia the revolution of 1905 and 1906 also formed the starting-point of a national reawakening. The small educated classes formed national organizations and tended to make cultural demands, which were not infrequently linked to social and general political aims. Of the non-Muslim ethnic groups of the middle Volga, the Chuvash were particularly active in 1905. This was demonstrated by the activities of a

Chuvash teachers' association, whose members also campaigned among the peasants. The first weekly newspaper in Chuvash, *Khypar* (News) began to be published in January 1906.[25] In Vladikavkaz members of the Ossetian intelligentsia published two periodicals with a national slant.[26] In Siberia the Iakuts and Buriats in particular continued to develop their existing national movements. Individual intellectuals published works in the Iakut language and founded an 'Association of Iakuts'. At the beginning of 1906 about 400 Iakut delegates met and made radical political and social demands. However, after a short time its leading members were arrested. This put an end to the activities of the Association.[27] The Buriats – and the Tungus of the region – protested against the recent administrative reforms, which had curtailed their system of self-government, and against the persistent encroachments on their land. In 1905 the lamaist clergy and the Buriat upper class organized assemblies in Chita and Irkutsk.[28] They decided to introduce a system of national self-government, a native-language educational system and land reform. A group of 'Buriat progressives', which came into being in 1906, further developed the national movement, which sought to combine populism and lamaism.

The revolution of 1905 was a failure, and what it achieved was partly overturned after 1907 by new reactionary forces and policies. As we shall see in the following section, this was also true of its national element. Yet 'Bloody Sunday', the general strike and the October manifesto led to the social and political mobilization of Russian society. This could, it is true, be contained, though not reversed. Similarly, the national mobilization of numerous ethnic groups of the Empire had a permanent effect. The mixture of social, political and national tinder which had ignited in certain peripheral areas in 1905 and 1906 clearly demonstrated the explosive power of the national movements. Although the revolution was not a 'dress rehearsal' for 1917, in the sense in which Lenin declared it to be, it was nonetheless an important precursor of the national revolutionary and separatist movements of 1917. From a modern vantage point it is noticeable that, in the national movement of 1905, the same ethnic groups as those in the new national movement of the perestroika era took the lead, almost without exception: the Poles, who were the most important catalyst; the Transcaucasians (Armenians, Azerbaidzhanis and Georgians), where inter-ethnic conflicts mingled with movements seeking emancipation from the centre; and the Estonians and Latvians with their central European character. At the beginning and at the end of the twentieth century the Muslims reacted to the upheaval later and in a politically less radical manner.

2. Political Participation and Reactionary Backlash in the Duma Period

After Nicholas II had dissolved the first elected Russian parliament on 8 July 1906 there were once again major uprisings in the army and later among the peasants. Their suppression also marked the end of the revolution. Yet for the time being the government's concessions as laid down in the 'Fundamental Laws' of April 1906 were not revoked. In addition to the guarantee of civil rights and freedoms, they included the parliament, the Duma.[29] It is true that the elections to the Duma were not based on universal, equal or direct suffrage, since they consisted of a multi-tier electoral college which gave only men the right to vote, and accorded preferential treatment to the property-owning classes. For this reason they were boycotted by most of the left-wing parties. Nonetheless the majority of the deputies who assembled on 27 April 1906 opposed the government. The two most important groups were the Constitutional Democrats (Cadets), who had about 40 per cent of the seats, and the populist peasant Trudoviki with about 20 per cent. In addition there were a number of non-Russian groups which in part joined the loose group of Autonomists, which comprised between sixty and seventy deputies. In the second Duma, which assembled on 20 February 1907, the opposition was even more vigorous. Whilst it is true that the Cadets had been weakened, the socialist parties, most of whom had participated in the election on this occasion, had considerably more deputies.

It is impossible to determine the precise ethnic composition of the parliament in view of the fact that the ethnic origin of certain deputies is uncertain. A total of about 220 non-Russians was elected to the first Duma.[30] About 270 Russians formed a small majority of about 55 per cent, which meant that with a share of the total population of 44 per cent they were clearly overrepresented. In practice they dominated in an even more overwhelming manner, since the deputies from the periphery arrived in St Petersburg late, or not at all. After the Russians came the Ukrainians with sixty-three deputies and the Poles (who, going by their share of the population, were clearly overrepresented), with fifty to sixty deputies. From the west of the Empire there were also twelve Jews, twelve Belorussians, seven Lithuanians, six Latvians, five Estonians, and four to six Germans. From the Caucasus there were eight Azerbaidzhanis, seven Georgians, four Armenians and a Chechen. From the Volga-Urals area there were eight Tatars, four Bashkirs, two Mordvinians and two Votiaks and a Chuvash. From Middle Asia, on the basis of predetermined quotas, there were four Kazakhs and, at least in theory, six Muslims from Turkestan, though at the time of the dissolution of the first Duma it had proved possible to elect only one. There were also one Romanian (Moldavian), one Bulgar and one Kalmyk. In the second Duma the percentage of non-Russians was slightly smaller, for the Ukrainians and Poles each had only forty-seven deputies and the Jews only four to six. However, on this occasion the 6 Muslims from Turkestan and a Buriat were able to attend.

Although most of the non-Russians were not represented in the first two dumas wholly in accordance with their percentage of the population, the two parliaments nevertheless reflected the ethnic composition of the Empire rather well. It is a remarkable fact that all of the ethnic groups, even the legally excluded inorodtsy and Jews, were given the right to vote. However, the political importance of the non-Russians did not correspond to the number of their deputies, since they did not constitute a united bloc. Separate parties were formed by the Ukrainian deputies, most of whom were peasants, and had a Duma Hromada which was close to the Trudoviki; by the Poles, who were virtually all members of the middle-class National Democrats, with a Polish club (kolo); and by the majority of the Muslims, who belonged to the Ittifak, and worked together closely with the Cadets, whereas a smaller group consisting of five Tatars and an Azerbaidzhani was close to the Trudoviki. The deputies of the other ethnic groups attached themselves directly to the large Russian parties. Thus all the Georgians joined the Social Democrats, whose party leader, Irakli Tsereteli, came from their ranks, whereas the Armenians, Lithuanians, Jews, Estonians and Latvians were distributed among different parties. The radicalization of the second Duma was demonstrated, for example, by the fact that five of the seven Lithuanians were now Social Democrats, and that the majority of the Armenian delegates came from the ranks of the Dashnaks, and joined the Socialist Revolutionaries.

The first two Dumas were hardly able to have an influence on government policy, since the council of ministers was only responsible to the tsar, and their lawmaking competency was blocked by a conservative second chamber (the State Council) and the tsar's right of veto, and undermined by emergency laws. They were nevertheless an important forum for political discussions. In the forefront of the debates was the agrarian question, whereas the specific problems of the nationalities were only discussed sporadically. At any rate, the question of equal rights for the Jews, and the responsibility of the authorities for their part in the pogroms was discussed. The Ukrainian Duma group combined demands for more land for the peasants with calls for native-language schools, and more autonomy for Ukraine. Muslim deputies spoke out in favour of equal rights for their religion and culture, whereas the Kazakh Karataev called for restrictions on the Russian settlement of the steppes. The Polish National Democrats under Dmowski considered the German Empire to be the principal enemy of Poland, and thus placed their hopes in cooperation with the Russian government. However, the demands for a restitution of an autonomous Congress Poland were rejected, as were the suggestions of other non-Russian groups.

What were considered to be unheard-of demands from the non-Russians in the eyes of the government under prime minister Stolypin with its increasingly Russian national stance was, in addition to the unbridgeable differences of opinion in regard to the agrarian question, one of the main reasons for the dissolution of the second Duma on 3 June 1907 and the promulgation of a new electoral law designed to ensure a loyal composition of the Duma. This motive is clearly enunciated in the manifesto of 3 June.

> The Imperial Duma, which was established for the greater stability of the Russian state, must also be Russian in spirit. The other peoples which belong to our Empire shall have representatives for their needs in the Imperial Duma, but they shall and will not appear in such numbers as to enable them to tip the scales on purely Russian matters. Yet in the border marches of the Empire, where the population as yet has insufficient experience of citizenship, the elections for the Imperial duma must for a time be suspended.[31]

Thus the new electoral law not only ensured that, by means of a new electoral college system, the noble and upper middle classes and their parties were able to retain the majority. By means of special regulations it also drastically diminished the share of non-Russians. The Muslims of the steppe regions and of Turkestan were even excluded completely. Thus in the third Duma (1907–12) the non-Russians had only slightly more than one hundred (24 per cent) deputies and in the fourth Duma (1912–17) seventy-six deputies (19 per cent).[32] Only the Germans, and especially the Baltic German elite, profited from the new electoral law, and were able to increase their representation in the third Duma to thirteen deputies. The numerically greatly reduced Polish club continued to pin its hopes on cooperation with Russia, and attempted once again with the help of the Octobrists to have the cultural and administrative restrictions in the Kingdom of Poland repealed, though once again it met with little success. Thereupon, in 1909, the leader of the National Democrats, R. Dmowski, resigned and gave up his seat in the Duma. The Muslim party, which now had only nine deputies instead of thirty-three, was just as unsuccessful in the Duma when it once more raised the question of religious rights and the issue of the ownership of the nomads' land. The twenty Ukrainians, who were now dominated by priests rather than by peasants, no longer formed a party of their own. Their petitions for some kind of status for the Ukrainian language in schools and in the courts were repeatedly rejected on account of the Russian majority in the Duma. In the course of the discussions about a reform of the educational system nearly all of the non-Russian deputies in the Duma came out in favour of native-language tuition. Yet even this concerted action did not meet with success.

In the third and fourth Dumas nationalist trends among the Russian deputies, with parties such as the 'Nationalists' and the 'Union of the Russian People', became increasingly important. They were opposed to the remaining special rights of the peripheral areas, against Jews, Poles, Germans, Finlanders and, in fact, against all non-Russians, and were in favour of strengthening the Russian nation, the predominance of the Russian language and the Orthodox church.[33] As early as 1907 a brochure had asked 'Can Russia leave its peripheral areas to the inorodtsy [used here in a general and pejorative sense for non-Russians]?' The general answer to this question was 'Russia for the Russians!'[34] Nationalist tendencies were also in the ascendant in the moderate parties of the Octobrists and the Cadets. The 'constitutional nationalism' of people such as P. Struve also favoured a Greater Russia to which most of the nationalities would have to assimilate. And the government made increasing use of Russian nationalism as an instrument with which to preserve its power. 'On this firm foundation the government institutions are called to the unswerving defence of . . . the hallowed unity and indivisibility of the empire, the predominance of the Russian nationality within it, and of the Orthodox faith', the new prime minister, V. Kokovtsov declared to the Duma in 1912.[35] The policy on nationalities, which reversed some of the concessions made at the time of the revolution, was also influenced by this nationalist tendency.

The very first three articles of the 'Fundamental Laws' of 23 April 1906 in themselves mapped out the overall framework:

1. The Russian state is one and indivisible.
2. The Grand Duchy of Finland, which is an indivisible part of the Russian state, shall be administered in internal affairs through special regulations on the basis of special laws.
3. The Russian language is the language of the state and obligatory in the army, the fleet, and all state and societal institutions. The use of local languages and dialects in state institutions shall be governed by special laws.[36]

After the 1907 coup d'état the policy on nationalities focussed on the same problems as before the revolution.[37] Thus the special status of Finland, which had been largely restored in 1905 and guaranteed in the 'Fundamental Laws', was largely abolished. A new diet had been elected as late as 1907, after the introduction of reforms which had also given the women of Finland, as the first in the world, the active and passive right to vote. Its radical composition, with the Social Democrats as the most important force (and strongest Socialist party in Europe), provided the excuse for its dissolution. In 1910 Finland, in all important areas, was placed under Imperial jurisdiction. The diet, whose competencies were thus considerably curtailed, used obstruction to delay the implementation of this and other drastic measures, which were not introduced with any great vigour by the Russian government.[38] Nevertheless the renewed attack on the traditional autonomy made a significant contribution to the further alienation of the Finlanders from Russia.

Similarly, the modest concessions (when compared to Finland) made to the Kingdom of Poland were soon abrogated. As early as December 1907 the Polish school association (Macierz Szkolna), which consisted of 781 departments and hundreds of thousands of members, was shut down. New assaults on the position of the Poles followed. A new province of Kholm (with a Ukrainian majority) was established in 1912, and prised out of the land of the Kingdom. And in 1913 the Warsaw–Vienna railway, which had hitherto been owned by Polish companies, was nationalized. The introduction of zemstvo self-government in six provinces of the 'western areas' in 1911, which also led to controversy in the Duma, strengthened the position of the Russians at the expense of the Poles by means of national electoral colleges. It is obvious that such a policy did not weaken the Polish national movement. Rather, it strengthened its resistance to Russia.

For the Russian nationalists the movement of the Ukrainians, whom they regarded as being Russian, constituted a serious provocation. The modest and incipient network of national communication which had arisen after 1905 was once again abolished, and by 1910 the local branches of the Prosvita association and most of the Ukrainian-language periodicals had been banned. The festivities marking the hundredth anniversary of the birth of the national poet Shevchenko in March 1914 were also banned. The fact that tens of thousands of Ukrainians gathered in Kiev nonetheless shows that it had proved impossible to strangle the Ukrainian movement. In the period immediately before the First World War the Ukrainian question became increasingly a function of the relationship to Austro-Hungary, where the Ukrainian national movement had developed more freely. Austria was believed to be behind the Ukrainian movement, and the Ukrainians in Russia were accused by Russian nationalists of being separatists (Mazepism). Russia's deteriorating relations with the German Empire now increasingly affected the Germans in Russia, who became the targets of nationalist attacks. After 1909 the question of restricting German ownership of land in Russia was a permanent subject for debate in the Duma, though it did not crystallize into a law.

Anti-semitism continued to be an important component of the extreme kind of Russian nationalism. The revolution had only marginally improved the position of the Jews. Discriminatory measures such as the pale of settlement, the restricted number of places in middle and higher schools, restrictions on the purchase of land and on professional mobility remained in place. True, after 1907 there were no further large-scale pogroms against Jews. However, the climax of Russian anti-semitism was marked by the Beilis case, which opened in a Kiev court in 1911. M. Beilis, a Jew, was accused of having committed ritual murder on a Christian boy. The charge was a fabrication by local right-wing extremists which received support from the Justice and Interior ministries and the local authorities, and was evidently designed to mobilize religious and national emotions, and to neutralize revolutionary tendencies. Russian public opinion took a great interest in the case, which ended in September 1913 with Beilis being acquitted by the jury.[39]

It would be an impermissible simplification to reduce Russian policy on nationalities between 1906 and 1914 to nationalism and repression, for it still continued to be illogical and inconsistent.[40] Thus the Ministry of Finance, whose aim was the modernization of the Empire, was not infrequently in favour of cooperating with non-Russians, and also with Jews. And the leading political figures, who mistrusted the extreme Russian nationalists, continued in certain areas to pursue traditionally cautious and pragmatic policies, and resort repeatedly to the pre-national imperial patriotism which was intended to integrate the non-Russians under the protection of the tsar. Some of the radical integrational measures enacted as a result of pressure from the Russian national public and the majority in the Duma were only implemented haltingly, and other projects were never put into practice. Some attempts were once again made to cooperate with loyal non-Russian elites, for example, the Baltic Germans, or the Muslim clergy. In Transcaucasia viceroy I. Vorontsov-Dashkov went back to cooperating with the Armenians, who were to be instrumentalized for the foreign policy pursued towards the Ottoman Empire. The fundamental toleration of Islamic schools and clergymen continued, whereby, as in the past, the conservatives received more support than the reformers. However, of considerably greater importance for relations with the ethnic groups of Middle Asia was the deliberate support for eastern Slav colonization contained in Stolypin's reforms. The continual decrease in the land owned by the nomads and the influx of Russian and Ukrainian settlers increased the potential for conflict in the northern areas of the steppes.

Thus the Russian policy on nationalities continued to be contradictory before the First World War. The tsarist state often sought answers to the problems of the day using old recipes, though it was unable to pursue one-dimensional policies without undermining the foundations of its very existence. Neither the solution proffered by a Russian nation state nor by a loose federation came into question. The renewed recourse to a reactionary policy on nationalities after 1907 meant that the national movements did in fact suffer some setbacks. However, it was impossible to turn the clock back to the time before 1905. Some of the achievements of the revolution such as the freedom of the press and the right of association were preserved, albeit in a restricted manner, and made national communication and agitation with the help of associations and native-language periodicals possible. Thus in these years some of the ethnic groups which had first awakened politically in 1905 in fact continued to expand their movements. In the case of the Ukrainian peasants the cooperative system was making progress, whereas the intelligentsia under the leadership of the Ukrainian historian M. Hrushevsky reorganized itself within the 'Society of Progressive Ukrainians'. The press and the publishing trade of the Muslims continued to flourish, and Jadidism gradually made its way to Middle Asia and even to the Emirate of Bukhara. The Azerbaidzhanis, who were strongly influenced by the revolution of the Young Turks, in 1912 founded the new Musavat (Equality) Party, which combined Islamic with secular pan-Turkish ideas, and soon assumed the leadership of the national movement.

3. Territorial Changes and Destabilization in the First World War

The protracted war which broke out in July 1914 subjected the Russian Empire to strains that exceeded its ability to deal with them.[41] A number of defeats at the hands of the German armies led, for the first time for 300 years, to significant territorial losses. Internally the war effort helped to exacerbate political and social tensions, and these finally erupted in February 1917.

As in other European states, the outbreak of the war initially led to a patriotic closing of ranks. 'Imperial loyalty' united the population behind the tsar, and demonstrated that the Russian Empire still had integrational powers at its disposal.[42] In the session of the Duma of 26 July only the Social Democrats protested against the war. The non-Russian delegates also declared their loyalty, and in the weeks that followed hundreds of thousands of non-Russians went to war as soldiers and officers of the tsar. Even the Poles expressed their loyalty via the Duma club. On 15 August the Commander-in-Chief of the Russian Army promised the Poles reunification under the tsar whilst preserving their religion, language and self-government, and a Polish National Committee established by Dmowski's National Democrats came out in favour of such a solution in November 1914. The Baltic Germans and the German colonists also declared their loyalty in the war against the German Empire.

The Germans of the Russian Empire were nonetheless subjected to discriminatory measures. German schools and associations were closed, and this was followed by a ban on speaking German in public.[43] In 1915 the liquidation of German ownership of land in Russia was once again discussed, and a decision was taken to do so in the case of German citizens who had immigrated after 1871, and those who lived in the western border area (especially in Volhynia), although this was only partially implemented. The Jews were also suspected of spying for the Central Powers, and in 1915, in addition to Germans and Poles, hundreds of thousands of Jews were forcibly resettled away from the border area.[44] In order to provide accommodation for all these people and to give a stimulus to the Russian economy, the pale of settlement was enlarged in August 1915, and Jews were allowed to settle in the towns of Russia proper.

In the Austrian territories in eastern Galicia and the Bukovina, which had been occupied by Russian troops in the autumn of 1914, the Jews were treated in a ruthless manner. The Ukrainians, who had expected a change in the policy on nationalities, were also disappointed. The government treated Galicia, which had never been part of Russia, as 'ancient Russian land'; Ukrainian schools and periodicals were closed down, the Uniate clergy were persecuted and numerous politically active Ukrainians and Poles arrested and deported to Russia, including the Metropolitan of the Greek-Catholic church, A. Sheptytsky.

The Austro-German offensive in the spring and summer of 1915 not only made up for Austria's territorial losses, but also took from the Russian Empire the whole of Congress Poland and large parts of the Lithuanian-Belorussian 'western provinces' and of Kurland. With this almost all of the Poles and Lithuanians and numerous Latvians, Belorussians, Ukrainians and Baltic Germans were no longer subjects of the Russian tsar. Renewed Russian promises to the Poles now came too late, for the initiative had already passed to the Central Powers. J. Piłsudski, who had fought against Russia from Galicia in a military and political capacity since the beginning of the war, now extended his activities, which were devoted to the reestablishment of an independent Poland, to Congress Poland. On 5 November 1916 a Kingdom of Poland allied with the Central Powers was proclaimed. The status of the former 'Western Provinces', of the 'Upper East Land', which was under German control, remained unclear. A 'Confederation of the Grand Duchy of Lithuania' formed by Lithuanians and Belorussians sought to reestablish a Lithuanian-Belorussian state, and competed with the claims of the Poles and of those Lithuanians who wished to establish a nation state. The German occupation of Kurland, which was placed under a germanizing military administration, led to a mass exodus of about half a million Latvians to the Russian Empire, where a national military unit, the 'Latvian Riflemen', which used Latvian as the command language, was established.

Russia's military conflict with the Ottoman Empire was also linked to the nationalities problem. On the one hand Turkic-speaking Muslims in Russia were suspected of constituting a pan-Islamic or pan-Turkish fifth column. A number of Tatar and Azerbaidzhani emigrants, including J. Akchura, were politically active in Istanbul, and in 1915 founded a 'Committee for the Defence of the Rights of the Muslim Turkic-Tatar Peoples in Russia'. The Ottoman Empire reckoned on an uprising by the Caucasian Muslims, and a revolt by the Adshars, which was put down by Russian troops, seemed to confirm these expectations.

On the other hand Russia made use of the Armenian question for its own purposes. Before the outbreak of the war it had, with the support of the Armenian church, begun to play the role of the protector of the Armenians in the Ottoman Empire, and for the war it commissioned units of Armenian volunteers from the Ottoman Empire and from Russia.[45] The Ottoman counter-offensive under Enver Pasha, which followed upon a Russian attack, ended in defeat in January 1915, and as the army retreated there were the first instances of Armenians being massacred. The conflict with Russia thus became the motive and the charge of collaboration the justification for the mass deportation and the genocide inflicted on about one million Armenians in 1915. However, the real reason lay in the transformational crisis of the declining Ottoman Empire, whose Young Turk power elites wished to mobilize the population with the help of national slogans, and used the Armenians as scapegoats. About 300,000 Armenians were able to reach the safety of Transcaucasia under the protection of Russian troops. When Russia, after a temporary setback, occupied large parts of Ottoman Armenia in 1916, there were practically no Armenians left in the area. To this day the massacres of 1915–16 continue to be the central historical point of reference for the Armenians, and one which determines their basic opposition to Turkey or to the Turkic-speaking Azerbaidzhanis, whom they regard as its representatives.

The First World War confronted a whole series of the Russian

Empire's nationalities with the question of whether they should ally themselves with the Central Powers against Russia. In addition to ethnic groups living under German occupation, some Finlander activists also turned to the German Empire, and numerous volunteers from Finland joined the Prussian Jägerbataillon 27, which was sent to the Baltic front. The 'Union for the Liberation of Ukraine', which had been founded in Lviv by emigrants from Russia at the beginning of the war, sought support from the Central Powers; and Germany also supported the 'League of the Foreign Peoples of Russia', which in May 1916 sent an appeal from Stockholm to US President Wilson, signed by representatives of the Finlanders, the Poles, the Baltic Germans, the Jews, the Ukrainians, the Lithuanians, the Latvians, the Belorussians, Georgians and Muslims in which they attacked the oppression of nationalities in the Russian Empire. At a conference on nationalities held in Lausanne the numerous representatives from Russia drew attention to their plight, and from September 1916 to February 1917 a *Bulletin des Nationalités de Russie* was published in Berne.[46]

Defeats and wartime economic problems, especially the badly organized food supplies in the cities, reinforced the political and social tensions within the interior of Russia. The gap between organized 'society' and the political leadership increased when the government reacted to the foundation of a moderate reformist 'Progressive Bloc' in the Duma in September 1915 by shifting to the right of the political spectrum. From the summer of 1915 onwards strikes by industrial workers once again began to increase, and now, in addition to Petrograd and the central Russian industrial zone, spread to southern Ukraine and Baku. Yet it is impossible to say that the most important centres of social unrest – as had been the case before the revolution of 1905 – were in the non-Russian periphery. The three main regions of national and social resistance were missing: Poland was in the hands of the Germans and the Baltic provinces and Transcaucasia were directly on the front line.

Nevertheless, what was by far the largest insurrectionary movement in the Russian Empire between the revolutions of 1905 and 1917 emanated from non-Russians and not from Russians. The background for the uprising, which in 1916 spread over large parts of Middle Asia, was Russian colonial rule in general and in particular the conflicts, which had increased dramatically since the end of the nineteenth century and were centred on the fertile northern areas of the steppe that the nomads used as summer pastures, between the nomadic herdsmen and the European settlers supported by the government. The immediate reason for the uprising was a government decree issued on 25 June 1916 which called up 390,000 inorodtsy for service in the army. It is true that they were merely being asked to do work behind the front lines, and there were no plans to send them into action. But the new decree infringed upon the exemption from military service the Asiatic inorodtsy had traditionally enjoyed.[47]

In the summer of 1916, in various towns and villages in southern Middle Asia, there were initially a number of uprisings by the sedentary population which were primarily directed against Russian bureaucrats and also against the railway. Subsequently the insurrection spread to virtually all of Middle Asia, from the mountains of Kirgizia to the western part of Kazakhstan and to the Turkmen of Transcaspia. Groups of up to several thousand rebels attacked towns and Russian troops, and to some extent the insurrection acquired the character of a 'Holy War' against the Russian infidels, and of an anti-colonial struggle for independence. The north-eastern steppe and mountain region of the Semireche district (the land of the seven rivers), where eastern Slav colonization was particularly intense, witnessed the most violent armed clashes between Kirgiz and Kazakhs on the one hand, and Russian settlers, administrators, policemen and soldiers on the other. In the course of this more than 3,000 Russians and an unknown and considerably higher number of non-Russians were killed, and about 10,000 Russian farms were pillaged and burnt. In certain districts within the region, the Kirgiz destroyed practically all of the European settlements. The consequences for the local Kirgiz and Kazakhs were catastrophic. Probably over 100,000 Kazakhs and Kirgiz were killed, and 200,000 fled to the mountains and to Chinese Eastern Turkestan. The decimation of the nomadic population and their herds not only ended their resistance, but also created space for new settlements inhabited by European peasants engaged in arable farming. Thus, in the unique confrontation between sedentary settlers and nomads, the inhabitants of Middle Asia had lost even more ground. Yet the decisive strike against the nomads first came under Stalin.

4. The Revolution of 1917 and the Disintegration of the Russian Empire

The fate of tsarist power in Russia was decided in the capital. Trotsky later commented: 'It would not be an exaggeration to say that Petrograd accomplished the February revolution. The rest of the country followed suit'.[48] The peripheral areas inhabited by non-Russians had already played a more minor role in the build-up to the revolution than in 1905. It was the workers, soldiers and women of Petrograd who, in conjunction with the democratic intelligentsia, toppled the ancien régime. However, that the revolution triumphed in such a swift and effortless manner throughout the country was also due to the fact that the tsarist autocracy had forfeited the support of both the Russians and the non-Russians. Nevertheless, in 1917 the revolutionary élan emanated to a greater extent than in 1905 from Russian workers, soldiers and peasants. The lesser importance of the peripheral areas inhabited by non-Russians was largely due to the fact that Poland and Kurland, which had been particularly active regions in the first revolution, had been occupied by troops of the Central Powers.

In 1917 the workers' movement was concentrated in the two capitals and in the Russian industrial areas. Workers' soviets were established at an early stage in towns on the periphery such as Helsinki, Tallinn (Reval), Riga, Minsk, Kiev, Odessa, Ufa, Tiflis, Baku and Tashkent, and in most regions there were strikes. In the peripheral areas it was often Russian workers and soldiers who seized the initiative with regard to protests and revolutionary organizations. In such cases there was a possibility of confrontation between revolutionary Russian workers and moderate national forces. When the initiative came from non-Russian workers, as in Finland and the Baltic provinces, clashes with the national movement were a foregone conclusion.

In the course of the year, as they had already done in the first revolution, the peasants of the Russian Empire confiscated increasingly large tracts of noble lands. For this reason the regional distribution of agrarian unrest shows that it was concentrated in areas in which the peasants lived almost exclusively from arable farming, and where a great deal of land was not in their hands. In addition to the Russian black earth provinces, they also included regions inhabited by non-Russians, especially the western part of Ukraine, and Belorussia, which, it is true, possessed a different structure.[49] The landowners in these areas were

Poles and Russians, and belonged to a different ethnic group to the Belorussian and Ukrainian peasants. This meant that social antagonisms were reinforced by ethnic ones. Here, near the front line, soldiers, the third carrier group of the revolution, also contributed to the radicalization of the peasants. Non-Russian soldiers, for example, Ukrainians, Estonians and Latvians, formed ethnically distinct military units. The Latvian riflemen, who had already seen service before 1917 in the war against Germany, became radical in the course of the year, and proved to be one of the Bolsheviks' most important military units.[50]

The revolution of 1917 was a social revolution, and the national movements unleashed in February combined national and social demands. As in the case of the Russians, the peasants constituted by far the largest social group in most of the non-Russian peoples, and for this reason the question of land was at the top of the agenda. The combination of social and national factors became particularly explosive whenever the lower classes of one ethnic group laid claim to the land of another ethnic group. The movements of the peasant peoples in the west were often directed not against Russian elites, but against Baltic German and Polish ones, whereas the nomads of the east came into conflict with what were mainly Russian settlers. The social tinder was also reinforced by national antagonisms among the multi-ethnic urban population in the peripheral areas. Socially mobilized peasants poured into the towns, and here they came upon foreign ethnic groups which constituted an obstacle to their social advancement. The classical pattern was found in the cities in the west and in the south, in which the ethno-religious diaspora groups of the Jews and the Armenians made up the mass of the commercial middle class. Here again the conflicts which arose were often not between non-Russians and Russians, so that cooperation between an ethno-social group and sections of the Russian population against another ethnic group was certainly a possibility. On the other hand, in the eastern areas of the Russian Empire the conflict between the non-Russian rural population and the Russian towns tended to be the rule. Although inter-ethnic conflicts predominated in the peripheral areas of the Russian Empire as a result of their ethno-social mixture, there were also profound social antagonisms within the various ethnic groups, particularly when, as in Transcaucasia or Finland, they were more obviously differentiated in social terms.

In keeping with the socio-ethnic structure, the revolution of 1917 was a complicated web of social and national antagonisms. Opinions among historians about the relative importance of the two factors differ. This is also due to the fact that to date most of the research within the Soviet Union and in other countries has been devoted to either the social *or* the national revolution, and has largely tended to exclude the other aspect. In place of this kind of polarization I have preferred to rely on an integrational approach which emphasizes the interplay of social and national factors, and the simultaneity of social and national movements.[51]

Some sections of the opposition had expected that the national question in the Russian Empire would automatically be solved with the end of tsarist rule. However, the opposite was the case. The February revolution unleashed the national movements to an extent that no one had foreseen. The question was whether the Provisional Government, which was weighed down with the problems of the war and the internal reorganization of Russia, would be able to satisfy the demands of the peripheral peoples without endangering the existence of the Russian state. For it soon became clear that the Provisional Government continued to subscribe to the ideal of a Russia which was 'one and indivisible', and saw its principal task to be the defence of the Russian borders in the war with the Central Powers.[52]

Yet the February Revolution led to a liberalization of the policy on nationalities which surpassed any of the concessions made in 1905. All citizens of Russia were granted civil rights and liberties, and individual national and cultural rights. The discriminatory exclusion laws, especially the ones which applied to the Jews and the inorodtsy, were repealed. Autonomy was restored to Finland and to the Kingdom of Poland (which, admittedly, was occupied by German troops). However, the other nations of the Russian Empire were not granted collective territorial rights. The Provisional Government (like the second power-sharing pillar, the Petrograd Soviet) underestimated the explosive power of the nationalities question. It was preoccupied with the conduct of the war, with maintaining law and order, and with feeding the population. Demands for autonomy were rejected, and a solution of the problem deferred to the Constituent Assembly, which had still to be elected. This, it was thought, would subsequently resolve the national question together with basic social and political problems in a democratic manner. However, it was just as impossible to keep the national forces which had been unleashed in February under control as it was to contain the social revolution in Russia. On the contrary, these delaying tactics led to a continual and growing radicalization of the social and national movements on the periphery. By the time the Provisional Government managed to make a half-hearted concession at the end of September and, pending the approval of the Constituent Assembly, granted the peoples of the Empire the right to self-determination, it had already lost most of the trust that had once been placed in it.

The national revolution on the periphery, even more than the revolution in Russia, was determined by the war. The supply problems and the general war-weariness reinforced the mistrust of the centre, and a series of national army units was established. On top of this the peripheral areas in the west and in the south were directly a theatre of war. In fact, the front remained fairly stable throughout 1917. The Poles and Lithuanians, and some of the Belorussians, Ukrainians, Latvians and Baltic Germans continued to be under the control of the Central Powers. And the seizure of Riga by German troops towards the end of August enlarged still further the proportion of non-Russian ethnic groups living under German occupation.

Throughout 1917 the national movements in the Russian Empire developed with different degrees of intensity, and this depended on the historical preconditions, the social and political antagonisms and the influence of the war.[53] Although the circumstances were very different, there were attempts to take joint action. At the end of May the representatives of the national socialist parties met in Petrograd, and in September there was a congress of the peoples of Russia in Kiev. The assembled ninety-three representatives of all the larger groups with the exception of the Poles and the Finlanders agreed that Russia should be reorganized into a democratic federal republic. Yet these endeavours produced no tangible results. The national interests proved to be greater than the things they had in common.

It is no accident that this congress was held in Kiev, for in 1917 the Ukrainian movement expanded with remarkable speed and now also embarked on the mass movement phase in Russia itself. In view of the fact that the Ukrainians were very numerous, and that the area in which they lived was of great strategic and economic significance, the Ukrainian question advanced to become a central problem for the Provisional Government, and later for the Bolsheviks.

In Kiev, a mere week after the February Revolution, representatives of various different social groups founded the Ukrainian Central

Council (Rada), a proto-parliament presided over by the historian M. Hrushevsky which a few weeks later was legitimated by a National Congress, and expressed its loyalty to the Provisional Government.[54] The political leadership was at first in the hands of the Ukrainian Progressists, though they were soon replaced by the Ukrainian Social Democratic Workers' Party, which pursued national and moderate social goals. In June the writer V. Vynnychenko, who was a member of this party, was the first to be appointed chairman of the General Secretariat of the Rada, the first Ukrainian government. However, the movements of the peasants and the soldiers determined the dynamic course of events, and not the Rada or the parties, which merely represented a small class of the intelligentsia. The decisive factor was that, after the February revolution, the peasants, who comprised about 90 per cent of the Ukrainians in Russia, were mobilized in social and to some extent in national terms. They organized themselves in a Peasants' Union and in peasant soviets, and in June more than 2,000 delegates took part in a Ukrainian peasants' congress. Their most important demands were a specific solution for the land question in Ukraine, the establishment of a Ukrainian land trust and political autonomy.

Acting under pressure from the mass movement, the Central Rada made more radical demands, and on 10 June declared Ukraine to be autonomous. The decree was entitled the '1st Universal', a term with which the Rada harked back to the edicts of the hetmans in the seventeenth century and thus to the 'Golden Age' of Ukrainian statehood.[55] The Provisional Government was forced to relent and recognized the Rada and its General Secretariat as *de facto* representatives of the Ukrainian nation. With this a Russian government had for the first time surrendered a part of its power to a national body, and recognized the national principle as the basis of administrative division. For the Cadets this concession was unacceptable, so that they withdrew their members from the government. However, in the summer of 1917 these concessions were no longer enough for the mobilized Ukrainian masses. They wanted to see solutions for their pressing social problems, and in their eyes the Rada had discredited itself by making a pact with the Provisional Government. Conflicts erupted within the Ukrainian national movement, and the populist radical Ukrainian Social Revolutionary Party, which combined revolutionary agrarian and national demands, quickly became increasingly influential, and by the autumn had become the leading political force. Furthermore, the tensions between the small

THE RUSSIAN MULTI-ETHNIC EMPIRE

intellectual political elite and the peasants and workers increased, as did those between the Ukrainians and the Russians in Ukraine, whose parties still dominated political life in the towns.

In the case of the Belorussians, who were partly under German occupation, events took a less dramatic turn. The sole national party, the Belorussian Socialist Hramada, did not have mass support among the peasants, who comprised 90 per cent of the Belorussians. Following the example of the Ukrainian movement, intellectuals and soldiers established a Belorussian Rada in July, but it received little support. For this reason the socialist parties active among the urban population, the majority of which was Russian and Jewish, continued to determine the political course of events in Belorussia.

The Baltic provinces were also partly occupied by German troops. In the area of Livonia, which was still under Russian control, and in Estonia, Latvians and Estonians were encouraged by the February Revolution to engage in political activity. They held a number of congresses, and founded new parties, which mainly demanded cultural self-government and political autonomy.[56] With their internationalist stance, the Bolsheviks were able to improve their position among Latvian workers, agricultural labourers and soldiers (the Latvian riflemen), and thus became the largest political force in this area. In the autumn they also gained ground in Estonia.

In Finland the diet, which had a Social Democrat majority, and was once again in a position to take decisions, had declared itself to be the 'supreme power' in July, leaving only foreign policy and the army under the control of the Russian centre. The Provisional Government would not accept this substantial increase in the autonomy of Finland, and dissolved the parliament. New elections in October led to a victory for the bourgeois parties which cooperated with the Provisional Government. This set the scene for the civil war.[57]

The Romanians of Bessarabia had also been drawn into the war in 1916. A Moldavian National Party was founded after the February Revolution. It made demands for autonomy, and in the autumn there was an upsurge in irredentist activities which sought to bring about reunification with Romania. The German colonists continued to be loyal subjects under the Provisional Government, especially since the anti-German laws had been lifted as early as March 1917. They used the new freedoms to establish a large number of cultural and political organizations which as a rule pursued moderate aims.

The Jews of the Russian Empire welcomed the February Revolution and the Provisional Government, which at long last accorded them equal rights.[58] Their cultural and political life began to revive, though political fragmentation persisted, and the projected All-Russian Jewish Congress failed to materialize. Among the numerous parties, almost all of which demanded extraterritorial cultural autonomy for the Jews, the most important continued to be the Zionists and the Social Democratic 'Bund', which was close to the Mensheviks. By and large there were hardly any anti-Jewish pogroms in 1917, such as those which had been staged by reactionary forces in 1905. There were merely a handful of anti-Jewish riots in Ukraine when, towards the end of the year, public order collapsed. Far more terrible ones were to follow in the Civil War.

The year 1917 was relatively quiet in Transcaucasia, which also lay in the vicinity of the front against the Ottoman Empire.[59] As in Russia itself a system of power-sharing emerged. On the one hand there was a Special Committee for Transcaucasia consisting largely of Georgians and Russians, which was set up by the Provisional Government. However, it did not come up with any solutions for the pressing social and political problems. On the other hand workers' soviets were set up in Tiflis and Baku. Whereas the Tiflis soviet was fundamentally Menshevik, Mensheviks, Bolsheviks, Social Revolutionaries, the Armenian Dashnaks and the Azerbaidzhani Musavat party cooperated in the Baku soviet. The Georgian Mensheviks continued to pursue supranational policies, and remained loyal to the Provisional Government. They contributed several of its ministers, and N. Chkheidze and I. Tsereteli were leading figures in the Petrograd soviet. The anti-Turkish Dashnaks also remained loyal to the Provisional Government, if only because it was still pursuing the war against the Ottoman Empire. The Musavat Party, which was dominated by the intelligentsia and the middle classes, was in favour of a federal structure for Russia, and gained mass support in 1917. Until October the Bolsheviks were in the minority everywhere, though their influence increased in the Baku soviet.

The Muslims of Russia continued to sustain the moderate movement which they had embraced in 1905.[60] The Union of Muslims (Ittifak) with its liberal and pan-Islamic orientation initially continued to be the most important force. It was confronted with a conservative religious movement, which received support from the clergy and the old elite, and a radical group which came from the left-wing intelligentsia and favoured the Social Revolutionaries. In May 1917 about a thousand elected delegates (including 200 women) met in Moscow at the First All-Russian Congress of Muslims. A majority decided in favour of gender equality (and were the first in the Islamic world to do so), and to support the federal programme advocated by the Azerbaidzhani delegates. The second congress, which took place in Kazan in July, led to the triumph of the more radical Volga Tatars, who placed social problems at the top of the agenda, and came out in favour of setting up a 'National Assembly' of the Muslims. Thus the gradual radicalization of political life, which gripped Russia in the course of the summer, also became apparent in the Muslim movement. At the same time the particularist tendencies of the various national movements became more visible.

The Muslims of Turkestan were also mobilized politically in 1917. Among the various organizations with differing political aims, the most important was the Muslim Central Council of Turkestan, which was under the aegis of the reformist Jadidists. However, the most radical movement emanated from the Russian population, which, in the autumn of 1917, organized the Tashkent soviet. The nomads were mobilized to an even greater extent, and their traditional conflicts with eastern Slav settlers flared up yet again. The Kazakhs had assembled at a congress in Orenburg as early as April 1917, and in the summer had founded a political party, the Alash Orda. They demanded autonomy, an end to colonization, and even the expulsion of new settlers. The violent clashes around the northern area of the steppe reached a new climax in the summer of 1917, when numerous Kirgiz and Kazakhs, who had fled to China in 1916, returned and laid claim to their former pastures. There were also conflicts between Bashkirs, and Russian and Tatar settlers. The Bashkirs also made demands for autonomy which conflicted with the programme proposed by the Tatars.

In 1917, as had been the case in 1905, numerous small non-Russian ethnic groups were once again mobilized in political and social terms. The Crimean Tatars founded a national party (Milli Firka) which demanded autonomy and soon clashed with the Russians and Ukrainians, who were more numerous in the Crimea. The moderate movement of the northern Caucasian 'gortsy' sought to cooperate with the conservative Russian Cossacks against the Russian colonists, the majority of whom were Social Revolutionaries. The small group of intellectuals of the ethnically diverse mountain peoples founded national soviets and a 'Federation of United Gortsy', and held two congresses at which demands for autonomy were made. In the summer the conservative

Islamic wing, which was preparing a 'Holy War' against the Russians in the manner of Shamil, received increasing support.

In May there was a congress of small peoples on the middle Volga. It was attended by more than 500 representatives from the Chuvash, Cheremis, Votiaks, Mordvinians, Zyrians, Kalmyks and baptized Tatars. The delegates declared their solidarity with the Provisional Government, and placed the emphasis on cultural and linguistic demands. There followed a series of meetings of the various ethnic groups, some of whom made national and cultural demands for the very first time. In Siberia the Buriats and Iakuts started from where they had left off in 1905. A national Buriat duma and a Iakut committee called for the introduction of native languages in schools and government offices, and demanded social reforms. Russian regionalists in Siberia attempted to combat colonial dependence on the centre together with non-Russian ethnic groups. However, social antagonisms between eastern Slav settlers and native ethnic groups made closer cooperation impossible.

Thus almost all of the non-Russians of the Russian Empire witnessed an explosion of national movements in 1917. Their forms and aims reflected the degree of social and political mobilization of the various ethnic groups, and the specific social antagonisms of the region. As in the case of the workers', peasants' and soldiers' movements, there was a noticeable radicalization in the course of the summer. This did not concern the political goals, which, with the exception of the Poles and Finns, never went beyond demands for autonomy. Rather, it applied to social matters. The national movements led by intellectuals were forced by the mass of the peasants to take greater note of socialist agrarian aims. A whole series of national parties which earlier in the year had inclined more to the liberal Cadets were thus close to the Russian Socialist Revolutionaries by the autumn. The Socialist Revolutionaries were also welcome as alliance partners because, unlike the centralist liberals, they had for a long time subscribed to the principle of federalism. True, the Russian Social Democrats had included the right to self-determination for the peoples in their programme since 1903. However, the national question was of minor importance for the workers' party with its internationalist policies. In 1917 the Mensheviks, among whom Georgians and Jews played an important role, came out in favour of extraterritorial autonomy, whereas the Bolsheviks, who hoped to exploit the revolutionary potential of the national movements, came out in favour of the right to self-determination and secession. Although this meant that they had the most radical national progamme of all the Russian parties, the situation in the mainly peasant non-Russian periphery remained difficult for them as well. In addition to the large Russian cities, in which they were able to enlarge their base considerably during the summer and the autumn, they made gains only among the Latvians, Finns and Estonians.

A snapshot of the political balance of power in the areas controlled by Russian troops (with the exception of Finland) shortly after the October Revolution is provided by the results of the elections to the Constituent Assembly in November 1917. It would certainly be true to say that the circumstances under which they were held – war, revolution and organizational problems – led to lacunae and distortions. Yet on the whole the results as reconstructed by Radkey are rather telling.[61] After the elections the Russian Socialist Revolutionaries, who received over 40 per cent, and the Bolsheviks, who received 23.8 per cent of the votes cast, emerged as the two most powerful political parties. The Russian Socialist Revolutionaries, whose share of the vote cannot be precisely ascertained on account of electoral pacts with national parties, were ahead in the black earth areas, in the Volga provinces and in Siberia, whereas the Bolsheviks took the lead in the centre, in the industrial areas and among the soldiers. The other Russian parties, the Mensheviks, the Cadets, and the nationalist right, together received less than 10 per cent of the vote.

The majority of non-Russians did not vote for Russian parties, preferring to elect their national parties instead. However, the Bolsheviks were able to achieve notable successes in the north-west. In Estonia they received 40 per cent of the vote compared with 59 per cent for the Estonian parties, in the part of Livonia not occupied by German troops (without Riga) as much as 72 per cent (the best result in the whole empire) and in the two provinces of Minsk and Vitebsk, in which the majority of the population was Belorussian, 63 and 51 per cent respectively. It is a remarkable fact that the majority of the Latvian and Belorussian peasants decided to vote for the Bolshevik workers' party.

The share of the national parties was about 22 per cent of the total number of votes known to have been cast. Since we do not have results from certain non-Russian regions, including virtually all of the provinces of Middle Asia, the northern Caucasus and Iakutia, and in view of the fact that there were some electoral alliances with Russian parties, the share of potential voters of national parties must have been at least 6 per cent higher. Although it is true that these parties did not form a single entity, they were largely of a social revolutionary nature. This was primarily true of the Ukrainian parties, for which the overwhelming majority of the Ukrainian peasants voted. They received more than 70 per cent of the votes in four provinces, the lion's share falling to the Ukrainian social revolutionaries. Although the largely non-Ukrainian inhabitants of the cities and the southern industrial areas voted for Russian parties, the elections for the Constituent Assembly documented the impressive surge in political and social mobilization which the Ukrainians had experienced in 1917. The picture was very different indeed in the case of the Belorussians, whose parties obtained less than 1 per cent of the votes in Belorussia. On the other hand, the ethnic minorities of the Jews, the Poles and the Germans voted almost unanimously for national parties, with the Zionists clearly defeating the 'Bund'.

In Transcaucasia the three main ethnic groups also voted for their traditional parties, the Georgians for the Mensheviks, the Armenians for the Dashnaks and the Azerbaidzhanis for the Musavatists and other Muslim groups. Here the Social Revolutionaries and Bolsheviks both only received about 5 per cent of the vote. The other Muslims in Russia also decided in favour of their national parties. In the Volga-Urals area the Tatars and Bashkirs had separate lists which together received more than 55 per cent of the vote in the province of Ufa. In Middle Asia the Muslims also voted for their own parties, as is demonstrated by the results from the only area whose results are known. Thus in the province of Uralsk the Kazakh parties received three-quarters of the votes cast. That some of the small ethnic groups were politically mobilized in the course of the year is documented by the Chuvash, who in the province of Kazan voted unanimously for a national bloc, and by the Buriats, whose parties received about 18 per cent of the votes cast in two provinces.

Thus the elections to the Constituent Assembly showed that the majority of the non-Russians in the Empire decided to vote for national parties in November 1917. This does not necessarily mean that the national factors had everywhere become more important than the social ones. Rather, it underlines the fact that in 1917 the national and social movements developed simultaneously and intermingled on numerous occasions. The programmes of most of the national parties assigned a great deal of importance to social aims. Without the incorporation of social demands they ran the risk, as the civil war was to demonstrate, of forfeiting the support of the mass of the peasants. Some, such as the leading parties of the Ukrainians, the Armenians and the Chuvash, were close to the Social Revolutionaries, who together with them commanded a clear majority of the deputies. The majority of the Muslims continued to favour the liberal and moderate camp, whereas the Kazakhs and Kirgiz in the 'land of the seven rivers' (Semireche) entered into an electoral alliance with the Russian Cossacks that was opposed to the eastern Slav settlers, the majority of whom were in favour of the Social Revolutionaries. Of decisive importance was the fact that the Bolsheviks had a very small electoral base in all of the regions inhabited primarily by non-Russians, with the exception of the Baltic provinces and Belorussia.

The significance of the national movements and, in more general terms, of the notion that the unsolved nationalities question was one of the reasons for the October Revolution, is a contentious issue. Since social and national factors intermingled in most of the national movements, it is virtually impossible to isolate the specifically national element. Yet it is certain that national autonomy movements weakened the position of the Provisional Government, which considered itself to be the champion of Russian unity. Its intransigence towards national and social demands and its support for the war meant that many non-Russians were willing to believe the Bolshevik slogans – land, peace and the peoples' right to self-determination. And for a time, at least, these suggested that it was possible to enter into alliances with them.

For this reason most of the national parties of the non-Russian periphery initially adopted a wait-and-see attitude after the Bolsheviks had seized power in Petrograd and the large Russian cities at the end of October and at the beginning of November 1917. The decrees concerning land and peace, and the declaration of the rights of the peoples of Russia issued on 2 November, in which the formula of the right to self-determination and even secession was restated, once again raised their hopes. However, it proved impossible to cooperate with the party of Lenin, which strove for centralization and unrivalled power, and subordinated national self-determination to the principle of class struggle. A clear sign of this was the dissolution of the Constituent Assembly on 5–6 January 1918. The victory of the Bolsheviks was now construed by many non-Russians as a triumph of towns over villages, of workers over peasants, of Russians over non-Russians.[62] For this reason the centrifugal movements gained momentum from the end of 1917 onwards, and by February 1918 Finland, Estonia, Lithuania, Ukraine and the Moldavian Republic (Bessarabia) had declared themselves independent. Belorussia followed – with no more than temporary success – in March, and the Transcaucasian Federation (without Baku, where the Bolsheviks were now in the majority) in April. In Turkestan a provisional Moslem government, in Kazakhstan the Alash Orda, in Bashkiria a central council, and in the northern Caucasus the coalition between the mountain peoples and the Cossacks proclaimed their territorial autonomy at the end of 1917.

In addition to the policies pursued by the Bolsheviks, the war made a significant contribution to the disintegration of Russia, since Germany and the Ottoman Empire took advantage of Russia's weakness to launch a new offensive. Among other things, it led to the occupation of Ukraine and the rest of the Baltic provinces. On 3 March 1918 this forced the Soviet leadership to conclude the Treaty of Brest-Litovsk with the Central Powers. As a result the Russian state lost a third of its population and a significant proportion of its sources of raw materials and industrial potential.

Thus it was a combination of internal and external factors which led to the rapid disintegration of the empire. By the summer of 1918 the following areas had seceded from Russia: Poland, Lithuania and Ukraine as new nation states under the protection of Germany; Estonia, Latvia and the larger part of Belorussia, which were also occupied by Germany; Finland (under German protection); Bessarabia (now within a Romanian framework); and Georgia, Armenia and Azerbaidzhan (after the dissolution of the Transcaucasian Federation). The situation was confused in the northern Caucasus, in Middle Asia, and in Siberia. In these areas national autonomy movements, Bolsheviks and Russian counter-revolutionary forces continued to confront each other.

Six months after the October Revolution Bolshevik Russia had lost almost all of the peripheral areas of the Russian Empire in the west and in the south. However, most of the secessionist movements had been considerably strengthened by the war. Thus, after the end of the First World War, the Bolsheviks attempted to recover control of the lost peripheral areas by means of uprisings and with armed force. Nonetheless their situation continued to deteriorate until the late summer of 1919. National governments, the counter-revolutionary 'Whites' and foreign interventionist powers, which, in addition to the Allies, included

Poland and Romania, now had even more areas of the old Russian Empire under their control. For its part, Soviet Russia had lost almost all of the territories which had been acquired since the seventeenth century: Siberia, the Baltic provinces, Ukraine, large parts of Belorussia, Lithuania, Poland, Finland, Bessarabia, almost the whole of the steppe, the Caucasus region and Middle Asia. It now seemed as if the end of the Russian multi-ethnic empire had finally come.

Notes

1. See the problem-oriented accounts by Geyer (1985); Hildermeier (1989); and Bernd Bonwetsch, *Die Russische Revolution 1917. Eine Sozialgeschichte von der Bauernbefreiung bis zum Oktoberumsturz* (Darmstadt, 1991).

2. The first edition of Pipes (1964) was published in 1954. It concentrates on the years between 1917 and 1922, and continues to be the only comprehensive account of this period.

3. On the revolution of 1905 see Ascher (1988); Shanin (1986); *Die Revolution* (1980); *Handbuch* III (1982), pp. 338–78.

4. Iu. I. Kir'ianov, 'Ulichnye demonstratsii rabochikh v Rossii v 1895–1900 gg.', *Rabochii klass Urala v period kapitalizma (1861–1917). Sbornik nauchnykh trudov* (Sverdlovsk, 1988), pp. 45–62.

5. With regard to the events in the different regions the reader is referred to the accounts of the history of the ethnic groups and regions of Russia cited in the preceding chapters. See also Kasteliansky (1910); *Revolutsiia 1905–1907 gg. v natsional'nykh raionakh Rossii. Sbornik statei* (Moscow, 1955); I. D. Kuznetsov (ed.), *Natsional'nye dvizheniia v period pervoi revoliutsii v Rossii. Sbornik dokumentov iz arkhiva byv. Departamenta Politsii* (Cheboksary, 1935).

6. See the summaries in Ascher (1988), pp. 152–62, and Seton-Watson (1967), pp. 607–12.

7. Kalabiński-Tych (1969); Anna Żarnowska and Janusz Żarnowski, 'La classe ouvrière du Royaume de Pologne dans la révolution de 1905–1907', in Coquin (1986), pp. 229–40; M. K. Dziewanowski 'The Polish Revolutionary Movement and Russia, 1904–1907', *Russian Thought and Politics. Harvard Slavic Studies* 4 ('s-Gravenhage, 1957), pp. 375–94.

8. Anahide Ter Minassian, 'Particularités de la révolution de 1905 en Transcaucasie', in Coquin (1986), pp. 315–37; Jones (1989); Leon Der Megrian, 'Tiflis during the Russian Revolution of 1905', Ph.D. thesis, University of California, Berkeley, 1968; E. L. Keenan, 'Remarques sur l'histoire du mouvement révolutionnaire à Bakou (1904–1905)', in *Sur 1905* (Paris, 1974), pp. 49–97; Jacques Baynac, 'Aspects caucasiens', idem, pp. 99–153. On the peasants' movement in Guria see also the memoirs of Grigorii Uratadze, *Vospominaniia gruzinskogo sotsial-demokrata* (Stanford, 1968).

9. See the contemporary account by Luigi Villari, *Fire and Sword in the Caucasus* (London, 1906).

10. Raun (1984); Trapans (1979), pp. 876–1153; *Die Lettische Revolution*, vol. II (Berlin, 1907) (tends to be pro-German and anti-Latvian).

11. Frankel (1981), pp. 134–49.

12. Robert Edelman, *Proletarian Peasants. The Revolution of 1905 in Russia's Southwest* (Ithaca and London, 1987).

13. A. S. Amal'rik, 'K vosprosu o chislennosti i geograficheskom razmeshchenii stachechnikov v Evropeiskoi Rossii v 1905 godu', *IZ* 52 (1955), 142–85.

14. Hoetzsch (1917), p. 337.

15. See Kalabiński-Tych (1969), p. 413; Jones (1989), p. 430.

16. German translation in *Die Orthodoxe Kirche* (1988), pp. 588–92.

17. Céline Gervais-Francelle, 'La grève scolaire dans le royaume de Pologne', in Coquin (1986), pp. 261–98.

18. Cited in S. Dubnov, 'Evrei', in Kasteliansky (1910), p. 406.

19. *Die Judenpogrome in Rußland*, vols I–II (Cologne, 1910). See the different interpretations in Rogger (1986); Löwe (1978); Baron (1964); and Asher (1988), pp. 129–31 and 253–62.

20. See Frankel (1981).

21. See Löwe (1990); Hans Rogger, 'Was There a Russian Fascism? The Union of Russian People', in Rogger (1986), pp. 212–32; Ferenczi (1984).

22. On the following see Mende (1936); Zenkovsky (1960); Arsharuni and Gabidullin (1931); Rorlich (1986); Swietochowski (1985); Scheibert (1972), pp. 91 f.

23. Bennigsen and Lemercier-Quelquejay (1964).

24. Boshyk (1981); Kappeler (1992b).

25. *Istoriia chuvash.* I (1966), pp. 189, 194 f., 201, 227–9.

26. Bennigsen and Lemercier-Quelquejay (1964), pp. 136 f.

27. On the following see L. Shternberg, 'Inorodtsy', in Kasteliansky (1910), pp. 534–63; *Istoriia Sib.* III (1969), pp. 291–8.

28. N.P. Egunov, *Pervaia russkaia revoliutsiia i vtoroi etap natsional'nogo dvizheniia v Buriatii* (Ulan Ude, 1970).

29. In general see *Handbuch* III, pp. 378–437; Seton-Watson (1967), pp. 621–76; F. Dan, 'Obshchaia politika pravitel'stva i izmeneniia v gosudarstvennoi organizatsii v period 1905–1907 gg', *Obshchestvennoe dvizh.*, 4 (1912), ch. 1, pp. 365–92; ch. 2, pp. 1–148; S.M. Sidel'nikov, *Obrazovanie i deiatel'nost pervoi Gosudarstvennoi dumy* (Moscow, 1962); Alfred Levin, *The Second Duma. A Study of the Social-Democratic Party and the Russian Constitutional Experiment*, 2nd edn (Hamden, Ct, 1966). The most important documents are given in Kalinychev (1957).

30. M. Boyovich, *Chleny Gosudarstvennoi Dumy (Portrety i biografii). Pervyi sozyv 1906–1911 g.* (Moscow, 1906); *Chleny 2-oi Gosudarsvennoi Dumy* (St Petersburg, 1907). The figures given by Hoetzsch (1917, pp. 112 f.), which scholars have occasionally accepted at face value, are incomplete and do not take into account the deputies from the periphery who arrived later. With regard to the representation of the non-Russians in the Duma see the general works cited above and in

previous chapters. See also the following special studies: Oleh W. Gerus, 'The Ukrainian Question in the Russian Duma, 1906–1917: An Overview, *Studia Ucrainica* 2 (Ottawa, 1984), pp. 157–73; *Zygmunt Lukawski, Koło polskie w Rosyjskiej Dumie Panstwowej w latach 1906–1909* (Wrocław, 1967); Edward Chmielewski, *The Polish Question in the Russian State Duma* (Knoxville, 1970).

31. Kalinychev (1957), p. 273, German in Hoetzsch (1917), p. 120.

32. Hoetzsch (1917), pp. 120–3, and 130 f.; Tiander (1934), pp. 40–9; Manfred Hagen, *Die Entfaltung politischer Öffentlichkeit in Rußland 1906–1914* (Wiesbaden, 1982), p. 84, see also pp. 307–18; Coonrod (1954), pp. 29 f.

33. On this subect see Löwe (1990); Ferenczi (1984); Avrekh (1968); Geoffrey A. Hosking, *The Russian Constitutional Experiment. Government and Duma, 1907–1914* (Cambridge, 1973). See two 1906 party manifestos in Scheibert (1972), pp. 81–8.

34. Budilovich (1907).

35. Cited after Hoetzsch (1917), p. 132.

36. Kalinychev (1957), p. 141.

37. On the policy on nationalities pursued after 1906 in general see Hoetzsch (1917); Avrekh (1968), and the individual studies on the various regions cited above.

38. See Avrekh (1968), pp. 44–91; Manfred Hagen, '*Edinenie* und *obnovlenie*: Traditionale und modernistische Züge in Stolypins Staatsnationalismus gegenüber Finland', *JBS* 15 (1984), 148–70.

39. Hans Rogger, 'The Beilis Case: Anti–Semitism and Politics in the Reign of Nicholas II', in Rogger (1986), pp. 40–55.

40. In general see Thaden (1981); Hagen, '*Edinenie* und *obnovlenie*', in note 38.

41. In general see *Handbuch* III, pp. 489–538.

42. On the following, in addition to the general works on the history of the various regions and peoples, see Coonrod (1954); von Rauch (1953), pp. 176–89.

43. Fleischhauer (1986), pp. 440–523.

44. Löwe (1978), pp. 146–91.

45. Hovannisian (1967), pp. 30–68.

46. On the various activities of the nationalities in Russia during the First World War see Tiander (1934), pp. 52–69; *Kennen Sie Rußland? Verfaßt von zwölf russischen Untertanen* (Berlin, 1916); Seppo Zetterberg, 'Die Tätigkeit der Liga der Fremdvölker Rußlands in Stockholm während der Jahre 1916–1918', *Acta Baltica* 10 (1970), 211–57; Ferro (1961), pp. 132–8; Oleh Fedyshyn, 'The Germans and the Union for the Liberation of the Ukraine, 1914–1917' in Hunczak (1977), pp. 305–22.

47. On the 1916 uprising see Edward Dennis Sokol, *The Revolt of 1916 in Russian Central Asia* (Baltimore, 1954); *Vosstanie 1916 goda v Srednei Azii i Kazakhstane. Sbornik dokumentov* (Moscow, 1960); Kh. Tursunov, *Vosstanie 1916 goda v Srednei Azii i Kazakhstane* (Tashkent, 1962); Pierce (1960), pp. 271–96; Olcott (1987), pp. 118–27.

48. Leo Trotzki, *Geschichte der Russischen Revolution. Februarrevolution* (Berlin, 1931), p. 144. On the revolution of 1917 see also Geyer (1985); Hildermeier (1989); *Handbuch* III (1982–83), pp. 538–622.

49. Graeme J. Gill, *Peasants and Government in the Russian Revolution* (London, 1979), especially pp. 157–69; Sergei M. Dubrowski, *Die Bauernbewegung in der russischen Revolution* (Berlin, 1929), including p. 90.

50. Allan K. Wildman, *The End of the Russian Imperial Army*, vols I–II (Princeton, 1980, 1987); Uldis Germanis, *Oberst Vacietis und die lettischen Schützen im Weltkrieg und in der Oktoberrevolution* (Stockholm, 1974).

51. See Ronald R. Suny, 'Nationalism and Class as Factors in the Revolution of 1917', Center for Research on Social Organization Working Paper 365, Ann Arbor, 1988.

52. On the following see Ferro (1961). The most important documents on the national question in 1917 are reproduced in *The Russian Provisional Government. Documents.* Selected and edited by R. P. Browder and A. F. Kerensky, vol. I (Stanford, 1961), pp. 317–472.

53. On the various regions see the general accounts cited in earlier chapters, and in general Pipes (1964). In the following I cite only specialist literature on the revolutionary period.

54. On the following see Hunczak (1977); John Reshetar, *The Ukrainian Revolution 1917–1920: A Study in Nationalism* (Princeton, 1952); Dietrich Geyer, 'Die Ukraine im Jahre 1917. Russische Revolution und nationale Bewegung', *Geschichte in Wissenschaft und Unterricht* 8 (1957), 670–87; Steven L. Guthier, 'The Popular Base of Ukrainian Nationalism in 1917', *SR* 38 (1979), 30–47.

55. In English in Hunczak (1977), pp. 382–5, in German in Manfred Hellmann (ed.), *Die russische Revolution 1917* (Munich, 1964), pp. 237–40.

56. *Von den baltischen Provinzen zu den baltischen Staaten. Beiträge zur Entstehungsgeschichte der Republiken Estland und Lettland 1917–1918* (Marburg, Lahn, 1971); Andrew Ezergailis, *The 1917 Revolution in Latvia* (Boulder, 1974); Andrew Ezergailis, *The Latvian Impact on the Bolshevik Revolution. The First Phase: September 1917 to April 1918* (Boulder, 1983).

57. Anthony F. Upton, *The Finnish Revolution 1917–1918* (Minneapolis, 1980); Alapuro (1988).

58. Zvi Y. Gitelman, *Jewish Nationality and Soviet Politics. The Jewish Sections of the CPSU, 1917–1930* (Princeton, 1972), pp. 69–101.

59. Firuz Kazemzadeh, *The Struggle for Transcaucasia (1917–1921)* (New York and Oxford, 1951); Hovannisian (1967); Swietochowski (1985); Ronald Grigor Suny, *The Baku Commune 1917–1918. Class and Nationality in the Russian Revolution* (Princeton, 1972); Suny, 'Nationality and Social Class in the Russian Revolution. The Cases of Baku and Tiflis' in Suny (1983), pp. 239–58.

60. See Mende (1936), pp. 120–49; Bennigsen and Lemercier-Quelquejay (1960), pp. 63–92; Zenkovsky (1960), pp. 139–78; Hayit (1971), pp. 206–52.

61. Oliver H. Radkey, *Russia goes to the Polls. The Election to the All-Russian Constituent Assembly, 1917* (Ithaca and London, 1990). This is also of relevance to what follows. See also the tables, pp. 148–60.

62. The phrase is taken from Pipes (1964), p. 53.

10

Aftermath: Change and Continuity in the Soviet Multi-ethnic Empire

THE RUSSIAN Empire fell apart as a result of the upheavals of the First World War and the Revolution, being reduced to all intents and purposes to the Great Russian core area.[1] The parallels to the collapse of the Soviet multi-ethnic empire at the beginning of the 1990s are obvious, even if the external factor of war was missing. Apart from Poland and Finland, the territories which seceded from Russia in 1918–19 – the three Baltic states, Ukraine, Bessarabia and Transcaucasia – were again among the leading secessionist forces seven decades later, whereas the autonomy movements in Belorussia, Middle Asia, the northern Caucasus, the Volga-Urals area and Siberia again pursued less radical goals, at least initially. Thus the course of history resumed where it had left off in 1918–19, bringing about the end of the Russian Empire that had been deferred for more than seven decades.

1. The Reorganization of the Multi-ethnic Empire

The year 1919 did not signal the end of the Russian multi-ethnic empire, though the new Soviet state, after the failure of abortive Bolshevik coups, had to relinquish important territories in the west. For this reason the empire's centre of gravity shifted even further in the direction of Asia. However, only Poland and Finland were lost in the long term, whereas the Baltic states, western Belorussia and Bessarabia were reincorporated during the Second World War. The other secessionist territories on the periphery that had been part of the tsarist empire were retaken by the Bolsheviks between 1919 and 1921, and in the east the territory of the empire was enlarged in 1924 to include the protectorates of Bukhara and Khiva.[2]

There are many reasons why the new Soviet state managed to defeat a seemingly superior coalition of enemies and was able once again

370

to consolidate the multinational empire. They included the disunity and the primarily Russian national and socially reactionary programmes of the 'Whites' and of the foreign interventionist powers, who had little to offer when compared to the Bolsheviks, who held out the promise of social justice, and also displayed increasing flexibility in the face of national demands; the attendant support for the Bolsheviks that was forthcoming from the majority of the largely Russian industrial proletariat, and the fact that they were tolerated as the lesser evil by large sections of the peasantry; the organization of the Communist Party and the effectiveness of the Red Army, whose power was used in a relentless manner; and the backward character of the national movements in Ukraine, in Belorussia and in the east, which received only qualified support from the masses.

The gathering of the lands of the tsarist empire by the Bolsheviks was carried out with the well-tried methods of the carrot and the stick and *divide et impera* (that is, by exploiting social and ethnic antagonisms). That their actions were primarily determined by power politics and global revolutionary expansionism, and not by the slogans of the social liberation of the proletariat and the peoples' right to self-determination was demonstrated in a particularly striking manner by the brutal conquest of the democratically legitimated and internationally recognized (also by Soviet Russia) Menshevik Republic of Georgia in 1921. It made little difference that in the following year Lenin criticized what the Bolsheviks, and especially Stalin, had done in Georgia, warning of the 'Great Russians, chauvinists, and in fact scoundrels and violent criminals, which is what the typical Russian bureaucrat is', who, 'having been taken over from the tsarist state, had merely been anointed with a little Soviet oil'.[3]

At the beginning of the 1920s the new Soviet state had consolidated itself as a multi-ethnic empire with a reduced western section, and the question now arose of the principles on which it should be organized. In Marxist thinking the national issue always played a subordinate role. It was linked to the bourgeois and capitalist world, and thus, once this had been superseded by socialism, the social reasons for national antagonisms would be removed and the way would be open for a supranational global society.[4] Although Lenin, unlike Marx and Engels, had recognized the revolutionary potential of the oppressed national ethnic groups at an early stage, and had included in the Bolshevik party manifesto the right to self-determination of the peoples, even the right to secede and form an independent state, he also adhered to the primacy of class struggle and the belief that in a socialist Russia the national problems would disappear automatically. Thus the Bolsheviks sought to replace the pre-national legitimated order of the tsarist empire with a post-national, proletarian and internationalist one, and to omit the intermediate stage of the nation state.

However, faced with the practical task of organizing the multi-ethnic state, they soon departed from their ideological premises. As early as 1918 Lenin returned to the principle of federalism, which had hitherto been propagated by his arch enemies, the Social Revolutionaries, and Russia was proclaimed to be a Socialist Federal Soviet Republic (RSFSR). The peripheral regions initially continued to be formally independent republics that were linked to Russia by military alliances and economic agreements. Not until 30 December 1922 were the areas controlled by the Bolsheviks united to form a federal state, the Union of Socialist Soviet Republics, which initially consisted of four republics, the RSFSR (with eight autonomous republics and 13 autonomous regions), and the Ukrainian, Belorussian and Federative Transcaucasian Republics. The borders in Middle Asia were redrawn two years later. The legally independent people's republics of Bukhara and Choresm, which had succeeded the Emirate of Bukhara and the Khanate of Khiva in 1920, and the Autonomous Republic of Turkestan, which had been proclaimed as early as 1918, were abolished and replaced by new national units, of which only Uzbekistan and Turkmenistan initially received the status of Soviet republics. The Transcaucasian Republic was dissolved in 1936, and the Stalinist constitution finally confirmed the division into 11 Soviet republics (Russia, Ukraine, Belorussia, Georgia, Armenia, Azerbaidzhan, Uzbekistan, Turkmenistan, Tadzhikistan, Kazakhstan, Kirgizia). Thereafter changes on the level of the Soviet republics were merely the result of the annexation of new territories.

The order of the new federal state was based on territories defined by language and nationality. This not only went against the tenets of communist ideology, which were non-nationalist, it also ignored the demographic realities of the Russian empire and its ethnic composition, for which the principle of personal cultural autonomy that was developed by the Austro-Marxists and later adopted by the Jewish Bund would have been much more appropriate. In Middle Asia the purpose of linguistic and national demarcation was also to destroy the ancient religious and cultural unity of Turkestan. However, it proved impossible to assign the ethnically mixed and frequently multilingual population to territories that were supposedly homogeneous with regard to language and ethnic composition.

2. The 'Golden' Twenties

In the early years of the Soviet Union it at first proved possible to deal with these problems. On the one hand, the centralist party organization and army had a unifying effect, and, on the other, the ethnic minorities in the republics were granted wide-ranging cultural rights on a regional and local level. The New Economic Policy introduced in 1921, which tried to appease the peasants and to reach a compromise with bourgeois and capitalist elements of society, was accompanied by a flexible policy on nationalities which was designed to induce the non-Russians to support the Soviet state. During the second stage of the civil war Lenin had already begun to move from unyielding dogmatism to a kind of flexible pragmatism that in some respects took its bearings from the pre-modern Russian policy on nationalities. As in the past, the retention of power and socio-political stability defined the boundaries within which the various ethnic groups were granted a fairly large degree of freedom.

Early Soviet policy on nationalities, for which Stalin, a Georgian, was responsible as people's commissar, replaced the principle of self-determination with that of the equality of the peoples within the federal union. In contrast to the late tsarist state, which discriminated against numerous non-Russian ethnic groups, the peoples were all now to enjoy equal political and cultural rights. Furthermore, the aim was also to achieve equality on a socio-economic and socio-cultural level in order to overcome the backwardness of the less developed ethnic groups. In this way, so the Communists thought, the national antagonisms that still existed would disappear, and the national question would be solved. To this end, as the Party and even Stalin himself emphasized, the remnants of Russian imperial chauvinism in the Soviet bureaucracy would have to be combated rather energetically.

As had already been the case under the tsars, the central government sought to cooperate with the loyal non-Russian elites, which were co-opted into the new Communist leadership. And it became necessary to make up for the enormous losses that the educated elite had sustained as a result of war, revolution, emigration and the civil war. As the number of available Russian cadres was insufficient, the government, as in the tsarist era, had recourse to mobilized diaspora groups. Since the educated elites of the Baltic Germans, the German urban population, and the Poles were no longer available, it was now primarily the turn of the Jews. Because restrictions on Jews had been lifted, they streamed into Russian cities in large numbers and attended the local educational institutions. After decades of discrimination and persecution, many of them looked forward to a new and better life and thus were loyal to the new Soviet regime. Secondly, some use was also made of Armenians and Georgians, who, like the Jews, had been active in the socialist movement, and possessed a fairly high standard of education. Jews, Armenians and Georgians (who, admittedly, had often been russified) were very much over-represented in the 1920s and 1930s in party and state organizations, especially in their upper echelons, and among the new intelligentsia in science, scholarship and culture.

On the other hand, the late tsarist practice of assigning the administration of the peripheral areas to Russians was abandoned, and the government returned to the traditional method of consigning it to loyal non-Russian elites. It was here that the policy of what was known as 'indigenization' (korenizatsiia) came into play: the systematic increase in the number of local inhabitants in a republic's party and government organizations. Although the low level of education and the dearth of pro-Soviet industrial workers impeded the process of 'indigenization', the percentage of Russians in the membership of the Communist Party decreased between 1922 and 1927 from 72 per cent to 65 per cent (they constituted 53 per cent of the population), whereas that of the Ukrainians and Belorussians in the party organizations of their republics between 1922 and 1932 rose from 24 per cent and 21 per cent to 59 per cent and 60 per cent. Even the nations of Middle Asia contributed more than half of the party members in their republics in 1932. In 1929 the nation which gave its name to the republic in Ukraine already provided 59 per cent of the bureaucrats; in Belorussia it was 66 per cent, and in Armenia it was as much as 95 per cent. However, in Middle Asia, where there was still a dearth of educated cadres, and Europeans continued to predominate in the state adminstration.

In the 1920s the policy on nationalities also returned to the prenational tradition of tolerance towards non-Russian languages and cultures. Indeed, by deliberately encouraging the development of smaller languages it went even further. For 48 ethnic groups a new written language was devised for the very first time, for example, for the Turkmen, Bashkirs, Chechens and for the smaller ethnic groups in Siberia. Non-Russian languages began increasingly to be used in the administration and the courts (especially at the lower levels of government), and in educational institutions. Yet some things continued to be purely theoretical, for at least at the higher levels it was impossible to do without Russian as a lingua franca. Towards the end of the 1920s the spirit of internationalism and modernization led to the introduction of Latin characters for 70 languages, especially those of the Muslim, lamaist and certain Christianized animist ethnic groups. Although attempts were made to introduce Latin characters in the case of the eastern Slavs, Armenians, Georgians and Jews, they retained their own characters. The preference for Latin as opposed to Cyrillic characters marked a break with the late tsarist period, which had encouraged Russian one-sidedly; secondly, it was in keeping with contemporary expectations concerning the world revolution; and, thirdly, by abolishing Arabic and Mongol characters, Muslims and Buddhists were cut off from their cultural heritage and religion.

Schools using native languages were established everywhere in order to combat illiteracy. In spite of immense difficulties the programme was implemented successfully: as early as 1927 90 per cent of Belorussian, 94 per cent of Kirgiz and almost 96 per cent of Tatar schoolchildren went to native language elementary schools in their respective republics. Schools were also set up for ethnic groups which did not have a republic of their own. Thus half of the Jews in Ukraine went to schools at which Yiddish was the principal language. In 1935 no less than 80 languages were used in the primary schools of the RSFSR. In the Uzbek Republic the total was 22, and in Dagestan 12. Yet the quality of the teaching left much to be desired, and the level of literacy increased very slowly. A breakthrough was first achieved in the 1930s. Local languages also began to be used in intermediate schools and higher education, and this increased the size of non-Russian elites. At the same time there was support for publications in the national languages. In 1933 37 per cent of the total number of newspapers were published in a non-Russian language, and in 1938 newspapers appeared in 66 languages. There was a flowering of literature, art and scholarship within the individual republics and national entities. Non-Communists also played a role in this process. For example, M. Hrushevsky, the former leader of the Ukrainian Rada, became the first chairman of the department of history of the Ukrainian Academy of Sciences.

The Soviet government did not consider this liberal policy on language and culture to be an end in itself. On the one hand, it was designed to ensure the stability of the multi-ethnic empire, and, on the other, it was supposed to eliminate discrimination against non-Russians and thus to defuse national tensions. Third, such liberal policies served as a positive advertisment for those foreign countries to which the revolution was later to be exported. This was also the function of the policies pursued with regard to the Muslims of Middle Asia, which were portrayed as being a model for the whole of Asia. Fourth, native language schools and publications were designed to spread Communist ideology among non-Russians; this was summed up by the slogan 'national in form, socialist in content'. Yet as early as the second half of the 1920s the liberal policy on nationalities came up against ideological barriers. This showed itself clearly in policy on religion, which began to become inflexible at an early stage. The campaigns against Islam were particularly dramatic, and were based on the Marxist belief in progress. Thus the jurisdiction of Islamic law was curtailed, Islamic schools and the property of the clergy were abolished, and a campaign against the wearing of veils sought – unsuccessfully, as it turned out – to mobilize Muslim women, a substitute for the non-existent proletariat, against their menfolk.

The policy of indigenization and the liberal policy on language, which lasted until the mid 1930s, had profound consequences. They certainly fulfilled their purpose, which was to win over large groups of non-Russians to the revolution and the party after the event, or at least to neutralize them. More important still was the fact that they speeded up the nation building of the large ethnic groups and first set in motion that of the smaller groups. Thus the Ukrainians consolidated themselves as a nation in the 1920s. The Ukrainian language began to be used almost everywhere in schools and in the administration, and for the first time there arose a broadly based Ukrainian-speaking elite, urban population and industrial workforce. In the case of the Belorussians this process happened rather more slowly, and met with resistance. In the case of the smaller ethnic groups it had only just begun.

Both this kind of consolidation of nations and the spread of national ideologies ran counter to the expectations of the central authorities, who had hoped that such measures would lead to a decrease in national sentiment and enhance the unity of the Soviet Union. It became increasingly apparent that in the medium term the new national elites would not be satisfied with formal equality and cultural and linguistic rights, and indeed that they would also formulate political demands. National Communists called for an increase in the responsibilities allotted to their republics, and strove for greater political participation. As early as 1923 the Volga Tatar Sultan-Galiev, who had declared the anti-colonial liberation struggle of the Muslims to be his most important task, was the first high-ranking Communist official to be expelled from the party. He was arrested in 1928, sentenced in 1929, and then sent to the labour camp of Solovki. Purges among the Muslim and Ukrainian Communists and intellectuals followed. They were harbingers of the Stalinist terror.

3. Gleichschaltung, Terror and the Partial Return to Pre-revolutionary Traditions under Stalin

The change from a pragmatic and flexible to a repressive policy on nationalities, which took place at the end of the 1920s, cannot simply be interpreted as a change of course of the kind that occurred at regular intervals in the tsarist empire. True, modernization, systematization and greater homogeneity were aims which coincided with those of the late tsarist policy on nationalities; however, Stalin's revolution from above implied a fundamental transformation of societies of a kind that traditionalist Russia had never sought to implement, and for which it had not possessed the means. Now the aim was to destroy the traditional social order and at the same time to eliminate potential resistance. The non-Russians, whose nation building had been arousing the suspicions of the central authorities for a long time, and most of whose societies were still more rooted in pre-modern traditions than that of Russia, suffered particularly under the Stalinist terror.

The New Economic Policy achieved the reconstruction of the economy in a remarkably short space of time. However, the levels reached by the various regions and ethnic groups of the Soviet Union continued to differ. The process of forced industrialization which Stalin introduced with the first Five-Year Plan (1929–33) did not alter the fact that heavy industry increased primarily in the old centres and in new ones in the Urals, in western Siberia and northern Kazakhstan, in other words, in regions inhabited mainly by Russians. More than a fair share of the necessary cadres and skilled workers were of Russian origin, and the Russian part of the urban population of all the eastern regions increased rapidly.

The forced collectivization of the agricultural sector had more serious consequences in the case of the majority of non-Russians, and led to a larger number of casualties than among the Russians themselves. In southern Middle Asia Moscow established cotton plantations and a single-crop economy against the will of the local population. For example, collectivization forced the nomads to become sedentary and destroyed their traditional clan structures. Yet the inhabitants of Middle Asia resisted these massive intrusions of the state into their lives. This was especially true of the nomads, who fled in droves to China or slaughtered their animals, which in turn led to a famine. The population losses as a result of emigration and hunger were highest in the case of the Kazakhs, where they amounted to a third of the population. In Ukraine and in the ethnically mixed areas to the north of the Caucasus and on the lower Volga, forced collectivization and the requisitioning of grain led to a famine between 1932 and 1934 as a result of which 3–7 million people died, many of them Ukrainians. This was preceded throughout the whole country by the brutal 'liquidation of the kulaks as a class', the expropriation and deportation of the wealthier peasants who had resisted collectivization.

At the same time the purges of the Ukrainian elite, who were suspected of harbouring National Communist sympathies, began. Thereafter, in the much more comprehensive wave of terror between 1936 and 1938, the whole leadership, not only in Ukraine, but in all non-Russian republics, was removed and executed. Thus all the members of the Ukrainian politburo disappeared, and of 102 members and candidates of the Ukrainian central committee, only three survived. However, not only the political elites of the non-Russian peoples were decimated; so were the intellectual elites. A large number of Russian Communists and intellectuals also perished in the purges, though the proportion of survivors was greater in the case of the Russians than in that of the non-Russians, who were additionally persecuted as potential nationalists and separatists.

At the end of the 1930s the republics were placed under the full control of the central government, and Soviet federalism, which had already been restricted by the centralized organization of the party, became a total sham. The top positions that had become vacant were now mainly filled with loyal Russians such as Nikita Khrushchev in Ukraine. The policy of 'indigenization', and cooperation with non-Russian elites was discontinued, and the share of native inhabitants in the party and Soviet organizations of the republics once again declined. In any case, the new economic bureaucracy was largely made up of Russian cadres.

Liberal cultural policies were terminated, the educational system was unified, socialist realism also appeared in Georgia and Uzbekistan, and the 'friendship of the peoples of the Soviet Union', and in particular 'the friendship for the great Russian people' were gradually raised to the status of an axiom. The main danger was now perceived to be 'local nationalism', and not 'Great Russian chauvinism'. In accordance with Stalin's slogan of 'socialism in one country', a new ideology of integration was now created in the shape of Soviet patriotism, and this increasingly had recourse to pre-revolutionary roots. Appealing to the international solidarity of the proletariat was replaced by love of one's native land and the cult of Stalin. The ideologies of nationalism and belief in the tsar, which had been declared obsolete, now came back to haunt the Bolsheviks. Soviet patriotism was increasingly enriched with elements of Russian nationalism. From the end of the 1930s onwards the Russian language was deliberately encouraged and introduced as a compulsory subject in schools throughout the Soviet Union. At the same time the use of the Latin alphabet, which had been introduced a few years earlier for a large number of number of languages, was abolished. It was replaced by Cyrillic. However, the clear predominance of Russian national ideas first occurred during and after the Second World War, and in the Zhdanov era, as had been the case before 1917, it was accompanied by anti-Semitism.

Such Soviet patriotism and Russian nationalism prescribed from above had a base in Russian society, which, as a result of industrialization and the expansion of the education system, witnessed massive social mobilization. Largely of rural origin, the newly emerging group of Russian industrial workers and cadres who were favoured by the regime, and can be regarded as the most important social basis of Stalinism, became the representatives of a new Russian national movement which the state sought to bring under its control. As had been the case before the revolution, it was also directed against the mobilized diaspora groups, and especially against the Jews, who were disproportionately represented in leading positions. Thereafter their importance decreased rapidly, and after the Second World War the government used them as scapegoats.

The non-Russian peoples participated less than the Russians in the increasingly swift modernization of the Soviet Union. However, in their case the size of the urban population, the number of industrial workers and the level of literacy also increased. The economy and administration were centralized, the control exercised by the party and the secret police grew unceasingly, the national cultures were forced to toe the line, and free speech was crushed by terror. Practically the whole of the new political and intellectual elite of the non-Russian nations was eradicated by means of forcible collectivization and purges. Since the vast majority of the non-Russian nations possessed only a relatively small number of educated people, they were once again largely without a native elite by the end of the 1930s, and as a result at the mercy of the Russian cadres. Thus Stalin's policy of force partly reversed the process which led to nation building in the 1920s.

The deportations during the Second World War constituted a new climax in the repressive policy on nationalities. Numerous non-Russians and Russians who had suffered under the Stalinist dictatorship (and hoped that their new masters would ameliorate their position) co-operated with the Germans until the majority had their eyes opened by the brutal occupation policies pursued by the National Socialist master race. The Soviet state responded to the collaboration of certain groups with the collective and exemplary punishment of whole ethnic groups. As a preventive measure the Koreans were deported before the war began (from the border in the Far East to Middle Asia), and in 1941 it was the turn of the Germans in the Soviet Union (who were sent to Asia). In 1943–44 they were followed by the Kalmyks, the northern Caucasian ethnic groups of the Balkars, the Ingush, Karachaians and the Chechens, the Crimean Tatars and the Turkic-speaking population of southern Georgia, the Meshketians. All in all about two million people were transported in cattle trucks to Asia, where they were settled as forced labour.[5] During the deportation and in the initial years in Asia about a third of them died. The autonomous republics and districts of these ethnic groups were dissolved, and their names expunged from statistics, reference books and historical works. That a state which derived its legitimacy from Marxism should collectively punish whole peoples with all their children, old people, party members and soldiers demonstrates the extent to which Stalinism had departed from its ideological premises and had turned to nationalistic thought patterns, quite apart from the fact that the charges levied against these people were largely unfounded. When selecting the ethnic groups concerned, Stalin had recourse to Russian national traditions. In the national view of history, all of them were seen to be traitors and sworn enemies of the Russians. Thus the Muslims of the northern Caucasus and the Crimean Tatars had already been forced to emigrate in large numbers in the nineteenth century, whereas the Germans had been moved from the border areas in the First World War.

Following in the footsteps of the tsarist empire, the Hitler–Stalin pact and the Soviet Union's victory in the Second World War enabled it to complete the gathering of the lands of Rus by recovering not only the areas of the tsarist empire inhabited by eastern Slavs, but also eastern Galicia, the northern part of the Bukovina and sub-Carpathian Ukraine, the majority of whose inhabitants were Ukrainians of the Uniate faith, although it had never formed part of the Russian Empire. In the case of Lithuania, Latvia, Estonia, Bessarabia and large parts of Karelia (the attempt to incorporate the rest of Finland was a failure) further territories of the tsarist empire were 'reunited' with the Soviet Union. To this were added the northern part of East Prussia, and Tannu-Tuva in the east. In this way the empire's centre of gravity shifted strongly towards Europe for the first time in a century. Between 1939 and 1941, and especially after they had been reconquered in 1944, the new territories were forced into the Soviet straitjacket. Large parts of the non-Russian elite in the annexed territories were deported, and their place was taken by Russian immigrants, especially cadres and industrial workers.

Thus for the non-Russians of the Soviet Union, the Stalinist period marked a greater break with the past than the revolution, for their traditional social orders and cultures were now destroyed. Stalinist policies departed from the old patterns of cooperation with non-Russian elites and cultural tolerance, taking their bearings more from the late tsarist era by emphasizing modernization, centralization and unification. They once again played the Russian national card, and were also influenced by national currents in Russian society. However, the dilemma remained. The multi-ethnic population of the empire could not be integrated with the help of Russian national ideology, and it could not be assimilated either. And terror could do no more than sweep it under the carpet. Whereas it is true that the nation building and the national movements of the non-Russians had once again received a setback, the Soviet empire was further away than ever from a permanent solution of the national question, which is what the party claimed to have achieved.

4. Destalinization and the Formation of New National Elites

After the death of Stalin the excesses of his nationalities policy were revoked, though his successors, in this as in other respects, did not totally reject Stalinism. At least in part they returned to the methods of the 1920s: 'indigenization', cooperation with non-Russian communists in the republics of the Union, partial decentralization and a tolerant policy on language and culture. To be sure, the concessions remained half-hearted, and later the policy on nationalities veered briefly from a more flexible to a more repressive line, and between concessions and oppression.

Around 1972, after a phase of greater flexibility, there was a more repressive policy which went hand in hand with a general hardening of internal policy, and this continued until the early 1980s. There were several purges in Ukraine, in Georgia and other republics. The political participation of non-Russians in the central government decreased. Russian tuition now received much greater support, and the Russian language was supposed to become the 'second mother tongue' of all of the peoples of the Soviet Union. As in the late tsarist period, official policy acquired Russian national and anti-Jewish traits, though it kept its distance from extremist nationalist and anti-Semitic currents in Russian society.

In the three decades after the death of Stalin societal, economic and cultural developments were of greater importance than policy on nationalities. Since the end of the tsarist era the Russians had had very high population growth rates, and had settled in non-Russian peripheral areas in increasing numbers. This tendency was now reversed in the east of the empire. Whereas in most European nations the natural increase in the population went into swift decline, it increased dramatically in the case of the Asiatic peoples, and especially in that of the Muslims. Their share of the total population rose to reach almost 20 per cent in 1989 (see Table 3). Russian migration continued until the 1960s, especially to Kazakhstan, where in 1979 the Kazakhs constituted no more than 36 per cent of the population. However, from the 1970s onwards the number of Russians and other immigrants in Middle Asia and Transcaucasia began to decrease. The influx of Russian industrial workers and cadres in the west continued unabated, and in a small country like Estonia the Russians already constituted 28 per cent of the population in 1979. In Latvia the figure was 33 per cent.

The industrial development of the Soviet Union and with it the process of urbanization continued to make progress in every region. However, the majority of non-Russians, especially the inhabitants of Middle Asia and the northern Caucasus, the Romanians, Georgians, Lithuanians, Belorussians and Ukrainians remained more closely tied to the land than the Russians. Numerous areas primarily inhabited by non-Russians, such as southern Middle Asia, Transcaucasia and Bessarabia, continued to be suppliers of agricultural products, whereas industry was concentrated in the Russian Republic and the western regions. Although the levels of economic development had evened out somewhat since the 1930s, the gap between these areas and the Asiatic republics once again began to widen in the 1960s. Thus the gradient from the north-west to the south-east, which had already existed prior to 1917, remained, from the Baltic provinces, which were quite clearly at the top of the list, via Russia, Belorussia and Ukraine to the regions in the south and the east. With its single-crop and cotton-based economy, Middle Asia, which was particularly backward, remained dependent on the centre in a wholly colonial manner. As had already been the case in the tsarist empire, the Baltic republics were assigned the function of being a 'window on Europe', for example as an experimental field for innovation. The centre deliberately emphasized the division of labour between the republics, and thus their mutual economic interaction and dependence.

It is a noteworthy fact that from the 1960s to the 1980s the Russian centre in the Soviet Union lagged behind the north-west of the country in economic terms. Thus a basic feature of the Russian multi-ethnic empire continued to remain in existence, albeit in a slightly less pronounced manner, that is, Russia, which dominated in military and political terms, ruled areas in the west where, with regard to sociopolitical organization, the economy and culture were more developed than in the capital. Thus, if one takes living standards as one's yardstick, they were still considerably lower in the case of the Russians, especially those in the provinces, than they were for the numerous non-Russians of the peripheral areas. As in the case of the tsarist government, the Soviet government in the post-Stalinist era was less concerned with the welfare of the mass of the Russians (who formed the basis of the state) than with the power and privileges of the ruling elites and the empire's great power status. As in the second half of the nineteenth century a part of the Russian population saw itself as an 'unprivileged majority' which had to shoulder the main burden of Soviet striving for world power, and it reacted with increasing aversion to the imagined or real privileges accorded to non-Russians.

Continuing economic development changed the social structure of the peoples of the Soviet Union. Above all it was the expansion of the educational system which led to the creation of sizeable and educated elites. The differences in the levels of education diminished, and Muslims and the traditional peasant nations began to catch up rather quickly. According to statistics published in 1980–81, at least ten nationalities had a higher percentage of students than the Russians, among them the Buriats, Iakuts, Kalmyks, Kabardinians and Kazakhs.[6] The social mobilization of non-Russians made the Russian cadres, who had been sent to the peripheral areas ever since the time of Stalin, more and more superfluous. In fact, they impeded the social mobility of non-Russians. It is true that many of these upwardly mobile people were acculturated in what was (with the exception of Estonia, Lithuania, Georgia and Armenia) a largely russified higher education system. However, hopes of rapid internationalization and the formation of 'a new historic community, the Soviet people' remained unfulfilled. The opposite was the case, for the nation-building processes impeded under Stalin took on a new lease of life. Yet there continued to be significant differences between the various nations. Whereas the Estonians, Latvians, Lithuanians, Georgians, Armenians and also the majority of the Muslim groups displayed a high degree of ethnic stability, Russification was more pronounced in the case of the Ukrainians, the Belorussians, the Tatars, the Jews and the Germans. In the case of certain smaller ethnic groups, such as the Mordvinians and the Karelians, the speed of assimilation led to a quantitative decline. However, most of the non-Russian intellectuals were very active, reviving national languages, literature and scholarship, the national cultural heritage and national consciousness, insofar as this was possible within the limits set by the official ideology, and above all by the axiom of 'the friendship of the peoples'. In the course of time the new national elites, who increasingly came up against the limits set by Moscow, and against Russian cadres who observed national ambitions with suspicion, became more and more frustrated.

However, non-Russians were now once again able to make better use of the USSR's federal structure. Since the 1960s they had been appropriately represented in the party and state leadership of their republics, and had also sent representatives to the centre of power. In certain republics, such as Kazakhstan, Azerbaidzhan, Georgia and Latvia, the titular nation was even over-represented in the leading positions. Yet in the central committees Russians continued to predominate, and all important decisions were taken in Moscow, as had always been the case. Protests against this kind of political paternalism by the Russian centre were repeatedly voiced by the regional party leaders. This inherent systemic opposition called for a greater say in local affairs, more autonomy and greater investment in one's own republic. It was opposed to the unchecked influx of Russians into the republics, and the russifying tendencies with regard to the question of language. There were examples of this in almost all of the republics. As far back as 1958 to 1961 the party leaders in Turkmenistan, Uzbekistan, Kirgizia, Tadzhikistan, Azerbaidzhan, Latvia and Moldavia had been accused of nationalistic tendencies and deposed. At the beginning of the 1970s they were followed by the Ukrainian party leader P. Shelest.

As in the nineteenth century the greater speed of modernization led to the social mobilization of new social groups, and these, from the 1960s onwards, began to be those who supported the national movements. As in the past they were spearheaded by parts of the intellectual elite. These illegal movements reached different levels of intensity in the various nations. In political terms the Crimean Tatars were mobilized earliest and most intensively. Since the 1960s they had sought to return to their homeland and had tried to achieve the reestablishment of their republic. For this purpose they organized numerous demonstrations. Petitions to the government in Moscow were signed by a large proportion of adult Crimean Tatars. Thus it comes as no surprise that in the 1970s they contributed more than their fair share of political prisoners in the USSR. Similar demands were made by the Germans, whose less radical movement turned out to be more successful on account of the support they received from the Federal Republic. Although the Volga republic was not reestablished, tens of thousands of Germans were able to leave and settle in the Federal Republic as early as the 1970s. Similar results were achieved by the Jewish movement, which had intensified since the Six-Day War of 1967. With American support it made possible the emigration of over 200,000 Jews by 1981.

The three movements mentioned above were special cases. Of the nations which had their own republic, only the Lithuanians had a mass movement in the 1960s and the 1970s. It was based, as in the nineteenth century, on the identity of national and religious demands, and had the support of the Catholic clergy. The *Chronicle of the Lithuanian Catholic Church* became one of the most important regular samizdat publications, and certain Lithuanian petitions had more than 100,000 signatures. In the case of the other nations smaller circles of intellectuals organized national activities. Of the Ukrainians, the western Ukrainians, who had first been 'reunited' in the Second World War, took the lead, and continued in secret to organize the Uniate church, which had been banned in 1946. In eastern Ukraine, however, protests against Russification predominated. As in tsarist times, the Soviet government reacted in a particularly repressive manner to the national ambitions of the Ukrainians, who, in view of their numbers and the economic and strategic significance of their republic, were of far greater importance than all the other non-Russians of the empire. Opposition groups in Georgia, Armenia, Estonia and Latvia concentrated primarily on cultural and linguistic problems. At the beginning of the 1980s there were open demonstrations in Estonia and Georgia against linguistic Russification, and these showed that here national resistance also had a mass following. Among the Muslim nations, however, national movements played a minor role, though their resistance manifested itself in adherence to Islamic lifestyles, and in part in the revival of Sufic brotherhoods. However, until the middle of the 1980s none of the national movements seemed capable of bringing down the system. Most observers at the time were of the opinion that the Soviet regime, despite increasing economic difficulties and political ossification, had the nationalities of the empire firmly under control.

5. Perestroika and the Collapse of the Soviet Union

As has almost always been the case in the history of Russia and the Soviet Union, the impulse for a revolutionary upheaval in the multi-ethnic empire did not come from the periphery: it came from the centre. In 1985 Mikhail Gorbachev, who had been elected to the post of General Secretary of the Communist Party, used the slogans perestroika (restructuring) and glasnost (transparency) to initiate a reform of the Soviet Union's economic and political system. Six years later it had become clear that he had not initiated a reform of the Soviet Union, but its demise. As had already been the case in 1917/18, the movements of the non-Russian nations made a significant contribution to the disintegration of the old order, and also to the formation of new structures.[7]

However, Gorbachev, whose thinking was rooted in Marxism, had for a long time underestimated the explosive nature of the national emancipation movements. This became clearly apparent towards the end of 1986, when, as part of the purge of the corrupt power elite in Middle Asia, the party leader in Kazakhstan, Kunaev, a Kazakh, was replaced by a Russian. As a result there were violent demonstrations by Kazakhs in Almaty. These were the first openly national disturbances. Thereafter the nationalities policy of the government in Moscow continued to lag behind the events as they unfolded, and it attempted unsuccessfully to regain control of the situation using the traditional methods of the carrot and the stick.

The year 1988 witnessed an explosion of national conflicts that for a long time had been smouldering beneath the surface. The Armenians, whose large demonstrations called for the annexation of the autonomous district of Nagorny Karabakh, which was part of the Republic of Azerbaidzhan, though inhabited largely by Armenians, triggered off a whole series of national mass movements. The Azerbaidzhanis reacted violently, and there was a repetition of the bitter civil wars of 1905 and 1917–18. There were deportations, economic blockades, pogroms against Armenians, a bloody use of military force in Baku and partisan warfare. The Georgians also reacted at an early stage, though it was only the brutal suppression by troops of a demonstration in Tiflis which, in April 1989, led to a swift radicalization of the national movement. This in turn soon came into conflict with the claims of the non-Georgian minorities of the republic, the Ossetians and Abkhaz.

In the course of 1988 the Estonians, Latvians and Lithuanians took over the leadership of the emancipation movements. Their popular fronts, which were characterized by democratic procedures, demanded economic, linguistic and cultural autonomy, and protested against further Russian immigration. The movements of the Baltic nations received a great impetus from the discussion of the illegal annexation of their states (in terms of international law) by the Soviet Union in 1940, which implied the restoration of independent states. Estonia was the first of the republics to declare itself to be a sovereign state in the autumn of 1988. The rapidly radicalized movement of the Romanians in the Moldavian Republic also based its claims on the annexation of 1940, and initially succeeded in reestablishing the use of the Romanian language (in Latin characters). It was opposed by the Ukrainian, Russian and Gagauz minorities.

In Ukraine the national movement needed slightly more time in order to mobilize the masses. Only the west Ukrainians, who had also only been part of the Soviet Union since 1939 or 1944, reacted swiftly, and openly demonstrated their allegiance to the Greek Catholic (Uniate) church, which was soon once again officially recognized. The Ukrainian movement, which was led by the democratic organization 'Rukh', devoted most of its energies to the question of language and attempted with mixed success to mobilize the population in the east and the south of the republic. That the Belorussian national movement had acquired a fairly large following by 1988 was a surprise. Here the discovery of mass graves of the victims of Stalin's secret police played a crucial role.

In Middle Asia the national and Islamic movements remained largely beneath the surface, and here initiatives which aimed at achieving national emancipation came from above. The extent of the ethno-social conflicts in Middle Asia, which was overpopulated, economically under-developed and an ecological disaster, was emphasized by a series of violent clashes. As early as 1989 there were pogroms in the Uzbek section of the Fergana valley directed against the Meskhetians, who had been deported to the area by Stalin. In the following year there were inter-ethnic conflicts in Tadzhikistan, and, again in the Fergana valley, particularly bloody clashes between Kirgiz and Uzbeks.

All the republics of the Union had declared themselves to be sovereign states by the end of 1990. As a rule this meant political and economic autonomy and the upgrading of their languages and culture. They were joined by a whole series of autonomous republics. Thus in the Russian Republic Chechens and Ingush, Volga Tatars, Bashkirs, Mordvinians, Udmurts (the former Votiaks), Komi (the former Zyrians), Kalmyks, Iakuts, Buriats and other small ethnic groups, such as the Chukchi and the Koriaks, made far-reaching demands for autonomy. There was renewed activity among the Germans and the Crimean Tatars, who demanded the restoration of their autonomous republics, and the Jews, who emigrated in large numbers. It is hardly possible to overestimate the significance of the fact that the Russian Republic also emancipated itself from central Soviet control and declared itself a sovereign state in June 1990. And it was of some importance that the democratic wing of the Russian national movement headed by Boris Yeltsin, and not the national bolshevik and reactionary anti-Semitic one, took over the leadership.[8]

The national movements which arose among almost all of the ethnic groups in the Soviet Union in 1988 and 1990 were linked to a whole series of other conflicts that had already been building up for some time. The clearly visible crisis in the economy, which had manifested itself since the end of the 1970s in declining standards of living, lent especial weight to economic demands. They were linked to social protest that was partly the result of a rise in unemployment and in ecological awareness, for example, protests against nuclear power stations (particularly after the Chernobyl disaster) or against the ecological catastrophes in Siberia and in Middle Asia (for example, the dried-up Aral Sea). The national movements in the west were not only opposed by the central government in Moscow and its power apparatus, but increasingly by the Communist parties in the republics. The crisis of the party and its ideology became increasingly apparent.

After 1988 the leading national movements existed in nations which had already reached the mass movement stage before 1917. Apart from the Poles, who had earlier given a decisive impetus to the disintegration of the Soviet system through the Solidarity movement, national sentiment was mobilized most easily and successfully in the case of the Estonians, Latvians, Lithuanians, Georgians and Armenians. As in the past they were followed by the Ukrainians, the Azerbaidzhanis and to varying extents by a series of other nations. These included the Muslims of Middle Asia, where the mobilization of national sentiment was still rather weak. The most important difference, when compared with the period between 1917 and 1920, was that the Russians now no longer identified themselves with the imperial state. This was something that neither the reactionary nor the liberal and constitutional national movements, nor the post-national communists had done. More and more Russians came to realize that the imperial policy, both in domestic and foreign policy terms, cost more than it was worth, and that it merely benefited the ruling elite and not the mass of the Russian people.

The Belorussian and Romanian national movements were considerably stronger after 1989 than they had been before 1917. Precisely these examples demonstrate that the situation had changed during the seven decades of Soviet rule. The framework of nationally defined republics, the results of the nation building in the 1920s and early 1930s that Stalin's regime of terror had been unable to destroy completely, and the social mobility of large sections of the population as a result of rapid change in the economy and in the educational system, had considerably improved the preconditions for the national movements. The fact that they had not been part of the Soviet Union in the inter-war period was of decisive importance for the Romanians in Bessarabia. Of course, this was also true of the Baltic nations, which until 1940 had been independent nation states. This tradition of statehood is an important explanation for the fact that the striving for independence was strongest in the Baltic states, but also for the unexpectedly radical movements of the Romanians and the Georgians, who also remembered the illegal annexation, in terms of international law, of their nation state in 1921. Other national movements also referred back to the short period of (usually precarious) independence after the October Revolution, and attempted in this way to establish a direct link with the pre-Soviet era. Apart from this, the rehabilitation of 'bourgeois' national movements of the tsarist period, which had long been taboo, and the national renaissance of the 1920s helped to crystallize national identity.

As after the October Revolution, the declarations of autonomy or sovereignty were followed by declarations of independence. A start was made by Lithuania in March 1990, whereas Estonia, Latvia, Georgia and Armenia at first only embarked on the transition to independence. In April 1991 Georgia also declared itself independent. The final collapse of the Soviet empire came about as a result of the abortive coup organized by reactionary forces in August 1991. Almost all of the Union's republics now declared themselves independent. Lithuania, Latvia and Estonia left the Soviet Union and were once again recognized as independent states. A referendum on 1 December 1991 returned a great majority for the independence of Ukraine, which, next to Russia, was the most important of the republics. This sealed the fate of the Soviet Union, which ceased to exist as a state at the end of 1991 when President Gorbachev resigned. Its place was taken by a loose 'Commonwealth of Independent States' (which did not include the Baltic republics).

The ideological vacuum that was created by the collapse of communism has been filled by national concepts. New nation states have taken the place of the Soviet Union, which was supranational in theory, though Russian-dominated in practice. In view of the fact that these nation states, the successors of the various Soviet republics, define themselves not only in political terms, but also on the basis of language and ethnicity, it will be of decisive importance to see how national ideologies develop when they are no longer an emancipatory force in the service of liberation from Soviet rule, and when their task is to integrate the various states. As all of the republics are a mixture in ethnic terms, the relationship between the main nations in the states and their ethnic minorities (and in all cases these also include Russians) will become a question of primary importance. Thus nationality problems will remain, though on a different level. Will the new nation states become genuine constitutional democracies by guaranteeing the rights of minorities, or will a reactionary kind of nationalism that is aggressive both without and within gain the upper hand?

What will remain of the Russian multi-ethnic empire, which existed for more than four centuries? Whether the Soviet Union, considerably reduced in size, will survive in the shape of a loose association of states is difficult to predict. Once the individual nations have achieved independence as nation states, they may well wish to reestablish a supranational community. What will certainly remain for the foreseeable future is the multi-ethnic empire of the Russian Federation, in which, in 1989, Russians only constituted 81.6 per cent of the total population. Whether non-Russians will continue to be part of this empire is doubtful in the case of the northern Caucasian Muslims. However, the other regions and ethnic groups, the Volga Tatars, the Bashkirs, Chuvash, Mordvinians, Mari (the former Cheremis), Udmurts, Komi, Karelians, Kalmyks, Buriats, Iakuts and the other even smaller groups stand little chance of achieving independent statehood on account of the fact that they live in the middle of areas inhabited by Russians. This suggests that the Russian multi-ethnic empire will continue to exist within the boundaries that it had in the middle of the seventeenth century, and once more during the civil war.

The other nations will also find it difficult to divest themselves of the legacy of the multi-ethnic empire overnight. Thus the ethno-demographic mixture and mutual economic relations will continue to be of importance, as will the formative power of political culture and mentalities. It is now the hour of nation states in which thinking will be determined by the memory of the tsarist 'prison of the peoples'; of a prison that became a torture chamber under Stalin; of political and military oppression; of economic exploitation; and of the imposition of a foreign culture by the Russian centre. It may well be that in the future people will remember the cosmopolitan tsarist world in which, admittedly, there was social injustice and political oppression, but in which cosmopolitan bureaucrats and intellectuals, Russians and Poles, Germans and Tatars, Finns and Georgians nevertheless thought and worked in a supranational context. As in the successor states of the Habsburg Empire, there may even come a time when people will idealize and look back nostalgically at the Russian multi-ethnic empire, whose geographical borders and intellectual horizons far exceeded those of the ethnic nation states.

Notes

1   This chapter is based on Simon (1986), the standard work on Soviet nationalities up to 1985. See also Nahaylo and Swoboda (1990) and Walter Kolarz, *Die Nationalitätenpolitik der Sowjetunion* (Frankfurt am Main, 1956).

2   Pipes (1964) continues to be the standard work on the civil war period. On the years prior to 1930 see Hélène Carrère d'Encausse, *Le gran défi. Bolchéviks et Nations 1917–1930* (Paris, 1987).

3   Lenin, *Studienausgabe*, vol. II (Frankfurt am Main, 1970), p. 275.

4   Hans Mommsen and Albrecht Martiny, 'Nationalismus, Nationalitätenfrage', *Sowjetsystem und demokratische Gesellschaft. Eine vergleichende Enzyklopädie*, vol. IV (Freiburg im Breisgau, 1971), pp. 623–95.

5   A frightening insight into the mechanism of terror is provided by the recently published correspondence between Beria and Stalin concerning the deportations. See 'Deportatsiia. Beria dokladyvaet Stalinu', *Kommunist* (1991/3), 101–12.

6   See table in Simon (1986), pp. 443 f.

7   On the following see Gerhard Simon 'Die Nationalbewegungen und das Ende des Sowjetsystems', *Osteuropa* 41 (1991), 774–90; Gerhard Simon, 'Die nationale Frage – Motor oder Bremse der Perestrojka?', in Andreas Kappeler (ed.), *Umbau des Sowjetsystems. Sieben Aspekte eines Experiments* (Stuttgart and Bonn, 1990), pp. 80–110; Erhard Stölting, *Eine Weltmacht zerbricht. Nationalitäten und Religionen in der UdSSR* (Frankfurt am Main, 1990).

8   See Kappeler (1990).

Appendices

Table 1: *Ethnic Groups of the Russian Empire by Linguistic Affiliation (c 1900)*

A. Indo-European Languages

1. Slav Languages
   - Eastern Slavs   Russians, Ukrainians, Belorussians
   - Western Slavs   Poles
   - Southern Slavs   Bulgars
2. Baltic Languages   Lithuanians, Latvians
3. Iranian Languages   Tadzhiks, Ossetians, Kurds, Gypsies
4. Armenian   Armenians
5. Romance Languages   Romanians (Moldavians)
6. Germanic Languages   Germans, Jews (Yiddish), Swedes

B. Uralic Languages

1. Finnish Languages   Finns, Estonians, Mordvinians, Votiaks (Udmurts) Cheremis (Mari), Zyrians (Komi and Komi-Permiaks), Karelians, Izhora (Ingrians), Veps, Lapps
2. Ugric Languages   Ostiaks (Khanty), Voguls (Mansi)
3. Samoed Languages   Samoyeds (Nentsy, etc.)

C. Altaic Languages

1. Turkic-Tatar Languages   Chuvash, Azerbaidzhanis, Turkmen, Turks, Gagauz, Kazakhs, Karakalpaks, Tatars, Bashkirs, Nogai, Kumyks, Balkars, Karachaians, Uzbeks ('Sarts'), Kirgiz, Uigurs, Khakassians, Shor, Iakuts, Altaians
2. Mongol Languages   Buriats, Kalmyks
3. Manchurian-Tungus Languages   Tungus (Evenks), etc.

D. Caucasian Languages

1. Southern Group   Georgians, Mingrelians, Svanetians, Adzhars
2. North-western Group   Kabardinians, Circassians (with Adygei), Abkhaz
3. North-eastern Group   Chechens, Ingushetians
4. Dagestan Group   Avars, Lezgians, Darginians, Laks, etc.

E. Palaeo-Asiatic Group   Chukchi, Koriaks, Iukagir, etc.

Table 2: *Ethnic Groups of the Russian Empire by Religion (around 1900)*

A. Christianity		
1.	Russian Orthodox Church	Russians, Ukrainians (majority), Belorussians (majority), Romanians (Moldavians), Bulgars, Greeks, Georgians, Chuvash, Mordvinians, Cheremis (majority), Votiaks, Karelians, Izhora, Veps, Lapps, Zyrians, Voguls, Ostiaks, Samoyeds (majority), Iakuts, Khakassians, Shor, Altai, Ossetians (majority), Gagauz, Gypsies
2.	Catholic Church	Poles, Lithuanians, Germans (some), Belorussians (some)
	– Uniate Church	Ukrainians (some), Belorussians (some), Armenians (some)
3.	Protestants	Finns, Estonians, Latvians, Germans (majority), Swedes
4.	Armenian Gregorian Church	Armenians
B. Judaism		Jews, Karaim, Tats
C. Islam		
1.	Sunnites	Tatars, Azerbaidzhanis (some), Kazakhs, Uzbeks, Tadzhiks, Turkmen, Kirgiz, Karakalpaks, Uigurs, Bashkirs, Nogai, Kumyks, Chechens, Ingushetians, Kabardinians, Circassians, Abkhaz, Avars, Lezgians, Darginians, Laks, Karachai, Balkars
2.	Shiites	Azerbaidzhanis (majority)
D. Buddhism (lamaism)		Buriats, Kalmyks
E. Animist religions		Numerous ethnic groups of the north and Siberia (some of them nominally Russian Orthodox) such as the Tungus, Chukchi, Samoyeds, etc.

Table 3: *Ethnic Groups of the Russian Empire and the Soviet Union (in their respective boundaries)*[1]

	1719		1897		1989	
	in 1000	%	in 1000	%	in 1000	%
Total	15764.8	100.00	125640.0	100.00	285743	100.00
Russians	11127.5	70.58	55667.5	44.31	145155	50.80
Ukrainians	2025.8	12.85	22380.6	17.81	44186	15.46
Belorussians	382.7	2.43	5885.6	4.68	10036	3.51
Eastern Slavs	13536.0	85.86	83933.7	66.80	199377	69.77
Karelians	80.9	0.51	208.1	0.17	131	0.05
Izhora	14.9	0.09	13.8	0.01	0.8	0.00
Veps	8.3	0.05	25.8	0.02	13	0.00
Lapps	1.5	0.01	1.8	0.00	1.9	0.00
Zyrians[2]	50.6	0.32	258.3	0.20	497	0.17
Samoyeds	6.0	0.04	15.9	0.01	35	0.01
The North	161.9	1.03	523.7	0.42	678.7	0.24
Volga Tatars	293.1	1.86	1834.2	1.46	6649	2.33
Chuvash	217.9	1.38	843.8	0.67	1842	0.64
Mordvinians	107.4	0.68	1023.8	0.81	1154	0.40
Cheremis	61.9	0.39	375.4	0.30	671	0.23
Votiaks	48.1	0.31	420.8	0.33	747	0.26
Bashkirs	171.9	1.09	1321.4	1.05	1449	0.51
Teptiars	22.6	0.14	117.8	0.09		
Volga/Urals	922.9	5.85	5937.2	4.73	12512	4.37
Siberian Tatars	15.3	0.10	50.0	0.04	?	
Ostiaks	16.7	0.11	19.7	0.02	23	0.01
Voguls	2.0	0.01	7.7	0.01	8.5	0.00
Khakassians *et al.*	13.1	0.08	37.7	0.03	80	0.03
Shor			12.0	0.01	17	0.01
Altaians			40.0	0.03	71	0.02
Buriats	47.8	0.30	288.7	0.23	421	0.15
Tungus	17.7	0.11	65.5	0.05	47	0.02
Iakuts	35.2	0.22	227.4	0.18	382	0.13
Chukchi			11.8	0.01	15	0.01
Others	7.9	0.05	21.6	0.02	244	0.09
Siberia	155.7	0.99	782.1	0.62	1308.5	0.46

Table 3 (*continued*)

	1719		1897		1989	
	in 1000	*%*	*in 1000*	*%*	*in 1000*	*%*
Kalmyks	*200.0*	1.27	190.6	0.15	174	0.06
Nogai	113.6	0.72	64.1	0.05	75	0.03
Crimean Tatars			_220.0_	_0.18_	_272_	_0.10_
Steppe	_313.6_	_1.99_	_474.7_	_0.38_	_521_	_0.19_
Estonians	309.2	1.96	1002.7	0.80	1027	0.36
Latvians	162.2	1.03	1435.3	1.14	1459	0.51
Finns	164.2	1.04	143.1[3]	0.11	67	0.02
Swedes	8.0	0.05	14.2[4]	0.01		
Poles			*7931.3*	6.31	1126	0.39
Lithuanians			1659.1[5]	1.32	3067	1.07
Jews			5063.2	4.03	1449	0.51
Romanians (Moldavians)			1121.7	0.89	3498	1.22
Bulgars			172.5	0.14	373	0.13
Gagauz			_55.8_	_0.04_	_198_	_0.07_
West	_643.6_	_4.08_	_18598.9_	_14.81_	_12264_	_4.29_
Georgians			1352.5	1.08	3981	1.39
Armenians			1173.1	0.93	4623	1.62
Azerbaidzhanis			*1440*	1.15	6770	2.37
Kurds			99.9	0.08	152	0.05
Abkhaz			72.1	0.06	105	0.04
Others			_302.2_	_0.24_	_50_	_0.02_
Transcaucasia			_4439.8_	_3.53_	_15681_	_5.49_
Chechens			226.5	0.18	957	0.33
Avars			212.7	0.17	601	0.21
Ossetians			171.7	0.14	598	0.21
Lezgians			159.2	0.13	466	0.16
Kabardinians			98.6	0.08	391	0.14
Darginians			130.2	0.10	365	0.13
Kumyks			83.4	0.07	282	0.10
Ingushetians			47.4	0.04	237	0.08
Laks + Tabasaranians			90.8	0.07	216	0.08
Circassians			44.7	0.04	177[6]	0.06

Table 3 (*continued*)

	1719		1897		1989	
	in 1000	*%*	*in 1000*	*%*	*in 1000*	*%*
Karachaians			27.2	0.02	156	0.05
Balkars			27.1	0.02	85	0.03
Others			1.6	0.00	104	0.04
Caucasus			1321.1	1.05	4635	1.62
Kazakhs			*3881.8*[7]	3.09	8136	2.85
Kirgiz			*634.8*	0.51	2529	0.89
Uzbeks			*1800*[8]	1.43	16698	5.84
Tadzhiks			350.4	0.28	4215	1.48
Turkmen			281.4	0.22	2729	0.96
Karakalpaks			104.3	0.08	424	0.15
Uigurs			100	0.08	263	0.09
Others					112	0.04
Middle Asia			7152.8	5.69	35106	12.29
Germans	31.1	0.20	1790.5	1.43	2039	0.71
Greeks			186.9	0.15	358	0.13
Gypsies			*44.5*[9]	0.04	262	0.09
Koreans			26.0	0.02	439	0.15
Others			334	0.27	340	0.12
Diaspora Groups			2470.9	1.91	3438	1.20

1 Figures for 1719 from Kabuzan (1990); for 1897 (without the Grand Duchy of Finland, the Emirate of Bukhara, and the Khanate of Khiva) from *Die Nationalitäten* (1991), vol. 2; for 1989 *Narodnoe Khoziaistvo SSSR v 1989 g. Statisticheskii ezhegodnik* (Moscow, 1990), pp. 30-33. The figures for 1719 and those for the other two censuses given in italics are doubtful. On the various ethnic groups see also Mark (1989).

2 Together with Permiaks.

3 Without the Grand Duchy of Finland, where 2.2 million Finns lived around 1900, who comprised about 1.75% (and together with the Finns outside of the Grand Duchy 1.83%) of the population of the Russian Empire (Kastelianskii, 1910, p. 627).

4 Without the Swedes in the Grand Duchy of Finland, who around 1897 comprised about 300,000, that is, about 0.24% of the total population of the empire (with Finland).

5 With those who spoke Zhmud.

6 Adygei and Circassians.

7 To some extent no distinction was made in 1897 between Kazakhs and Kirgiz. The data from Bekmakhanova (1986), p. 175, 182.

8 Uzbeks and Sarts

9 The number of Gypsies was in fact much higher in 1897, for the census only recorded people who stated that their native language was Roma.

Table 4: *Degree of urbanization of individual ethnic groups of the Russian Empire 1897 (as a % of the total of the ethnic group)*[1]

Russian Empire	13.4		
Jews	49.42	Romanians	5.72
Tadzhiks	29.50	Ukrainians	5.61
Germans	23.38	Lithuanians	3.16
Armenians	23.25	Belorussians	2.91
Sarts	21.06	Caucasian Mountain Peoples	1.96
Poles	18.35	Iakuts	1.71
Greeks	17.99	Karelians	1.34
Latvians	16.05	Kazakhs	1.17
Russians	15.85	Bashkirs	1.05
Estonians	13.92	Ethnic Groups Middle Volga	0.92
Uzbeks	12.63	Buriats	0.71
Tatars and Azerbaidzhanis	11.29	Kalmyks	0.66
Georgians	9.41	Tungus	0.29
Bulgarians	8.32	Chukchi	0.07

1   Data from *Die Nationalitäten* (1991), vol. 2

Table 5: *Ethnic composition of the principal cities of the Russian Empire 1897*[1]

City	Inhabitants (in 1000)	Russians %	Ukrainians %	Poles %	Jews %	Germans %	Armenians %	Muslims %	Others %	
St Petersburg	1264	86.5	0.4	2.9	1.0	4.0	0.1	0.4	1.7	Finns
Moscow	1039	95.0	0.4	0.9	0.5	1.7	0.2	0.5	0.2	French
Warsaw	684	7.3	1.3	61.7	27.1	1.7	0.0	0.1	0.2	Romanians
Odessa	404	49.1	9.4	4.3	30.8	2.5	0.4	0.5	1.3	Greeks
Łódź	314	2.2	0.1	46.4	29.4	21.4	0.0	0.0	–	
Riga	282	15.8	0.1	4.8	6.0	23.8	0.0	0.2	45.0	Latvians
Kiev	248	54.2	22.2	6.7	12.1	1.8	0.0	0.8	1.1	Belorussians
Kharkov	174	63.2	25.9	2.3	5.7	1.4	0.3	0.5	0.4	Belorussians
Tiflis	160	28.1	1.7	2.6	1.8	1.8	29.5	5.4	26.4	Georgians
Tashkent	156	9.6	1.7	1.4	0.9	0.4	0.0	85.8	–	
Vilna	155	20.0	0.33	0.9	40.0	1.4	0.0	0.5	2.0	Lithuanians
Saratov	137	88.8	0.9	1.3	0.9	6.1	0.0	1.3	0.3	Mordvinians
Kazan	130	73.4	0.5	1.1	1.0	0.8	0.0	22.0	0.4	Chuvash
Rostov	119	79.2	4.7	1.2	9.4	1.0	1.9	1.1	0.6	Greeks
Tula	115	95.9	0.8	0.6	2.0	0.4	0.0	0.1	0.1	Belorussians
Astrakhan	113	76.7	0.4	0.6	1.9	1.4	3.6	14.8	0.1	Mordvinians
Ekaterinoslav	113	41.8	15.8	3.0	35.4	1.3	0.0	0.8	1.2	Belorussians
Baku	112	33.4	0.8	0.8	1.7	2.2	17.1	40.6	0.9	Georgians
Kishinev	108	27.0	3.1	3.0	45.9	1.2	0.3	0.2	17.6	Romanians

1 Data from *Die Nationalitäten* (1991), vol. 2

Table 6: *Major ethnic groups of the Russian Empire on the basis of selected estates (1897, in percentage of group total)*[1]

	Her Nobility	Per Nobility	Clergy Cbr	Mer + Hon	Meshchane	Peasants	Cossacks	Inorodtsy	Foreigners
Total Population	0.97	0.50	0.47	0.49	10.66	77.13	2.33	6.60	0.51
Russians	0.87	0.84	0.82	0.73	8.24	83.71	4.15	0.04	0.53
Ukrainians	0.30	0.16	0.26	0.19	5.69	90.94	2.21	0.00	0.07
Belorussians	1.50	0.16	0.17	0.10	5.73	92.16	0.06	0.00	0.02
Poles	4.41	0.78	0.04	0.11	15.28	77.70	0.00	0.00	1.45
Lithuanians	2.41	0.08	0.04	0.00	3.95	93.34	0.00	0.00	0.09
Latvians	0.03	0.08	0.02	0.08	4.70	94.86	0.00	0.00	0.05
Estonians	0.03	0.05	0.04	0.06	4.38	95.01	0.00	0.00	0.05
Germans	1.39	0.96	0.14	1.49	18.12	70.72	0.01	0.00	6.77
Jews	0.00	0.07	0.00	1.54	94.16	3.90	0.00	0.01	0.13
Greeks	0.37	0.30	0.83	0.73	6.94	65.23	0.02	0.02	25.32
Romanians	0.26	0.17	0.58	1.13	8.02	89.29	0.01	0.00	0.40
Georgians	5.29	1.04	2.18	0.38	3.55	87.33	0.05	0.00	0.09
Armenians	0.83	0.55	1.30	1.68	15.00	76.06	0.01	0.00	4.45
Cauc Mt Peoples	0.58	0.20	0.04	0.03	0.29	92.65	0.30	5.78	0.04
Tatars+Azerbds	1.60	0.09	0.03	0.17	7.28	83.29	1.17	4.73	1.36
Eth Grp Mid Vga	0.00	0.00	0.02	0.00	0.52	99.03	0.38	0.00	0.00
Eth Grp Urals	0.07	0.03	0.00	0.12	0.17	99.50	0.07	0.04	0.00
Kalmyks	0.01	0.02	0.00	1.21	0.15	0.36	15.23	83.01	0.00
Eth Grp Md Asia	0.03	0.01	0.00	0.01	0.14	0.67	0.02	98.92	0.19
Eth Grp Siberia	0.02	0.01	0.01	0.04	0.06	0.50	3.91	95.38	0.01

1 Data from *Die Nationalitäten* (1991), vol. 2

The above estate categories always include families (see *Die Nationalitäten* (1991), vol. 1, pp. 392–429)

– Her(editary) and per(sonal) nobility – Clergy Chr: Clergy of Christian denominations – Mer + Hon: Merchants (kuptsy), hereditary and personal honorary citizens – Also meshchane (petit bourgeois), peasants, Cossacks (Army Cossacks), inorodtsy (allogeneous) and foreigners.

Composition of the language groups comprising several languages as listed in Tables 7 to 9:

– Cauc Mt Peoples: Ossetians, Lezgians, Avars, Chechens, Ingushetians, Circassians, Kabardinians, Abkhaz, Kumyks, Nogai, etc. – Ethnic Groups Middle Volga: Cheremis, Chuvash, Mordvinians, Votiaks – Ethnic Groups Urals: Bashkirs, Teptiars, Mishars – Ethnic Groups Middle Asia: Tadzhiks, Turkmen, Kazakhs, Kirgiz, Uzbeks, Sarts, Karakalpaks, Uigurs, etc. – Ethnic Groups Siberia: Iakuts, Buriats, Voguls, Ostiaks, Samoyeds, etc.

Table 7: *Ethnic groups of the Russian Empire on the basis of selected professions 1897 (with families, as % of total ethnic group)*[1]

	Agriculture	Manufacture	Trade	Service	Servants	Freelance	Rentier	Administration	Military	Church
Total Population	74.6	9.5	3.3	2.2	4.6	0.7	1.2	0.8	1.0	0.6
Russians	71.6	11.0	2.5	2.9	4.4	0.8	1.3	1.1	1.4	0.9
Ukrainians	87.2	4.8	0.7	1.0	3.5	0.2	0.4	0.4	0.8	0.3
Belorussians	90.9	2.8	0.2	0.9	2.8	0.2	0.5	0.4	0.5	0.5
Poles	63.0	13.0	1.3	2.8	12.0	0.9	2.5	1.2	1.2	0.3
Lithuanians	85.8	4.1	0.3	0.9	5.6	0.1	0.7	0.4	0.4	0.3
Latvians	69.4	13.3	1.2	2.8	8.2	0.6	1.2	0.7	0.5	0.1
Estonians	68.3	13.5	1.4	2.8	8.7	0.6	1.4	0.7	0.5	0.1
Germans	57.7	20.9	3.3	2.4	6.3	2.3	3.5	1.0	1.0	0.3
Jews	3.8	34.5	36.7	6.5	6.6	3.3	3.4	0.2	1.1	1.8
Greeks	73.0	9.0	6.7	3.2	2.9	0.5	1.7	0.4	0.4	0.7
Romanians	92.9	1.9	0.3	0.4	1.9	0.1	0.3	0.2	0.7	0.5
Georgians	82.5	4.0	1.9	2.1	3.3	0.3	2.6	0.6	0.5	1.0
Armenians	71.4	9.6	6.4	2.6	4.1	0.4	1.8	0.7	0.5	0.8
Cauc Mt Peoples	89.3	3.2	0.7	0.4	3.2	0.1	0.5	0.4	0.2	0.3
Tatars+Azerbds	81.7	4.2	3.9	2.0	4.0	0.2	0.7	0.4	0.7	0.6
Eth Grp Mid Vga	97.4	0.6	0.1	0.1	0.5	0.1	0.1	0.1	0.3	0.1
Eth Grp Urals	92.4	2.0	0.8	0.4	1.5	0.1	0.1	0.1	0.2	0.6
Kalmyks	71.2	1.1	0.3	0.2	23.4	0.1	0.2	0.3	0.1	1.2
Eth Grp Md Asia	86.0	5.7	2.8	0.8	2.8	0.2	0.1	0.2	0.1	0.4
Eth Grp Siberia	96.0	0.7	0.3	0.4	1.1	0.0	0.1	0.1	0.1	0.1

1 Data from *Die Nationalitäten* (1991), vol. 2

The professions comprise the following occupations (see more detailed list in *Die Nationalitäten* (1991), vol. 2, pp. 26–9; vol. 1, pp. 466–88):

– Agriculture: farming, beekeeping, silkworm, animal husbandry, forestry, hunting and fishing. – Manufacturing goods from metal, animal products, wood, textiles, etc. – Trade: All kinds of trade and banking. – Service: Transport, post, inns, etc. – Servants – Freelance: private lawyers, health service, education, scholarship, and art. – Rentier: People living on the proceeds of capital and property, or with the financial support of parents or relatives. – Administration: administration, courts, police, public and estate–based service. – Military: Armed forces. – Church: Christian and non–Christian worship, holders of ecclesiastical offices, etc.

For the composition of the ethnic groups see Table 6, note 1.

Table 8: *Ethnic groups of the Russian Empire on the basis of selected professions 1897 (as percentage of the working population of an ethnic group, without families)*[1]

	Agriculture	Industry	Trade	Service	Servants	Freelance	Rentier	Administration	Military	Church
Total Population	54.9	15.0	3.8	3.3	10.0	1.1	2.0	1.0	3.4	0.9
Russians	47.3	18.3	3.2	4.4	10.3	1.4	2.4	1.4	4.3	1.3
Ukrainians	73.1	7.3	1.0	1.6	9.0	0.5	0.8	0.6	3.4	0.5
Belorussians	77.8	5.3	0.4	1.7	7.3	0.5	0.9	0.6	2.2	0.3
Poles	48.6	15.8	1.4	3.0	17.9	1.3	3.3	1.2	3.5	0.4
Lithuanians	73.7	6.6	0.4	1.3	10.5	0.3	1.1	0.5	1.2	0.4
Latvians	58.4	15.6	1.4	3.1	12.2	0.8	2.0	0.7	1.4	0.1
Estonians	56.4	17.4	1.5	3.0	12.6	0.7	2.1	0.7	1.2	0.1
Germans	39.0	25.0	4.0	2.8	11.7	3.8	5.8	1.0	2.9	0.3
Jews	2.7	35.4	29.6	5.1	11.5	3.2	3.8	0.2	3.5	1.3
Greeks	50.1	15.4	11.7	5.8	6.9	1.0	3.0	0.6	1.5	0.8
Romanians	82.4	3.2	0.5	0.8	5.2	0.3	0.8	0.3	3.2	1.1
Georgians	66.2	7.7	2.8	4.2	8.3	0.6	3.6	0.9	1.6	1.1
Armenians	48.1	16.4	9.6	4.7	9.0	0.9	3.2	1.1	1.9	1.0
Cauc Mt Peoples	80.7	5.2	0.9	0.6	5.3	0.2	1.1	0.6	0.7	0.3
Tatars+Azerbds	67.2	7.2	5.1	3.0	7.6	0.4	1.0	0.5	3.1	0.6
Eth Grp Mid Vga	90.6	1.7	0.3	0.4	1.6	0.2	0.4	0.3	1.4	0.5
Eth Grp Urals	83.7	3.1	0.9	0.6	2.8	0.2	0.3	0.1	1.1	0.7
Eth Grp Md Asia	74.9	11.4	3.5	1.2	5.4	0.3	0.3	0.2	0.5	0.5
Eth Grp Siberia	90.2	1.5	0.4	0.7	3.0	0.1	0.3	0.1	0.2	0.2

1   Data from *Die Nationalitäten* (1991), vol. 2
With regard to the professional groups see Table 7, note 1. On the composition of the language groups see Table 6, note 1.

Table 9: *Educational level of the principal ethnic groups of the Empire 1897 (people over the age of ten as a percentage of everyone over the age of ten)*[1]

	Reading Skills			More than primary school education		
	Total	Male	Female	Total	Male	Female
Total Population	27.7	38.6	17.0	1.51	1.87	1.14
Russians	29.3	44.9	14.7	2.28	2.80	1.78
Ukrainians	18.9	32.4	5.3	0.36	0.47	0.25
Belorussians	20.3	31.0	9.8	0.49	0.83	0.15
Poles	41.8	44.7	38.9	2.77	3.96	1.60
Lithuanians	48.4	49.3	47.6	0.27	0.54	0.02
Latvians	85.0	84.8	85.3	0.63	1.13	0.17
Estonians	94.1	93.8	94.4	0.59	0.98	0.23
Germans	78.5	79.7	77.3	6.37	7.51	5.26
Jews	50.1	64.6	36.6	1.20	1.18	1.22
Greeks	36.7	51.8	17.7	2.10	2.66	1.39
Bulgars	29.8	47.7	10.5	1.26	1.40	1.10
Romanians	8.8	15.1	2.2	0.43	0.55	0.30
Georgians	19.5	23.9	14.6	1.45	2.19	0.64
Armenians	18.3	25.7	9.8	2.27	3.07	1.35
Cauc Mt Peoples	7.1	12.2	1.8	0.13	0.23	0.02
Tatars+Azerbds	16.5	19.1	13.5	0.12	0.16	0.07
Eth Grp Mid Vga	9.8	18.1	1.8	0.04	0.07	0.01
Eth Grp Urals	26.2	30.3	21.8	0.01	0.02	0.00
Kalmyks	4.1	7.6	0.3	0.03	0.05	0.00
Eth Grp Md Asia	3.4	5.7	0.7	0.02	0.03	0.01
Eth Grp Siberia	5.0	9.3	0.6	0.05	0.09	0.01

1   Data from *Die Nationalitäten* (1991), vol. 2

The 'reading skills' category comprises those individuals who were recorded as having these skills in Russian or in another language, in addition to those individuals who had more than a primary school education (including those who had not completed their studies). These individuals are included in the 'more than primary school education' category.

On the composition of the language categories see Table 6, note 1.

Glossary

Autocracy (samoderzhavie): political system of the Muscovite and Russian Empires, in which limitless power (in theory) was given to the tsar.

Beg (Bäy, Bey, Bei): honorary Turkish title for tribal chieftains and aristocrats.

Bund: Jewish General Workers' Association in Lithuania, Poland and Russia.

Cadets: abbreviation for Constitutional Democratic (CD) Party, also known as Party of Popular Freedom, which had a radical and liberal programme.

Colleges: central government departments introduced by Peter the Great to succeed the prikazy, replaced by ministries in the nineteenth century.

Colonists: foreign settlers in the Russian Empire who, until 1871, were distinct from the rural Russian population as a group with legal and social privileges.

Cossacks:

1. population group consisting primarily of eastern Slavs which settled on the steppe frontier in the sixteenth and seventeenth centuries mainly along the rivers (Dnepr, Don, Volga, Terek, Iaik); lived by raiding, looting and pillage, fishing and animal husbandry, had a specific military–democratic constitution and performed border defence functions for the rulers of Poland-Lithuania and Russia.

2. service Cossacks: a category of 'chosen service men' (sluzhilye liudi po priboru) in Muscovy usually deployed in the garrisons of frontier fortresses.

3. in the armed forces of the Russian Empire in the eighteenth and nineteenth centuries, a separate estate organized into Cossack hosts.

Dashnaks (Dashnaktseutiun): Party of the Revolutionary Armenian Federalists.

Duma (Gosudarstvennaia duma, state duma): elected parliament conceded by the tsarist government during the revolution of 1905/1906. The electoral laws for the first and second dumas (1906–07) were fairly democratic, whereas those of the third and fourth dumas were very disadvantageous to the lower classes.

Estates (sosloviia, sostoianiia): legal categories created by the government in the course of the eighteenth and nineteenth centuries: hereditary nobility, personal nobility, clergy, hereditary honorary citizens, personal honorary citizens, merchants, meshchane, peasants and the special groups of inorodtsy and Cossacks.

Golden Horde (Ulus Juchi): successor state of the Mongolian empire in western Eurasia from the thirteenth to the late fifteenth century. Its centre was at Sarai on the lower Volga.

Gortsy (mountain people): collective Russian term for the ethnic groups of the Caucasus mountains.

Guild merchants (kupcy): estate of the Russian Empire comprising the more prosperous merchants, divided on the basis of wealth into three and after 1863 into two guilds.

Haskalah: Jewish enlightenment movement.

Hetmanate: a polity in Ukraine founded by hetman B. Khmelnytsky and the Dnepr Cossacks in 1648. From 1667 onwards area in Ukraine on the left bank of the Dnepr (with Kiev), which until 1764 possessed wide-ranging autonomy within Muscovy and the Russian Empire.

Honorary citizen (pochetnii grazhdanin): privileged urban estate created in 1831–32, divided into hereditary and personal honorary citizens.

Householders (odnodvortsy): demoted lower service men, subcategory of state peasants.

Hromada (community): Ukrainian national movement organization.

Iasak: (Mongolian and Tatar) tribute; in Muscovy tax imposed on taxable men (iasak men) who had formerly been under Mongolian rule; subsequently also imposed on all Siberian tribes.

Inorodtsy (of foreign origin, allogeneous):

1. legal estate category which excluded numerous non-Russian ethnic groups from the ranks of full citizens (prirodnye), and gave them a special status and local self-administration. Created in 1822 for the non-sedentary ethnic groups of Siberia, the term was subsequently

applied to other ethnic groups in the Asiatic part of Russia, and to the Jews.

2. from the middle of the nineteenth century pejorative term for all non-Russians in the tsarist empire.

Ittifak: Union of the Muslims of Russia.

Jadidism: Islamic reform movement which sought to renew the traditional educational system and subsequently the whole of Islamic culture by infusing them with Western thought.

Kahal (kehilla): self-administrative body of the Jewish community in Poland-Lithuania and the Russian Empire.

Khan: Turkish title; ruler of part of the Mongolian empire.

Khanate: realm (Turkish), successor state of the Mongolian empire.

Kholop: slave (servant) in the Muscovite polity.

Little Russia (Malorossiia): initially ecclesiastical and subsequently official Russian term for Ukraine.

Maloliud'e (maloliudstvo): 'dearth of people', the lack of educated specialists.

Merchants see Guild Merchants.

Meshchane ('petit bourgeois'): estate introduced in Russia in 1785 comprising the personally free basic layer of the urban population which engaged in trade and commerce.

Meshcheriaki (mishari, Mishars): Tatar service men in the Urals, subsequently regional group of Volga Tatars.

Metropolitan: Head of the church of Rus and of Muscovy until the establishment of the Moscow patriarchate in 1589.

Muridism: Islamic teaching of Sufic brotherhoods involving the unconditional loyalty of pupils (murids).

Narodniki (populists): members of the Russian agrarian socialist movement in the second half of the nineteenth century.

New Russia (Novorossiia): contemporary term for south Ukraine, the steppe area to the north of the Black Sea.

Oblast (area): administrative unit in peripheral areas of the Russian Empire (instead of province).

Octobrists (Soiuz 17 oktiabria, Union of 17 October): right-wing liberal party.

Pale of settlement (cherta osedlosti): the regions of the Russian Empire (fifteen provinces in the west, and ten in the Kingdom of Poland) in which Jews were permitted to live.

PPS (Polska Partia Socjalistyczna): Polish Socialist Party.

Prikaz: central authority in Muscovy. — Prikaz Kazanskogo Dvortsa: Chancellery for the Khanate of Kazan, which was responsible for all newly acquired territories in the east until the establishment of the Sibirskii (Siberian) Prikaz (1637).

Province (guberniia): basic administrative unit of the Russian Empire.

Revision: census of the taxable population of Russia, 1719–1858.

Ritterschaft: corporation of the Baltic German nobility in the Baltic provinces.

Rus: term used in the Middle Ages by the eastern Slavs to describe themselves.

Sejm: diet in Poland-Lithuania.

Sejmik: regional diet in Poland-Lithuania.

Senate: highest authority in Russia created by Peter the Great; importance subsequently declined, in the nineteenth century was primarily a supervisory body and the supreme court.

Sloboda Ukraine: region of eastern Ukraine around Kharkhov.

Smuta: time of disturbances in Muscovy at the beginning of the seventeenth century.

Starshyna: officers, and subsequently upper class of the Dnepr Cossacks.

State Council (gosudarstvennii sovet, also Imperial Council): highest authority in Russia in the nineteenth century; from 1906 onwards the upper chamber of the Russian parliament (above the Duma).

State peasants: category of taxable peasants created by Peter the Great who were dependent directly on the state and not on private landowners, and in contrast to serfs remained personally free. A whole series of former population groups were incorporated into the category, including the so-called 'black peasants', the 'householders', the Russian peasants in Siberia, and the sedentary iasak men.

Sufism: mystical Islamic teaching whose adherents formed fraternities and orders.

Szlachta: nobility in Poland-Lithuania.

Table of Ranks: stepladder of all the ranks and offices in the army, the navy, the civil service and at court introduced by Peter the Great.

Tayshi: title of Mongolian nobles.

Teptiars and bobyls: immigrant non-Russian iasak men in the Urals who were dependent on the Bashkirs.

Trudoviki: 'Group of Workers' in the Duma who were in favour of agrarian socialism.

Uezd: administrative unit (county, district), a subdivision of a province in the Russian Empire.

Uniate church: Roman Catholic church of the Orthodox rite founded at the Union of Brest (1596) which recognizes the Pope and Roman Catholic dogmas, but has retained Orthodox rites and Church Slavonic. Also know as Greek Catholic church.

Union of the Russian People (Soiuz russkogo naroda): extreme right-wing Russian party.

Voevoda: military leader, head of the regional administration in Muscovy and the Russian Empire from the sixteenth to eighteenth centuries.

Votchina: patrimony, inheritance, inherited property.

Zaporozhian Sich: fortified centre of the Dnepr Cossacks, where their traditional lifestyle and military-democratic order survived until its dissolution in 1775.

Zemstvo: term used for the system of regional and local self-administration introduced in the central regions of the empire in 1864.

Bibliography

Collective Works and Periodicals Referred to by Initials

AAE Akty, sobrannye v bibliotekakh i arkhivakh Rossiiskoi Imperii Arkheograficheskoi Ekspeditsiei Imperatorskoi Akademii Nauk. 1–4. St Petersburg, 1836.

APH Acta Poloniae Historica

ASEER The American Slavic and East European Review

CAS Central Asian Survey

CMRS Cahiers du monde russe et soviétique

ES Entsiklopedicheskii slovar' (F.A. Brokgauz and I.A. Efron). Vols 1–41 (1–82) St Petersburg, 1890–1904.

FOG Forschungen zur osteuropäischen Geschichte

HUS Harvard Ukrainian Studies

ISSSR Istoriia SSSR

IZ Istoricheskie Zapiski

JbbGO Jahrbücher für Geschichte Osteuropas

JBS Journal of Baltic Studies

MERSH Modern Encyclopedia of Russian and Soviet History. Ed. Joseph L. Wieczynski. Vol. 1 ff., Gulf Breeze, 1976 ff.

PSZ Polnoe Sobranie Zakonov Rossiiskoi imperii. Sobranie pervoe (I). Vols 1–50. St Petersburg, 1830; *Sobranie vtoroe* (II). Vols 1–55. St Petersburg, 1830–1884.

RH Russian History

RR The Russian Review

SE Sovetskaia Etnografiia

SEER Slavonic and East European Review

SIRIO Sbornik Imperatorskogo russkogo istoricheskogo obshchestva. Vols 1–148. St Petersburg, 1867–1916.

SR Slavic Review

SZ Svod zakonov

VIst Voprosy istorii

ZfO Zeitschrift für Ostforschung

Sources and Literature

Akiner, Shirin (1983) *Islamic Peoples of the Soviet Union*, London.

Alapuro, Risto (1988) *State and Revolution in Finland*, Berkeley.

Albertini, Rudolf von (1976) *Europäische Kolonialherrschaft 1880–1940*, Zürich, Freiburg i. Br.

Alekseev, A. I. (1982) *Osvoenie russkimi liud'mi Dal'nego Vostoka i Russkoi Ameriki (do kontsa XIX veka)*, Moscow.

Alishev, S. Kh (1990) *Istoricheskie sud'by narodov Srednego Povolzhia XVI – nachalo XIX v.* Moscow.

Allworth, Edward (ed.) (1989) *Central Asia. 120 Years of Russian Rule*, Durham and London.

Allworth, Edward (ed.) (1990) *The Modern Uzbeks. From the Fourteenth Century to the Present. A Cultural History*, Stanford.

Alston, Patrick L. (1969) *Education and the State in Tsarist Russia*, Stanford.

Amburger, Erik (1961) *Geschichte des Protestantismus in Rußland*, Stuttgart.

Amburger, Erik (1966) *Geschichte der Behördenorganisation Rußlands von Peter dem Großen bis 1917*, Leiden.

Ammann, Albert M. S.J. (1950) *Abriß der ostslawischen Kirchengeschichte*, Wien.

Apollova, N.G. (1964) 'K voprosu o politike absoliutizma v natsional'nykh raionakh Rossii v XVIII v.', *Absoliutizm v Rossii (XVII–XVIII vv.). Sbornik Statei k semidesiatiletiiu so dnia rozhdeniia . . . V. K. Kafengauza*, Moscow, pp. 355–88.

Armstrong, John A. (1976) 'Mobilized and Proletarian Diasporas', *The American Political Science Review* 70, 393–408.

Armstrong, John A (1978) 'Mobilized Diaspora in Tsarist Russia: The Case of the Baltic Germans', in Jeremy R. Azrael (ed.), *Soviet Nationality Policies and Practices*, New York, pp. 63–104.

Arsharuni, A. and Gabidullin, Kh. (1931) *Ocherki panislamizma i panturkizma v Rossii*, Moscow.

Ascher, Abraham (1988) *The Revolution of 1905. Russia in Disarray*, Stanford.

Atkin, Muriel (1980) *Russia and Iran 1780–1828*, Minneapolis.

Atkin, Muriel (1988) 'Russian Expansion in the Caucasus to 1813', in Rywkin, pp. 139–87.

Avrekh, A. Ia. (1968) *Stolypin i tret'ia Duma*, Moscow.

Babel, Antony (1926) *La Bessarabie. Étude historique, ethnographique et économique*, Paris.

Bacon, Elizabeth E. (1966) *Central Asians under Russian Rule. A Study in Cultural Change*, Ithaca, NY.

Baron, Salo W. (1964) *The Russian Jew under Tsars and Soviets*, New York and London.

Basarab, John (1982) *Pereiaslav 1654: A Historiographical Study*, Edmonton.

Batunsky, Mark (1987) 'Imperial Pragmatism, Liberalistic Culture Relativism and Assimilatively Christianizing Dogmatism in Colonial Central Asia: Parallels, Divergencies, Mergences', *Utrecht Papers on Central Asia. Proceedings of the First European Seminar on Central Asian Studies*, Utrecht, pp. 95–122.

Batunsky, Mark (1990) 'Islam and Russian Culture in the First Half of the 19th Century', *CAS* 9 (4), 1–27.

Baumann, Robert F. (1987) 'Subject Nationalities in the Military Service of Imperial Russia: The Case of the Bashkirs', *SR* 46, 489–502.

Bazylow, Ludwik (1984) *Polacy w Petersburgu*, Wrocław.

Beauvois, Daniel (1985) *Le noble, le serf et le revizor. La noblesse polonaise entre le tsarisme et les masses ukrainiennes (1831–1863)*, Paris.

Becker, Seymour (1986) 'The Muslim East in Nineteenth-Century Russian Popular Historiography', *CAS* 5 (3/4), 25–47.

Bekmakhanova, N. E. (1986) *Mnogonatsional'noe naselenie Kazakhstana i Kirgizii v epokhu kapitalizma*, Moscow.

Bennigsen, Alexandre (1972) 'The Muslims of European Russia and the Caucasus', in Vucinich, pp. 135–66.

Bennigsen, Alexandre and Chantal Lemercier-Quelquejay (1960) *La presse et mouvement national chez les musulmans de Russie avant 1920*, Paris and The Hague.

Bennigsen, Alexandre and Chantal Lemercier-Quelquejay (1964) *Les mouvements nationaux chez les musulmans de Russie. Le 'Sultangalievisme' au Tatarstan*, Paris and The Hague.

Bennigsen, Alexandre and Chantal Lemercier-Quelquejay (1981) *Les musulmans oubliés. L'Islam en Union soviétique*, Paris.

Bennigsen, Alexandre and S. Enders Wimbush (1985) *Muslims of the Soviet Empire. A Guide*, London.

Bitterli, Urs (1986) *Alte Welt – neue Welt. Formen des europäisch-überseeischen Kulturkontakts vom 15. bis zum 18. Jahrhundert*, Munich.

Blackwell, William L. (1959) 'Alexander I and Poland: The Foundations of his Polish Policy and its Repercussions in Russia, 1801–1825', Ph. D. thesis, Princeton.

Blackwell, William L. (1968) *The Beginnings of Russian Industrialization 1800–1860*, Princeton.

Bonwetsch, Gerhard (1919) *Geschichte der deutschen Kolonien an der Wolga*, Stuttgart.

Boshyk, George Y. (1981) 'The Rise of Ukrainian Political Parties in Russia, 1900–1907: With Special Reference to Social Democracy', D. Phil. thesis, Oxford.

Bruk, S. I. and V. M. Kabuzan (1980) 'Etnicheskii sostav naseleniia Rossii (1719–1917 gg.)', *SE*, 6, 18–34.

Bruk, S. I. and V. M. Kabuzan (1981) 'Chislennost' i rasselenie ukrainskogo etnosa v XVIII – nachale XX v.', *SE*, 5, 15–31.

Bruk, S. I. and V. M. Kabuzan (1982) 'Dinamika chislennosti i rasseleniia russkogo etnosa (1678–1917 gg)', *SE* 4, 9–25.

Bruk, S. I. and V. M. Kabuzan (1984) 'Migratsiia naseleniia v Rossii v XVIII – nachale XX veka (Chislennost', struktura, geografiia)', *ISSSR*, 4, 41–59.

Brutskus, B. D. (1908) *Professional'nyi sostav Evreiskogo naseleniia Rossii po materialam pervoi vseobchshei perepisi naseleniia 1897 goda*, St Petersburg.

Brutskus, B. D. (1909) *Statistika evreiskogo naseleniia. Raspredelenie po territorii, demograficheskie i kul'turnye priznaki evreiskogo naseleniia po dannym perepisi 1897 g*, St Petersburg.

Budilovich, A. S. (1907) *Mozhet-li Rossiia otdat' inorodtsam svoi okrainy?*, St Petersburg.

Byelorussian Statehood. Reader and Bibliography (1988), ed. Vitaut and Zora Kipel, New York.

Carrère d'Encausse, Hélène (1988) *Islam and the Russian Empire. Reform and Revolution in Central Asia*, Berkeley.

Čeginskas, K. J. (1959) *Die Russifizierung und ihre Folgen in Litauen unter zaristischer Herrschaft*, Bonn.

Civil Rights in Imperial Russia (1989), ed. Olga Crisp and Linda Edmondson, Oxford.

Coonrod, Robert W. (1954) 'The Duma's Attitude toward War-Time Problems of Minority Groups', *ASEER*, 13, 29–46.

Coquin, François-Xavier and Céline Gervais-Francelle (eds) (1986) *1905. La première révolution russe*, Paris.

Curtiss, John Shelton (1965) *The Russian Army under Nicholas I, 1825–1855*, Durham.

Curzon, George N. (1967) *Russia in Central Asia in 1889 and the Anglo-Russian Question*, London (reprint of 1889 edn).

Dameshek, L. M. (1986) *Vnutrenniaia politika tsarizma i narody Sibiri. XIX – nachalo XX veka*, Irkutsk.

Dann, Otto (ed.) (1978) *Nationalismus und sozialer Wandel*, Hamburg.

Davies, Norman (1981) *God's Playground. A History of Poland*, vols I–II, Oxford.

Demko, George J. (1969) *The Russian Colonization of Kazakhstan 1896–1916*, Bloomington.

Dokumente zur Geschichte der europäischen Expansion (1984–8), ed. Eberhard Schmitt *et al.*, vols II–IV, Munich.

Donnelly, Alton S. (1968) *The Russian Conquest of Bashkiria 1552–1740. A Case Study in Imperialism*, New Haven.

Drabkina, El. (1930) *Natsional'nyi i kolonial'nyi vopros v Tsarskoi Rossii. Posobie dlia vuzov, komvuzov i samoobrazovaniia*, Moscow.

Dubnow, S. M. (1916–20) *History of the Jews in Russia and Poland from the Earliest Times until the Present Day*, vols I–III. Philadelphia (reprint 1946).

Duffy, Christopher (1981) *Russia's Military Way to the West. Origins and Nature of Russian Military Power 1700–1800*, London.

Egunov, N. P. (1963) *Kolonial'naia politika tsarizma i pervyi etap natsional'nogo dvizheniia v Buriatii v epokhu imperializma*, Ulan Ude.

Ehrt, Adolf (1932) *Das Mennonitentum in Rußland von seiner Einwanderung bis zur Gegenwart*, Berlin and Leipzig.

Erdmann, Johann Friedrich (1822–26) *Beiträge zur Kenntnis des Innern von Rußland*, vols 1 and 2 (1–2), Riga, Dorpat and Leipzig.

Etnicheskaia istoriia narodov severa (1982), Moscow.

Etnicheskie gruppy v gorodakh Evropeiskoi chasti SSSR (formirovanie, rasselenie, dinamika, kultury) (1987), Moscow.

Etnokontaktnye zony v Evropeiskoi chasti SSSR (geografiia, dinamika, metody izucheniia) (1989), Moscow.

Fadeev, A. V. (1960) *Rossiia i Kavkaz v pervoi treti XIX v*, Moscow.

Fedorov, M. M. (1978) *Pravovoe polozhenie narodov Vostochnoi Sibiri (XVII – nachalo XX veka)*, Iakutsk.

Ferenczi, Casper (1984) 'Nationalismus und Neoslavismus in Rußland vor dem Ersten Weltkrieg', *FOG* 34, 7–128.

Ferro, Marc (1961) 'La politique des nationalités du gouvernement provisoire (février–octobre 1917)', *CMRS* 2, 131–65.

Fisher, Alan W. (1968) 'Enlightened Despotism and Islam under Catherine II', *SR* 27, 542–53.

Fisher, Alan W. (1978) *The Crimean Tatars*, Stanford.

Fisher, Raymond H. (1943) *The Russian Fur Trade 1550–1700*, Berkeley, Los Angeles.

Fleischhacker, Hedwig (1941) *Russische Antworten auf die polnische Frage 1795–1917*, Munich and Berlin.

Fleischhauer, Ingeborg (1986) *Die Deutschen im Zarenreich. Zwei Jahrhunderte deutsch-russische Kulturgemeinschaft*, Stuttgart.

Frankel, Jonathan (1981) *Prophecy und Politics. Socialism, Nationalism, and the Russian Jews, 1862–1917*, Cambridge.

Galoian, G. A. (1976) *Rossiia i narody Zakavkaz'ia. Ocherki politicheskoi istorii ikh vzaimootnoshenii s drevnikh vremen do pobedy Velikoi Oktyabr'skoi sotsialisticheskoi revoliutsii*, Moscow.

Galuzo, P. G. (1929) *Turkestan – koloniia (Ocherki po istorii Turkestana ot zavoevaniia russkimi do revoliutsii 1917 goda)*, Moscow.

Garve, Horst (1978) *Konfession und Nationalität. Ein Beitrag zum Verhältnis von Kirche und Gesellschaft in Livland im 19. Jahrhundert*, Marburg.

Georgi, Johann Gottlieb (1776–80) *Beschreibung aller Nationen des Russischen Reiches, ihrer Lebensart, Religion, Gebräuche, Wohnungen, Kleidungen und übrigen Merkwürdigkeiten*, vols I–IV, St Petersburg.

Geyer, Dietrich (1977) *Der russische Imperialismus. Studien über den Zusammenhang von innerer und auswärtiger Politik 1860–1914*, Göttingen.

Geyer, Dietrich (1985) *Die Russische Revolution. Probleme und Perspektiven*, 5th edn, Göttingen.

Gierowski, Józef Andrzej (1988) *Historia Polski 1764–1864*, Warsaw.

Glazik, Josef (1954) *Die russisch-orthodoxe Heidenmission seit Peter dem Großen. Ein missionsgeschichtlicher Versuch*, Münster.

Glazik, Josef (1959) *Die Islammission der russisch-orthodoxen Kirche. Eine missionsgeschichtliche Untersuchung nach russischen Quellen und Darstellungen*, Münster.

Golikova, N. B. (1982) *Ocherki po istorii gorodov Rossii kontsa XVII – nachala XVIII v*, Moscow.

Gregorian, Vartan (1972) 'The Impact of Russia on the Armenians and Armenia', in Vucinich, pp. 167–218.

Halbach, Uwe (1989) '"Heiliger Krieg" gegen den Zarismus. Zur Verbindung von Sufismus und Djihad im antikolonialen Widerstand gegen Rußland im 19. Jahrhundert', *Die Muslime*, pp. 213–34.

Halbach, Uwe (1991) 'Die Bergvölker (gorcy) als Gegner und Opfer: Der Kaukasus in der Wahrnehmung Rußlands (Ende des 18. Jahrhunderts bis 1864)', *Kleine Völker*, pp. 52– 65.

Haltzel, Michael (1977) *Der Abbau der deutschen ständischen Selbstverwaltung in den Ostseeprovinzen Rußlands. Ein Beitrag zur Geschichte der russischen Unifizierungspolitik 1855–1905*, Marburg.

Hambly, Gavin (ed.) (1966) *Zentralasien*. Frankfurt am Main.

Hamm, Michael F. (ed.) (1986) *The City in Late Imperial Russia*, Bloomington.

Handbuch der Geschichte Rußlands (1976ff), eds Manfred Hellmann, Klaus Zernack and Gottfried Schramm, vols I–III, Stuttgart.

Haumann, Heiko (1990) *Geschichte der Ostjuden*, Munich.

Hayit, Baymirza (1971) *Turkestan zwischen Rußland und China. Eine ethnographische, kulturelle und politische Darstellung zur Geschichte der nationalen Staaten und des nationalen Kampfes Turkestans im Zeitalter der russischen und chinesischen Expansion vom 18. bis ins 20. Jahrhundert*, Amsterdam.

Hellmann, Manfred (1966) *Grundzüge der Geschichte Litauens*, Darmstadt.

Hensel, Jürgen (1983) 'Polnische Adelsnation und jüdische Vermittler 1815– 1830. Über den vergeblichen Versuch einer Judenemanzipation in einer noch nicht emanzipierten Gesellschaft', *FOG* 32, 7–227.

Herberstein, Sigmund von (1984) *Das alte Rußland*, Zurich.

Hildermeier, Manfred (1984) 'Die jüdische Frage im Zarenreich. Zum Problem der unterbliebenen Emanzipation', *JbbGO* 32, 321–43.

Hildermeier, Manfred (1989) *Die Russische Revolution 1905–1921*, Frankfurt am Main.

Histoire des Arméniens (1982), ed. Gérard Dédéyan, Toulouse.

Historia państwa i prawa Polski (1981–2), vols III–IV, Warsaw.

Historyia Belaruskay SSR (1972), vols I–II, Minsk.

Hoensch, Jörg K. (1983) *Geschichte Polens*, Stuttgart.

Hösch, Edgar (1991) 'Die kleinen Völker und ihre Geschichte: Zur Diskussion über Nationwerdung und Staat in Finland', *Kleine Völker*, pp. 22–32.

Hoetzsch, Otto (1917) *Rußland. Eine Einführung auf Grund seiner Geschichte vom Japanischen bis zum Weltkrieg*, 2nd edn, Berlin.

Hoetzsch, Otto (1966) *Rußland in Asien. Geschichte einer Expansion*, Stuttgart.

Horak, Stephen M. (ed.) (1982) *Guide to the Study of Soviet Nationalities. Non-Russian Peoples of the USSR*. Littleton, Colorado.

Hovannisian, Richard G. (1967) *Armenia on the Road to Independence*, Berkeley, Los Angeles.

Hroch, Miroslav (1963) *Die Vorkämpfer der nationalen Bewegung bei den kleinen Völkern Europas. Eine vergleichende Analyse zur gesellschaftlichen Entwicklung der patriotischen Gruppen*, Prague.

Hroch, Miroslav (1985) *Social Preconditions of National Revival in Europe. A Comparative Analysis of the Social Composition of Patriotic Groups among the Smaller European Nations*, Cambridge.

Hrushevsky, Michael (1941) *A History of Ukraine*, New Haven.

Hunczak, Taras (ed.) (1974) *Russian Imperialism from Ivan the Great to the Revolution*, New Brunswick.

Hunczak, Taras (ed.) (1977) *The Ukraine 1917–1921: A Study in Revolution*, Cambridge, Mass.

Hundley, Helen Sharon (1984) 'Speransky and the Buriats: Administrative Reform in Nineteenth Century Russia,' Ph.D. thesis, University of Illinois.

Iablochkov, Mikhail (1876) *Istoriia dvorianskogo sosloviia v Rossii*, St Petersburg.

Istoriia Azerbaidzhana (1958–60) I–III, Baku.

Istoriia Buriat-Mongol'skoi ASSR (1954) I, Ulan Ude.

Istoriia Chuvashskoi ASSR (1966) I, Cheboksary.

Istoriia Dagestana (1968) II, Moscow.

Istoriia Estonskoi SSR (1961–74) I–III, Tallinn.

Istoriia Iakutskoi ASSR (1957) II, Moscow.

Istoriia Kazakhskoi SSR (1975–9) I–II, Alma Ata.

Istoriia Kirgizii (1963) I, Frunze.

Istoriia Latviiskoi SSR (1952–8) I–III, Riga.

Istoriia Moldavskoi SSR s drevneishikh vremen do nashikh dnei (1982), Kishinev.

Istoriia narodov Severnogo Kavkaza (konets XVIII v. – 1917 g.) (1988), Moscow.

Istoriia Sibiri s drevneishikh vremen do nashikh dnei (1968–9) I–V, Leningrad.

Istoriia SSSR s drevneishikh vremen do nashikh dnei. Pervaia seriia, (1966–68) I–VI, Moscow.

Istoriia tadzhikskogo naroda (1964) II(2), Moscow.

Istoriia Tatarskoi ASSR (S drevneishikh vremen do nashikh dnei) (1968), Kazan.

Istoriia Turkmenskoi SSR (1957) I(2), Ashkhabad.

Istoriia Ukrains'koi RSR (1977–9) I–VIII, Kiev.

Istoriia Uzbekskoi SSR (1968) II, Tashkent.

Iukhneva, N. V. (1984) *Etnicheskii sostav i etnosotsial'naia struktura naseleniia Peterburga. Vtoraia polovina XIX – nachalo XX veka. Statisticheskii analiz,* Leningrad.

Ivancevich, Anthony (1976) 'The Ukrainian National Movement and Russification'. Ph.D. thesis, Northwestern University.

Jadrinzew, N. (1886) *Sibirien. Geographische, ethnographische und historische Studien,* Jena.

Jewsbury, George F. (1976) *The Russian Annexation of Bessarabia: 1774–1828. A Study of Imperial Expansion,* Boulder and New York.

Jones, S. F. (1989) 'Marxism and Peasant Revolt in the Russian Empire: The Case of the Gurian Republic', *SEER* 67, 403–34.

Jurgela, Constantine R. (1948) *History of the Lithuanian Nation,* New York.

Jutikkala, Eino (with Kauko Pirinen) (1964) *Geschichte Finnlands,* Stuttgart.

Kabuzan, V. M. (1963) *Narodonaselenie Rossii v XVIII – pervoi polovine XIX v. (po materialam revizii),* Moscow.

Kabuzan, V. M. (1971) *Izmeneniia v razmeshchenii naseleniia Rossii v XVIII – pervoi polovine XIX v. (po materialam revizii),* Moscow.

Kabuzan, V. M. (1984) 'Zahl und Siedlungsgebiete der Deutschen im Russischen Reich (1796–1917)', *Zeitschrift für Geschichtswissenschaft* 32, 866–74.

Kabuzan, V. M. (1990) *Narody Rossii v XVIII veke. Chislennost' i etnicheskii sostav,* Moscow.

Kabuzan, V.M. and S. M. Troitskii (1971) 'Izmeneniia v chislennosti, udel'nom vese i razmeshchenii dvoryanstva v Rossii v 1782–1858 gg.', *ISSSR,* 4, 153–69.

Kahan, Arcadius (1983) 'Notes on Jewish Entrepreneurship in Tsarist Russia', in Gregory Guroff and Fred V. Carstensen (eds), *Entrepreneurship in Imperial Russia and the Soviet Union,* Princeton, pp. 104–24.

Kahan, Arcadius (1985) *The Plow, the Hammer and the Knout. An Economic History of Eighteenth-Century Russia,* Chicago and London.

Kalabiński, Stanisław and Feliks Tych (1969) *Czwarte powstanie czy pierwsza rewolucja. Lata 1905–1907 na ziemiach polskich,* Warsaw.

Kalinychev, F. I. (ed.) (1957) *Gosudarstvennaia duma v Rossii v dokumentakh i materialakh,* Moscow.

Kappeler, Andreas (ed.) (1982a) 'Historische Voraussetzungen des Nationalitätenproblems im russischen Vielvölkerreich', in *Geschichte und Gesellschaft* 8, 159–83.

Kappeler, Andreas (1982b) *Rußlands erste Nationalitäten. Das Zarenreich und die Völker der Mittleren Wolga vom 16. bis 19. Jahrhundert,* Cologne and Vienna.

Kappeler, Andreas (1986) 'Ethnische Minderheiten im alten Rußland (14.–16. Jahrhundert): Regierungspolitik und Funktionen', *FOG* 38, 131–51.

Kappeler, Andreas (1990) *Die Russen. Ihr Nationalbewußtsein in Geschichte und Gegenwart*, Cologne.

Kappeler, Andreas (1992a) 'Moskau und die Steppe. Das Verhältnis zu den Nogai-Tataren im 16. Jahrhundert', *FOG* 46, 87–105.

Kappeler, Andreas (1992b) 'The Ukrainians of the Russian Empire 1860–1914', in A. Kappeler (ed.) *The Formation of National Elites*, Aldershot, pp. 105–32 (vol. VI of *Comparative Studies on Governments and Non-dominant Ethnic Groups in Europe, 1850–1940*).

Kasteliansky, A. I. (ed.) (1910) *Formy natsional'nogo dvizheniia v sovremennykh gosudarstvakh. Avstro-Vengriia. Rossiia. Germaniia*, St Petersburg.

Katz, Martin (1966) *Mikhail N. Katkov. A Political Biography 1818–1887*, The Hague and Paris.

Keep, John L. H. (1985) *Soldiers of the Tsar. Army and Society in Russia 1462–1874*, Oxford.

Kharlampovich, K. V. (1914) *Malorossiiskoe vliianie na velikorusskuiu tserkovnuiu zhizn'*, I, Kazan (reprint 1968)

Kirby, D. G. (ed.) (1975) *Finland and Russia 1808–1920. From Autonomy to Independence*. London and Basingstoke.

Kleine Völker in der Geschichte Osteuropas (1991) *Festschrift für Günther Stökl zum 75. Geburtstag*. Eds M. Alexander, F. Kämpfer und A. Kappeler, Stuttgart.

Klier, John Doyle (1986) *Russia Gathers her Jews. The Origins of the 'Jewish Question' in Russia, 1772–1825*, Dekalb.

Kochekaev, B-A. B. (1988) *Nogaisko-russkie otnosheniia v XV–XVIII vv.*, Alma Ata.

Kohut, Zenon E. (1982) *Russian Centralism and Ukrainian Autonomy. Imperial Absorption of the Hetmanate. 1760s–1830s*, Cambridge, Mass.

Kolonial'naia politika rossiiskogo tsarizma v Azerbaidzhane v 20–60-kh gg. 19 v. (1936), vols I–II, Moscow and Leningrad.

Kononenko, Konstantyn (1958) *Ukraine and Russia. A History of the Economic Relations Between Ukraine and Russia (1654–1917)*, Milwaukee.

Korelin, A. P. (1979) *Dvorianstvo v poreformennoi Rossii 1861–1904 gg. Sostav, chislennost', korporativnaia organizatsiia*, Moscow.

Kosman, Marceli (1979) *Historia Białorusi*, Wrocław.

Krawchenko, Bohdan (1985) *Social Change and National Consciousness in Twentieth-Century Ukraine*, Basingstoke and London.

Kreindler, Isabelle (ed.) (1985) *Sociolinguistic Perspectives on Soviet National Languages. Their Past, Present and Future*, Berlin.

Krupnyckyj, Borys (1943) *Geschichte der Ukraine von den Anfängen bis zum Jahre 1920*, Leipzig.

Kruus, Hans (1932) *Grundriß der Geschichte des estnischen Volkes*, Tartu.

Kumor, Bolesław (1980) *Ustrój i organizacja kościoła polskiego w okresie niewoli narodowej (1772–1918)*, Cracow.

Lang, David Marshall (1957) *The Last Years of the Georgian Monarchy 1658–1832*, New York.

Lang, David Marshall (1962) *A Modern History of Georgia*, London.

Lantzeff, George V. and Richard A. Pierce (1973) *Eastward to Empire. Exploration and Conquest on the Russian Open Frontier, to 1750*, Montreal and London.

LeDonne, John P. (1984) *Ruling Russia. Politics and Administration in the Age of Absolutism 1762–1796*, Princeton.

Lemberg, Eugen (1964) *Nationalismus*, I–II, Reinbek.

Lemercier-Quelquejay, Chantal (1967) 'Les missions orthodoxes en pays musulmans de Moyenne- et Basse-Volga, 1552–1865', *CMRS* 8, 369–403.

Leslie, R. F. (1956) *Polish Politics and the Revolution of November 1830*, London.

Levin, M. G. and Potapov, L. P. (eds) (1964) *The Peoples of Siberia*, Chicago and London.

Löwe, Heinz-Dietrich (1978) *Antisemitismus und reaktionäre Utopie. Russischer Konservatismus im Kampf gegen den Wandel von Staat und Gesellschaft, 1890–1917*, Hamburg.

Löwe, Heinz-Dietrich (1990) 'Nationalismus und Nationalitätenpolitik als Integrationsstrategie im zarischen Rußland', in Kappeler, pp. 55–79.

Loit, Alexander (ed.) (1985) *National Movements in the Baltic Countries during the 19th Century*, Stockholm.

Long, James W. (1988) *From Privileged to Dispossessed. The Volga Germans 1860–1917*, Lincoln, Nebraska and London.

Lorenz, Richard (1988) 'Die Turkmenen. Zum historischen Schicksal eines mittelasiatischen Volkes', in Erling von Mende (ed.) *Turkestan als historischer Faktor und politische Idee. Festschrift für Baymirza Hayit zu seinem 70. Geburtstag. 17 Dezember 1987*, Cologne, pp. 120–48.

Lorenz, Richard (1989) 'Die Basmatschen-Bewegung', *Die Muslime*, pp. 235–56.

Lukashevich, Stephen (1965) *Ivan Aksakov (1823–1886). A Study in Russian Thought and Politics*, Cambridge, Mass.

Lukawski, Zygmunt (1978) *Ludnosc polska w Rosji 1863–1914*, Wroclaw.

Madariaga, Isabel de (1981) *Russia in the Age of Catherine the Great*, New Haven and London.

Makhmedov, Ekhtibar Selidar ogly (1987) 'Tsarizm i vysshee musul'manskoe soslovie Zakavkaz'ia (Problema soslovno-zemel'nykh otnoshenii. Nachalo XIX veka – 1917 g.)' Diss. na soisk. uch. step. kandidata istoricheskikh nauk, Baku.

Mal'tsev, A. N. (1974) *Rossiia i Belorossiia v seredine XVII veka*, Moscow.

Mark, Rudolf A. (1989) *Die Völker der Sowjetunion. Ein Lexikon*, Opladen.

Martens, F. de (reprint 1969) *Recueil des traités et conventions conclus par la Russie avec les puissances étrangères* vols I–XV. St Petersburg, 1874–1909.

Meehan-Waters, Brenda (1982) *Autocracy and Aristocracy. The Russian Service Elite of 1730*, New Brunswick.

Mende, Gerhard von (1936) *Der nationale Kampf der Rußlandtürken. Ein Beitrag zur nationalen Frage in der Sowjetunion*, Berlin.

Milman, A. Sh. (1966) *Politicheskii stroi Azerbaidzhana v XIX – nachale XX vekov (administrativnyi apparat i sud, formy i metody kolonial'nogo upravleniia)*, Baku.

Mironov, B. N. (1981) *Vnutrennii rynok Rossii vo vtoroi polovine XVIII – pervoi polovine XIX v.*, Leningrad.

Müller, Michael G. (1984) *Die Teilungen Polens 1772, 1793, 1795*, Munich.

Die Muslime in der Sowjetunion und in Jugoslawien. Identität, Politik, Widerstand (1989) eds A. Kappeler, G. Simon and G. Brunner, Cologne.

Nahaylo, Bohdan and Victor Swoboda (1990) *Soviet Disunion. A History of the Nationality Problem in the USSR*, London.

Die Nationalitäten des Russischen Reiches in der Volkszählung von 1897 (1991), eds H. Bauer, A. Kappeler and B. Roth, vols 1–2. Stuttgart.

Neutatz, Dietmar (1993) *Die 'deutsche Frage' im Schwarzmeergebiet und in Wolhynien. Politik, Wirtschaft, Mentalitäten und Alltag im Spannungsfeld von Nationalismus und Modernisierung (1856–1914)*, Stuttgart.

Nolde, B. F. (1911) *Ocherki russkogo gosudarstvennogo prava*, St Petersburg.

Nolde, Boris (1952–53) *La Formation de l'Empire russe. Études, notes et documents*, vols I–II, Paris.

Nolte, Hans-Heinrich (1969a) *Religiöse Toleranz in Rußland 1600–1725*, Göttingen.

Nolte, Hans-Heinrich (1969b) 'Verständnis und Bedeutung der religiösen Toleranz in Rußland 1600–1725', *JbbGO* 17, 494–530.

Obshchestvennoe dvizhenie v Rossii v nachale XX–go veka (1912), IV, St Petersburg.

Ocherki istorii Kalmytskoi ASSR. Dooktyabr'skii period (1967) Moscow.

Ocherki istorii Udmurtskoi ASSR (1958) I, Izhevsk.

Ocherki po istorii Bashkirskoi ASSR (1956–9) I (1–2), Ufa.

Ocherki po istorii Komi ASSR (1955) I, Syktyvkar.

Ochmański, Jerzy (1967) *Historia Litwy*, Wrodaw.

Olcott, Martha Brill (1987) *The Kazakhs*, Stanford.

Die Orthodoxe Kirche in Rußland. Dokumente ihrer Geschichte (1860–1980) (1988), eds Peter Hauptmann and Gerd Stricker, Göttingen.

Parsamyan, V. A. (1972) *Istoriia armianskogo naroda 1801–1900 gg. Kniga pervaia*, Erevan.

Passé turco-tatar – présent soviétique. Études offertes à Alexandre Bennigsen (1986), eds C. Lemercier-Quelquejay, G. Veinstein and S. E. Wimbush, Louvain and Paris.

Pelesz, Julian (1880) *Geschichte der Union der ruthenischen Kirche mit Rom von den ältesten Zeiten bis auf die Gegenwart*, vol. II, Vienna.

Picht, Ulrich (1969) *M. P. Pogodin und die Slavische Frage*, Stuttgart.

Pierce, Richard A. (1960) *Russian Central Asia 1867–1917. A Study in Colonial Rule*, Berkeley, Los Angeles.

Pipes, Richard (1964) *The Formation of the Soviet Union. Communism and Nationalism 1917–1923*, 2nd edn, Cambridge, Mass.

Polonska-Vasylenko, Natalija (1988) *Geschichte der Ukraine. Von den Anfängen bis 1923*, Munich.

Przemiany społeczne w Królestwie Polskim 1815–1864 (1979), Wrocław.

Raeff, Marc (1971) 'Patterns of Russian Imperial Policy Toward the Nationalities', in Edward Allworth (ed.), *Soviet Nationality Problems*, New York and London, pp. 22–42.

Rauch, Georg von (1953) *Rußland: Staatliche Einheit und nationale Vielfalt. Föderalistische Kräfte und Ideen in der russischen Geschichte*, Munich.

Raun, Toivo U. (1979) 'The Development of Estonian Literacy in the 18th and 19th Centuries', *JBS* 10, pp. 113–26.

Raun, Toivo U. (1984) 'The Revolution of 1905 in the Baltic Provinces and Finland', *SK* 43, 453–67.

Raun, Toivo U. (1987) *Estonia and the Estonians*, Stanford.

Recueil de matériaux sur la situation économique des Israélites de Russie d'après l'enquête de la Jewish Colonization Association (1906–8), vols I–II, Paris.

Recueil des traités, conventions et actes diplomatiques concernant la Pologne 1762–1882 par le comte d'Angeberg (1862), Paris.

Reinhard, Wolfgang (1983–8) *Geschichte der Europäischen Expansion*, vols I–III, Stuttgart.

Rest, Matthias (1975) *Die russische Judengesetzgebung von der ersten Polnischen Teilung bis zum 'Polozhenie dlya evreev' (1804)*, Wiesbaden.

Die Revolution von 1905–1907 in Rußland. Translated from the Russian, East Berlin (1980).

Rhinelander, Laurens Hamilton Jr (1975) 'The Incorporation of the Caucasus into the Russian Empire: The Case of Georgia, 1801–1854'. Ph.D. thesis, Columbia University.

Rhode, Gotthold (1980) *Geschichte Polens. Ein Überblick*, 3rd edn, Darmstadt.

Riasanovsky, Nicholas V. (1959) *Nicholas I and Official Nationality in Russia 1825–1855*, Berkeley, Los Angeles.

Rieber, Alfred J. (1982) *Merchants and Entrepreneurs in Imperial Russia*, Chapel Hill.

Rogger, Hans (1961/62) 'Nationalism and the State. A Russian Dilemma', *Comparative Studies in Society and History* 4, 253–64.

Rogger, Hans (1986) *Jewish Policies and Right-Wing Politics in Imperial Russia*, Basingstoke, London.

Romanovich-Slavatinskii, A. (1912) *Dvorianstvo v Rossii ot nachala XVIII veka do otmeny krepostnogo prava. Svod materialov i priugotovitel'nye etiudy dlia istoricheskogo issledovaniia. Izd. 2-oe*, Kiev.

Rorlich, Azade-Ayshe (1986) *The Volga Tatars. A Profile in National Resilience*, Stanford.

Russian Jewry (1860–1917) (1966), eds J. Frumkin, G. Aronson, A. Goldenweiser, New York and London.

Rußlands Aufbruch ins 20. Jahrhundert. Politik – Gesellschaft – Kultur 1894–1917 (1970), Olten and Freiburg.

Rywkin, Michael (ed.) (1988) *Russian Colonial Expansion to 1917*, London and New York.

Salia, Kalistrat (1983) *History of the Georgian Nation*, Paris.

Sambuk, S. M. (1980) *Politika tsarizma v Belorussii vo vtoroi polovine XIX veka*, Minsk.

Sarkisyanz, Emanuel (1961) *Geschichte der orientalischen Völker Rußlands bis 1917. Eine Ergänzung zur ostslawischen Geschichte Rußlands*, Munich.

Saunders, David (1985) *The Ukrainian Impact on Russian Culture 1750–1850*, Edmonton.

Scharf, Claus (1988) 'Konfessionelle Vielfalt und orthodoxe Autokratie im frühneuzeitlichen Rußland', in *Deutschland und Europa in der Neuzeit. Festschrift für Karl Otmar Freiherr von Aretin zum 65. Geburtstag*, Stuttgart, pp. 179–92.

Scheibert, Peter (ed.) (1972) *Die russischen politischen Parteien von 1905 bis 1917. Ein Dokumentationsband*, Darmstadt.

Schweitzer, Robert (1978) *Autonomie und Autokratie. Die Stellung des Großfürstentums Finnland im russischen Reich in der zweiten Hälfte des 19. Jahrhunderts (1863–1899)*, Gießen.

Schweitzer, Robert (1984) 'Die "Baltische Parallele": Gemeinsame Konzeption oder zufällige Koinzidenz in der russischen Finnland- und Baltikumpolitik im 19. Jahrhundert?', *ZfO* 33, 551–76.

Screen, J. E. 0. (1976) 'The Entry of Finnish Officers into Russian Military Service 1809–1917', Ph.D. thesis, London.

Seton-Watson, Hugh (1967) *The Russian Empire 1801–1917*. Oxford.

Seton-Watson, Hugh (1977) *Nations and States. An Enquiry into the Origins of Nations and the Politics of Nationalism*, London.

Seton-Watson, R. W. (1934) *A History of the Roumanians. From Roman Times to the Completion of Unity*, Cambridge (reprint 1963).

Shanin, Teodor (1986) *Russia, 1905–1907. Revolution as a Moment of Truth*, Basingstoke and London.

Simon, Gerhard (1969) *Konstantin Petrovich Pobedonoscev und die Kirchenpolitik des Heiligen Sinod 1880–1905*, Göttingen.

Simon, Gerhard (1986) *Nationalismus und Nationalitätenpolitik in der Sowjetunion. Von der totalitären Diktatur zur nachstalinschen Gesellschaft*, Baden-Baden.

Smolitsch, Igor (1964, 1991) *Geschichte der russischen Kirche 1700–1917*, vol. I (Leiden, 1964); vol. II, (Berlin, 1991) (*FOG* 45).

Die sozialen Verhältnisse der Juden in Rußland. Auf Grund des Amtlichen statistischen Materials bearbeitet (1906), Berlin.

Spekke, Arnolds (1951) *History of Latvia. An Outline*, Stockholm.

Starr, S. Frederick (1978) 'Tsarist Government: The Imperial Dimension', in Jeremy R. Azrael (ed.), *Soviet Nationality Policies and Practices*, New York, pp. 3–38.

Stein, Hans-Peter (1967) 'Der Offizier des russischen Heeres im Zeitalter zwischen Reform und Revolution (1861–1905)', *FOG* 13, 346–507.

Stökl, Günther (1990) *Russische Geschichte. Von den Anfängen bis zur Gegenwart.* 5th edn, Stuttgart.

Storch, Heinrich (1795) *Statistische Übersicht der Statthalterschaften des Russischen Reiches nach ihren merkwürdigen Kulturverhältnissen. In Tabellen*, Riga.

Storch, Heinrich (1797–99) *Historisch-Statistisches Gemälde des Russischen Reiches am Ende des achtzehnten Jahrhunderts*, vols I–II (Riga, 1797); vol. III, (Leipzig, 1799).

Studies in Russian Historical Geography (1983), ed. J. H. Bater and R. A. French, vol. I, London.

Subtelny, Orest (1988) *Ukraine. A History*, Toronto, Buffalo and London.

Suny, Ronald Grigor (1989) *The Making of the Georgian Nation*, London.

Suny, Ronald Grigor (ed.) (1983) *Transcaucasia. Nationalism and Social Change. Essays in the History of Armenia, Azerbaijan, and Georgia*, Ann Arbor.

Svod statisticheskikh dannykh o naselenii Zakavkazskago kraia, izvlechennykh iz posemeinykh spiskov 1886 g. (1893), Tiflis.

Swietochowski, Tadeusz (1985) *Russian Azerbaijan 1905–1920. The Shaping of National Identity in a Muslim Community*, Cambridge.

Thackeray, Frank W. (1980) *Antecedents of Revolution: Alexander I und the Polish Kingdom, 1815–1825*, Boulder.

Thaden, Edward C. (1984) *Russia's Western Borderlands, 1710–1870*. With the Collaboration of Marianna Forster Thaden, Princeton.

Thaden, Edward C. (ed.) (1981) *Russification in the Baltic Provinces and Finland, 1855–1914*, Princeton.

Tiander, Karl (1934) *Das Erwachen Osteuropas. Die Nationalitätenbewegung in Rußland und der Weltkrieg. Erinnerungen und Ausblicke*, Vienna and Leipzig.

Tillett, Lowell (1969) *The Great Friendship. Soviet Historians on the Non-Russian Nationalities*, Chapel Hill.

To Siberia and Russian America: Three Centuries of Russian Eastward Expansion, 1558–1867 (1985–9), ed. Basil Dmytryshyn *et al.*, vols I–III, Portland.

Trapans, Janis Arveds (1979) 'The Emergence of a Modern Latvian Nation: 1764–1914', Ph.D. thesis, University of California, Berkeley.

Troitsky, S. M. (1974) *Russkii absoliutizm i dvorianstvo v XVIII v. Formirovanie biurokratii*, Moscow.

Ulashchik, N. N. (1965) *Predposylki krestianskoi reformy 1861 g. v Litve i zapadnoi Belorussii*, Moscow.

Vakar, Nicholas P. (1956) *Belorussia. The Making of a Nation. A Case Study*, Cambridge, Mass.

Volkova, N. G. (1974) *Etnicheskii sostav naseleniia Severnogo Kavkaza v XVIII – nachale XX veka*, Moscow.

Vucinich, Wayne S. (ed.) (1972) *Russia and Asia. Essays on the Influence of Russia on the Asian Peoples*, Stanford.

Wandycz, Piotr S. (1974) *The Lands of Partitioned Poland 1795–1918*, Seattle and London.

Wasilewski, Leon (1916) *Die Ostprovinzen des alten Polenreiches (Litauen u. Weißruthenien – die Landschaft Chełm – Ostgalizien – die Ukraina)*, Cracow.

Wasilewski, Leon (1925) *Litwa i Białoruś. Przeszłość, terazniejszość, tendencje rozwojowe*, Cracow.

Weinryb, Bernard D. (1972) *Neueste Wirtschaftsgeschichte der Juden in Rußland und Polen. Von der I. polnischen Teilung bis zum Tode Alexanders II. (1772–1881)*, 2nd edn Hildesheim and New York.

Wheeler, Geoffrey (1964) *The Modern History of Soviet Central Asia*, London.

Winiarski, Bohdan (1924) *Les institutions politiques en Pologne au XIXe siècle*, Paris.

Wittram, Reinhard (1954) *Baltische Geschichte. Die Ostseelande Livland, Estland, Kurland 1180–1918. Grundzüge und Durchblicke*, Munich.

Wittram, Reinhard (1964) *Peter I., Czar und Kaiser. Zur Geschichte Peters des Großen in seiner Zeit*. Göttingen.

Wixman, Ronald (1980) *Language Aspects of Ethnic Patterns and Processes in the North Caucasus*, Chicago.

Wixman, Ronald (1984) *The Peoples of the USSR. An Ethnographic Handbook*, London.

Wood, Alan (ed.) (1991) *The History of Siberia. From Russian Conquest to Revolution*, London and New York.

Wuorinen, John H. (1965) *A History of Finland*, New York and London.

Yaroshevsky, Dov B. (1989) *The Attitude of Catherine II toward Nomads of the Russian Empire*, paper given at the Fourth International Conference on Eighteenth-Century Russia, Hoddesdon.

Zaionchkovskii, P. A. (1978) *Pravitel'stvennyi apparat samoderzhavnoi Rossii v XIX v.*, Moscow.

Zakonodatel'stvo perioda rastsveta absoliutizma (1987), Moscow (= *Rossiiskoe zakonodatel'stvo X–XX vekov*, vol.V).

Zelenchuk, V.S. (1979) *Naselenie Bessarabii i Podnestrov'ia v XIX v. (Etnicheskie i sotsial'no-demograficheskie protsessy)*, Kishinev.

Zenkovsky, Serge A. (1960) *Pan-Turkism and Islam in Russia*, Cambridge, Mass.

Zhukovich, P. (1915), 'Soslovnyi sostav naseleniia Zapadnoi Rossii v tsarstvovanie Ekateriny II.', *Zhurnal ministerstva narodnogo prosveshcheniia*, new series, ch. LV, January, pp. 76–109; February, pp. 171–321; ch. LVII, May, pp. 130–78.

Ziablovsky, E. (1815) *Statisticheskoe opisanie Rossiiskoi imperii v nyneshnem ee sostoianii*, chs 1–3, 2nd edn, St Petersburg.

Index

Crimean Tatars (*continued*)
population, 286
religion, 148
Crimean War, 193
cultural development, 322, 382, 383
cultural diversity, 141–53
culture, 88, 135–6, 137, 151, 317, 318
Armenia, 267, 317
Georgian, 178
German, 250–1, 317
Middle Asia, 190
in national movements, 225, 227, 230
Polish, 84, 252, 317
Curtiss, J. S., 163, 164, 210
Curzon, Viscount, 198, 211, 212
customs barriers, 88, 96, 128
Cyrillic alphabet, 230, 238, 256, 262, 375, 379
Czacki, Tadeusz, 84
Czartoryski, Adam Jerzy, 84, 86, 89, 132, 136, 217
Russian Foreign Minister, 81
Czepulis-Rastenis, R., 165

Dabrowa basin, 303
Dagestan, 179, 180, 181, 182, 184, 185
literacy, 313
Dameshek, L. M., 208, 281
Danilevsky, N. Ia., 241, 318
Dan, F., 367
Dann, O., 11, 243, 244
Danube, 99
Darginians, 179
Darien, 204
Dashnak party, 233, 337, 342, 359, 363
Davies, N., 110, 111, 244
Davletbaev, B. S., 162
Decembrist uprising (1825), 88, 240
Demidova, N. F., 57
Demko, G. J., 210, 325
demography, 199, 200, 203
demonstrations, 330, 386, 387
Denmark, 72
deportation, 45, 185, 253, 256, 380, 381
Crimean Tatars, 45, 185, 380
Derbent, 172, 176
Derzhavin, Gavril R., 91
Desna, 19
despotism, 192
destabilization, 348–52
destalinization, 382–6
Deutsch, K. W., 243
diaspora groups, 137–41, 232, 374, 379
Diebitsch, 131
Dima, N., 112
diplomacy, 134–5, 137, 140, 141
discrimination, 92, 94, 138, 267–73, 349, 355

disintegration of Russian Empire, 353–66, 387
division of labour, 126–41, 303–9, 383
Dmowski, Roman, 219, 343, 344, 348
Dnepr, 51, 65–6, 79, 104, 114, 155, 291, 294, 304
Dnepr Cossacks, 51, 61–4, 77
Dnestr, 43, 80, 99
Dolgikh, O., 57
domestic trade, 128, 139
Don, 45, 49, 50, 62, 114, 139
Donnelly, A. S., 57, 212
Doroshenko, Petro, 65
Dorpat, 71
Dorpat, University of, 46, 72, 136, 143, 146, 221, 258–9
Dostoevsky, Fyodor Mikhailovich, 196, 208, 211, 212, 237
Drabkina, E., 13, 324
Drahomanov, M., 228
Druzhinina, E. I., 58
Dubnov, S., 367
Dubnow, S. M., 110, 111, 112, 281
Dubrowski, S. M., 369
Duchy of Kurland, 71, 72, 76, 80, 145, 349, 353
Duchy of Warsaw, 85, 93, 224
Duffy, C., 163
Duma, 341–8, 351
Dvina, western, 79, 114
Dzhugashvili, I. V. *see* Stalin, Josef
Dzhungaria, 44
Dziewanowski, M. K., 366

eastern Slavs, 14, 54, 221, 285
East India Company, 201
East Prussia, 381
ecology, 35, 389
economic development, 220, 382, 383, 384
economy, 126, 128, 196, 198, 387, 389
Edelman, R., 367
educated people *see* intelligentsia
education, 66, 72, 84, 136, 254, 345
Armenian, 178, 233
Bukhara, 197
and clergy, 143, 173, 185, 192
Estonia, 146
Finland, 95, 98, 136, 146, 221
foreign workers in, 135
German, 349
higher education, 136, 252, 270, 375, 384
Islam, 185, 192
Jesuit, 144
Jews, 147, 270
language, 86, 254, 255, 259
see also language
literacy *see* literacy

nature religions, 142, 149
Negidal, 203
Nerchinsk agreement, 35, 202
Nesselrode, Karl, 133, 152
Neutatz, D., 281
Neva, 72
Nevelskoi, 202
New Economic Policy, 373, 377
New Nakhichevan, 139
new nation states, 391
new national elites, 377, 382–6
New Russia, 51, 118, 127, 140, 213, 296,
    307
  1767 commission, 156
  grain products, 305
  Romanians in, 123, 296
newspapers, 339, 340, 375
  see also press and publishing
Nicholas I, 84, 88, 89, 93, 97, 98, 107, 131,
    133, 134, 175, 183, 207, 248, 250, 251,
    252, 257, 265, 266, 268, 269, 270, 273
Nicholas II, 257, 259, 260, 261, 273, 300, 341
Nieroth, Magnus W., 132
Nifontov, A. S., 326
Nikolaevsk, 202
Nimaev, D. D., 324
Nizhnii Novgorod, 337
Nizhyn, 128, 140
Nobel, 304
nobility, 70, 71, 137, 176–7, 289, 319
  Armenian, 172, 173
  Azerbaidzhani, 173
  Baltic German, 73, 74, 223
  in Caucasus, 184–5
  Finnish, 95
  Georgian, 172, 231, 232, 289, 299
  German, 72, 289, 299
  hereditary, 289, 294, 296, 299
  Kingdom of Poland, 291
  New Russian, 296
  non-Russian, 299
  Poland-Lithuanian, 77
  Polish see Polish nobility
  Romanian-speaking, 99, 100, 101, 294
  Russian, 82–3, 88, 289, 296, 299, 302
  in Russian empire, 117, 123, 124, 158
  Shemaitic minor, 227
  Slavonic, 62
  Tatars, 152, 299
Nogai Horde, 23
Nogai Tatars, 26, 40, 42–3, 46, 53–4, 100,
    179, 206
  allies, 45
  emigration, 47, 48
  migration, 118, 184
  resistance, 153

Nolde, B., 9, 12, 56–8, 109, 110, 111,
    112,0209
Nolte, H-H., 57, 113, 165, 166, 208
nomadic herdsmen, 43, 189, 351–2
nomadic horseman, 38, 39, 40, 42, 43
nomads, 41, 49, 121, 128, 159, 378
  in Afghanistan, 191
  Kirgiz, 195
  Lapps, 15, 16, 17, 121
  excluded from Legal Commission (1767),
    169
  migration, 118
  population, 116, 288, 352
  protests, 154, 195
  Uzbek, 195
non-Orthodox faiths, 142, 300
non-Russians, 126–41, 158, 159–60, 199, 264,
    387
  in Duma, 341, 342, 343–4
  elites, 124, 129, 136, 150–1, 301, 319
  ethnic groups, 16–17, 332, 360–1
  intellectuals, 384
  languages, 374–5, 376
  modernization, 380
  national movements, 361
  nobility, 299
  peasantry, 124, 125
  population, 116, 295, 320–1, 326n
  regions, 121
  resistance, 153–7, 159, 161–2, 200
  voting preferences, 362, 363
North American, fur trade, 200, 201
northern Russia, 229, 295
northern Urals, 295
Northern Wars, 66, 69, 72, 79
November insurrection, Polish, 89, 155, 217,
    239, 248, 252
Novgorod, 14, 15, 18, 27, 37, 52, 53
Novo-Arkhangelsk, 201
Novorossiia see New Russia
Novoselskii, A. A., 57
Novosiltsev, N.N., 87, 93
nuclear power, 389

oaths, 39, 43, 86–7, 97, 187, 260
Ob, 33
O'Brien, C. B., 109
Ochmański, J., 244
October Manifesto, 332, 334, 336, 340
October Revolution, 362, 364, 390
Octobrists, 337, 344
Odessa, 51, 123, 140, 153, 269, 288, 296, 324,
    331, 353
Ogiński, Michał, 81
Ogloblin, A. P.
oil industry, 304, 321

population (*continued*)
St Petersburg, 152
Siberia, 286, 295, 298
urban *see* urban population
Populists, 302
Portal, R., 326
Port Arthur, 204
Porvoo, 96
Pososhkov, I. T., 106, 113
Potapov, L. P., 57, 212
Potemkin, battleship, 331
Potemkin, Grigorii, 70
Potichnyi, P. J., 108
Potocki, Prince Seweryn, 84, 132, 136
power, stabilization of, 248–52
PPS (Polish Socialist Party), 219, 330, 332, 335
Prague, 258
pre-modern Russia, 114–62
precious metals, 35
prejudice, anti-Jewish, 91, 93
press and publishing, 256, 338, 339, 347, 348, 375
Russian national press, 257, 260, 265, 266
printing ban, 334
Pritsak, O., 281
Prokopovych, Feofan, 132, 136
Protestant ethnic groups, 310
Protestant Germans, 317
Protestantism, 51, 73, 131, 145–6, 258, 313
elites, 152, 301
protests, 28, 153, 154, 161, 195
anti-colonial, 179, 185
Armenian, 233
Cheremis, 28, 230, 251
Chuvash, 251
Mordvinians, 230
see also insurrection; rebellions; resistance
Protocols of the Elders of Zion, 271
Prousis, T. C., 165
province system, 176
provincial order (1775), 81–2
Provisional Government, 355, 356, 358, 359, 361
see also government; local government; self-government
Prussia, 60, 79, 80, 83, 216, 257, 351
Prussian Jägerbataillon, 27 351
Pruth, 99, 100
Pshavians, 172
Pskov, 18, 114
Ptukha, M., 327
publications *see* press and publishing
Pugachev, E., 107,
Pugachev uprising, 154, 156, 187
purges, 378, 380, 382

Pushkin, Alexander S., 71, 185, 249, 279

Quested, R. K. I., 212

Rabinovich, M. D., 163
Rada *see* Ukrainian Central Council (Rada)
Radkey, O. H., 362, 369
Raeff, M., 9, 12, 58, 106, 113, 208
railways, 199, 303, 304, 345, 352
Rainis, Janis, 224
Rakhmatullin, U. Kh., 57
Ranum, O., 167
Rauch, Georg von, 9, 12, 113, 279, 368
Raun, T. U., 13, 109, 166, 244, 325, 326, 367
Razin, Stepan, 30, 154
rebellions, 35, 41, 153, 154, 200, 202–3
see also insurrection; protest; resistance
Red Army, 371
Reddel, C., 12
reform, 85, 86, 221, 231, 267, 275, 276, 347
administrative, 75
agrarian, 74, 197, 218, 221
education, 344
Islam, 238, 263
Reinhard, W., 12, 59, 167, 212
religion, 136, 138, 141–53, 248, 287, 376
animism, 203
Armenians, 147, 286, 317
brotherhoods, 182, 200, 226, 262, 386
Catholicism, Lithuanian, 228
Chukchi, 37, 149, 287
conversions, 143, 250, 254
Germans, 76, 145, 286, 317
Greeks, 142, 225
Lithuanian, 145, 225, 228
Lutheran, 221
missionaries, 198
Muslim, 267
in national movements, 225, 227, 228, 235
Ossetian, 180
in Russia, 158, 160, 180
in Transcaucasia, 178
Renvall, P., 244
resettlement, 270, 349
Reshetar, J., 369
resistance, 153–7, 179, 182, 330, 335
Finnish, 155, 261, 330
Iakut, 35, 153
Kirgiz, 44, 195, 352
Lithuanian, 256
Muslim, 161, 179, 180
non-Russian, 153–7, 159, 161–2, 200
see also insurrection; protests; rebellions
Rest, M., 111, 112
Reutern, M. von, 300
Reval, 71, 73, 353

sable, 15, 35, 127
Sacke, G., 167
St Petersburg, 50, 72, 97, 304, 320–1, 324,
    326, 329, 336, 338
  migration, 74
  population, 152
  Revolution (1905), 330, 333
St Petersburg Cadet Corps, 130
Sakhalin island, 203
Salia, K., 208, 245
salt trade, 34
Samanid dynasty, 190
Samara, 41
Samarin, Iurii, 133, 253, 257, 258, 280
Samarkand, 190, 191, 195, 197
Sambuk, S. M., 280
Samoyeds, 15, 16, 17, 34, 121, 149
San Francisco, 201
Sarkisyanz, E., 9, 12, 57, 166, 208, 209, 210,
    211, 245, 246, 281
Sarts, 308, 309
Saunders, D., ix, 164
Saussay, J., 280
Savchenko, F., 280
Scharf, C., 58, 113, 165
Scheibert, P., 112, 245, 367, 368
Schieder, T., 244
Schirren, Carl, 109, 257, 258, 280
Schlüsselburg, 182
scholarship, 137, 141
schools see education
Schumann, H., 109
Schweitzer, R., 112, 279, 280, 282
'Schwertbrüderorden', 71
Schulin, E., 281
science, 135, 141, 376
Screen, J. E. O., 163, 325
secret police, 380
secret societies, 88
Sejm, 78, 82, 86, 87, 249
self-government, 90, 91, 93, 94, 270
  see also government; Provisional
      Government
Semipalatinsk, administrative units, 188
Semipalatinsk, fortress, 187
Seraphim, A., 109
Serbs, 50
Serczyk, W. A., 108
serfdom, 124, 218, 220, 221, 224, 231
serfs, 124, 224
Seton-Watson, H., 279, 366, 367
Seton-Watson, R. W., 12, 112, 244, 281
settlement, 40, 203, 222, 299, 352
  pale of settlement, 125, 138, 268, 270, 346,
      349
  see also emigration; immigration; migration

Seven Years War, 79, 129
Shafirov, 132
Shaibanid dynasty, 191
shamanism, 34, 36, 37, 149
Shamil, Caucasian chief, 179, 182–3, 185, 188,
    361
Shanin, T., 366
Shapiro, L., 325
Sheki, 172
Shelest, P., 385
Shelikhov, Grigorii, 201
Shelikhova, N. A., 212
Shemaitic minor nobility, 227
Shemakha, 176
Sheptytsky, A., Metropolitan, 349
Shevchenko, Taras, 225, 226, 228, 229, 346
Shiite Muslims, 172, 178, 191
Shirvan, 172
Shishmarev, V. F., 279
Shopen, I., 209
Shor, 34
Shternberg, L., 246, 367
Sibelius, Jean, 224
Siberia, 15, 33–8, 52, 55, 114, 116, 127, 156,
    161, 298, 361
  ethnic groups, 229, 288, 298
  inorodtsy, 264
  literacy, 312
  national movements, 340
  population, 286, 295, 298
  religion, 147, 149
  socio-ethnic structure, 121, 293, 295,
      298
  Tatars, 36, 147, 295
Siberian Kirgiz, 188
Sibir, Khanate of, 16, 23, 35, 40
Sibirskii Prikaz, chancellery for Siberia, 38
Sidelnikov, S. M., 367
Sievers, Johann J., 132
silk manufactories, 139
Silvester, archbishop of Novgorod, 27
Simon, G., 11, 12, 280, 281, 392
Sinkiang, 190, 196
Sitka, 200, 201
Six-Day War (1967), 386
Skobelev, General Mikhail D., 193, 195, 196
Slabchenko, M. E., 163
slavery, 45, 46, 125, 192, 197, 201
Slavinsky, M., 282
Slavs, 62, 150, 221, 285
  peasantry, 45, 199, 203
Slavynetsky, Epifanii, 135
Sloboda Ukraine, 65, 68, 156
Słowacki, Juliusz, 217
Small Nogai Horde, 42
'small' or 'young' nations, 214, 215

Smith, A. D., 12
Smolensk, 19, 69–71, 81, 104, 114, 116, 120,
    132, 152, 156, 295
Smolitsch, I., 57, 111, 165, 209, 279
smuta (civil war), 63
Smykov, Iu. I., 324
Snellman, J. V., 222
soap production, 140
Social Democratic Party, 227
Social Democrats, 222, 345
    'Himmat' group in Azerbaidzhan, 338
Social Democrats of the Kingdom of Poland
    and Lithuania (SDKPil), 335
Social Revolutionaries, 302, 363, 364
social development, 382, 383, 384
social integration, 31
social mobilization, 319, 360, 374, 379, 385,
    389
social order in Bessarabia, 100
social structure, 115–25, 180
Society for Popular Enlightenment, 338
Society of Progressive Ukrainians, 348
Society for the Promotion of Literacy in
    Georgia, 231
socio-ethnic composition, 34, 119, 121, 122
socio-ethnic structure, 34, 117–25, 180,
    285–302, 322
socio-political organization, 49, 61, 75, 97,
    180, 186
Sokol, E. D., 58, 368
Sokolovskii, S. V., 166
Solchanyk, R., 280
soldiers see armed forces
Solidarity movement, Polish, 389
Solomon II, king of Imeretia, 176
Soloviev, S. M., 8
Solovki, labour camp, 377
southern Urals, 41, 122–3, 126, 127, 297
    Cheremis, 123, 297
sovereignty, 197, 213, 229, 389
Soviet federalism, 378–9
Soviet multi-ethnic empire, 370
    destalinization, 382–6
    Gleichschaltung, 377–82
    Golden 20's, 373–7
    perestroika, 386–92
    reorganization, 370–3
Soviet Union, 1, 2, 53, 61, 329, 355, 373,
    382–92
Spiess, K., 212
Spekke, A., 109, 244
Speransky, M. M., 169, 170, 187
Sprengtporten, Colonel G. M., 95
Spuler, B., 56
Stackelberg, 135
Stadelbauer, J., 212

Stalin, Josef, 3, 10, 99, 185, 190, 352, 371, 373,
    377–82, 390, 392
Stalinism, 379, 380–1, 382, 390
standard of living, declining, 389
Stanislawski, M., 112
Stankevich, J. P., 109
Starr, S. F., 9, 12, 58, 113, 163, 167, 273, 282
starshyna, 66
State Council, 343
Statute of 1804 on Jews, 92
Stavropol, 297
Stebelsky, I., 210
Stein, H-P., 163, 325
Stephen of Perm, Bishop, 16, 262
steppes, 10, 38–51, 99, 118, 123, 124,
    185–90
    code of conduct, 23
Stockholm, 95, 97, 351
Stölting, E., 12, 392
Stökl, G., 20, 58
Stolypin, P., 343, 347
Storch, Heinrich, 8, 12, 141, 144, 157, 159,
    165, 166, 167
street demonstrations, 330
strikes, 331, 332, 333, 335, 340, 351
Stroganov family, 34
Struve, P., 344
Stumpp, K., 58
Subtelny, O., 108, 244, 279, 280
Sufic brotherhoods, 182, 192, 200, 236, 386
Sugar, P. F., 244
sugar beet, 305
sugar industry, 127, 138, 303, 304
Sultan-Galiev, 377
Sunni Muslims, 148, 191
Suny, R. G., 13, 208, 209, 245, 246, 281, 369
Suvalkiia, 80
Svanetians, 172
Svekomanes, Swedish, 222
Svensson, F., 57
Sviiazhsk, 25
Sweden, 8, 16, 60, 64, 66, 71, 72, 94–6
    battle of Poltava, 66
    Charles XII, 66
    language, 95, 96, 98, 152, 290
Swedes, 71, 95, 98, 221, 222, 310
    migration, 51
Swet, G., 281
Swietochowski, T., 209, 246, 367, 369
Switzerland, 51
Swoboda, V., 12, 392
Sysyn, F. E., 108
szlachta, Polish, 216, 217

Table of Ranks, 132
Tabriz, 174